ACCA

PAPER P3

BUSINESS ANALYSIS

PRACTICE & REVISION KIT

BPP Learning Media is an **ACCA Approved Content Provider** for the ACCA qualification. This means we work closely with ACCA to ensure our products fully prepare you for your ACCA exams.

In this Practice and Revision Kit, which has been reviewed by the **ACCA examination team,** we:

- Discuss the **best strategies** for revising and taking your ACCA exams

- Ensure you are well **prepared** for your exam

- Provide you with **lots of great guidance** on tackling questions

- Provide you with **three** mock exams

- Provide **ACCA exam answers** as well as our own for selected questions

Our **Passcard** product also supports this paper.

FOR EXAMS FROM 1 SEPTEMBER 2015 TO 31 AUGUST 2016

BPP
LEARNING MEDIA

First edition 2007
Ninth edition April 2015

ISBN 9781 4727 2694 0
(previous ISBN 97814727 11090)

e-ISBN 9781 4727 2746 6

British Library Cataloguing-in-Publication Data
A catalogue record for this book
is available from the British Library

Published by

BPP Learning Media Ltd
BPP House, Aldine Place
London W12 8AA

www.bpp.com/learningmedia

Printed in the United Kingdom by Polestar Wheatons

Hennock Road
Marsh Barton
Exeter
EX2 8RP

We are grateful to the Association of Chartered Certified
Accountants for permission to reproduce past
examination questions. The suggested solutions in the
practice answer bank have been prepared by BPP
Learning Media Ltd, except where otherwise stated.

BPP
LEARNING MEDIA

Contents

Page

Finding questions
Question index v
Topic index vii

Helping you with your revision viii

Revising P3
Topics to revise ix
Reading articles x
Question practice x
Passing the P3 exam xi
Exam information xvi
Useful websites xix

Questions and answers
Questions 3
Answers 103

Exam practice
Mock exam 1
- Questions 339
- Plan of attack 349
- Answers 350

Mock exam 2
- Questions 367
- Plan of attack 377
- Answers 379

Mock exam 3 (December 2014)
- Questions 395
- Plan of attack 407
- Answers 408

ACCA's exam answers
- June 2014 431
- December 2014 441

Review Form

A note about copyright

Dear Customer

What does the little © mean and why does it matter?

Your market-leading BPP books, course materials and e-learning materials do not write and update themselves. People write them: on their own behalf or as employees of an organisation that invests in this activity. Copyright law protects their livelihoods. It does so by creating rights over the use of the content.

Breach of copyright is a form of theft – as well as being a criminal offence in some jurisdictions, it is potentially a serious breach of professional ethics.

With current technology, things might seem a bit hazy but, basically, without the express permission of BPP Learning Media:

- Photocopying our materials is a breach of copyright

- Scanning, ripcasting or conversion of our digital materials into different file formats, uploading them to Facebook or emailing them to your friends is a breach of copyright

You can, of course, sell your books, in the form in which you have bought them – once you have finished with them. (Is this fair to your fellow students? We update for a reason.) Please note the e-products are sold on a single user licence basis: we do not supply 'unlock' codes to people who have bought them second-hand.

And what about outside the UK? BPP Learning Media strives to make our materials available at prices students can afford by local printing arrangements, pricing policies and partnerships which are clearly listed on our website. A tiny minority ignore this and indulge in criminal activity by illegally photocopying our material or supporting organisations that do. If they act illegally and unethically in one area, can you really trust them?

Question index

The headings in this checklist/index indicate the main topics of questions, but questions are expected to cover several different topics.

		Marks	Time allocation Mins	Page number Question	Answer
Part A: The overall strategic perspective					
1	Nesta (6/13)	25	45	3	103
2	Airtite (3.5, 6/06, amended)	25	45	4	105
3	The Management Press (12/10)	25	45	5	109
4	Rock Bottom (6/09)	25	45	6	111
5	Jayne Cox Direct (6/12)	25	45	7	114
6	Marlow Fashion (amended)	25	45	8	118
7	Frigate(12/10)	25	45	9	122
8	Alpha Software	25	45	10	124
9	AutoFone (6/08)	25	45	11	128
Part B: Options and organisation					
10	8-Hats (6/11)	25	45	13	133
11	Joe Swift Transport (6/10)	25	45	14	135
12	MMI (12/08)	25	45	16	138
13	The Environment Management Society (Pilot Paper)	25	45	18	142
Part C: Strategic implementation					
14	Country Car Club (6/08)	25	45	19	145
15	The Missing Link	25	45	20	148
16	Ergo City (6/10, amended)	25	45	21	151
17	Cronin Auto Retail (6/11)	25	45	22	153
18	Fresh 'n' Frozen	25	45	23	156
19	The BA Times (12/13)	25	45	24	161
20	Housham Garden (12/13)	25	45	25	165
21	iTTrain (6/14)	25	45	27	168
22	BeauCo	25	45	28	173
23	Finch Co	25	45	29	176
24	Chemical Transport (6/13)	25	45	30	179
25	DRB (Pilot Paper)	25	45	31	182
26	Perfect Shopper (12/07)	25	45	32	186
27	Independent Living (12/09)	25	45	33	190
28	Accounting Education Consortium (6/08)	25	45	34	192
29	ATD (12/13)	25	45	35	196
30	CoolFreeze (Pilot Paper)	25	45	37	200
31	Clothing Company (12/07)	25	45	39	202
32	Tillo Community Centre (6/12)	25	45	40	207
33	Lowlands Bank (12/09)	25	45	42	210
34	OneEnergy plc (6/09)	25	45	43	212

BPP
LEARNING MEDIA

	Marks	Time allocation Mins	Page number Question	Page number Answer
35 Bridge Co (6/14)	25	45	45	214
36 ASW (6/10, amended)	25	45	46	218
37 The Institute of Independent Analysts (IIA) (6/14)	25	45	48	222
38 Flexipipe (6/12)	25	45	49	226
39 Institute of Administrative Accountants (12/10)	25	45	50	228
40 Institute of Analytical Accountants (6/11)	25	45	51	230
41 Pharmacy Systems International (6/08)	25	45	53	233
42 Academic Recycling Company (6/13)	25	45	54	237

Part D: Case studies

	Marks	Time allocation Mins	Page number Question	Page number Answer
43 ReInk Co (6/14)	50	90	56	241
44 MachineShop (12/13)	50	90	58	247
45 Network Management Systems (Pilot Paper)	50	90	61	253
46 The Ace Bicycle Company	50	90	63	258
47 MidShire Health (6/13)	50	90	65	264
48 Polymat Tapes (3.5, 12/03, amended)	50	90	68	269
49 Shoal plc (12/10)	50	90	70	273
50 Bonar Paint (3.5, 6/07, amended)	50	90	73	278
51 Hammond Shoes (6/12)	50	90	75	284
52 EcoCar (6/11)	50	90	77	289
53 Oceania National Airlines (12/07)	50	90	80	294
54 ABCL (12/09)	50	90	83	303
55 Wetland Trust (6/10)	50	90	86	309
56 Institute of Information Systems Architects	50	90	90	316
57 The National Museum	50	90	93	321
58 Green Tech (6/09)	50	90	96	328

Mock exam 1

Mock exam 2

Mock exam 3 (December 2014)

Topic index

Listed below are the key Paper P3 syllabus topics and the numbers of the questions in this Kit covering those topics.

If you need to concentrate your practice and revision on certain topics or if you want to attempt all available questions that refer to a particular subject, you will find this index useful.

Syllabus topic	Question numbers
Benchmarking	Mock 2 Q1
Big Data	18
Business Process Change	23
Capabilities and competences	12, 16
Change management & the context of change	16, 41, 48, Mock 2 Q1, 49, 54, 57
Corporate appraisal (SWOT)	43, 50, Mock 1 Q1, 53, 55, 58
Critical success factors	Mock 1 Q1
Culture	Mock 1 Q2, 7,47, 48
Diamond model	11
e-business	3, 17
e-Marketing	17, 24, Mock 1 Q4, 55
Environmental analysis	2, Mock 1 Q1
Five forces	1,9 50,54, 55
Integrated reporting	8
Investment appraisal	10, Mock 2 Q3, 34, 37, Mock 2 Q4,51,54
Marketing mix	3, 21, 28, Mock 1 Q4
IT controls and continuity planning	22
Mission statement and organisational objectives	50, 51, 55
Organisation structure	4, 7, 10, 56
Outsourcing	14, 16, 52
People	42
PESTEL	50, 52, 55, 56, 57
Process-strategy matrix	Mock 1 Q2, 14, 24, 33, 56
Product Life Cycle	48
Project management	31, 32,33, Mock 1 Q3, 36, 39, 47
Software	34, 35, 37, 38, 40
Stakeholders	16, Mock 2 Q2, 54,55
Strategic capabilities	9
Strategic change	16, 41
Strategic options	11, 12, Mock 2 Q3, 48, 50, 51, Mock 1 Q1
Strategy development	9, 12, 57
Supply chain management	5, 25, 26
Value chain	5, 26, 27

Helping you with your revision

BPP Learning Media – ACCA Approved Content Provider

As an ACCA **Approved Content Provider**, BPP Learning Media gives you the **opportunity** to use **exam team reviewed** revision materials. By incorporating the examination team's comments and suggestions regarding syllabus coverage, the BPP Learning Media Practice and Revision Kit provides excellent, **ACCA-approved** support for your revision.

Tackling revision and the exam

Using feedback obtained from the ACCA exam team review:

- We look at the dos and don'ts of revising for, and taking, ACCA exams
- We focus on Paper P3; we discuss revising the syllabus, what to do (and what not to do) in the exam, how to approach different types of question and ways of obtaining easy marks

Selecting questions

We provide signposts to help you plan your revision.

- A full **question index**
- A **topic index** listing all the questions that cover key topics, so that you can locate the questions that provide practice on these topics, and see the different ways in which they might be examined

Making the most of question practice

At BPP Learning Media we realise that you need more than just questions and model answers to get the most from your question practice.

- Our **Top tips** included for certain questions provide essential advice on tackling questions, presenting answers and the key points that answers need to include
- We show you how you can pick up **Easy marks** on some questions, as we know that picking up all readily available marks often can make the difference between passing and failing
- We include **marking guides** to show you what the examiner rewards
- We include **comments from the examiners** to show you where students struggled or performed well in the actual exam
- We refer to the **BPP Study Text** for exams from 1 September 2015 to 31 August 2016 for detailed coverage of the topics covered in questions
- In a bank at the end of this Kit we include the **official ACCA answers** to the June and December 2014 papers. Used in conjunction with our answers they provide an indication of all possible points that could be made, issues that could be covered and approaches to adopt.

Attempting mock exams

There are three mock exams that provide practice at coping with the pressures of the exam day. We strongly recommend that you attempt them under exam conditions. **Mock exams 1 and 2** reflect the question styles and syllabus coverage of the exam; **Mock exam 3** is the December 2014 paper.

Revising P3

Firstly we must emphasise that you will need a good knowledge of the **whole syllabus**. Any part of the syllabus could be tested within compulsory Question 1. Having to choose two out of three optional questions does not really represent much choice if there are areas of the syllabus you are keen to avoid. There are certain topics that are stressed in the syllabus and therefore are core:

Strategic position

- The need for and purpose of business analysis (rational model, levels of strategy, strategic lenses)

- The internal resources, capabilities and competences of an organisation (value chain and corporate appraisal)

- Setting critical success factors (CSF) and key performance indicators (KPI)

- Environmental issues affecting the strategic position of an organisation (PESTEL and Porter's Diamond)

- Stakeholders, ethics culture and integrated reporting (stakeholder mapping, scope of corporate social responsibility and cultural web)

Strategic choices

- Portfolio models; the Boston Consulting Group (BCG) matrix, public sector, parenting matrix and Ashridge Portfolio display

- Approaches to achieving competitive advantage (strategy clock and generic options)

- Methods of development (Ansoff's matrix, internal development, mergers, acquisitions)

- Criteria to assess strategic options (suitability, acceptability and feasibility)

Strategic action

- Organisational set up (boundary-less organisations, hollow, modular and virtual) and strategic alliances (joint ventures, networks, franchising, licensing) and concepts of outsourcing, offshoring and shared services

- Organisational configurations (Mintzberg)

- Managing strategic change

- Organisational context of change (Balogun, Hope and Hailey)

- Different approaches to strategic development (emergent strategies)

Business and process change

- Assess the stages of the business change lifecycle and the four view model

- The role of Harmon's process strategy matrix

- Software solutions

Information technology

- Analyse IT and application controls and evaluate controls for safeguarding IT assets

- Principles of e-business including upstream and downstream supply chain management

- Understand the characteristics of e-marketing using the 6I's and the use of customer relationship management software (CRM)

Project management

- The nature of projects (building the business case and managing projects)

Financial analysis

- Understand the impact of financing decisions on strategy setting

- The role of the budgetary process and evaluating strategic options (use of resources, make or buy decisions)

People

- Relationship between strategy and people (leadership traits, classical and modern theories)

Reading articles

The examining team have stressed the importance of reading the technical articles published on the ACCA website that relate to P3. Some of the articles are written by the examining team.

It's also useful to keep reading the business press during your revision period and not just narrowly focus on the syllabus. Remember that this paper is about how organisations respond to real-world issues, so the more you read, the more practical examples you will have of how organisations have tackled real-life situations.

Question practice

You should use the Passcards and any brief notes you have to revise these topics, but you mustn't spend all your revision time passively reading. **Question practice is vital**; doing as many questions as you can in full will help develop your ability to analyse scenarios and produce relevant discussion and recommendations.

You should make sure you leave yourself enough time during your revision to practise 50 mark Section A questions as you cannot avoid them, and the scenarios and requirements of Section A questions are more complex. You should also leave yourself enough time to do the three mock exams.

BPP
LEARNING MEDIA

Passing the P3 exam

Displaying the right qualities

The examining team will expect you to display the following qualities.

Qualities required	
Fulfilling the higher level question requirements	This means that when you are asked to show higher level skills such as **assessment or evaluation**, you will only score well if you demonstrate them. Merely describing something when you are asked to evaluate it will not earn you the marks you need.
Identifying the most important features of the organisation and its environment	You must use your **technical knowledge and business awareness** to identify the key features of the scenario.
Applying your knowledge to the scenario	You should apply relevant theoretical models to the information presented in the scenario. However, your answer should not simply describe theoretical models. You need to employ two different skills here: • Use relevant theory to provide a framework or model for your answer • Use the scenario to answer the question The examining team frequently comment that students fail to use the information in the scenarios properly. Answers that are too general, or lack appropriate context as provided by the scenario, will not score well.
Selecting relevant real-life examples	You may gain credit for using **good examples**, providing you use the examples to illustrate your understanding of the points in the scenario.
Arguing well	You may be expected to discuss both sides of a case, or present an argument in favour or against something. You will gain marks for the **quality** and **logical flow of your arguments**.
Making reasonable recommendations	The measures you recommend must be **appropriate** for the organisation; you may need to discuss their strengths and weaknesses, as there may be costs of adopting them. The recommendations should clearly state what has to be done.

Avoiding weaknesses

Our experience of, and examining team feedback from, other higher level exams enables us to predict a number of weaknesses that are likely to occur in many students' answers. You will enhance your chances significantly if you ensure you avoid these mistakes:

- **Failing to provide what the question verbs require** (discussion, evaluation, recommendation) or to write about the topics specified in the question requirements

- **Repeating the same material** in different parts of answers

- **Stating theories and concepts** rather than applying them

- **Quoting chunks of detail** from the question that don't add any value

- **Forcing irrelevancies into answers**, for example irrelevant definitions or theories, or examples that don't relate to the scenario

- **Giving long lists or writing down all that's known** about a broad subject area, and not caring whether it's relevant or not

- **Focusing too narrowly on one area** – for example only covering financial risks when other risks are also important

- **Letting your personal views prevent you from answering the question** – the question may require you to construct an argument with which you personally don't agree

- **Unrealistic or impractical recommendations**

- **Vague recommendations** – instead of just saying improve risk management procedures, you should discuss precisely **how** you would improve them

- **Failing to answer sufficient questions**, or all parts of a question, because of poor time management

Using the reading time

We recommend that you spend the first part of the 15 minutes reading time choosing the Section B questions you will do, on the basis of your knowledge of the syllabus areas being tested and whether you can fulfil all the question requirements. Remember that Section B questions can cover different parts of the syllabus, and you should be happy with all the areas that the questions you choose cover. We suggest that you should note on the paper any ideas that come to you about these questions.

However don't spend all the reading time going through and analysing the Section B question requirements in detail; leave that until the three hours' writing time. Instead you should be looking to spend as much of the reading time as possible looking at the Section A scenario, as this will be longer and more complex than the Section B scenarios and cover more of the syllabus. You should highlight and annotate the key points of the scenario on the question paper.

Choosing which questions to answer first

Spending most of your reading time on the compulsory Section A question will mean that you can get underway with planning and writing your answer to the Section A question as soon as the three hours start. It will give you more actual writing time during the one and a half hours you should allocate to it and it's writing time that you'll need. Comments from examiners of other syllabuses that have similar exam formats suggest that students appear less time-pressured if they do the big compulsory questions first.

During the second half of the exam, you can put Section A aside and concentrate on the two Section B questions you've chosen.

However our recommendations are not inflexible. If you really think the Section A question looks a lot harder than the Section B questions you've chosen, then do those first, but **DON'T run over time on them.** You must leave yourself at least one hour and 30 minutes to tackle the Section A question. When you come back to it, having had initial thoughts during the reading time, you should be able to generate more ideas and find the question is not as bad as it looks.

Remember also that small overruns of time during the first half of the exam can add up to your being very short of time towards the end.

Tackling questions

You'll improve your chances by following a step-by-step approach to Section A scenarios along the following lines.

Step 1   **Read the background**

Usually the first couple of paragraphs will give some background on the company and what it is aiming to achieve. By reading this carefully you will be better equipped to relate your answers to the company as much as possible.

Step 2   **Read the requirements**

There is no point reading the detailed information in the question until you know what it is going to be used for. Don't panic if some of the requirements look challenging – identify the elements you are able to do and look for links between requirements, as well as possible indications of the syllabus areas the question is covering.

Step 3   **Identify the action verbs**

These convey the level of skill you need to exhibit and also the structure your answer should have. A lower level verb such as define will require a more descriptive answer; a higher level verb such as evaluate will require a more applied, critical answer. It should be stressed that **higher level requirements and verbs** are likely to be most significant in this paper.

Action verbs that are likely to be frequently used in this exam are listed below, together with their intellectual levels and guidance on their meaning.

Intellectual level		
1	Define	Give the meaning of
1	Explain	Make clear
1	Identify	Recognise or select
1	Describe	Give the key features
2	Distinguish	Define two different terms, viewpoints or concepts on the basis of the differences between them
2	Compare and contrast	Explain the similarities and differences between two different terms, viewpoints or concepts
2	Contrast	Explain the differences between two different terms, viewpoints or concepts
2	Analyse	Give reasons for the current situation or what has happened
3	Assess	Determine the strengths/weaknesses/ importance/significance/ability to contribute
3	Examine	Critically review in detail
3	Discuss	Examine by using arguments for and against
3	Explore	Examine or discuss in a wide-ranging manner
3	Criticise	Present the weaknesses of/problems with the actions taken or viewpoint expressed, supported by evidence

Intellectual level		
3	Evaluate/critically evaluate	Determine the value of in the light of the arguments for and against (critically evaluate means weighting the answer towards criticisms/arguments against).
3	Construct the case	Present the arguments in favour or against, supported by evidence
3	Recommend	Advise the appropriate actions to pursue in terms the recipient will understand

Also make sure you identify all the action verbs; some question parts may have more than one.

Step 4   Identify what each part of the question requires

Think about what frameworks or theories you could choose if the question doesn't specify which one to use.

When planning, you will need to make sure that you aren't reproducing the same material in more than one part of the question.

Also you're likely to come across part questions with two requirements that may be at different levels; a part question may for example ask you to explain X and discuss Y. You must ensure that you **fulfill both requirements** and that your discussion of Y shows greater depth than your explanation of X (for example by identifying problems with Y or putting the case for and against Y).

Step 5   Check the mark allocation to each part

This shows you the depth anticipated and helps allocate time.

Step 6   Read the whole scenario through, highlighting key data

Put points under headings related to requirements (eg by noting in the margin to what part of the question the scenario detail relates).

Step 7   Consider the consequences of the points you've identified

Remember that you will often have to provide recommendations based on the information you've been given. Consider that you may have to criticise the code, framework or model that you've been told to use. You may also have to bring in wider issues or viewpoints, for example the views of different stakeholders.

Step 8   Write a brief plan

You may be able to do this on the question paper as often there will be at least one blank page in the question booklet. However any plan you make should be reproduced in the answer booklet when writing time begins.

Make sure you identify all the requirements of the question in your plan – each requirement may have sub-requirements that must also be addressed. If there are professional marks available, highlight in your plan where these may be gained (such as preparing a report).

Step 9   Write the answer

Make every effort to present your answer clearly. The pilot paper and exam papers so far indicate that the examining team will be looking for you to make a number of clear points. The best way to demonstrate what you're doing is to put points into separate paragraphs with clear headers.

Remember that **depth of discussion** will be important. Discussions will often consist of paragraphs containing 2-3 sentences. Each paragraph should:

- **Make a point**

- **Explain the point** (you must demonstrate why the point is important)

- **Illustrate the point** (with material or analysis from the scenario, perhaps an example from real-life)

In this exam a number of requirement verbs will expect you to express a viewpoint or opinion, for example construct an argument, criticise, evaluate. When expressing an opinion, you need to provide:

- **What the question wants**. For instance, if you are asked to criticise something, don't spend time discussing its advantages. In addition if a scenario provides a lot of information about a situation, and you are (say) asked to assess that situation in the light of good practice, your assessment is unlikely to be favourable.

- **Evidence** from theory or the scenario – again we stress that the majority of marks in most questions will be given for applying your knowledge to the scenario.

Gaining the easy marks

As P3 is a Professional level paper, 4 or 5 **professional level marks** will be awarded in the compulsory question. Some of these should be easy to obtain. The examining team has stated that some marks may be available for presenting your answer in the form of formal business letters, briefing notes, memos, presentations, press releases, narratives in an annual report and so on. You may also be able to obtain marks for the format, layout, logical flow and persuasiveness of your answer.

What you write should always sound professional, and you will be awarded marks for good introductions and conclusions. You must use the format the question requires. You must also lay your answer out so that somebody could actually read it and use it. A good way to end all documents is to invite further communication.

How you make the document persuasive will depend on who you are and who the recipients are. If you are writing to management you should consider how much information you need to provide. If you are trying to convince the reader that a decision is right, you should focus on the benefits.

Exam information

Format of the exam

Section A: 1 compulsory case study   50

Section B: Choice of 2 from 3 questions (25 marks each)   50

    100

Time: 3 hours plus 15 minutes reading time

Section A will be a compulsory case study question with several requirements relating to the same scenario information. The question will usually assess and link a range of subject areas across the syllabus. It will require students to demonstrate high-level capabilities to understand the complexities of the case and evaluate, relate and apply the information in the case study to the requirements.

The examining team have stressed the importance of reading the case in detail, taking notes as appropriate and getting a feel for what the issues are.

Section B questions are more likely to assess a range of discrete subject areas from the main syllabus section headings; they may require evaluation and synthesis of information contained within short scenarios and application of this information to the question requirements.

Although one subject area is likely to be emphasised in each Section B question, students should not assume that questions will be solely about content from that area. Each question will be based on a shorter case scenario to contextualise the question.

The paper will have a global focus.

Analysis of past papers

The table below provides details of when each element of the syllabus has been examined and the question number and section in which each element appeared.

Covered in Text chapter		Dec 2014	June 2014	Dec 2013	June 2013	Dec 2012	June 2012	Dec 2011	June 2011	Dec 2010	June 2010	Dec 2009	June 2009	Dec 2008	June 2008	Dec 2007	Pilot Paper
	STRATEGIC POSITION																
1	Business strategy	C				O	C	C	C		C						
1	Strategy lenses				C								C	C			
2	PESTEL analysis							C	C		C			C			C
2	National competitiveness			C							O						
2	Competitive forces						O		C			C			C		C
2	Business scenario building & forecasting			O	O			O	O								O
3	Marketing and market segmentation		O	O					O								
3	Industry lifecycle																
4	Value chain; supply chain management	O				O						O				O	O
4	SWOT analysis	O	C				C	C			C		C		C		
4	Benchmarking					C											
5	Stakeholders											C					
5	Culture and the cultural web			O	C				O	O				C			
	STRATEGIC CHOICES																
6	Generic strategies													C	C		
6	Product-market strategy														O		
	BCG	C				C											
6	Methods of growth			C		O							C	O			O
6	Corporate parents										C				O		
6	SAF	C		C													
	ORGANISING AND ENABLING SUCCESS																
7	Organisational structures									O	O						

Covered in Text chapter		Dec 2014	June 2014	Dec 2013	June 2013	Dec 2012	June 2012	Dec 2011	June 2011	Dec 2010	June 2010	Dec 2009	June 2009	Dec 2008	June 2008	Dec 2007	Pilot Paper
8	Managing strategic change		C			C				C					O		
	BUSINESS PROCESS CHANGE																
9	Process-strategy matrix				O		O	O					O		O		
9	Outsourcing	O						C			O				O		
9	Business process redesign	O							O	O	C		C				
10	Managing risk					O											
	INFORMATION TECHNOLOGY																
11	E-business and upstream supply chain management								O	O						O	O
11	E-business and downstream supply chain management									O						O	O
12	E-marketing		O	O		O			O	O	C				O		
12	Customer relationship marketing				O												
	PROJECT MANAGEMENT																
13	Project management	O	O		C		O	O	O		O		O		O		
	FINANCE																
14	Finance					O			O		O						C
	PEOPLE																
15	Leadership				O								O				
15	Job design				O												
15	Staff development																
	STRATEGIC DEVELOPMENT																
16	Developing strategies																

IMPORTANT!

The table above gives a broad idea of how frequently major topics in the syllabus are examined. It should not be used to question spot and predict for example that Topic X will not be examined because it came up two sittings ago.

Useful websites

The websites below provide additional sources of information of relevance to your studies for *Business Analysis*.

- www.accaglobal.com

  ACCA's website. The students' section of the website is invaluable for detailed information about the qualification, past issues of *Student Accountant* (including technical articles) and a free downloadable Student Planner App.

- www.bpp.com

  Our website provides information about BPP products and services, with a link to ACCA's website.

- www.ft.com

  This website provides information about current international business. You can search for information and articles on specific industry groups as well as individual companies.

- www.economist.com

  Here you can search for business information on a week-by-week basis, search articles by business subject and use the resources of the Economist Intelligence Unit to research sectors, companies or countries.

- www.invweek.co.uk

  This site carries business news and articles on markets from *Investment Week* and *International Investment*.

- www.pwc.com

  The PricewaterhouseCoopers website includes UK Economic Outlook.

- www.cfo.com

  Good website for financial officers.

- www.bankofengland.co.uk

  This website is useful for sourcing Bank of England publications

- www.bbc.co.uk

  This website of the BBC carries general business information as well as programme-related content.

- www.strategy-business.com

  This website includes articles from Strategy and Business

Questions

THE OVERALL STRATEGIC PERSPECTIVE

Questions 1 to 9 cover the overall strategic perspective, the subject of Parts A, B and C of the BPP Study Text for Paper P3.

1 Nesta (6/13)   45 marks

NESTA is a large chain of fixed-price discount stores based in the country of Eyanke. Its stores offer ambient goods (goods that require no cold storage and can be kept at room temperature, such as cleaning products, stationery, biscuits and plastic storage units) at a fixed price of one dollar. Everything in the store retails at this price. Fixed-price discount chains focus on unbranded commodity goods which they buy from a number of small suppliers, for which the dollar shops are the most significant customers. Profit margins on the products they sell are low and overheads are kept to a minimum. The target price is fixed. The products tend to be functional, standardised and undifferentiated.

NESTA has observed the long-term economic decline in the neighbouring country of Eurobia, where a prolonged economic recession has led to the growth of so-called 'dollar shops'. Three significant dollar shop chains have developed: ItzaDollar, DAIAD and DollaFellas (see Table One). The shops of these three chains are particularly found on the high streets of towns and cities where there is significant financial hardship. Many of these towns and cities have empty stores which are relatively cheap to rent. Furthermore, landlords who once required high rents and long leases are increasingly willing to rent these stores for a relatively short fixed-term lease. The fixed-price dollar shop chains in Eurobia advertise extensively and continually stress their expansion plans. Few weeks go by without one of the chains announcing plans for a significant number of new shops throughout the country.

NESTA has recognised the growth of fixed-price discount retailers in Eurobia and is considering entering this market.

NESTA recently commissioned a brand awareness survey in Eurobia. The survey results showed that NESTA was relatively well-known to respondents who work in the consumer goods retail market. Most of these respondents correctly identified the company as a discount fixed-price company with a significant presence in Eyanke. However, amongst general consumers, only 5% of the respondents had heard of NESTA. In contrast, the three current fixed-price dollar shop discounters in Eurobia were recognised by more than 90% of the respondents.

NESTA itself has revenue of $120,000 million. It has cash reserves which could allow it to lease a significant number of shops in Eurobia and establish a credible market presence. It has recognised competencies in effective supplier selection and management, supported by effective procurement systems. Its logistics systems and methods are core strengths of the company.

There are also many conventional supermarket chains operating in Eurobia. The largest of these has annual revenue of $42,500 million. Supermarkets in Eurobia tend to increasingly favour out-of-town sites which allow the stores to stock a wide range and quantity of products. Customer car parking is plentiful and it is relatively easy for supplying vehicles to access such sites. As well as stocking non-ambient goods, most supermarkets do also stock a very wide range of ambient goods, often with competing brands on offer. However, prices for such goods vary and no supermarkets have yet adopted the discount fixed-price sales approach. In general, the large supermarket chains largely compete with each other and pay little attention to the fixed-price dollar shop discounters. Many supermarkets also have internet-based home ordering systems, offering (usually for a fee of $10) deliveries to customers who are unable or unwilling to visit the supermarket.

Table One shows the relative revenue of the three main discount fixed-price chains in Eurobia.

	2012 ($million)	2011 ($million)	2010 ($million)
ItzaDollar	330	300	275
DAIAD*	310	290	250
DollaFellas	290	235	200
Total	930	825	725

*Don't Ask It's A Dollar

Table One: Revenue of three main discount fixed-price chains in Eurobia

Required

(a) Use Porter's five forces framework to assess the attractiveness, to NESTA, of entering the discount fixed-price retail market in Eurobia. **(15 marks)**

(b) Discuss the potential use of scenarios by NESTA's managers as part of their analysis of NESTA's possible entry into the discount fixed-price retail market in Eurobia. **(10 marks)**

(Total = 25 marks)

2 Airtite (3.5, 6/06, amended) 45 mins

Airtite was set up in 2000 as a low cost airline operating from a number of regional airports in Europe. Using these less popular airports was a much cheaper alternative to the major city airports and supported Airtite's low cost service, modelled on existing low cost competitors. These providers had effectively transformed air travel in Europe and, in so doing, contributed to an unparalleled expansion in airline travel by both business and leisure passengers. Airtite used one type of aircraft, tightly controlled staffing levels and costs, relied entirely on online bookings and achieved high levels of capacity utilisation and punctuality. Its route network had grown each year and included new routes to some of the 15 countries that had joined the EU in 2004. Airtite's founder and Chief Executive, John Sykes, was an aggressive businessman ever willing to challenge governments and competitors wherever they impeded his airline and looking to generate positive publicity whenever possible.

John is now looking to develop a strategy which will secure Airtite's growth and development over the next 10 years. He can see a number of environmental trends emerging which could significantly affect the success or otherwise of any developed strategy. Airtite has seen its fuel costs continuing to rise reflecting the uncertainty over global fuel supplies. Fuel costs currently account for 25% of Airtite's operating costs. Conversely, the improving efficiency of aircraft engines and the next generation of larger aircraft are increasing the operating efficiency of newer aircraft and reducing harmful emissions. Concern with fuel also extends to pollution effects on global warming and climate change. Co-ordinated global action on aircraft emissions cannot be ruled out, either in the form of higher taxes on pollution or limits on the growth in air travel. On the positive side European governments are anxious to continue to support increased competition in air travel and to encourage low cost operators competing against the over-staffed and loss-making national flag carriers.

The signals for future passenger demand are also confused. Much of the increased demand for low cost air travel to date has come from increased leisure travel by families and retired people. However families are predicted to become smaller and the population increasingly aged. In addition there are concerns over the ability of countries to support the increasing number of one-parent families with limited incomes and an ageing population dependent on state pensions. There is a distinct possibility of the retirement age being increased and governments demanding a higher level of personal contribution towards an individual's retirement pension. Such a change will have a significant impact on an individual's disposable income and with people working longer reduce the numbers able to enjoy leisure travel.

Finally, air travel will continue to reflect global economic activity and associated economic booms and slumps together with global political instability in the shape of wars, terrorism and natural disasters.

John is uncertain as to how to take account of these conflicting trends in the development of Airtite's 10-year strategy and has asked for your advice.

Required

(a) Using models where appropriate, provide John with an environmental analysis of the conditions affecting the low cost air travel industry. **(15 marks)**

(b) Explain how the process of developing scenarios might help John better understand the macro-environmental factors influencing Airtite's future strategy. **(10 marks)**

(Total = 25 marks)

3 The Management Press (12/10)

Introduction

TMP (The Management Press) is a specialist business publisher; commissioning, printing and distributing books on financial and business management. It is based in a small town in Arcadia, a high-cost economy, where their printing works were established fifty years ago. 60% of the company's sales are made through bookshops in Arcadia. In these bookshops TMP's books are displayed in a custom-built display case specifically designed for TMP. 30% of TMP's sales are through mail order generated by full-page display advertisements in magazines and journals. Most of these sales are to customers based outside Arcadia. The final 10% of sales are made through a newly established website which offers a restricted range of books. These books are typically very specialised and are rarely featured in display advertising or stocked by general bookshops. The books available on the website are selected to avoid conflict with established supply channels. Most of the online sales are to customers based in Arcadia. High selling prices and high distribution costs makes TMP's books expensive to buy outside Arcadia.

Business changes

In the last decade costs have increased as the raw materials (particularly timber) used in book production have become dearer. Paper is extremely expensive in Arcadia and the trees used to produce it are becoming scarcer. Online book sellers have also emerged who are able to discount prices by exploiting economies of scale and eliminating bookshop costs. In Arcadia, it is estimated that three bookshops go out of business every week. Furthermore, the influential journal 'Management Focus', one of the journals where TMP advertised their books, also recently ceased production. TMP itself has suffered three years of declining sales and profits. Expenditure on marketing has been reduced significantly in this period and further reductions in the marketing budget are likely because of the weak financial position of the company. Overall, there is increasing pressure on the company to increase profit margins and sales.

Despite the poor financial results, the directors of TMP are keen to maintain the established supply channels. One of them, the son of the founder of the company, has stated that 'bookshops need all the help they can get and management journals are the heart of our industry'.

However, the marketing director is keen for the company to re-visit its business model. He increasingly believes that TMP's conventional approach to book production, distribution and marketing is not sustainable. He wishes to re-examine certain elements of the marketing mix in the context of the opportunities offered by e-business.

A young marketing graduate has been appointed by the marketing director to develop and maintain the website. However, further development of the website has not been sanctioned by the Board. Other directors have given two main reasons for blocking further development of this site. Firstly, they believe that the company does not have sufficient expertise to continue developing and maintaining its own website. It is solely dependent on the marketing graduate. Secondly, they feel that the website will compete with the established supply channels which they are keen to preserve.

However, the marketing director is convinced that investing in e-business is essential for the survival of TMP. 'We need to consider what unique opportunities it offers for pricing the product, promoting the product, placing the product and providing physical evidence of the quality of the product. Finally, we might even re-define the product itself'. He feels if the company fails to grasp these opportunities, then one of its competitors will, and 'that will be the end of us'.

Required

(a) Determine the main drivers for the adoption of e-business at TMP and identify potential barriers to its adoption. **(5 marks)**

(b) Evaluate how e-business might help TMP exploit each of the five elements of the marketing mix (price, product, promotion, place and physical evidence) identified by the marketing director. **(20 marks)**

(Total = 25 marks)

4 Rock Bottom (06/09)

This scenario summarises the development of a company called Rock Bottom through three phases, from its founding in 1965 to 2008 when it ceased trading.

Phase 1 (1965–1988)

In 1965 customers usually purchased branded electrical goods, largely produced by well-established domestic companies, from general stores that stocked a wide range of household products. However, in that year, a recent university graduate, Rick Hein, established his first shop specialising solely in the sale of electrical goods. In contrast to the general stores, Rick Hein's shop predominantly sold imported Japanese products which were smaller, more reliable and more sophisticated than the products of domestic competitors. Rick Hein quickly established a chain of shops, staffed by young people who understood the capabilities of the products they were selling. He backed this up with national advertising in the press, an innovation at the time for such a specialist shop. He branded his shops as 'Rock Bottom', a name which specifically referred to his cheap prices, but also alluded to the growing importance of rock music and its influence on product sales. In 1969, 80% of sales were of music centres, turntables, amplifiers and speakers, bought by the newly affluent young. Rock Bottom began increasingly to specialise in selling audio equipment.

Hein also developed a high public profile. He dressed unconventionally and performed a number of outrageous stunts that publicised his company. He also encouraged the managers of his stores to be equally outrageous. He rewarded their individuality with high salaries, generous bonus schemes and autonomy. Many of the shops were extremely successful, making their managers (and some of their staff) relatively wealthy people.

However, by 1980 the profitability of the Rock Bottom shops began to decline significantly. Direct competitors using a similar approach had emerged, including specialist sections in the large general stores that had initially failed to react to the challenge of Rock Bottom. The buying public now expected its electrical products to be cheap and reliable. Hein himself became less flamboyant and toned down his appearance and actions to satisfy the banks who were becoming an increasingly important source of the finance required to expand and support his chain of shops.

Phase 2 (1989–2002)

In 1988 Hein considered changing the Rock Bottom shops into a franchise, inviting managers to buy their own shops (which at this time were still profitable) and pursuing expansion though opening new shops with franchisees from outside the company. However, instead, he floated the company on the country's stock exchange. He used some of the capital raised to expand the business. However, he also sold shares to help him throw the 'party of a lifetime' and to purchase expensive goods and gifts for his family. Hein became Chairman and Chief Executive Officer (CEO) of the newly quoted company, but over the next thirteen years his relationship with his board and shareholders became increasingly difficult. Gradually new financial controls and reporting systems were put in place. Most of the established managers left as controls became more centralised and formal. The company's performance was solid but unspectacular. Hein complained that 'business was not fun any more'. The company was legally required to publish directors' salaries in its annual report and the generous salary package enjoyed by the Chairman and CEO increasingly became an issue and it dominated the 2002 Annual General Meeting (AGM). Hein was embarrassed by its publication and the discussion it led to in the national media. He felt that it was an infringement of his privacy and civil liberties.

Phase 3 (2003–2008)

In 2003 Hein found the substantial private equity investment necessary to take Rock Bottom private again. He also used all of his personal fortune to help re-acquire the company from the shareholders. He celebrated 'freeing Rock Bottom from its shackles' by throwing a large celebration party. Celebrities were flown in from all over the world to attend. However, most of the new generation of store managers found Hein's style to be too loose and unfocused. He became rude and angry about their lack of entrepreneurial spirit. Furthermore, changes in products and how they were purchased meant that fewer people bought conventional audio products from specialist shops. The reliability of these products now meant that they were replaced relatively infrequently. Hein, belatedly, started to consider selling via an Internet site. Turnover and profitability plummeted. In 2007 Hein again considered franchising the company, but he realised that this was unlikely to be successful. In early 2008 the company ceased trading and Hein himself, now increasingly vilified and attacked by the press, filed for personal bankruptcy.

(a)   Analyse the reasons for Rock Bottom's success or failure in each of the three phases identified in the scenario. Evaluate how Rick Hein's leadership style contributed to the success or failure of each phase.

(18 marks)

(b)   Rick Hein considered franchising the Rock Bottom brand at two points in its history – 1988 and 2007.

Explain the key factors that would have made franchising Rock Bottom feasible in 1988, but would have made it 'unlikely to be successful' in 2007.   **(7 marks)**

(Total = 25 marks)

5 Jayne Cox Direct (6/12)   45 mins

Jayne Cox Direct is a company that specialises in the production of bespoke sofas and chairs. Its products are advertised in most quality lifestyle magazines. The company was started ten years ago. It grew out of a desire to provide customers with the chance to specify their own bespoke furniture at a cost that compared favourably with standard products available from high street retailers. It sells furniture directly to the end customer. Its website allows customers to select the style of furniture, the wood it is to be made from, the type of upholstery used in cushion and seat fillings and the textile composition and pattern of the covering. The current website has over 60 textile patterns which can be selected by the customer. Once the customer has finished specifying the kind of furniture they want, a price is given. If this price is acceptable to the customer, then an order is placed and an estimated delivery date is given. Most delivery dates are ten weeks after the order has been placed. This relatively long delivery time is unacceptable to some customers and so they cancel the order immediately, citing the quoted long delivery time as their reason for cancellation.

Jayne Cox Direct orders wood, upholstery and textiles from long-established suppliers. About 95% of its wood is currently supplied by three timber suppliers, all of whom supplied the company in its first year of operation. Purchase orders with suppliers are placed by the procurement section. Until last year, they faxed purchase orders through to suppliers. They now email these orders. Recently, an expected order was not delivered because the supplier claimed that no email was received. This caused production delays. Although suppliers like working with Jayne Cox Direct, they are often critical of payment processing. On a number of occasions the accounts section at Jayne Cox Direct has been unable to match supplier invoices with purchase orders, leading to long delays in the payment of suppliers.

The sofas and chairs are built in Jayne Cox Direct's factory. Relatively high inventory levels and a relaxed production process means that production is rarely disrupted. Despite this, the company is unable to meet 45% of the estimated delivery dates given when the order was placed, due to the required goods not being finished in time. Consequently, a member of the sales team has to telephone the customer and discuss an alternative delivery date.

Telephoning the customer to change the delivery date presents a number of problems. Firstly, contacting the customer by telephone can be difficult and costly. Secondly, many customers are disappointed that the original, promised delivery date can no longer be met. Finally, customers often have to agree a delivery date much later than the new delivery date suggested by Jayne Cox Direct. This is because customers often get less than one week's notice of the new date and so they have to defer delivery to much later. This means that the goods have to remain in the warehouse for longer.

A separate delivery problem arises because of the bulky and high value nature of the product. Jayne Cox Direct requires someone to be available at the delivery address to sign for its safe receipt and to put the goods somewhere secure and dry. About 30% of intended deliveries do not take place because there is no-one at the address to accept delivery. Consequently, furniture has to be returned and stored at the factory. A member of the sales staff will subsequently telephone the customer and negotiate a new delivery date but, again, contacting the customer by telephone can be difficult and costly.

Delivery of furniture is made using the company's own vans. Each of these vans follow a defined route each day of the week, irrespective of demand.

The company's original growth was primarily due to the innovative business idea behind specifying competitively priced bespoke furniture. However, established rivals are now offering a similar service. In the face of this competition the managing director of Jayne Cox Direct has urged a thorough review of the supply chain. She feels that costs and inventory levels are too high and that the time taken from order to delivery is too long. Furthermore, in a recent customer satisfaction survey there was major criticism about the lack of information about the progress of the order after it was placed. One commented that 'as soon as Jayne Cox Direct got my order and my money they seemed to forget about me. For ten weeks I heard nothing. Then, just three days before my estimated delivery date, I received a phone call telling me that the order had been delayed and that the estimated delivery date was now 17 June. I had already taken a day off work for 10 June, my original delivery date. I could not re-arrange this day off and so I had to agree a delivery date of 24 June when my mother would be here to receive it'.

People were also critical about after-sales service. One commented 'I accidentally stained my sofa. Nobody at Jayne Cox Direct could tell me how to clean it or how to order replacement fabrics for my sofa'. Another said 'organising the return of a faulty chair was very difficult'.

When the managing director of Jayne Cox Direct saw the results of the survey she understood 'why our customer retention rate is so low'.

Required

(a)   Analyse the existing value chain, using it to highlight areas of weakness at Jayne Cox Direct.   **(12 marks)**

(b)   Evaluate how technology could be used in both the upstream and the downstream supply chain to address the problems identified at Jayne Cox Direct.   **(13 marks)**

(Total = 25 marks)

6 Marlow Fashion (amended)   45 mins

Susan Grant is in something of a dilemma. She has been invited to join the board of the troubled Marlow Fashion Group as a non-executive director, but is uncertain as to the level and nature of her contribution to the strategic thinking of the Group.

The Marlow Fashion Group was set up by a husband and wife team a number of years ago in an economically depressed part of the UK. They produced a comprehensive range of women's clothing built round the theme of traditional English style and elegance. The Group had the necessary skills to design, manufacture and retail its product range. The Marlow brand was quickly established and the company built up a loyal network of suppliers, workers in the company factory and franchised retailers spread around the world. Marlow Fashion Group's products were able to command premium prices in the world of fashion. Rodney and Betty Marlow ensured that their commitment to traditional values created a strong family atmosphere in its network of partners and were reluctant to change this. The Group continues to operate a traditional finance function, which is responsible for overseeing all financial matters affecting the business. Tasks undertaken by the finance team commonly involve the processing of accounting transactions, maintaining records and preparing month end reports.

Unfortunately, changes in the market for women's wear presented a major threat to Marlow Fashion. Firstly, women had become a much more active part of the workforce and demanded smarter, more functional outfits to wear at work. Marlow Fashion's emphasis on soft, feminine styles became increasingly dated. Secondly, the tight control exercised by Betty and Rodney Marlow and their commitment to control of design, manufacturing and retailing left them vulnerable to competitors who focused on just one of these core activities. Thirdly, there was a reluctance by the Marlows and their management team to acknowledge that a significant fall in sales and profits were as a result of a fundamental shift in demand for women's clothing. Finally, the share price of the company fell dramatically. Betty and Rodney Marlow retained a significant minority ownership stake, but the company has had a new Chief Executive Officer every year since.

Required

(a)   Write a short report to Susan Grant identifying and explaining the strategic strengths and weaknesses in the Marlow Fashion Group.   **(13 marks)**

Susan is aware of benchmarking as a useful input into performance measurement and strategic change.

(b)   Assess the contribution benchmarking could make to improving the position of the Marlow Fashion Group.   **(7 marks)**

(c)   Susan Grant recently read an article about the changing role of the finance function in modern business and the rise of the business partner model.

Briefly explain the meaning of the 'finance function as a business partner' and outline the potential benefits of making the finance function a business partner at the Marlow Fashion Group.   **(5 marks)**

(Total = 25 marks)

7 Frigate (12/10)

Introduction

Frigate Limited is based in the country of Egdon. It imports electrical components from other countries and distributes them throughout the domestic market. The company was formed twenty years ago by Ron Frew, who now owns 80% of the shares. A further 10% of the company is owned by his wife and 5% each by his two daughters.

Although he has never been in the navy, Ron is obsessed by ships, sailing and naval history. He is known to everyone as 'The Commander' and this is how he expects his employees to address him. He increasingly spends time on his own boat, an expensive motor cruiser, which is moored in the local harbour twenty minutes drive away. When he is not on holiday, Ron is always at work at 8.00 am in the morning to make sure that employees arrive on time and he is also there at 5.30 pm to ensure that they do not leave early. However, he spends large parts of the working day on his boat, although he can be contacted by mobile telephone. Employees who arrive late for work have to immediately explain the circumstances to Ron. If he feels that the explanation is unacceptable then he makes an appropriate deduction from their wages. Wages, like all costs in the company, are closely monitored by Ron.

Employees, customers and suppliers

Frigate currently has 25 employees primarily undertaking sales, warehousing, accounts and administration. Although employees are nominally allocated to one role, they are required to work anywhere in the company as required by Ron. They are also expected to help Ron in personal tasks, such as booking holidays for his family, filling in his personal tax returns and organising social events.

Egdon has laws concerning minimum wages and holidays. All employees at Frigate Ltd are only given the minimum holiday allocation. They have to use this allocation not only for holidays but also for events such as visiting the doctor, attending funerals and dealing with domestic problems and emergencies. Ron is particularly inflexible about holidays and work hours. He has even turned down requests for unpaid leave. In contrast, Ron is often away from work for long periods, sailing in various parts of the world.

Ron is increasingly critical of suppliers ('trying to sell me inferior quality goods for higher prices'), customers ('moaning about prices and paying later and later') and society in general ('a period working in the navy would do everyone good'). He has also been in dispute with the tax authority who he accused of squandering his 'hard-earned' money. An investigation by the tax authority led to him being fined for not disclosing the fact that significant family expenditure (such as a holiday for his daughters overseas) had been declared as company expenditure.

Company accountant

It was this action by the tax authority that prompted Ron to appoint Ann Li as company accountant. Ann had previously worked as an accountant in a number of public sector organisations, culminating in a role as a compliance officer in the tax authority itself. Ron felt that 'recruiting someone like Ann should help keep the tax authorities happy. After all, she is one of them'.

Ann was used to working in organisations which had formal organisational hierarchies, specialised roles and formal controls and systems. She tried to install such formal arrangements within Frigate. As she said to Ron 'we cannot have everyone working as if they were just your personal assistants. We need structure, standardised processes and accountability'. Ron resisted her plans, at first through delaying tactics and then through explicit opposition, tearing up her proposed organisational chart and budget in front of other employees. 'I regret the day I ever made that appointment', he said. After six months he terminated her contract. Ann returned to the tax authority as a tax inspector.

Required

The cultural web allows the business analyst to explore 'the way things are done around here'.

(a) Analyse Frigate Ltd using the cultural web or any other appropriate framework for understanding organisational culture.

(15 marks)

(b) Using appropriate organisation configuration stereotypes identified by Henry Mintzberg, explain how an understanding of organisation configuration could have helped predict the failure of Ann Li's proposed formalisation of structure, controls and processes at Frigate Ltd.

(10 marks)

(Total = 25 marks)

8 Alpha Software

Gemma Murphy has recently been appointed as the CEO of Alpha Software plc. The company develops specialist software for use by accountancy professionals. The specialist software market is particularly dynamic and fast changing. It is common for competitors to drop out of the market place. The most successful companies have been particularly focused on enhancing their offering to customers through creating innovative products and investing heavily in training and development for their employees.

Turbulent times

Alpha has been through a turbulent time over the last three years. During this time there have been significant senior management changes which resulted in confusion among shareholders and employees as to the strategic direction of the company. One investor complained that the annual accounts made it hard to know where the company was headed.

The last CEO introduced an aggressive cost-cutting programme aimed at improving profitability. At the beginning of the financial year the annual staff training and development budget was significantly reduced and has not been reviewed since the change in management.

Future direction

In response to the confusion surrounding the company's strategic direction, Gemma and the board published a new mission, the primary focus of which centres on making Alpha the market leader of specialist accountancy software. Gemma was appointed as the CEO having undertaken a similar role at a competitor. The board were keen on her appointment as she is renowned in the industry for her creativity and willingness to introduce 'fresh ideas'. In her previous role Gemma oversaw the introduction of an integrated approach to reporting performance. This is something she is particularly keen to introduce at Alpha.

During the company's last board meeting, Gemma was dismayed by the finance director's reaction when she proposed introducing integrated reporting at Alpha Software. The finance director made it clear that he was not convinced of the need for such a change, arguing that 'all this talk of integrated reporting in the business press is just a fad, requiring a lot more work, simply to report on things people do not care about. Shareholders are only interested in the bottom line'.

Required

(a)   Discuss what is meant by 'integrated reporting', highlighting how it differs from traditional performance reporting.   **(10 marks)**

(b)   How may integrated reporting help Alpha Software to communicate its strategy and improve the company's strategic performance. Your answer should make reference to the concerns raised by the finance director.
                                                                                                                                                (10 marks)

(c)   Advise on the likely implications of introducing 'integrated reporting' which Alpha should consider before deciding to proceed with its adoption.   **(5 marks)**

                                                                                                                                    (Total = 25 marks)

9 AutoFone (6/08)

Introduction

AutoFone was established at the beginning of the mobile telephone boom by a dynamic CEO who still remains a major shareholder of the company. It brought two new concepts to the market. Firstly, it established retail shops where customers could handle the products and discuss options with trained sales people rather than directly contacting the telephone network provider. Secondly, AutoFone sold products and services from all four major network providers (customers were previously restricted to one network provider's range). This was reflected in their motto 'ethical advice: the customer's choice'.

In 1990, AutoFone signed a thirty-year supply contract with each provider. The four network providers themselves had re-signed twenty-five year license deals with the government in 1995. Under the terms of these deals, licences will be restricted to the four current providers until their renewal date of 2020.

Retail shops Division

AutoFone now has 415 shops around the country located near (but not in) the main shopping area of the town they serve. AutoFone usually sign a fifty-year shop lease in return for low initial annual rental. In 1997, AutoFone floated on the country's stock market to fund more shops and so continue its organic growth. The strategy continues to focus on the central business idea of giving independent and impartial advice to customers.

Marketplace trends

Since AutoFone's arrival into the market, two significant trends have emerged:

(i)   The licensed network providers have opened their own retail stores, usually in city centres. AutoFone has reacted by stressing AutoFone's independence and impartiality, which the CEO now refers to as 'our central business idea'. This is core to their strategy and heavily emphasised in all their promotional material.

(ii)   Mobile phones have become vastly more sophisticated.

AutoFone has itself established its own Internet division, AFDirect, as a separate division within the group. Revenue earned from each division, analysed by the age of the customer, is shown in Table 1.

Table 1: Analysis of AutoFone Sales: 2007 (all figures in $m)

		Age of customer					
		Under 15	15-25	26-40	41-60	Over 60	Total
Division	AutoFone retail shops	5	90	60	120	65	340
	AFDirect	0	15	20	8	2	45
	Total sales of mobile phones						385

Analysts agree that growth in the mobile phone business is slowing down and this is supported by the figures given in Table 2 showing revenue from sales (both retail and Internet) for AutoFone and its competitors, the four licensed network providers, for the period 2003–2007.

Table 2: Market Analysis (all figures in $m) of sales of mobile phones

Company	2007	2006	2005	2004	2003
AutoFone	385	377	367	340	320
NetAG	350	348	345	340	305
09Net	390	388	380	365	350
PhoneLine	315	315	315	305	300
NetConned	295	295	294	290	285
Total	**1,735**	**1,723**	**1,701**	**1,640**	**1,560**

However, while AFDirect is prospering, there are increasing problems in the retail shops division. Profitability has been declining over the last few years (see Table 3) and this has had a demoralising effect on shop employees.

Future strategy

Two long serving directors on the strategic planning committee are increasingly concerned about the company's decline in profitability and have written an internal paper suggesting that the retail division is sold off and that AutoFone re-position itself as an online phone retailer. The CEO is strongly opposed to this suggestion as it was the shop-based approach that formed the company's original business model. He has a strong emotional attachment to the retail business which the two directors claim is clouding his judgement and hence he is unable to see the logic of an 'economically justifiable exit from the retail business'.

Table 3: Extracted Financial Information for AutoFone (retail shops division only)

Extracted Financial Information (all figures in $m)

Extracted from the Balance Sheet

	2007	2006	2005	2004	2003
Total non-current assets	143	140	134	128	123
Current assets:					
Inventories	345	340	335	320	298
Trade receivables	1,386	1,258	1,216	1,174	1,120
Cash and cash equivalents	345	375	390	400	414
Total current assets	2,076	1,973	1,941	1,894	1,832
Total assets	**2,219**	**2,113**	**2,075**	**2,022**	**1,955**
Total shareholder's equity	150	155	160	165	169
Non-current liabilities:					
Interest bearing long-term loans	55	50	45	40	35
Other provisions	16	15	13	13	10
Total non-current liabilties	71	65	58	53	45
Total current liabilities	1,998	1,893	1,857	1,804	1,741
Total equity and liabilities	**2,219**	**2,113**	**2,075**	**2,022**	**1,955**

Extracted from the Income Statement

		2007	2006	2005	2004	2003
Revenue		340	337	332	320	305
Cost of sales		250	252	230	220	205
Gross profit		90	85	102	100	100
Wages & salaries		39	38	37	35	33
Other expenses		40	38	35	30	30
Interest payable		4	4	3	3	3
	Total	83	80	75	68	66
Net profit before tax		7	5	27	32	34
Tax		2	3	5	4	4
Net profit after tax		5	2	22	28	30

Extracted from annual reports

	2007	2006	2005	2004	2003
Number of employees	1,400	1,375	1,325	1,300	1,275

Required

(a) Using an appropriate model or models, analyse the competitive environment of AutoFone's retail shops division. **(16 marks)**

(b) AutoFone's CEO is anxious to develop a rational and well argued case for retaining the retail shops division.

Write a briefing paper for the CEO to submit to the strategy planning committee explaining why the retail shops division should continue to form a key part of AutoFone's future strategy.

(9 marks)

(Total = 25 marks)

OPTIONS AND ORGANISATION

Questions 10 to13 review options and organisation, as covered in Parts B and C of the BPP Study Text for Paper P3.

10 8-Hats (06/11)

45 mins

8-Hats Promotions was formed twenty years ago by Barry Gorkov to plan, organise and run folk festivals in Arcadia. It soon established itself as a major events organiser and diversified into running events for the staff and customers of major companies. For example, for many years it has organised launch events, staff reward days and customer experiences for Kuizan, the car manufacturer. 8-Hats has grown through a combination of organic growth and acquiring similar and complementary companies. Recently, it purchased a travel agent (now operated as the travel department of 8-Hats) to provide travel to and from the events that it organised.

Barry Gorkov is himself a flamboyant figure who, in the early years of the company, changed his name to Barry Blunt to reflect his image and approach. He calls all the events 'jobs', a terminology used throughout the company. A distinction is made between external jobs (for customers) and internal jobs (within 8-Hats itself). The company is organised on functional lines. The sales and marketing department tenders for external jobs and negotiates contracts. Sales managers receive turnover-related bonuses and 8-Hats is known in the industry for its aggressive pricing policies. Once a contract is signed, responsibility for the job is passed to the events department which actually organises the event. It is known for its creativity and passion. The operations department has responsibility for running the event (job) on the day and for delivering the vision defined by the events department. The travel department is responsible for any travel arrangements associated with the job. Finally, the finance department is responsible for managing cash flow throughout the job, raising customer invoices, paying supplier invoices and chasing any late payments.

However, there is increasing friction between the departments. The operations department is often unable to deliver the features and functionality defined by the events department within the budget agreed by the sales manager. Finance is unaware of the cash flow implications of the job. Recently, an event was in jeopardy because suppliers had not been paid. They threatened to withdraw their services from the event. Eventually, Barry Blunt had to resolve friction between finance and other departments by acquiring further funding from the bank. The event went ahead, but it unsettled Kuizan which had commissioned the job. The sales and marketing department has also complained about the margins expected by the travel department, claiming that they are making the company uncompetitive.

There has been a considerable amount of discussion at 8-Hats about the investment appraisal approach used to evaluate internal jobs. The company does not have sufficient money and resources to carry out all the internal jobs that need doing. Consequently, the finance department has used the Net Present Value (NPV) technique as a way of choosing which jobs should be undertaken. Figure 1 shows an example comparison of two computer system applications that had been under consideration. Job One was selected because its Net Present Value (NPV) was higher ($25,015) than Job Two ($2,090).

'I don't want to tell you about the specific details of the two applications, so I have called them Job One and Job Two' said Barry. 'However, in the end, Job One was a disaster. Looking back, we should have gone with Job Two, not Job One. We should have used simple payback, as I am certain that Job Two, even on the initial figures, paid back much sooner than Job One. That approach would have suited our mentality at the time – quick wins. Whoever chose a discount rate of 8% should be fired – inflation has been well below this for the last five years. We should have used 3% or 4%. Also, calculating the IRR would have been useful, as I am sure that Job Two would have shown a better IRR than Job One, particularly as the intangible benefits of improved staff morale appear to be underestimated. Intangible benefits are just as important as tangible benefits. Finally, we should definitely have performed a benefits realisation analysis at the end of the feasibility study. Leaving it to after the project had ended was a ridiculous idea.'

Job 1				$000s		
Costs		Year 0	Year 1	Year 2	Year 3	Year 4
	Hardware costs	50	0	0	0	0
	Software costs	50	0	0	0	0
	Maintenance costs	10	10	10	10	10
	Total	110	10	10	10	10
Benefits	Staff savings	0	40	5	0	0
	Contractor savings	0	20	10	10	10
	Better information	0	0	0	20	30
	Improved staff morale	0	0	10	20	30
	Total	0	60	25	50	70
	Cash flows	-110	50	15	40	60
	Discount factor at 8%	1.000	0.926	0.857	0.794	0.735
	Discounted CF	-110.00	46.300	12.855	31.760	44.100
Job 2				$000s		
Costs		Year 0	Year 1	Year 2	Year 3	Year 4
	Hardware costs	50	0	0	0	0
	Software costs	30	10	10	0	0
	Maintenance costs	10	10	10	10	10
	Total	90	20	20	10	10
Benefits	Staff savings	0	30	10	5	0
	Contractor savings	0	30	15	15	15
	Better information	0	0	0	10	10
	Improved staff morale	0	0	10	10	10
	Total	0	60	35	40	35
	Cash flows	-90	40	15	30	25
	Discount factor at 8%	1.000	0.926	0.857	0.794	0.735
	Discounted CF	-90.000	37.040	12.855	23.820	18.375

Figure 1: NPV calculation for two projects at 8-Hats (with a discount rate of 8%)

Required

(a) Barry Blunt has criticised the investment appraisal approach used at 8-Hats to evaluate internal jobs. He has made specific comments on payback, discount rate, IRR, intangible benefits and benefits realisation.

Critically evaluate Barry's comments on the investment appraisal approach used at 8-Hats to evaluate internal jobs. **(15 marks)**

(b) Discuss the principles, benefits and problems of introducing a matrix management structure at 8-Hats.

(10 marks)

(Total = 25 marks)

11 Joe Swift Transport (06/10)   45 mins

Ambion is the third largest industrial country in the world. It is densely populated with a high standard of living. Joe Swift Transport (known as Swift) is the largest logistics company in Ambion, owning 1500 trucks. It is a private limited company with all shares held by the Swift family. It has significant haulage and storage contracts with retail and supermarket chains in Ambion. The logistics market-place is mature and extremely competitive and Swift has become market leader through a combination of economies of scale, cost efficiencies, innovative IT solutions and clever branding. However, the profitability of the sector is under increased pressure from a recently elected government that is committed to heavily taxing fuel and reducing expenditure on roads in favour of alternative forms of transport.

It has also announced a number of taxes on vehicles which have high carbon emission levels as well as reducing the maximum working hours and increasing the national minimum wage for employees. The company is perceived as a good performer in its sector. The 2009 financial results reported a Return on Capital Employed of 18%, a gross profit margin of 17% and a net profit margin of 9·15%. The accounts also showed a current liquidity ratio of 1·55 and an acid test ratio of 1·15. The gearing ratio is currently 60% with an interest cover ratio of 8.

10 years ago the northern political bloc split up and nine new independent states were formed. One of these states was Ecuria. The people of Ecuria (known as Ecurians) traditionally have a strong work ethic and a passion for precision and promptness. Since the formation of the state, their hard work has been rewarded by strong economic growth, a higher standard of living and an increased demand for goods which were once perceived as unobtainable luxuries. Since the formation of the state, the government of Ecuria has pursued a policy of privatisation. It has also invested heavily in infrastructure, particularly the road transport system, required to support the increased economic activity in the country.

The state haulage operator (EVM) was sold off to two Ecurian investors who raised the finance to buy it from a foreign bank. The capital markets in Ecuria are still immature and the government has not wished to interfere with or bolster them. EVM now has 700 modern trucks and holds all the major logistics contracts in the country. It is praised for its prompt delivery of goods. Problems in raising finance have made it difficult for significant competitors to emerge. Most are family firms, each of which operates about 20 trucks making local deliveries within one of Ecuria's 20 regions.

These two investors now wish to realise their investment in EVM and have announced that it is for sale. In principle, Swift are keen to buy the company and are currently evaluating its possible acquisition. Swift's management perceive that their capabilities in logistics will greatly enhance the profitability of EVM. The financial results for EVM are shown in Figure 1. Swift has acquired a number of smaller Ambion companies in the last decade, but has no experience of acquiring foreign companies, or indeed, working in Ecuria. Joe Swift is also contemplating a more radical change. He is becoming progressively disillusioned with Ambion. In a recent interview he said that 'trading here is becoming impossible. The government is more interested in over regulating enterprise than stimulating growth'. He is considering moving large parts of his logistics operation to another country and Ecuria is one of the possibilities he is considering.

2009

Figure 1 – Extract from financial results: EMV

Extract from the statement of financial position

	$million
Assets	
Non-current assets	
Intangible assets	2,000
Property, plant and equipment	6,100
	8,100
Current assets	
Inventories	100
Trade receivables	900
Cash and cash equivalents	200
	1,200
Total assets	9,300

	$million
Equity and liabilities	
Equity	
Share capital	5,700
Retained earnings	50
Total equity	5,750

Non-current liabilities

Long-term borrowings	2,500

Current liabilities

Trade payables	1,000
Current tax payable	50
	1,050
Total liabilities	3,550
Total equity and liabilities	9,300

Extract from the statement of comprehensive income

	$million
Revenue	20,000
Cost of sales	(16,000)
Gross profit	4,000
Administrative expenses	(2,500)
Finance cost	(300)
Profit before tax	1,200
Income tax expense	(50)
Profit for the year	1,150

Required

(a) Assess, using both financial and non-financial measures, the attractiveness, from Swift's perspective, of EVM as an acquisition target. **(15 marks)**

(b) Porter's Diamond can be used to explore the competitive advantage of nations and could be a useful model for Joe Swift to use in his analysis of countries that he might move his company to.

Examine using Porter's Diamond (or an appropriate alternative model/framework) the factors which could influence Swift's decision to move a large part of its logistics business to Ecuria. **(10 marks)**

(Total = 25 marks)

12 MMI (12/08)   45 mins

In 2002 the board of MMI met to discuss the strategic direction of the company. Established in 1952, MMI specialised in mineral quarrying and opencast mining and in 2002 it owned fifteen quarries and mines throughout the country. However, three of these quarries were closed and two others were nearing exhaustion. Increased costs and falling reserves meant that there was little chance of finding new sites in the country which were economically viable. Furthermore, there was significant security costs associated with keeping the closed quarries safe and secure.

Consequently the Chief Executive Officer (CEO) of MMI suggested that the company should pursue a corporate-level strategy of diversification, building up a portfolio of acquisitions that would 'maintain returns to shareholders over the next fifty years'. In October 2002 MMI, using cash generated from their quarrying operations, acquired First Leisure, a company that owned five leisure parks throughout the country. These leisure parks provided a range of accommodation where guests could stay while they enjoyed sports and leisure activities. The parks were all in relatively isolated country areas and provided a safe, car-free environment for guests.

The acquisition was initially criticised by certain financial analysts who questioned what a quarrying company could possibly contribute to a profitable leisure group. For two years MMI left First Leisure managers alone, letting them get on with running the company. However, in 2004 a First Leisure manager commented on the difficulty of developing new leisure parks due to increasingly restrictive government planning legislation. This gave the CEO of MMI an inspired idea and over the next three years the five quarries which were either closed or near exhaustion were transferred to First Leisure and developed as new leisure parks. Because these were developments of 'brown field' sites they were exempted from the government's planning legislation. The development of these new parks has helped First Leisure to expand considerably (see table 1). The company is still run by the managers who were in place when MMI acquired the company in 2002 and MMI plays very little role in the day-to-day running of the company.

In 2004 MMI acquired two of its smaller mining and quarrying competitors, bringing a further five mines or quarries into the group. MMI introduced its own managers into these companies resulting in a spectacular rise in revenues and profits that caused the CEO of MMI to claim that *corporate management capabilities* were now an important asset of MMI.

In 2006 MMI acquired Boatland, a specialist boat maker constructing river and canal boats. The primary rationale behind the acquisition was the potential synergies with First Leisure. First Leisure had experienced difficulties in obtaining and maintaining boats for its leisure parks and it was expected that Boatland would take on construction and maintenance of these boats. Cost savings for First Leisure were also expected and it was felt that income from the First Leisure contract would also allow Boatland to expand its production of boats for other customers. MMI perceived that Boatland was underperforming and it replaced the current management team with its own managers. However, by 2008 Boatland was reporting poorer results (see Table 1). The work force had been used to producing expensive, high quality boats to discerning customers who looked after their valued boats. In contrast, the boats required by First Leisure were for the casual use of holiday makers who often ill-treated them and certainly had no long-term investment in their ownership. Managers at First Leisure complained that the new boats were 'too delicate' for their intended purpose and unreliability had led to high maintenance costs. This increase in maintenance also put Boatland under strain and its other customers complained about poor quality workmanship and delays in completing work. These delays were compounded by managers at Boatland declaring First Leisure as a preferred customer, requiring that work for First Leisure should take precedence over that for established customers. Since the company was acquired almost half of the skilled boat builders employed by the company have left to take up jobs elsewhere in the industry.

Three months ago, InfoTech – an information technology solutions company approached MMI with a proposal for MMI to acquire them. The failure of certain contracts has led to falling revenues and profits and the company needs new investment. The Managing Director (MD) of InfoTech has proposed that MMI should acquire InfoTech for a nominal sum and then substantially invest in the company so that it can regain its previous profitability and revenue levels. However, after its experience with Boatland, the CEO of MMI is cautious about any further diversification of the group.

Table 1: Financial and market data for selected companies (all figures in $millions)

MMI quarrying and mining	2008	2006	2004	2002
Revenue	1,680	1,675	1,250	1,275
Gross profit	305	295	205	220
Net profit	110	105	40	45
* Estimated market revenue	6015	6050	6200	6300
First Leisure	2008	2006	2004	2002
Revenue	200	160	110	100
Gross profit	42	34	23	21
Net profit	21	17	10	9
* Estimated market revenue	950	850	770	750
Boatland	2008	2006	2004	2002
Revenue	2.10	2.40	2.40	2.30
Gross profit	0.30	0.50	0.50	0.60
Net profit	0.09	0.25	0.30	0.30
* Estimated market revenue	201	201	199	198
InfoTech	2008	2006	2004	2002
Revenue	21	24	26	25
Gross profit	0.9	3	4	4
Net profit	−0.2	2	3	3
* Estimated market revenue	560	540	475	450

* The estimated size of the market (estimated market revenue) is taken from Slott's Economic Yearbooks, 2002–2008.

Required

(a)   In the context of MMI's corporate-level strategy, explain the rationale for MMI acquiring *First Leisure* and *Boatland* and assess the subsequent performance of the two companies.   **(15 marks)**

(b)   Assess the extent to which the proposed acquisition of *InfoTech* represents an appropriate addition to the MMI portfolio.   **(10 marks)**

                                                                                                            (Total = 25 marks)

13 The Environmental Management Society (Pilot paper) 45 mins

The Environment Management Society (EMS) was established in 1999 by environment practitioners who felt that environmental management and audit should have its own qualification. EMS has its own Board who report to a Council of eight members. Policy is made by the Board and ratified by Council. EMS is registered as a private limited entity.

EMS employs staff to administer its qualification and to provide services to its members. The qualification began as one certificate, developed by the original founding members of the Society. It has since been developed, by members and officers of the EMS, into a four certificate scheme leading to a Diploma. EMS employs a full-time chief examiner who is responsible for setting the certificate examinations which take place monthly in training centres throughout the country. No examinations are currently held in other countries.

If candidates pass all four papers they can undertake an oral Diploma examination. If they pass this oral they are eligible to become members. All examinations are open-book one hour examinations, preceded by 15 minutes' reading time. At a recent meeting, EMS Council rejected the concept of computer-based assessment. They felt that competence in this area was best assessed by written examination answers.

Candidate numbers for the qualification have fallen dramatically in the last two years. The Board of EMS has concluded that this drop reflects the maturing marketplace in the country. Many people who were practitioners in environmental management and audit when the qualification was introduced have now gained their Diploma. The stream of new candidates and hence members is relatively small.

Consequently, the EMS Board has suggested that they should now look to attract international candidates and it has targeted countries where environmental management and audit is becoming more important. It is now formulating a strategy to launch the qualification in India, China and Russia.

However, any strategy has to recognise that both the EMS Board and the Council are very cautious and notably risk averse. EMS is only confident about its technical capability within a restricted definition of environmental management and audit. Attempts to look at complementary qualification areas (such as soil and water conservation) have been swiftly rejected by the Council as being non-core areas and therefore outside the scope of their expertise.

Required

Internal development, acquisitions and strategic alliances are three development methods by which an organisation's strategic direction can be pursued.

(a)   Explain the principles of internal development and discuss how appropriate this development method is to EMS.   **(8 marks)**

(b)   Explain the principles of acquisitions and discuss how appropriate this development method is to EMS.   **(8 marks)**

(c)   Explain the principles of strategic alliances and discuss how appropriate this development method is to EMS.   **(9 marks)**

                                                                                                            (Total = 25 marks)

STRATEGIC IMPLEMENTATION

Questions 14 to 42 cover strategic implementation, the subject of Parts D to I of the BPP Study Text for Paper P3.

14 Country Car Club (6/08)

45 mins

Introduction

The Country Car Club (3C) was established fifty years ago to offer breakdown assistance to motorists. In return for an annual membership fee, members of 3C are able to phone for immediate assistance if their vehicle breaks down anywhere in the country. Assistance is provided by 'service patrol engineers' who are located throughout the country and who are specialists in vehicle repair and maintenance. If they cannot fix the problem immediately then the vehicle (and its occupants) are transported by a 3C recovery vehicle back to the member's home address free of charge.

Over the last fifteen years 3C has rapidly expanded its services. It now offers vehicle insurance, vehicle history checks (to check for previous accident damage or theft) as well as offering a comprehensive advice centre where trained staff answer a wide range of vehicle-related queries. It also provides route maps, endorses hotels by giving them a 3C starred rating and lobbies the government on issues such as taxation, vehicle emissions and toll road charging. All of these services are provided by permanent 3C employees and all growth has been organic culminating in a listing on the country's stock exchange three years ago.

However, since its stock market listing, the company has posted disappointing results and a falling share price has spurred managers to review internal processes and functions. A Business Architecture Committee (BAC) made up of senior managers has been charged with reviewing the scope of the company's business activities. It has been asked to examine the importance of certain activities and to make recommendations on the sourcing of these activities (in-house or outsourced). The BAC has also been asked to identify technological implications or opportunities for the activities that they recommend should remain in-house.

First review

The BAC's first review included an assessment of the supply and maintenance of 3C's company vehicles. 3C has traditionally purchased its own fleet of vehicles and maintained them in a central garage. When a vehicle needed servicing or maintenance it was returned to this central garage. Last year, 3C had seven hundred vehicles (breakdown recovery vehicles, service patrol engineer vans, company cars for senior staff etc) all maintained by thirty staff permanently employed in this garage. A further three permanent employees were employed at the garage site with responsibility for the purchasing and disposal of vehicles. The garage was in a residential area of a major town, with major parking problems and no room for expansion.

The BAC concluded that the garage was of low strategic importance to the company and, although most of the processes it involved were straightforward, its remoteness from the home base of some vehicles made undertaking such processes unnecessarily complicated. Consequently, it recommended outsourcing vehicle acquisition, disposal and maintenance to a specialist company. Two months ago 3C's existing vehicle fleet was acquired by AutoDirect, a company with service and repair centres nationwide, which currently supplies 45,000 vehicles to companies throughout the country. It now leases vehicles back to 3C for a monthly payment. In the next ten years (the duration of the contract) all vehicles will be leased from AutoDirect on a full maintenance basis that includes the replacement of tyres and exhausts. 3C's garage is now surplus to requirements and all the employees that worked there have been made redundant, except for one employee who has been retained to manage the relationship with AutoDirect.

Second review

The BAC has now been asked to look at the following activities and their supporting processes. All of these are currently performed in-house by permanent 3C employees.

- *Attendance of repair staff at breakdowns* – currently undertaken by permanent 'service patrol engineers' employed at locations throughout the country from where they attend local breakdowns.

- *Membership renewal* – members must renew every year. Currently renewals are sent out by staff using a bespoke computer system. Receipts are processed when members confirm that they will be renewing for a further year.

- *Vehicle insurance services* providing accident insurance which every motorist legally requires.

- *Membership queries* handled by a call-centre. Members can use the service for a wide range of vehicle-related problems and issues.

- *Vehicle history checks.* These are primarily used to provide 'peace of mind' to a potential purchaser of a vehicle. The vehicle is checked to see if it has ever been in an accident or if it has been stolen. The check also makes sure that the car is not currently part of a loan agreement.

Required

(a) The Business Architecture Committee (BAC) has been asked to make recommendations on the sourcing of activities (in-house or outsourced). The BAC has also been asked to identify technological implications or opportunities for the activities that they recommend should remain in-house.

Suggest and justify recommendations to the BAC for each of the following major process areas:

(i) Attendance of repair staff at breakdowns
(ii) Membership renewal
(iii) Vehicle insurance services
(iv) Membership queries
(v) Vehicle history checks   **(15 marks)**

(b) Analyse the advantages that 3C will gain from the decision to outsource the purchase and maintenance of their own vehicles.   **(10 marks)**

(Total = 25 marks)

15 The Missing Link   45 mins

The Missing Link (ML) is a small manufacturing company based in Arcadia. It manufactures replacement components for machinery used in the construction industry. Much of the machinery used by ML's customers is quite old so components are no longer available from the original manufacturers, most of which are large multinational companies.

The business model is very traditional. The sales manager receives orders by telephone or fax and if the required component has been supplied before, the sales manager checks the price list and informs the customer. ML holds very low levels of finished goods inventory of only of the most popular components.

If the component has not been made before, an ML engineer obtains the original component drawings (from ML archives or the original manufacturer, produces detailed engineering drawings, a list of materials required, and an estimate of the labour hours needed. The estimate is passed to a costing clerk in the accounts department who calculates the likely product cost (labour, materials and overheads), adds a 'mark-up' of 40%, and advises the sales manager of the price. If the customer accepts the price, an order is passed to the production department, which schedules and completes the work. If the actual cost of production is significantly different from that estimated, the price list is amended to reflect the actual manufacturing cost.

Occasionally a component cannot be traced back to an original manufacturer. When this happens, the engineer produces a customised component by dismantling the original and producing the relevant engineering drawings himself. Customised components such as these currently account for about 10% of ML's business.

When an order is fulfilled, the component and invoice are delivered to the customer. Most customers pay within 30 days, by cash or cheque. ML does not have a problem with bad debts. An increasing proportion of ML's business is now transacted in US dollars, as Arcadian currencies tend to be unstable.

ML prides itself on customer service and receives lots of repeat business. ML grew significantly for a number of years as a result of 'word of mouth' recommendations but has not experienced growth for the last two years, although turnover and profit have remained stable.

ML uses only very basic Information Systems (IS), and reports its performance using a simple comparison between budget and actual, which is produced using a spreadsheet package. ML's accounting system is not automated, and transactions are recorded in traditional ledgers.

The sales manager of ML has noticed increasing customer demand for online ordering and a growing trend towards business-to-business (B2B) e-commerce. To make e-commerce possible, ML's accounting system will also have to be computerised.

The sales manager believes that e-commerce should lead to an increase in the company's turnover by 10% each year for the foreseeable future, and also that any increase in indirect costs as a result of this higher volume of business will be fully offset by a reduction in administration workload as a result of the new computerised accounting system.

Required

(a)   Describe the impact that e-commerce has had on the way business is conducted.   **(5 marks)**

(b)   Analyse the potential benefits to ML of the proposed e-commerce system.   **(15 marks)**

(c)   Discuss how ML might use its e-commerce system to increase the volume of business related to customised components.   **(5 marks)**

(Total = 25 marks)

16 Ergo City (6/10, amended)   45 mins

Ergo city authority administers environmental, social care, housing and cultural services to the city of Ergo. The city itself has many social problems and a recent report from the local government auditor criticised the Chief Executive Officer (CEO) for not spending enough time and money addressing the pressing housing problems of the city.

Since 1970 the authority has had its own internal Information Technology (IT) department. However, there has been increasing criticism of the cost and performance of this department. The CEO has commented that 'we seem to expand the department to cope with special demands (such as the millennium bug) but the department never seems to shrink back to its original size when the need has passed'. Some employees are lost through natural wastage, but there have never been any redundancies in IT and the labour laws of the nation, and strong trade unions within the authority, make it difficult to make staff redundant.

In the last few years there has been an on-going dispute between managers in the IT department and managers in the finance function. The dispute started due to claims about the falsification of expenses but has since escalated into a personal battle between the director of IT and the finance director. The CEO has had to intervene personally in this dispute and has spent many hours trying to reconcile the two sides. However, issues still remain and there is still tension between the managers of the two departments.

A recent internal human resources (HR) survey of the IT department found that, despite acknowledging that they received above average pay, employees were not very satisfied. The main complaints were about poor management, the ingratitude of user departments, ('we are always being told that we are overheads, and are not core to the business of the authority') and the absence of promotion opportunities within the department. The ingratitude of users is despite the IT department running a relatively flexible approach to fulfilling users' needs. There is no cross-charging for IT services provided and changes to user requirements are accommodated right up to the release of the software. The director of IT is also critical of the staffing constraints imposed on him. He has recently tried to recruit specialists in web services and 'cloud computing' without any success. He also says that 'there are probably other technologies that I have not even heard of that we should be exploring and exploiting'.

The CEO has been approached by a large established IT service company, ProTech, to form a new company ProTech-Public that combines the public sector IT expertise of the authority with the commercial and IT knowledge of ProTech. The joint company will be a private limited company, owned 51% by ProTech and 49% by the city authority. All existing employees in the IT department and the IT technology of the city authority will be transferred to ProTech who will then enter into a 10 year outsourcing arrangement with the city authority. The CEO is very keen on the idea and he sees many other authorities following this route.

The only exception to this transfer of resources concerns the business analysts who are currently in the IT department. They will be retained by the authority and located in a new business analysis department reporting directly to the CEO.

The CEO has suggested that the business analysts have the brief to 'deliver solutions that demonstrably offer benefits to the authority and to the people of the city, using information technology where appropriate'. They need to be 'outward looking and not constrained by current processes and technology'. They will also be responsible for liaising between users and the newly outsourced IT company and, for the first time, defining business cases with users.

In principle, the creation of the new company and the outsourcing deal has been agreed.

Required

(a)   Evaluate the potential benefits to the city authority and its IT employees, of outsourcing IT to Pro-Tech Public.   **(12 marks)**

(b)   The role of the business analyst is currently being redesigned.

        Analyse what new or enhanced competencies the business analysts will require to undertake their proposed new role in the city authority.   **(7 marks)**

(c)   Identify the main stakeholders that would be affected by the planned changes at the city authority. **(6 marks)**

(Total = 25 marks)

17 Cronin Auto Retail (06/11)   45 mins

Cronin Auto Retail (CAR) is a car dealer that sells used cars bought at auctions by its experienced team of buyers. Every car for sale is less than two years old and has a full service history. The company concentrates on small family cars and, at any one time, there are about 120 on display at its purpose-built premises. The premises were acquired five years ago on a 25 year lease and they include a workshop, a small cafe and a children's playroom. All vehicles are selected by one of five experienced buyers who attend auctions throughout the country. Each attendance costs CAR about $500 per day in staff and travelling costs and usually leads to the purchase of five cars. On average, each car costs CAR $10,000 and is sold to the customer for $12,000. The company has a good sales and profitability record, although a recent economic recession has led the managing director to question 'whether we are selling the right type of cars. Recently, I wonder if we have been buying cars that our team of buyers would like to drive, not what our customers want to buy?' However, the personal selection of quality cars has been an important part of CAR's business model and it is stressed in their marketing literature and website.

Sales records show that 90% of all sales are to customers who live within two hours' drive of CAR's base. This is to be expected as there are many competitors and most customers want to buy from a garage that they can easily return the car to if it needs inspection, a service or repair. Consequently, CAR concentrates on display advertising in newspapers in this geographical area. It also has a customer database containing the records of people who have bought cars in the last three years. All customers receive a regular mail-shot, listing the cars for sale and highlighting any special offers or promotions. The company has a website where all the cars are listed with a series of photographs showing each car from a variety of angles. The website also contains general information about the company, special offers and promotions, and information about its service, maintenance and repair service.

CAR is keen to expand the service and mechanical repair side of its business. It would particularly like customers who have purchased cars from them to bring them back for servicing or for any mechanical repairs that are subsequently required. However, although CAR holds basic spare parts in stock, it has to order many parts from specialist parts companies (called motor factors) or from the manufacturers directly. Mechanics have to raise paper requisitions which are passed to the procurement manager for reviewing, agreeing and sourcing. Most parts are ordered from regular suppliers, but there is an increasing backlog and this can cause a particular problem if the customer's car is in the garage waiting for the part to arrive. Customers are increasingly frustrated and annoyed by repairs taking much longer than they were led to expect. Another source of frustration is that the procurement manager only works from 10.00 to 16.00. The mechanics work on shifts and so the garage is staffed from 07.00 to 19.00. Urgent requisitions cannot be processed when the procurement manager is not at work. The backlog of requisitions is placing increased strain on the procurement manager who has recently made a number of clerical mistakes when raising a purchase order.

Requests for stationery and other office supplies also go through the same requisitioning process, with orders placed with the office supplier who is offering the best current deal. Finding this deal can be time consuming and so employees are increasingly submitting requisitions earlier so that they can be sure that new supplies will be received in time.

The managing director is aware of the problems of the requisitioning system but is reluctant to appoint a second procurement manager because he is trying to keep staff overheads down during a difficult trading period. He is keen to address 'more fundamental issues in the marketing and procurement processes'. He is particularly interested in how the 'interactivity, intelligence, individualisation and independence of location offered by e-marketing media can help us at CAR'.

Required

(a)   Evaluate how the principles of interactivity, intelligence, individualisation and independence of location might be applied in the e-marketing of the products and services of CAR.   **(16 marks)**

(b)   Explain the principles of e-procurement and evaluate its potential application to CAR.   **(9 marks)**

(Total = 25 marks)

18 Fresh 'n' Frozen   45 mins

Company background

Fresh 'n' Frozen Co (FF) was set up 7 years ago by Russell Beaumont. The company specialises in the delivery of frozen foods including ready meals, fruit, meat and fish products. Deliveries are made to the homes of private individuals by FF's fleet of 75 specially modified vans. Each van has been fitted with a freezer unit allowing frozen goods to be transported at very low temperatures. Ensuring that the food does not spoil while in transit after leaving the company's depot is of critical importance. Although, FF is based in a developed country with a good infrastructure increasing road congestion presents a growing challenge for the company's drivers. FF currently serves customers based in the southern regions of its country with deliveries made to customers in a 150 mile radius of the company's depot.

Online ordering

FF buys in frozen food products from a number of suppliers which are packaged and marketed under the FF brand. Customers can place orders by calling FF's main depot or via the company's website. Today the majority of orders are placed through the company's website. Orders through the website require customers to provide very few details, these include recording the customers name, address, contact details and payment. Customers are currently unable to request a time of delivery. Once an order has been received the Head of Delivery will allocate a driver to make the delivery on a specific day. The customer is notified of the delivery date and time by the company's small customer service team who often contact customers via landline telephone or text message.

In the event that a customer is not home to take the call informing them of delivery a voice mail message and a text message is left (only when the customer has provided mobile phone contact details). In the event that the customer does not respond to the message, it is assumed that the allocated delivery slot is to the customers liking and no further action is taken. Russell Beaumont has made it a company objective that all deliveries must be fulfilled within 4 days.

Delivery route management

When every new driver starts working at FF they are allocated a particular route from which deliveries are made. Most routes were determined by the previous Head of Delivery who retired from FF nearly 4 years ago. The routes were based on historic patterns of deliveries made at the time and also took into account the anticipated mileage covered to make a delivery. Mileage was determined by using a well-known website which provided approximate distances between any two locations. Since the previous Head of Delivery retired, the delivery routes have not been updated.

On recent occasions there have been instances where drivers have been sent out to make a small number of deliveries (2-3) on their assigned route, while at the same time other drivers have had a full day of deliveries to make, meaning that some of the hourly delivery slots have been missed. When delivery slots are missed this requires alternative arrangements to be made with the customer, with goods often being redelivered when the driver is next out on the same route.

Management meeting

Due to a recent dip in FF's performance, Russell Beaumont held a meeting with his management team, during which the Head of Delivery raised some concerns. She noted 'over the past few months I have noticed an increase in the amount of fuel that our older vans have started to use, I believe this is linked to the amount of power the freezer units consume. My team carry out regular physical inspections of all delivery vans once a month and we noticed that a number of these older vehicles are running at colder temperatures than is required to keep the food frozen. Last week I also identified a couple of vans where the freezer was not actually working at all!

Furthermore, my team of drivers have started to experience an increase in the number of delivery slots being missed, due to increasing road congestion. Customers appear to be unwilling to wait in to take receipt of a delivery much beyond the allocated time slot. This generates a lot of extra work for us, as the depot staff have to unload the undelivered food and make alternative arrangements for delivery'.

At this point the Head of Customer Services added, 'The points being raised here would support the findings from some recent customer research that I carried out. A number of customers have started to complain about the service they receive from us, with one vocal customer stating 'I have used FF for a number of years, however the fact that I cannot specify a delivery time to fit around my work commitments simply means I can no longer use this service. I have recently started using the home delivery service of a well known supermarket due to the flexibility this offers'. Another, customer said 'I am sick of waiting for my delivery to turn up only for it not to turn up at all. When I contact FF I get told that my delivery driver was held up in traffic and that my delivery will be dispatched again the following week'. The Head of Customer Service finished by highlighting the key findings from a business news article he had read. 'This article mentioned something called 'Big Data' and 'Big Data Analytics'. The journalist seemed to suggest that the widening use of data has now become as important as the internet has become in modern business. I wonder if this could help us here at FF?'.

Intrigued by the Head of Customer Service's suggestion, Russell Beaumont has contacted a firm of business advisors to prepare a report on the role of Big Data and its potential use at FF.

Required

Acting as a consultant write a report to Russell Beaumont which outlines the following:

(a)   Briefly discuss what is meant by the term 'Big Data'.   **(4 marks)**

(b)   Explain how the management at FF could make use of Big Data and Big Data analytics to improve the company's performance.   **(13 marks)**

(c)   Discuss the practical implications that FF would need to consider before attempting to capture more data about its customers.   **(8 marks)**

(Total = 25 marks)

19 The BA Times (12/13)   **45 mins**

The country of Umboria has two professional business analysis associations, both running certification examination schemes for business analysts worldwide. These are the Association of Benefits Consultants (ABC) and the Institute of Consultants, Finance and Commerce (ICFC). Many private and public sector learning providers run accredited training courses to prepare candidates for the examinations. Some learning providers provide courses for both associations, whilst others focus on niche markets. Umboria itself is a wealthy country with high labour costs and property prices, particularly in the capital city of Ambosium.

Victor is the editor of the *BA Times*, a subscription magazine, published once a month, which provides news and articles preparing students for the examinations of both business analysis associations. The magazine is edited and printed in offices and an adjoining factory in Ambosium. The offices and factory are leased and the magazine currently employs 20 people, all of whom live close to the offices. It is the only independent magazine in the sector. Each association has its own magazine and website, but relatively tight control is maintained over their editorial policy. Victor was the editor of the ABC magazine (*Business Analysis Today*) for 16 years before establishing the *BA Times* nine years ago. Because of its independence, the *BA Times* can be a little more controversial and provocative than its rivals and it is popular with students and well respected by the profession.

However, despite such recognition, the magazine is currently unprofitable due to increased production, distribution and office costs, falling subscriptions and reduced advertising. Changing reading habits in Umboria, particularly amongst the young, has led to less reading of printed media. All of the traditional media providers are experiencing financial problems. The sales of printed magazines and the profits of publishers are both falling dramatically throughout Umboria. Furthermore, advertisers are increasingly unconvinced about the effectiveness of advertising in printed magazines and so the advertising revenues of these magazines are also falling.

The *BA Times* currently has a website but its role is to convince the visitor to order the printed magazine. The website offers extracts of news and articles, often with provocative headlines, which may only be read in full in the printed magazine.

Recent survey

A recent survey of people who had decided not to renew their *BA Times* subscription revealed the following comments:

I am studying the ABC syllabus and so in-depth articles on ICFC topics and examinations are not relevant to me. I quite enjoy reading the news parts, but not the in-depth analysis of examinations that I am not taking.

ABC student

I have reached the final stage of my examinations. I do not want to read articles about the stages I have already passed. I reckon only about 15% of *BA Times* is relevant to me now. *ABC Final Stage student*

Some of the readers' letters are really irritating or just plain wrong, but the editor seldom makes a comment! It really annoys me! *ICFC student*

I became a business analyst to get a job, not just to sit examinations and read about examining bodies.

ICFC student

The examinations are getting more demanding and Victor is under pressure to increase the number of technical examination articles in the magazine, despite the fact that this will make the magazine longer and heavier and so increase print and distribution costs.

Victor is aware that new technology and new media offer opportunities for changing the business model and the financial performance of the *BA Times*. However, he likes the physical, tactile feel of printed magazines and he feels that some of his subscribers do as well. Also, he cannot see how harnessing new technology will make him money, particularly if it leads to decreasing sales of the printed magazine. He is also concerned about how his subscribers and advertisers will react to technological change. He feels that some subscribers will not have access to online technology and that many advertisers would prefer to continue with display advertisements in a printed magazine.

Required

(a) Analyse how the principles of interactivity, individualisation, intelligence and independence of location offered by the internet and other new media could be exploited by Victor in his development of a new business model for the *BA Times*. **(15 marks)**

(b) Write a short report which addresses the specific concerns Victor has about the effect of any potential technology or media change on his subscribers, on his advertisers and on the financial viability of his company. **(10 marks)**

(Total = 25 marks)

20 Housham Garden (12/13) 45 mins

Housham Garden is a large garden in the country of Euphorbia, where gardening and visiting gardens is a popular pastime. For many years the garden was neglected, until bought by the Popper family who painstakingly restored the garden and four years ago opened it to the public. The garden is now owned and operated by a charitable trust set up by the Popper family – the Housham Garden Trust (HGT) – with initial funding provided by a legacy from the late Clive Popper.

However, HGT is finding it difficult to meet its costs and it is gradually spending the legacy. It is estimated that fixed costs are currently $60,000 per annum. The price of entry into the garden is $5 per visit. At present, there are approximately 1,000 visits per month and the garden is open for eight months a year. It is closed for a period when the weather is usually much colder and few plants are flowering. HGT feels that few people would wish to visit the garden and so they have always closed it for the four 'cold' months.

There is a café in the garden and it is estimated that 60% of visitors visit the café and buy drinks and food. However, each purchase is relatively modest. The current trust administrator estimates that the average contribution is $1.25 per visitor using the café.

A recent survey undertaken by a local university revealed that most consumers felt that the admission price for a garden such as Housham was too high. It revealed that the average consumer would be willing to pay an entry fee of $3.25, and indeed similar gardens in Euphorbia charge about this amount.

HGT currently advertises the garden in the monthly magazine *Heritage Gardens*. Each display advertisement costs $500 per issue. Adverts have been booked for the next six months, but it is possible to cancel the last three of these without incurring cancellation charges. The advertisements, like HGT's brochure, stress the historical nature of the garden (it is the only surviving garden designed by William Wessex) and the painstaking nature of the restoration. However, these were not factors that figured highly in a recent visitor survey. Table 1 shows the most common primary reasons for visitors visiting the garden. 200 visitors were surveyed and they were only allowed to choose one reason for visiting Housham Gardens.

Table 1: Primary reasons for visiting the gardens: one day survey on 13 March 2012

Reason for visiting Housham Garden	Number of respondents
To walk in a peaceful, beautiful, safe environment	100
To enjoy the plants and flowers of the garden	70
To see the restoration work carried out by the trust	20
To visit the café and shop	5
To observe the work of William Wessex	5

Respondents were critical of the food offered by the café. One respondent commented that quality 'had gone down since the café was moved into the garden. Really, there is very little choice, and I could not find anything substantial enough for lunch'. Her reference to the relocation of the café into the garden refers to the fact that the café used to be in the gatehouse of the garden. At this time, many people just visited Housham to use the café and did not pay for admission into the garden. It was decided that moving the café inside the garden would encourage people to pay for garden entry. However, this has not occurred. It is estimated that the café has lost about 500 visits per month and this has had an adverse effect on staff morale and food quality. The gatehouse area where the café was originally situated is still empty.

In the recent consumer survey, 20% of the respondents said that they would buy an annual (calendar year) ticket giving access to the garden for eight months if it were offered for $9. The customer survey also asked visitors where they had heard of the garden. Table 2 summarises their responses. Again, the 200 respondents were only allowed to make one choice for how they heard about Housham Gardens.

Table 2: How visitors heard about the gardens: one day survey on 13 March 2012

How did you hear of Housham Gardens?	Number of respondents
Personal recommendation from a friend	110
Recent articles in the local newspaper	50
Internet	10
Heritage Gardens magazine	10
Other	20

The reference in Table 2 to recent articles in the local newspaper concerns a series of articles written by the HGT administrator outlining the problems of the trust and the fact that short-term cash flow problems might cause the garden's temporary closure. One visitor commented that 'we had never heard of Housham Gardens until then, and we only live four kilometres away'.

HGT also has a simple informative website showing the location of the garden, giving opening times, showing pictures of the restoration and providing a biography of William Wessex. You are a business analyst who undertakes voluntary work for the trust. You have been asked to suggest immediate short-term changes as well as long-term marketing initiatives for the trust. Short-term changes should be proposals which can be implemented immediately or within three months and will generate quantifiable income or savings. Long-term marketing initiatives are proposals which will take longer than three months to implement.

Required

(a)   Using the data provided, show why HGT is losing money and recommend immediate and other short-term (within three months) changes for HGT, quantifying the increased income or cost savings that these changes should bring.

(15 marks)

(b)   Recommend, with justifications, longer-term marketing strategies (longer than three months) for HGT.

(10 marks)

(Total = 25 marks)

21 iTTrain (06/14)

45 mins

For 11 years, Marco was a senior salesman at AQT, a company specialising in IT certification courses. During that time, AQT became the most successful and dominant training provider in the market.

Marco has now left AQT and established his own training company, iTTrain, aimed at the same IT certification market as his former employers. He wishes to offer premium quality courses in a high quality environment with high quality teaching. He has selected a number of self-employed lecturers and he has agreed a daily lecturing fee of $450 per day with them. He has also selected the prestigious CityCentre training centre as his course venue. It has a number of training rooms which hold up to nine delegates. Each training room costs $250 per day to hire. There is also a $10 per day per delegate charge for lunch and other refreshments. Although not a lecturer, Marco is an IT expert and he has already produced the relevant documentation for the courses iTTrain will run. He sees this as a sunk cost and is not concerned about recovering it. However, printing costs mean that there is also a $20 cost for the course manual which is given to every course delegate.

Marco has scheduled 40 courses next year, as he is limited by the availability of lecturers. Each course will have a maximum of nine delegates (determined by the room size) and a minimum of three delegates. Each course is three days long.

iTTrain has been set up with $70,000 of Marco's own money. He currently estimates that fixed annual costs will be $65,000 (which includes his own salary) and he would like the company to return a modest profit in its first year of operation as it establishes itself in the market.

Marco is currently considering the price he wishes to charge for his courses. AQT charges $900 per delegate for a three-day course, but he knows that it discounts this by up to 10% and a similar discount is also offered to training brokers or intermediaries who advertise AQT courses on their own websites. Some of these intermediaries have already been in touch with Marco to ask if he would be prepared to offer them similar discounts in return for iTTrain courses being advertised on their websites. There are also a number of cheaper training providers who offer the same courses for as little as $550 per delegate. However, these tend to focus on self-financing candidates for whom price is an issue. These courses are often given in poor quality training premises by poorly motivated lecturers. Marco is not really interested in this market. He wants to target the corporate business market, where quality is as important as price and the course fee is paid by the delegate's employer. He is currently considering a price of $750 per delegate.

During his employment at AQT, Marco collected statistics about courses and delegates. Figure 1 shows the data he collected showing the attendance pattern over 1,000 courses.

Number of delegates attending the course	Number of courses
3	150
4	210
5	250
6	190
7	70
8	80
9	50
Total	**1,000**

Figure 1: Analysis of attendance at 1,000 AQT courses

Required

(a) Suggest a pricing strategy for iTTrain, including an evaluation of the initial price of $750 per delegate suggested by Marco. Your strategy should include both financial and non-financial considerations.

(16 marks)

(b) Physical evidence, people and process are three important elements of the marketing mix for services.

Analyse the contribution each of these three elements could make to the success of iTTrain's entry into the IT certification market.

(9 marks)

(Total = 25 marks)

22 BeauCo

45 mins

BeauCo is a medium sized manufacturer of specialist computer components. The market has become particularly competitive in recent years, with competitors vying to sell products to large blue chip organisations. BeauCo's operations are heavily dependent on IT. Production materials are purchased through the company's state of the art online procurement and inventory management systems, and all sales are made via the company's website. A back-up of all information stored across BeauCo's IT systems is taken every three months.

Component parts department

BeauCo pays engineers working in the component parts department a generous salary. This is due to the specialist nature of the work undertaken and long hours worked. Frequently engineers are required to work overtime in order to meet customer orders. During the company's most recent board meeting, BeauCo's managing director Thomas Gethings revealed a fraud that had been uncovered by the assistant head of human resources.

Fraud

The fraud was carried out by two employees. Alice Perkin, the payroll officer, had recently been left in charge of the payroll department as the payroll supervisor was on maternity leave. The payroll supervisor always reviewed and signed off the payroll data produced by Alice prior to finance releasing payments. Due to the supervisor's absence, Alice had taken over both roles.

Adam Thomas, operations manager of the component parts department was responsible for producing and authorising the overtime worked by the engineers each month. He would send Alice the approved monthly overtime figures to enter onto the payroll system.

BeauCo's human resources department maintains standing data on all employees. The standing data is updated when an employee joins or leaves the organisation. This data contains each employee's personal bank details used by the finance department in paying the monthly staff salaries. The assistant head of human resources was designated to update the standing data stored on her computer. Late one evening, Alice was able to access the data where she added three fictitious engineers with the same bank account details. The human resources department had disabled the required security settings on all computers as many in the department regarded the need to continually update their passwords to be too cumbersome.

In a bid to improve security on site all internal doors leading to areas containing confidential information, including finance and human resources, had been fitted with a pass code entry system. To gain access, authorised staff were required to enter a four digit code to unlock the doors. Due to early glitches with the system, all internal entrances had been left unlocked.

Adam submitted false overtime claims to the payroll department in respect of the fictitious employees. Using the company's payroll processing system Alice was able to put through significant monthly payments per rogue employee.

Initially, a member of the finance department queried the sudden rise in overtime payments with Adam, who downplayed the concern, exclaiming that 'the overtime had been needed to meet a shortage of staff'. No further action was taken. Company policy requires that significant deviations in staff costs should be taken up with the head of production prior to payments being made.

As a result Alice and Adam were able to amass a significant amount of additional pay, which was received into a new bank account operated by both fraudsters. The fraud was uncovered five months later when the assistant head of HR conducted a review of the standing data and noticed the three fictitious employees entered all had the same bank account details.

IT review

In response, Thomas Gethings ordered a full review of the company's IT and information systems to ensure that a similar event does not occur again. To support the board an external IT consultancy firm has been approached to recommend improvements to help safeguard BeauCo's IT systems and processes. During one meeting with the BeauCo board one consultant made reference to the importance of continuity planning and disaster recovery.

Required

(a) Analyse the adequacy of BeauCo's internal control processes. (You should give particular consideration to the IT controls and payroll processes in place at the company and suggest practical recommendations on how these could be improved.)

(16 marks)

(b) The board of BeauCo would like to gain a better understanding of the terms continuity planning and disaster recovery. Acting as an IT consultant advise the board why both continuity planning and disaster recovery activities are likely to be significant to BeauCo.

(9 marks)

(Total = 25 marks)

23 Finch Co

45 mins

The company

Finch Co is a national grocery retailer, consisting of 230 stores throughout the country. The company has a strong reputation for selling quality food and drink products, supported by excellent standards of customer service. The company is regarded as a relatively small player in the market. Finch Co has a loyal customer and staff base, and many employees have worked for the company for a number of years.

Historically, the company has limited its use of IT in its operations. The company does have a small IT team based at head office. The current information system allows for weekly sales reports to be generated per store. All inventory ordering for stores is done manually at head office. Six years ago Finch Co developed its first website. The site offered basic information such as opening times and store locations.

Trading conditions

In recent years Finch Co has suffered from a drop in profits and seen its market share fall. The CEO, Andrew Finch, identified rising store costs and technological developments by competitors as being the two main causes behind the company's dip in performance. In response, two years ago he established a project to generate proposals to address the company's declining performance. The project was overseen by a project committee consisting of the CEO, Operations Director, and the Customer Service Director – none of whom had been involved in any similar projects in the past.

Project proposals

The project committee agreed to the implementation of two new systems without delay.

New checkout system

The first new system saw Finch Co scrap its staffed checkouts in all of its stores and introduce a 'state of the art' scanner system. As a result, a significant number of the company's checkout operators have been made redundant. The scanner system works by allowing shoppers to scan product barcodes using a hand-held scanning device as they pass around the store. Once scanned these items can then be placed in the shopper's trolley. At the checkout, the customer then attaches the device to a small docking port which downloads the scanned items, removing the need to physically move items from the trolley to conveyor belt. The customer then pays for their items using a self-service payment function. To reduce the scope for product theft, where items are put in a trolley without being scanned, the retained checkout operators have been assigned to assisting customers download their scanned items at the checkouts. Andrew Finch believes this should help deter customers from leaving the store without paying for all of the items in the trolley as staff should be able to clearly identify such disparities between the downloaded data and the physical items in the trolley or basket.

The project committee were particularly attracted by the hardware suppliers promise that the new system would on average cut the amount of time customers spend queuing at the checkout from 5 minutes to 2 minutes. Andrew Finch decided to limit amount of training all store staff would receive regarding the usage of the scanner system before the it went live, insisting that 'staff learn best by simply getting stuck in and learning as they go'.

The new system can generate 'real time' sales reports per store and has been integrated into the company's inventory ordering system to remove the need for manual ordering.

'Click and collect'

The second development introduced was based upon systems which are already used by Finch Co's competitors. A 'click and collect' feature was added to Finch Co's existing website. The system allowed shoppers to order goods online to be collected from their nearest store arranged at a time to suit. All stores have been fitted with a new customer service counter where customers collect their orders at the designated time slot. Prior to the implementation of the service, the Operations Director anticipated online orders to be in the region of 3,000 orders each month per store.

Unveiling the developments to Finch Co's store staff, Andrew Finch stated that 'the new systems represent a bold move for our company. For too long we have believed that the key to our success was only selling good quality products. The world has moved on and we need to evolve if we are to remain a competitive player. Customers now expect more from us, convenience is what people want. If we don't adapt, our customers will shop with our rivals. I hope you will all get behind these changes and support each other through this time'.

Post-implementation

Since the introduction of the new systems, things have not gone smoothly. Finch Co has seen a dramatic increase in the number of customer complaints it receives.

A significant number of customers have complained about not understanding how the in-store scanner system operates. This has caused delays at the checkouts, with many customers queuing up the aisles to pay for their goods. Store managers have complained that some loyal shoppers have started to walk out of the store when noticing the growing queues. One comment left on an online shopping forum claimed that 'customers were struggling to connect the scanners to the checkout. When I asked a member of staff for help he just looked at me blankly and said I'm not too sure, I only had 10 minutes training this morning'.

Actual orders through the 'click and collect' service have been much higher than anticipated. On average 8,000 orders each month per store have been received since the system went live. This has resulted in numerous cases of online orders not being ready when due for collection. One shop worker complained that 'no one knows what they are doing. I not sure if I am supposed to be stocking items on the shop floor or preparing click and collect orders for collection or helping customers with the scanners. It's a mess.'

Required

(a)   In support of the CEO's comments that Finch Co needs to evolve and adapt to remain competitive, evaluate why the new systems are necessary in helping Finch Co to address the issue of strategic alignment.

(7 marks)

(b)   Using the four views model as a framework, evaluate the extent to which these four views led to the failure of the new systems.

(18 marks)

(Total = 25 marks)

24 Chemical Transport (6/13)   45 mins

Chemical Transport (CT) is a specialist haulage company providing transport services for several chemical wholesalers. Despite these wholesalers being in competition with each other, many of them have outsourced their distribution to CT, recognising the company's expertise in this area and its compliance with stringent and emerging legislation. This legislation is at both national and international level and concerns the transportation and handling of chemicals, as well as the maintenance of trucks and trailers and the health, competencies, safety and driving hours of drivers. There are also chemical wholesalers in the country who either organise their own distribution or outsource to one of CT's competitors.

CT handles the distribution of chemicals from either the port of importation or point of production to the wholesaler's depots or directly to the end customers of the wholesaler. The chemical wholesalers are increasingly attempting to minimise their own storage costs, so many of CT's deliveries are now directly from the point of production (or port of importation) to the end customer. Most of these end customers are manufacturing companies with limited chemical storage capacity.

The complex and changing nature of legislation has led to CT engaging a specialist legal consultancy to provide it with advice. They have found this advice to be both useful and proactive. The consultancy has identified the potential effect of employment, tax and health and safety legislation in advance and has notified CT of its likely implications. CT has benefited from this advice but it is concerned that it is expensive and it is considering employing a full-time legal expert, instead of using the legal consultancy.

The chemical wholesalers have asked CT to provide an internet-based system which would allow them to request and track deliveries. CT does currently have a website, but it only contains information about the company: its structures, history, key contacts and case studies. CT has agreed to provide such a system because it is aware that failure to do so will lead to wholesalers looking for an alternative distributor. CT does have an internal IT capability with some expertise in building web-based systems.

The internal IT team have also developed a bespoke payroll system. Drivers at CT are rewarded with basic pay, together with a complex set of bonuses and deductions which have been developed and enhanced over the last few years. There are bonuses for certain skills and attainments and deductions for missed or delayed deliveries or mistakes. The drivers themselves find the pay arrangements very confusing. One commented that 'we find it almost impossible to check if we have been paid correctly and it confuses us rather than motivates us!' Changes in national tax legislation are also continually affecting the payroll calculation. Indeed, recent changes in legislation led to the IT team being fully occupied for three months, developing and testing the required modifications to the payroll system.

Required

(a)   Three significant business process areas have been identified in the scenario: (1) payroll, (2) legal advice and (3) an enhanced web service allowing wholesalers to request and track deliveries.

        Use Harmon's process-strategy matrix to analyse the characteristics of each of the three process areas defined above and suggest how each should be sourced and implemented at CT.   **(15 marks)**

(b)   Requesting and tracking information could be the first part of a comprehensive customer relationship management (CRM) system.

        Evaluate how CT could use a CRM system to acquire and retain customers.   **(10 marks)**

        (Total = 25 marks)

25 DRB (Pilot Paper)   45 mins

DRB Electronic Services operates in a high labour cost environment in Western Europe and imports electronic products from the Republic of Korea. It re-brands and re-packages them as DRB products and then sells them to business and domestic customers in the local geographical region. Its only current source of supply is ISAS electronics based in a factory on the outskirts of Seoul, the capital of the Republic of Korea. DRB regularly places orders for ISAS products through the ISAS website and pays for them by credit card. As soon as the payment is confirmed ISAS automatically e-mails DRB a confirmation of order, an order reference number and likely shipping date. When the order is actually despatched, ISAS send DRB a notice of despatch e-mail and a container reference number. ISAS currently organises all the shipping of the products. The products are sent in containers and then trans-shipped to EIF, the logistics company used by ISAS to distribute its products. EIF then delivers the products to the DRB factory. Once they arrive, they are quality inspected and products that pass the inspection are re-branded as DRB products (by adding appropriate logos) and packaged in specially fabricated DRB boxes. These products are then stored ready for sale. All customer sales are from stock. Products that fail the inspection are returned to ISAS.

Currently 60% of sales are made to domestic customers and 40% to business customers. Most domestic customers pick up their products from DRB and set them up themselves. In contrast, most business customers ask DRB to set up the electronic equipment at their offices, for which DRB makes a small charge. DRB currently advertises its products in local and regional newspapers. DRB also has a website which provides product details. Potential customers can enquire about the specification and availability of products through an email facility in the website. DRB then e-mails an appropriate response directly to the person making the enquiry. Payment for products cannot currently be made through the website.

Feedback from existing customers suggests that they particularly value the installation and support offered by the company. The company employs specialist technicians who (for a fee) will install equipment in both homes and offices. They will also come out and troubleshoot problems with equipment that is still under warranty. DRB also offer a helpline and a back to base facility for customers whose products are out of warranty. Feedback from current customers suggests that this support is highly valued. One commented that 'it contrasts favourably with your large customers who offer support through impersonal off-shore call centres and a time-consuming returns policy'. Customers can also pay for technicians to come on-site to sort out problems with out-of-warranty equipment.

DRB now plans to increase their product range and market share. It plans to grow from its current turnover of £5m per annum to £12m per annum in two years' time. Dilip Masood, the owner of DRB, believes that DRB must change its business model if it is to achieve this growth. He believes that these changes will also have to tackle problems associated with:

- Missing, or potentially missing shipments. Shipments can only be tracked through contacting the shipment account holder, ISAS, and on occasions they have been reluctant or unable to help. The trans-shipment to EIF has also caused problems and this has usually been identified as the point where goods have been lost. ISAS does not appear to be able to reliably track the relationship between the container shipment and the Waybills used in the EIF system.

- The likely delivery dates of orders, the progress of orders and the progress of shipments is poorly specified and monitored. Hence deliveries are relatively unpredictable and this can cause congestion problems in the delivery bay.

Dilip also recognises that growth will mean that the company has to sell more products outside its region and the technical installation and support so valued by local customers will be difficult to maintain. He is also adamant that DRB will continue to import only fully configured products. It is not interested in importing components and assembling them. DRB also does not wish to build or invest in assembly plants overseas or to commit to a long-term contract with one supplier.

Required

(a) Draw the primary activities of DRB on a value chain. Comment on the significance of each of these activities and the value that they offer to customers. **(9 marks)**

(b) Explain how DRB might re-structure its upstream supply chain to achieve the growth required by DRB and to tackle the problems that Dilip Masood has identified. **(10 marks)**

(c) Explain how DRB might re-structure its downstream supply chain to achieve the growth required. **(6 marks)**

(Total = 25 marks)

26 Perfect Shopper (12/07)   45 mins

Local neighbourhood shops are finding it increasingly difficult to compete with supermarkets. However, three years ago, the *Perfect Shopper* franchise group was launched that allowed these neighbourhood shops to join the group and achieve cost savings on tinned and packaged goods, particularly groceries. *Perfect Shopper* purchases branded goods in bulk from established food suppliers and stores them in large purpose-built warehouses, each designed to serve a geographical region. When *Perfect Shopper* was established it decided that deliveries to these warehouses should be made by the food suppliers or by haulage contractors working on behalf of these suppliers. *Perfect Shopper* places orders with these suppliers and the supplier arranges the delivery to the warehouse. These arrangements are still in place. *Perfect Shopper* has no branded goods of its own.

Facilities are available in each warehouse to re-package goods into smaller units, more suitable for the requirements of the neighbourhood shop. These smaller units, typically containing 50–100 tins or packs, are usually small trays, sealed with strong transparent polythene. *Perfect Shopper* delivers these to its neighbourhood shops using specialist haulage contractors local to the regional warehouse. *Perfect Shopper* has negotiated significant discounts with suppliers, part of which it passes on to its franchisees. A recent survey in a national grocery magazine showed that franchisees saved an average of 10% on the prices they would have paid if they had purchased the products directly from the manufacturer or from an intermediary – such as cash and carry wholesalers.

As well as offering savings due to bulk buying, *Perfect Shopper* also provides, as part of its franchise:

(a) Personalised promotional material. This usually covers specific promotions and is distributed locally, either using specialist leaflet distributors or loosely inserted into local free papers or magazines.

(b)   Specialised signage for the shops to suggest the image of a national chain. The signs include the *Perfect Shopper* slogan 'the nation's local'.

(c)   Specialist in-store display units for certain goods, again branded with the *Perfect Shopper* logo.

Perfect Shopper does not provide all of the goods required by a neighbourhood shop. Consequently, it is not an exclusive franchise. Franchisees agree to purchase specific products through *Perfect Shopper*, but other goods, such as vegetables, fruit, stationery and newspapers they source from elsewhere. Deliveries are made every two weeks to franchisees using a standing order for products agreed between the franchisee and their *Perfect Shopper* sales representative at a meeting they hold every three months. Variations to this order can be made by telephone, but only if the order is increased. Downward variations are not allowed. Franchisees cannot reduce their standing order requirements until the next meeting with their representative.

Perfect Shopper was initially very successful, but its success has been questioned by a recent independent report that showed increasing discontent amongst franchisees. The following issues were documented.

(a)   The need to continually review prices to compete with supermarkets

(b)   Low brand recognition of *Perfect Shopper*

(c)   Inflexible ordering and delivery system based around forecasts and restricted ability to vary orders (see above)

As a result of this survey, *Perfect Shopper* has decided to review its business model. Part of this review is to re-examine the supply chain, to see if there are opportunities for addressing some of its problems.

Required

(a)   Describe the primary activities of the value chain of *Perfect Shopper*.   **(5 marks)**

(b)   Explain how *Perfect Shopper* might re-structure its upstream supply chain to address the problems identified in the scenario.   **(10 marks)**

(c)   Explain how *Perfect Shopper* might re-structure its downstream supply chain to address the problems identified in the scenario.   **(10 marks)**

(Total = 25 marks)

27 Independent Living (12/09)   **45 mins**

Introduction

IL (Independent Living) is a charity that provides living aids to help elderly and disabled people live independently in their own home. These aids include walkers, wheelchairs, walking frames, crutches, mobility scooters, bath lifts and bathroom and bedroom accessories.

IL aims to employ people who would find it difficult or impossible to work in a conventional office or factory. IL's charitable aim is to provide the opportunity for severely disabled people to 'work with dignity and achieve financial independence'. IL currently employs 200 severely disabled people and 25 able bodied people at its premises on an old disused airfield site. The former aircraft hangars have been turned into either production or storage facilities, all of which have been adapted for severely disabled people.

Smaller items (such as walking frames and crutches) are manufactured here. These are relatively unsophisticated products, manufactured from scrap metal bought from local scrap metal dealers and stored on-site. These products require no testing or training to use and they are packaged and stored after manufacture. IL uses its own lorry to make collections of scrap metal but the lorry is old, unreliable and will soon need replacing.

Larger and more complex items (such as mobility scooters and bath lifts) are bought in bulk from suppliers and stored in the hangars. Delivery of these items to IL is organised by their manufacturers. These products are stored until they are ordered. When an order is received for such products, the product is unpacked and tested. An IL transfer logo is then applied and the product is re-packaged in the original packing material with an IL label attached. It is then dispatched to the customer. Some inventory is never ordered and last year IL had to write-off a significant amount of obsolete inventory.

All goods are sold at cost plus a margin to cover wages and administrative costs. Prices charged are the same whether goods are ordered over the web or by telephone. Customers can also make a further voluntary donation to help support IL if they wish to. About 30% of customers do make such a donation.

Ordering and marketing

IL markets its products by placing single-sided promotional leaflets in hospitals, doctors' surgeries and local social welfare departments. This leaflet provides information about IL and gives a direct phone number and a web address. Customers may purchase products by ringing IL directly or by ordering over their website. The website provides product information and photos of the products which are supplied by IL. It also has a secure payment facility. However, customers who ring IL directly have to discuss product requirements and potential purchases with sales staff over the phone. Each sales discussion takes, on average, ten minutes and only one in two contacts results in a sale. 20% of sales are through their website (up from 15% last year), but many of their customers are unfamiliar with the Internet and do not have access to it.

Goods are delivered to customers by a national courier service. Service and support for the bought-in products (mobility scooters, bath lifts) are supplied by the original manufacturer.

Commercial competitors

IL is finding it increasingly difficult to compete with commercial firms offering independent living aids. Last year, the charity made a deficit of $160,000, and it had to sell some of its airfield land to cover this. Many of the commercial firms it is competing with have sophisticated sales and marketing operations and then arrange delivery to customers directly from manufacturers based in low labour cost countries.

Required

IL fears for its future and has decided to review its value chain to see how it can achieve competitive advantage.

(a)   Analyse the primary activities of the value chain for the product range at IL.   **(10 marks)**

(b)   Evaluate what changes IL might consider to the primary activities in the value chain to improve their competitiveness, whilst continuing to meet their charitable objectives.   **(15 marks)**

(Total = 25 marks)

28 Accounting Education Consortium (6/08)   45 mins

Introduction

The Accounting Education Consortium (AEC) offers professional accountancy education and training courses. It currently runs classroom-based training courses preparing candidates for professional examinations in eight worldwide centres. Three of these centres are also used for delivering continuing professional development (CPD) courses to qualified accountants. However, only about 30% of the advertised CPD courses and seminars actually run. The rest are cancelled through not having enough participants to make them economically viable.

AEC has developed a comprehensive set of course manuals to support the preparation of its candidates for professional examinations. There is a course manual for every examination paper in the professional examination scheme. As well as being used on its classroom-based courses, these course manuals are also available for purchase over the Internet. The complete set of manuals for a professional examinations scheme costs $180.00 and the website has a secure payment facility which allows this to be paid by credit card. Once purchased, the manuals may be downloaded or they may be sent on a CD to the home address of the purchaser. It is only possible to purchase the complete set of manuals for the scheme, not individual manuals for particular examinations. To help the student decide if he or she wishes to buy the complete manual set, the website has extracts from a sample course manual. This sample may be accessed, viewed and printed once a student has registered their email address, name and address on the website.

AEC has recently won a contract to supply professional accountancy training to a global accounting company. All students working for this company will now be trained by AEC at one of its worldwide centres.

Website

The AEC website has the following functionality:

Who we are: A short description of the company and its products and services.

Professional education courses: Course dates, locations and standard fees for professional examination courses. This schedule of courses is printable.

Continuing professional development: Course dates, locations and standard fees for CPD courses and seminars. This schedule is also printable.

CPD catalogue: Detailed course and seminar descriptions for CPD courses and seminars.

Downloadable study material: Extracts from a sample course manual. Visitors to the site wishing to access this material must register their email address, name and address. 5,500 people registered last year to download study material.

Purchase study material: Secure purchase of a complete manual set for the professional scheme. Payment is by credit card. On completion of successful payment, the visitor is able to download the manuals or to request them to be shipped to a certain address on a CD. At present, 10% of the people who view downloadable study material proceed to purchase.

Who to contact: Who to contact for booking professional training courses or CPD courses and seminars. It provides the name, email address, fax number, telephone number and address of a contact at each of the eight worldwide centres.

Marketing strategy

The marketing manager of AEC has traditionally used magazines, newspapers and direct mail to promote its courses and products. Direct mail is primarily used for sending printed course catalogues to potential customers for CPD courses and seminars. However, she is now keen to develop the potential of the Internet and to increase investment in this medium at the expense of the traditional marketing media. Table 1 shows the percentage allocation of her budget for 2008, compared with 2007. The actual budget has only been increased by 3% in 2008.

Table 1

Percentage allocation of marketing budget (2007–2008)

	2008	2007
Advertising	30%	40%
Direct mail	10%	30%
Sponsorship	10%	10%
Internet	50%	20%

Required

(a)   Explain, in the context of AEC, how the marketing characteristics of electronic media (such as the Internet) differ from those of traditional marketing media such as advertising and direct mail.   **(10 marks)**

(b)   Evaluate how the marketing manager might use electronic marketing (including the Internet) to vary the marketing mix at AEC.   **(15 marks)**

(Total = 25 marks)

29 ATD (12/13)   45 mins

ATD is a medium-sized engineering company providing specialist components for the marine engineering market. The sales manager is currently under pressure from the other departmental managers to explain why his sales revenue forecasts are becoming increasingly unreliable. Errors in his forecasts are having consequential effects on production, inventory control, raw materials purchasing and, ultimately, on the profitability of the company itself. He uses a 'combination of experience, intuition and guesswork' to produce his sales forecast, but even he accepts that his forecasts are increasingly inaccurate.

Consequently, he has asked a business analyst to investigate more rigorous, appropriate ways of forecasting. The business analyst has suggested two possible alternatives. The first (summarised in Figure 1) is least squares regression. The second (summarised in Figure 2) is time series analysis. The actual sales figures in both of these examples are for ATD, so the company is currently in quarter 3 – 2013. However, the business analyst has left the company before completing and explaining either the basis for, or implications of, these two alternative approaches to forecasting.

Figure 1: Least squares analysis

Year/quarter	Quarter	Sales ($'000)			
	x	y	x2	xy	y2
2010 quarter 1	1	110	1	110	12,100
2010 quarter 2	2	160	4	320	25,600
2010 quarter 3	3	155	9	465	24,025
2010 quarter 4	4	96	16	384	9,216
2011 quarter 1	5	116	25	580	13,456
2011 quarter 2	6	160	36	960	25,600
2011 quarter 3	7	153	49	1,071	23,409
2011 quarter 4	8	100	64	800	10,000
2012 quarter 1	9	128	81	1,152	16,384
2012 quarter 2	10	180	100	1,800	32,400
2012 quarter 3	11	169	121	1,859	28,561
2012 quarter 4	12	99	144	1,188	9,801
2013 quarter 1	13	137	169	1,781	18,769
2013 quarter 2	14	180	196	2,520	32,400
		1,943	1,015	14,990	281,721
			b	1.84	
			a	125.02	
			r	0.253	

The equation of a straight line is y = a + bx

Figure 2: Time series analysis

Quarter	Sales ($'000)	Trend	Deviation	Svar (1)	Residual	Sadj (2)
2010 quarter 1	110					124.70
2010 quarter 2	160					127.77
2010 quarter 3	155	131.00	24.00	22.55	1.45	132.45
2010 quarter 4	96	131.75	-35.75	-40.08	4.33	136.08
2011 quarter 1	116	131.50	-15.50	-14.70	-0.80	130.70
2011 quarter 2	160	131.75	28.25	32.23	-3.98	127.77
2011 quarter 3	153	133.75	19.25	22.55	-3.30	130.45
2011 quarter 4	100	137.75	-37.75	-40.08	2.33	140.08
2012 quarter 1	128	142.25	-14.25	-14.70	0.45	142.70
2012 quarter 2	180	144.13	35.88	32.23	3.64	147.77
2012 quarter 3	169	145.13	23.88	22.55	1.33	146.45
2012 quarter 4	99	146.25	-47.25	-40.08	-7.17	139.08
2013 quarter 1	137					151.70
2013 quarter 2	180					147.77

	1	2	3	4	
Analysis of seasonal variation			24.00	-35.75	
	-15.50	28.25	19.25	-37.75	
	-14.25	35.88	23.88	-47.25	
Totals	-29.75	64.13	67.13	-120.75	
Average	-14.88	32.06	22.38	-40.25	-0.69
Adjustment	0.17	0.17	0.17	0.17	
Svar (1)	-14.70	32.23	22.55	-40.08	

Note 1: Svar: seasonal variation

Note 2: Sadj: seasonally adjusted figures

The failure of the company to meet sales targets for quarters 1 and 2 of 2013 has prompted the Chief Executive Officer (CEO) to put into place a broad cost-cutting policy. He has banned business travel, cancelled a number of marketing initiatives and introduced a complete freeze on recruiting for posts which become vacant on the resignation of the current post holder. He claims that 'our failure to meet sales targets means we must ruthlessly cut costs'. However, many of the departmental managers are critical of such an indiscriminate approach and believe that the measures might be counter-productive.

This cost-cutting has particularly demotivated the production manager and the inventory manager, who both blame the sales director for setting unrealistic targets. The production manager has commented that, 'I am working tirelessly to keep costs down, but my only reward is that I cannot replace one of my best purchasing administrators who left last month'. In general, departmental managers at the company feel 'powerless and undervalued'.

The company currently does not have a formal budgeting process in place. The production manager is sure that such a process, particularly if senior managers were involved in the budget setting process, would help address issues around forecast reliability, the low morale of departmental managers and the seemingly indiscriminate cost-cutting of the CEO.

Required

(a) Explain and analyse the data in the least squares regression and time series analysis spreadsheets (Figure 1 and 2) left by the business analyst and evaluate the appropriateness of both techniques to sales forecasting at ATD. **(15 marks)**

(b) Analyse how introducing a formal budgeting process would address the issues of inaccurate forecasting, low morale and indiscriminate cost cutting at ATD. **(10 marks)**

(Total = 25 marks)

30 CoolFreeze (Pilot Paper)   45 mins

CoolFreeze construct refrigeration systems for supermarkets, food processing plants, warehouses and other industrial premises. It has a sales forecasting committee consisting of the company's sales manager, procurement manager, production manager and the head of administration. The committee produces annual sales forecasts for the company which they review quarterly. Historically, these forecasts have been reasonably accurate.

In the second quarter of 2009 they revised/produced their estimates for the next four quarters. The predicted unit sales volume and prices are given in Figure 1.

Figure 1: Sales forecast 2009-2010

Year	Quarter	Predicted sales	Predicted sales prices	Revenue
2009	3	81	$1,000	$81,000
	4	69	$1,000	$69,000
2010	1	62	$1,000	$62,000
	2	83	$1,000	$83,000

At the meeting that agreed this forecast the sales manager expressed some doubts about the figures. 'My team are telling me that it is very tough out there. Companies are not replacing old equipment or constructing new plants. Furthermore, cheaper foreign products are becoming available – undercutting our prices by 10%'. Despite these reservations, the sales manager agreed the sales forecasts produced by the committee.

Actual sales performance

The actual sale for the four projected quarters were as follows (Figure 2).

Figure 2: Actual sales 2009-2010

Year	Quarter	Predicted sales	Actual sales
2009	3	81	82
	4	69	68
2010	1	62	61
	2	83	50

The sudden drop in quarter 2 sales caused consternation in the boardroom, particularly as it was a quarter when high demand and profits were anticipated. An analysis of the quarter 2 trading is shown in Figure 3.

The managing director of CoolFreeze has called you in to review the forecasting model used by the sales forecasting team. 'It must be very flawed to go so badly wrong. I have the feeling that the model is not based on a well-accepted approach'. He has obtained a copy of the spreadsheet used by the sales forecasting team (see Figure 4) to help you in your analysis.

The managing director recognizes that the actual quarter 2 performance has to be analysed against the budgeted one. 'I think everyone here has made mistakes – the sales manager, procurement manager, production manager, administration manager. They all have to take responsibility. We are in this together and now we must pull together to get out of this mess'.

Figure 3: Analysis of quarter 2 trading; budget and actual

Quarter 2 – 2010	Budget	Actual
Units	83	50
Revenue	$83,000.00	$45,000.00
Raw materials	($29,050.00)	($15,000.00)
Labour	($26,975.00)	($15,750.00)
Fixed overheads	($18,000.00)	($18,000.00)
Operating profit	$8,975.00	($3,750.00)

Figure 4: Forecasting spreadsheet

A	B	C	D	E	F	G	H	I
Part 1								
Year	Quarter	Units		Trend	Variation	Seasonal	Residual	Check
2006	1	56						
	2	70						
	3	74	524	65.50	8.50	7.35	1.15	74.00
	4	60	538	67.25	-7.25	-4.73	-2.52	60.00
2007	1	60	554	69.25	-9.25	-11.65	2.4	60.00
	2	80	570	71.25	8.75	9.02	-0.27	80.00
	3	80	582	72.75	7.25	7.35	-0.10	80.00
	4	70	586	73.25	-3.25	-4.73	1.48	70.00
2008	1	62	588	73.50	-11.50	-11.65	0.15	62.00
	2	82	588	73.50	8.50	9.02	-0.52	82.00
	3	80	586	73.25	6.75	7.35	-0.60	80.00
	4	70	586	73.25	-3.25	-4.73	1.48	70.00
2009	1	60	590	73.75	-13.75	-11.65	-2.10	60.00
	2	84	590	73.75	10.25	9.02	1.23	84.00
	3	82						
	4	68						

Part 2				
	1	2	3	4
2006			8.50	-7.25
2007	-9.25	8.75	7.25	-3.25
2008	-11.50	8.50	6.75	-3.25
2009	-13.75	10.25		
Total	-34.50	27.50	22.50	-13.75
Average	-11.50	9.17	7.50	-4.58	0.58
Adj	0.15	0.15	0.15	0.15
New Avg	-11.65	9.02	7.35	-4.73	0.00

Forecast				
2009	3	73.50	7.35	**81**
	4	73.50	-4.73	**69**
2010	1	73.65	-11.65	**62**
	2	74.00	9.02	**83**

Required

Write a briefing paper for the managing director that:

(a) Explains and evaluates the spreadsheet used by the sales forecasting team. **(12 marks)**

(b) Analyses the quarter 2 – 2010 performance of CoolFreeze. **(13 marks)**

(Total = 25 marks)

31 Clothing Company (12/07)   **45 mins**

A clothing company sells 40% of its goods directly to customers through its website. The marketing manager of the company (MM) has decided that this is insufficient and has put a small team together to re-design the site. MM feels that the site looks 'amateur and old-fashioned and does not project the right image'. The board of the company has given the go-ahead for the MM 'to re-design the website'. The following notes summarise the outcomes of the meetings on the website re-design. The team consists of the marketing manager (MM), a product range manager (RP), a marketing image consultant (IC) and a technical developer (TD).

Meeting 1: 9 July attended by MM, RP, IC and TD

The need for a re-designed website to increase sales volume through the website and to 'improve our market visibility' was explained by MM. IC was asked to produce a draft design.

Meeting 2: 16 August attended by MM, RP, IC and TD

IC presented a draft design. MM and RP were happy with its image but not its functionality, suggesting that it was too similar to the current site. 'We expected it to do much more' was their view.

Meeting 3: 4 September attended by MM, RP and IC

IC produced a re-drafted design. This overall design was agreed and the go-ahead was given for TD to produce a prototype of the design to show to the board.

Meeting 4: 11 September attended by RP, IC and TD

TD explained that elements of the drafted re-design were not technically feasible to implement in the programming language being used. Changes to the design were agreed at the meeting to overcome these issues and signed off by RP.

Meeting 5: 13 October attended by MM, RP, IC and TD

The prototype re-design was demonstrated by TD. MM was unhappy with the re-design as it was 'moving too far away from the original objective and lacked functionality that should be there'. TD agreed to write a technical report to explain why the original design (agreed on 4 September) could not be adhered to.

Meeting 6: 9 November attended by MM, IC and TD

It was agreed to return to the 4 September design with slight alterations to make it technically feasible. TD expressed concerns that the suggested design would not work properly with all web browsers.

At the board meeting of 9 December the board expressed concern about the time taken to produce the re-design and the finance director highlighted the rising costs (currently $25,000) of the project. They asked MM to produce a formal cost-benefit of the re-design. The board were also concerned that the scope of the project, which they had felt to be about re-design, had somehow been interpreted as including development and implementation.

On 22 December MM produced the following cost-benefit analysis of the project and confirmed that the word 'redesign' had been interpreted as including the development and implementation of the website.

BPP
LEARNING MEDIA

	Year 1	Year 2	Year 3	Year 4	Year 5
Costs	$50,000	$10,000	$10,000	$10,000	$10,000
*Benefits	0	$15,000	$25,000	$35,000	$35,000

*These benefits are extra sales volumes created by the website's extra functionality and the company's increased visibility in the market place.

On 4 January the board gave the go ahead for the development and implementation of the website with a further budget of $25,000 and a delivery date of 1 March. TD expressed concern that he did not have enough developers to deliver the re-designed website on time.

Meeting 7: 24 February attended by MM, RP, IC and TD

A partial prototype system was demonstrated by TD. RP felt that the functionality of the re-design was too limited and that the software was not robust enough. It had crashed twice during the demonstration. He suggested that the company delay the introduction of the re-designed website until it was complete and robust. MM declared this to be impossible.

Conclusion

The re-designed website was launched on 1 March. MM declared the re-design a success that 'had come in on time and under budget'. On 2 and 3 March, numerous complaints were received from customers. The website was unreliable and did not work with a particular popular web browser. On 4 March an emergency board meeting decided to withdraw the site and reinstate the old one. On 5 March, MM resigned.

Required

Most project management methods have an initiation or definition stage which includes the production of a document that serves as an agreement between the sponsors and deliverers of the project. This may be called a project initiation document or a project charter. Defining the business case is also an important part of the initiation or definition stage of the project.

(a)   Explain how a business case and a project initiation document would have helped prevent some of the problems that emerged during the conduct of the website re-design project.   **(15 marks)**

(b)   Analyse how effective project management could have **further** improved both the process and the outcomes of the website re-design project.   **(10 marks)**

(Total = 25 marks)

32 Tillo Community Centre (6/12)   45 mins

Introduction

The country of Mahem is in a long and deep economic recession with unemployment at its highest since the country became an independent nation. In an attempt to stimulate the economy the government has launched a Private/Public investment policy where the government invests in capital projects with the aim of stimulating the involvement of private sector firms. The building of a new community centre in the industrial city of Tillo is an example of such an initiative. Community centres are central to the culture of Mahem. They are designed as places where people can meet socially, local organisations can hold conferences and meetings and farmers can sell their produce to the local community. The centres are seen as contributing to a vibrant community life. The community centre in Tillo is in a sprawling old building rented (at $12,000 per month) from a local landowner. The current community centre is also relatively energy inefficient.

In 2010 a business case was put forward to build a new centre on local authority owned land on the outskirts of Tillo. The costs and benefits of the business case are shown in Figure 1. As required by the Private/Public investment policy the project showed payback during year four of the investment.

All figures in $	Year 1	Year 2	Year 3	Year 4	Year 5
Costs: Initial	600,000				
Costs: Recurring	60,000	60,000	60,000	60,000	60,000
Benefits: Rental savings	144,000	144,000	144,000	144,000	144,000
Benefits: Energy savings	30,000	30,000	30,000	30,000	30,000
Benefits: Increased income	20,000	20,000	70,000	90,000	90,000
Benefits: Better staff morale	25,000	25,000	25,000	25,000	25,000
Cumulative net benefits	(441,000)	(282,000)	(73,000)	156,000	385,000

Figure 1: Costs and benefits of the business case for the community centre at Tillo

New buildings built under the Private/Public investment policy must attain energy level targets and this is the basis for the estimation, above, of the *energy savings*. It is expected that the new centre will attract more customers who will pay for the centre's use as well as increasing the use of facilities such as the cafeteria, shop and business centre. These benefits are estimated, above, under *increased income*. Finally, it is felt that staff will be happier in the new building and their motivation and morale will increase. The centre currently employs 20 staff, 16 of whom have been with the centre for more than five years. All employees were transferred from the old to the new centre. These benefits are shown as *better staff morale* in Figure 1.

Construction of the centre 2010–2011

In October 2010 the centre was commissioned with a planned delivery date of June 2011 at a cost of $600,000 (as per Figure 1). Building the centre went relatively smoothly. Progress was monitored and issues resolved in monthly meetings between the company constructing the centre and representatives of the local authority. These meetings focused on the building of the centre, monitoring progress and resolving issues. Most of these issues were relatively minor because requirements were well specified in standard architectural drawings originally agreed between the project sponsor and the company constructing the centre. Unfortunately, the original project sponsor (an employee of the local authority) who had been heavily involved in the initial design, suffered ill health and died in April 2011. The new project sponsor (again an employee of the local authority) was less enthusiastic about the project and began to raise a number of objections. Her first concern was that the construction company had used sub-contracted labour and had sourced less than 80% of timber used in the building from sustainable resources. She pointed out the contractual terms of supply for the Private/Public policy investment initiatives mandated that sub-contracting was not allowed without the local authority's permission and that at least 80% of the timber used must come from sustainable forests. The company said that this had not been brought to their attention at the start of the project. However, they would try to comply with these requirements for the rest of the contract. The new sponsor also refused to sign off acceptance of the centre because of the poor quality of the internal paintwork. The construction company explained that this was the intended finish quality of the centre and had been agreed with the previous sponsor. They produced a letter to verify this. However, the letter was not counter-signed by the sponsor and so its validity was questioned. In the end, the construction company agreed to improve the internal painting at their own cost. The new sponsor felt that she had delivered 'value for money' by challenging the construction company. Despite this problem with the internal painting, the centre was finished in May 2011 at a cost of $600,000. The centre also included disability access built at the initiative of the construction company. It had found it difficult to find local authority staff willing and able to discuss disability access and so it was therefore left alone to interpret relevant legal requirements. Fortunately, their interpretation was correct and the new centre was deemed, by an independent assessor, to meet accessibility requirements.

Unfortunately, the new centre was not as successful as had been predicted, with income in the first year well below expectations. The project sponsor began to be increasingly critical of the builders of the centre and questioned the whole value of the project. She was openly sceptical of the project to her fellow local authority employees. She suggested that the project to build a cost-effective centre had failed and called for an inquiry into the performance of the project manager of the construction company who was responsible for building the centre. 'We need him to explain to us why the centre is not delivering the benefits we expected', she explained.

Required

(a)   The local authority has commissioned the independent Project Audit Agency (PAA) to look into how the project had been commissioned and managed. The PAA believes that a formal 'terms of reference' or 'project initiation document' would have resolved or clarified some of the problems and issues encountered in the project. It also feels that there are important lessons to be learnt by both the local authority and the construction company.

Analyse how a formal 'terms of reference' (project initiation document) would have helped address problems encountered in the project to construct the community centre and lead to improved project management in future projects. **(13 marks)**

(b) The PAA also believes that the four sets of benefits identified in the original business case (rental savings, energy savings, increased income and better staff morale) should have been justified more explicitly.

Draft an analysis for the PAA that formally categorises and critically evaluates each of the four sets of proposed benefits defined in the original business case. **(12 marks)**

(Total = 25 marks)

33 Lowlands Bank (12/09)

45 mins

Branch rationalisation project

Four years ago Lowlands Bank acquired Doe Bank, one of its smaller rivals. Both had relatively large local branch bank networks and the newly merged bank (now called LDB) found that it now had duplicated branches in many towns. One year after the takeover was finalised, LDB set up a project to review the branch bank network and carry out a rationalisation that aimed to cut the number of branches by at least 20% and branch employment costs by at least 10%. It was agreed that the project should be completed in two years. There were to be no compulsory staff redundancies. All branch employment savings would have to be realised through voluntary redundancy and natural wastage.

LDB appointed its operations director, Len Peters as the sponsor of the project. The designated project manager was Glenys Hopkins, an experienced project manager who had worked for Lowlands Bank for over fifteen years. The project team consisted of six employees who formerly worked for Lowlands Bank and six employees who formerly worked for Doe Bank. They were seconded full-time to the project.

Project issues and conclusion

During the project there were two major issues. The first concerned the precise terms of the voluntary redundancy arrangements. The terms of the offer were quickly specified by Len Peters. The second issue arose one year into the project and it concerned the amount of time it took to dispose of unwanted branches. The original project estimates had underestimated how long it would take to sell property the bank owned or to re-assign or terminate the leases for branches it rented. The project board overseeing the project agreed to the project manager's submission that the estimates had been too optimistic and they extended the project deadline for a further six months.

The project team completed the required changes one week before the rearranged deadline. Glenys Hopkins was able to confirm that the branch network had been cut by 23%. Six months later, in a benefits realisation review, she was also able to confirm that branch employment costs had been reduced by 12%. At a post-project review the project support office of the bank confirmed that they had changed their project estimating assumptions to reflect the experience of the project team.

Potential process initiatives

LDB is now ready to undertake three process initiatives in the Information Technology area. The IT departments and systems of the two banks are still separate. The three process initiatives under consideration are:

(a) The integration of the two bespoke payroll systems currently operated by the two banks into one consolidated payroll system. This will save the costs of updating and maintaining two separate systems.

(b) The updating of all personal desktop computer hardware and software to reflect contemporary technologies and the subsequent maintenance of that hardware. This will allow the desktop to be standardised and bring staff efficiency savings.

(c) The bank has recently identified the need for a private personal banking service for wealthy customers. Processes, systems and software have to be developed to support this new service. High net worth customers have been identified by the bank as an important growth area.

The bank will consider three solution options for each initiative. These are outsourcing or software package solution or bespoke development.

Required

(a) The branch rationalisation was a successful project.

Identify and analyse the elements of good project management that helped make the branch rationalisation project successful. **(12 marks)**

(b) The bank has identified three further desirable process initiatives (see above).

(i) Explain, using Harmon's process-strategy matrix, how the complexity and strategic importance of process initiatives can be classified. **(4 marks)**

(ii) Recommend and justify a solution option for each of the three process initiatives. **(9 marks)**

(Total = 25 marks)

34 OneEnergy plc (06/09)   45 mins

OneEnergy plc supplies over half of the electricity and gas in the country. It is an expanding, aggressive company which has recently acquired two smaller, but significant, competitors.

Just over a year ago, OneEnergy purchased the RitePay payroll software package from RiteSoftware. The recently appointed Human Resources (HR) director of OneEnergy recommended the package because he had used it successfully at his previous employer – a major charity. His unreserved recommendation was welcomed by the board because the company was currently running three incompatible payroll systems. The purchase of the RitePay payroll system appeared to offer the opportunity to quickly consolidate the three separate payroll systems into one improved solution. The board decided to purchase the software without evaluating alternative solutions. It was felt that payroll rules and processes were relatively standard and so there was no need to look further than a package recommended by the HR director. The software was purchased and a project initiated for converting the data from the current systems and for training users in the features and functions of the new software.

However, it soon became apparent that there were problems with the suitability of the RitePay software package. Firstly, OneEnergy had a wide variety of reward and pay schemes to reflect previous employment in the acquired companies and to accommodate a wide range of different skills and grades. Not all of these variations could be handled by the package. Consequently, amendments had to be commissioned from the software house. This led to unplanned costs and also to delays in implementation. Secondly, it also became clear that the software was not as user-friendly as the previous systems. Users had problems understanding some of the terminology and structure of the software. 'It just does not work like we do', commented one frustrated user. Consequently users made more errors than expected and training costs exceeded their budget.

Three months ago, another set of amendments was requested from RiteSoftware to allow one of the acquired companies in OneEnergy to pay bonuses to lorry drivers in a certain way. Despite repeated requests, the amendments were not received. Two weeks ago, it was announced that RiteSoftware had filed for bankruptcy and all software support was suspended. Just before this was announced the HR director of OneEnergy left the company to take up a similar post in the public sector.

OneEnergy has engaged W&P consultants to advise them on the RitePay project. An interim report from W&P suggests that OneEnergy should abandon the RitePay package. 'It is clear to us that RitePay never had the functionality required to fulfil the variety of requirements inevitable in a company the size of OneEnergy.' They also commented that this could have been avoided if the project had followed the competitive procurement policy defined in company operating procedures.

W&P also reports that:

- The procurement department at OneEnergy had requested two years of accounts from RiteSoftware. These were provided (see Figure 1) but not interpreted or used in the selection process in any way. W&P concluded 'that there were clear signs that the company was in difficulty and this should have led to further investigation'.

- They discovered that the former HR director of OneEnergy was the brother of the managing director of RiteSoftware.

Figure 1: RiteSoftware Accounts

Extract from the statement of financial position $000

Assets	2008	2007
Non-current assets		
Property, plant and equipment	30	25
Goodwill	215	133
	245	158
Current assets		
Inventories	3	2
Trade receivables	205	185
	208	187
Total assets	453	345
Liabilities		
Current liabilities		
Trade payables	257	178
Current tax payable	1	2
Bank overdraft	10	25
	268	205
Non-current liabilities		
Long-term borrowings	80	35
Total liabilities	348	240
Equity		
Share capital	105	105
Total equity and liabilities	453	345

Extract from the statement of comprehensive income		
Revenue	2,650	2,350
Cost of sales	(2,600)	(2,300)
Gross profit	50	50
Other costs	(30)	(20)
Finance costs	(10)	(4)
Profit before tax	10	26
Income tax expense	(1)	(2)
Profit for the year	9	24

Extract from the annual report		
Number of staff	90	70

Required

(a) W&P concluded in their report 'that there were clear signs that the company (RiteSoftware) was in difficulty and this should have led to further investigation'.

Assess, using the financial information available, the validity of W&P's conclusion. **(13 marks)**

(b) Examine **four** ways in which OneEnergy failed to follow a proper evaluation procedure in the selection of the RitePay software package. Include in your examination a discussion of the implication of each failing.

(12 marks)

(Total = 25 marks)

35 Bridge Co (06/14)

45 mins

Introduction

The following is an interview with Mick Kazinski, a senior marketing executive with Bridge Co, a Deeland-based construction company. It concerns their purchase of Custcare, a Customer Relationship Management (CRM) software package written by the Custcare Corporation, a software company based in Solland, a country some 4,000 km away from Deeland. The interview was originally published in the *Management Experiences* magazine.

Interviewer: Thanks for talking to us today Mick. Can you tell us how Bridge Co came to choose the Custcare software package?

Mick: Well, we didn't choose it really. Teri Porter had just joined the company as sales and marketing director. She had recently implemented the Custcare package at her previous company and she was very enthusiastic about it. When she found out that we did not have a CRM package at Bridge Co, she suggested that we should also buy the Custcare package as she felt that our requirements were very similar to those of her previous company. We told her that any purchase would have to go through our capex (capital expenditure) system as the package cost over $20,000. Here at Bridge Co, all capex applications have to be accompanied by a formal business case and an Invitation to Tender (ITT) has to be sent out to at least three potential suppliers. However, Teri is a very clever lady. She managed to do a deal with Custcare and they agreed to supply the package at a cost of $19,995, just under the capex threshold. Teri had to cut a few things out. For example, we declined the training courses (Teri said the package was an easy one to use and she would show us how to use it) and also we opted for the lowest level of support, something we later came to regret. Overall, we were happy. We knew that Custcare was a popular and successful CRM package.

Interviewer: So, did you have a demonstration of the software before you bought it?

Mick: Oh yes, and everyone was very impressed. It seemed to do all the things we would ever want it to do and, in fact, it gave us some ideas about possibilities that we would never have thought of. Also, by then, it was clear that our internal IT department could not provide us with a bespoke solution. Teri had spoken to them informally and she was told that they could not even look at our requirements for 18 months. In contrast, we could be up and running with the Custcare package within three months. Also, IT quoted an internal transfer cost of $18,000 for just defining our requirements. This was almost as much as we were paying for the whole software solution!

Interviewer: When did things begin to go wrong?

Mick: Well, the implementation was not straightforward. We needed to migrate some data from our current established systems and we had no-one who could do it. We tried to recruit some local technical experts, but Custcare pointed out that we had signed their standard contract which only permitted Custcare consultants to work on such tasks. We had not realised this, as nobody had read the contract carefully. In the end, we had to give in and it cost us $10,000 in fees to migrate the data from some of our internal systems to the new package. Teri managed to get the money out of the operational budget, but we weren't happy.

We then tried to share data between the Custcare software and our existing order processing system. We thought this would be easy, but apparently the file formats are incompatible. Thus we have to enter customer information into two systems and we are unable to exploit the customer order analysis facility of the Custcare CRM.

Finally, although we were happy with the functionality and reliability of the Custcare software, it works very slowly. This is really very disappointing. Some reports and queries have to be aborted because the software appears to have hung. The software worked very quickly in the demonstration, but it is painfully slow now that it is installed on our IT platform.

Interviewer: What is the current situation?

Mick: Well, we are all a bit deflated and disappointed in the package. The software seems reasonable enough, but its poor performance and our inability to interface it to the order processing system have reduced users' confidence in the system. Because users have not been adequately trained, we have had to phone Custcare's support desk more than we should. However, as I said before, we took the cheapest option. This is for a help line to be available from 8.00 hrs to 17.00 hrs Solland time. As you know, Solland is in a completely different time zone and so we have had to stay behind at work and contact them in the late evening. Again, nobody had closely read the terms of the contract. We have taken legal advice, but we have also found that, for dispute resolution, the contract uses the commercial contract laws of Solland. Nobody in Bridge Co knows what these are! Our solicitor said that we should

 BPP
LEARNING MEDIA

Questions 45

have asked for this specification to be changed when the contract was drawn up. I just wish we had chosen a product produced by a company here in Deeland. It would have made it much easier to resolve issues and disputes.

Interviewer: What does Teri think?

Mick: Not a lot! She has left us to rejoin her old company in a more senior position. The board did ask her to justify her purchase of the Custcare CRM package, but I don't think she ever did. I am not sure that she could!

Required

(a)   Suggest a process for evaluating, selecting and implementing a software package solution and explain how this process would have prevented the problems experienced at Bridge Co in the Custcare CRM application.

(15 marks)

(b)   The CEO of Bridge Co now questions whether buying a software package was the wrong approach to meeting the CRM requirements at Bridge Co. He wonders whether they should have commissioned a bespoke software system instead.

Explain, with reference to the CRM project at Bridge Co, the advantages of adopting a software package approach to fulfilling business system requirements compared with a bespoke software solution.

(10 marks)

(Total = 25 marks)

36 ASW (06/10, amended)   45 mins

ASW is a software house which specialises in producing software packages for insurance companies. ASW has a basic software package for the insurance industry that can be used immediately out of the box. However, most customers wish ASW to tailor the package to reflect their own products and requirements. In a typical ASW project, ASW's business analysts define the gap between the customer's requirements and the basic package. These business analysts then specify the complete software requirement in a system specification. This specification is used by its programmers to produce a customised version of the software. It is also used by the system testers at ASW to perform their system tests before releasing it to the customer for acceptance testing.

One of ASW's new customers is CaetInsure. Initially CaetInsure sent ASW a set of requirements for their proposed new system. Business analysts from ASW then worked with CaetInsure staff to produce a full system specification for CaetInsure's specific requirements. ASW do not begin any development until this system specification is signed off. After some delay (see below), the system specification was eventually signed off by CaetInsure.

Since sign-off, ASW developers have been working on tailoring the product to obtain an appropriate software solution. The project is currently at week 16 and the software is ready for system testing. The remaining activities in the project are shown in Figure 1. This simple plan has been put together by the project manager. It also shows who has responsibility for undertaking the activities shown on the plan.

The problem that the project manager faces is that the plan now suggests that implementation (parallel running) cannot take place until part way through week 28. The original plan was for implementation in week 23. Three weeks of the delay were due to problems in signing off the system specification. Key CaetInsure employees were unavailable to make decisions about requirements, particularly in the re-insurance part of the system. Too many requirements in this module were either unclear or kept changing as users sought clarification from their managers. There have also been two further weeks of slippage since the sign-off of the system specification.

The CaetInsure contract had been won in the face of stiff competition. As part of securing the deal, the ASW sales account manager responsible for the CaetInsure contract agreed that penalty clauses could be inserted into the contract. The financial penalty for late delivery of the software increases with every week's delay. CaetInsure had insisted on these clauses as they have tied the delivery of the software in with the launch of a new product. Although the delay in signing off the system specification was due to CaetInsure, the penalty clauses still remain in the contract. When the delay was discussed with the customer and ASW's project manager, the sales account manager assured CaetInsure that the 'time could be made up in programming'.

The initial planned delivery date (week 23) is now only seven weeks away. The project manager is now under intense pressure to come up with solutions which address the project slippage.

Required

(a) Evaluate the alternative strategies available to ASW's project manager to address the slippage problem in the CaetInsure project. **(10 marks)**

(b) As a result of your evaluation, recommend and justify your preferred solution to the slippage problem in the CaetInsure project. **(6 marks)**

(c) Explain what is meant by a post-project review and demonstrate how carrying out such a review could be of benefit to ASW. **(9 marks)**

(Total = 25 marks)

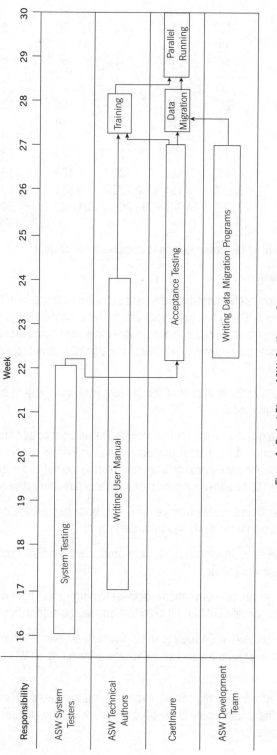

Figure 1: Project Plan – ASW: CaetInsure Contract

37 The Institute of Independent Analysts (IIA) (6/14)   45 mins

The Institute of Independent Analysts (IIA), an examining body, is considering replacing its conventional assessment process with computer-based assessment which produces instant results to the candidate. A business case has been developed for the computer-based assessment project. Figure 1, extracted from the business case, shows the financial appraisal of the project. It uses a discount rate of 8%. The NPV of the project is $10,925.

All figures in $'000s				Year				
	0	1	2	3	4	5	6	7
Costs								
Initial software	200	200						
Software maintenance			40	40	40	40	40	40
Question bank	50	50	5	5	5	5	5	5
Security			20	20	20	20	20	20
Disruption		15	15					
Total costs	250	265	80	65	65	65	65	65
Income/Savings								
Marker fees			125	125	125	125	125	125
Admin saving		20	30	30	30	30	30	30
Extra income			10	20	30	30	40	40
Total benefits		20	165	175	185	185	195	195
Benefits – costs	(250)	(245)	85	110	120	120	130	130
Discount factor	1	0.926	0.857	0.794	0.735	0.681	0.630	0.583
Present value	(250)	(226.870)	72.845	87.340	88.200	81.720	81.900	75.790
							NPV	10.925

Figure 1: Financial cost/benefit of the computer-based assessment project

An explanation of the costs and benefits is given below.

Initial software – refers to the cost of buying the computer-based assessment software package from the vendor. The software actually costs $375,000, but a further $25,000 has been added to reflect bespoke changes which the IIA requires. These changes are not yet agreed, or defined in detail. Indeed, there have been some problems in actually specifying these requirements and understanding how they will affect the administrative processes of the IIA.

Software maintenance – This will be priced at 10% of the final cost of the delivered software. This is currently estimated at $400,000; hence a cost of $40,000 per annum.

Question bank – refers to the cost of developing a question bank for the project. This is a set of questions which the software package stores and selects from when producing an examination for an individual candidate. Questions will be set by external consultants at $50 for each question they successfully deliver to the question bank. It is expected that further questions will need to be added (and current ones amended) in subsequent years.

Security – refers to security provided at computer-based assessment centres. This price has already been agreed with an established security firm who have guaranteed it for the duration of the project.

Disruption – refers to an expected temporary decline in IIA examinations staff productivity and staff morale during the implementation of the computer-based assessment solution.

Marker fees – manual marking is undertaken in the current conventional assessment process. There will no longer be any requirement for markers to undertake this manual marking. All examinations will be automatically marked.

Admin saving – concerns reduction in examinations staff at IIA headquarters. The actual savings will partly depend on the detailed requirements currently being discussed with the software package provider. It is still unclear how this will affect the administrative process.

Extra income – the IIA expects candidates to be attracted by the convenience of computer-based assessment. Other competing institutions do not offer this service. The extra income is the IIA's best guess at the amount of income which will result from this new assessment initiative.

The IIA is also putting in place a benefits management process for all projects. The IIA director is concerned that project managers are just moving on to other projects and not taking responsibility for the benefits initially established in the business case.

Required

(a)   Critically evaluate the financial case (cost/benefit) of the computer-based assessment project.   **(15 marks)**

(b)   Benefit owners, benefits maps and benefits realisation are important concepts in benefits management process.

Explain each of these concepts and their potential application to the computer-based assessment project.

(10 marks)

(Total = 25 marks)

38 Flexipipe (6/12)   45 mins

Introduction

Flexipipe is a successful company supplying flexible pipes to a wide range of industries. Its success is based on a very innovative production process which allows the company to produce relatively small batches of flexible pipes at very competitive prices. This has given Flexipipe a significant competitive edge over most of its competitors whose batch set-up costs are higher and whose lead times are longer. Flexipipe's innovative process is partly automated and partly reliant on experienced managers and supervisors on the factory floor. These managers efficiently schedule jobs from different customers to achieve economies of scale and throughput times that profitably deliver high quality products and service to Flexipipe's customers.

A year ago, the Chief Executive Officer (CEO) at Flexipipe decided that he wanted to extend the automated part of the production process by purchasing a software package that promised even further benefits, including the automation of some of the decision-making tasks currently undertaken by the factory managers and supervisors. He had seen this package at a software exhibition and was so impressed that he placed an order immediately. He stated that the package was 'ahead of its time, and I have seen nothing else like it on the market'.

This was the first time that the company had bought a software package for something that was not to be used in a standard application, such as payroll or accounts. Most other software applications in the company, such as the automated part of the current production process, have been developed in-house by a small programming team. The CEO felt that there was, on this occasion, insufficient time and money to develop a bespoke in-house solution. He accepted that there was no formal process for software package procurement 'but perhaps we can put one in place as this project progresses'.

This relaxed approach to procurement is not unusual at Flexipipe, where many of the purchasing decisions are taken unilaterally by senior managers. There is a small procurement section with two full-time administrators, but they only become involved once purchasing decisions have been made. It is felt that they are not technically proficient enough to get involved earlier in the purchasing lifecycle and, in any case, they are already very busy with purchase order administration and accounts payable. This approach to procurement has caused problems in the past. For example, the company had problems when a key supplier of raw materials unexpectedly went out of business. This caused short-term production problems, although the CEO has now found an acceptable alternative supplier.

The automation project

On returning to the company from the exhibition, the CEO commissioned a business analyst to investigate the current production process system so that the transition from the current system to the new software package solution could be properly planned. The business analyst found that some of the decisions made in the current production process were difficult to define and it was often hard for managers to explain how they had taken effective action. They tended to use their experience, memory and judgement and were still innovating in their control of the process. One commented that 'what we do today, we might not do tomorrow; requirements are constantly evolving'.

When the software package was delivered there were immediate difficulties in technically migrating some of the data from the current automated part of the production process software to the software package solution.

However, after some difficulties, it was possible to hold trials with experienced users. The CEO was confident that these users did not need training and would be 'able to learn the software as they went along'. However, in reality, they found the software very difficult to use and they reported that certain key functions were missing. One of the supervisors commented that 'the monitoring process variance facility is missing completely. Yet we had this in the old automated system'. Despite these reservations, the software package solution was implemented, but results were disappointing. Overall, it was impossible to replicate the success of the old production process and early results showed that costs had increased and lead times had become longer.

After struggling with the system for a few months, support from the software supplier began to become erratic. Eventually, the supplier notified Flexipipe that it had gone into administration and that it was withdrawing support for its product. Fortunately, Flexipipe were able to revert to the original production process software, but the ill-fated package selection exercise had cost it over $3m in costs and lost profits. The CEO commissioned a post-project review which showed that the supplier, prior to the purchase of the software package, had been very highly geared and had very poor liquidity. Also, contrary to the statement of the CEO, the post-project review team reported that there were at least three other packages currently available in the market that could have potentially fulfilled the requirements of the company. The CEO now accepts that using a software package to automate the production process was an inappropriate approach and that a bespoke in-house solution should have been commissioned.

Required

(a)   Critically evaluate the decision made by the CEO to use a software package approach to automating the production process at Flexipipe, and explain why this approach was unlikely to succeed.   **(12 marks)**

(b)   The CEO recommends that the company now adopts a formal process for procuring, evaluating and implementing software packages which they can use in the future when a software package approach appears to be more appropriate.

Analyse how a formal process for software package procurement, evaluation and implementation would have addressed the problems experienced at Flexipipe in the production process project.   **(13 marks)**

(Total = 25 marks)

39 Institute of Administrative Accountants (12/10)   45 mins

Introduction

The Institute of Administrative Accountants (IAA) has a professional scheme of examinations leading to certification. The scheme consists of six examinations (three foundation and three advanced) all of which are currently assessed using conventional paper-based, written examinations. The majority of the candidates are at the foundation level and they currently account for 70% of the IAA's venue and invigilation costs.

There are two examination sittings per year and these sittings are held in 320 centres all over the world. Each centre is administered by a paid invigilation team who give out the examination paper, monitor the conduct of the examination and take in completed scripts at the end. Invigilators are also responsible for validating the identity of candidates who must bring along appropriate identification documents. At over half of the centres there are usually less than ten candidates taking the foundation level examination and no candidates at all at the advanced level. However, the IAA strives to be a worldwide examination body and so continues to run examinations at these centres, even though they make a financial loss at these centres by doing so.

Recent increases in invigilation costs have made the situation even worse. However, the principles of equality and access are important to the IAA and the IAA would like to increase the availability of their examinations, not reduce it. Furthermore, the IAA is under increased financial pressure. The twice-yearly examination schedule creates peaks and troughs in cash flow which the Institute finds increasingly hard to manage. The Institute uses its $5m loan and overdraft facility for at least four months every year and incurred bank charges of $350,000 in the last financial year.

Examinations

All examinations are set in English by contracted examiners who are paid for each examination they write. All examinations are three-hour, closed-book examinations marked by contracted markers at $10 per script. Invigilators send completed scripts directly to markers by courier. Once scripts have been marked they are sent (again by courier) to a centralised IAA checking team who check the arithmetic accuracy of the marking. Any marking errors are resolved by the examiner. Once all marks have been verified, the examination results are released. This usually takes place 16 weeks after the examination date and candidates are critical of this long delay. The arithmetic checking of scripts and the production of examination results places significant demands on IAA full-time administrative staff, with many being asked to work unpaid overtime. The IAA also employs a significant number of temporary staff during the results processing period.

E-assessment

The new head of education at the IAA has suggested e-assessment initiatives at both the foundation and advanced levels.

He has suggested that all foundation level examinations should be assessed by multiple-choice examinations delivered over the Internet. They can be sat anytime, anyday, anywhere. 'Candidates can sit these examinations at home or at college. Anywhere where there is a personal computer and a reliable broadband connection.'

Advanced-level examinations will continue to be held twice-yearly at designated examination centres. However, candidates will be provided with personal computers which they will use to type in their answers. These answers will then be electronically sent to markers who will use online marking software to mark these answers on the screen. The software also has arithmetic checking facilities that mean that marks are automatically totalled for each question. '100% arithmetic accuracy of marking is guaranteed.'

He has also suggested that there is no need to make a formal business case for the adoption of the new technology. 'Its justification is so self-evident that defining a business case, managing benefits and undertaking benefits realisation would just be a pointless exercise. It would slow us down at a time when we need to speed up.'

Required

(a)   Evaluate the perceived benefits and costs of adopting e-assessment at the IAA.   **(15 marks)**

(b)   Explain why establishing a business case, managing benefits and undertaking benefits realisation are essential requirements despite the claimed 'self-evident' justification of adopting e-assessment at the IAA.

(10 marks)

(Total = 25 marks)

40 Institute of Analytical Accountants (6/11)   45 mins

The institute of Analytical Accountants (IAA) offers three certification programmes which are assessed through examinations using multiple choice questions. These questions are maintained in a computerised question bank. The handling process for these questions is documented in Figure 1 and described in detail below. The IAA is currently analysing all its processes seeking possible business process re-design opportunities. It is considering commissioning a bespoke computer system to support any agreed re-design of the business process. The IAA is keen to implement a new solution fairly quickly because competitors are threatening to move into their established market.

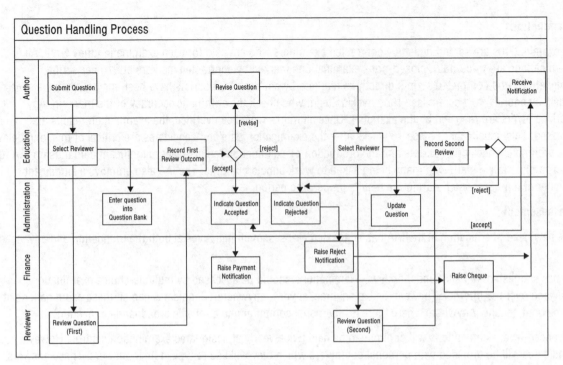

Figure 1: Question Handling Process at IAA

The author (the question originator) submits the question to the IAA as a password protected document attached to an email. The education department of the IAA (which is staffed by subject matter experts) select an appropriate reviewer and forward the email to him or her. At no point in the process does the author know the identity of the reviewer. A copy of the email is sent to the administration department where administrators enter the question in a standard format into a computerised question bank. These administrators are not subject matter experts and sometimes make mistakes when entering the questions and answers. A recent spot-check identified that one in ten questions contained an error. Furthermore, there is a significant delay in entering questions. Although five administrators are assigned to this task, they also have other duties to perform and so a backlog of questions has built up. Administrators are paid less than education staff.

The reviewer decides whether the question should be accepted as it is, rejected completely, or returned to the author for amendment. This first review outcome is recorded by the education department before the administration department updates the database with whether the question was accepted or rejected. On some occasions it is not possible to find the question which needs to be updated because it is still in the backlog of questions waiting to be entered into the system. This causes further delay and frustration.

The finance department is notified of all accepted questions and a payment notification is raised which eventually leads to a cheque being issued and sent to the author.

The amended question is returned by the author to the education department who forward this onto the reviewer. A copy is again sent to the administration department so that they can amend the question held on the database.

On the second review, the question is accepted or rejected. Rejected questions (irrespective of when they are rejected) are notified to the finance department who raise a reject notification and send it back to the author.

Currently, 20% of questions are immediately rejected by the reviewer and a further 15% are sent back to the author for revision. Of these, 30% are rejected on the second review.

Required

(a) The IAA would like to consider a number of re-design options, ranging from very simple improvements to radical solutions.

Identify a range of re-design options the IAA could consider for improving their question handling process. Evaluate the benefits of each option. **(15 marks)**

(b) Eventually, the IAA decided not to develop a bespoke solution but to use an established software package to implement its multiple choice question management and examination requirements. The selected package, chosen from a shortlist of three, includes the delivery of tests, question analysis, student invoicing and student records. It is already used by several significant examination boards in the country.

Explain the advantages of fulfilling users' requirements using a software package solution and discuss the implications of this solution for process re-design at IAA. **(10 marks)**

(Total = 25 marks)

41 Pharmacy Systems International (6/08) 45 mins

Introduction

Retail pharmacies supply branded medicinal products, such as headache and cold remedies, as well as medicines prescribed by doctors. Customers expect both types of product to be immediately available and so this demands efficient purchasing and stock control in each pharmacy. The retail pharmacy industry is increasingly concentrated in a small number of nationwide pharmacy chains, although independent pharmacies continue to survive. The pharmacy chains are increasingly encouraging their customers to order medicinal products online and the doctors are being encouraged to electronically send their prescriptions to the pharmacy so that they can be prepared ready for the patient to collect.

Pharmacy Systems International (PSI)

Pharmacy Systems International (PSI) is a privately owned software company which has successfully developed and sold a specialised software package meeting the specific needs of retail pharmacies. PSI's stated objective is to be a 'highly skilled professional company providing quality software services to the retail pharmacy industry'. Over the last three years PSI has experienced gradual growth in turnover, profitability and market share (see Figure 1).

Figure 1: PSI Financial information

	2007	2006	2005
Turnover ($'000)	11,700	10,760	10,350
Profits ($'000) (pre-tax)	975	945	875
Estimated market share	26%	24%	23%
Number of employees	120	117	115

PSI has three directors, each of whom has a significant ownership stake in the business. The chief executive is a natural entrepreneur with a past record of identifying opportunities and taking the necessary risks to exploit them. In the last three years he has curbed his natural enthusiasm for growth as PSI has consolidated its position in the market place. However, he now feels the time is right to expand the business to a size and profitability that makes PSI an attractive acquisition target and enables the directors to realise their investment in the company. He has a natural ally in the sales and marketing director and both feel that PSI needs to find new national and international markets to fuel its growth. The software development director, however, does not share the chief executive's enthusiasm for this expansion.

The chief executive has proposed that growth can best be achieved by developing a generic software package which can be used by the wider, general retail industry. His plan is for the company to take the current software package and take out any specific references to the pharmaceutical industry. This generic package could then be extended and configured for other retail sectors. The pharmaceutical package would be retained but it would be perceived and marketed as a specialised implementation of the new generic package.

This proposed change in strategic direction is strongly resisted by the software development director. He and his team of software developers are under constant pressure to meet the demands of the existing retail pharmacy customers. Online ordering of medicinal products and electronic despatch of prescriptions are just two examples of the constant pressure PSI is under from their retail customers to continuously update its software package to enable the pharmacies to implement technical innovations that improve customer service.

Ideally, the software development director would like to acquire further resources to develop a more standardised software package for their current customers. He is particularly annoyed by PSI's salesmen continually committing the company to producing a customised software solution for each customer and promising delivery dates that the software delivery team struggle to meet. Frequently, the software contains faults that require expensive and time consuming maintenance. Consequently, PSI is being increasingly criticised by customers. A recent user group

conference expressed considerable dissatisfaction with the quality of the PSI package and doubted the company's ability to meet the published deadline for a new release of the software.

Required

(a) The proposal to develop and sell a software package for the retail industry represents a major change in strategy for PSI.

Analyse the nature, scope and type of this proposed strategic change for PSI. **(10 marks)**

(b) The success of any attempt at managing change will be dependent on the context in which that change takes place.

Identify and analyse, using an appropriate model, the *internal contextual features* that could influence the success or failure of the chief executive's proposed strategic change for PSI. **(15 marks)**

(Total = 25 marks)

42 Academic Recycling Company (6/13)   45 mins

Ten years ago Sully Truin formed the Academic Recycling Company (ARC) to offer a specialised waste recycling service to schools and colleges. The company has been very successful and has expanded rapidly. To cope with this expansion, Sully has implemented a tight administrative process for operating and monitoring contracts. This administrative procedure is undertaken by the Contracts Office, who track that collections have been made by the field recycling teams. Sully has sole responsibility for obtaining and establishing recycling contracts, but he leaves the day-to-day responsibility for administering and monitoring the contracts to the Contracts Office. He has closely defined what needs to be done for each contract and how this should be monitored. 'I needed to do this', he said, 'because workers in this country are naturally lazy and lack initiative. I have found that if you don't tell them exactly what to do and how to do it, then it won't get done properly.' Most of the employees working in the Contracts Office like and respect Sully for his business success and ability to take instant decisions when they refer a problem to him. Some of ARC's employees have complained about his autocratic style of leadership, but most of these have now left the company to work for other organisations.

A few months ago, conscious that he was a self-taught manager, Sully enrolled himself on a week's course with Gapminding, a training consultancy which actively advocates and promotes a democratic style of management. The course caused Sully to question his previous approach to leadership. It was also the first time, for three years, that Sully had been out of the office during working hours for a prolonged period of time. However, each night, while he was attending the course, he had to deal with emails from the Contracts Office listing problems with contracts and asking him what action they should take. He became exasperated by his employees' inability to take actions to resolve these issues. He discussed this problem with his course tutors. They suggested that his employees would be more effective and motivated if their jobs were enriched and that they were empowered to make decisions themselves.

On his return from the course, Sully called a staff meeting with the Contracts Office where he announced that, from now on, employees would have responsibility for taking control actions themselves, rather than referring the problem to him. Sully, in turn, was to focus on gaining more contracts and setting them up. However, problems with the new arrangements arose very quickly. Fearful of making mistakes and unsure about what they were doing led to employees discussing issues amongst themselves at length before coming to a tentative decision. The operational (field) recycling teams were particularly critical of the new approach. One commented that 'before, we got a clear decision very quickly. Now decisions can take several days and appear to lack authority.' The new approach also caused tensions and stress within the Contracts Office and absenteeism increased.

At the next staff meeting, employees in the Contracts Office asked Sully to return to his old management style and job responsibilities. 'We prefer the old Sully Truin', they said, 'the training course has spoilt you.' Reluctantly, Sully agreed to their requests and so all problems are again referred up to him. However, he is unhappy with this return to the previous way of working. He is working long hours and is concerned about his health. Also, he realises that he has little time for obtaining and planning contracts and this is severely restricting the capacity of the company to expand.

Required

(a) Analyse Sully Truin's leadership style before and immediately after the training course and explain why the change of leadership style at ARC was unsuccessful. **(15 marks)**

(b) Describe the principles of job enrichment and evaluate its potential application in the Contracts Office at ARC. **(10 marks)**

(Total = 25 marks)

CASE STUDIES

The 50 mark case study is compulsory. It is likely that it will always include a part-question on mainstream strategy, plus two or three other part-questions that could be drawn from any area of the syllabus.

43 ReInk Co (6/14)   90 mins

Eland – the country

Eland is an industrial country with a relatively high standard of living. Most commercial and domestic consumers have computers and printers. However, the economic performance of the country has declined for the last seven years and there are large areas of unemployment and poverty. The economic problems of the country have led to a significant decline in tax revenues and so the government has asked its own departments (and the public sector as a whole) to demonstrate value-for-money in their purchases. The government is also considering privatising some of its departments to save money. The Department of Revenue Collections (DoRC), which is responsible for collecting tax payments in the country, has been identified as a possible candidate for future privatisation.

The people of Eland are enthusiastic about the principles of reuse and recycling. There has been a notable rise in the number of green consumers. Mindful of this, and aware of the economic benefits it delivers, the government is also encouraging its departments (and the economy as a whole) to recycle and reuse products.

The printer consumables market

There is a significant computer printer market in Eland, dominated by Original Equipment Manufacturers (OEMs). Many of these are household names such as Landy, IPD and Bell-Tech. OEMs also dominate the printer consumables market, which is worth about $200m per year. However, there are also independent companies who only supply the printer consumables (printer cartridges and toner cartridges) market, offering prices which significantly undercut the OEMs. The printer and printer consumables markets are both technology driven, with companies constantly looking for innovations which make printing better and cheaper.

The emergence of independent printer consumables suppliers has not been welcomed by the OEMs. They have brought legal actions against the independents in an attempt to make refilling their branded products illegal. However, they have not succeeded. The government in Eland has ruled this to be anti-competitive. However, the OEMs continue to promote their case with political parties, claiming that they need the revenues from printer consumables to fund innovations and advances in printer technology. They also regularly issue statements which worry consumers, claiming that printers may be harmed by using ink which is not from the OEM. Landy has been particularly aggressive in this regard. It continues to pursue legal claims against the independents and has also issued a statement which makes clear that if one of their printers is found to be faulty whilst using non-Landy ink, then the printer's warranty will be void.

It is relatively easy to enter the independent printer consumables market and so companies tend to compete on price. There is little brand loyalty amongst consumers, who regularly change their choice of brand. The independent companies constantly focus on finding technologies which make the print cartridges cheaper to buy and are of better quality. Used print cartridges can be reused for their material alone (recycled), or reused by being refilled with ink. However, there are still printing products on the market which can only be used once, or are expensive to recycle.

ReInk Co

ReInk Co (ReInk) was formed five years ago by Dexter Black, a technology entrepreneur with expertise in printer technologies. He still remains the only shareholder. He set up ReInk to produce and market his designs for reusable ink systems. ReInk is focused primarily on the reuse of printer cartridges by using a process to refill them with ink. Key technical elements of ReInk's innovative process for refilling cartridges have been patented, but in Eland, such patents only last for eight years. The current patent has a further six years to run.

The company was established in a declining industrial town in Eland with high unemployment. Government grants were available for two years to help support hi-tech industry and purpose built factories were cheap, readily available and, initially, rent free. Although the company now pays rent for its factory and offices, the annual rent is relatively low. The area has a good supply of people suitable for administrative and factory jobs in the company. ReInk's location is also close to an attractive area of countryside, which Dexter felt would appeal to the technology experts needed to help him exploit and develop his printer technology ideas. It would help provide a good standard of living and relatively cheap property and so he could attract good staff for modest salaries. His assumption proved correct. He has been able to attract an expert team of technologists who have helped him develop a unique approach to printer cartridge reuse. As one of them commented, 'I took a pay cut to come here. But now I can afford a bigger house and my children can breathe fresh country air.'

ReInk is an attractive company to work for and the team of technologists are enthusiastic about working with such an acknowledged industry expert, where technical innovation is recognised and rewarded. Both his staff and competitors acknowledge Dexter's technical expertise, but his commercial expertise is less well regarded. Dexter recognised this as a weakness and it was the prime driver behind his decision to recruit two new directors to the company.

To fund the development of the printer refilling technology, ReInk has needed significant bank loans and a substantial overdraft. Although the company has made a small operating profit for the last three years, interest repayments have meant that it has recorded a loss every year. It currently has revenues of $6m per year, 20% of which are derived from a long-term contract with the DoRC. ReInk is not one of the independent companies currently being sued by Landy.

To help him address these continuing financial losses, Dexter recently recruited a sales director to attempt to increase revenue through improved sales and marketing and a human resources (HR) director to review and improve staffing practices. Together with the financial director and Dexter himself, they make up the board of ReInk.

Although both of these recently appointed directors had the commercial expertise which Dexter lacked, neither has been a success. The technologists within the company are particularly scathing about the two new appointments. They claim that the sales director has never really made the effort to understand the market and that 'he does not really understand the product we are selling'. There has been no evidence so far that he has been able to generate more sales revenue. The HR director upset the whole company by introducing indiscriminate cost cutting and attempting to regrade staff to reduce staff costs. The technologists believe that the HR director 'clearly has no experience of dealing with professional staff'.

Despite the appointment of the new sales director, ReInk is still not recognised by the majority of the consumers who were surveyed in a recent brand awareness survey. No significant marketing is undertaken outside of the development and promotion of ReInk's website. In search results, it often appears alongside companies which appear to offer similar services and usually have very similar trading names.

ReInk continues to struggle financially, and its bank, Firmsure, in response to its own financial difficulties, has recently reduced ReInk's overdraft facility, creating a cash flow crisis which threatens the company's very existence. At present, it does not have enough cash to meet next month's payroll payments.

The employees of the company are well aware of the company's financial position and although they are proud of the company's technical achievements, they believe that the company may soon go into administration and so many are actively looking for other jobs in the industry or in the area. A combination of poor management (particularly from the new directors) and the company's uncertain financial position has demotivated many of the employees, particularly the technologists who have created the company's vital technical edge over its competitors.

Vi Ventures (VV)

Vi Ventures are venture capitalists who inject money and management expertise into struggling companies, in exchange for a certain degree of control, ownership and dividend reward. They have acknowledged financial and management competencies which they have used in a variety of commercial environments. They are experienced change managers.

VV have been introduced to ReInk by Firmsure and they are considering some form of involvement. Actual arrangements are still under consideration and will only be discussed after they have made their standard assessment of ReInk's strategic position. This standard assessment report contains three elements:

- A SWOT analysis

- An assessment of the contextual factors of strategic change. They need to understand what factors will affect the change which they may need to bring to the company. The framework they use is shown in Figure 1 and is derived from the work of Balogun and Hope Hailey.

- A TOWS matrix analysis to identify strategic options which might be pursued if VV invest in the company.

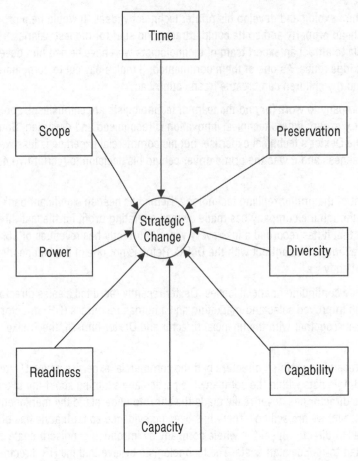

Figure 1: Contextual features in strategic change

Required

You have been asked to write the standard assessment report of the strategic position of ReInk required by Vi Ventures. Write a report for Vi Ventures which:

(a) Undertakes a SWOT analysis of ReInk Co. **(20 marks)**

(b) Evaluates the effect of contextual features on the introduction of strategic change at ReInk Co. **(14 marks)**

(c) And, in the light of your analysis above, recommends possible strategic options for each quadrant of a TOWS matrix of ReInk Co. **(12 marks)**

Professional marks will be awarded in question 1 for the overall quality, construction, fluency and professionalism of the complete standard assessment report required by Vi Ventures. **(4 marks)**

(50 marks)

44 MachineShop (12/13)   90 mins

Arboria is a prosperous industrial country with an established consumer culture that is distinguished by demanding and assertive consumers. Many companies find it difficult to compete successfully in the country but MachineShop is a notable exception. MachineShop sells small electrical machines and tools to both trade (people who use the machines/tools in their work) and domestic customers (people who use the machines/tools at home). For example, it sells a range of paint strippers retailing from $100 to $3,500. These paint strippers are bought by both tradesmen (for example, decorators) and ordinary domestic customers who use them to maintain their own home. It is estimated that 65% of sales are to domestic customers. MachineShop currently has 50 brightly decorated stores throughout Arboria. On average, a further two stores are opened every month. The company has no direct competitors. Most firms offering similar machines only sell them to tradesmen. In many respects MachineShop has defined a new market and it is the only company which, at present, seems to understand the dynamics of this market.

MachineShop is a private company still wholly owned by its directors. The board is headed by Dave Deen, a dynamic entrepreneur who enjoys a high national media profile. He likes the excitement of business and is determined to rapidly grow MachineShop – an ambition shared by his fellow directors. In 2012, on a turnover of $50m, MachineShop recorded a gross profit margin of 28% and an operating margin of 17%. It delivered a Return on Capital Employed (ROCE) of 17.5%. It currently has a gearing ratio (defined as long-term loans/capital employed) of 15% and an interest cover ratio of 3.5.

Dave Deen has an ambitious growth plan, which he intends to achieve through a combination of internal growth, acquisition and, possibly, strategic alliances. The opening of further stores in Arboria is providing internal (organic) growth. Much of this drive for growth is fuelled by a desire to exploit MachineShop's unique competencies before the idea is copied, both within Arboria and elsewhere in the world. However, the company is having difficultly finding companies to acquire, as there are few equivalent companies to target, either in Arboria or elsewhere in the world. Although MachineShop has never traded outside Arboria, the search for acquisitions is worldwide, with Dave Deen particularly keen to explore international markets in his desire to build a worldwide brand. He has specifically identified the developing country of Ceeland as a potential target, because macroeconomic trends suggest that a consumer society is emerging there, which is similar to the one in Arboria.

Ceeland

The government of Ceeland has spent the last decade building an effective road transport system, supported by low fuel and road taxes which make it cheap to use. The government has also installed a fast digital communication network, providing broadband internet access to all of the population. This is important to MachineShop because internet order placement (either for collection or delivery) is an important part of their business model. The government has also lifted certain restrictions which had been in place under its predecessor. For example, it has removed the need for companies trading in the country to be registered in Ceeland and to have at least one Ceelander citizen on the board. Until recently, there were restrictions on what machines could be used by domestic customers. However, these restrictions have also been removed, as part of a government initiative to encourage the development of light manufacturing in the country. Indeed, one brand of products already stocked by MachineShop is made by a company based in Ceeland.

Fabrique Regle de Garrido (FRG)

Dave Deen has identified Fabrique Regle de Garrido (FRG) as a potential acquisition or strategic partner. FRG currently has 30 depots in Ceeland supplying large machine tools solely to trade customers. It does not sell products to domestic customers. It has an effective distribution network and a sales team which is experienced in selling to Ceeland businesses. MachineShop has the finance (in the form of bank loans and retained earnings) in place for an acquisition or a strategic partnership. Dave Deen has not yet opened up negotiations with FRG, but he has extracted some financial information from the company's most recently filed accounts (see Figure 1). He has also discovered that FRG is a privately owned company, with 30 shareholders, including a local trade union. Dave Deen sees the potential acquisition of FRG as an opportunity to introduce the MachineShop business model into Ceeland. He fully expects the country to become increasingly similar to Arboria and so it will be suitable for the sort of service and products which MachineShop offers. 'Achieving quick, substantial growth through acquisition will give us a powerful bargaining position. It will allow us to develop economies of scale, including purchasing in bulk to further drive down product prices. This will help us erect barriers to potential competition', he said.

Figure 1 – Extracted financial information for FRG

All figures in $'000	2012
Revenue	9,000
Cost of sales	(7,500)
Gross profit	1,500
Other expenses	(700)
Finance costs	(300)
Profit before tax	500
Income tax expense	(100)
Profit for the year	400
Non-current liabilities	
Share capital	9,500
Retained profit	400
Long-term loans	2,500

MachineShop acquisitions

MachineShop does have some experience in acquisitions. In 2010 it acquired two companies based in Arboria which still trade as independent companies. The purchase of LogTrans was prompted by the need for MachineShop to have a dedicated and reliable logistics supplier. The post-acquisition performance of the company was spoilt by a dispute between Dave Deen and the senior management of LogTrans. This was due to a personality clash, caused by a different way of doing business. Eventually, the senior management of LogTrans was removed and replaced by people more aligned with the corporate culture of MachineShop. EngSup was also acquired in 2010 to provide an enhanced service facility to people who had purchased machines from MachineShop. Customer feedback showed that many customers were unimpressed by MachineShop's after sales service. EngSup already provided support for many domestic electrical products and so MachineShop bought the company with the intention of using it to provide support for MachineShop's customers. However, initial feedback was negative because EngSup's service engineers provided a poor level of service, coupled with an arrogant approach to the customer. A retraining scheme, together with selected redundancies, has now addressed these problems. Extracts from the current year's figures for both companies, compared with the last full pre-acquisition period of the company, are shown in Figure 2.

Figure 2 – Extracted financial information for LogTrans and EngSup

All figures in $'000	LogTrans		EngSup	
Extracted data	2012	2009	2012	2009
Revenue	700	650	350	325
Cost of sales	(575)	(510)	(275)	(250)
Gross profit	125	140	75	75
Other expenses	(60)	(70)	(35)	(30)
Finance costs	(30)	(15)	(10)	(8)
Profit before tax	35	55	30	37
Income tax expense	(15)	(10)	(7)	(10)
Profit for the year	20	45	23	27
Non-current liabilities				
Share capital	500	400	250	100
Retained profit	80	70	40	170
Long-term loans	100	50	30	20

Required

(a) Internal growth, acquisition and strategic alliances are three methods of pursuing growth.

Explain and evaluate each of these three methods of pursuing growth in the context of MachineShop's development to date and its ambitions for future growth and development. **(18 marks)**

(b) MachineShop is considering the acquisition of FRG. They have asked you, as a business analyst, to write a report which advises them on this potential acquisition.

Write a report, using the criteria of suitability, acceptability and feasibility, which evaluates the potential acquisition of FRG, concluding with whether you would recommend MachineShop to acquire FRG.

(18 marks)

Professional marks will be awarded in part (b) for the structure of the report, the clarity of the analysis and the soundness of the conclusion or recommendation. **(4 marks)**

(c) Dave Deen has heard about Porter's 'diamond' and wants an explanation of the principles, relevance and application of this model.

Explain the principles of Porter's 'diamond' and use it to assess the relative attractiveness of Ceeland and Arboria in providing an environment in which MachineShop's growth ambitions could be achieved.

(10 marks)

(Total = 50 marks)

45 Network Management Systems (Pilot Paper)

Introduction

Network Management Systems (NMS) is a privately owned high technology company established in 1997 by computer engineer, Ray Edwards. It is situated in the country of Elsidor, a prosperous developed nation with a stable well-established political system. Successive governments in Elsidor have promoted technology by providing grants and tax incentives. Tax credits are also provided to offset company investment in research and development. The government, like many governments worldwide, has invested heavily in a national telecommunications infrastructure. However, in 2010 the country suffered an economic downturn that led many companies to postpone technological investment.

By 2010 NMS employed 75 full-time employees in a new, purpose-built factory and office unit. These employees were a mixture of technically qualified engineers, working in research and development (R&D), factory staff manufacturing and assembling products and a small sales and service support team.

Product areas

In 2010, NMS had three distinct product/service areas – data communication components, network management systems and, finally, technical support.

NMS sells data communication components to original equipment manufacturers (OEMs), who use these components in their hardware. Both the OEMs and their customers are predominantly large international companies. NMS has established a good reputation for the quality and performance of its components, which are competitively priced. However, NMS has less than 1% of the domestic marketplace and faces competition from more than twenty suppliers, most of whom also compete internationally. Furthermore, one of the company's OEM customers accounts for 40% of its sales in this area. The international market for data communication components had increased from $33 billion in 2001 to $81 billion in 2010. Forecasts for 2011 and beyond, predict growth from increased sales to currently installed networks rather than from the installation of new networks. The maturity of the technology means that product lifecycles are becoming shorter. Success comes from producing high volumes of reliable components at relatively low prices. NMS produces components in a relatively prosperous country where there is significant legislation defining maximum work hours and minimum wage rates. All new components have to be approved by an appropriate government approval body in each country that NMS supplies. This approval process is both costly and time consuming.

The second product area is network management systems. NMS originally supplied fault detection systems to a small number of large end users such as banks, public utility providers and global manufacturers. NMS recognised the unique requirements of each customer and so it customised its product to meet specific needs and requirements. They pioneered a modular design which allowed customers to adapt standard system modules to fit their exact networking requirements. The success of their product led to it being awarded a prestigious government technology award for 'technological innovation in data communications'. This further enhanced the company's reputation and enabled it to become a successful niche player in a relatively low volume market with gross margins in excess of 40%. They only have two or three competitors in this specialist market. Unlike component manufacture, there is no need to seek government approval for new network products.

Finally, the complexity of NMS products means that technical support is a third key business area. It has an excellent reputation for this support. However, it is increasingly difficult and costly to maintain the required level of support because the company does not have a geographically distributed network of support engineers. All technical support is provided from its headquarters. This contrasts with the national and international support services of their large competitors.

Current issues

NMS currently manufactures 40% of the components used in its products. The rest of the components, including semiconductors and microprocessors, are bought in from a few selected global suppliers. Serious production problems have resulted from periodic component shortages, creating significant delays in manufacturing, assembly, and customer deliveries.

NMS is still a relatively immature organisation. There are small functional departments for sales and marketing, technical research and development, manufacturing and procurement. Ray still personally undertakes all staff recruitment and staff development. He is finding the recruitment of high calibre staff a problem, with NMS' small size and geographical location making it difficult to attract the key personnel necessary for future growth.

Financial situation

In response to poor internal investment decisions, Ray has introduced a more formal approach to quantifying costs and benefits in an attempt to prioritise projects that compete for his limited funds and time. His first formal cost-benefit analysis helped him select a new machine for producing certain components in his factory. The results of his analysis are shown in Figure 1. The cost of the machine was $90,000, with annual maintenance fees of $5,000. Ray has seen the machine working and he believes that he can save the cost of one technician straight away. These savings are shown as reduced staff costs. The manufacture of the machine claims that the accuracy of the machine leads to reduced wastage of 'up to 10%'. NMS has detailed measures of the wastage of the current machine and Ray has used this to estimate wastage savings. The increased accuracy of the machine over time is reflected in his estimates. Finally, the manufacture claims 'energy savings'. NMS currently knows the energy costs of the whole factory – but not of individual machines. However, Ray thinks that his estimates for energy savings are realistic. He concludes that 'over five years the machine breaks even, so this seems a reasonable business case to me'. Overall summary financial data for NMS is presented in Figure 2.

Figure 1: Business case for new machine

Year	0	1	2	3	4
All figures in $'000					
Cost of the machine	90				
Maintenance costs	5	5	5	5	5
Reduced staff costs	15	15	15	15	15
Reduced wastage	2	4	6	8	10
Energy savings	2	2	2	2	2

Figure 2: Financial analysis NMS 2007-2010

All figures in $'000	2010	2009	2008	2007
Revenue				
Domestic	6,235	6,930	6,300	4,500
International	520	650	500	300
Total	6,755	7,580	6,800	4,800
Cost of sales	4,700	5,000	4,200	2,850
Gross profit	2,055	2,580	2,600	1,950
Overhead expenses	1,900	2,010	1,900	1,400
Profit before tax and finance costs	155	570	700	550
Finance costs	165	150	120	25
Tax expense	17	62	75	60
Profit for the year	-27	358	505	465

Extracted from internal statistical reports

Employees	75	75	60	45
% of orders late	6	10	7	5
Order book	2,500	3,750	4,150	3,505

Required

(a) Evaluate the macro-environment of NMS by undertaking a PESTEL analysis. **(15 marks)**

(b) Analyse the industry or marketplace environment that NMS is competing in. **(16 marks)**

Professional marks will be awarded in part (b) for clarity, structure and an appropriate approach. **(4 marks)**

(c) Figures 1 and 2 summarise two financial aspects of NMS.

(i) Analyse the financial position of NMS. **(9 marks)**

(ii) Evaluate the cost-benefit analysis used to justify the purchase of the new machine. **(6 marks)**

(Total = 50 marks)

46 The Ace Bicycle Company

The Ace Bicycle Company (ABC) is a private UK company, based within the United Kingdom and managed by Colin Doncroft, the grandson of its founder. The shares are totally owned by the family, with Colin and his wife controlling just under half of the shares, the rest being held by other members of the family. The company was started in 1935, producing bicycles for the general market. These bicycles were targeted mainly at people who could not afford to buy motor vehicles – then a relative luxury – but who needed transportation to get them to work or for local travel. Initially the company was a regional producer focusing on markets in Central England but over the next 70 years ABC transformed itself into a national company. ABC took advantage of changes in fashion and periodically introduced new models focusing on different market segments. Its first diversification was into making racing bicycles, which still account for 20% of its volume output. Most of these bicycles are very expensive to produce. They are made of specialist light-weight metals and are often custom-built for specific riders, most of the sales being made on a direct basis. Members of amateur cycling clubs contact the company directly with their orders and this minimises distribution costs, so making these machines more affordable to the customers. ABC's reputation has been enhanced by this highly profitable product. The company has seen no reason to change its branding policy and these products are still sold under the 'ABC' brand name.

During the 1980s the company responded to the demand for more sporty leisure machines. Mountain bikes had become the fashion and ABC designed and produced some models which appealed to the cheaper end of the market. These products, although robust and stylish, were relatively cheap and were aimed at families with teenage children and who could not afford to spend large sums of money on the more sophisticated models. The company is currently selling nearly 30% of its output to this market segment. Most of the sales are through specialist bicycle shops, although about 25% of these mountain bikes sales are made through a national retail chain of bicycle and motor vehicle accessories stores. Apart from those sold via this retail network, under the retail brand name, the mountain bikes were also sold under the ABC brand. With the advent of fitness clubs the company saw an opening for the provision of cycling machines for the health club and gymnasium market. These machines were sold at a premium price but they still accounted for less than 5% of total volume sales of the company. The main product group for the company was still its basic bicycle – it is the entry model for most families who are buying bicycles for teenagers and for those people who still use bicycles as a means of transportation as distinct from seeing them as entertainment or fun machines. The product is standardised, with few differentiating features, and as such can be produced relatively cheaply. About 75% of this segment is sold through the same national retail chain mentioned above with reference to mountain bike sales. These bicycles in fact are built for the retail chain and marketed under their brand name. This appears to be advantageous to ABC because it guarantees them a given level of business without their being responsible for either distribution or promotion. This segment, however, is now seeing increasing competition from cheaper overseas imports.

The company had historically made reasonable profits and most of these were re-invested in the company's production facilities, increasing capacity substantially. However, since the late 1990s, ABC has seen its market being eroded. Sales have fallen gradually, mainly because the total United Kingdom market for bicycles has been in decline, but also because of increased competition from foreign suppliers. The high value of sterling has encouraged imports. Surprisingly, during this period ABC actually increased its share of domestic output. This is due to the fact that it has been prepared to accept lower margins so as to maintain sales and, in addition, a few UK producers had decided to exit the market and move into other, more attractive product lines.

By early in the year 2008 the company has seen its profits continue to fall. It now has a debt to the bank of £4 million, having been unable to pay for all recent, new capital expenditure out of retained earnings. (Table I gives some financial information about the recent performance of ABC.)

There are now very few UK manufacturers of bicycles who concentrate solely on producing bicycles. Most have a diversified portfolio and can count on other product groups to support the bicycle sector when demand is poor. However, ABC has continued to focus entirely on this specialised product range. It is surviving basically because it has built up a strong reputation for reliable products and because the Doncroft family has, until recently, been content with a level of profits which would be unacceptable to a public company that had external shareholders to consider. However, it is now becoming apparent that unless some radical action is taken the company cannot hope to survive. The bank will now only make loans if ABC can find a suitable strategy to provide it with a higher and more acceptable level of profit. If the company is to retain its independence (and it is questionable whether any company will really want to acquire it in its current position) it has to consider radical change. Its only experience is within the bicycle industry and therefore it appears to be logical that it should stay in this field in some form or other.

Colin Doncroft has examined ways to improve the profitability of the company. He is of the opinion that if ABC becomes more successful it could become a desirable acquisition for other companies. However, currently the company will not attract bidders unless it is at a low price. Doncroft has looked at the profile of his products and wonders whether any rationalisation could help to improve performance. He has also decided to look at the potential for overseas marketing. Having examined statistics on current world production and sales statistics he has identified that the real growth areas for bicycles are in the Far East. China alone supports a bigger market for bicycles than the whole of Europe and North America. India and Pakistan have also developed a significant demand for bicycles. Doncroft decided to visit some of these markets and he has returned full of enthusiasm for committing ABC to operate in these Far Eastern markets or in India and Pakistan. Whilst Doncroft considers that exporting from the UK might be a viable option, he has become increasingly attracted to manufacturing in the Far East, particularly in China. He believes that transportation costs could prove to be a disadvantage to exporting for ABC. He estimates that costs for shipping and insurance could add about 15% to the final selling price. Furthermore, he is concerned about the discrepancy between labour costs in the United Kingdom and in China. Wage rates, including social costs in China appear to be about 30% of those in the UK and these costs account for approximately 25% of the total production costs.

Colin Doncroft has summoned a meeting of all the shareholders to persuade them to agree to plan to manufacture, or at least assemble bicycles in the Far East. The other shareholders are not quite so enthusiastic. They feel that this strategy is too risky. The company has never been involved in overseas business and now they are being asked to sanction a strategy which by-passes the exporting stage and commits them to significant expenditure overseas. Colin is convinced that the bank will loan them the necessary capital, given the attractiveness of these overseas markets. The other shareholders are more in favour of a gradual process. They want to improve the position within the United Kingdom market first rather than leap into the unknown. They also believe that diversification into other non-bicycle products might be less risky than venturing overseas. They know the UK market but overseas is an unknown area. Colin has decided that it is time he sought some professional advice for the company. A management consultant, Simon Gaskell, has been retained. He is a qualified accountant who also has an MBA from a prestigious business school.

Table I: Information concerning ABC's current sales and financial performance

Financial Year April/March	2006/2007	2007/2008	2008/2009 (forecast)
Mountain bikes			
Volume	18,000	17,500	16,500
Direct costs £'000	2,070	2,187.5	2,145
Revenue £'000	2,610	2,625	2,475
Standard bicycles			
Volume	27,000	26,200	25,000
Direct costs £'000	2,160	2,096	2,075
Revenue £'000	2,430	2,227	2,125
Racing bicycles			
Volume	11,000	11,500	11,750
Direct costs £'000	4,950	5,750	6,227.5
Revenue £'000	6,875	7,475	7,931.25
Exercise bicycles			
Volume	2,800	2,800	2,700
Direct costs £'000	756	840	837
Revenue £'000	910	980	945
Indirect costs £'000: inc.	1,225	1,730	1,890
Distribution	175	200	250
Promotion	300	280	240
Administration and other	750	850	1,000
Interest on loan	-	400	400
Profit before tax £'000	1,664	703.5	301.75

Required

Acting in the role of Simon Gaskell:

(a) Write a report, evaluating the current strategies being pursued by the Ace Bicycle Company (ABC) for its different market segments, using appropriate theoretical models to support your analysis. **(25 marks)**

(b) Identify and explain the key factors which should be taken into consideration before ABC decide on developing manufacturing/assembly facilities in China. **(13 marks)**

(c) Using the example of the ACE Bicycle Company to support your views, identify the benefits of:

(i) Organic growth **(4 marks)**
(ii) Acquisitions **(4 marks)**
(iii) Joint developments **(4 marks)**

As a preferred means of developing the business in China.

(Total = 50 marks)

47 MidShire Health (6/13)   90 mins

Introduction

In 2011 Terry Nagov was appointed as Chief Executive Officer (CEO) of MidShire Health, a public authority with responsibility for health services in Midshire, a region with a population of five million people in the country of Etopia. Like all health services in Etopia, MidShire Health is funded out of general taxation and is delivered free of charge. Terry Nagov was previously the CEO of a large private company making mobility appliances for disabled people. He had successfully held a number of similar executive positions in companies producing consumer products and goods for the consumer market. He was appointed to bring successful private sector practices and procedures to MidShire Health.

Etopia had experienced a prolonged economic recession and such appointments were encouraged by the government of Etopia who were faced with funding increased healthcare costs. They perceived that private sector expertise could bring some order and greater control to the functioning of public sector services. One of the government ministers publicly commented on the apparent 'anarchy of the health service' and its tendency to consume a disproportionate amount of the money collected through general taxation. The government was keen on establishing efficiencies in the public sector, by demonstrating 'value for money' principles.

Vision and strategic planning

Terry Nagov believed that all organisations need to be firmly focused on a visionary objective. He stated that 'our (MidShire Health) mission is to deliver health to the people of Midshire and, by that, I don't just mean hospital services for the sick, but a wider vision, where health is a state of complete physical, mental and social well-being and not merely the absence of disease or infirmity.'

He believed that this vision could only be achieved through a comprehensive strategic planning process which set objectives, policies and standards at a number of levels in the organisation. In the strategic plan, the high-level objectives and policies of the organisation would be cascaded down to operational levels in a series of lower-level plans, where departments and functions had specific objectives that all contributed to the overall strategic vision. Terry Nagov had successfully implemented such strategic planning systems at previous organisations he had worked for. He believed that centralised, senior management should decide strategy, and that line managers should be given power and responsibility to achieve their defined objectives. This approach had worked well in the heavily automated industries he had worked in, with semiskilled employees closely following standards and procedures defined by senior managers in the organisation.

Terry Nagov believed that a project should be put in place to establish a formal strategic planning system at MidShire Health and that this should be supported by a comprehensive computer-based information system which recorded the outcomes and activities of the organisation. He immediately engaged the commercial IT consultants, Eurotek, to develop and implement this information system using a standard software package that they had originally developed for the banking sector. The overall strategic planning system project itself would be owned by a small steering group of two senior hospital doctors, two hospital nursing managers and two workers from the health service support sector. Health service support employees provide health services to the wider community in the form of health education and public health information and initiatives. Their inclusion in the steering group was not welcomed by the hospital doctors, but the CEO wanted a wide range of professional input. 'Collectively', Terry declared, 'the steering group has responsibility for delivering health to the Midshire community'.

Initial meeting of the steering group (meeting 1)

The initial meeting of the steering group was not attended by the two senior hospital doctors. In Etopia, it is accepted that hospital doctors, although employed by the health authority on full-time contracts, also have the right to undertake paid private work (practice) where they deliver services for private hospitals to fee-paying patients. This right was negotiated by their professional body, the Institute of Hospital Doctors (IOHD), many years ago. Many of the patients they treat in private practice have paid for private health insurance so that they can be treated quickly and thus avoid the long waiting times associated with the free, public service. The initial meeting of the steering group coincided with a day when both doctors were undertaking private work. In their absence, the steering group approved the overall vision of the CEO and agreed to the initiation of an information system project to generate the detailed planning and control information to support this vision. The exact nature and contents of this information system would be determined by a small multi-disciplinary team reporting to the steering group and referred to as the 'implementation team'. It was made up of three administrative staff employed by MidShire Health supported by four technical consultants from Eurotek, experienced in implementing their software package solution. The composition of the implementation team and steering group is shown in Figure 1.

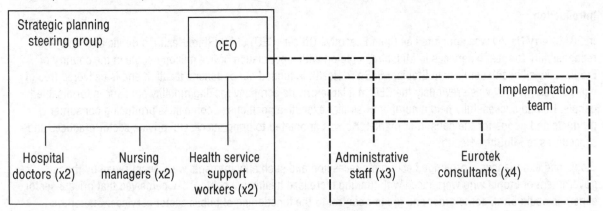

Figure 1: Composition of the steering group and the implementation team

Second meeting of the steering group (meeting 2)

The second meeting was attended by the two senior hospital doctors, but one of the health service support sector workers could not attend. At the start of the meeting, the two hospital doctors questioned the wide definition of health agreed at the previous meeting. One of the hospital doctors suggested that delivering health in this wider context was completely beyond the resources and capabilities of MidShire Health. 'You have to realise', he said, 'that poor health is often caused by poverty, bad housing and social dislocation. You cannot expect MidShire Health to solve such problems. We can advise and also treat the symptoms, but prevention and cure for these wider issues are well beyond us.' The nursing managers, who had previously approved the wider definition of health, now voiced their support for a narrower definition of health and sided with the hospital doctors. One of them commented that 'our real work is treating the sick and we must recognise this'. The CEO, outnumbered and outmanoeuvred in the meeting, had to agree to a modification of his initial vision, narrowing the overall objective to 'effectively and efficiently treating disease'. 'And, as we all know', stated one of the doctors, 'efficiency can only be achieved through giving control and budgets to the doctors, not to the administrators who are an unwanted overhead. This is the very first step we should take.' The nursing managers agreed and the meeting came to a slightly acrimonious and early conclusion.

Meeting three of the steering group (meeting 3)

At the third meeting, a presentation was made by the IT consultants, Eurotek, where they demonstrated their software for recording business activities and showed how these activities could be measured against agreed targets. A great deal of discussion took place on the targets that could be set for measuring health efficiency. After a long heated debate, three measures were agreed for hospitals. It was suggested that similar measures should be discussed and developed for health service support services, such as health education. However, at this point, the two senior doctors declared that they had to leave the meeting to 'return to our real job of treating patients'. The CEO agreed that the health service support workers could establish their own measures before the next meeting.

One of these representatives commented that 'in my day-to-day job I am confronted by many people who have preventable illnesses. Their problems are due to poor diet and unhealthy habits. Preventing such problems must be better than curing them!' The CEO agreed; this was what he wanted to hear!

Meeting four of the steering group (meeting 4)

The fourth meeting of the steering group began with a discussion of the preventative perspective of health raised by one of the health service support workers at the end of the previous meeting. Both the hospital doctors and nursing managers suggested that this did not come under the revised definition of health used by the steering group, and the CEO quickly agreed. The rest of the meeting was dominated by a discussion of the costs of the Eurotek software solution. A local newspaper had run the headline 'spending money on computers – not patients' and it included a number of quotes attributed to one of the hospital doctors on the strategic steering group where he criticised the appointment of Eurotek and the attitude of the MidShire Health CEO. 'Running a manufacturing company is very different from running a health service', he said. 'We are motivated by service, not products and profit.' Terry Nagov as CEO, openly questioned the ethics of members of the steering group discussing confidential internal matters with the press. The hospital doctors and the nursing managers fiercely defended their right to do so. 'You have to understand', they said, 'our loyalty is to the profession and to the public. We must act in the public interest.' Nevertheless, the CEO raised the possibility of disciplinary action against the hospital doctor. At this point, the senior hospital doctors and the nursing managers left the meeting. The health service support workers stayed and pledged their support to the CEO. They revealed that the autocratic behaviour of hospital doctors often resulted in their work being both unrewarding and unrecognised. One commented, 'We have little professional autonomy, we feel controlled by the agenda of the hospital doctors.'

Meeting five of the steering group (meeting 5)

The possibility of disciplinary action against the hospital doctor had been published in the press and the Institute of Hospital Doctors (IOHD) had made a formal complaint about the CEO's behaviour to Etopia's health minister. Faced with pressure from within the hospital sector, Terry Nagov was forced to retract his threat of disciplinary action and to issue a public apology, but meeting five was boycotted by the hospital doctors and nursing manager representatives due to 'the lack of respect shown by the CEO'. Consequently, meeting five was cancelled.

Meeting six of the steering group (meeting 6)

This meeting received a report from the implementation team working on the specification of the information system for MidShire Health. They reported that the software suggested by Eurotek was excellent for time recording, analysis and reporting, but had very few features to aid the planning and control of activities. 'I suspected this all along', said one of the hospital doctors. 'I think this report shows that you are more interested in finding out what we are doing.The strategic planning exercise is really about cost reduction.' It was agreed that Eurotek should be contacted to provide a price for developing a bespoke solution for the information system requirements envisaged by the MidShire implementation team. 'I realise', the CEO said, 'this will affect the viability of the whole strategic planning project but I ask you all to pull together for the good of MidShire Health and its image within the community.'

Just prior to the next planned meeting, the implementation team specifying the information system reported that Eurotek had quoted a price of $600,000 to develop a software solution that integrated planning and control of hospital activities into their software package solution. This was additional to the $450,000 it was charging for the basic software package. The CEO reacted immediately by cancelling the information system project 'on cost grounds' and disbanding the steering group. He stated that 'from now on, I will personally specify and develop the targets required to bring health to the people of Midshire. I will focus on using the current systems to bring these into place'. Emails were sent to the steering committee members informing them of the dissolution of the steering group, stating that no further meetings would be held and no comments were invited. However, the costs of paying penalty charges to Eurotek were soon released to the press and Terry Nagov resigned from his post as CEO of MidShire Health to return to his previous company as chairman. The Institute of Hospital Doctors (IOHD) took the opportunity to issue the following press release:

'Once again, the government has failed to realise that managing public sector services is not the same as managing a private sector profit making company. Money and time have been wasted, and reputations needlessly damaged. Doctors and nurses, people at the cutting edge of the service, know what needs to be done. But time after time our views are disregarded by professional managers and administrators who have little understanding of healthcare delivery. The public deserve better and we, the IOHD, remain committed to delivering services in the public interest.'

Required

(a) (i)   Identify and analyse mistakes made by the CEO in the project management process (initiation, conduct and termination) in his attempt to introduce strategic planning, and an associated information system, at MidShire Health.   **(18 marks)**

(ii) Explain how an understanding of organisational culture and organisational configuration would have helped the CEO anticipate the problems encountered in introducing a strategic planning system, and an associated information system, at MidShire Health.   **(18 marks)**

Professional marks will be allocated in part (a) for the clarity, structure and logical flow of your answer.   **(4 marks)**

(b) Johnson, Scholes and Whittington identify three strategy lenses: design, experience and ideas.

Evaluate the strategic planning project at MidShire Health through each of these three strategy lenses.   **(10 marks)**

(Total = 50 marks)

48 Polymat Tapes (3.5, 12/03, amended)   90 mins

Introduction

Richard Johnson, Managing Director of Polymat Industrial Tapes Limited (PIT), was worried. The global economic slowdown following the events of 11 September 2001, and subsequent Stock Market falls had meant 2002 had been a difficult year for the company. The company manufactured a range of industrial tapes for sale to a wide range of customers, from masking tape used by individual Do-It-Yourself (DIY) enthusiasts through to high performance tapes for the major automotive and aerospace companies. The origins of the company were in the late 1920s when PIT set up as a private company making tapes for use by cable manufacturers who were meeting the growing needs of the National Grid (a Government owned electricity supply network). The technology for making its products was, therefore, reasonably mature though breakthrough products did occasionally occur – as witnessed by the explosive demand for optic fibre cable and PIT's hi-tech cable jointing tapes. The tapes were mainly produced by a process that coats adhesive on to a variety of materials, including PVC, textiles and paper.

Product range and competitive environment

PIT had grown up in close proximity to some of its much larger cable manufacturing and automotive customers. There were currently three factories manufacturing its product range. Its original factory concentrates on cable jointing products supplied to the large UK cable manufacturers. These manufacturers are exerting strong pressure for price reductions on their suppliers in order to prevent entry into the market by large US global cable manufacturers. PIT's products need to respond to any significant product developments by the UK cable manufacturers and by its US tape competitors. Johnson is very aware of the global brand recognition of one of its major US competitors, which has a strong consumer products division and a reputation for aggressive product innovation.

At its second factory PIT produces PVC tapes, mainly standardised products with a typical 30-year product life cycle. Distribution is primarily through electrical wholesalers with an extremely wide customer base. PIT's main UK competition is of a similar size and not regarded as being particularly innovative. PIT has also had some success in meeting the particular tape needs of car makers in their new car model programmes. PIT has had to satisfy the demanding quality standards required by each car manufacturer of their suppliers. The main competition comes from low cost base manufacturers from Europe and the Far East.

At its third factory PIT produces paper masking tape. The move into paper masking tape is a more recent move aimed at the apparently ever-increasing market for masking tape with particularly heavy demands by the car industry for use in paint spraying and in the domestic market by DIY customers. The technology to produce the tape was imported from the USA under licence with a very modern factory being built to manufacture these products. Unfortunately, PIT's masking tape capacity became available just as there was a significant slow down in global car sales. Tape manufacturers such as PIT are faced with the dual problem of excess industry capacity and sales of low priced tape in Europe by low cost North American producers. The main competitor is an American company with access to lower cost raw materials and a 35% share of the UK market compared to PIT's 20% share.

PIT's difficulties were further exacerbated by its inability to achieve efficient low cost operation, partly due to a high level of fixed overhead cost for the company as a whole. The fixed overhead had been significantly increased by an investment in, and operation of, a centralised warehouse facility. This warehouse and distribution facility had been designed to alleviate major space problems at the factories and improve service to all of the key clients, but in practice has merely added to overhead costs and working capital levels with little added value to the company's activities. Safety stocks of finished products continue to be held at the three factories. Distribution to the customers is through the company's own transport system.

Current situation and financial performance

PIT had been acquired by one of the UK's largest cable manufacturers during the Second World War. However, the recession of the early 1990s had seen the parent company look to concentrate on its core product – cable manufacture – and dispose of non-core activities including PIT's industrial tapes. Thus an opportunity was presented to the three senior directors to buy out the company. The subsequent buyout had, to use Richard Johnson's words, given them 'a company with a mature product range produced by outdated equipment'. Each of the directors has spent the majority of their careers in the industry and recognises the challenge of competing in markets that are dominated by large customers looking to drive prices down and rationalise their supplier base. The directors are committed to securing the future of the business and saving as many jobs as possible.

PIT is very much a product led as opposed to a marketing led company. The nature of its products mean that it employs a significant number of chemistry graduates at its three factories and each factory pursues a separate R & D strategy. Recognition of the changing marketplace had come with the appointment of Paul Wright, an economics graduate, as Marketing Manager. Paul soon recognised that the company lacked key information on its customers, the products they bought and which were profitable. To use Paul's words, there were some 'little gems' where the product was generating good margins from a small number of industrial customers. But identifying them is the problem. Many of its customers are small DIY retailers and information on the profitability of such orders was less than impressive. Equally worrying is the lack of any process through which the ideas for new or improved products brought back by its sales force are effectively considered in terms of PIT's ability to develop, make and then sell them at a profit. The dominance of the company by technologists means that there is a real gap between understanding market opportunities and the products developed in the company. There is also a failure to identify the key decision makers in their larger cable manufacture and automotive customers and little external recognition of the technological advances made by PIT's R & D activity.

Table 1: Information on PIT's current sales and financial performance (£'000) (where appropriate)

	2001/02 £'000	2002/03 £'000	2003/04 (forecast) £'000
Product group			
Cable Jointing Tapes			
Sales	4,000	4,510	5,100
Cost of sales	2,400	2,593	2,805
Gross profit	1,600	1,917	2,295
Transport costs	120	135	153
R & D	High	High	High
Market share	25%	25%	25%
Sales volume index	100	110	121
Product range	Narrow	Narrow	Medium
PVC Industrial Tapes	£'000	£'000	£'000
Sales	3,000	3,100	3,200
Cost of sales	1,650	1,705	1,760
Gross profit	1,350	1,395	1,440
Transport costs	150	155	160
R & D	Low	Low	Low
Market share	10%	9%	8%
Sales volume index	100	103	106
Product range	Wide	Wide	Wide

	2001/02	2002/03	2003/04 (forecast)
Paper Masking Tapes	£'000	£'000	£'000
Sales	2,500	2,400	2,300
Cost of sales	1,625	1,680	1,725
Gross profit	875	720	575
Transport costs	150	192	230
R & D	Moderate	Moderate	Moderate
Market share	20%	20%	20%
Sales volume index	100	106	112
Product range	Narrow	Medium	Medium
Company	£'000	£'000	£'000
Sales	9,500	10,010	10,600
Cost of sales	5,675	5,978	6,290
Gross profit	3,825	4,032	4,310
Transport costs	420	482	543
Other fixed costs	3,080	3,270	3,500
Operating profit	325	280	267
ROS	3.4%	2.8%	2.5%

Retardon

Indicative of the problems PIT faces, is its one and only breakthrough product 'Retardon'. This tape had been developed some five years earlier and offered significant fire resistant properties over the normal tapes supplied to cable manufacturers installing their cables in high risk environments, such as underground railway systems, airports and high rise buildings. Environmental conditions are favourable for a product with the ability to both reduce the risk of fire and the toxic fumes given off should a fire occur. However, despite significant R & D investment, the lack of adequate patent protection, a deficient product design and a failure to stimulate the market means that the threat of competition from more effectively organised competitors is increasingly likely.

Outlook for the future

Richard is sympathetic to Paul's concern over the lack of marketing information and the consequent failure to generate new products. Equally concerning is the speed at which many of its products are becoming commodity products in which price is the key factor influencing supplier choice. Certainly there are opportunities to work with the large automotive companies in their development of new models, but such projects were typically of five years duration and PIT's lack of market presence is not helping it secure these long-term contracts. Richard has now decided to get an external assessment of the company's position.

Required

(a) Assuming the role of an external consultant, prepare a report for Richard evaluating the performance of the three product groups and their contribution to overall company results. Use appropriate models to support your analysis. **(25 marks)**

(b) Assess the main strategic options open to PIT and recommend a preferred strategy. **(15 marks)**

(c) Explain how PIT might change from a technology driven culture to a marketing led one. **(10 marks)**

(Total = 50 marks)

49 Shoal plc (12/10) 90 mins

Introduction

Shoal plc is a well-known corporate organisation in the fish industry. It owns 14 companies concerned with fishing and related industries.

This scenario focuses on three of these companies:

ShoalFish Ltd – a fishing feet operating in the western oceans ShoalPro Ltd – a company concerned with processing and canning fish ShoalFarm Ltd – a company with saltwater fish farms.

Shoal plc is also finalising the purchase of the Captain Haddock chain of fish restaurants.

ShoalFish

Shoal plc formed ShoalFish in 2002 when it bought three small fishing feets and consolidated them into one feet. The primary objective of the acquisition was to secure supplies for ShoalPro. 40% of the fish caught by ShoalFish are currently processed in the ShoalPro factories. The rest are sold in wholesale fish markets. ShoalFish has recorded modest profits since its formation but it is operating in a challenging market-place. The western oceans where it operates have suffered from many years of over-fishing and the government has recently introduced quotas in an attempt to conserve fish stocks.

ShoalFish has 35 boats and this makes it the sixth largest feet in the western oceans. Almost half of the total number of boats operating in the western oceans are individually owned and independently operated by the boat's captain. Recent information for ShoalFish is given in Figure 1.

ShoalPro

ShoalPro was acquired in 1992 when Shoal plc bought the assets of the Trevarez Canning and Processing Company. Just after the acquisition of the company, the government declared the area around Trevarez a 'zone of industrial assistance'. Grants were made available to develop industry in an attempt to address the economic decline and high unemployment of the area. ShoalPro benefited from these grants, developing a major fish processing and canning capability in the area. However, despite this initiative and investment, unemployment in the area still remains above the average for the country as a whole.

ShoalPro's modern facilities and relatively low costs have made it attractive to many fishing companies. The fish received from ShoalFish now accounts for a declining percentage of the total amount of fish processed and canned in its factories in the Trevarez area. Recent information for ShoalPro is given in Figure 1.

ShoalFarm

ShoalFarm was acquired in 2004 as a response by Shoal plc to the declining fish stocks in the western oceans. It owns and operates saltwater fish farms. These are in areas of the ocean close to land where fish are protected from both fishermen and natural prey, such as sea birds. Fish stocks can be built up quickly and then harvested by the fish farm owner. Shoal plc originally saw this acquisition as a way of maintaining supply to ShoalPro.

Operating costs at ShoalFarm have been higher than expected and securing areas for new fish farms has been difficult and has required greater investment than expected. Recent information for ShoalFarm is given in Figure 1.

All figures in $m

	2007	2008	2009
ShoalFish			
Turnover of market sector	200.00	198.50	190.00
Turnover of ShoalFish	24.00	23.50	21.50
Gross profit	1.20	1.10	1.05
ShoalPro			
Turnover of market sector	40.00	40.10	40.80
Turnover of ShoalPro	16.00	16.20	16.50
Gross profit	1.60	1.65	1.75
ShoalFarm			
Turnover of market sector	10.00	11.00	12.00
Turnover of ShoalFarm	1.00	1.10	1.12
Gross profit	0.14	0.14	0.15

Figure 1: Financial data on individual companies 2007–2009

Captain Haddock

The Captain Haddock chain of restaurants was founded in 1992 by John Dory. It currently operates one hundred and thirty restaurants in the country serving high quality fish meals. Much of Captain Haddock's success has been built on the quality of its food and service. Captain Haddock has a tradition of recruiting staff directly from schools and universities and providing them with excellent training in the Captain Haddock academy. The academy ensures that employees are aware of the 'Captain Haddock way' and is dedicated to the continuation of the quality service

and practices developed by John Dory when he launched the first restaurant. All management posts are filled by recruiting from within the company, and all members of the Captain Haddock board originally joined the company as trainees. In 1999 the Prime Minister of the country identified Captain Haddock academy as an example of high quality in-service training. In 2000, Captain Haddock became one of the thirty best regarded brands in the country.

In the past few years, the financial performance of Captain Haddock has declined significantly (see Figure 2) and the company has had difficulty in meeting its bank covenants. This decline is partly due to economic recession in the country and partly due to a disastrous diversification into commercial real estate and currency dealing. The chairman and managing director of the company both resigned nine months ago as a result of concern over the breaking of banking covenants and shareholder criticism of the diversification policy. Some of the real estate bought during this period is still owned by the company. In the last nine months the company has been run by an interim management team, whilst looking for prospective buyers. At restaurant level, employee performance still remains relatively good and the public still highly rate the brand. However, at a recent meeting one of the employee representatives called for a management that can 'effectively lead employees who are increasingly demoralised by the decline of the company'.

Shoal plc is currently finalising their takeover of the Captain Haddock business. The company is being bought for a notional $1 on the understanding that $15 million is invested into the company to meet short-term cash flow problems and to improve liquidity. Shoal plc's assessment is that there is nothing fundamentally wrong with the company and that the current financial situation is caused by the failed diversification policy and the cost of financing this. The gross profit margin in the sector averages 10%.

Captain Haddock currently buys its fish and fish products from wholesalers. It is the intention of Shoal plc to look at sourcing most of the dishes and ingredients from its own companies; specifically ShoalFish, ShoalPro and ShoalFarm. Once the takeover is complete (and this should be within the next month), Shoal plc intends to implement significant strategic change at Captain Haddock so that it can return to profitability as soon as possible. Shoal plc has implemented strategic change at a number of its acquisitions. The company explicitly recognises that there is no 'one right way' to manage change. It believes that the success of any planned change programme depends on an understanding of the context in which the change is taking place.

Captain Haddock (all figures in $m)	2007	2008	2009
Turnover	115.00	114.50	114.00
Gross profit (loss)	0.20	(5.10)	(6.20)

Figure 2: Financial information for Captain Haddock 2007–2009

Required

(a) In the context of Shoal plc's corporate-level strategy, assess the contribution and performance of ShoalFish, ShoalPro and ShoalFarm. Your assessment should include an analysis of the position of each company in the Shoal plc portfolio. **(15 marks)**

Shoal plc explicitly recognises that there is no 'one right way' to manage change. It believes that the success of any planned change programme will depend on a clear understanding of the context within which change will take place.

(b) (i) Identify and analyse, using an appropriate model, the contextual factors that will influence how strategic change should be managed at Captain Haddock. **(13 marks)**

Professional marks will be awarded in part (b)(i) for the identification and justification of an appropriate model. **(2 marks)**

Once the acquisition is complete, Shoal plc wish to quickly turnaround Captain Haddock and return it to profitability.

(ii) Identify and analyse the main elements of strategic change required to achieve this goal. **(8 marks)**

Professional marks will be awarded in part (b)(ii) for the cogency of the analysis and for the overall relevance of the answer to the case study scenario. **(2 marks)**

Portfolio managers, synergy managers and parental developers are three corporate rationales for adding value.

(c) Explain each of these separate rationales for adding value and their relevance to understanding the overall corporate rationale of Shoal plc. **(10 marks)**

(Total = 50 marks)

BPP
LEARNING MEDIA

50 Bonar Paint (3.5, 6/07, amended)   90 mins

Introduction

Bonar Paint is a medium-sized paint manufacturer set up by two brothers, Jim and Bill Bonar. Turnover has been static for some years and both brothers are now wanting to retire from the business. The brothers have created a loyal workforce and feel that this loyalty will be strengthened if they sell the business to the three senior managers: Roy Crawford, production manager, Tony Edmunds, sales and marketing manager and Vernon Smith, chief accountant. The three managers recognise that this is a major opportunity for them to change the direction and growth of the company, but one that will involve the raising of significant loan and equity finance to buy the business. Equally significant are the equity stakes of £100,000 from each of them, which the banks will require to show the senior managers' personal commitment.

Company product range and processes

Bonar Paint makes high quality specialist paints for a range of industrial customers. Its major customers include car manufacturers, steel makers and the oil companies investing heavily in offshore oil rigs. Bonar Paint also supplies many smaller industrial customers. Raw materials are sourced from large chemical companies. Jim Bonar has the necessary chemical expertise and Bill has the complementary sales skills to meet the specialised paint needs of their demanding customers. Bonar Paint has a good reputation for product innovation and its product range of over 200 paints include paints able to tolerate harsh and demanding conditions. The small research and development team, headed by Jim, has an excellent track record of meeting the technical demands and timescales for developing new high performance paints. New paints are normally developed in response to customer demand and, consequently, there is no formal process for new product development. Replacing Jim's technical skills and leadership will undoubtedly create problems for the senior management buyout team. Jim and Bill have taken all the key strategic decisions to date with little reference to the senior management team.

Bonar Paint's product innovation success has come at a price. Its product range is far too extensive to sustain with the majority of the paints produced infrequently and in small batches. As a consequence, customers often experience long lead times when ordering a particular paint. This results in higher than necessary inventory levels, much of which is unlikely to be bought. Paints are supplied directly to each and every customer. Unfortunately, Bonar Paint's management information systems fail to show the profitability or otherwise of individual paints and the future demand for the paint. There is little communication between sales and the research and development part of the business. Roy Crawford has consistently argued for the benefits of reducing the product range and increasing the size of the batches produced. Such a policy would give him more control over production, and lower costs. Higher volumes would also justify investment in new production technology, which would bring labour savings with fewer and less skilled workers needed to operate the new machinery. There has been little recent investment in new plant or machinery. Simplifying the product range would also improve quality and reduce expensive warranty claims when paints fail to perform in a hostile environment. Such claims require extensive investigation to determine where the responsibility lies.

Competitive environment

Tony Edmunds, as sales and marketing manager, is very resistant to any attempt to reduce the product range. Such a move, he feels, would upset customers and lead to their defection to competitors. The UK paint industry is very fragmented – at the top end of the industry are large international paint manufacturers with significant brands and supplying both industrial and domestic paint customers. They produce in high volumes and offer a comprehensive but limited range of paints. At the bottom end of the industry are many small and medium-sized paint makers. Many have chosen to produce own label paints for the large Do-It-Yourself (DIY) retailers. Specialist paint makers, such as Bonar Paint, are finding it increasingly difficult to survive with neither the sales volumes nor brands to compete with their larger competitors. The industry as a whole is seen as mature and lacking in innovation. There is increased environmental concern about the toxic by-products of lead-based paints and the development of less toxic water-based paints is only slowly emerging. Even more worrying is the increased usage of plastics and other materials, which do not require painting. The DIY market is dominated by the same large international paint makers and the market for industrial paint is vulnerable to the usage of alternative materials and entry into the UK market by large European paint makers.

Future strategy

Each of the prospective buyout managers has a different view of how Bonar Paints should develop after the buyout takes place. Roy Crawford sees his proposed reduction of the product range and increased investment in new production technology as a means of reducing costs, improving margins and focusing on getting a larger share of their current large industrial paint customers' needs. Product innovation should only come when there is a clear and profitable need for a new paint. He argues for a critical review of their smaller customers, believing them to be unprofitable.

Tony Edmunds, however, sees an extension of the customer base as a necessary step in securing the future of the firm. The product range should be extended to meet the needs of the professional painters and decorators looking for high performance paints for use in both domestic and industrial applications. Tony also feels they should begin to make their paints available to the general public. He has seen the success of factory shops in other industries, whereby manufacturers sell unwanted and outdated inventory to customers at heavily discounted prices at an outlet on the firm's premises. Such a shop would be relatively simple and inexpensive to set up and bring Bonar Paint's products to a wider public. It would require either the production, or buying in, of a range of the most popular paint colours used in home decoration.

Finally, Vernon Smith is anxious that the internal control systems be improved to establish which paints are, or are not, making money. Investment in new paint ranges or technology should be resisted until the buyout has been successfully completed. In the longer term he feels that Bonar Paint is vulnerable because of its small size and that increasing size through merger and acquisition of similar sized firms is a sensible strategy. Vernon is also anxious that a fair valuation is made of the business and that the sales forecasts for 2007 and 2008, made by Bill Bonar, are realistic.

Table 1: Financial information on Bonar Paint (£'000)

	2004	2005	2006	2007 (estimate)	2008 (forecast)
Sales	10,500	10,250	10,000	10,500	11,000
Cost of sales	5,250	5,400	5,500	5,460	5,500
Gross profit	5,250	4,850	4,500	5,040	5,500
Marketing	100	100	100	150	150
Distribution	1,575	1,650	1,700	1,785	1,650
Administration	2,100	2,150	2,200	2,250	2,200
Research and Development	105	100	100	105	110
Net profit	1,370	850	400	750	1,390
Return on sales (%)	13.0	8.3	4.0	7.1	12.6
Net assets	2,500	2,350	2,200	2,200	2,200
Inventory	1,450	1,750	2,000	1,650	1,200
Warranty costs	100	150	150	125	100
Employees	250	264	262	275	280
Product range (units)	204	210	212	220	230

Customer analysis:

Sales to large industrial companies	75%
Sales to small industrial companies	25%

Required

The senior management team has asked for your advice in evaluating the current position of Bonar Paint and its attractiveness for a management buyout.

(a)   Using models where appropriate, provide the senior management team at Bonar Paint with an assessment of its strategic position and its attractiveness, or otherwise, for a management buyout.   **(20 marks)**

Roy Crawford has argued for a reduction in both the product range and customer base to improve company performance.

(b)   Assess the advantages and disadvantages to Bonar Paint of choosing such a strategy.   **(15 marks)**

Bonar Paint to date has had no formal strategic planning process.

(c) What are the advantages and disadvantages of developing a formal mission statement to guide Bonar Paint's future direction after the buyout and what role could the mission statement play in the strategic planning process? **(15 marks)**

(Total = 50 marks)

51 Hammond Shoes (6/12)   90 mins

Introduction

Hammond Shoes was formed in 1895 by Richard and William Hammond, two brothers who owned and farmed land in Petatown, in the country of Arnland. At this time, Arnland was undergoing a period of rapid industrial growth and many companies were established that paid low wages and expected employees to work long hours in dangerous and dirty conditions. Workers lived in poor housing, were largely illiterate and had a life expectancy of less than forty years.

The Hammond brothers held a set of beliefs that stressed the social obligations of employers. Their beliefs guided their employment principles – education and housing for employees, secure jobs and good working conditions. Hammond Shoes expanded quickly, but it still retained its principles. Today, the company is a private limited company whose shares are wholly owned by the Hammond family. Hammond Shoes still produce footwear in Petatown, but they now also own almost one hundred retail shops throughout Arnland selling their shoes and boots. The factory (and surrounding land) in Petatown is owned by the company and so are the shops, which is unusual in a country where most commercial properties are leased. In many respects this policy reflects the principles of the family. They are keen to promote ownership and are averse to risk and borrowing. They believe that all stakeholders should be treated fairly. Reflecting this, the company aims to pay all suppliers within 30 days of the invoice date. These are the standard terms of supply in Arnland, although many companies do, in reality, take much longer to pay their creditors.

The current Hammond family are still passionate about the beliefs and principles that inspired the founders of the company.

Recent history

Although the Hammond family still own the company, it is now totally run by professional managers. The last Hammond to have operational responsibility was Jock Hammond, who commissioned and implemented the last upgrade of the production facilities in 1991. In the past five years the Hammond family has taken substantial dividends from the company, whilst leaving the running of the company to the professional managers that they had appointed. During this period the company has been under increased competitive pressure from overseas suppliers who have much lower labour rates and more efficient production facilities. The financial performance of the company has declined rapidly and as a result the Hammond family has recently commissioned a firm of business analysts to undertake a SWOT analysis to help them understand the strategic position of the company.

SWOT analysis: Here is the summary SWOT analysis from the business analysts' report.

Strengths

Significant retail expertise: Hammond Shoes is recognised as a successful retailer with excellent supply systems, bright and welcoming shops and shop employees who are regularly recognised, in independent surveys, for their excellent customer care and extensive product knowledge.

Excellent computer systems/software expertise: Some of the success of Hammond Shoes as a retailer is due to its innovative computer systems developed in-house by the company's information systems department. These systems not only concern the distribution of footwear, but also its design and development. Hammond is acknowledged, by the rest of the industry, as a leader in computer-aided footwear design and distribution.

Significant property portfolio: The factory in Petatown is owned by the company and so is a significant amount of the surrounding land. All the retail shops are owned by the company. The company also owns a disused factory in the north of Arnland. This was originally bought as a potential production site, but increasingly competitive imports made its development unviable. The Petatown factory site incorporates a retail shop, but none of the remaining retail shops are near to this factory, or indeed to the disused factory site in the north of the country.

Weaknesses

High production costs: Arnland is a high labour cost economy.

Out-dated production facilities: The actual production facilities were last updated in 1991. Current equipment is not efficient in its use of either labour, materials or energy.

Restricted internet site: Software development has focused on internal systems, rather than internet development. The current website only provides information about Hammond Shoes; it is not possible to buy footwear from the company's website.

Opportunities

Increased consumer spending and consumerism: Despite the decline of its manufacturing industries, Arnland remains a prosperous country with high consumer spending. Consumers generally have a high disposable income and are fashion conscious. Parents spend a lot of money on their children, with the aim of 'making sure that they get a good start in life'.

Increased desire for safe family shopping environment: A recent trend is for consumers to prefer shopping in safe, car-free environments where they can visit a variety of shops and restaurants. These shopping villages are increasingly popular.

Growth of the green consumer: The numbers of 'green consumers' is increasing in Arnland. They are conscious of the energy used in the production and distribution of the products they buy. These consumers also expect suppliers to be socially responsible. A recent television programme on the use of cheap and exploited labour in Orietaria was greeted with a call for a boycott of goods from that country. One of the political parties in Arnland has emphasised environmentally responsible purchasing in its manifesto. It suggests that 'shorter shipping distances reduce energy use and pollution. Purchasing locally supports communities and local jobs'.

Threats

Cheap imports: The lower production costs of overseas countries provide a constant threat. It is still much cheaper to make shoes in Orietaria, 4000 kilometres away, and transport the shoes by sea, road and train to shops in Arnland, where they can be offered at prices that are still significantly lower than the footwear produced by Hammond Shoes.

Legislation within Arnland: Arnland has comprehensive legislation on health and safety as well as a statutory minimum wage and generous redundancy rights and payments for employees. The government is likely to extend its employment legislation programme.

Recent strategies

Senior management at Hammond Shoes have recently suggested that the company should consider closing its Petatown production plant and move production overseas, perhaps outsourcing to established suppliers in Orietaria and elsewhere. This suggestion was immediately rejected by the Hammond family, who questioned the values of the senior management. The family issued a press release with the aim of re-affirming the core values which underpinned their business. The press release stated that 'in our view, the day that Hammond Shoes ceases to be a Petatown company, is the day that it closes'. Consequently, the senior management team was asked to propose an alternative strategic direction.

The senior management team's alternative is for the company to upgrade its production facilities to gain labour and energy efficiencies. The cost of this proposal is $37.5m. At a recent scenario planning workshop the management team developed what they considered to be two realistic scenarios. Both scenarios predict that demand for Hammond Shoes' footwear would be low for the next three years. However, increased productivity and lower labour costs would bring net benefits of $5m in each of these years. After three years the two scenarios differ. The first scenario predicts a continued low demand for the next three years with net benefits still running at $5m per year. The team felt that this option had a probability of 0.7. The alternative scenario (with a probability of 0.3) predicts a higher demand for Hammond's products due to changes in the external environment. This would lead to net benefits of $10m per year in years four, five and six. All estimated net benefits are based on the discounted future cash flows.

Financial information: The following financial information (see Figure 1) is also available for selected recent years for Hammond Shoes manufacturing division.

Figure 1: Extracts from the financial statements of Hammond Shoes (2007–2011)

Extracted from the income statements (all figures in $m)	2011	2009	2007
Revenue	700	750	850
Cost of sales	(575)	(600)	(650)
Gross profit	125	150	200
Administration expenses	(95)	(100)	(110)
Other expenses	(10)	(15)	(20)
Finance costs	(15)	(10)	(5)
Profit before tax	5	25	65
Income tax expense	(3)	(7)	(10)
Profit for the year	2	18	55

Extracted from statements of financial position (all figures in $m)			
Trade receivables	70	80	90
Share capital	100	100	100
Retained earnings	140	160	170
Long term borrowings	70	50	20

In 2007, Hammond Shoes paid, on average, their supplier invoices 28 days after the date of invoice. In 2009 this had risen to 43 days and in 2011, the average time to pay a supplier invoice stood at 63 days.

Required

(a) Analyse the financial position of Hammond Shoes and evaluate the proposed investment of $37.5 million in upgrading its production facilities. **(14 marks)**

(b) Using an appropriate framework (or frameworks) examine the alternative strategic options that Hammond Shoes could consider to secure its future position. **(20 marks)**

Professional marks will be awarded in part (b) for the clarity, structure and style of the answer. **(4 marks)**

(c) Advise the Hammond family on the importance of mission, values and objectives in defining and communicating the strategy of Hammond Shoes. **(12 marks)**

(Total = 50 marks)

52 EcoCar (06/11)   90 mins

The EcoCar company was formed six years ago to commercially exploit the pioneering work of Professor Jacques of Midshire University, a university in the country of Erewhon. Over a number of years he had patented processes that allowed him to use Lithium-ion batteries to power an electric car, which could travel up to 160 kilometres before it needed recharging. Together with two colleagues from the university, he set up EcoCar to put the car into commercial production.

Coincidentally, an area in the south of Midshire was suffering from major industrial decline. This area was centred on the former Lags Lane factory of Leopard Cars, which had recently been shut down by its parent company, bringing to an end 60 years of continuous vehicle manufacture on that site. Many skilled car production workers had been made redundant in an area that already suffered significant unemployment. Grants from the regional council and interest-free loans from the government allowed EcoCar to purchase and re-furbish part of the Lags Lane site and take on a hundred of the skilled workers made redundant by Leopard Cars.

The company now manufactures three car models: the original Eco, the EcoPlus, and the EcoLite. The EcoPlus is a luxury version of the Eco and shares 95% of the same components. The EcoLite is a cheaper town car and uses only 70% of the components used in the Eco. The rest of the components are unique to the EcoLite. A comparison of an Eco with a similar petrol-fuelled car (Kyutia 215) is given in Figure 1. This table also gives a comparison with a hybrid car (Xdos-Hybrid C) where the petrol engine is supplemented by power from an electric motor. Hybrids are a popular way of reducing emissions and fuel consumption. Petrol currently costs $5 per litre in Erewhon. There are

also experimental cars, not yet in production, which are fuelled by other low-emission alternatives to petrol such as hydrogen.

Model	Eco	Kyutia 215	Xdos-HybridC
Power source	Lithium-ion batteries, electric motor	Petrol	Petrol with assistance from an electric motor
Price	$9,999	$7,999	$9,500
Emissions (CO_2)	Zero	180 gram/kilometre	95 gram/kilometre
Economy	Approximately $1 per 20 kilometres (electricity charge)	8 litres/100km	5 litres/100km
Performance	0-100 kph: 18 seconds Max speed: 120kph	0-100 kph: 10 seconds Max speed: 180kph	0-100 kph: 12 seconds Max speed: 170kph
Range	160 kilometres until the battery needs recharging	550 kilometres on a tank full of petrol	1,200 kilometres on a tank full of petrol

Figure 1: Comparison of the Eco with comparable conventional and hybrid cars

The Eco model range can be re-charged from a domestic electricity supply. However, to supplement this, the government has recently funded the development of 130 charging stations for electric cars spread throughout the country. It has also given business tax incentives to switch to electric cars and is heavily taxing cars with high CO_2 emissions because of the detrimental effect of excess CO_2 on the environment. It has also enacted a number of laws on car safety which EcoCar has to comply with. Erewhon itself remains a prosperous, developed country with a well-educated population. The government is committed to tackling social and economic problems in areas such as South Midshire. EcoCar still receives significant government grants to help keep the company financially viable.

The EcoCar model range is largely bought by 'green' consumers in Erewhon, who are prepared to pay a price premium for such a car. They are also popular in the Midshire region, where the residents are proud of their car making tradition and grateful to Professor Jacques and the government for ensuring its survival, albeit at a reduced level. Only 5% of EcoCar's production is exported.

Universal Motors

One year ago, EcoCar was bought by Universal Motors, the second largest car manufacturer in the world. Professor Jacques and his two colleagues remain as senior managers and board members of the company. Car production of electric cars is still very low (see Figure 2), but Universal Motors believes that demand for electric cars will be very significant in the future and purchased EcoCar as a way of entering this market. They believe that Lithium-ion batteries (the power source for the EcoCar range) will eventually become lighter, cheaper and give better performance and range.

Since purchasing the company Universal Motors have undertaken an external and internal analysis of EcoCar and invested further capital into the business.

Their analysis identified four main areas of weakness. These are given below:

(1) **High cost of labour, skills shortage and production capacity problems**

Although EcoCar was established in an area where there already existed a pool of skilled car workers, the subsequent retirement of many of these workers has left a skills gap. Although unemployment remains high in the area, applicants for jobs appear to lack the skills and motivation of the older workers. EcoCar is finding it difficult to recruit skilled labour and this shortage is being reflected in increased wages and staff costs at the Lags Lane site. The urban location of the Lags Lane site also causes a problem. Inbound logisitics are made expensive by the relative inaccessibility of the site and the general congestion on Midshire's main roads. Finally, there is insufficient production capacity at the Lags Lane site to meet the current demand for EcoCar's products. EcoCar attempts to produce the most profitable combination of its products within this constraint. However, it is unable to completely satisfy market demand.

(2)   **Lack of control and co-ordination**

The individual departments and functions of the company are poorly integrated. Although budgets are agreed annually, they are not properly co-ordinated or monitored. Recently, car production was halted by the shortage of an important sub-assembly. Components for this sub-assembly had to be purchased quickly at a cost 10% above the normal purchase price. Overtime also had to be paid to employees to minimise the delay in restarting car production. A similar lack of co-ordination appears to exist within bought-in inventory items. A recent purchase order for superior quality car seats was agreed by senior management, despite the fact that few customers had ever specified this option on the EcoPlus model. The seats were delivered and stored, but the finance department was unable to pay for them within the supplier's agreed payment terms. This failure was leaked to a newspaper and a very public row took place between EcoCar and the supplier. Eventually short-term financing (at a premium interest rate) was agreed with one of the banks and the seat manufacturer was paid.

(3)   **Research and Development – succession and learning**

In the initial growth of EcoCar, the technical capabilities of the three founding senior managers were very significant. However, these three managers are now aged 50 or over. There is concern that their technical expertise and thirst for innovation is diminishing. To some extent the senior managers recognised this themselves two years ago and instigated a graduate training scheme with the aim of 'bringing new thinking into the company and ensuring its future'. Four graduates were taken on and a graduate training scheme agreed. However, it was cut within a year because 'training costs got out of control' and all four graduates have subsequently left the firm. A resignation letter from one of the graduates criticised the 'poor management skills of senior managers'. Universal Motors is concerned that the research and management culture is inappropriate and outdated. As a result, the graduates were not properly managed or motivated and there is evidence that their contribution was not welcomed or recognised.

(4)   **The understanding of risk**

Universal Motors is concerned that decisions are taken by the senior managers of EcoCar without a proper analysis of the associated risks. Although the three senior managers are individually quite risk averse, as a team they make quite risky decisions. At a recent meeting to discuss entering a car in an economy car rally (accompanied by a mobile charging system) various risks were discussed at length but not documented or analysed. After two hours of exhaustive discussion the three senior managers decided to vote on the decision. They all voted in favour. No further discussion was held about the risks they had just discussed. Furthermore, the risk of an employee leaving to join a competitor and taking valuable information with them is discussed at every board meeting. However, no action is taken to address the risk. There just seems to be a general expectation that it will not occur.

Outsourcing

To address the first internal weakness, Universal Motors is considering outsourcing the manufacture of the EcoLite model to an overseas company. Information relevant to this decision is presented in Figure 2. The potential manufacturer has quoted a production price to Universal Motors of $3,500 per car. The manufacturing plant is approximately 300 miles from Erewhon, which includes crossing the 40 mile wide Gulf of Berang.

There are 112 production hours available in total per week at the Lags Lane site (seven days per week, two eight hour shifts) which can be used for a combination of the three product lines.

The weekly overhead costs are $35,000 per week at Lags Lane. If the production of the EcoLite model is outsourced, it is forecast that overhead costs will fall by $1,250 per week. The transportation cost is estimated at $250 for each outsourced EcoLite produced

	Eco	EcoPlus	EcoLite
Selling price per car ($)	9,999	12,999	6,999
Variable cost per car ($)	7,000	10,000	4,500
Weekly demand (cars)	6	5	6
Production time per car (hrs)	9	10	8

Figure 2: Information relevant to the outsourcing decision

Required

(a) Universal Motors have explicitly recognised the need for analysing the external macro-environment and marketplace (industry) environment of EcoCar.

Analyse the external macro-environment and marketplace (industry) environment of EcoCar. **(16 marks)**

Professional marks will be awarded in part (a) for the inclusion of appropriate model(s) and the overall structure and clarity of the analysis. **(4 marks)**

(b) Universal motors is considering outsourcing the EcoLite model to an overseas manufacturer, whilst retaining in-house production of the Eco and EcoPlus models.

Evaluate the financial and non-financial case for and against the outsourcing option. **(15 marks)**

(c) Three weaknesses identified by Universal Motors are (1) lack of control and co-ordination, (2) research & development – succession and learning and (3) the understanding of risk.

Analyse how each of these three weaknesses might be addressed at EcoCar. **(15 marks)**

(Total = 50 marks)

53 Oceania National Airlines (12/07)   90 mins

Introduction

The island of Oceania attracts thousands of tourists every year. They come to enjoy the beaches, the climate and to explore the architecture and history of this ancient island. Oceania is also an important trading nation in the region and it enjoys close economic links with neighbouring countries. Oceania has four main airports and until 1997 had two airlines, one based in the west (OceaniaAir) and one based in the east (Transport Oceania) of the island. However, in 1997 these two airlines merged into one airline – Oceania National Airlines (ONA) with the intention of exploiting the booming growth in business and leisure travel to and from Oceania.

Market sectors

ONA serves two main sectors. The first sector is a network of routes to the major cities of neighbouring countries. ONA management refer to this as the regional sector. The average flight time in this sector is one and a half hours and most flights are timed to allow business people to arrive in time to attend a meeting and then to return to their homes in the evening. Twenty five major cities are served in the regional sector with, on average, three return flights per day. There is also significant leisure travel, with many families visiting relatives in the region. The second sector is what ONA management refer to as the international sector. This is a network of flights to continental capitals. The average flight time in this sector is four hours. These flights attract both business and leisure travellers. The leisure travellers are primarily holiday-makers from the continent. Twenty cities are served in this sector with, on average, one return flight per day to each city.

Image, service and employment

ONA is the airline of choice for most of the citizens of Oceania. A recent survey suggested that 90% of people preferred to travel ONA for regional flights and 70% preferred to travel with ONA for international flights. 85% of the respondents were proud of their airline and felt that it projected a positive image of Oceania. The company also has an excellent safety record, with no fatal accident recorded since the merging of the airlines in 1997. The customer service of ONA has also been recognised by the airline industry itself. In 2005 it was voted Regional Airline of the Year by the International Passenger Group (IPG) and one year later the IPG awarded the ONA catering department the prestigious Golden Bowl as provider of the best airline food in the world. The courtesy and motivation of its employees (mainly Oceanic residents) is recognised throughout the region. 95% of ONA employees belong to recognised trade unions. ONA is perceived as an excellent employer. It pays above industry average salaries, offers excellent benefits (such as free healthcare) and has a generous non-contributory pension scheme. In 2004 ONA employed 5400 people, rising to 5600 in 2005 and 5800 in 2006.

Fleet

Fleet details are given in Table 1. Nineteen of the Boeing 737s were originally in the fleet of OceaniaAir. Boeing 737s are primarily used in the international sector. Twenty-three of the Airbus A320s were originally part of the Transport Oceania fleet. Airbuses are primarily used in the regional sector. ONA also used three Embraer RJ145 jets in the regional sector.

Table 1: Fleet details

	Boeing 737	Airbus A320	Embraer RJ145
Total aircraft in service			
2006	21	27	3
2005	21	27	3
2004	20	26	2
Capacity (passengers)	147	149	50
Introduced	October 1991	November 1988	January 1999
Average age	12.1 years	12.9 years	6.5 years
Utilisation (hrs per day)	8.70	7.41	7.50

Performance

Since 2004 ONA has begun to experience significant competition from 'no frills' low-cost budget airlines, particularly in the international sector. Established continental operators now each offer, on average, three low fares flights to Oceania every day. 'No frills' low-cost budget airlines are also having some impact on the regional sector. A number of very small airlines (some with only one aircraft) have been established in some regional capitals and a few of these are offering low-cost flights to Oceania. A recent survey for ONA showed that its average international fare was double that of its low-cost competitors. Some of the key operational statistics for 2006 are summarised in Table 2.

Table 2: Key operational statistics for ONA in 2006

	Regional	International	Low-cost competitor average
Contribution to revenue ($m)			
Passenger	400	280	Not applicable
Cargo	35	15	Not applicable
Passenger load factor			
Standard class	73%	67%	87%
Business class	90%	74%	75%
Average annual pilot salary	$106,700	$112,500	$96,500
Source of revenue			
Online sales	40%	60%	84%
Direct sales	10%	5%	12%
Commission sales	50%	35%	4%
Average age of aircraft	See Table 1		4.5 years
Utilisation (hrs per day)	See Table 1		now allows 9.10

ONA have made a number of operational changes in the last few years. Their website, for example, passengers to book over the internet and to either have their tickets posted to them or to pick them up at the airport prior to travelling. Special promotional fares are also available for customers who book online. However, the website does not currently allow passengers to check-in online, a facility provided by some competitors. Furthermore, as Table 2 shows, a large percentage of sales are still commission sales made through travel agents. Direct sales are those sales made over the telephone or at the airport itself. Most leisure travellers pay standard or economy fares and travel in the standard class section of the plane. Although many business travellers also travel in standard class, some of them choose to travel business class for which they pay a price premium.

In the last three years, the financial performance of ONA has not matched its operational success. The main financial indicators have been extracted and are presented in Table 3. In a period (2004–2006) when worldwide passenger air travel revenue increased by 12% (and revenue from air travel to Oceania by 15%) and cargo revenue by 10%, ONA only recorded a 4·6% increase in passenger revenue.

Table 3: Extracted Financial Information

All figures in $m

Extracted from the statement of financial position

		2006	2005	2004
Non-current assets				
Property, plant and equipment		788	785	775
Other non-current assets		60	56	64
	Total	848	841	839
Current assets				
Inventories		8	7	7
Trade receivables		68	71	69
Cash and cash equivalents		289	291	299
	Total	365	369	375
Total assets		**1213**	**1210**	**1214**
Total shareholders' equity		250	259	264
Non-current liabilties				
Interest bearing long-term loans		310	325	335
Employee benefit obligations		180	178	170
Other provisions		126	145	143
Total current liabilities		616	648	648
Current liabilities				
Trade payables		282	265	255
Current tax payable		9	12	12
Other current liabilities		56	26	35
Total current liabilities		347	303	302
Total equity and liabilities		**1213**	**1210**	**1214**

Extracted from the income statement

		2006	2005	2004
Revenue				
Passenger		680	675	650
Cargo		50	48	45
Other revenue		119	112	115
	Total	849	835	810
Cost of sales				
Purchases		535	525	510
	Total	535	525	510
Gross profit		314	310	300

		2006	2005	2004
Wages & salaries		215	198	187
Directors' salaries		17	16	15
Interest payable		22	21	18
	Total	254	235	220
Net profit before tax		60	75	80
Tax expense		18	23	24
Net profit after tax		42	52	56

Future strategy

The management team at ONA are keen to develop a strategy to address the airline's financial and operational weaknesses. One suggestion has been to re-position ONA itself as a 'no frills' low-cost budget airline. However, this has been angrily dismissed by the CEO as likely to lead 'to an unnecessary and bloody revolution that could cause the death of the airline itself'.

Required

(a) Using the information provided in the scenario, evaluate the strengths and weaknesses of ONA and their impact on its performance. Please note that opportunities and threats are **not** required in your evaluation.

(20 marks)

(b) The CEO of Oceania National Airways (ONA) has already strongly rejected the re-positioning of ONA as a 'no frills' low-cost budget airline.

   (i)   Explain the key features of a 'no frills' low-cost strategy. **(4 marks)**

   (ii) Analyse why moving to a 'no frills' low-cost strategy would be inappropriate for ONA.

   Note: requirement (b) (ii) includes 3 professional marks. **(16 marks)**

(c) Identify and evaluate other strategic options ONA could consider to address the airline's current financial and operational weaknesses.

   Note: requirement (c) includes 2 professional marks. **(10 marks)**

(Total = 50 marks)

54 ABCL (12/09) 90 mins

Introduction

ABC Learning plc (ABCL) is a large training company based in Arcadia. It specialises in professional certification training for accountants, lawyers, business analysts and business consultants. ABCL delivers training through face-to-face courses and e-learning, mainly using full-time lecturing staff. Thirty percent of its revenue is from e-learning solutions. It is constantly seeking new markets and acquisitions to improve shareholder value. It has become aware of the expanding business analysis certification training industry (BACTI) in the neighbouring country of Erewhon. ABCL has commissioned Xenon, a market intelligence company to undertake an analysis of the BACTI market in Erewhon with the aim of assessing its attractiveness and profitability before deciding whether or not to expand into Erewhon. ABCL is aware that an Arcadian competitor, Megatrain, has previously tried to establish itself in this market in Erewhon. Established providers in the BACTI industry in Erewhon responded by price cutting and strengthened promotional campaigns. This was supported by a campaign to discredit the CEO of Megatrain and to highlight its foreign ownership. Within six months Megatrain had withdrawn from the market in Erewhon.

Xenon interim report on the BACTI market in Erewhon – January 2009

Introduction

The BACTI market in Erewhon is dominated by three suppliers; CATalyst, Batrain and Ecoba (collectively known as the 'big three'). CATalyst is a wholly owned subsidiary of the Tuition Group, a public limited company quoted on the Erewhon stock market. The last annual report of the Tuition Group identified CATalyst as core to their strategy and a source of significant growth. Batrain is a private limited company, with the shares equally divided between the eight founding directors. Four of these directors are under 40. Ecoba is also a private limited company with 95% of the shares owned by Gillian Vari. The other 5% are owned by her business partner Willy Senterit. Gillian is approaching retirement age.

Delivery model

Both CATalyst and Batrain have similar delivery models. They employ mainly full-time lecturing staff who are offered attractive salary packages, share options and generous benefits; such as ten weeks paid holiday. Even with these packages they find it hard to recruit. Teaching vacancies are advertised on both of their websites. CATalyst and Batrain both stress their 'brand' in their marketing material. On their websites there is no specific reference to the lecturers who will present each module. In contrast, Ecoba specifically identifies lecturers in both its advertisements (supported by photographs of the lecturers) and on their website, where the lecturer taking the module is specified. All the lecturers are 'high profile' names in the business analysis training community. None of these are directly employed by Ecoba. They are all on fixed-term contracts and are paid a premium daily rate for lecturing and assignment marking. Xenon interviewed Mike Wilson, a named management lecturer and asked him about the arrangement. He said that he felt relatively secure about it. 'Students are attracted to Ecoba because they know I will be teaching a particular module. I suppose I could be substituted by a cheaper lecturer but the students would soon complain that they had been misled.' Mike had also worked as a sub-contractor for CATalyst but no longer did so because he found that a booking could be cancelled at short notice if full-time staff became available.

'Gillian Vari (the MD of Ecoba) is much more transparent and straightforward in her treatment of sub-contract staff. The only problem is the time it takes to pay our invoices. We are always complaining about that.'

The 'big three' are recognised and established brands in the industry. Although the 'big three' are competitors there does appear to be a degree of mutual tolerance of each other. For example, they appear to have co-ordinated their response to the attempted entry of Megatrain into the industry. Three of the directors of Batrain used to work as lecturers for CATalyst and Gillian Vari (the MD of Ecoba) was a director of the company that spawned CATalyst. Mike Wilson has lectured for all of the 'big three' providers. However, there are also, approximately, twenty other providers in the industry in Erewhon (accounting for 20% of the total industry revenue).

Students and providers

The fees of 60% of students are paid for by their employers. There are around 15 major corporate clients who place significant contracts for certification training with providers. Most (but not all) of these are placed with the 'big three'. CATalyst is particularly strong in managing these contracts, setting up dedicated training sessions and a personalised website to support each contract. However, there is increasing evidence that providers are being played off against each other by the major corporate customers who are seeking to drive down costs. One of the large insurance companies recently moved all of its training to Ecoba after several years of using CATalyst as its sole provider. Another large customer has also recently moved their training contract to Ecoba because they were impressed by the 'named' lecturers that Ecoba used. Interestingly, in a new move for the industry, WAC, a major supplier of business analysis consultancy services, recently bought one of the smaller business analysis training providers and thus is now able to deliver all of its business analysis training in-house for its own staff.

Business Analysis certification in Erewhon is administered by the EIoBA (Erewhon Institute of Business Analysts) which sets the examination. There is no requirement for students to attend a certified training course. In fact 40% of students prepare themselves for the examinations using self-study. One of the smaller BACTI providers has gained some success by offering a blended learning solution that combines tutor support with e-learning modules. Interestingly, the 'big three' all appear to acknowledge the possibilities of e-learning but do not promote it. All three have invested money in specially designed training venues and so they seem committed, at least in the short term, to their classroom-based model.

EIoBA runs a certification scheme for providers of training. This operates at three levels; bronze, silver and gold. The 'big three' all have the highest level of certification (gold). Xenon recognises that gold certification offers a significant competitive advantage and that it will take any new entrant more than one year to achieve this level of certification.

Ecoba Ltd: background

Ecoba is a private limited company. As well as being its managing director and majority shareholder, Gillian Vari is the only full-time lecturer. Mike Wilson told Xenon that Gillian is averse to employing full-time lecturing staff because 'they have to be paid if courses do not run and also during the long vacations'. Her policy appears to be to minimise overhead training and administrative costs. This may contribute to the slow payment of lecturers. Mike Wilson did comment that the 'full-time administrative staff seem to be under increasing pressure'.

Figure 1 provides comparative data for CATalyst and Batrain. Financial information for Ecoba is presented in Figure 2.

Figure 1: Financial Analysis (all 2008)

	CATalyst	Batrain
Revenue	$35,000,000	$25,000,000
Cost of sales as a percentage of revenue	65%	63%
Average payables settlement period	65 days	60 days
Average receivables settlement period	30 days	35 days
Sales revenue to capital employed	3·36	3·19
Gross profit margin	35%	37%
Net profit margin	6%	8%
Liquidity ratio	0·92	0·93
Gearing ratio	30%	25%
Interest cover ratio	3.25	4.75

Figure 2: Financial Analysis: Ecoba Ltd

(All figures in $'000)

Extract from the statement of financial position

	2008	2007
Assets		
Non-current assets		
Intangible assets	5,800	5,200
Property, plant, equipment	500	520
Total	6,300	5,720
Current assets		
Inventories	70	90
Trade receivables	4,300	3,000
Cash and cash equivalents	2,100	1,500
Total	6,470	4,590
Total assets	12,770	10,310
Current liabilities		
Trade payables	6,900	4,920
Current tax payable	20	15
Total	6,920	4,935
Non-current liabilities		
Long-term borrowings	200	225
Total	7,120	5,160
Equity		
Share capital	5,100	5,100
Retained earnings	550	50
Total equity and liabilities	12,770	10,310

Extract from the statement of comprehensive income

	2008	2007
Revenue	22,000	17,000
Cost of sales	(17,500)	(13,750)
Gross profit	4,500	3,250
Overhead expenses	(3,500)	(2,500)
Profit before tax and finance costs	1,000	750
Finance costs	(20)	(20)
Profit before tax	980	730
Tax expense	(30)	(25)
Profit for the year	950	705

Required

Xenon usually analyses an industry using Porter's five forces framework.

(a)　Using Porter's framework, analyse the business analysis certification industry (BACTI) in Erewhon and assess whether it is an attractive market for ABCL to enter. **(20 marks)**

After considering Xenon's interim report, ABCL decided to enter the business analysis certification training industry (BACTI) in Erewhon through the acquisition of one of the three main providers. In March 2009 they asked Xenon to write a short report to evaluate Ecoba Ltd and to analyse whether it was the most appropriate and attractive of the three possible acquisition targets. You are a business analyst with Xenon and were given the task of writing this report.

(b)   Write the requested short report evaluating Ecoba Ltd and analysing whether it was the most appropriate and attractive of the three possible acquisition targets for ABCL.   **(16 marks)**

Professional marks will be awarded in part (b) for clarity and format of your report.   **(4 marks)**

In November 2009 ABCL acquired Ecoba Ltd. Gillian Vari agreed to stay on for two years to assist the management of the ownership transition. However, her business partner became seriously ill and ABCL have agreed, on compassionate terms, for her to leave the company immediately. ABCL, from experience, know that they must manage stakeholders very carefully during this transition stage.

(c)   Identify the stakeholders in Ecoba Ltd and analyse how ABCL could successfully manage them during the ownership transition.   **(10 marks)**

(Total = 50 marks)

55 Wetland Trust (6/10)   90 mins

Introduction

Aradia is a country with great mineral wealth and a hard-working, well educated population. It has recently enjoyed sustained economic growth generated by the expansion of its manufacturing industry. The population has grown as well and, as a result, agricultural output has increased to satisfy this problem, with much previously marginal land converted to arable and pasture land. However, after 10 years of sustained economic growth the country, in 2009, began to experience economic problems. Gross Domestic Product (GDP) has declined for three successive quarters and there are increasing problems with servicing both personal and business debt leading to business bankruptcy and homelessness.

The climate of the country is also changing, becoming drier and widier. Last year, for the first time, the government had to ration water supply to domestic homes.

The formation of WET

In 2002, the environmental campaigner Zohail Abbas published a book on the Wetlands of Arcadia. The Wetlands of Arcadia are areas of natural habitat made up of land that is saturated with moisture, such as swamp, marsh or bog. Dr Abbas' book chronicled the systematic destruction of the wetlands due to population growth, increased economic development and climate change. Water had been progressively drained from the wetlands to provide land for farming and to provide water for the increasing population and industry of the country. Wetlands also provide an important habitat for wildlife. Dr Abbas showed that in the period from 1970 to 2000, there had been a dramatic decline in birds, mammals and fish dependent upon the wetland habitat. Some species had become extinct.

In 2003, Dr Abbas formed the WEtland Trust (WET), with the aim of preserving, restoring and managing wetlands in Arcadia. Since its formation, the Trust has acquired the four remaining wetland sites left in the country. The Trust's work is funded through donations and membership fees. Donations are one-off contributions. Membership is through an annual subscription which gives members the right to visit the wetlands. Each wetland is managed by volunteers who provide access and guidance to members. The wetlands are not currently open to the general public. Dr Abbas' work on the wetlands has brought him to the attention of the Arcadian public and he is now a popular television presenter. WET is also a strong brand, recognised by 85% of Arcadians in a recent green consumer survey.

GiftHelp

WET is a registered charity. Charities within Arcadia have to be registered with the Commission of Charities which regulates charities within the country. The number of charities has increased significantly in the last few years leading to widespread criticism from established charities, politicians and the public, who believe that many of these charities have been formed to exploit taxation advantages. Dr Abbas is a vociferous critic, particularly after the Commission of Charities gave permission for the establishment of a rival wetland charity (WWTFT) despite the fact that all wetlands in Arcadia are under WET's control. WWTFT promised to create new wetlands artificially in Arcadia. They have so far only raised $90,000 of the $151,000,000 required for a pilot site. Dr Abbas was part of a group that lobbied the government for the reform of the Commission of Charities, but the government has rejected their advice.

The government of Arcadia has recently changed the rules on charity taxation. Previously, once the charity's accounts had been audited, the government paid the charity a sum of 20% of the total value of donations and memberships. This reflected the income tax the donor would have paid on the amount they had given to the charity. However, the government has now declared that this is unfair as not all donations or membership fees are from Arcadian taxpayers or from people in Arcadia who actually pay tax. Consequently, in the future, charities will have to prove that a donation or membership fee was from an Arcadian tax payer. Only donations or fees supported by this proof will receive the 20%, so called GiftHelp, refund. Research and evidence from other countries suggests that 30% of donors will not give the GiftHelp details required and so the charity will not be able to reclaim tax from these donors. An analysis of WET's income for 2008 is given in Figure 1 and an analysis of income for all charities is given in Figure 2. Research has also shown that 55% of members and 85% of donors also give money to other charities.

Figure 1 – WET's income sources; year 2008

	Members	Donors
Arcadian Taxpayers	$650,000	$100,000
Arcadian Non-taxpayers	$100,000	$50,000
Non-Arcadian	$50,000	$50,000
Total	$800,000	$200,000

Figure 2 – Income for all Arcadian charities; year 2008 (in $millions)

	Amount donated to charity
Health charities	775.0
Social care charities	275.5
International charities	149.8
Environmental charities (including WET)	45.6

WET 2003–2009

WET was originally a vehicle for promoting the vision and ideology of Dr Abbas. Volunteers were recruited to manage and administer the wetland sites and the number of members gradually increased (see Figure 3). Many of these volunteers have become acknowledged experts in wetlands and their knowledge and experience is valued by members. However, as the charity expanded a number of issues emerged.

1. Administrative costs rose at a faster rate than subscriptions and donations. Administrative staff are all full-time paid employees of the charity. However, despite an increase in staff numbers, there is a substantial backlog of cleared applications in the Membership Department which have not yet been entered into the membership computer system. The membership computer system is one of the systems used to support administration. However, the functionality of this software is relatively restricted and cumbersome and there have been complaints about its accuracy. For example, members claim that renewal reminders are often sent out to people who have already paid and that members who should have received renewal invoices have never received them. As a result 'we seem to be wasting money and losing members'.

2. Members have become increasingly frustrated by their limited access to the wetlands and many wish to participate more in determining the policies of the organisation. They feel that the wetland sites should also have better facilities, such as toilets and concealed positions for bird watching. There were increasing criticisms of Dr Abbas' domineering style and cavalier disregard for the members. Membership is currently falling and very little money is spent on sales and marketing to arrest this fall.

3. Volunteers have also become disgruntled with Dr Abbas' management style. They feel patronised and undervalued. The number of volunteers is declining (see Figure 3) which in itself is reducing the access of members to the wetlands. A recent decision not to pay travelling expenses to volunteers led to further resignations.

Figure 3 – Membership and volunteer statistics WET 2002–2009

	2002	2003	2004	2005	2006	2007	2008	2009
Members	12,000	14,000	15,000	20,000	22,000	25,000	23,000	20,000
Volunteers	30	35	35	45	50	52	50	40

At the 2009 Annual General Meeting (AGM) Dr Abbas stood down and announced the appointment of a new Chief Executive Officer (CEO). Dr Abbas admitted in an emotional resignation speech that he had not sufficiently taken into account the views of members, donors or volunteers. 'It is a matter of deep regret that I spent more time focusing on wetlands rather than people'. He was made honorary president of WET in recognition of his work in establishing and expanding the charity.

The new CEO, Sheila Jenkins, wishes to pursue a more inclusive strategy, and immediately set about consulting the membership and voluntary staff about what they expected from WET. The two clearest messages that came from this consultation exercise were that:

- Members wanted much better access to wetlands and they were more interested in the wildlife that used the wetlands (particularly the birds) than the wetlands sites themselves. This was not a view shared by Dr Abbas who wanted the wetlands preserved for their own sake.

- Volunteers wished to be much more involved in the running of the organisation and wanted to be treated by management in a way that recognised their voluntary commitment.

System review

Sheila Jenkins is particularly keen to improve the technology that supports WET. She has stated that the better acquisition and management of members, volunteers and donors is an important objective of WET. WET's current website is very rudimentary, but she sees 'email and website technology as facilitating the acquisition, retention and satisfaction of our customers' needs. And by customers, I mean both prospective and existing members, volunteers and donors of WET.' She also wishes to gain increased revenue from each member and donor.

The current membership renewal process has come under instant review and it is shown in the swim lane diagram (flowchart) of Figure 4. A narrative to support this diagram is given below.

Membership renewal process

One month before the date of membership renewal, the computer system (Membership System) sends a renewal invoice to a current (not lapsed) member giving subscription details and asking for payment. A copy of this invoice is sent to the Membership Department who file it away. Approximately 80% of members decide to renew and send their payment (either by providing credit card details (60%) or as a cheque (40%)) to WET. The Membership Department matches the payment with the renewal invoice copy. The invoice copy (stamped paid) is sent to Sales and Marketing who use it to produce a membership card and send this card together with a Guide to Sites booklet, to the member. The Membership Department passes the payment to the Finance Department.

Finance now submits payments to the bank. It currently takes the Finance Department an average of five days from the receipt of renewal to notifying the Membership Department of the cleared payment. Once cleared, Finance notifies the Membership Department by email and they update the Membership System to record that the payment has been made. As mentioned before, there is a backlog in entering these details into the computer system.

Some cheques do not clear, often because they are filled in incorrectly (for example, they are unsigned or wrongly dated). In these circumstances, Finance raises a payment request and sends it to the member. Once the member re-submits a replacement cheque, it again goes through the clearing process.

Credit card payments are cleared instantly, but again there may be problems with the details. For example, incorrect numbers and incorrect expiry dates will lead to the transaction not being authorised and so, in these circumstances, Finance again raises a payment request.

The members' response to payment requests is very low (about 5%). The finance manager has described this as scandalous and 'an unethical response from supposedly ethical people'.

Also, not shown on the diagram: One week before renewal, the Membership System produces a renewal reminder and sends it to the member. Some members pay as a result of this reminder. If payment is not received then the member details are recorded as 'lapsed'.

Figure 4 – membership renewal process

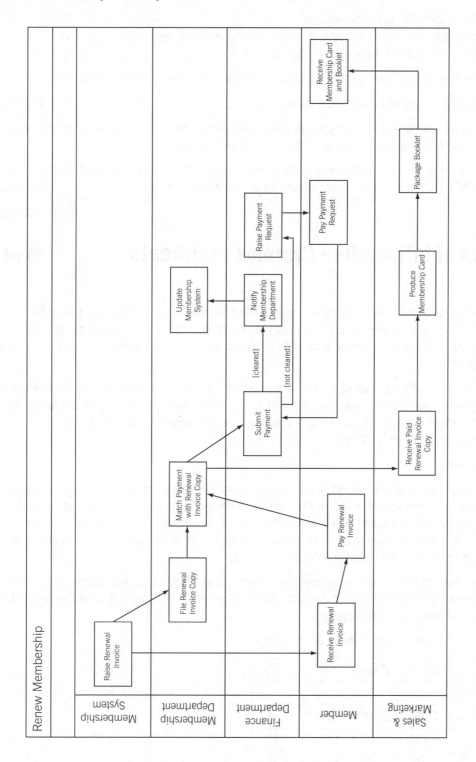

Required

(a) The new CEO, Sheila Jenkins, recognises that she should understand the strategic position of WET before considering strategic options and changes. She wants a concise assessment of the strategic position; covering environment, strategic capability, stakeholder expectations and organisational mission.

Undertake the assessment, required by Sheila Jenkins, of the strategic position of WET. **(21 marks)**

Professional marks will be awarded in part (a) for the scope, structure and tone of the answer. **(4 marks)**

(b)   Problems with the current membership renewal process include:

- The low response to payment requests
- The despatch of renewal reminders for people who have already paid
- The failure to send renewal invoices to some members

Analyse faults in the current membership renewal process that cause the problems identified above.

Suggest solutions that would remedy these faults.   **(15 marks)**

(c)   Sheila Jenkins sees customers as 'both prospective and existing members, volunteers and donors of WET'. She also wishes to gain increased revenue from each member and donor.

Evaluate how email and website technology might facilitate the acquisition and retention of WET's customers and support WET's aim to gain increased revenues from members and donors.   **(10 marks)**

(Total = 50 marks)

56 Institute of Information Systems Architects   90 mins

Case study

The Institute of Information Systems Architects (IISA) was founded in 1999 by representatives of a number of organisations who felt that systems architecture should have its own qualification. The Institute has its own Board who report to a Council of 13 members. Policy is made by the Board and ratified by Council. The IISA is registered as a private limited company.

The IISA is based in London where it employs staff to administer its examination scheme and provide services to its members. It also employs two chief examiners on a full-time basis. These examiners are responsible for setting the IISA certificate examinations which take place monthly in training and conference centres around the UK. No examinations are currently held outside the UK.

The examination scheme

The IISA examination scheme contains four examinations. If candidates pass all four papers they can undertake an oral diploma examination. If they pass this oral they are eligible to become members. Each examination costs £42. The oral examination costs £60 and is conducted by two members of the Institute. The current membership fee is £30 per year. Many training companies run courses to help candidates prepare for the IISA examinations, however, it is possible to sit an examination without attending such a course.

All the examinations are open book, one-hour examinations, preceded by 15 minutes' reading time. At a recent meeting, the IISA Board rejected the concept of computer-based assessment. They felt that competence in this area was best assessed by written examination answers.

Candidate numbers for the last four years are given in Figure 1:

	2003	2004	2005	2006
Number of Candidates				
Paper 1	2,897	2,800	2,600	2,215
Paper 2	2,649	2,300	2,115	1,879
Paper 3	3,450	1,908	1,975	1,750
Paper 4	3,210	3,012	1,790	1,600
Diploma	3,015	2,985	1,690	1,550
Members	17,050	19,115	19,350	19,715

Figure 1: Candidate numbers for 2003–2006

The Board of the IISA is concerned about falling candidate numbers. They have concluded that this drop reflects the maturing marketplace in the UK and that they should now look overseas for candidates. The Board has targeted India, Singapore and China as countries with a large number of IT professionals who would be interested in the qualification. It is now formulating a strategy to launch the qualification in these three countries.

Eighty percent of IISA candidates already have a degree. However, they perceive that getting the IISA Diploma will enhance their career prospects. Many employers specify the Diploma in Information Systems Architecture in their job advertisements for system architects. IISA promotes events to communicate the fact that the IISA Diploma is the primary qualification for system architects.

The examinations system

The examination script handling system requires markers, invigilators and auditors. These are all employed by the IISA on a contract basis and are usually practising or retired information system architects. Many have taken early retirement from colleges and universities. They are paid hourly fees for undertaking invigilation, marking and auditing as requested by the IISA. The administrative employees of the IISA must check marker and auditor availability before sending scripts to them to mark or audit. It is increasingly difficult to find people to undertake marking (and, to a lesser extent, invigilation and auditing) and the IISA is currently considering raising marking fees and undertaking a recruitment drive. The marking load per marker is not particularly onerous. The most prolific marker last year marked 900 scripts at an average of 10 per day. Each script is normally four to six pages long.

In recent years, there have been a number of problems with the script handling system:

The cost of couriers has increased substantially.

Some scripts have been lost by couriers and candidates have had to be compensated.

It has proved difficult to keep marker, auditor and invigilator details up to date. Some scripts have been sent to out of date addresses and it has been difficult (and on one occasion, impossible) to recover the scripts.

Candidates increasingly expect their results to be processed more quickly. At a recent feedback seminar, the slow publishing of results was heavily criticised.

The cost of secure storage and secure disposal has increased.

The script handling system

The examinations are held in conference centres and training rooms around the country. The open-book nature of the examination means that many of the security measures surrounding closed-book examinations are no longer required. However, examinations are invigilated by an external invigilator employed by the IISA on a contract basis. The invigilator hands out the examination scripts at the start of the examination and collects them at the end. He or she then takes them home and arranges for a secure designated courier to collect the scripts and take them to the IISA headquarters in London. When they arrive in London, administrative employees identify the appropriate and available markers and send the scripts, by secure designated courier, to these markers. The markers then mark the scripts and return them (again by secure courier) to the IISA headquarters. The administrative employees then review the need to audit selected scripts. All scripts with a mark between 45 and 55 are sent to an auditor for second marking. The auditor (like the marker and the invigilator) is employed by the IISA on a contract basis. Once audited, the scripts are returned with a recommended mark. Again, transport between the auditor and the headquarters is only through secure, designated couriers. If the candidate has scored less than 45 or greater than 55 their results are published straight away. The candidate is notified by e-mail or by surface post of their actual mark. Candidates whose scripts were audited are sent their marks after the audit has been completed.

It has been suggested that changes in the script handling system should be made before the organisation attempts to expand overseas. Before discussing possible changes, it has been agreed that a process diagram should be drawn of the current script handling system at the IISA. The diagram is shown in Figure 2.

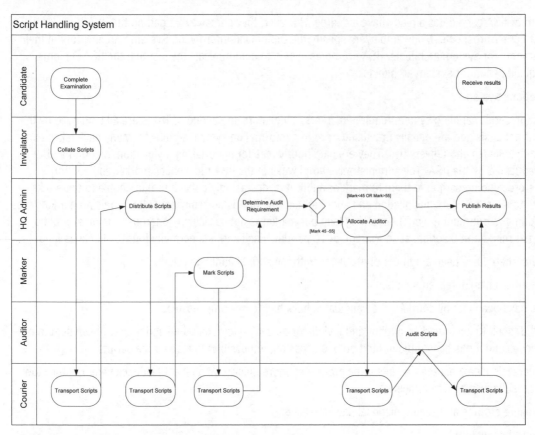

Figure 2: The current script handling system at the IISA

The nature of the Board and its relationship with Council make it a very conservative organisation. It is notably risk averse and is only confident about its expertise within the fairly restricted bounds of information system architecture. Attempts to look at complementary qualifications (such as software engineering) have been swiftly rejected by Council. However, at a recent Council meeting, internal development, acquisitions and strategic alliances were all discussed as possible development methods by which the organisation's strategic direction could be pursued. After much discussion it was agreed that strategic alliances appeared to offer the best way forward, and so the Board were asked to favour this approach when formulating their strategy for India, Singapore and China.

Required

(a) Analyse the macro-environment of the IISA. Use this analysis to highlight the key drivers of change that are likely to affect the IISA in the future.

Note: requirement (a) includes 3 professional marks. **(20 marks)**

(b) Explain the principles of strategic alliances and assess how appropriate this development method is to the IISA. **(10 marks)**

(c) Evaluate the significance of the script handling system in the context of Harmon's process-strategy matrix. **(10 marks)**

(d) Define **two** options for the redesign of the current script handling system at the IISA. Explain the advantages and disadvantages of each option.

Note: requirement (d) includes 2 professional marks. **(10 marks)**

(Total = 50 marks)

57 The National Museum   90 mins

The National Museum (NM) was established in 1857 to house collections of art, textiles and metalware for the nation. It remains in its original building which is itself of architectural importance. Unfortunately, the passage of time has meant that the condition of the building has deteriorated and so it requires continual repair and maintenance. Alterations have also been made to ensure that the building complies with the disability access and health and safety laws of the country. However, these alterations have been criticised as being unsympathetic and out of character with the rest of the building. The building is in a previously affluent area of the capital city. However, what were once large middle-class family houses have now become multi-occupied apartments and the socio-economic structure of the area has radically changed. The area also suffers from an increasing crime rate. A visitor to the museum was recently assaulted whilst waiting for a bus to take her home. The assault was reported in both local and national newspapers.

Thirty years ago, the government identified museums that held significant Heritage Collections. These are collections that are deemed to be very significant to the country. Three Heritage Collections were identified at the NM, a figure that has risen to seven in the intervening years as the museum has acquired new items.

Funding and structure

The NM is currently 90% funded by direct grants from government. The rest of its income comes from a nominal admission charge and from private sponsorship of exhibitions. The direct funding from the government is based on a number of factors, but the number of Heritage Collections held by the museum is a significant funding influence. The Board of Trustees of the NM divide the museum's income between departments roughly on the basis of the previous year's budget plus an inflation percentage. The division of money between departments is heavily influenced by the Heritage Collections. Departments with Heritage Collections tend to be allocated a larger budget. The budgets for 2008 and 2009 are shown in Figure 1.

Collection sections	Number of Heritage collections	Budget ($'000) – 2008	Budget ($'000) – 2009
Architecture	2	120.00	125.00
Art	2	135.00	140.00
Metalwork	1	37.50	39.00
Glass		23.00	24.00
Textiles	1	45.00	47.50
Ceramics		35.00	36.00
Furniture		30.00	31.50
Print and books		35.00	36.50
Photography		15.00	15.50
Fashion		10.00	10.50
Jewellery	1	50.00	52.50
Sculpture		25.00	26.00
Administration		60.50	63.00
Total		621.00	647.00

Figure 1: Section budgets; 2008 and 2009

The head of each collection section is an important position and enjoys many privileges, including a large office, a special section heads' dining room and a dedicated personal assistant (PA). The heads of sections which have 'Heritage Collections' also hold the title of professor from the National University.

The departmental structure of the NM (see Figure 2) is largely built around the twelve main sections of the collection. These sections are grouped into three departments, each of which has a Director. The Board of Directors is made up of the three directors of these departments, together with the Director of Administration and the Director General. The museum is a charity run by a Board of Trustees. There are currently eight trustees, two of whom have been recently appointed by the government. The other six trustees are people well-known and respected in academic fields relevant to the museum's collections.

BPP LEARNING MEDIA

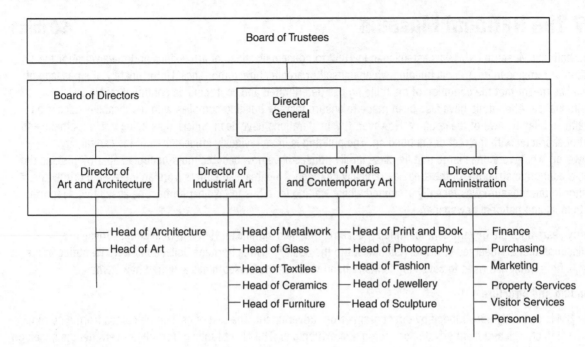

Figure 2: Current Organisational Structure

Government change

One year ago, a new national government was elected. The newly appointed Minister for Culture implemented the government's election manifesto commitment to make museums more self-funding. The minister has declared that in five year's time the museum must cover 60% of its own costs and only 40% will be directly funded by government. This change in funding will gradually be phased in over the next five years. The 40% government grant will be linked to the museum achieving specified targets for disability access, social inclusion and electronic commerce and access. The government is committed to increasing museum attendance by lower socio-economic classes and younger people so that they are more aware of their heritage. Furthermore, it also wishes to give increasing access to museum exhibits to disabled people who cannot physically visit the museum site. The government have asked all museums to produce a strategy document showing how they intend to meet these financial, accessibility and technological objectives. The government's opposition has, since the election, also agreed that the reliance of museums on government funding should be reduced.

Traditionally, the NM has provided administrative support for sections and departments, grouped together beneath a Director of Administration. The role of the Director General has been a part-time post. However, the funding changes introduced by the government and the need to produce a strategy document, has spurred the Board of Trustees to appoint a full-time Director General from the private sector. The trustees felt they needed private industry expertise to develop and implement a strategy to achieve the government's objectives. The new Director General was previously the CEO of a major chain of supermarkets.

Director General's proposal

The new Director General has produced a strategic planning document showing how the NM intends to meet the government's objectives. Proposals in this document include:

(1)   Allocating budgets (from 2010) to sections based on visitor popularity. The most visited collections will receive the most money. The idea is to stimulate sections to come up with innovative ideas that will attract more visitors to the museum. Visitor numbers have been declining (see Figure 3) since 2004.

Visitor numbers (000s)	2007	2006	2005	2004
Age 17 or less	10	12	15	15
Age 18-22	5	8	12	10
Age 23-30	10	15	20	20
Age 31-45	20	20	18	25
Age 46-59	35	35	30	30
Age 60 or more	40	35	35	30
Total	120	125	130	130

Figure 3: Visitor numbers 2004–2007

(2)   Increasing entrance charges to increase income, but to make entry free to pensioners, students, children and people receiving government benefit payments.

(3)   Removing the head of sections' dining room and turning this into a restaurant for visitors. An increase in income from catering is also proposed in the document.

(4)   Removing the head of sections' personal assistants and introducing a support staff pool to reduce administrative costs.

(5)   Increasing the display of exhibits. Only 10% of the museum's collection is open to the public. The rest is held in storage.

(6)   Increasing commercial income from selling posters, postcards and other souvenirs.

The Director General has also suggested a major re-structuring of the organisation as shown in Figure 4.

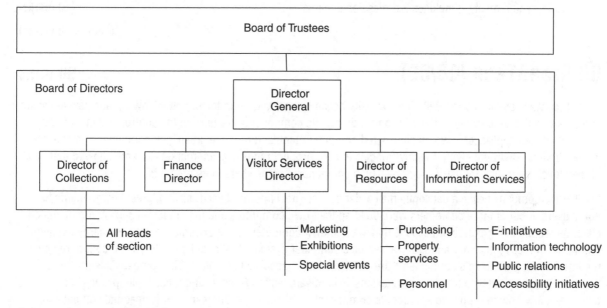

Figure 4: Proposed Organisational Structure

Reaction to the proposals

Employees have reacted furiously to the Director General's suggestions. The idea of linking budgets to visitor numbers has been greeted with dismay by the Director of Art and Architecture. 'This is a dreadful idea and confuses popularity with historical significance. As previous governments have realised, what is important is the value of the collection. Heritage Collections recognise this significance by putting the nation's interests before those of an undiscerning public. As far as I am concerned, if they want to see fashion, they can look in the high street shops. Unlike fashion, great art and architecture remains.' The Director of Art and Architecture and the two professors who hold the Head of Architecture and Head of Art posts have also lobbied individual members of the Board of Trustees with their concerns about the Director General's proposals.

The Director of Industrial Arts and the Director of Media and Contemporary Art have contacted powerful figures in both television and the press and as a result a number of articles and letters critical of the Director General's proposals have appeared. A recent television programme called 'Strife at the NM' also featured interviews with

various heads of collections criticising the proposed changes. They were particularly critical of the lack of consultation; 'these proposals have been produced with no input from museum staff. They have been handed down from on high by an ex-grocer', said one anonymous contributor.

Eventually, the criticism of staff and their lack of cooperation prompted the Director General to ask the Board of Trustees to publicly back him. However, only the two trustees appointed by the government were prepared to do so. Consequently, the Director General resigned. This has prompted an angry response from the government which has now threatened to cut the museum's funding dramatically next year and to change the composition of the Board of Trustees so that the majority of trustees are appointed directly by the government. The Minister of Culture has asked the museum to develop and recommend a new strategy within one month.

Required

(a)   Analyse the macro-environment of the National Museum using a PESTEL analysis.   **(20 marks)**

(b)   The failure of the Director General's strategy has been explained by one of the trustees as 'a failure to understand our organisational culture; the way we do things around here'.

        Assess the underlying organisational cultural issues that would explain the failure of the Director General's strategy at the National Museum.

        Note: requirement (b) includes 2 professional marks.   **(20 marks)**

(c)   Johnson, Scholes and Whittington identify three strategy lenses; design, experience and ideas.

        Examine the different insights each of these lenses gives to understanding the process of strategy development at the National Museum.

        Note: requirement (c) includes 2 professional marks.   **(10 marks)**

        (Total = 50 marks)

58 GreenTech (06/09)   90 mins

GreenTech was established in 1990. The company began by specialising in the supply of low voltage, low emission, quiet, recyclable components to the electronic industry. Its components are used in the control systems of lifts, cars and kitchen appliances. Two medium-sized computer manufacturers use greenTech components in selected 'green' (that is, environmentally-friendly) models in their product range. Recent market research showed that 70% of the global electronics industry used greenTech components somewhere in its products.

In 1993 the company began a catalogue mail order service (now Internet-based) selling 'green' components to home users. Most of these customers were building their own computers and they required such components on either environmental grounds or because they wanted their computers to be extremely quiet and energy efficient. From 2005, greenTech also offered fully assembled computer systems that could be ordered and configured over the Internet. All greenTech's components are purchased from specialist suppliers. The company has no manufacturing capability, but it does have extensive hardware testing facilities and it has built up significant technical know-how in supplying appropriate components. The management team that formed the company in 1990 still runs the company.

Finance and revenue

The company has traded profitably since its foundation and has grown steadily in size and revenues. In 2008, its revenues were $64 million, with a pre-tax profit of $10 million. The spread across the three revenue streams is shown in Figure 1:

All figures in $million	2008	2007	2006
Component sales to electronics industry	40	36	34
Component sales to home users	20	18	16
Fully assembled green computers	4	3	2
Total	64	57	52

Figure 1: Turnover by revenue stream 2006–2008

The company has gradually accumulated a sizeable cash surplus. The board cannot agree on how this cash should be used. One beneficiary has been the marketing budget (see Figure 2), but the overall spend on marketing still remains relatively modest and, by April 2008, the cash surplus stood at $17 million.

All figures in $	2008	2007	2006
Internet development & marketing	100,000	70,000	60,000
Display advertising (manufacturers)	50,000	40,000	30,000
Display advertising (domestic customers)	20,000	15,000	15,000
Exhibitions & conferences	30,000	20,000	15,000
Marketing literature	10,000	5,000	5,000
Total	210,000	150,000	125,000

Figure 2: Marketing budget 2006–2008

Company Doctor

In 2008 a television company wrote to greenTech to ask whether it would consider taking part in a television programme called 'Company Doctor'. In this programme three teams of consultants spend a week at a chosen company working on a solution to a problem identified by the company. At the end of the week all three teams present their proposal for dealing with the problem. A panel of experts, including representatives from the company, pick the winner and, in theory, implement the winning proposal. greenTech agreed to take part in the programme and selected their future strategic direction as the problem area to be analysed. Their cash surplus would then be used to fund the preferred option. The show was recorded in September 2008 to be transmitted later in the year. A brief summary of the conclusions of each team of consultants is given below.

- The accountants Lewis-Read suggested a strategic direction that planned to protect and build on greenTech's current strategic position. They believed that the company should invest in marketing the fully assembled 'green' computers to both commercial and home customers. They pointed out that the government had just agreed a preferential procurement policy for energy efficient computers with high recyclable content. 'This segment of the market is rapidly expanding and is completely under-exploited by greenTech at the moment', Lewis-Read concluded.

- The corporate recovery specialists, Fenix, put forward a strategic direction that essentially offered more services to greenTech's current customers in the electronics industry. They suggested that the company should expand its product range as well as being able to manufacture components to respond to special requirements. They also believed that potential supply problems could be avoided and supply costs could be cut if greenTech acquired its own manufacturing capability. 'You need to secure the supply chain, to protect your future position.' They felt that the surplus cash in the company should be used to acquire companies that already had these manufacturing capabilities.

- The third team was led by Professor Ag Wan from MidShire University. Their main recommendation was that greenTech should not see itself as a supplier of components and computers but as a supplier of green technology. They suggested that the company should look at many other sectors (not just electronics) where quietness, low emissions and recyclable technology were important. 'The company needs to exploit its capabilities, not its products. It is looking too narrowly at the future. To compete in the future you need to develop your markets, not your products', concluded the professor.

Figure 3, which was shown on the television show, illustrates how each solution came from a different part of an amended Ansoff product/market matrix.

Markets		Products	
		Existing	**New**
	Existing	Project/Build *Lewis-Read (option 1)*	Product development with new capabilities *Fenix (option 2)*
	New	Market Development with new uses and capabilities *Professor Ag Wan (option 3)*	No team chose this option Diversification

Figure 3: Adapted Ansoff matrix showing the position of the three solutions

In the television programme, the panel chose option 3 (as suggested by Professor Ag Wan's team) as being the most appropriate strategic direction and, much to everyone's surprise, the company began to pursue this direction with much vigour. Objectives and goals were established and a set of processes was designed to facilitate business-to-business transactions with potential new customers. These processes allow customers, by using computer-aided design software, to view the specification of products available, to assemble them and to integrate their own components into the design. This means that they are able to construct virtual prototypes of machines and equipment. This process design, delivered through a web service, is still under development.

Tackling operational problems

In parallel, greenTech has decided to make tactical changes to current processes where the company has received poor customer feedback. One of these is the ordering of fully assembled green computers. The current Internet-based process for ordering and configuring these computers is described below. A swim-lane diagram (flowchart) showing the process is also included as Figure 4.

Online customers use the greenTech website to enter the specific computer configuration they require. These details are fed through to the sales department at greenTech which then e-mails Xsys – greenTech's Korean manufacturer – to ask for a delivery date for the requested computer. Xsys e-mails the date back to greenTech which then e-mails the customer with delivery and cost details. The customer then decides whether they wish to proceed with their order. Currently, 40% of enquiries proceed no further, which is of concern to greenTech as it means that time and effort have been wasted.

For those enquiries that do proceed, customers are invited to enter their payment details (credit card only). These details are sent directly to Equicheck – a specialist credit checking agency. About 20% of orders are rejected at this point because the potential customer has a poor credit rating. For orders that pass the credit check, a payment confirmation is raised by greenTech and sent to the customer and greenTech place a confirmed order with Xsys for the computer.

Ordering and configuring computer

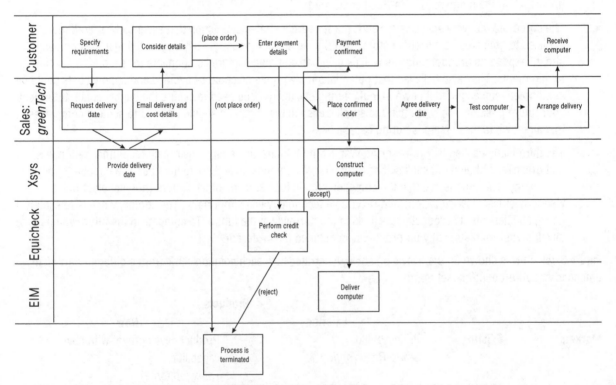

Figure 4: The process of ordering and configuring a computer

When Xsys has completed the construction of the computer it arranges for the international logistics company EIM to deliver the machine to greenTech for testing. After acceptance testing the machine, greenTech e-mails the customer, agrees a delivery date and arranges for delivery by courier.

Recent feedback from customers suggests that missing promised delivery dates is their biggest complaint. This is because the delivery date agreed early in the order process cannot necessarily be matched by Xsys when it actually receives the confirmed order. Figure 4 shows the process involved.

Required

(a) Evaluate the current strategic position of greenTech using a SWOT analysis. **(12 marks)**

(b) The panel selected the proposal of Professor Ag Wan as the winning proposal.

Write a briefing paper evaluating the three proposals and justifying the selection of the proposal of Professor Ag Wan as the best strategic option for greenTech to pursue.
Note: requirement (b) includes 2 professional marks. **(20 marks)**

(c) (i) Identify deficiencies in the current Internet-based process for ordering and configuring fully assembled green computers. Recommend a new process, together with its implications, for remedying these deficiencies. **(10 marks)**

(ii) The board is determined to link strategy with current and future processes.

Analyse the relationship between process design and strategic planning using the context of greenTech to illustrate your analysis.

Note: requirement (c)(ii) includes 2 professional marks. **(8 marks)**

(Total = 50 marks)

Answers

1 Nesta

Text reference. Porter's five forces framework and scenario planning are both covered in Chapter 2 of your BPP Study Text for exams from September 2015 to 31 August 2016.

Top tips.

Part (a) – there was the opportunity to gain a significant number of easy marks in this part of the question. The requirement tells you which model to apply, so you do not need to spend time considering which model would be the most suitable, and by this stage in your studies you should be very familiar with the five forces framework. The scenario given also clearly details many points which can be used in your answer. By taking the time to read the scenario carefully you should easily be able to identify enough points to allow you to pass this requirement.

Easy marks. These were available for illustrating an understanding of Porter's five forces model.

Examiner's comments. This question specifically asked for the application of Porter's five forces framework to the fixed-price retail market in the fictional country of Eurobia.

Candidates scored well in this part question, with some getting full marks. The only slight disappointment here was candidate's reluctance to use the financial data provided in Figure One of the scenario. This data was important because it revealed two things. Firstly, that the three companies in the industry were of a very similar size and, secondly, that the market they were participating in was growing.

Part (b) – this part question, on the whole, was answered very poorly and it would appear that many candidates were unclear about this area of the syllabus. Ensure that you cover the entire syllabus as part of your revision and do not overlook the smaller syllabus areas.

Many candidates simply repeated points from part (a) again in this part question, while others chose to undertake a similar activity as in part (a) using a different model (eg Porter's Diamond or PESTEL). Such answers did not address the requirement at all and, on the whole, gained few, if any, marks.

Another common error was to look at different ways that NESTA could enter the market, such as acquisitions, mergers, franchises etc. Again, such answers failed to generate any marks.

A possible approach to this question could have been to think through the logic of the scenario: NESTA is considering whether or not to invest in a new country. There is inevitably uncertainty around such a decision, and uncertainty about what might happen if/when it has entered the market. Therefore, before making any decision about whether or not to invest, NESTA should look at the impact difference scenarios could have on its future performance in the country.

Easy marks. As the requirement is focused on the use of scenarios, set the scene by explaining the purpose of using a scenario.

Examiner's comments. It was clear that most candidates were unfamiliar with the concept of scenarios, producing answers using a variety of perspectives and frameworks. Porter's diamond, the suitability, feasibility and acceptability criteria and SWOT analysis were just three of the inappropriate approaches used, and all usually resulted in candidates scoring no marks for this part question. The Study Guide forms the basis of the questions asked in the examination, and so candidates should be familiar with all aspects of it.

Marking scheme

		Marks
(a)	1 mark for each relevant point up to a maximum of 15 marks	15
(b)	1 mark for each relevant point up to a maximum of 10 marks	10
		Total = 25

(a) **Existing rivalry**

There are three existing rivals in the market and competition would appear to be strong. It is likely these companies would resist a new entrant in this market, in particular a well known rival such as NESTA. This would probably be achieved via rapid store expansion, increased marketing and the tightening of supplier contracts.

However, the information given in the scenario suggests that the dollar shop market sector is still growing, even though the economy is in recession. This would mean that competitors need only keep up with industry performance in order to improve their results, therefore giving the competitors room to breathe. The market may even gain legitimacy and continue to grow as a result of NESTA entering the market as more geographical areas can be exploited which are not yet fully served by the existing competitors.

Bargaining power of suppliers

NESTA's suppliers have low bargaining power. There are a number of small suppliers and the dollar shops are their main customers. The products are also undifferentiated and so the dollar shops can switch suppliers very easily. It is unlikely that any of these suppliers could become competitors of their current customers by applying forward integration.

In addition, NESTA has recognised competencies in effective supplier management, supported by effective procurement system. These core strengths, combined with the low bargaining power of the suppliers, make this market in Eurobia very attractive to NESTA.

Landlords could also be considered to be suppliers in this case. The bargaining power of these suppliers is also low due to the number of empty properties and the low rents and short leases offered in order to fill them.

Bargaining power of customers

NESTA's customers have strong bargaining power. This is due to a number of factors:

- There is a low profit margin on the products which provide an incentive for buyers seeking lower purchasing costs.

- NESTA sells unbranded commodity goods and so it would be easy for the buyer to switch to an alternative supplier. The switching costs are therefore low.

- Standard, undifferentiated products can be easily provided by other suppliers. Buyers can therefore choose which supplier to use and can play the companies off against each other in order to obtain the best terms of supply.

- Buyers are likely to be very price sensitive and so will invest a lot into trying to ensure the best terms of supply.

Threat of substitutes

The conventional supermarkets are potential substitutes to the dollar shops as they offer a wide range of ambient goods, often with competing brands on offer. However, the prices vary and no supermarkets have yet adopted the discount fixed-price sale approach, choosing instead to differentiate using known brands. Location is also a key differentiator as the supermarkets are located out of town with plentiful parking and vehicle access. However, NESTA is an established global player in the fixed-price market and as such its arrival in Eurobia may lead supermarkets to reconsider their approach.

Conventional supermarkets also offer internet shopping and home delivery options. Ambient goods such as those offered by the dollar shops are well suited to this approach and so the internet could also be considered to be a substitute channel. However the $10 delivery charge might reduce this threat. NESTA could consider making use of the internet in this way as a way of differentiating itself on entry to the market.

Potential entrants and barriers to entry

A significant barrier to entry to this market is the high level of capital that is required in order to establish a credible presence. However, for NESTA this is unlikely to be a problem as it has the cash reserves available to allow it to lease a significant number of shops in Eurobia, and establish a credible market presence there.

Capital costs are also lowered by the reduced rental costs that are now available in Eurobia as many of the towns and cities now have empty stores which are relatively cheap to rent. In addition, landlords who once required high rents and long leases are increasingly willing to rent these stores for a relatively short fixed-term lease. This reduces the exit costs that are faced by this market.

One barrier to entry which may be a problem for NESTA is brand awareness. The existing competitors have very high levels of brand recognition (90%), whereas NESTA is only recognised by 5% of general consumers. NESTA may have to commit significant resources to a large scale marketing campaign if it is to successfully break into this market.

(b) Scenarios are a tool to allow managers to envisage alternative futures in highly uncertain business environments.

A scenario is a detailed and consistent view of how the business environment of an organisation might develop in the future. Scenarios are built with reference to key influences and change drivers in the environment. They inevitably deal with conditions of high uncertainty, so they are not forecasts: instead, they are internally consistent views of potential future conditions.

For the scenarios to be most use the influencing factors should be:

- Limited to a few significant ones

- Largely out of the control of the organisation. Macroeconomic forces are usually outside the control of the organisation and it can only react to, not influence, them

Factors which could be used to develop scenarios in NESTA could be:

- **Change to the economic climate**. The success of the dollar shops seems to have been built on the economic recession being experienced in Eurobia. An improvement in the economy may lead to a loss of customers as branded products and more upmarket suppliers are sought out. Scenarios should be prepared for the economic situation improving, declining and remaining constant.

- **Competitor response**. It is not easy to predict how the existing competitors will react to NESTA's entry to the market place. Therefore, scenarios should consider the possibility of an aggressive response, a muted response and no response.

- **Conventional supermarket approach**. The conventional supermarkets have not currently adopted a fixed-price discount approach. However, they may decide to establish outlet style stores to allow it to do so. They could also acquire one of the established dollar stores (competitors) and enter the market this way.

- **Internet shopping**. Many customers are now choosing to shop online rather than visit physical shops and the effect of this has been significant in many areas of retail. The implications of this trend could be considered within the scenarios.

These factors would then be combined into scenarios. The attractiveness of the Eurobia market would then be assessed for each scenario along with tactics for entering the market under those circumstances.

2 Airtite

Text reference. The topics mentioned in this answer are discussed in Chapter 2 of your BPP Study Text for exams from September 2015 to 31 August 2016.

Top tips. The requirement asks you to use models where appropriate, but does not specify which model(s) to use.

The material in the scenario should have pointed you towards using PESTEL analysis – a number of political/legal, economic, social, technological and ecological factors were highlighted in the scenario.

However, the requirement did not limit you to using PESTEL analysis, and applying Porter's five forces could also have helped you identify some important environmental factors.

The answer below is based primarily on PESTEL analysis, but in the text box at the end of the answer we have also included some equally valid points derived from five forces analysis.

Don't forget that all versions of the PESTEL model are fairly arbitrary in the way they analyse the general environment into sectors. It doesn't really matter whether you cover the demographic issues from the scenario under the economic heading or the society one, for instance, as long as you cover it.

Easy marks. As mentioned above, a reasonably competent discussion of the relevant PESTEL items should score well.

Examiner's comments. The important factors in the setting included the key drivers of change.

		Marks
(a)	2 marks for each relevant point up to a maximum of 12 marks for PESTEL analysis Analysis should include: Political – increasing government control Economic – trends in disposable income Social – ageing population Technological – more efficient aircraft Environmental – tighter emission control Legal – global agreement on emissions 1 mark for each relevant point up to a maximum of 3 marks for assessing impact and uncertainty	
	Max	15
(b)	2 marks for each relevant point up to maximum of 5 marks for issues that developing a scenario would highlight These could include: Identifying high impact/high uncertainty factors in environment Identifying different possible futures by factor Building scenarios of plausible configurations of factors	
	Max	5
	2 marks for each relevant point up to maximum of 5 marks for linking issues to Airtite's strategy	
	Max	5
		25

Part (a)

Airtite – the general environment

Political factors

EU expansion – The number of states in the EU is continuing to rise and this offers growth opportunities for Airtite. Airtite has already opened up routes to some of the countries that joined in 2004, and as additional states join they provide additional potential destinations for Airtite to fly to.

Competition policy – Moreover, European governments are keen to **support the competition** low-cost airlines provide for national flag carriers, so this reinforce the opportunities EU expansion offers the low-cost airlines.

Legal factors

Government legislation – However, if the potential government legislation to increase retirement age and to demand a higher level of personal contributions to pension schemes goes ahead this will be a threat to the travel industry. Both aspects of the legislation will lead to a demand for air travel because people will either have less leisure time (reducing retirement age) or less disposable income (increasing pension contributions).

Environment and pollution – There is becoming increasing public awareness of the impact of pollution and harmful emissions on the environment and the earth's climate. While air travel companies should be looking at ways of **reducing their harmful emissions** to display their **corporate social responsibilities**, the level of concern about the environment means that co-ordinated government action to reduce emissions is becoming increasingly likely.

Taxes on aircraft emissions – Governments, globally, are looking at ways to control harmful aircraft emissions, either by restricting the number of flights or by imposing higher taxes on pollution. If aircraft taxes are increased, the low cost airlines will either have to **pass these costs on to consumers** – which could see demand fall – or **absorb the costs themselves**, seeing their margins reduced.

The scale of the impact legislative changes as a whole could have on the industry means that **governments are key stakeholders** for Airtite, because they could exert significant power over Airtite's future business decisions.

Social factors

Perception of travel – The expansion in airline travel for both business and leisure passengers has created an environment in which people are more willing and keen to travel than they historically have been. People now perceive travelling by air to be easy, so this provides ongoing opportunities for the growth of the industry.

At the moment, the **threat of terrorist activity** does not appear to have had a major impact on demand for air travel, but if the threat increases then demand is likely to suffer.

New market segments – The relative ease and cheapness of low cost airline travel could allow the industry to create new market segments. For example, an increasing number of people are now having overseas stag parties or hen parties, which suggests that there are opportunities for growth in leisure travel among young, single people, instead of the family market which has been a major source of growth previously.

Demographic changes – However, changing population structures could affect the demand for travel overall. A significant part of the recent growth in the industry has come from leisure travel by families, but the increasing number of one-parent families within limited incomes could jeopardise this growth. Similarly, the increasing proportion of retired people in the population, dependent on state pensions, could also limit the opportunities for further growth.

Economic factors

Reduced disposable incomes – Changes in general economic conditions and people's disposable incomes will have an impact on the demand for air travel. For example, the current (2008) global financial crisis, rising inflation and rising interest rates are squeezing disposable income levels. Coupled with lower levels of job security, these economic conditions are likely to cause people to **reduce their leisure spending**, which in turn may lead them to **spend less on foreign holidays**.

Switching to lower cost brands – However, this desire to spend less on foreign holidays could be either a threat or an opportunity for the low cost airlines. While some people may decide not to have a foreign holiday at all, there are others who have previously flown with a national carrier who might now fly with a low cost carrier instead.

Business passengers will face similar choices. In an economic downturn, companies are have to be more **prudent with their spending**, and so some may cut back on air travel altogether, while others will redirect their spending from premium airlines to low cost airlines.

Fuel costs – Fuel costs are continuing to rise over due to uncertainty over supplies and increasing global demand. As fuel costs currently account for 25% of Airtite's operating costs, changing fuel costs could have a significant impact on its business. As with taxes discussed above, low cost airlines will be faced with the dilemma of whether to pass on the increased costs to their consumers (thereby possibly reducing demand) or to absorb the costs themselves leading to significantly reduced margins.

Technological factors

Online bookings – The growth of e-commerce and online bookings are essential to Airtite's business model because it relies entirely on online bookings. Therefore the spread of internet access, and in particular broadband access to the internet, will increase the size of Airtite's potential market and in turn its potential revenues.

Engine efficiency – One of the key challenges facing the industry is **reducing aircraft emissions**. In this respect, technological advances are important because the improving efficiency of aircraft engines is reducing harmful emissions. By implementing the reductions themselves, airlines may be able to reduce the threat of political or environmental lobbyists calling for air travel to be subject to higher taxes.

Engine efficiency also has an important economic impact, because reduced **fuel consumption** will help the airlines reduce their fuel costs.

However, technological change may have some short term costs for the airlines if it means they have to **upgrade their fleets**, and have to either buy or lease the next generation of aircraft.

Environmental uncertainty

The analysis above shows that the European air travel industry is both complex and dynamic. A number of the factors we have identified **could be either opportunities or threats**.

The effect of this is to create a high level of uncertainty, which **makes long-term strategic planning difficult**. Consequently, Airtite must remain alert to all the environmental factors which could affect them, and be innovative and flexible in their responses to changes in those environmental factors.

Experience in the industry is likely to be very important in assessing the importance of future environmental developments, due to the complexity of the interactions between them.

Alternative issues which are also relevant (using Porter's five forces):

Competition – The airline industry has experienced a period of rapid growth in both business and leisure passengers, as low cost airlines have joined the market alongside the traditional flag carriers.

The market can support an increasing number of players as it is growing rapidly, but as growth starts to slow down, industry rivalry will become increasingly competitive, meaning it could become harder to sustain profit levels.

The European governments have indicated that they support this increased competition, and are encouraging low cost operators to compete against the national flag carriers which they feel are inefficient.

New Entrants – Airtite was able to join the industry successfully in 2000, and if new entrants continue to join then the competition will be intensified still further.

Although there are barriers to entry – for example, securing routes in and out of airports, and raising the funds required to lease or buy planes – Airtite's successful entry into the industry suggests that these barriers to entry can be overcome.

Consequently, Airtite should start consider ways of protecting its existing market share against possible new entrants as well as continuing to challenge its existing competitors.

Suppliers – Fuel costs are a significant operating cost for airlines, and fuel suppliers – for example, the OPEC countries – have considerable power to increase fuel costs. In effect, **airlines have no bargaining power** to challenge the suppliers' fuel price rises, and have no alternative means of fuelling their planes, so if the oil producers continue to increase prices the airlines' margins are going to continue to suffer.

Part (b)

Top tips. We all know what scenarios are, more or less, but many of us are unsure about both when it would be a good idea to prepare one and how to go about doing it.

The clue to the first problem – when scenarios are a good idea – lies in **environmental uncertainty**. A high degree of uncertainty limits to usefulness of techniques based on extrapolation: the possibility of a transformational change must be considered.

The scenario-writing process then requires a consideration of potential **impact** on the organisation and what it does.

A scenario is an internally consistent view of how the future might turn out to be. Scenarios are useful when there is **high environmental uncertainty** as a result of complexity or rapid change, or both and thus difficulty in forecasting how a range of important influences might affect the future.

Scenario building is not an attempt to foretell the future. It is rather an attempt to **identify critical outcomes or branching points** that may arise at some future time and to work out how to deal with the various possible future states that they imply.

A very large number of factors may influence the way future events develop. *Johnson, Scholes and Whittington* suggest that only a few of them should be considered so as to reduce the complexity that is likely to arise from a large number of assumptions and uncertainties. This can be done by basing scenario development on those factors that display both **high uncertainty** and the **potential for major impact** on the industry in question. Such an approach would concentrate John's mind on the most important environmental features. Fuel prices and taxation are both important in this context, combining a high degree of uncertainty and high potential to disrupt Airtite's budgets.

The chosen factors, or **drivers of change** are assessed for the ways in which they might interact and a small number of different but equally logically consistent scenarios are created. A **time horizon** of perhaps ten years is used, partly to enhance the usefulness of the scenarios that are developed and partly to discourage simple extrapolation from the present. No attempt is made to allocate probabilities to the various future states envisioned: this would lend them a spurious accuracy and would detract from their utility.

The process of writing scenarios depends on an ability to discern patterns and a general awareness of the potential significance of widely disparate data. It can be taken in stages, with the initial production of up to a dozen mini scenarios, each dealing with a restricted set of factors and interactions. These can then be combined into, say, three larger scenarios dealing with all of the drivers.

The preparation and discussion of scenarios would contributes to **organisational learning** in Airtite by developing its senior managers' awareness of the environmental factors influencing the airline's development. This awareness should lead to **more informed environmental monitoring** and prompt the development of appropriate **contingency plans**.

3 The Management Press

Text reference. E-commerce is covered in Chapters 11 and 12 of the BPP Study Text for exams from September 2015 to 31 August 2016.

Top tips. Make sure you read the scenario very carefully and understand exactly what business is described in the scenario. TMP is actually a publisher, **not** a bookshop like many students appear to have thought.

Notice the mark allocation in this question and how it is split between parts (a) and (b) and allocate your own time accordingly. Don't spend too long in part (a) talking about things that would better be discussed in part (b).

Easy marks. Part (a) offers five very easy marks. The scenario clearly states a number of drivers and barriers for e-commerce that you should be able to identify and describe.

Make sure you highlight these drivers and barriers that have been handed to you and don't waste time listing every possible generic benefit and limitation of e-commerce that you can possibly think of.

The list of drivers and barriers given in the suggested answer are provided for tuition purposes only and you would not be expected to identify all of these in order to score the five marks available. Five clearly stated relevant issues would have been enough to score full marks on this requirement.

			Marks
(a)	1 mark for each relevant point up to a maximum of 5 marks	Max	5
(b)	1 mark for each appropriate point up to a maximum of 20 marks	Max	20
			25

Part (a)

Drivers for e-commerce

- Reduction in costs, including the cost of raw materials and bookshop distribution

- Increased profit margin as physical bookshop no longer required.

- Increased revenue due to increased sales. E-commerce allows TMP to market to and sell to an extended customer base.

- The need to keep up to date to avoid falling behind the competitors, which the marketing director claims 'would be the end of us'.

- The marketing director is a driving force for the change.

- A graduate has been taken on to develop and maintain the website.

- Ecological awareness is a driving force as there is an acceptance that timber is becoming scarce and the earth's resources should be protected.

Barriers to the adoption of e-commerce

- TMP 'does not have sufficient expertise to continue developing and maintaining its own website', therefore costs would be incurred in getting someone to do this on their behalf. This has a significant impact on the long term viability of the project.

- Profits and revenue are declining and so TMP will struggle to meet the costs involved in developing the website.

- The website will compete with existing supply channels that they are keen to preserve.

- Fraud risks associated with electronic financial transactions.

- Piracy risks may arise if the online books are not carefully protected. They could potentially be illegitimately copied and sold on.

- Resistance from the other directors.

Part (b)

> **Top tips.** With strong knowledge of the marketing mix and the benefits of e-business you should be able answer this question very well. Remember, as ever, to relate everything you say back to the scenario in question and keep your answers in context.
>
> Many students failed to mention the possibility of introducing e-books (such as those for Kindle). Applying practical examples such as this to the scenario will score far more marks that theoretical examples about the 6 I's for instance.
>
> A number of students struggled with the physical evidence section of this requirement. Physical evidence should relate to the content of the books, not the content of the website itself.

Product

TMP currently sells physical books. E-business would allow them to either **replace** the product with an electronic equivalent (ebook) or to **augment** the products by adding additional services such as an associated website which offers further case studies and questions etc.

Replacing the product with eBooks may allow the product range to be increased as it allows books to be introduced that would otherwise be uneconomical to print. This method would reduce the cost of raw materials and assist in meeting environmental targets, therefore reinforcing two of the drivers noted in part (a).

Augmenting the product would improve the product the customer receives and enhance their experience.

E-business could also be used to extend the product range, eg training or financial advice could be offered by an intermediary.

Price

E-business should involve lower costs than those incurred selling physical books in physical shops. By eliminating bookshops (and the commission payable to them) the price could be lowered, yet TMP's profit margin could still be increased.

Current high prices means that overseas sales have been low. This could be addressed by combining differential pricing (in local currencies) with electronic alternatives.

TMP will have to monitor competitor costs and react accordingly due to the existence of price comparison websites. They will also have to be aware of large existing channels (eg Amazon) that pay commission on books sold through their site.

Alternative pricing strategies, such as subscribing to the site rather than purchasing individual books, could also be explored.

Direct pricing to customers, such as pre-publication deals and other special offers could be made to existing customers.

Promotion

Currently, promotion involves bookshop displays and full-page adverts in magazines/journals. This is a classic 'push' approach as it focuses on the product, not the customers.

E-business allows information, such as customer details, to be recorded so TMP can then target them specifically, for example online suggestions at the check out stage ('people who bought this book also bought the following') and next time they visit (welcome page of tailored suggestions based on previous activity).

Banner adverts on associated websites, such as sites that provide management advice. Links to academic websites could also be established via their reading list. Commission will be payable for this.

TMP will also have to develop their website carefully to ensure it features prominently in search engines.

In order to develop these new promotion methods, expenditure on offline advertising may need to be scaled back.

Place

Bookshops have limited reach, and although circulation figures for magazines/journals are provided it is unclear how many people read the adverts, therefore their reach is difficult to predict. The scenario also indicates the reach of both bookshops and magazines/journals is in decline.

The internet, by contrast, has unlimited (global) reach. Few books are currently sold outside Arcadia, however this may be simply down to unfamiliarity with TMP. The internet could address this easily.

Arcadia is a high-cost economy and it is likely that printing and distributing the books in lower labour cost countries could lead to significant cost savings.

Physical evidence

Bookshops have an advantage over the internet (and journal advertisements) in that they allow customers to inspect books properly to ensure they meet their needs before deciding to purchase them.

This can be partially addressed online by providing a 'look inside' facility. This allows the customer to view key pages such as contents list, index and the first few pages or chapter.

Customer reviews, feedback and ratings can provide customers with a form of physical evidence that they are unlikely to obtain from any bookshop.

By providing books online, possibly through subscription, much of the need for physical evidence is removed.

4 Rock Bottom

Text reference. Leadership is covered in Chapter 15 of the BPP Study Text for exams from September 2015 to 31 August 2016.

Chapter 6 covers franchising.

Marking scheme

			Marks
(a)	Up to 1 mark for each relevant point up to a maximum of 6 marks for each phase Three phases required, giving a maximum of 18 marks		18
		Max	
(b)	Up to 1 mark for each relevant point up to a maximum of 7 marks		7
		Max	
			25

(a)

Phase I

Growth phase – When Rock Bottom first opened it offered a significant contrast to the general stores which sold domestically produced electrical goods alongside other household goods. Rock Bottom specialised solely in selling electrical goods, and sold imported Japanese goods.

The Japanese goods were new to the country, but they were more sophisticated and more reliable than their domestic equivalents.

The new products were therefore in the introduction and growth phases of their product life cycles at this time.

Similarly, the new store format which Rock Bottom used also suggests an introduction and growth stage of the stores' own lifecycle.

Marketing – The innovative way Rock Bottom marketed goods, distinguished it from potential competitors.

The stores were set up as specialist shops which were very different from the general stores where customers usually bought the type of goods offered by Rock Bottom, possibility allowing Rock Bottom to enjoy a first mover advantage in this market.

He also made sure customers knew about Rock Bottom by developing a high public profile, unique image and staged stunts to publicise the company.

Customer lifestyle – Rick Hein recognised the growing spending power of young people, who wanted to spend disposable income on high-tech electrical goods to allow them to enjoy popular music. The way that Rock Bottom was set up catered directly to those needs.

Technological change – Rock Bottom exploited the opportunities offered by the advance of the Japanese electronics industry.

Leadership style - The aspects of Rock Bottom's success described above come from the market/environment. But Rick's leadership style also help contribute to the success in Phase I.

- He was a charismatic leader and entrepreneur, building a vision for the organisation, and then encouraging staff to achieve it.

- Rick was also a motivator. He appointed staff who were young and understood the products they were selling. Rick appreciated that the skills and knowledge of his staff were important to Rock Bottom's success, and staff were well rewarded for success.

Phase II

Increased competition – By the late 1980s, a number of competitors had entered the market.

Distinctive advantage eroded – Competitors enter the market that are able to imitate Rock Bottom's product offering and service approach. As a result, Rock Bottom cannot preserve its unique competitive advantage.

Correspondingly, it cannot maintain sales and profit growth as customers are shared between an increasing number of competitors.

Rock Bottom is now entering **maturity phase** of industry life cycle, and the leadership needs to match this change in product life cycle. Rick's approach was to float the company on the stock exchange and use the capital raised to expand the business. This decision, however, created several problems for the company:

- *Returns to shareholders* – The company was now under pressure to provide acceptable returns to shareholders. The company would now have to pay dividends to external shareholders, and monitor and maintain the quoted share price.

- *Organisational culture* – In an attempt to establish the company so that it could deliver value to its shareholders, Rick changed the organisational structure and style of the company. The increased level of control meant there was less freedom and flexibility for managers. In addition, the reward packages more tightly controlled. The managers were not impressed with the changes, and so many left.

- *Transparency* – As a public company, Rock Bottom had to disclose information about its **directors' remuneration**. Rick's personal image and lifestyle appeared excessive and indulgent to shareholders.

- *Corporate governance* – The idea of combining roles of Chairman and CEO is unlikely to be best practice for a public company.

- *Leadership style* – Ultimately, Rick failed to adapt to a maturing marketplace and a maturing organisational structure. His personal image and lifestyle were now damaging the company and he found it difficult to accept that he now had to abide by rules and governance, and to service stakeholders/shareholders rather than doing what he wanted.

Phase III

Declining product – Whereas in Phase I, Rock Bottom was offering new and exciting products, by the start of the 21st century music is increasingly played from downloaded computer files or through MP3 players, rather than through hi-fi systems. Unfortunately, Rock Bottom's product range had not changed to reflect this.

Product reliability – By the start of the 21st century, hi-fi systems are much more reliable than they were in the 1960s and so last longer. Consequently, people have to replace their equipment less frequently, further reducing demand for Rock Bottom's products.

Sales channels – Also, Rock Bottom has continued to operate only as a high street retailer, without developing an online shop. The operating costs associated with a high street shop, compared to an internet shop, mean that Rock Bottom no longer has the low cost advantage which it enjoyed in Phase I.

Bargaining power of consumers – The internet also makes pricing more transparent and allows consumers to compare different retailers and products before deciding what to buy and where to buy them. This empowered customers giving them a much wider choice of products and suppliers. If Rock Bottom were unable to operate at costs low enough to keep their prices competitive, they could be forced out of the market.

Leadership style – as was the case phases 1 and 2, Rick's leadership style also affected Rock Bottom in phase 3.

- Rick alienated his managers with his loose and unfocused approach, and he further distanced himself from them by becoming angry and rude towards them.

- He reacted to the freedom gained from no longer being a public company by spending a large amount of money on a celebration party, further devaluing the already damaged image of the company.

(b)

> **Top tips.** Part (b) asks you to identify why franchising would have been successful in 1988 (the end of phase 1) and unlikely to succeed in 2007 (phase 3). It is very clear from the scenario that Rock Bottom is a successful, profitable company in 1988 and an unsuccessful company in 2007.

There are two key reasons that franchising Rock Bottom would have been feasible in 1988 and unlikely to succeed in 2007:

Brand image

When a franchisee invests in a company, a significant chunk of what they are buying is the brand itself, therefore the stronger a brand is, the more likely the franchise is to succeed.

1988: The brand was strong and perceived to be youthful and innovative. It was a first mover in the market, and as such it is likely to have retained customer loyalty even once other competitors entered the market. This would be attractive to potential franchisees.

2007: The brand image was low. Rick's extravagant lifestyle had damaged customer perceptions, and the company itself was now out of date for the modern market, for example, it still had no online store. Potential franchisees would not be attracted to this company and would invest their funds elsewhere, in a company with a stronger, more positive brand image.

Financial success

The more financially successful a company is, the more appealing it is to potential franchisees. They invest in the company in the hope to gain a share of the profits.

1988: Rock Bottom was still financially successful, and so would be attractive to franchisees. Rick would have generated funds from the franchise fees which he could have used to build the brand image. He would not have needed to float the company on the stock exchange to raise funds, and the brand may not have become damaged. In addition, a large proportion of the future risk would have been transferred from the company to the franchisees. Franchising clearly would have been a sensible strategy at this point in time.

2007: Most of Rock Bottom's shops were now trading at a loss. It is very unlikely that franchisees would want to invest in a loss making company.

5 Jayne Cox Direct

(a)   1 mark for each appropriate point up to a maximum of 12 marks   Max   12

(b)   1 mark for each appropriate point up to a maximum of 13 marks   Max   13

(Total = 25 marks)

(a)

Porter's value chain groups the various activities of an organisation into value activities in order to illustrate how the organisation creates value.

If the organisation is successful, it will create a margin. This margin is the excess that the customer is prepared to pay over the cost to the firm of obtaining resource inputs and providing value activities. It represents the value created by the value activities themselves and the linkages between them.

Primary activities are the activities involved in making the product, selling it, and providing the customer with the product and after-sales service and assistance.

Support activities provide purchased inputs, human resources, technology and infrastructural functions to support the primary activities. These activities are involved at each stage of the value creation process and support the entire value chain.

The primary activities of the value chain, and the associated weaknesses at Jayne Cox Direct (JCD) are considered below.

Inbound logistics relates to the receiving, handling and storing of inputs to the production system. The inputs at JCD include wood, upholstery, textiles and other raw materials and the inbound logistics relates to the storage and inventory of these items prior to their use in production.

A key weakness in this area of the value chain relates to the issues with the e-mail purchase order system. At least one large order was not received due to a failure of this system.

The high levels of inventory indicated in the scenario may indicate a further weakness and the rationale for this should be investigated.

Operations relates to the processes of converting the resource inputs (including materials and human resources) into finished products. At JCD this is the manufacturing processes used to make the furniture. JCD keep high levels of inventory, and run a relaxed and relatively undisturbed production process, yet they still fail to meet 45% of their estimated delivery dates due to products running late. This could be caused by inefficiencies in the production process, or simply be down to over-optimistic quoting of delivery dates. Investigations into the cause of this failure should be carried out as it causes increased administrative costs to be incurred as well as causing disappoint and disruption to the customer.

Outbound logistics includes the storing of the finished product, ie the completed furniture and distributing it to customers. This will include the safe packaging of the furniture for transit and delivering it in their vans to the customer on the specified date.

JCD has several weaknesses in this area. First, the failure of JCD to provide sufficient notice to customers of a revised delivery date means that customers have to defer this date yet further to a more suitable date. This causes their completed item of furniture to remain in storage longer than necessary causing an increase in inventory holding costs. A second cause of increased storage requirement results from the return of delivered goods where no-one was available to collect the delivery. This again causes an increase in the cost of holding inventory, as well as increases in both administrative and transport costs as the delivery date has to be once again re-arranged.

Marketing and sales involves informing customers about the product, convincing them to buy it, and enabling them to do so. At JCD this relates to their advertisements in quality lifestyle magazines and online ordering system.

The main weakness here is that the website does not give any indication of the length of time a customer can expect to wait for their furniture to be delivered until after their order has been placed. This results in a significant number of cancelled orders at this stage. This is likely to leave the customer feeling frustrated with the company for wasting their time and are therefore unlikely to return to JCD in the future. A simple indication that orders take 'on average 10 weeks', with an explanation as to why (bespoke nature, high quality etc) would no doubt greatly reduce this problem.

After-sales service relates to those activities which continue to add value after the sale has been made and the product delivered. For JCD after-sales service might include the replacement of faulty or damaged goods, a guarantee lasting for a set time after delivery, complaints handling and product care advice.

A recent customer satisfaction survey identified a number of criticisms of the after-sales services offered by JCD and it is thought this may be a factor in their low customer retention rate.

Procurement, a support activity, is also relevant for JCD. This activity and the associated weaknesses are as follows.

Procurement includes all of the processes involved in acquiring the resource inputs to the primary activities, eg purchase of materials, subcomponents and equipment. The effectiveness of these processes will have a significant impact on both the cost and the quality of the finished products. For JCD, the price paid for wood, textiles and upholstery will have a direct effect on the cost charged for the final product. The company currently source 95% of its wood from three timber suppliers and the company has used the same suppliers since its first year of business. Long-term relationships such as this may mean that JCD are no longer benefiting from the best prices due to the complacency and un-competitiveness this may bring about in the suppliers. This should be further investigated to determine if savings could be made with alternate suppliers.

(b)

> **Top tips.** Note that this part of the question requires you to evaluate how **technology** can be used to address the weaknesses you have identified in part (a) above. You must therefore ensure that you restrict your answer to technology rather than general ways in which the value chain weaknesses can be addressed.
>
> As ever, make sure you relate your answer directly to the organisation and only give answers that are actually relevant to this company and its products. Vague or generic answers are unlikely to score highly.

Upstream supply chain

Upstream activities in the supply chain are those that relate to suppliers and the obtaining and storing of raw material. Therefore, the problems identified above that can be addressed via technology in the upstream supply chain are those relating to procurement and inbound logistics.

Problems	Suggested solutions
Long-term supplier relationships may have created uncompetitive, complacent suppliers	Use e-procurement websites to identify a broader range of suppliers. The suppliers which may offer the best balance of quality and cost can then be more easily selected and cost savings can be made.
Cumbersome ordering process leading to the occasional failure to receive deliveries	The occasional failure of payment system to correctly match purchase orders to supplier invoices has led to payment delays and criticism from suppliers. JCD could implement a linked procurement and payment system which connects via electronic data interchange to their suppliers. This would allow orders to be automatically entered into the supplier's system and all invoicing an payments would occur electronically. This system may not be compatible with the above suggestion as it may be necessary to retain a smaller supplier base in order to implement such a system. However it would reduce administrative costs, improve the relationship with suppliers and solve the non-delivery problem the company has experienced.

Problems	Suggested solutions
Delays as a result of inventory shortage	An integrated system could be installed which allows suppliers to view demand for particular products. This might allow them to anticipate demand and therefore supply materials to JCD quicker. This could help JCD to meet a greater proportion of estimated customer delivery dates and reduce delivery lead time. This is most likely to work with trend-driven demand such as that for particular textiles and the usefulness of such linkages should be investigated.
Poor inventory management	JCD currently stock high levels of inventory. This could be addressed via integration between the stock system, the ordering system, and the suppliers' systems. This would allow suppliers to produce to order (rather than to stock) and JCD could move towards a just-in-time system so that stock is only ordered just before it is needed. This would also enhance the suppliers' understanding of demand allowing them to improve their own inventory management. This could create cost savings which may be reflected in the prices charged to JCD and therefore lowering input costs. JCD should also be able to implement systems that optimise the quantities of products ordered as a result of the improved understanding of demand and the costs of ordering and storing inventory.

Downstream supply chain

As JCD sells directly to the customers, the downstream supply chain is reasonably straight-forward. The main weaknesses identified in part (a) that could be addressed by technology in the downstream supply chain are therefore the ones relating to outbound logistics and after-sales support.

Problems	Suggested solutions
Failed deliveries	30% of deliveries currently fail causing an increase in the cost of storing finished goods, increased administrative costs, and the costs of repeat deliveries. Route planning software could improve van utilisation, while the use of automated emails/text messages and updates on delivery slots would increase the chances of customers being at home when the delivery is made.
Failure to update customers on order status	Following the initial delivery estimate provided at the time of ordering, customers receive no more updates or communication from JCD until a week before the delivery is due to take place. This date is often different from that originally quoted as a result of issues with JCD's procurement processes. This date is often not-suitable for the customer (who has often planned to be available on the date previously quoted). Yet another date then has to be arranged and the completed product must be stored until that date. JCD could address this by implementing an 'order tracking' facility on their website. This involvement would enhance customer satisfaction and also leave them more informed and more likely to be available on the date of delivery as they can now better plan for this. This would reduce storage costs as well as the costs associated with multiple delivery attempts.

Problems	Suggested solutions
Poor/limited after-sales service	An FAQ section could be provided on JCD's website, eg 'how do I clean my new sofa?' and 'how do I order replacement materials?' For questions relating to replacements a link can be provided to the relevant page where such orders can be made quickly and directly on line.
	To improve customer retention, targeted emails, newsletters and 'existing customer only' special offers could be sent out on a regular basis.

6 Marlow Fashion

Text reference. Chapters 4 and 14(SWOT analysis; Benchmarking and the finance function as a business partner)

Top tips. Requirement (a) asks you to identify and explain strategic strengths and weaknesses. Note strengths and weaknesses are factors which are internal to a business. You must restrict your answer to these internal factors alone. If you include external factors (opportunities and threats) in your answer you will get no marks for these.

Note also the requirement is to identify and explain; so for each strength or weakness you identify you must explain its strategic significance.

When answering requirement (b), it will be useful to consider what types of benchmarking Marlow could use. The contribution benchmarking can make to the Group is likely to depend on the type of benchmarking it uses, and the examiner's marking scheme indicates that there are marks available for assessing the different types of benchmarking.

Part (c) is only worth 5 marks so you needed to be careful to not spend too much time on this requirement. It is important that you apply your knowledge of the business partner model to the scenario and avoid simply generating a list of generic benefits that this approach can bring.

Easy marks. The scenario provides some useful context for (a) so you should be able to identify a number of strengths and weaknesses from it.

Requirement (b) focuses more narrowly a single topic – benchmarking. If you have a good knowledge of this topic, you should be able to score well here.

In part (c) there was a mark available for explaining the meaning of 'the finance function as a business partner'. This should have been easily attainable provided you had read through Chapter 14 in your BPP Study Text and the section on the changing role of the finance function.

Marking scheme

			Marks
(a)	Up to 3 marks each for relevant strategic strength and weakness identified and explained	Max	13
(b)	Up to 2 marks for each relevant point about the contribution benchmarking could make improving Marlow's strategic position		_7_
(c)	1 mark for explaining the meaning of the 'finance function as a business partner'		
	1 mark per benefit of the business partner model applied to Marlow Fashion		5
			_25_

(a) To: Susan Grant

From: Accountant

Strategic strengths and weaknesses in Marlow Fashion Group

This report looks at the strengths which are helping Marlow Fashion Group achieve its commercial success, and the weakness that are hindering it.

It is important to note that an analysis of strengths and weaknesses looks only at **factors which are internal to the business**. It does not in itself look at the external opportunities which are available to a business or the threats facing it, although these should also be considered in due course to get a full understanding of Marlow's strategic position.

It is also important to note that features of a company that have historically been **strengths can shift to become weaknesses as the competitive environment changes** over time, meaning that the company needs a strategic turnaround in order to survive. This appears to be the case with Marlow.

Strengths

Market position and reputation. Marlow has successfully **developed a niche market** for its products, based around traditional English style and elegance. This enabled it to expand successfully, and developed Marlow as a **worldwide brand with a reputation for design excellence and quality.**

Premium prices. Because Marlow has developed a reputation for quality, it has been able to charge premium prices for its clothes. The ability to sustain a high price premium is important in retaining the profitability of the company.

Supplier relationships. Marlow has built up a strong relationship with its suppliers. This relationship with the suppliers is important in maintaining the quality of the clothes produced, and so has facilitated the brand's reputation and global expansion of the group.

Loyal network of franchise partners. Marlow has created a strong family atmosphere among its network of retail partners around the world. As with the strong supplier relationships, this network has also helped facilitate the global expansion of the group.

Weaknesses

Outdated business model. The business model which has served Marlow well in the past is no longer appropriate to the fashion world in which they are now competing.

Lack of outsourcing, and high cost base. The competitive environment in which Marlow operates is becoming increasingly competitive. Therefore clothing retailers are increasingly looking to outsource the manufacture of their clothes. However, the **vertically integrated model** which Marlow uses prevents this, and means that **Marlow's cost base is higher** than it should be, because the company is failing to benefit from any economies of scale which outsourced providers enjoy. Consequently, Marlow's costs are also likely to be higher than its competitors, reducing its profitability.

Unclear strategy. One of Marlow's strengths was the niche position and brand reputation is established for itself. However, the changes in its environment have now led to some uncertainty as to whether Marlow Fashion is a brand, a manufacturer, a retailer or an integrated fashion company. It is likely that to be successful in the future, Marlow will need to **identify its core competencies** and focus only on its core activities.

Outdated styles. Women's tastes in clothing have also changed and Marlow's emphasis on soft, feminine styles has become outdated. Consequently, demand for the clothes they sell has declined, and this has prompted a **significant fall in Marlow's sales and profits**.

Narrow product range. Although Marlow produces a comprehensive range of women's clothing, it is all built round the theme of traditional English style and elegance. This means that Marlow's products are **overconcentrated** in one style, and therefore extremely vulnerable to a fall in demand as styles change.

Resistance to change. The tight control which Rodney and Betty Marlow exerted over product design has **prevented recognition of the changes in consumer tastes**, meaning the company has continued to produce the type of designs that served it well in the past, rather than the designs which consumers now want.

BPP
LEARNING MEDIA

This resistance to change can also be seen in the management team's reluctance to accept that the significant fall in sales and profits reflects the shift in demand for women's clothing.

Lack of awareness of competitive environment. It is possible that the failure to adapt product design and manufacturing processes to keep pace with current trends may be as much due to Rodney and Betty Marlow not being aware of the current trends as them resisting change. Either way, the failure to produce clothes which current tastes demand is causing a significant fall in sales.

Rapid turnover of CEO's. Marlow has had a new Chief Executive Officer every year. A succession of CEOs of this nature is indicative of a company which is performing poorly – with each new CEO being brought in to try to turn around its fortunes.

Conclusion

The changes in the market for women's wear have caused Marlow to move from a strategically sound position to one where it now needs a swift strategic turnaround. Its products and markets have changed, and its value chain no longer delivers any distinctive value to its customers. These issues need addressing urgently to try to reverse the decline in the company's sales and profitability.

(b) **Benchmarking**

> **Top tips.** Note there are only 7 marks available for this question, with up to 2 marks available for each relevant point about the contribution benchmarking could make to improving Marlow's strategic position.
>
> For tutorial purposes, the answer below includes a number of possible ways Marlow could benefit from benchmarking.
>
> However, as the marking guide illustrates, you would not need to include all these points to score well on this question. But you would need to make relevant points, and relate them directly back to Marlow's specific circumstances.

Benchmarking at Marlow Fashion will not be an easy exercise. Marlow has developed a distinctive way of reaching its markets, and this means direct comparisons with other companies could be hard to make. However, there are still ways it can use benchmarking to assess its current position with a view to improving it.

Best-in-class benchmarking. Marlow should be looking to compare the performance of its own key operations against the 'best in class' performers with similar features or processes, regardless of which industry the leading performer comes from.

Marlow could, and should, have been carrying out competitive benchmarking on the retail side of its business, because information should be relatively easily available there.

The indicators for Marlow's performance should have a shock on their managers, and lead to dramatic performance improvements.

The contribution benchmarking could make to improving the position of the Marlow Fashion Group:

Challenging existing processes. Some of the key questions which Marlow should be asking when carrying out a benchmarking exercise are:

- Why are these products or services provided in this particular way?
- What are the examples of best practice elsewhere?
- How could our activities be reshaped in the light of these comparisons?

This third question could be crucial in helping improve Marlow's strategic position.

One of Marlow's key weaknesses is that its processes are lagging behind its competitors, due to the vertically integrated model which Rodney and Betty have imposed. If the benchmarking exercise can show that Marlow's business model is now less effective than other models being adopted by competitors this should **facilitate the change towards a more flexible model**.

In Marlow Fashion, the **acceptance that things have to be done differently will be the first stage in the turnaround** the business needs.

Motivation for change. There has traditionally been a **reluctance to change** things at Marlow fashion. However, by comparing its performance against competitors, Marlow may be able to identify **motivating, achievable targets of improved performance** to aim for.

Accepting responsibility for change

The benchmarking comparisons should be carried out by the managers who are responsible for each key area of performance. Consequently, benchmarking should also **encourage the managers to take responsibility for any changes necessary** to improve the performance in that area.

Moreover, by comparing its performance in key areas against 'best-in-class' indicators, Marlow will have some performance targets to aim for. Benchmarking can have a significant benefit to Marlow's turnaround if it prompts challenging, but achievable, **targets to be set in all key performance areas**.

Compare to other turnaround companies

As well as comparing itself to best-in-class performers, Marlow could also use external benchmarking to see how **other struggling companies have managed to turn around their fortunes**. For example, this might highlight the importance of focusing on just one of design, manufacturing or retailer, whereas Marlow has continued to try to do all three.

Insights into technology

It appears that Marlow's organisation is rather 'traditional' and 'dated.' Therefore it is likely that its design and production technology could also be dated, meaning it is less efficient than many of its competitors.

Through external benchmarking, Marlow may be able to identify possible **improvements to the technology used its design and manufacturing process**. For example, it may be possible to implement some computer-aided design (CAD) or computer-aided manufacturing (CAM) systems.

(c) **The finance function as a business partner**

In recent times there has been a shift in the role of the modern finance function. An increasing number of organisations now expect the finance function to take on a more commercially-focused role than it had done in the past. Finance professionals are now expected to participate as members of operational teams and to bring greater financial expertise to the management process.

Benefits to the Marlow Group

At present the finance function at the Marlow Group fulfil the traditional role expected of finance professionals (processing accounting transactions and preparing month end reports). The group's recent performance indicates that it may benefit from pursuing the business partner model. Marlow Fashion has suffered from a lack of understanding of the changes in its business environment and has seen its performance fall. The introduction of the business partner model should help to improve managements understanding of environmental changes through enhancing the information used for decision-making at both a strategic and operational level. In essence, improved information for decision-making should contribute to improved performance.

Improved information for strategic decision-making

The management team at Marlow Fashion have been reluctant to accept that the drop in profits was due to changes in the clothing market. This ignorance may have been partly borne out of the quality of the information that management received about market trends. The finance function as a business partner could enhance the quality of information provided to the board when making strategic decisions by combining internal financial details such as profit forecasts with external data relating to key movements in fashion products and customer trends. Improved information for decision-making is also likely to lead to the setting of better quality strategic objectives.

Improved information for operational decision-making

The business partner model should also allow finance professionals to provide financial expertise to operational managers. For example, helping managers involved in the manufacturing of clothes to better understand the causes of production and labour variances as opposed to only reporting the results. Furthermore, in the event that operational managers prepare departmental budgets they could look to draw on the expertise of the finance team during the budgeting process in order to make their budgets more realistic.

Improved communication

The Marlow Fashion Group's commitment to its workers, retailers and suppliers makes them important stakeholders. Each stakeholder group is likely to require different information about Marlow Fashion's performance. The establishment of the finance function as a business partner may help the group to better communicate with such stakeholders as relevant financial and non-financial information can be prepared and interpreted for different stakeholder groups to suit their needs. The reporting of performance by the traditional finance function is likely to have focused solely on financial aspects which non-finance professionals may have struggled to understand.

7 Frigate

Text reference. The cultural web is covered in Chapter 5 of the BPP Study Text for exams from September 2015 to 31 August 2016. Project management is covered in Chapter 13.

Top tips. There is lots of information in the scenario that can be applied to the cultural web and if you have a good understanding of this model it should not be too difficult. Remember to apply the information from the scenario to the model rather than just describing the model itself.

Also, make sure you do link your point back to the model rather than just repeating the information given to you in the scenario without going on to explain what this means in respect of the culture of Frigate.

Marking scheme

			Marks
(a)	1 mark for each relevant point up to a maximum of 15 marks		
		Max	15
(b)	1 mark for each relevant point up to a maximum of 10 marks		
		Max	10
			25

Part (a)

The cultural web illustrates the combination of assumptions that make up the **paradigm**, together with the **physical manifestation** of culture. It is applied to Frigate below.

Symbols

Organisations are represented by symbols such as logos, offices, dress, language and titles. Symbols at Frigate that indicate how the managing director wishes the company to be perceived and run include:

- Ron's nickname 'The Commander'
- Ron's use of naval terminology
- The naval inspired name of the company

Ron's motor cruiser is the main symbol of his success.

Power structures

Power structures look at who holds the real power within an organisation. At Frigate the power comes from one person, Ron, whose leadership style is based on his strong opinions and beliefs.

Organisational structures

The structure of the organisation often reflects the power structure. There is little formal structure at Frigate, and the attempt to install a formal organisational structure failed.

Control systems

Organisations are controlled through a number of systems including financial systems, quality systems and rewards. The areas that are controlled closest indicate the priorities of the organisation. The focus in Frigate is on cost control and the emphasis is on punishment (such as wage deductions for being late) rather than reward.

There are few formal process controls at Frigate, and the attempt to install such controls was heavily resisted.

Routines and rituals

The daily behaviour and actions of staff signal what the organisation considers to be 'acceptable', expectations and management values. At Frigate, there is one rule for the managing director (flexible hours, extended holidays etc) and another for everyone else (minimum holiday, no flexibility, wage deductions for arriving late).

Stories

The people and past events talked about in an organisation can illustrate the values of the organisation and the behaviour it encourages. Stories at Frigate relate to the managing director as 'The Commander'. He is the hero of the organisation who constantly has to deal with numerous villains – lazy staff, poor quality suppliers, customers who delay paying, the tax authority, and society in general (who he believes all need to do a stint in the navy).

Paradigm

The paradigm signifies the basic assumptions and beliefs that an organisation's decision makers hold in common and take for granted. It summarises and reinforces the rest of the cultural web. The paradigm at Frigate shows a company run for the personal gratification of the managing director and his family. Ron believes that his lifestyle and benefits are the reward for taking risks in a hostile environment.

Part (b)

> **Top tips.** Don't spend too much time describing in detail the entire of Mintzberg's theory. Although referencing the six stereotypes is useful, a detailed explanation of each is not.
>
> Focus your efforts on describing the two stereotypes relevant to this question (Entrepreneurial and Machine bureaucracy), explaining what they are, which of the two organisations in the scenario they describe and the clearly incompatible nature of one with the other.
>
> Many students did not answer this requirement well and appeared to have little understanding of Mintzberg's theory. This once again highlights the importance of revising all areas of the syllabus in your preparation for this exam.

Henry Mintzberg's theory of organisational culture expresses the main features through which formal structure and power relationships are expressed in organisations. He identifies six configuration stereotypes.

Two of these configurations are relevant for Frigate Limited.

Entrepreneurial

Frigate Ltd displays the characteristics of a machine bureaucracy. These characteristics include:

- Simple, flexible structure made up of few staff of a similar authority level
- Activities revolve around a 'hands on' chief executive
- Simple dynamic environment
- Small organisation with a strong leader.

At Frigate, power is centred around Ron, the managing director and he exercises control via informal, direct supervision.

Machine bureaucracy

Ann Li has joined Frigate Ltd from the Tax Authority – an organisation which is likely to have the characteristics of a machine bureaucracy. These characteristics include:

- Formal and heavily defined processes
- Clear division of labour and defined hierarchy

- Often larger or mature organisation
- Processes are rationalised and standardised
- Environment is simple and stable

Operations in such organisations are routine, simple and repetitive and so processes are highly standardised. Ann has tried to implement this at Frigate stating that 'we need structure, standardised processes and accountability'.

This was destined to fail in a CEO-controlled environment in which flexible processes are dictated by the leader. There is a clear mismatch between structure, processes and context. This could have been predicted if Ann had understood the importance of matching the processes to the culture, and had appreciated the importance that Ron places on the fact that he has absolute power and is in absolute control.

8 Alpha Software

Text reference. The concept of integrated reporting is covered in Chapter 5 of your BPP Study Text for exams from September 2015 to 31 August 2016.

Top tips. Part (a). A good technique to answering part (a) was to consider the key differences between integrated reporting and traditional approaches to reporting performance. Remember the aim of integrated reporting is to show users how the company has created value using the resources at its disposal. By contrast traditional methods of reporting performance are focused on financial metrics such as profitability. Part (b): The second requirement builds upon part (a). Part (a) requires you to illustrate that you understand the theory of integrated reporting in general. There were easy marks going for this part of the question provided you had read Chapter 5 of your BPP Study Text which explores the role of integrated reporting. Part (b) required the application of these points to the scenario, with particular emphasis on how integrated reporting could help Alpha improve its strategic performance.

To score well on this requirement it is critical that your answer is related to Alpha Software. The scenario is provided to give you the opportunity to show two things. Firstly, that you understand the theory – ie what integrated reporting is – and secondly, for you to show that you can apply your knowledge. A good approach to dealing with such questions is to set the scene by identifying what has gone wrong in the scenario. In this case stakeholders (shareholders and employees) are confused as to the strategic direction that Alpha is trying to pursue.

Next, use your knowledge to explain how integrated reporting can help Alpha to communicate its strategy. Integrated reporting places a strong emphasis on relaying what the company stands for through setting out its objectives and strategy to realise these. The introduction of integrated reporting would therefore provide the company with a great opportunity to convey Gemma Murphy's new mission.

Easy marks. Three marks were available for incorporating a discussion of the finance directors views. Failure to comment on a particular matter when a question directs you – in this case, making reference to the finance directors statement – loses you easy marks.

Part (c). Was a fairly straightforward requirement. Provided you were able to generate a range of practical implications you should have picked up the 5 easy marks on offer.

Marking scheme

	Marks
Part (a)	
Integrated reporting:	
Up to 2 marks for a discussion of how integrated reporting allows for a wider performance appraisal	2
Up to 3 marks for a discussion of value creation	3
Up to 2 marks for a discussion on how short term decisions have long term implications	2
Up to 2 marks for a discussion of monetary values and the use of KPIs in integrated reporting	2
1 mark for a discussion of materiality	1
	10

	Marks
Part (b)	
1 mark for explaining the current stakeholder confusion at Alpha	1
Up to 3 marks for a discussion on how integrated reporting may help communicate strategy	3
Up to 3 marks for a discussion on how integrated reporting may improve Alpha's performance	3
Up to 3 marks for a discussion of the finance director's comments	3
	10
Part (c)	
1 mark per implication raised related to Alpha	5
	25

Part (a)

Integrated reporting

Wider performance appraisal

Integrated reporting is concerned with conveying a wider message on an entity's performance. It is not solely centred on profit and the company's financial position but aims to focus on how the organisations activities interact to create value over the short, medium and long term. It is thought that by producing a holistic view of organisational performance that this will lead to improved management decision making as business decisions are not taken in isolation.

Value creation

In the context of integrated reporting an organisation's resources are referred to as 'capitals'. The International Integrated Reporting Council have identified six capitals which can be used to assess value creation. Increases or decreases in these capitals indicate the level of value created or lost over a period. Capitals cover various types of resources found in a standard organisation. These may include financial capitals, such as the entity's financial reserves, through to its intellectual capital which is concerned with intellectual property and staff knowledge.

Performance evaluation of the six capitals is central to integrated reporting. Throughout time these capitals continually interact with one another, an increase in one may lead to a decrease in another. A decision to purchase a new IT system would improve an entity's 'manufactured' capital while decreasing its financial capital. By contrast the decision to purchase a patent for a new production technology would increase intellectual capital and may also boost financial capital if it reduces costs and increases output. It is important to note that due to the voluntary nature of integrated reporting, organisations are free to report only on those 'capitals' felt to be most relevant.

Short term v long term

In many ways, integrated reporting forces management to balance its short term objectives against its longer term plans. Business decisions which are solely dedicated to the pursuit of increasing profit (financial capital) at the expense of building good relations with key stakeholders such as customers (social capital) are likely to hinder value creation in the longer term.

Performance measures

Integrated reporting is not aimed at attaching a monetary value to every aspect of the organisation's operations. It is fundamentally concerned with evaluating value creation, and uses qualitative and quantitative performance measures to help stakeholders assess how well an organisation is creating value.

The use of KPIs to convey performance is an effective way of reporting. For example when providing detail on customer satisfaction, this can be communicated as the number of customers retained compared to the previous year. Best practice in integrated reporting requires organisations to report on both positive and negative movements in 'capital'. This ensures the entity's performance is fully communicated and not just those favourable movements. Stakeholders are likely to be as interested (if not more so) in understanding what an organisation has not done well as opposed to only considering the entity's achievements. Integrated reporting ensures that a balanced view of performance is presented.

Materiality

When preparing an integrated report, management should disclose matters which are likely to impact on an organisation's ability to create value. Internal weaknesses and external threats regarded as being materially important are evaluated and quantified. This provides users with an indication of how management intend to combat such instances should they materialise.

Part (b)

Integrated reporting at Alpha Software

Confusion

As a result of the recent management changes at Alpha Software, the company has struggled to communicate its 'strategic direction' to key stakeholders. The company's annual accounts have made it hard for shareholders to understand Alpha's strategy which in turn has led to confusion. Uncertainty among shareholders and employees is likely to increase the risk of investors selling their shares and talented IT developers seeking employment with competitors.

Communicating strategy

The introduction of integrated reporting may help Alpha to overcome these issues as it places a strong focus on the organisation's future orientation. An integrated report should detail the company's mission and values, the nature of its operations, along with features on how it differentiates itself from its competitors.

Including Alpha's new mission to become the market leader in the specialist accountancy software industry would instantly convey what the organisation stands for.

In line with best practice in integrated reporting, Alpha could supplement its mission with how the board intend to achieve this strategy. Such detail could focus on resource allocations over the short to medium term. For example, plans to improve the company's human capital through hiring innovative software developers working at competing firms would help to support the company's long term mission. To assist users in appraising the company's performance, Alpha should provide details on how it will measure value creation in each 'capital'. 'Human capital' could be measured by the net movement in new joiners to the organisation compared to the previous year.

A key feature of integrated reporting focuses on the need for organisations to use non-financial customer-oriented performance measures (KPIs) to help communicate the entity's strategy. The most successful companies in Alpha's industry are committed to enhancing their offering to customers through producing innovative products. Alpha could report through the use of KPIs how it is delivering on this objective, measures could be set which for example measure the number of new software programs developed in the last two years or report on the number of customer complaints concerning newly released software programs over the period.

Improving long term performance

The introduction of integrated reporting may also help Alpha to enhance its performance. Historically, the company has not given consideration to how decisions in one area have impacted on other areas. This is clearly indicated by former CEO's cost cutting programme which served to reduce the staff training budget. Although, this move may have enhanced the company's short term profitability, boosting financial capital, it has damaged long term value creation.

The nature of the software industry requires successful organisations to invest in staff training to ensure that the products they develop remain innovative in order to attract customers. The decision to reduce the training budget will most likely impact on future profitability if Alpha is unable to produce software customers' demand.

Finance director's comments

As illustrated in the scenario, the finance director's comments indicate a very narrow understanding of how the company's activities and 'capitals' interact with each other in delivering value. To dismiss developments in integrated reporting as simply being a 'fad', suggest that the finance director is unaware of the commitment of ACCA in promoting its introduction. The ACCA's support for integrated reporting may lead to backing from other global accountancy bodies thereby reducing the scope for it be regarded as a passing 'fad'.

However, some critics refute this and argue that the voluntary nature of integrated reporting increases the likelihood that companies will choose not to pursue its adoption. Such individuals highlight that until companies are legally required to comply with integrated reporting guidelines, many will simply regard it as an unnecessary effort and cost.

The finance director's assertion regarding shareholders is likely to some degree to be correct. Investors looking for short term results from an investment might assess Alpha's performance based on improvements in profitability. However, many shareholders will also be interested in how the board propose to create value in the future. Ultimately, Alpha's aim to appease both groups is its focus on maximising shareholder value, the achievement of which requires the successful implementation of both short and long term strategies.

Furthermore, unlike traditional annual accounts, integrated reports highlight the importance of considering a wider range of users. Key stakeholder groups such as Alpha's customers and suppliers are likely to be interested in assessing how the company has met or not met their needs beyond the 'bottom line'. Integrated reporting encourages companies to report performance measures which are closely aligned to the concepts of sustainability and corporate social responsibility. This is implied by the different capitals used: consideration of social relationships and natural capitals do not focus on financial performance but instead are concerned, for example, with the impact an organisation's activities have on the natural environment.

Ultimately as integrated reporting provides senior management with a greater quantity of organisational performance data this should help in identifying previously unrecognised areas which are in need of improvement.

Clearly, a major downside to generating extensive additional data concerns determining which areas to report on. This is made especially difficult as there is no recognised criteria for determining the level of importance of each 'capital'. As we shall explore in part (c), the finance director's remark regarding the increase in the Alpha's workload to comply with integrated reporting practices may have some merit.

It is debatable as to whether the production of an integrated report necessarily leads to an improvement in organisational performance or whether it simply leads to an improvement in the reporting of performance. However, focusing management's attention on the non-financial aspects of Alpha's performance as well as its purely financial performance, could be expected to lead to performance improvements in those areas. For example, if innovation is highlighted as a key factor in sustaining Alpha's long term value, a focus on innovation could help to encourage innovation within the company.

Part (c)

Implications of implementing integrated reporting

IT and IS costs

The introduction of integrated reporting at Alpha will most likely require significant upgrades to be made to the company's IT and information system infrastructure. Such developments will be needed to assist Alpha in capturing both financial and non-financial KPI data. Due to the broad range of business activities reported on using integrated reporting (customer, finance and human resources) the associated costs in improving the infrastructure to deliver relevant data about each area is likely to be significant. It may, however, be the case that Alpha's existing information systems are already capable of producing the required non-financial performance data needed in which case it is likely that the focus here will be on investigating which data sets should be included in the integrated report.

Time implications

The process of gathering and collating the data to include in an integrated report is likely to require a significant amount of staff time. This may serve to decrease staff morale especially if staff are expected to undertake this work in addition to completing existing duties. In some cases this may require Alpha to pay employees overtime to ensure all required information is published in the report on time.

Staff costs

To avoid overburdening existing staff the board may decide to appoint additional staff to undertake the work of analysing data for inclusion in the integrated report. This will invariably lead to an increase in staff costs.

Consultancy costs

As this will be Alpha's first integrated report the board may seek external guidance from an organisation which provides specialist consultancy on reporting. Any advice is likely to focus on the contents of the report. The consultant's fees are likely to be significant and will increase the associated implementation costs of introducing integrated reporting.

BPP
LEARNING MEDIA

Disclosure

A potential downside of adopting integrated reporting centres on Alpha potentially volunteering more information about its operations than was actually needed. In the event that Alpha fully disclosed the company's planned strategies it is likely that this could be used by competitors. Such a move is likely to undermine any future moves to out-manoeuvre other industry players. In the event that Alpha have hired an external consultant to support the introduction of integrated reporting it is likely that the advice given by the consultant will stress the need to avoid disclosure of commercially sensitive information.

9 AutoFone

Text reference: Porter's five forces model is covered in Chapter 2 of the BPP Study Text for exams from September 2015 to 31 August 2016; the industry life cycle is covered in Chapter 3 and strategic choices are covered in Chapter 6.

Top tips. Section (a) asked you to use an appropriate model or models to analyse the competitive environment of AutoFone's retail shops. The scenario was written to encourage you to identify Porter's five forces model as the appropriate model – for example, there were clear references to barriers to entry, and industry competitors.

When this exam was sat, some candidates used PESTEL as a model as an alternative, and the examiner acknowledged it did help candidates identify some relevant issues, although it didn't fit as neatly with the scenario as Five forces.

Although the question allowed you the opportunity of using more than one model you must remember that you do not score marks for duplicated points. Therefore, issues of government regulation identified under 'P' in PESTEL and 'threat of new entrants' in Porter's five forces only counted once.

Similarly, whichever model you chose, you should not have wasted time describing the model in detail. The marks were earned for the analysis of AutoFone's competitive environment, not describing the model.

Section (b) asked you to explain why AutoFone should not dispose of its retail shops. In this part, there isn't a model which you can use to structure your answer, but the scenario should have provided you with sufficient information to build a case: for example, financial exit barriers associated with terminating the shop leases; impact on the brand of closing the shops; value of cross-selling between the shops and the internet.

Also you must always make use of the financial data you were given in the scenario. For example, the figures indicate that the shops contribute 85% of group revenue. This in itself is a strong argument for not selling the shops! (We have included the calculations related to the financial data at the end of (b) for tutorial purposes only. You would not be expected to show workings in your briefing note.)

Easy marks. Porter's five forces model is a core model in the P3 syllabus, and by using this as a framework you should have been able to score well in (a).

The scenario highlighted a number of points which you could use in (b).

Examiner's comments. In (a) many candidates produced long answers using more than model, but with significant repetition. There is little to be gained by using different models to make the same points. Also, in P3 there are relatively few marks available for simply describing a model such as Porter's five competitive forces. The vast majority of marks are for recognising the presence and effect of the forces in the context of the scenario.

Marking scheme

		Marks
(a)	One mark for each relevant point up to a maximum of 16 marks	16
(b)	One mark for each relevant point up to a maximum of 9 marks	9
		25

(a)   Michael Porter suggests that the competitive environment of an industry, and hence its potential to earn profits, is determined by **five forces**: the threat of new entrants; the bargaining power of suppliers; the bargaining power of customers; threat of substitute products; and the level of rivalry among current competitors in the industry.

Each of these five forces affects the competitive environment of AutoFone's retail sales division.

The threat of new entrants

If new entrants join an industry they bring **extra capacity** and **increased competition** to that industry. However, whether potential new entrants choose to enter the market or not is likely to depend on the level of **barriers to entry** into the industry. In the case of AutoFone's retail sales division, there are some significant barriers to entry.

Access to networks – Government regulation has restricted the number of network providers supplying mobile telephone services to four, and each of these now has their own retail outlets. Consequently the **network providers are unlikely to sign deals with an alternative retailer** which would effectively become a competitor to their own shops.

Even if the network providers do offer deals to new entrants, the **commercial terms of any deal are** likely to be considerably less favourable than the terms which AutoFone secured. The network providers have now realised that AutoFone 'got away with incredible profit margins' when they signed their original deal in 1990, so any new deals offered will be on terms which are weighted much more favourably to the network providers. This will **restrict the potential profit** any new entrants could make, making them inherently less profitable than AutoFone.

The network providers themselves have signed **long-term licence deals** with the Government (to 2020) so it seems unlikely that any new network providers will be allowed to enter the market until after that point.

Economies of scale – The five existing retailers in the industry are all roughly the same size, with annual turnovers in the region of $300m. In AutoFone's case, this is achieved through a **network of 415 shops**. This size means that AutoFone is likely to benefit from economies of scale in purchasing, servicing and distribution of products. In order to achieve similar economies of scale, a new entrant would have to enter the market at a similar scale. This would require the new entrant to acquire (lease or buy) and fit-out a large number of stores, as well as purchasing the inventories to stock them. The **level of initial capital investment** needed to achieve this may prove another barrier to entry.

The bargaining power of suppliers

Suppliers can exert power by increasing the price of their goods and services. The relative power of suppliers is highest in industries dominated by a few suppliers, because customers have limited scope for purchasing from other suppliers.

The following factors affect the network providers' bargaining power:

Limited number of network providers – The bargaining power of suppliers is strong in the mobile phone industry because the market is limited to a small number of network providers.

Importance of product – If it did not have any phones to sell, AutoFone would not have a business.

Non-substitutability of product – The suppliers' position is also enhanced by the fact that there are few direct substitutes for mobile phones.

These three factors mean that the network providers have very strong bargaining power over retailers in the mobile phone industry. However, the relative strength of their bargaining power with AutoFone is reduced because of the beneficial long-term deals AutoFone signed in 1990.

Forward vertical integration – In industries where supplier power is high, the suppliers seek to increase the margins they make by looking to control as much of the value system as they can. When they realised how much margin AutoFone was making by retailing their phones they set up their own stores to compete with AutoFone.

Threat of substitutes

Substitutes to the mobile phone industry would be products from another industry which could perform the same function of mobile communication.

However, the threat of any such substitutes is currently low, especially as a number of mobile phones now allow email and internet access.

The bargaining power of customers

Number and size of buyers – Customers want better quality products and services at the lowest price possible. However, they are usually in a stronger position to achieve this when there are comparatively few buyers and each is large relative to the supplier. This is not the case in the mobile phone industry though, where sales are aimed primarily at individual customers so there are a very large number of buyers and each is small relative to the supplier.

Standardised products – Buyers do still have some bargaining power in the mobile phone industry. Because phone handsets are now very widely available, and different models are relatively standardised in terms of core functionality, customers can play one supplier off against another to try to get the best price possible.

Low switching costs – Moreover, buyers face few switching costs in moving from one phone to another. The only significant tie they have is their contract period with the network provider, which is usually for a minimum of twelve months. At the end of that contract period, a customer can move to a new provider at no cost.

Consequently, although customers are individuals rather than large corporate buyers they do still retain a degree of bargaining power.

Competitive rivalry

If competition between rivals is intense this may lower the profitability in an industry as competitors battle to increase their market share; for example, by lowering price, by advertising extensively, or by offering additional features at no extra cost.

Competitive rivalry in the mobile industry is caused by the following factors.

Number and size of competitors – Retail sales are divided relatively evenly between five main suppliers. Because each of the competitors is reasonably large they have the resources to sustain competitive actions against the others, as they try to increase their market share, and possibly as one seeks to become a clear market leader.

Slow market growth – The need to gain market share is reinforced by the slow growth of the overall market. The mobile phone market is now a **mature market**, with growth of less than 1% in 2007. Therefore, firms can only achieve significant growth by capturing market share from their rivals.

Lack of differentiation and ease of switching – Many customers now consider mobile phones as commodity products, so a large part of their buying decision will be based on price and service levels. This, in conjunction with the ease of switching between phones, will mean that there is intense price and service competition in the mobile phone market.

Exit barriers – Although growth is slowing, it is unlikely that firms will want to leave the industry. The level of **capital invested in their shops**, plus the potential **redundancy costs** if they lay staff off represent considerable barriers to exit. Therefore firms are likely to stay and fight for market share rather than leaving the industry to look for new opportunities elsewhere.

(b)   **Briefing paper – for Strategy Planning Committee**

Justification for keeping the retail sales division

Introduction

The directors have suggested that moving to a purely online business model will be more profitable for AutoFone. However, this paper will show that that suggestion is flawed, and AutoFone needs the retail sales division to remain central to its future strategy.

Industry life cycle

The growth in the market for mobile phones does appear to be slowing down, suggesting it has now reached the **mature phase** of its life cycle.

Intense competition – In its early years, the mobile phone industry enjoyed rapid growth as new customers bought phones for the first time. However, that **overall growth has now slowed**, and so companies are increasingly having to gain market share from their competitors in order to increase sales, rather than simply signing-up new customers.

In such a market, **operating efficiently** and **minimising costs** will be important, so that AutoFone can offer competitive deals to maintain its market position against its competitors. To this end, AutoFone may need to look at its shop processes to check they are as efficient as possible, but that is a very different issue than moving away from the retail sector altogether. Operating online may be seen as a way of minimising costs, but this overlooks the significant contribution the retail shops division makes to the group as a whole.

Financial analysis

The directors' suggestion is that AutoFone can operate more profitably without the retail sales division. However, while the underlying profitability of the retail division has fallen over the five year period 2003 – 2007, the shops are still making a **positive contribution to group profits**.

Margins – ROCE has fallen from 18.1% in 2003 to 5.3% in 2007, and operating profit has fallen from 12.1% to 3.2% over the same period (see workings at end). These tighter margins **reflect the intense competition** in the market, but both gross and net profit increased in 2007 compared to 2006 suggesting that the retail market can still be profitable.

Liquidity and gearing – Despite the lower margins, AutoFone's **liquidity position** has only changed slightly over the five year period. Also, although its **gearing ratio** has risen from 21% to 32% as its loan financing has increased, AutoFone remains relatively lightly geared.

Therefore, overall the financial position is not as poor as the directors may be suggesting.

Shops' contribution to group profit – Perhaps most importantly of all, the shops contribute **85% of the total group revenue**, so it is debatable whether AutoFone could continue to compete effectively in an industry dominated by a small number of big players if it reduced its operations so significantly. Admittedly, some retail shop customers may migrate to use AFDirect but there is no guarantee in this.

Impact of demographics on sales – Analysis of shop sales by age suggests that the face-to-face service available in the shops is valued by older customers. Over 50% of shop revenue is from customers over 40, while over 75% of AFDirect revenue is from customers under 40. This indicates that the retail shops and AFDirect have different customer profiles, and suggests that if the shop division were closed, a number of shop customers may choose to buy their phones from one of the network providers' retail shops rather than buying online through AFDirect.

Therefore, rather than selling off the retail sales division, AutoFone should recognise its longer-term strategic value to the group, even though its profit levels will be constrained as the market matures.

Competing in a mature market

Environmental analysis has suggested that customer bargaining power is relatively strong in the mobile phone market. Also, as the market matures **customers are likely to be increasingly selective** in their purchases.

In this respect, AutoFone has a **competitive advantage** because it is the only retail provider which can offer customers a choice from the full selection of phones across all the networks.

Importance of shops to group

If the shops division were closed, the brand's visibility to the public would be significantly reduced. Moreover, if customers see that AutoFone has closed its shops they may think the company is in financial difficulties. This could create damage the brand, and therefore have a negative impact on sales through the remaining Internet operations.

Exits barriers from the retail sales industry

As well as the potential negative consequences for the brand and for cross-selling, AutoFone could incur some significant costs from leaving the retail shop industry, depending on its exit strategy.

Leases – AutoFone has taken out long leases on its shops. The leases are not in prime shopping areas and so may be difficult to re-let. Consequently they are likely to include substantial break clauses which AutoFone will have to pay if it wants to terminate the lease.

Redundancies – AutoFone currently employs 1,400 staff who would be made redundant if the shops were closed down. The resulting redundancy payments would be a significant cost to the business.

AutoFone could avoid these costs by selling the shops division as a going concern, but any buyer would need to be satisfied that the network providers will allow them to inherit the remainder of the supply contracts. Moreover, if someone is prepared to buy the shops as a going concern, it suggests the new owners think they can run the shops profitably – which again questions the logic of AutoFone selling them.

Conclusion

The mobile phone market has matured in the last few years, reducing the opportunities for growth and profit. However, the market does remain profitable, and AutoFone is better placed to serve the market by offering both a retail shop division and an internet division. Closing the retail sales division could adversely affect AFDirect's sales, in effect undermining the alternative business model which the directors are proposing.

Workings for financial analysis *[included for tutorial purposes only]*		
	2007	2003
ROCE: [PBIT / (Equity + long-term debt)]	11/(150 + 55) = 5.3%	37/(169 + 35) = 18.1%
Operating profit margin: [PBIT / Revenue]	11/340 = 3.2%	37/305 = 12.1%
Gross profit margin:	90/340 = 26.5%	100/305 = 32.8%
Liquidity (Current ratio):	2,076/1,998 = 1.04	1,832/1,741 = 1.05
Capital Gearing	71/(71 + 150) = 32%	45/(45 + 169) = 21%

10 8-Hats

Marking scheme

			Marks
(a)	1 mark for each relevant point up to a maximum of 15 marks		
		Max	15
(b)	1 mark for each relevant point up to a maximum of 10 marks		
		Max	10
			25

(a) **Payback rate**

Job 1

All figures in $'000

C/F	0	-110	-60	-45	-5
	Year 0	Year 1	Year 2	Year 3	Year 4
Total costs	110	10	10	10	10
Total savings	0	60	25	50	70
Cumulative	-110	-60	-45	-5	55

Job 2

All figures in $'000

C/F	0	-90	-50	-30	-5
	Year 0	Year 1	Year 2	Year 3	Year 4
Total costs	90	20	20	10	10
Total savings	0	60	35	40	35
Cumulative	-90	-50	-30	-5	20

The calculations above show that both jobs would have had a payback period of 4 years, however, Job 1 ($55) would pay back more than Job 2 ($20) therefore Job 1 would still have been preferable and so selected.

Payback ignores any cashflows that would be received in the years after payback. With hindsight, we know Job 1 was a disaster, and it is possible Job 2 may have generated more revenue subsequent to payback.

However, had the payback method been used, any such future cashflows would not have been considered at the time of appraisal and so Job 1 would still have been selected over Job 2. Barry Blunt's assertion that this method would have led to the selection of Job 2 is therefore incorrect.

The discount rate

The discount rate is not the same as the inflation rate. Although inflation may be taken into account, other factors such as interest forgone (the opportunity cost of investing elsewhere), the cost of capital (the cost of borrowing to fund the investment) and risk are influential in determining the discount rate. The discount rate used will include a risk allowance which determines the required rate of return for a project to be considered to be viable.

To determine the appropriate discount rate to use, it would be useful to have further information about risk-free interest rates, the risk profile of the company and the company's cost of capital.

However, note that even if the discount rate was changed to 3% or 4%, this would make no difference as to which project was selected. It would in fact increase the attractiveness of Job 1 as there would be less discounting of the cash flows in years 3 and 4. This would actually increase the gap in the NVP between Jobs 1 and 2.

The internal rate of return (IRR)

The IRR is the discount rate that would give an NPV of zero for the net cash flows of the job as, and the two jobs are of a similar scale. Therefore, in this case the project with the greater NPV will produce the higher IRR, and so the result under IRR will the same as that selected under NPV (ie Job 1 would still have been selected).

IRR may have been important, however, if the company has to achieve an internal hurdle rate, or when different scales of investment are being compared. Neither of these situations exist at 8-Hats.

Tangible and intangible benefits

Both jobs allocate significant monetary benefits to intangible benefits such as 'better information' and 'improved staff morale'. However, it is unlikely that these benefits could be estimated before the project is carried out. Although these benefits are important, they should not be given artificial accuracy or inflated to make a business case as Barry suggests.

If intangible benefits are excluded from the business case, then Job 2 does have greater NPV than Job 1, however, in both cases the NPV is below zero and so neither project should be accepted. Therefore, if the benefits had been properly assessed then the disaster of Job 1 (and indeed Job 2) could have been predicted and avoided.

Benefits realisation

Barry has misunderstood the concept of benefits realisation.

The point of the feasibility study is to consider likely costs and benefits from the project for inclusion in the business case. The benefits realisation process determines whether the predicted benefits have been actually been delivered, therefore is must take place sometime after the project (or service) has been completed and has been in place long enough for the realised benefits to be evident. It compares the benefits actually realised to those outlined in the business case. It would not be possible to complete the benefit realisation process after the feasibility study as there would be no actual benefits to compare to the predictions.

(b)

Text reference. Organisational structure is covered in Chapter 7 of your BPP Study Text for exams from September 2015 to 31 August 2016.

Top tips. Make sure you are familiar with the entire P3 syllabus to ensure you are fully prepared for your exam, and do not overlook those areas you appear to be smaller, or less-examined. This is the first time that matrix management has been specifically examined and many candidates demonstrated that they are lacking the required knowledge in this area.

8-Hats is currently structured on a **functional** basis. There is a department for each activity of the company and each job is passed between functions. Each function is focused on optimising its part of the transaction, and has defined objectives sometimes reflecting the reward system in place. However, these objectives are not always aligned with those in other areas of the business and therefore objectives clash. For example the sales department are rewarded based on turnover (not profit) and so will try to win sales by heavily discounting the price, whereas the events department focus on providing the best client experience. This will cause problems for the operations department who then have the task of delivering the functionality promised by the events department at the price promised by the sales department whilst still making a profit.

Such clashes are typical of a silo mentality with functions (departments) sub-optimising based on their own interests at the detriment to the organisational overall objectives. These conflicts can only be resolved by referring upwards, as shown by the scenario where Barry Blunt had to arrange extra funding to ensure suppliers could be paid before their event was boycotted.

Implementing a matrix structure would be an attempt to manage the key 'jobs' (projects) across various the functional departments. Each job has the characteristics of a project – it has a start, runs for a specified time period, and then an end (often the actual event). Under the matrix structure the organisation would be split into **multi-disciplinary teams** drawn from the each of the functional departments. Each of these teams would focus on delivering a successful and profitable project. Decisions taken within that project will generally represent a consensus view of all those involved and so their objectives are brought back into line with the overall objectives of the organisation. Such focus on the event itself should greatly improve customer experience and satisfaction with 8-Hats.

A potential drawback of the matrix structure would be that decisions may take longer due to the need for consensus. This would perhaps create more conflict within the company, particularly if cost and profit responsibilities are either unclear or counter-productive. To minimise potential conflict, the reward systems at 8-Hats will probably have to be re-structured, particularly for sales managers (currently rewarded based on turnover).

Another matrix structure problem is that job and task responsibilities may not be clear, so 8-Hats will have to ensure these responsibilities are properly defined. This could be achieved by transferring responsibilities for profit and work allocation to the project, while maintaining technical support and employee appraisal and competency development within the departments. Changing to matrix management is a fundamental change for the organisation would therefore require significant cultural changes to take place at 8-Hats.

11 Joe Swift Transport

Text reference. The success criteria SAF is covered in Chapter 6 of your BPP Study Text for exams from September 2015 to 31 August 2016. Ratio analysis is dealt with in Chapter 14.

Top tips. Many students chose not to use the success criteria of SAF to structure their answer and as a result their answers lacked focus and direction. However, this question was a very popular choice and many students scored highly on this question.

Remember, you will earn few marks if you simply churn out every ratio you can think of. In order to score highly, limit the ratios you select to only those that are specifically relevant to the question and ensure you fully **explain** the results and how this affects the decision you are being asked to make.

Examiner's comments. Candidates answered part (a) relatively well, using appropriate calculations as well as describing the pull factors of Ecuria and the push factors of Ambion.

Marking scheme

		Marks
(a)	1 mark for each relevant point up to a maximum of 15 marks	15
(b)	1 mark for each relevant point up to a maximum of 10 marks	10
		25

(a) The suitability, feasibility, acceptability technique can be used to assess the attractiveness of EVM as an acquisition target.

Suitability

Suitability relate to the strategic logic of the strategy – it should fit the organisation's current strategic position and should satisfy a range of requirements.

Acquiring EVM would appear to be a suitable strategy for Swift. This is based on a number of considerations:

- The Ambion market is mature and highly competitive. This pushes down profit margins.

- The Ambion government is hostile to road transport. This has led to high taxes and restricted working practices which again push down margins.

- Acquiring EVM would provide Swift with access to a new market in which demand is growing, competition is immature and the government are investing in road transportation.

- Acquiring EVM will increase the overall size of the group, allowing increased economies of scale to be exploited which purchasing trucks and other equipment.

However, suitability of the acquisition may be reduced in light of any potential culture clash that may arise between the two companies involved. These may arise for a number of reasons:

- Swift has no experience of operating or acquiring foreign companies.

- Swift has no experience of trading in Ecuria.

- Although EVM is now a private company, the mindset may still be that of the government organisation it once was. Changing these practices, although potentially leading to higher profits, may be complex and could lead to reputation-damaging labour disputes. This may be unavoidable if Swift attempt to force the Ambion style working practices upon them, and may lead to conflict that could be impossible to resolve.

Acceptability

The acceptability of a strategy depends on expected performance outcomes and the extent to which these are acceptable to stakeholders. Acceptability can be evaluated by considering return, risk and shareholder reactions.

Return

- EVM delivers a Return on Capital Employed (ROCE) of 18.4%. This is very similar to the ROCE of Swift Transport and appears to be a strong performance for the sector. This should be acceptable to Swift shareholders.

- The gross profit margin at 20% is higher than that of Swift, however, its net profit margin of 7.5% is lower. This may raise concerns over suitability. The low net profit margin may be due to EVM still carrying high costs from its state owned days. However, it is possible that Swift will be able to improve the profit margin through economies of scale and by implementing competences gained at Albion. This would make the prospect more acceptable.

Risk

- Liquidity (as demonstrated by the current ratio of 1.14% and the acid test ratio of 1.05%) is much lower than that of Swift. Swift will have to determine why this is the case.

- Gearing (30.9%) is much lower for EVM than for Swift. This may indicate a more conservative approach to long-term lending.

- The interest cover ratio (5) is half that of Swift. This could indicate lower profitability and higher business taxation.

Stakeholders

- Swift is still a private run company and the family are major shareholders making opposition to the acquisition from the shareholders unlikely.

- Drivers may not be in full support of the acquisition.

- Joe has openly criticised the government who may now respond, for example they may impose taxes on foreign investment.

Feasibility

Feasibility is concerned with whether the strategy can be implemented and if the organisation has sufficient strategic capability (resources and competences) to deliver it. Swift has the funds in place and its competences are one of the main factors driving the acquisition. This would suggest that the acquisition is a feasible strategy for Swift to pursue.

(b)

Text reference. Porter's diamond is covered in Chapter 2 of your BPP Study Text for exams from September 2015 to 31 August 2016.

Top tips. This is the first time that the Diamond model has been specifically asked for in the P3 exam, however, many students demonstrated that they are reasonably confident with the model and made sensible points.

To score highly in this question you will need to do more than simply name the determinants. Strong candidates explained each quadrant, applied it to Ecuria with examples, and noted the interdependence of the quadrants along with other factors that sit outside the diamond.

Do not waste time drawing the model. This will gain you little, if any, marks. Only do this if you need to see it visually as part of your answer plan.

The question does allow for an alternative model to be used, however the highest marks will be earned if the specified model, ie the diamond is used. Some students used PESTEL to some effect in the exam, scoring reasonable marks and in some cases passing the question. Others used Porter's Five Forces and scored few marks. Some of these students seemed to be confused between the Diamond and the Five Forces models. A handful of students used the Value Chain; these students scored very badly in this question. Where possible, try to use the model requested, only use an alternative as a last resort.

Examiner's comments. Candidates answers this part question very well, not only showing knowledge of the model but were also confident in applying it to a case study scenario.

Porter suggests that some nation's industries are more internationally competitive than others and this is due to the **conditions** in that country that may help firms to compete. This means that the location of the company can play a big part in establishing international competitive advantage. Porter's Diamond consists of four main determinants of competitive advantage, along with chance and government which exist outside the diamond.

Factor conditions

These are factors, such as skilled labour and infrastructure, that are necessary for firms to compete in a given industry.

Significant factor conditions in Ecuria are the work ethic of the people, and the government investment in the transport infrastructure.

Demand conditions

The home demand conditions are how firms perceive, interpret and respond to buyer needs.

In Ecuria, there has been a rapid growth in the transport of goods due to the moved to a market economy. The people of Ecuria are traditionally demanding and have a passion for promptness and precision which has shaped the operations of EVM.

Related and supporting industries

Competitive success in one industry is often linked to success in related industries.

The case study does not provide any evidence that there are internationally competitive industries related to logistics. The absence of internationally successful related and supporting industries is an important factor to take into account when Swift decide whether to move a large part of its logistics business to Ecuria.

Firm strategy, structure and rivalry

Nations are likely to display competitive advantage in industries that are culturally suited to their normal management practices and industrial structures.

EVM was created by the nationalisation of the state-run haulage system. There were few competitors initially and raising finance is difficult due to the structure of the capital markets in Ecuria. As a result, most of EVM's competitors are small, family run firms that offer a local service.

Rivalry is also important as Porter suggested that there is a relationship between the creation and sustainability of competitive advantage and intense domestic rivalry. There is little evidence of rivalry in Ecuria. When there is little domestic rivalry, firms are generally happy to rely on the home market.

In addition to the four main determinants, competitive advantage will also be determined by chance and government. Chance factors are developments outside of the control of firms and the nation's government, such as wars or falls in foreign demand.

Government helps to shape the diamond overall by creating policies which affect all four of the determinants. Ecuria's government has influenced factor conditions by investing in infrastructure, and has influenced firm structure and rivalry via its policies on capital markets.

12 MMI

Text reference. Portfolio analysis and the role of the corporate parent are covered in Chapter 6 of the BPP Study Text for exams from September 2015 to 31 August 2016. Chapter 6 also explores the relationship between a corporate parent and its business units, and discusses the idea of synergies within groups.

Top tips. This question looks at MMI's role as a corporate parent and performance of its SBUs. This is a key area of the Business Analysis syllabus.

From the scenario you should have identified that MMI initially acquired First Leisure with a view to diversification, while the Boatland acquisition was intended to create synergies. However, the subsequent performance of First Leisure has been far better than Boatland's. Does this indicate anything about MMI's strategic rationale – is it a better portfolio manager than it is a synergy manager?

Note that part (a) in effect contains two requirements: (i) explain the rationale for the acquisitions; then (ii) assess the subsequent performance of the companies acquired. Remember to use the financial information provided in Table 1 to support your answer; there are marks specifically available for interpreting this data.

Although the requirement does not specify any models to use, the BCG matrix would have helped you consider how the SBUs fit into MMI's corporate portfolio. The Ashridge Portfolio Display would also have been useful in considering the fit between the SBUs and MMI's corporate parenting skills.

Your analysis in part (a) should help your answer to part (b). In part (a) you should have identified the strengths and weaknesses of MMI's corporate parenting skills, and you can use this to help assess how well it could manage the InfoTech acquisition. Does MMI have the competences required to make this acquisition successful?

The examiner also noted that suitability is one of the three criteria used for judging strategic options (suitability, acceptability, feasibility). So you could have answered this question by looking at the situation in which MMI and InfoTech are operating, and looking at the suitability of the proposal.

However, make sure you look at InfoTech's underlying performance in Table 1 – for example, it is a loss-making company. What will acquiring InfoTech contribute to MMI's portfolio? What value will InfoTech bring to the MMI group? And importantly, does MMI have any experience at turning around failing companies?

Easy marks. The marking scheme identifies that there are up to 7 marks available overall for interpreting the financial and market data. These are relatively easy marks looking at revenue and profitability trends and market share.

Marks

(a) **First Leisure**
Up to 2 marks for recognising that this unrelated diversification was driven by environmental change; supported by appropriate data
Up to 2 marks for issues concerning economies of scope
Up to 3 marks for interpreting the financial and market data
Up to 2 marks for recognising the likely parenting role and for locating First Leisure on an appropriate analysis matrix

Boatland
Up to 2 marks for recognising the synergies expected from Boatland
Up to 2 marks for interpreting the financial and market data
Up to 3 marks for explaining the failure of the acquisition
Up to 2 marks for recognising the likely parenting role and for locating Boatland in an appropriate analysis matrix

15

(b) Up to 3 marks for interpreting the financial performance of MMI and summarising its acquisition strategy
Up to 2 marks for recognising a 'hands-off' approach has been more successful when MMI has pursued unrelated diversification
Up to 2 marks for recognising the difficulty of pursuing this approach at InfoTech
Up to 2 marks for interpreting the financial and market data
Up to 2 marks for recognising the likely parenting role and for locating InfoTech in an appropriate analysis matrix

10
25

Part (a)

Rationale for acquiring First Leisure

Growing market – MMI's original business of quarrying and mining is a declining market place, whose total revenue fell 4.5% between 2002–8. Increased costs and falling reserves meant that industry profitability is likely to continue declining, and moreover meant that there was little chance of MMI finding new sites in its existing market in which to invest. Therefore, **MMI was forced to look for new investment opportunities**.

In contrast to the quarrying and mining market, the leisure market was growing rapidly, and its total revenue increased by 26.7% from 2002–8. Within this market, First Leisure was a profitable company.

So the original rationale for MMI acquiring First Leisure was to enable it to **diversify out of a declining market into an expanding market**.

Unrelated diversification – However, when MMI acquired First Leisure, there didn't appear to be any synergies between the two companies, and so MMI's strategy appeared to be one of unrelated diversification. This lack of synergy initially prompted some finance analysts to question the wisdom of the acquisition.

Economies of scope – After the acquisition, certain synergies between MMI and First Leisure emerged, resulting from the fact that **disused or unprofitable quarry sites could be converted into leisure parks**. These synergies had not been foreseen at the time of acquisition.

Converting quarry sites into leisure parks had two benefits:

(i)   MMI no longer had to incur the costs of running unprofitable mines or to maintain security and safety at disused sites.

BPP
LEARNING MEDIA

(ii)   First Leisure was able to acquire new sites easily and cheaply, in an environment where planning legislation was otherwise making it increasingly expensive and difficult to purchase new sites.

In this way, MMI was able to **benefit from economies of scope – **changing the use of under-utilised resources (from quarries to leisure parks) in a way which benefited the group overall.

Performance of First Leisure post-acquisition

Rapid growth – First Leisure's turnover has doubled from $100m in 2002 to $200m in 2008, and its market has increased from 13% to 21% over the same period. First Leisure's growth in an expanding market suggests that it is a **star business unit**, and so it is likely that **MMI will continue to encourage its growth**.

Stable profit margins – Gross profit margins have remained constant, suggesting that market conditions have allowed it to grow without having to offer any discounts. Furthermore, net profits have increased slightly, suggesting that First Leisure is **keeping its costs under control**, despite the recent reliability issues with the boats from Boatland, which are likely to have increased maintenance costs.

Portfolio management (Ashridge model) – MMI plays little role in the day-to-day running of First Leisure, and when MMI acquired the company it envisaged First Leisure remaining a **largely autonomous business unit**. This suggests MMI initially planned to play a **portfolio management role** at First Leisure. However, the **unexpected discovery of the synergies** between MMI and First Leisure has now prompted MMI to adopt a **synergy manager role**.

Rationale for acquiring Boatland

Expected synergy with First Leisure – The primary reason for MMI's acquisition of Boatland was the synergies it expected between Boatland and First Leisure. **First Leisure had experienced difficulties in obtaining and maintaining boats for its parks**, so acquiring a boat making company was seen as a way of overcoming these difficulties.

Backward integration and cost savings – MMI also felt that bringing Boatland into the Group would **provide cost savings for First Leisure**, through backward integration. First Leisure would **no longer need to buy boats from an external supplier**, because they would be provided by another group company.

Underperforming company – MMI perceived that Boatland was underperforming, so MMI felt it could **apply its managerial competencies to drive extra value from Boatland**. MMI felt that Boatland's existing management team had no ambitions to expand, but producing boats for First Leisure would provide a steady income and cash flow which Boatland could then use to help it expand.

Synergy management – It appears that MMI saw itself in a synergy manager role in relation to the Boatland acquisition. However, the **synergies it foresaw have not been realised**, because Boatland's specialist boats are not hard-wearing enough for the way they are used by First Leisure's customers. Unfortunately, this has meant that maintenance time and costs have increased, and because Boatland has had to spend more time repairing First Leisure's boats the quality of service it has been able to give its external customers has fallen.

Therefore, rather than providing an opportunity for it to expand, **the Boatland/First Leisure integration has actually damaged Boatland's business.**

Performance of Boatland post-acquisition

Declining revenue and market share – Although the total market size has remained constant between 2006-8, at $201m, Boatland's revenues have declined from $2.4m to $2.1m, rather than expanding as MMI had hoped.

Decline in profit margins – Gross profit has fallen from $0.5m (2006) to $0.3m (2008), and net profit has similarly fallen from $0.25m (2006) to $0.09m (2008). This means that Boatland's net profit margin is now only 4.3%, down from 10.4% in 2006.

Staff turnover – Alongside its poor financial performance, since the acquisition Boatland has also lost nearly half of its skilled boat builders. This suggests there is a problem of **cultural fit** with the acquisition. Boatland has historically made a small number of high quality boats, for customers who look after their boats. After the acquisition, Boatland has had to produce a larger number of robust boats which can be used by holiday makers. To this extent, the synergies which MMI had envisaged were an illusion, because the two boat markets are quite distinct from one another.

Value trap business – Consequently, the benefit opportunities from acquiring Boatland were significantly less than MMI had initially realised. Using the classifications from the Ashridge model, rather than being a **heartland business** as MMI had imagined, Boatland is actually a **value trap business**.

In this context, and given Boatland's small market share of a static market, MMI should consider **divesting the business**. However, divestment would mean that it has to find an alternative boat supplier for First Leisure, so it should look to find this replacement supplier before divesting of Boatland.

Part (b)

Composition of portfolio – Although MMI's portfolio only contains three businesses, they are strategically quite diverse, and have met with varying degrees of success.

MMI has consolidated its position in the quarrying marketplace by acquiring two of its smaller competitors, and its market share has increased from 20% (2002) to 28% (2008). MMI has also significantly increased its net profit margin, because it no longer has the costs of maintaining the redundant quarries or operating unprofitable ones it has redeployed as leisure resources for First Leisure.

First Leisure has turned out to be a very successful acquisition, due to the unexpected synergies between it and MMI.

However, the **Boatland** acquisition, which was expected to deliver synergies with First Leisure, has not been successful, and has actually destroyed value rather than creating it.

Corporate management capabilities - Following the acquisition of the two smaller mining and quarrying companies in 2004, MMI introduced its own managers to run the businesses, and this resulted in a spectacular rise in revenues. This success prompted MMI's CEO to claim that **corporate management capabilities are now an important strategic asset** for MMI.

However, the CEO's assessment is perhaps **too bullish**. MMI has successfully improved the performance of businesses in an industry it is familiar with. But, the post-acquisition performance of **Boatland has been much less successful**.

Because MMI did not really understand the boat industry, it did not appreciate the differences between Boatland and First Leisure, and **tried to create artificial synergies** between the two.

MMI's acquisition of First Leisure has been much more successful, but in this case MMI has left the day-to-day management of the business to First Leisure's own, experienced, managers.

So it appears MMI may **better to adopt a hands-off approach to corporate management**, except for acquisitions directly related to its own core business (quarrying and mining).

InfoTech

Current financial position – Although the information technology solutions market has grown by nearly 25% between 2002-8, InfoTech's **revenues have actually fallen**, meaning it has suffered a significant decline its market share. InfoTech's low market share in a growing market means it is a **question mark business unit** (BCG matrix).

Moreover, InfoTech has suffered a marked **decrease in both its gross and net profits**, especially over the two year period from 2006-8. The decline in profitability means that InfoTech actually made a **net loss of $0.2m in 2008**.

Corporate Management – InfoTech's recent results suggest that the current management team may not be able to turn around its financial performance, and therefore if MMI acquired it, **MMI would have to introduce a new management team**.

Industry experience – However, MMI needs to appreciate that the **information technology solutions industry is very different to the quarrying and mining industry**. Therefore despite the CEO's comments about MMI's corporate management capabilities, it is unlikely that MMI can successfully make up this new management team from within its existing staff.

The relative failure of the Boatland acquisition should alert MMI of the need to install managers who are experienced in the information technology solutions industry, and understand its culture.

Financial risk – When MMI acquired First Leisure and Boatland they were both relatively successful, profitable companies in their own right. However, InfoTech is loss-making, and so is likely to need a considerable **cash investment to support it**. InfoTech's classification as a question mark also suggests it could require investment in order to try to increase its market share.

However, **MMI doesn't have any experience of acquiring a failing company and turning it round**. This suggests InfoTech is not an appropriate choice for acquisition, especially if MMI basically adopts a portfolio manager role due to its lack of experience in the information technology industry.

13 The Environmental Management Society

Text reference. Chapter 6 of the BPP Study Text for exams from September 2015 to 31 August 2016 covers strategic options.

Top tips. The three requirements to this question ask you to explain three different methods of strategic growth by a company, and to compare their appropriateness to a specified scenario.

Each requirement looks both at the principles of a type of strategic development, and its suitability to the scenario presented in the question. If you only address either principles or suitability, you would not have scored more than half the marks available.

The key issues here were that any strategic development initiative needs to fit with EMS risk-averse culture, and also provide access to new markets.

Given the context of the question, you should identify that requirement (a) was talking about organic growth, even though the requirement used the alternative title of 'internal development'.

Whilst internal development fits with EMS's risk-averse nature, will it really allow entry into the new markets it wishes to target?

An acquisition strategy (requirement (b)) presents the opposite issues: it will provide fast entry into new markets, but will it be deemed too high risk for the Board and the Council? Remember that EMS is a private limited entity rather than a public company. Therefore the Board and the Council are the key stakeholders.

Strategic alliances (requirement (c)) can be seen as a middle ground between the two strategies considered in (a) and (b). Again, you need to consider whether they will provide the entry required into new markets, and what risks are associated with them.

Note that although an alliance is strictly just an agreement between the parties with no formal requirements on either side, the examiner's answer also includes joint ventures so he has taken a broader interpretation of the word alliance. You should always be alert to the breadth of interpretations available in the P3 exam.

Easy marks. Half the marks for each requirement were available for explaining the principles of each means of strategic development. This is mainstream textbook knowledge, so you should be able to score a good proportion of these marks.

There should also have been some easy marks available for consider these principles in the context of the scenario. For example, the scenario clearly indicated that EMS was risk-averse: so you should use this to consider how acceptable each strategy was for the society.

		Marks
This question asks for principles and suitability.		
(a)	1 mark for each relevant point up to a maximum of 8 marks for internal development	
	There is a maximum of 4 marks for points relating to principles	8
(b)	1 mark for each relevant point up to a maximum of 8 marks for acquisitions	
	There is a maximum of 4 marks for point relating to principles	8
(c)	1 mark for each relevant point up to a maximum of 9 marks for strategic alliances	9
	There is a maximum of 5 marks for points relating to principles	25

(a) **Internal development**

Internal development – also known as **organic growth** – is achieved through an organisation **developing its own internal resources.**

This is the way EMS has grown up until now. After the original certificates were developed by the founders of the society, the qualification has been enhanced by adding additional certificates and then the Diploma programme. These changes have all be developed by the members and officers of the Society.

Advantages

Low risk. As a means of growth, organic growth involves much less risk than an acquisition. Therefore it is likely to be suited to the culture of the Society, which is notably risk-averse and cautious.

Economies of scale. The organic approach spreads cost and risk over time and may allow an organisation to benefit from economies of scale. However, these economies may be limited if growth is too slow.

Easier to plan. Growth is much easier to manage and plan and offers less disruption than an acquisition.

Disadvantages

However, there are some problems with organic growth as a means of development.

Slow growth. Growth can be very slow, and the problems which EMS is currently facing reflect that current growth has ceased altogether.

Constrained by resources. Because growth is driven from within an organisation, it is restricted by the breadth of the organisation's capabilities. EMS is currently constrained by its narrow product range, but if it continues a policy of internal development it cannot expand this product range because its members and officers do not have any expertise in other subject areas.

Equally, EMS is **constrained by its narrow scope**, and constraint will remain all the time it grows through internal development. Attempts to move into complementary qualification areas (such as soil conservation) have been rejected by the council as being non-core areas, and therefore outside the scope of EMS's expertise.

Barriers to entry. Internal development is an appropriate method for market development in EMS's home country but it is less appropriate for breaking into new market places and countries. It will be difficult for EMS to establish itself as a brand in India, China and Russia.

The problems of EMS trying to expand overseas using organic growth will be exacerbated because none of its members have any previous experience of developing products in overseas markets.

Internal development has been the method which EMS has used to grow up until now, based on consolidation of the market and market penetration. Internal development is the **ideal means of implementing a market penetration strategy**.

However, EMS is now looking to **pursue a market development strategy,** by expanding into India, China and Russia. It seems unlikely that internal development will be an appropriate method of pursuing this new strategic direction.

(b) **Acquisitions**

A strategy of acquisition is one where one organisation (such as EMS) takes ownership of another existing organisation.

Speed of growth. One of the most important advantages of growth by acquisition is that it allows the acquiring company **very fast access to a new market area** or product range.

In this case, EMS might look to acquire organisations already offering professional examination qualifications and certificates in its target markets of India, China and Russia. It could then use these existing organisations as a mechanism for launching the EMS qualifications in these markets. In this way, EMS has effectively acquired the infrastructure it needs to operate in its target markets, **overcoming any geographical barriers to entry.**

New products. The organisation EMS acquires **will already offer qualifications of their own**, and it is likely that these will be ones which EMS does not currently offer. Therefore there is an opportunity that **EMS could offer these qualifications in its home market**, thereby increasing the range of products it can offer in its home market. In effect, it has acquired new competencies in these new subjects and so they are now within the scope of its expertise.

However, EMS will face some issues with acquisition as a method of growth.

Cost. Acquiring an organisation usually **requires considerable expenditure**, and evidence suggests that the returns delivered from the organisation acquired are often less than promised in the takeover process. Given the risk-averse nature of EMS, the Board and the Council may not want to spend a large amount of money when the returns are not guaranteed.

Access to funds. Although we are not told anything about EMS income or financial position, it is unlikely that EMS will have enough money to fund the acquisition without looking for external financing. However, because **it is a private company it cannot use a share issue on the stock markets to raise additional finance**. It will either have to seek a bank loan, or seek funding from private equity investment or the society members themselves.

Incompatibility. Acquisitions can bring **problems of assimilating employees and different operating systems**. This is likely to be the case here since this is an international acquisition, so there could well be problems of cultural fit between EMS and the companies acquired. Again, given EMS's cautious and risk-averse nature it is unlikely they will be prepared to jeopardise the **corporate culture** through acquiring new companies.

Therefore, although acquisitions are a popular way of fuelling rapid growth, it is **unlikely that EMS will have either the cash or the desire to pursue this method** of strategic development. As EMS has grown organically until now, it is **unlikely that it has any experience of acquisitions** – even in its home market. Therefore moving to make an acquisition overseas would be very risky. Consequently, the Board and Council are unlikely to approve such a venture.

(c)   **Strategic alliances**

A strategic alliance takes place when two or more organisations share resources and activities to pursue a particular strategic objective.

Cost. One of the major advantages of a strategic alliance compared to an acquisition is that it allows an organisation to enter into a new marketplace **without the large financial outlay required to acquire a local organisation**. This could be important for EMS, given the difficulties it may face in trying to finance an acquisition.

Corporate culture. A strategic alliance allows each of the partner organisations to **maintain its own corporate culture**, and so it will avoid the cultural dislocation of either acquiring or merging with another organisation.

Core competencies. The motive for the alliance would be **co-specialisation**, with each partner concentrating on the activities that best match their capabilities. Johnson, Scholes and Whittington suggest that co-specialisation alliances 'are used to enter new geographic markets where an organisation needs local knowledge and expertise.' This meets EMS's requirements exactly.

The exact nature of the alliance would need to be considered carefully, and it may be that different types of alliances are established in the three new markets which EMS is targeting.

Joint Venture. A joint venture occurs where two (or more) parent organisations set up a new organisation and **each has a share in the equity and the management of the new venture**. This is a formal alliance and will take time to establish. EMS will have to contribute to the costs and resources needed by the newly established organisation, but such **cost and resource requirements should be less than those needed for an acquisition**.

However, the **time taken to establish the joint venture may be a problem** if EMS wants to move quickly into a target marketplace to attract new students. When setting up the joint venture, EMS will have to agree with its venture partner who contributes what in terms of time and resources, and how future profits will be shared. This could take time to agree if any points are disputed.

Licence agreement. EMS could licence the use of its qualification in the target markets. Two ways this could be arranged are:

(i)   A **local organisation could market the EMS qualification as its own** and pay EMS a fee or each certificate and diploma issued.

(ii)   The **qualification could be marketed by the local organisation as an EMS qualification**, and EMS pays the local organisation a commission for every certificate and diploma it issues in that country.

The licence agreement will **require less commitment from EMS than an acquisition**, but it will also **bring less financial return** because EMS has to split the revenues with the licensees in the three target countries.

Also, by relying on licence partners to market the qualification for them, EMS will have **less control over how it is marketed**. The Board and Council may consider that this loss of control is undesirable.

Furthermore, if the qualification is successful, there is a risk that the **local organisation will develop its own alternative to EMS qualification**. It could then promote its own qualification instead of EMS's, thereby keeping all the revenue from its own certificates rather than just the percentage of the fee it receives on EMS's qualification.

A strategic alliance initially appears the most appropriate method of development for EMS. Licensing agreements seem particularly attractive because they **offer quick access to new markets without requiring any significant financial commitment** from EMS or causing any cultural change within EMS. However, EMS will **only receive a proportion of the income generated**.

Importantly though, entering a licensing agreement would mean that the **marketing and promotion of the qualification is outside EMS's control**, and this may prove difficult for EMS to accept. To date, EMS has only grown by internal development and has had full control over all the delivery of its qualifications. If EMS enters an alliance, it will have to **trust its partner organisation to manage its service delivery for it**.

Ultimately, whether or not the Board and Council are prepared to place the necessary trust in a partner organisation may well determine whether this method is acceptable to EMS or not.

14 Country Car Club

Text reference. Harmon's process-strategy matrix and outsourcing are both covered in Chapter 9 of the BPP Study Text for exams from September 2015 to 31 August 2016.

Top tips. Part (a) required you to suggest and justify recommendations for outsourcing or improvement in five different process areas. There were 15 marks available, meaning three marks for each process area.

Although you did not need to mention it by name, the framework for this question was Harmon's process-strategy matrix, which looks at process in terms of their strategic importance and process complexity. Analysing the five processes against these criteria would allow you to make sensible recommendations for all of them. There is no definitive right answer here; so if your justification is logical and supports your recommendation you would score marks.

Part (b) is a fairly simple question about the advantages of outsourcing. However, to score well you needed to make your points relevant to the scenario, rather than making general points about the advantages of outsourcing. And remember to think through the implications of any scenario fully – for example, by outsourcing its vehicle maintenance, 3C no longer needs its garage facilities meaning it could sell them for development. The scenario told you the garage was in a residential area of the town.

Note the examiner's comments below which reiterate the importance of reading the question carefully: part (b) was looking at the outsourcing of 3C's own fleet, not outsourcing the maintenance of members' cars. So some candidates lost marks by not reading the question properly.

Easy marks. If you were familiar with Harmon's process-strategy matrix, you should have found part (a) very approachable because the matrix is an ideal framework for answering the question.

Examiner's comments. Many candidates provided excellent answers to part (a), often using Harmon's framework as a reference point. Part (b) was also answered reasonably well, although some candidates confused 3C's own vehicles with the vehicles of the club's members.

Marks

(a) Up to 3 marks for the recommendation and its justification in each of the
process areas required by the question
Five process areas required, giving a maximum of 15 marks · 15

(b) Up to 2 marks for each appropriate advantage identified, up to a
maximum of 10 marks · 10
___
25
___

(a) When analysing 3C's processes, the BAC should consider the **complexity of the processes** and the value
they add to the business – their **strategic importance**.

As a general rule, 3C should aim to retain processes with high strategic importance in-house, and should
consider **outsourcing processes of less strategic importance** or ones which fall outside its core
competences.

Equally, where possible 3C should look to **automate straightforward processes** to improve efficiency, and
concentrate its business process improvement efforts on its complex, dynamic processes.

(i) **Attendance at breakdowns**

Strategic importance – This is the most strategically important of all 3C's processes, and so should
definitely be retained in-house.

Process complexity – Although some breakdowns may be easy to fix, others may be more
complicated. The service patrol engineers need to be capable of dealing with the full range of
breakdowns, as well as providing a good quality of service to customers. The range of possible
situations engineers face makes this a complex process.

It appears that the speed with which engineers can attend breakdowns has already been addressed
by having a range of locations across the country. However, 3C should ensure that the engineers'
efficiency in solving breakdowns is maintained by ensuring they have up-to-date equipment for
diagnosing and fixing faults. The engineers may also be given laptops with a database of previously
observed faults for each make of car, and ways of fixing them, so that the engineers have an easily
accessible reference point if they cannot immediately fix the problem themselves.

(ii) **Membership renewal**

Strategic importance – Although the membership renewal process is not strategically as important
as attendance at breakdowns **it is still strategically important** for 3C because it underpins 3C's core
revenue stream. Therefore, it should continue to be managed in-house rather than outsourced.

Process complexity – Membership renewal should be a **relatively straightforward process**, so
should be automated as far as possible to maximise efficiency.

3C already has a **bespoke computer system** for dealing with membership renewals which indicates
the process is already automated. However, the **design of the system could be changed** to improve
efficiency. Currently, members have to renew every year, and receipts are only processed when
members confirm they will be renewing. A more efficient alternative would be to assume that
members are continuing their membership unless they inform 3C they wish to cancel. In this way, all
the routine membership renewals and receipts can be **processed automatically**, and the only
transactions which require attention from staff are those where members which to cancel their
membership.

(iii) **Vehicle insurance services**

Strategic importance – Insurance is one of the new services 3C has added to its product portfolio over the last fifteen years, rather than being a core product. Consequently, it is likely to have relatively low strategic importance.

Process complexity – Providing insurance services involves a number of potentially **complex processes;** most notably **assessing risks** in order to determine premiums. Providing insurance services also requires very **different skills** from those which 3C needs for its core business of breakdown assistance.

In addition, insurance business is subject to significant regulatory requirements. Consequently, 3C should look to **outsource the provision of vehicle insurance services** to a specialist insurance company. Insurance could still be offered in 3C's name, but the policies and risks would be administered and managed by the insurance company. An additional benefit of this is that the insurance company will benefit from **economies of scale** and **specialist knowledge** which 3C are unlikely to have.

(iv) **Membership queries**

Strategic importance – The quality of service which members receive is very important, because if members are not satisfied with the way their queries are handled this could lead them to cancel their membership. Phone calls about membership queries are therefore a very **important contact point between 3C and its customers**, and a fall in service levels could also affect revenues if customers do not renew their memberships. To this end, membership queries are strategically important, and the queries process should be **retained in-house**.

All the same, 3C may wish to review the **location of the call centre**, because it may be able to move it to an area where property rents are lower and/or wages are cheaper than 3C is currently paying.

Process complexity – As with breakdown assistance itself, the complexity of queries is likely to vary – some will be easy, some much more complicated. Therefore, the process should be considered as **potentially complex**. Although 3C may consider having a **'Frequently Asked Questions'** section on a website customers can refer to, the main focus of the queries process needs to be on the staff working in the call centre. It will be important to ensure that **staffing levels** are sufficient to ensure customers to receive a prompt response to their queries. However, it will also be important to ensure that the call centre is not over-staffed leading to unnecessary costs.

Staff training is another key issue. 3C needs to ensure that staff are properly trained and briefed so that they can deal accurately and courteously with a wide range of queries.

(v) **Vehicle history check**

Strategic importance – Vehicle history checks, like insurance services, **do not appear to be central to 3C's business**, and require **different competences** to the core business of breakdown assistance. Therefore they appear to have **relatively low strategic importance**.

Process complexity – The basic history check initially appears to be a relatively simple process, comparing registration details against a database of vehicle records. However, obtaining the vehicle history **may be more complicated than it first seems**, and may also have some **risks attached to it**. For example, if a vehicle has been damaged and 3C doesn't identify this, this may lead to someone buying a vehicle on the basis of inaccurate information. If the damage subsequently does come to light, the purchaser might be able to make a claim against 3C, particularly if the vehicle has been involved in an accident caused by the damage.

Consequently, 3C may be better advised to **outsource the history checks** to a specialist organisation in this field, who can operate the checks on their behalf.

(b) 3C will gain a number of advantages 3C from outsourcing the purchase and maintenance of their own vehicles. These are as follows:

Economies of scale – AutoDirect currently supplies 45,000 vehicles to companies throughout the country. This volume should allow them to negotiate discounts on the price, meaning they can buy the vehicles more cheaply than 3C could in their own name.

Also, AutoDirect may **replace vehicles more frequently** that 3C historically used to. This may have an added benefit for 3C because **fuel consumption** should be lower in the newer vehicles, thereby reducing 3C's fuel costs.

Quicker repairs and maintenance – Because 3C only had one garage from which to service its nationwide fleet of vehicles, any vehicle needing a repair had to be brought to the garage before it could be worked on. AutoDirect has nationwide repair centres, which should reduce the overall time which 3C's vehicles are out of action while being repaired.

Easier to budget costs – The lease deal means that 3C pays a single lease payment to AutoDirect each month, and 3C knows in advance what the payment will be. When 3C maintained its own vehicles, costs could vary from one month to the next depending on the level of repairs and maintenance required. The new arrangement means that 3C can budget its costs and associated cash flows more accurately, which should assist with its working capital management.

Reduced capital requirements – Traditionally, 3C purchased its own vehicles. This is likely to have required significant levels of capital, invested in assets which only have short economic lives. Under the lease scheme with AutoDirect, 3C will be able to invest the capital elsewhere in the business.

Reduced overhead costs – 3C used to employ 30 staff in its garage to maintain its vehicle fleet, and a further 3 staff to purchase and dispose of vehicles. However, it no longer needs these staff, so the outsourcing deal should have generated significant savings in wage costs.

Profit on sale of garage – Similarly, 3C no longer needs its garage site. Given that the garage was in a residential area of a major town, 3C should seek to sell the garage site for residential development – thereby hopefully making a significant profit on the sale

15 The Missing Link

Part (a)

> **Text reference.** E-commerce is covered in Chapters 11 and 12 of the BPP Study Text for exams from September 2015 to 31 August 2016.
>
> **Top tips.** Requirement (a) is a general requirement about e-commerce and does not relate specifically to ML or the scenario.
>
> **Easy marks.** Requirement (a) offers some relatively easy marks for factual knowledge.

Marking scheme

		Marks
(a)	1 mark for each relevant point up to a maximum of 5 marks in respect of the impact of e-commerce on business	5
(b)	1 mark for each relevant point up to a maximum of 15 marks for an analysis of the benefits to ML of introducing e-commerce	15
(c)	1 mark for each relevant point up to a maximum of 5 marks for a discussion of the use of e-commerce at ML in respect of customised components	5
		25

E-commerce consists of the buying and selling of products and services over electronic systems like the internet. E-commerce has challenged traditional business models and has changed the way businesses and their customers inter-relate, both in terms of the way goods are bought and sold, and also the way information is communicated.

New business model – E-commerce enables the suppliers of products and services to interact directly with their customers instead of using **intermediaries** (for example, hotels can now sell rooms directly to overseas holiday makers rather than going through a tour operator or a travel agent). In this way, e-commerce has enabled business to improve the effectiveness of their downstream **supply chain management**.

Opening up global markets – The internet is global in its operation; and so e-commerce allows small companies to access the global market place, whereas previously they would have been restricted by their physical infrastructure.

New online marketplaces – The emergence of online marketplaces (such as Amazon.com) means that small enterprises can now gain access to customers on far greater scale than the previously could.

Increases speed and scope of communication – The internet allows online transactions to be completed very quickly. It also allows new networks of communication – between businesses and their customers (most notably through e-mail); and between customers themselves (for example, discussing product features or quality through chat rooms, and forums).

Increased price transparency – Potential customers can readily compare prices from a range of suppliers before making a purchase, thereby increasing the level of price competition in the market.

Part (b)

> **Top tips.** Requirement (b) has the highest mark allocation in the question, so make sure that you allow sufficient time to answer it thoroughly.
>
> Note that you are asked to **analyse** the potential benefits of the proposed systems, so you need to present a balanced answer, including any limitations to the system's benefits as well as the benefits themselves.

International marketplace – Possibly the most significant strategic benefit of the e-commerce system is that it will enable ML to reach an international, potentially global, audience. This offers ML significant opportunities in terms of market development.

Construction is a global business, and so being able to sell to new customers outside Arcadia should allow ML to achieve the **sales growth** which it has been unable to do over the last two years. The sales manager expects the introduction of e-commerce to generate turnover growth of 10% each year for the foreseeable future.

However, in order to realise this benefit, ML will need to ensure that it has the **operational resources** (production capacity, distribution networks etc) to **cope with any increase in demand**. This will include making sure that ML's upstream supply chain can cope with any increase in demand.

One of ML's strengths at the moment is the level of service it offers customers. If the drive for expansion means it is unable to fulfil customer orders or to **meet customer expectations**, then its reputation (and then potentially also its sales) will suffer.

Equally, if the development of the international business means that prices all become quoted in US dollars with **no option for local currency**, this may mean that Arcadian customers who used to pay in local currency may move their custom elsewhere (especially if the local currency weakens against the dollar).

Commercial image – If ML wants to expand and serve an international marketplace, it needs to present an image which supports that ambition. Potential customers will want to be able find out about the company, its capabilities and credentials, and the website will allow them to do so.

The interactivity of the website should also help improve the levels of customer service ML can offer its customers, so is a competitive benefit as well as a strategic one.

Improved customer service and customer information – The sales manager has noted that customers are increasingly mentioning that they would like to be able to order online. Therefore, if the new system showed a list of all previously supplied components, and a price, they would be able to do this without having to phone or fax their order in. Moreover, the customer would be able to **get the information immediately** without waiting to design a price as they do at the moment. This will support ML's aim to provide the highest levels of customer service.

The online ordering would also **support the international growth**, because the website could take orders 24 hours a day.

We are not told anything about ML's competitors in the scenario, but to a degree the extent to which the online ordering facility is a competitive benefit will depend on the **comparative levels of service** offered by ML's competitors. It may be that some of them already offer a similar service, which is why customers have mentioned it to the sales manager.

Also, ML will need to review its **customer service arrangements** to ensure that it has enough staff on hand to deal with any queries. It is likely that queries will now be more complex. Simple orders will be processed on the e-commerce system, so the ones which require assistance are likely to be more complex. As ML prides itself on the personal service is provides, it will need to ensure that the e-commerce remains properly supported by customer service staff.

Moreover, online ordering would only be available for previously ordered products. Unique customised products would still need to be ordered in person, and will continue to take longer to price up due to the complexity of the design process involved.

Internal information management – ML should be able to **reduce the costs** currently incurred by the engineer in creating paper-based drawings of the components, and in the **time taken** for these drawings to be passed to the costing clerk and then priced up.

As noted from the customer's perspective in the previous point, if the new e-commerce system contains a database of previous orders, component specifications, and technical drawings this would allow ML to standardise, and therefore speed up, its order preparation process.

However, this standardised process would not be possible for customised products as each job is unique and so there wouldn't be any information in the database to help with such jobs.

Improved cash collection times – At the moment customers pay by cash or cheque usually within 30 days of an order being fulfilled. ML could investigate the possibility that customers who order online pay, (either in part or in full) at the **moment they make the order**. This will be beneficial to ML's cash flow management.

However, as ML is a relatively small company it may find that trade customers do not want to change their credit terms, especially as they will still have to wait for ML to produce the goods after the order is made. In which case, the e-commerce system will not generate any significant benefits in this area.

Moreover, ML does not currently have a problem with bad debts, which again reduces the upside potential from improving cash collection processes.

Improved inventory management – One of the theoretical benefits of e-commerce is that it allows a business to reduce its inventory levels; instead of producing goods and then trying to sell them, the business responds to demand 'pull' and produces on demand. However, this appears to already be the way ML operates and it only holds very low levels of finished goods inventory. Therefore, there are unlikely to be any significant benefits from the e-commerce system in this respect.

Part (c)

> **Top tips.** When tackling requirement (c) it is important that you appreciate the difference between ML's customised components and its standard products. Customised components are unique, and so it is unlikely they can be sold via the website using a standard price list in the way that standard products can. Therefore, the benefits will accrue from marketing and making existing customers aware of the customisation side of the business, rather than direct online sales.

The e-commerce project is aimed at directly increasing the volume of business ML generates from 'standard' product sales. The complex, one-off nature of customised components means ML will not be able to sell them directly online in the same way, but instead ML could use the e-commerce platform to generate extra demand for these components.

Cross-selling – At the moment, ML does not advertise its services. However, it could use the e-commerce platform to advertise and promote the full range of services it offers. Therefore, customers who are looking initially to purchase standard components without realising ML also offer a customising service may subsequently also purchase customised components.

Direct marketing – ML could also email customers who have purchased standard components, informing them about the additional range of services it offers. The e-commerce system should have a database which gathers all the email addresses of customers, and ML can use this to send subsequent marketing messages.

Some customers may not wish to receive these e-mails, viewing them as junk mail, and so customers need to be offered the option of not receiving any subsequent marketing mail from ML when they make a purchase.

Online questions – ML could offer a facility for potential customers to contact an engineer to discuss potential work, and may also show some of the more frequently asked questions pre-answered. Equally, ML could host a forum for customers to discuss issues among themselves. Either of these options should help create 'noise' about ML's products and services which in turn should help promote demand.

16 Ergo City

Text reference. Outsourcing is covered in Chapter 9 of your BPP Study Text for exams from September 2015 to 31 August 2016.

Top tips. Remember to relate your answer to the scenario, rather than just list every generic benefit of outsourcing you can think of. Candidates who scored highly on this question took a broader approach and recognised that the city authority has a major stake in the company.

Examiner's comments. Most candidates answered part (a) relatively well, although many did not recognise that the formation of a joint company might itself bring significant advantages to the city authority.

Marking scheme

		Marks
(a)	1 mark for each relevant point up to a maximum of 12 marks	12
(b)	1 mark for each relevant point up to a maximum of 7 marks	7
(c)	1 mark for each relevant point up to a maximum of 6 marks	6
		25

(a)   Outsourcing could be beneficial to the city authority for a number of reasons:

Reduction in staffing costs

The City Authority has well documented problems in shedding labour that once short-term demands are over. This means that IT staff costs are currently too high. Outsourcing would allow demand to be matched to supply and so IT staff costs would only be incurred as and when they are required. Furthermore there would be a significant reduction in fixed costs as the employees would be transferred to the semi-state company.

Internal conflicts

Over the last few years there have been conflicts between managers in the finance department and managers in the IT department and the dispute has still not been resolved. Outsourcing would resolve this problem for the City Authority or, if resolution is impossible, it would at least be passed on to the outsource provider.

Outsourcing would also release the CEO, who has had to personally intervene, from resolving these internal conflicts.

Core business

The core business of the Authority is addressing the housing problems of the city, and they have come under recent criticism for not spending enough time and money doing this. Outsourcing a non-core activity, such as IT, would allow the City Authority to focus more on their core business.

Technological opportunities

The outsourced IT provider should be at the leading edge of technology and have highly skilled and knowledgeable staff. This should allow authority access to the new technical opportunities that the director of IT wishes to explore and exploit.

Staff morale

There is an issue of low staff morale at the authority which is partly influenced by the ingratitude of users. In the outsourced company, IT would be the core-business function and so it is likely the staff will feel higher valued and their morale would improve.

In addition, the outsourced company may provide employees with better promotion and development opportunities. The case study notes there are no such opportunities at the authority.

Stake in new company

The City Authority will hold a significant stake in the new company and the CEO has observed that is it likely that other authorities will follow the outsourcing route in the future. The stake in the new company may help to gain contracts with those authorities due to their extensive public sector experience.

In addition the new company may bring in income, reducing taxes and improving the services offered by the authority.

(b)

> **Top tips.** Don't miss the competencies that are clearly signposted in the scenario, such a business case development and strategy analysis. You need to identify the key points made in the scenario relating to the analysts and develop them using your own thought processes to determine skills you would expect these people to need in order to carry out their new role.
>
> **Examiner's comments.** Many candidates failed to identify any relevant competencies (falling back on generalisations such as 'good communication skills') and hence did not score well.

The business analysts will require a number of new competencies in order to carry out their new role, including:

- **Negotiation with users** – the business analysts will be responsible for liaising between users and the newly outsourced IT company. They will have to have strong communication and negotiation skills in order to carry this out effectively.

- **Strategic analysis techniques** – the case study states that the business analysts should be 'outward looking and unconstrained by current process and technology'. To do this they need to have an external business focus and apply strategic analysis such as SWOT to help them to identify opportunities in the wider environment.

- **Business case development** – the business analysts will be responsible for agreeing the business case, so they will have to liaise with users to ensure the business cases are properly defined.

- **Benefits realisation** – the business analysts will have to ensure that the promised benefits are actually delivered in line with the costs described in the original proposal.

- **Business process modelling** – the business analysts should be able to come up with solutions beyond those of IT, such as changes to processes that will deliver benefits. To do this they will require business process modelling and redesign skills.

- **Requirements definition** – changes to the requirements will be charged for under the new arrangement so it is important that the business analysts have the skills to ensure requirements are properly defined at the outset. They will also have to be able to manage any changes that do need to be made to requirements.

- **Procurement** – the relationship between the city authority and the IT provider has changed to become a supplier-customer relationship. Procurement and contract management skills will be important for the business analysts to manage this relationship.

(c)

The key stakeholders that would have to be considered are:

The **local government** is a key stakeholder that is likely to be very supportive of these changes. They recently carried out an audit of the city authority which identified that the authority do not spend enough time and money addressing the pressing housing problems of the city. Outsourcing would allow the authority to focus on the core business and ideally the housing problems of the city would begin to improve.

Employees of the IT department. These employees are currently unsatisfied and have low morale despite receiving above average pay. They would be likely to be supportive of the move to outsourcing, presuming they were guaranteed employment in the newly formed company, as IT would be the core function of this company and their morale would improve. These employees would also want to see increased **opportunities** for development and promotion in the new role.

The **finance director** and **finance department** are currently involved in an ongoing dispute with the IT department. They will be affected by this change as once the IT staff move over to the outsourced company they will have to find a way of working with this newly formed company. The expectation is that they would be in favour of the move as it would ease the tension that has built up between the departments leading to an improved working atmosphere.

The **business analysts** will be greatly affected by the change as their whole role will be re-defined and they will report to a new area of the organisation. Their initial concerns may relate to concerns over redundancy, changes to their role specifically which they may not feel confident about, and new working relationships and business processes that will have to be established. They may feel some apprehension about these changes and will have to be carefully managed during the change process. Training and development should be provided to these employees to ensure they are properly prepared for their new role.

17 Cronin Auto Retail

Marking scheme

		Marks
(a)	Up to 1 mark for each point up to a maximum of 4 marks for each element	16
(b)	1 mark for each relevant point up to a maximum of 10 marks	9
		25

(a) **Interactivity**

Interactivity relates to the development of a two-way relationship between the customer and the supplier. Car currently uses a traditional 'push' method of advertising consisting of adverts in local newspapers and customer mail-shots. CAR have developed a website, however, this is currently used as an 'online catalogue' and so also represents 'push' media.

CAR could immediately save money by replacing their mail-shots with emails, however, this allows little consumer interaction and so is still a 'push' technique.

Moving to a 'pull' approach would increase the level of interactivity between CAR and the customers, and this could be done in a number of ways.

CAR could:

- Develop their website in such a way that allows customers to **book a test drive** or to **book their car in for a service/repair online**.

- Set up a **discussion thread** on the website to encourage potential buyers to discuss and ask questions about cars that interest them. This both increases the information available to customers which may lead to them purchasing the car, and also generates a buzz which may encourage potential buyers to proceed quickly for fear for 'losing out' should someone else purchase the car first.

- Encourage customers to provide **feedback** on the website following completion of their purchase. This provides customers with useful information and strong testimonials provide future buyers with confidence making it more likely they will go ahead with a planned purchase.

Intelligence

Intelligence is linked to market and marketing research. It involves identifying and understanding the needs of potential customers and how they wish to be communicated with. CAR does very little research about what its customers actually want. Instead, it relies on what their sales people **think** their customers want and a small database of historical data consisting only of people who have actually bought cars from CAR.

CAR could improve its interactivity by collecting email addresses through interactivity initiatives and promotions such as those described above. This would give CAR access to a wider pool of **potential customers** who then can be kept up to date via email.

Providing these potential customers with the ability to 'submit requests' either to the website or by email, or 'vote for your favourite car' would allow CAR to build up a better picture of what potential buyers are really interested in. This may support the concern that the buyers are making the wrong decisions at auctions and potentially lead to a change in buying policy.

Individualisation

In conventional media, such as that currently used by CAR, the same information tends to be sent to everyone. Individualisation relates to the tailoring of marketing information to each individual, and using personalisation to build up a relationship with the customer.
CAR could implement a **personalised** approach by selectively emailing individuals who have shown an interest in a certain model or type of car when a car that meets their requirements comes into stock. This approach could also be used with existing CAR customers, for example by emailing them two or three years after purchase with opportunities to upgrade to a newer or improved model.

After-sales service can also be improved via individualisation for example, if the correct details are kept, current customers can be emailed with an invite to book in for a service when their MOT is due to, and to send them updates on services for specific features relevant to their car (eg air-conditioning renewal would only be sent to customers who bought air-conditioned cars).

Individualisation only be successful, however, if **sufficient details** have been collected. The methods discussed under intelligence and interactivity above will be central in providing this information.

Independence of location

Independence of location relates to the geographical location of the company. This is of benefit to many organisations as the use of electronic media means that no matter where the organisation is physically located, it can potentially serve markets anywhere in the world.

However, independence of location is unlikely to be particularly useful to CAR as it is stated that the majority of customers live within 2 hours drive in order to benefit from local service and support. The type of cars sold by CAR are commodities with many competitors throughout the country selling similar models. Often these too will be garages that offer local service and support.

Independence of location would be more relevant to CAR were it to change focus and sell classic or rare, collectable cars as potential customers are more likely to travel a long distance for something they perceive to be a 'one-off'. However, the long lease on CARs premise means that any opportunity to relocate to a cheaper location that would allow CAR to take advantage of independence of location could not be taken.

One factor of independence of location that would be relevant to CAR is the fact that electronic media is available 24/7, and so is there whenever the customer wishes to make use of it. This means the buyers can access information at a time convenient to them and, if the suggestions made under interactivity are implemented, can book a test drive/service out of office hours and therefore begin the purchase process.

(b)

> **Text reference.** E-procurement is covered in Chapter 11 of your BPP Study Text for exams from September 2015 to 31 August 2016.
>
> **Top tips.** On the whole, candidates who chose this question did very well in this part requirement. This requirement is relatively straightforward and a number of marks can be gained simply from theoretical knowledge of e-procurement and its general application. However, don't forget that you will gain much higher marks by keeping the context of CAR in mind and tailoring your answer appropriately.

Procurement relates to organisational purchasing and involves locating items of the right **price**, that are available at the right **time**, of the right **quality**, in the right **quantity** and from the right **source**. E-procurement looks at the potential opportunities that can be gained from automating aspects of the procurement process.

CAR is involved in two very different procurement processes: production-related procurement (cars) and non-production procurement (office supplies etc).

Production-related procurement

The purchase of cars and parts is directly linked to the core activities of the organisation. CAR uses experienced buyers to purchase its cars in person at auctions at the cost of $500 per day. On average, 5 cars per day are purchased, therefore the purchasing cost of each car is $100 representing 5% of the average profit margin on each car.

This cost could be eliminated if cars were instead purchased through **e-auctions**, where bids made online with no need for a physical presence. However, this could be risky as it is not possible to physically inspect the car for quality prior to purchase. This risk could be minimised if this technique is only used to buy cars that are less than 2 years old with a full service history.

Non-production procurement

CAR currently orders parts needed for service and maintenance from motor factors or manufacturers. CAR has long-term relationships with a number of regular suppliers and employs a systematic sourcing method.

In the current process, all requisitions have to be passed through procurement manager incurring cost, delay and customer frustration. A backlog of requisitions has built up, which creates particular problems when a customer's car is in the garage awaiting a part. Not only is the customer annoyed by the delay, but the garage space cannot be put to other, more profitable use.

This is made worse by the restricted working hours of the manager. This means that urgent requisitions can only be processed when he is at work and the building backlog is placing him under increased strain, leading to increases in costly mistakes. This has also led to the increased frustration of the mechanics who, despite working longer hours, can only make orders when the procurement manager is also at work.

E-procurement could help reduce these problems by providing a procurement system and giving mechanics the authorisation to order parts up to a pre-defined limit through agreed internet channels. This should speed up repairs and services, reduce cost and lead to an increase in customer goodwill.

CAR could also use e-procurement to facilitate the competitive bidding for the supply of parts over the internet. They would do this by publishing their requirements on their website and inviting suppliers to bid. This would mean that parts could gain the lowest price for each part by using many different suppliers. If this is combined with just-in-time supply, the costs of holding stock could be significantly reduced.

Stationery and office supplies are also ordered regularly by CAR and fall into the category of non-production procurement. E-procurement can be equally helpful here to help CAR to lower the costs of the purchasing cycle and so improve profitability without selling more products.

With cheap, standardised items such as stationery, the cost of procurement can exceed the cost of the goods. E-procurement should provide better information leading to the easier identification of cheap suppliers and allowing spot sourcing to fulfil immediate needs.

Overall CAR can greatly benefit from e-procurement as it should reduce the burden on the procurement manager, allowing him to focus on more strategic aspects of the procurement process.

18 Fresh 'n' Frozen

Text reference. Big Data is covered in Chapter 11 of the BPP Study Text for exams from September 2015 to 31 August 2016.

Top tips.

Part (a)

A good approach to structuring your answer to requirement (a) is to start with a definition of what 'Big Data' means. Mentioning some of the key attributes associated with 'Big Data' helps to illustrate your understanding of the theory. In the answer below we have built our answer around the three constituent parts of Laney's 3 V model of 'Big Data', (volume, velocity and variety). However, you could have answered the question just as effectively without the use of a specific model. In either case, the use of headings as a basis for structuring your answer enables the marker to immediately see the points made and makes your work easier to mark.

It is important to note that the answer provided here in part (a) is longer than would be expected of a student attempting the question under exam conditions. It has been included to illustrate a range of points which could have been made to gain the 4 marks on offer.

Part (b)

The requirement asks for an explanation of how Fresh 'n' Frozen could make better use of Big Data and Big Data analytics to help improve performance. This question required the application of your knowledge to the scenario. As you can see from our answer a good approach to adopt when attempting this style of question is to firstly consider those factors in the scenario that explain in part Fresh 'n' Frozen's recent dip in performance, eg missing customer delivery time slots would appear to be due in part to the historic way in which routes have been scheduled. It is important that you then provide practical points showing how Big Data and Big Data analytics could help the company. Clearly, if Fresh 'n' Frozen keep on missing delivery times then analysing 'real time' data to plot out alternative routes for drivers should help improve customer satisfaction. As mentioned above it is often useful to put in headings to help you structure your answer, this should keep you focused and stop you from including unnecessary information which gains few marks.

Remember, 1) state the issue and 2) apply your knowledge.

Part (c)

Part (c) did not require the use of any theory. This requirement was an opportunity for you to show that you are confident in suggesting some of the practical implications that the company would need to consider before capturing greater quantities of customer data. Two considerations always worth mentioning in such a question if you are struggling for points to make concern time and cost. Time in this context could relate to the amount of management time that will be lost in implementing new databases to hold captured data, whereas cost is likely to concern the costs of establishing the IT architecture needed to support the database.

Easy marks. In part (a) the 4 marks on offer for providing a brief discussion of the term 'Big Data' should have been relatively easy to obtain. This was a straight knowledge based question, provided you had studied the material set out in Chapter 11 of the Study Text.

Marking scheme

			Marks
(a)	Up to 4 marks for a brief discussion on 'Big Data'	Max	4

(b) 1 mark per relevant point concerning the use of Big Data at FF (Up to 5 marks)
Points could include:
- Freezer units
- Install sensors
- Traffic congestion
- Customer satisfaction
- Poor route management
- Basic website

1 mark per relevant point concerning how Big Data analytics could improve
FF's performance (Up to 8 marks)
Points could include:
- Saves staff time
- Reduces cost
- Track deliveries in progress
- Improve customer care
- Improve staff morale
- Targeted marketing message
- Market segmentation
- Improved decision-making
- Gain customer feedback

Max   13

(c) 1 mark per relevant point (Up to 8 marks)
Points could include:
- Cost v benefit
- Management time
- Need for specialist skills
- Limited experience of technology
- Dangers of data overload
- Data security
- Capturing and storing data / capacity issues

Max   8
25

Report

To: Russell Beaumont (Fresh 'n' Frozen)

From: Business advisor

xx/xx/xx

Big Data

(a) **Introduction**

This report focuses on the role of 'Big Data' and the impact that it is having on modern business. Particular consideration is given to how FF could use data analytics to help improve performance. The report finishes by exploring the practical implications that the company should consider before capturing greater quantities of data about its customers.

Big Data

Data analytics firm SAS define Big Data as 'the exponential growth and availability of data, both structured and unstructured. Big data may be as important to business and society as the internet has become.'

Doug Laney at Gartner defines Big Data through the consideration of three V's: volume, velocity and variety.

Volume

Volume refers to the amount of data which is now available for organisations to access, store and use. One report suggests that as much as 90% of the data in existence today has been produced in the past few years. Increases in the volume of data produced has been proliferated by the widespread use of the internet, smart phones and social media. Many organisations have realised the potential benefits and insights that can be gained from processing vast quantities of data about their customers. The bigger the data, the more potential insights it can give in terms of identifying trends and patterns, in the context of getting a deeper understanding of customer requirements.

Velocity – refers to the speed at which 'real time' data is being streamed into and processed by modern organisations. Many online retailers compile records of each click and interaction a customer makes while visiting a website, rather than simply recording the final sale at the end of a customer transaction. The speed at which such retailers are able to utilise this data about customer clicks and interactions can be used to generate a competitive advantage. For example, by recommending additional purchases to a customer when they visit the company's website.

Variety (or variability) – Big data is associated with the diversity of source data. In many cases big data may come in unstructured form (ie not in a database). For example, keywords from conservations people have on Facebook or Twitter, and content they share through media files (tagged photographs, or online video postings) could be sources of unstructured data. This presents modern businesses with new challenges in how best to capture, store and process such data. If data is too big, moves too fast, or doesn't fit with the structures of an organisation's existing information systems, then in order to gain value from it, an organisation needs to find an alternative way to process that data.

(b) **Big Data at Fresh 'n' Frozen**

In the following section of the report we shall explore how the use of Big Data and Big Data analytics could help improve FF's performance.

Freezer units

Install sensors

The Head of Delivery has identified that a number of freezer units fitted in the company's older vans are running at temperatures below those required to keep the products suitably frozen, resulting in increased fuel costs. This issue could be addressed through the installation of sensors in FF's fleet of vans which could measure and monitor the temperature of the freezer units. Large retailers have taken to placing sensors into in-store refrigeration and freezer cabinets to assess whether such equipment is functioning correctly.

Saves staff time

The temperature of individual units could feedback 'real time' performance data to a central computer accessed by the Head of Delivery and her team. Any discrepancies could then be identified between the desired temperature and the actual temperature recorded by the sensors. This would remove in part, the need for regular physical inspections to be carried out on the vans and would save the time of the driver and depot workers, freeing them to undertake other tasks.

Reduce costs

Installing sensors should also allow the Head of Delivery to identify those units which require fixing immediately. In addition, during the recent management meeting it came to light that two vans had freezers which were not functioning at all. Obtaining this data sooner would have helped to ensure that these vehicles were not being used for deliveries until either mended or replaced. There may even be scope to install more advanced sensors which not only record the temperatures in the vans, but automatically adjust the freezer units settings to maintain the required temperature.

As this illustrates, the use of sensors could assist FF in reducing vehicle running costs, cut down on fuel usage and help to improve the company's financial performance.

Logistics and deliveries

Traffic congestion

It is evident that congestion on the roads is creating problems for FF's delivery drivers when completing their daily rounds. Heavy traffic congestion has started to result in drivers missing their agreed delivery slots. This has lead to an increase in the occurrences of no one being at home to accept the goods when the driver eventually arrives. This necessitates the need for the deliveries to be rearranged the following week. As the Head of Customer Services highlighted this is having a negative effect on customer satisfaction. One disgruntled customer commented that they had now switched to using an alternative retailer, with another adding 'I am sick of waiting for my delivery to turn up only for it not to turn up at all'.

Tracking deliveries

Big data analytics could be employed by FF to relay up to date travel information from the delivery van back to the depot to assist the Head of Delivery ensure all customer delivery time slots are met. This could be achieved through the installation of tracking devices which feedback 'real time' data about the driver's progress and the likelihood of meeting the delivery time. By capturing and relaying such data this should allow the team at the depot to plot alternative routes to those regularly used by the drivers while they are still out on their rounds. However, more fundamentally the use of such data should allow the Head of Delivery to re-design the drivers current routes to make them more realistic. The delivery routes currently used are evidently no longer viable as these were determined a number of years earlier by the previous Head of Delivery using a historic delivery data. This should help to increase the number of deliveries successfully made and reduce the need for return visits.

Customer care

In the event that the driver is unable to meet the required time slot, relaying the driver's progress will allow the customer service team to contact the customer and inform them of the delay. In some cases it may be possible that the delivery is arranged at a later point on the same day, as opposed to a number of days later. Such an approach should contribute to improving customer satisfaction when buying from FF.

Poor route management

In addition to road congestion it could be argued that FF's approach to route management has significantly increased the scope for busier drivers to miss their designated time slots. As those drivers with fewer deliveries to make on their daily rounds are potentially sitting around with little to do while their colleagues struggle to make their designated deliveries. As mentioned earlier the current situation has been compounded by the fact that historical delivery patterns were used in conjunction with an online mileage calculator to determine the delivery routes used. It is evident that this approach to route management has not been updated since the previous Head of Delivery retired.

Active data base management

The current situation could be improved if the company actively managed the data it receives about its customers. Enhancing the company's systems for analysing customer data, such as customer order details (eg delivery addresses) would allow FF to build up a historic pattern of the busiest day of the week for deliveries and those towns and cities where demand for the company's services is greatest. This could prove particularly beneficial for the Head of Delivery when planning the daily deliveries as more drivers could be assigned to make deliveries during busy times. This would overcome the current situation where drivers only make deliveries on their pre-assigned route and should ensure that customers receive their goods at the correct time.

Basic website

At the current time FF operates a very basic website which is capable of accepting customer orders. To place an order, customers are required to only provide limited details, including their name, address, contact and payment details. The company's management should look to collect greater quantities of better quality customer data with a view to maximising sales.

Market segmentation and customisation

Data analytics software could be used to analyse the type of purchases individual customers make, assess the frequency of purchases and the amounts typically spent. This data could be used to identify hidden patterns and trends in customer purchasing behaviour. This approach would allow FF to customise its marketing message by sending emails with special offers to customers based on their regular purchases. Complementary products to those purchased could also be promoted to appeal to individual customers when returning to the website.

Furthermore, if data can be captured which covers the age of customers, spend per shop as well as the areas in which existing customers live, then this should help FF to better direct its marketing efforts. It is likely that clusters of existing high spend customers identified as living in a particular town or region may live near other individuals with similar needs. In such cases FF could benefit from targeting adverts promoting it's service in local newspapers which cover these areas. Equally, there may be scope to purchase from a reputable source the names and addresses of people living in a target area to facilitate direct marketing.

Data analytics also help companies today by providing customers with recommendations of items to purchase based on the tastes of similar customers. Providing shoppers with recommendations while visiting the website may help to expand the range of products customers purchase.

Decision making

Data analytic tools could be used to improve decision making at FF. For example, trends (including seasonal trends) identified in online sales in real time could be used to determine inventory and pricing strategies. Decisions could be made using this analysis by management or even through the use of automated software. For example in the event that a particular line is not selling very well automated software using algorithms could be linked to the company's website to make decisions about inventory levels and pricing in response to current and predicted sales data.

Feedback

FF could also look to interact more closely with customers by providing them with the opportunity to leave feedback on the experience of shopping with the company (feedback could cover issues covering the quality of the company's products and delivery service). Capturing and analysing such feedback using sophisticated data analytic tools whether in structured or unstructured form (eg feedback from Twitter or Facebook) would allow FF to respond quickly to customer complaints. Analysing customer feedback may also prove insightful in identifying changes in the types of products customers demand from the company.

(c) **Practical implications**

The final part of this report explores the practical implications that the management at FF will need to consider before attempting to capture more data about customers.

Cost

Increasing the amount of data that FF captures and processes about its customers would require the company to improve its existing IT architecture and software applications. The associated costs of undertaking such an overhaul would most likely be significant, and would need to be fully considered against the expected benefits to be delivered. The management at FF would need to give careful consideration to the scope of the IT project required. The scope of the project is concerned with the determining the desired project outcomes eg to capture more meaningful customer data, and the necessary work needed to achieve this. Where the scope of the project has not been determined in advance there is a serious risk that the project will fail to deliver the intended result.

Important consideration must also be given to FF's ability to pay for an investment in a new IT system. Given the company's recent dip in performance coupled to problems with some of the older delivery vans, there may not be sufficient funds available to fully enhance the existing IT infrastructure at the current time.

Time

Closely connected to the issue of cost is the amount of management time that will be required to establish the necessary databases and the analytical software tools. This process is likely to consume a significant amount of the Customer Service Director's time (and the time of the IT and Marketing Directors, if FF has them) in determining the types of data needed to be captured. Furthermore, if capturing customer data is to be facilitated by upgrading FF's website, then consideration will need to be given to any potential disruption that this may cause the company. This is likely to be of significant importance as the majority of the company's sales are made through the website.

Specialist skills

Consideration needs to be given to whether the FF management team have the required skills to be able to extract meaningful insight from the data they capture and process. As FF is a relatively small entity it seems highly unlikely that any of the existing managers will have any experience in analysing large data sets. Employing additional experts with the required skills will increase costs.

Limited experience of using technology

Increasing the amount of customer data captured and analysed will make data management more of a strategic issue at FF. This focus is likely to require a change in the attitude of the management team towards the use of technology. Based on the fact that the company presently operates a basic website this may indicate that the management are somewhat reluctant to increase FF's dependency on the use of IT systems. Given the required investment needed to improve FF's IT infrastructure it is important that all members of the management team support the initiative. Failure to understand the benefits of capturing increased quantities of customer data increases the scope that this is simply viewed by some as following the latest 'fad'.

Data overload

Careful consideration needs to be given to which customer data sets are likely to be of use to FF. There is an inherent danger with data collection that too much of the wrong type of data may be captured if the needs of the business are not determined in advance. Too much data may lead to 'data overload'.

Data security

Holding increasing amounts of customer data raises some interesting questions including; the issue of who actually owns the data held? Whether customers consent to their data being held? What data is held? These points clearly raise legal and security concerns over the data held. The management team at FF will need to ensure that adequate measures are put in place to stop customer data falling into the wrong hands. Clear company policies on data handling and adequate password protection over systems holding personal data will need to be introduced.

I hope this report has been of some use to you, in the event that you wish to discuss any of the matters raised further please do not hesitate to contact me.

A BUSINESS ADVISOR

19 The BA Times

Text reference. The 6Is are covered in Chapter 12 of your BPP Study Text for exams from September 2015 to 31 August 2016.

Top tips. The survey mentioned in the scenario identifies a number of issues, which demonstrate a lack of interactivity, individualisation, intelligence and independence of location. These are parts of the 6Is model which students need to be familiar with.

A good approach to answering part (a) is to consider how the use of the internet could help *BA Times* address the issues raised by the survey.

Marking scheme

		Marks
(a)	1 mark for each relevant point up to a maximum of 15 marks, with a maximum of 5 marks for each individual 'I'.	15
(b)	1 mark for each relevant point up to a maximum of 10 marks.	10
		25

(a) **Issues facing *BA Times***

BA Times is facing difficult trading conditions arising from a number of issues. Victor has decided that *BA Times* will continue to operate as a printed magazine in the domestic market of Umboria. Umboria is suffering from high labour costs, increasing production and distribution costs, reducing advertising income and falling subscriptions.

Victor's views

Victor's experience as a print editor appears to have convinced him that his current business model is the most appropriate due to his preference for the tactile feel of printed magazines and a belief that subscribers and advertisers may not react positively to technological change.

Exploiting new media

The introduction of a new online presence will give *BA Times* the opportunity to reach out beyond their current physical magazine and exploit its current website. At present, the website is only used to encourage visitors to purchase a hard copy. *BA Times* has historically pursued a push media approach as it pushes its magazine directly onto final users through its online marketing message.

Interactivity

It is evident that *BA Times* is suffering from a lack of interaction with its customers. Customers are not able to comment on reader's letters published in the magazine as this is only carried out by the editor. It is evident that this is a source of irritation for some users. Interactivity on the website could be enhanced by developing threads which would allow users to comment on matters raised in the magazine. This could also be supplemented by setting up online communities which allow users to share their experiences of attempting ABC and ICFC exams.

Interactivity could be enhanced further by asking users to provide feedback on the quality of the articles in the magazine. This would also help *BA Times* to ensure it remains close to the needs of its users.

As events arise which miss the latest printed edition of the magazine these could be updated via the website, therefore further supporting the needs of subscribers. Such developments would allow *BA Times*' customers to 'pull' the information they require through the website to suit their own individual needs.

Individualisation

The recent survey of those individuals who chose not to renew their subscriptions indicates users have been deterred from continuing with their membership due to there being too many irrelevant articles, such as those not related to their studies. One respondent bemoans that too much of the magazine is concerned with articles covering topics relevant to examinations at the lower level stages of the qualification.

Through embracing new technologies *BA Times* could look to make the user experience of engaging with the magazine more individualised. Subscribers could register their details and set up their own personal accounts. Then once a database of study articles for both the ABC and ICFC qualifications has been uploaded onto the *BA Times* website, relevant articles could be recommended to individual subscribers according to the qualifications they are sitting and the stage they have reached. Similarly, subscribers could search for specific articles in the database, according to their individual needs.

Victor could also supplement the existing magazine offering through introducing exam focused podcasts and webcasts. This may help to act as a source of differentiation between the two associations' websites.

Intelligence

The use of the internet would allow *BA Times* to gain a better understanding of the subscribers' requirements to its magazine. For example, the details of the number of hits per page would be particularly useful for Victor when attempting to attract advertisers to the magazine, especially if the types of products and resources sought by students are known. In addition, this would be useful for indicating the types of articles students are most interested in.

User expectations of the magazine and website could be captured through the use of online surveys and feedback questionnaires. This would ensure that *BA Times* remains responsive to user needs.

Furthermore, capturing user details – such as understanding whether they prefer to study via distance learning or through attending tuition courses – could also be of commercial interest to Victor. It is not uncommon for organisations to hold such information in computerised databases, which can then be sold onto interested parties, eg employment agencies, the qualification associations and learning providers. However, such an initiative move would require *BA Times* to gain subscribers' permission to pass on their data to third parties.

Independence of location

Internet technologies have now made it easier than ever before for organisations to have independence of location, and to operate in a far more global manner than in the past. If Victor wishes to maintain his existing business model producing printed magazines, he could realise cost savings through sending digital versions of the finished magazine to low cost production facilities outside Umboria. This is likely to appeal to Victor as Umboria is currently suffering from high wage and production costs. Magazines produced overseas could then be distributed to subscribers located around the world.

Furthermore, offering online articles via the *BA Times* website would allow *BA Times* to reduce its print costs, similar in many ways to ACCA's monthly *Student Accountant*. This may be beneficial to Victor as the associated costs of physically printing the magazine can be passed onto the end user as they could download and print off editions themselves.

(b)

> **Top tips.** It is vital you read the question carefully. There are 10 marks available for this requirement and you have to consider the impact of a technological change on subscribers, advertisers and *BA Times*' financial viability. To perform well you need to aim to make three relevant points on each.

To: BA Times
From: An accountant
Date: 9 December 2013
Subject: Potential changes in technology

This report aims to explore the likely impact that potential technological changes could have on the operations of *BA Times* with particular consideration given to the magazine's financial viability, its subscribers and current advertisers.

Drivers and barriers to the introduction of new technologies and media

Drivers for change

BA Times is operating in a highly challenging climate. The magazine is currently experiencing increasing production and distribution costs in its home market of Umboria. Conditions are also worsening in part due to changes in reading habits, especially amongst younger readers of print media who no longer want hard copies. These drivers for change indicate that new technologies could offer *BA Times* the ability to address the threats it currently faces.

Barriers to change

Victor's attitude towards the introduction of new technology and media seems to be a potential barrier to embracing new processes at *BA Times*. Victor likes the physical, tactile feel of printed magazines. He is concerned that existing subscribers and advertisers will not react positively to any technological change. This indicates that business decisions at *BA Times* are predominantly based on Victor's personal preferences as opposed to commercial realities. The company's current position will make overcoming these issues even more important.

Impact of change on key stakeholders

Subscribers

The impact of an improved website may act to attract potential subscribers to the magazine. The ability to tailor online content is likely to be attractive to existing and prospective subscribers. Free articles focusing on forthcoming examinations could be posted. These may entice users to subscribe to the online content or to purchase the physical magazine.

The business would need to investigate Victor's concerns regarding the number of subscribers without internet access to ensure that any development of the magazine online would prove to be worthwhile. However, based on changing reading habits it appears likely that such a move would be well received by subscribers.

A stronger online presence may help *BA Times* to maintain its respected status among subscribers provided such a move is perceived as being innovative. This may act as a draw for potential subscribers too if they believe they are paying for something not available elsewhere.

Advertisers

Advertisers are increasingly unconvinced about the effectiveness of advertising in printed magazines, which has led to falling magazine advertising revenues. As fewer young people are choosing to purchase print media and traditional print advertising is reducing, it is increasingly likely that advertisers will need to adapt their methods of reaching their intended target market. Therefore developing the magazine's website to allow advertisers to reach subscribers seems a natural move that most advertisers are likely to support.

Online advertising may also allow advertisers greater scope to individualise and tailor their marketing message, thereby increasing the likelihood that the message is received and not ignored by the user. Based on these factors it seems unlikely that Victor's concerns regarding the advertiser's reaction to technological changes are justified.

BA Times – financial viability

Introducing new technology could help *BA Times* reduce its print production costs. The development of an enhanced website with more features would allow *BA Times* to extend its offering to its subscribers. This may serve to reduce the demand for the printed product thereby reducing the associated costs of production.

As the founder of *BA Times* any such changes would require Victor to 'buy in' to the developments. This may prove to be particularly difficult given his current concerns. Victor would need to be convinced that the business would benefit financially from any such move. However, introducing new technology may offer up new opportunities for revenue generation. For example, an enhanced *BA Times* website could be used to capture subscriber details which could then be sold onto interested third parties.

As illustrated by the survey, one of the respondents not choosing to renew his subscription to the magazine claims that he wanted to become a 'business analyst to get a job, not just sit examinations and read about examining bodies'. *BA Times* could therefore look to exploit the use of an enhanced website to offer a greater range of services. For example, recruitment agencies could be allowed to take out banner adverts on the website, advertising their services directly to the magazine's subscribers. The fees *BA Times* receive from the advertisers will, in turn, increase the revenue generated from the website.

I hope this report has been helpful in identifying the issues of technological advancement at *BA Times*.

20 Housham Garden

Text reference. The marketing mix is covered in Chapter 3 of your BPP Study Text for exams from September 2015 to 31 August 2016.

Top tips. Students need to be particularly careful when reading question requirements. Part (a) asked for recommendations to improve HGT's performance in the short term (within three months), so your answer to part (a) should have only included recommendations which could realistically have been introduced within three months.

There were 9 marks available out of 15 for calculations in part (a). When a question requirement states that students should 'use the data provided' it is critical that this is used if easy marks are not to be lost.

Tutorial note. It is important to note that the $1.75 average contribution generated from the café and the 75% usage rate are arbitrary figures. They are presented in the answer to quantify the possible impact of any changes should the quality of the café experience be improved. You could have used other figures here to illustrate this point, provided these were reasonable.

Marking scheme

		Marks
(a)	1 mark for each relevant point up to a maximum of 15 marks.	
	The answer might include certain calculations, which will be marked as follows:	
	– Calculation of direct income: 0.5 mark	
	– Calculation of financial shortfall: 1 mark	
	– Breakeven analysis for consumer price: 2 marks	
	– Calculation of income from annual subscriptions: 1 mark	
	– Income if café returns to previous level of use: 1 mark	
	– Calculations associated with increased café revenue: 1 mark	
	– Cost saving associated with display advert cancellation: 2 marks	9
	1 mark for each relevant point related to scenario	6
(b)	1 mark for each relevant point up to a maximum of 10 marks	10
		25

(a) Analysis of why HGT is running at a loss

HGT is currently making an annual loss of $14,000. This is illustrated by the following:

	$
Revenue ($5 per visit × 1,000 visits per month × 8 months)	40,000
Contribution from café ($1.25 per visitor × 1,000 visits per month × 8 months × 60%)	6,000
Fixed costs	(60,000)
Annual shortfall	(14,000)

Immediate action HGT could take

Reduce entry price

The recent survey conducted by the local university indicates that consumers regard the current entry fee of $5 to be too expensive. Many visitors have stated that they are only prepared to pay an entry fee of $3.25 on average. If HGT lowers the admission fee, this will result in a breakeven visitor volume of 15,000 visitors per annum (see Working).

The workings below are based on the assumption that 60% of visitors continue to use the café, and the average contribution generated per café sale remains at $1.25.

Working

$3.25 (revised admission fee) + 60% × $1.25 (café contribution) = $4

Fixed costs $60,000/$4 = 15,000 visitors per annum

Implications of change in visitor numbers

The proposed reduction in the admission fee may increase the visitor numbers by almost 90% of current levels. The trust will need to give consideration to the potential implications of increasing the number of visits by 7,000 per annum. Monitoring visitor satisfaction levels to ensure that any significant increase in numbers does not detract from the experience of visiting the gardens is likely to be key.

The decision is also complicated by the uncertainty of whether a reduction in the admission fee will translate to an increase in anticipated visitor numbers. A revised $3.25 admission fee may actually reduce the contribution to fixed costs.

Implications of introducing an annual ticket

The recent consumer survey conducted by the trust suggested that 20% of respondents would be prepared to purchase an annual ticket to gain admission to the gardens for a fee of $9 per annum. Such a move would prove beneficial as this would improve HGT's cash position, through a one-off inflow of money.

At present the gardens receive 8,000 visits per annum, however the number of actual visitors remains unknown. On the assumption that 5,000 visitors visit per annum and 20% of these individuals take up the annual pass ticket this would result in a cash inflow of $9,000 (5,000 visitors × 20% × $9). In evaluating the viability of this option the trust would need to consider the likely loss of repeat income from those visitors who currently pay $5 per visit, but will no longer pay when they visit because they hold an annual ticket.

Short term changes

Improve the café

The trust should consider enhancing the existing visitor experience when using the café. Recent visitors have been particularly critical of the food offered. Improvements to the menu, with an increased emphasis on quality, should help to address the current situation.

As it stands, only 60% of visitors buy food in the café, and the average contribution ($1.25) per visitor is also low.

If the quality of food was improved, this could lead to an increase in the usage rate and contribution per visitor. If, for example, average contribution increased to $1.75, coupled with 75% usage rate, this would result in additional contribution of $4,500 over the 8 month season ($1.75 × 8000 visits per annum × 75% − $6,000).

However, before making any changes, HGT should carry out a feasibility assessment. The lack of visitor support for the decision to move the café from the gatehouse site suggests a potential weakness in the trust's strategic approach to understanding what its visitors want.

Re-locate the café

HGT should also consider moving the café back to the gatehouse area. The recent visitor survey suggests that visitors have been deterred from visiting the café due to its relocation from outside the grounds to within the gardens. This has resulted in the café losing 500 visits per month, which in turn has impacted negatively on morale and food quality, as well as revenue.

Financially, moving the café into the garden has resulted in the loss of $625 worth of contribution per month or $5,000 per annum ($1.25 average contribution × 500 visits per month). As visitors now have to pay to gain access to the café this may also contribute to a greater expectation in terms of the quality of experience when they visit. Repositioning the café in the more popular gatehouse location may serve to address the issues identified. Furthermore, it is likely this could be achieved relatively quickly as the gatehouse area is still empty.

Advertising spend

The trust may also consider reducing its current advertising spend. Only 10 respondents from 200 (5%) claimed to have heard of Housham Gardens via through the advertisements placed in the '*Heritage Gardens*' magazine. This issue was further compounded by the fact that a recent visitor commented on having not heard of gardens, despite only living four kilometres away. Cancelling three months of the adverts currently booked will result in a saving of $1,500 and avoid incurring the associated cancellation charges should the decision to cancel be made later. The income generated each month by the advert stands at $287.50 (see Working) compared to expense of $500 a month to place the advertisement. The trust may decide to access the target market using a more appropriate medium eg regional newspaper advertising.

Working:

(1,000 visits per month × 5% = 50 visits × $5 admission fee = $250) + (50 café visits × 60% × $1.25 = $37.50)

(b)

> **Top tips.** As this part of the question required practical recommendations to HGT's longer term marketing strategies it is important that answers relate to the period beyond 3 months.
>
> It is also critical that the suggestions provided are realistic. Clearly a recommendation that HGT should undertake a TV advertising campaign is not realistic. Given that HGT spends $500 a month advertising in the monthly magazine '*Heritage Gardens*', a TV campaign will potentially cost many thousands of dollars, or more.

Product

Reasons for visiting the gardens

In the context of HGT, the gardens themselves are the product that visitors experience. The product to date has been marketed as a site of historical significance due to its association with the designer William Wessex. According to the recent survey, only 5 of the 200 respondents highlighted that their motivation for visiting the gardens was to 'observe the work of William Wessex'. Most visitors claimed they visited the gardens in order to go for a walk in a peaceful environment, or to enjoy the plants and flowers. This suggests that the focus of HGT's current marketing message may have been lost, by trying to attract visitors to the gardens for the wrong reason. Instead, HGT's marketing material should place stronger emphasis on the natural beauty of the environment.

Opening period

The reasons for visiting the gardens suggest that there could be potential to increase the number of months when the garden is open. The trust has historically closed the gardens during the winter months due to colder conditions and fewer flowering plants. However, there could be scope to keep the gardens open all year round.

The product itself could be enhanced through the planting of different plants to attract visitors at all times throughout the year, for example, the planting of winter flowers during the colder months.

The associated gardening costs would need to be carefully matched against any anticipated increase in income as a result of any decision to keep the gardens open all year round.

Local events

As it stands, the gardens do not appear to be used in any other capacity, which has restricted the ability to appeal to a wider target market. There could be scope to extend the product further through teaming up with local theatre groups to put on open air plays during the summer months and to open up the facilities during the colder months to outdoor skating.

This may help the trust to reach a wider range of potential visitors who may be tempted to return during the garden's normal opening hours. The viability of such a move would need to be contrasted against the potential impact on the garden's reputation of providing a peaceful environment.

Extensive use of the café

There may be some scope to complement the café via the opening of a small shop with a view to increase the range of items sold. This could include the option to sell a selection of plants to the general public or to provide gardening advice to visitors in exchange for a small fee.

Promotion

Reduce '*Heritage Gardens*' magazine advertisements

As mentioned in part (a) the trust should stop wasting money by advertising in the monthly magazine '*Heritage Gardens*', as there needs to be a focus on HGT's longer term marketing strategy. One solution which would help to reduce advertising spending would be to advertise the gardens in a local newspaper.

Website investment

HGT's website is currently very simple, providing users with basic information including details of the restoration work carried out on the gardens. The trust should look to enhance its website by introducing new features, such as allowing visitors to book tickets for future events at the gardens, along with a facility for visitors to make donations to the trust. A web page could be devoted to dealing with visitors' own gardening queries, which could be responded to by HGT's gardening team. Such a development would also provide an opportunity for HGT to capture the details of visitors to its site. This would allow for special online promotions to be targeted to those individuals who leave their details.

21 iTTrain

Part (a)

Text reference. Pricing strategies and the marketing mix are covered in Chapter 12 of your BPP Study Text for exams from September 2015 to 31 August 2016.

Top tips. The question requires students to suggest a pricing strategy and to evaluate of the proposed price to be charged to delegates of iTTrain's IT certification courses. As the requirement clearly states that answers should include both financial and non-financial considerations it is vitally important that you cover both aspects. Failure to make use of the financial data in the question restricts your ability to gain the full marks available. The number of marks available were equally split between the financial and non-financial considerations.

If you are ever unsure of where to start when faced with such financial data it is important that you attempt the bits that you think you can do first. In this case a good approach to adopt was to calculate the total costs of running the courses using the cost information given. As Table 1 in the suggested solution below illustrates it is important that you use the data obtained from AQT in respect of the number of delegates to determine the total associated lunch and course manual costs. It was important that you picked up on the fact that the cost given for lunch was a daily cost and not the cost per course.

The information concerning the number of delegates per course was also needed in calculating the fee income generated per course. This calculation allowed you to determine the level of contribution earned per the number of delegates attending courses which could then be used to calculate the expected average contribution using the expected values.

Easy marks. Easy marks were available for performing basic calculations using the information provided in the scenario. There were two marks on offer for calculating figures showing the values for different class sizes and with a further two marks available for determining the breakeven number of courses or breakeven course price from the data.

Examiner's comments. Most candidates elected to attempt this question, but it was not answered particularly well. Financial analysis was often very limited, with little use of expected values. The non-financial analysis was often very poorly structured and was not well integrated with the financial analysis. The examining team noted that better candidates identified that the proposed $750 delegate fee was slightly too low. Good candidates suggested that a higher price would have allowed the company to potentially make the required modest profit, and was more in line with the quality image that it wished to convey, thereby aligning financial and non-financial considerations. Very few candidates commented on the likelihood of the start-up IT training company achieving the course sizes of an established training provider, thus undermining the legitimacy of the expected values.

Marks

(a)   For the non-financial analysis 1 mark for an appropriate point up to a
maximum of 9 marks.

For the financial analysis up to a maximum of 10 marks:
– Table of figures showing values for different class sizes (2 marks)
– Expected contribution per course (2 marks)
– Breakeven analysis (2 marks)
– Course running value and implication (1 mark)
– Options for flexing (2 marks)
– Assumptions (2 marks)
   (The total number of marks for the question are capped at 16)

16

(b)   1 mark for each appropriate point up to a maximum of 3 marks for each
part of the marketing mix

<u>9</u>

<u>25</u>

Marketing objectives

The price that an organisation charges customers for its products or services are likely to form a key part of its strategy. Pricing is an essential component of how an organisation is positioned in its chosen market. Customer perception forms an important element in determining an appropriate selling price as the value a customer derives from using a particular service needs to be sufficiently attractive in light of the price demanded. Marco intends to position iTTrain as a quality provider of IT certification training.

Based on his understanding of prices charged by competing firms for similar training courses, Marco has proposed a price of $750 per delegate. This appears to represent a reasonable price given the high quality customer experience iTTrain is hoping to provide. Cheaper training providers offer courses for $550 per delegate, however such courses represent a 'no frills' offering with attendees tending to be self-financing 'for whom price is an issue'. This difference in focus suggests that Marco's higher price may be appropriate.

AQT offer similar types of courses for $900 per delegate for a three-day programme, however, this price is often discounted by up to 10%, resulting in an actual fee of $810. At a price of $750 per delegate, Marco is offering a better customer experience at a lower and more competitive price.

Pricing objectives

Ultimately, the prices set by Marco need to reflect his personal objectives. Marco has stated that he would like iTTrain to generate a modest profit in its first year in order for the company to establish itself. For some entities the need to survive in order to achieve short-term cash flows will lead to reduced pricing of products and services.

Financial analysis

The following financial analysis of iTTrain's proposal to run IT certification training is based upon the information provided. The expected contribution per course shown in Table 2 has been determined using probabilities based on the number of courses run at AQT. The income figures were calculated based on Marco's proposed price of $750 per delegate.

Workings

Table 1: Contribution generated per course

Number of delegates per course (based on AQT)	Number of courses run (based on AQT)	Lecturer costs per day ($450 × 3 days)	Training room costs per day ($250 × 3 days)	Course manual costs ($20 per manual per delegate)	Lunch cost per delegate ($10 per delegate per day)	Total Cost	Income ($750 per number of delegates)	Contribution
3	150	$1,350	$750	$60	$90	$2,250	$2,250	$0
4	210	$1,350	$750	$80	$120	$2,300	$3,000	$700
5	250	$1,350	$750	$100	$150	$2,350	$3,750	$1,400
6	190	$1,350	$750	$120	$180	$2,400	$4,500	$2,100
7	70	$1,350	$750	$140	$210	$2,450	$5,250	$2,800
8	80	$1,350	$750	$160	$240	$2,500	$6,000	$3,500
9	50	$1,350	$750	$180	$270	$2,550	$6,750	$4,200

Table 2: Expected contribution for class sizes of three to nine delegates

Probability	Contribution from above	Expected contribution
0.15	$0	$0
0.21	$700	$147
0.25	$1,400	$350
0.19	$2,100	$399
0.07	$2,800	$196
0.08	$3,500	$280
0.05	$4,200	$210
		$1,582

Total expected contribution per course is $1,582

Therefore, in order for iTTrain to breakeven the number of courses run would be:

$65,000 annual fixed costs / $1,582 per course = 41.09 courses per annum

Marco has planned to run 40 courses next year. Based on contribution of $1,582 per annum per course, iTTrain will make a small loss ($1,720) for the year.

Total contribution based on 40 courses:

40 courses × $1,582 = $63,280

Total contribution less annual fixed costs:

$63,280 – ($65,000) = ($1,720) Loss

Table 3: Operating profit or loss based on number of delegates attending

Number of delegates based on AQT	Contribution (contribution per course calculated in Table 1 × 40 courses per annum)	Fixed costs per annum	Operating profit or (loss)
3	$0	($65,000)	($65,000)
4	$28,000	($65,000)	($37,000)
5	$56,000	($65,000)	($9,000)
6	$84,000	($65,000)	$19,000
7	$112,000	($65,000)	$47,000
8	$140,000	($65,000)	$75,000
9	$168,000	($65,000)	$103,000

Table 3 illustrates that, based on the contribution calculated per course in Table 1, iTTrain will need to ensure that, on average, at least six delegates are on each of the 40 courses offered in order for it to generate a profit after taking into account annual fixed costs.

Options

Increase prices

In light of the above analysis, Marco may wish to consider amending the proposed price of $750. An increase in the price charged to, say, $800-$810 per delegate would bring iTTrain's fees nearer to the discounted fees charged by AQT. This option would allow iTTrain to preserve its competitive pricing approach and help Marco to achieve the modest profit he is seeking in year 1.

Decrease costs

Furthermore, Marco could explore the possibility of lowering the associated costs of running the courses. The costs of hiring the self-employed lecturers and of renting the training centre rooms are set as standard prices. There may be scope to realise discounted rates on such bookings if these are made in bulk. Discounted rates coupled to a selling price of $750 per delegate would help to improve the contribution and profits generated.

Financial analysis – the implications and assumptions

From the financial analysis conducted, it appears that Marco's proposed fee of $750 per delegate may be too low to guarantee a modest profit in the coming year. In addition, the analysis conducted was formed on the basis of probabilities derived from the results obtained from another company, AQT. It also seems unlikely that iTTrain would be able to immediately establish the same levels of trading as an existing, established IT certification training entity such as AQT. This raises further doubts over the viability of Marco achieving his profit objective.

Furthermore, Marco appears to have made some significant assumptions. Firstly he is assuming that all of the courses he planned will all run and secondly that these courses will not be under-subscribed at the proposed price of $750. Marco will need to give careful consideration to any associated costs that iTTrain may incur should scheduled courses have to be cancelled due to limited interest. Self-employed lecturers and the CityCentre training venue may require iTTrain to make penalty payments if insufficient notice of cancellation for previously booked services occurs.

Competition in the market

AQT is the most dominant training provider in the IT certification training market, with course prices running from $810 up to $900. As 'no frills' providers offer courses at significantly lower prices, ($550 per delegate), this indicates that price alone is not the only consideration for customers when choosing where to study. The low quality training premises and poorly motivated lecturers used by 'no frills' operators explains in part why such providers do not hold greater market share.

Marco's desire to offer a premium service at a higher price which principally targets the corporate business market may therefore prove successful, especially if customers are prepared to pay more for their delegates to benefit from enjoying a superior experience.

Intermediaries

The IT certification market is characterised by the role that intermediaries play in the supply chain. This is evident by the role of brokers which advertise AQT courses on their own websites in exchange for discounted prices. This potentially has implications for the course prices that Marco is attempting to determine. Some brokers have already approached Marco asking about the possibility of iTTrain offering similar 10% discounts to those received from AQT.

In the event Marco offered a similar level of discount on iTTrain's courses this would reduce the price per delegate from $750 to $675. Such a move would have to be fully considered prior to being accepted to assess the impact on contribution and profitability.

Pricing ploys

When setting a selling price most organisations use different types of tactics to attract customers. Approaches include; price penetration (where a low price is initially offered to gain market appeal), price skimming (is commonly used when marketing hi-tech products, this involves setting a high price when a new item is launched). Such approaches do not appear to be particularly applicable to iTTrain's business model. It may be more appropriate for iTTrain to offer 'early bird' schemes where customers benefit from a discount on the usual price in exchange for earlier payment. This approach is particularly effective at improving cash flows.

Summary

Based on the above analysis Marco's proposed fee price of $750 would be appear to be reasonable. However, the likely impact that setting this price would have on his modest profit ambitions would need to be more fully explored. Establishing a price slightly in excess of $800 per delegate may therefore prove to be more effective at ensuring a profit is realised. If Marco is required to offer discounts to intermediaries then a marginally higher selling price should help to offset the effects of discounting.

Part (b)

Top tips. The marketing mix is a key model in paper P3. It is important that you understand that physical evidence, people and processes relate predominantly to the provision of services. The question required candidates to analyse three elements of the marketing mix in relation to iTTrain's entry into the IT certification market. You are encouraged to draw upon your own practical experience when attempting such questions. You may have studied with an education provider as part of your ACCA studies to date which may have helped in answering the question. Many education providers operate websites which offer free sample lecture presentations and issue prospective students with sample course materials in the hope of attracting new customers.

Easy marks. There were three marks available in respect of the three marketing mix elements up to a total of 9 marks. Illustrating an understanding of how each element related to iTTrain would have gained some straightforward marks.

Examiner's comments. The examiner commented that this part of the question was poorly answered despite clear signposts in the scenario; the importance of the lectures (people), the significance of course material (physical evidence), the need for an easy transaction process.

Contribution of physical evidence, people and processes

Physical evidence

Physical evidence in the context of iTTrain relates to the actual environment in which a service is provided. The environment in which a service is received by a customer forms an important element in how that service is perceived in relation to its market positioning. Marco's decision to use the 'prestigious' CityCentre training venue appears to be directed towards enhancing the delegates' experience of studying with iTTrain.

The use of this venue helps to reinforce the quality teaching experience that prospective delegates can expect upon attending a course. This may help to attract customers from the targeted corporate business market who are keen for their employees to have access to the best possible training.

Marco could promote the location of iTTrain courses via the company's website where pictures and customer reviews of the facilities could be presented. Furthermore, the superior quality of iTTrain's offering could also be achieved by providing prospective customers with a sample set of course materials used on courses.

People

Organisations which are focused on the provision of services often invest heavily in those people (usually employees) who are involved directly in interacting with the end customer. Such investment commonly takes the form of employee development and training. This is particularly important for service sector organisations where no physical product is sold. It is the quality of the service customers receive which ultimately determines whether they return.

In the case of iTTrain people can be regarded as being of vital importance, as it is the self-employed lecturers that deliver the courses to delegates. As the self-employed lecturers are not employees of iTTrain Marco will need to ensure that those lecturers hired provide delegates with the level of service expected. People-related issues, such as poor reviews by delegates which threaten perception of the iTTrain brand as a quality provider must be dealt with immediately. Marco should monitor the performance of lecturers through the use of delegate feedback surveys, customer questionnaires and lesson observations. Positive delegate reviews can then be used in promotional marketing material.

Process

iTTrain provides IT certification training to delegates, as a result relevant processes are likely to include those related to booking a place on a course. Issues including the ease of paying for a place and the quality of the joining instructions prior to attendance will form a key part the customers' perception of the iTTrain brand. It is of critical importance that such features are adequately managed by Marco when establishing his new company.

22 BeauCo

Text reference. IT controls, continuity planning and disaster recovery are covered in Chapter 11 of the BPP Study Text for exams from September 2015 to 31 August 2016.

Top tips. Adopting a structured approach to answering this question was key. A good approach to use was to identify the different types of controls which should be in operation per the scenario. Discussing the weaknesses identified, supported by practical recommendations to overcome these, helped to avoid repetition of the same points.

When asked for practical recommendations ensure that these could be implemented in a real life situation. There were up to two marks per recommendation given.

Part (a)

Adequacy of BeauCo's internal controls

A number of weaknesses in BeauCo's internal controls significantly contributed to the payroll system fraud.

Operational controls

Operational controls are aimed at ensuring that an organisation's day to day activities run effectively. Most organisations establish operational controls aimed at influencing an individual's behaviour. Strong internal company policies often stop situations arising which lead to one individual having too much power over a particular function. This is often achieved through ensuring a segregation of duties.

Until recently there appears to have been a segregation of duties in the payroll department with the payroll supervisor reviewing the work processed by the payroll officer. This arrangement worked adequately until the supervisor went off on maturity leave, thereby giving the payroll officer complete control over the payroll system.

To compound matters, the finance department failed to follow company policy when querying the rise in staff costs. Such deviations should have been brought to the attention of the head of production, not the manager in charge of the component parts division. This failing represents a significant weakness in BeauCo's internal control environment which must be rectified to avoid similar instances arising in the future.

Recommendation

The board at BeauCo need to ensure that at all times two or more individuals are involved in the processing of key information such as the monthly payroll. During times of staff absence it is important that an appropriate individual is designated to fill in and conduct a review of any processing before payment is made.

As BeauCo is a medium sized company there may be some difficulty in assigning an individual to this role as there are less staff available to choose from than there might be if it was a large company. Ideally such a review should be carried out by an individual with no interest in the matter, however as this concerns pay it is likely that this task should be carried out by a member of senior management for example the HR or finance director.

Furthermore, the board should communicate the importance to the finance team of following company policy when it comes to approving deviations in expenses. This could be supplemented by providing a reminder of the management authority hierarchy.

Controls over physical access

Physical access controls are aimed at stopping unauthorised individuals from accessing an entity's assets, including its IT assets. Such measures are also directed at preventing physical damage to the IT infrastructure which may occur as a result of natural hazards, which include fires and flooding.

It is evident that BeauCo have been proactive in enhancing its physical access controls as the company has recently moved to install a pass code entry system on its internal doors. However, the effectiveness of these controls has been undermined as the glitches in the system have not been addressed meaning that doors to rooms containing servers and systems with confidential information on them have been left unlocked.

Recommendation

BeauCo should move to correct the current situation by ensuring that the pass code system is fixed. All staff requiring access to these areas should then be provided with their own personal entry number. To supplement this it is recommended that a log of all employee door codes is maintained. When an employee leaves BeauCo it is important that the individual's pass code is deactivated to prevent potential unauthorised access in the future.

To reduce the likely impact on BeauCo's IT assets in the event of a natural disaster such as a fire, it is recommended that if a ceiling sprinkler system has not already been installed, one should be introduced to prevent the spread of any potential fire damage. Other measures could include the installation of fire doors and air conditioned 'cold rooms' to help maintain IT servers in the event of a fire.

Control over logical access

Logical access controls are aimed at ensuring that only authorised users of IT systems are provided with access. Such measures are directed towards identifying and confirming the authenticity of the user. A common mechanism in protecting computerised data is through the use of passwords.

At BeauCo the ability to set passwords on the HR system was disabled as it was regarded as being too cumbersome. This played a significant part in the fraud as it allowed the payroll officer easy access to employee's standing data.

Recommendation

The password control mechanism was put in place to prevent unauthorised access to highly confidential information. The move to disable such a function should not be decided by staff and should not really be deactivated at all. Such decisions should only be determined by senior management. To overcome this issue it is recommended that passwords are used on all systems. It needs to become a matter of company policy that all employees are expected to use and regularly update their computer password. Breaches of policy should be treated as a disciplinary matter.

Controls over data input

Controls over data input are aimed at ensuring the quality of the system's output. The focus of such mechanisms is to ensure that only valid data is accepted by the system. Data validation is likely to centre upon ensuring that data entered into a system has been posted to the correct account codes, that only acceptable values are allowed, and that input data is in a suitable format.

A key failure in the controls over BeauCo's payroll system was that the payroll officer was able to input new overtime entries significantly higher than the average monthly amounts without the system flagging this. It is evident that no higher level permission was required to post these entries to the payroll.

However, the payroll system's most prominent failing was that the software actually allowed the entry of three bogus employees each with the same bank account details. Most modern payroll and accounting systems are designed to detect and reject duplicate entries. This underlying failure with BeauCo's payroll software suggests that the system perhaps lacks functionality due to its age or was not properly configured when initially installed.

Recommendation

It is recommended that the payroll system has predetermined entry limits. Therefore, any entries input which exceed the processing limit will require a user with a higher level of authority to approve the posting. Furthermore, it is highly recommended that management investigate the weaknesses in the actual software to prevent further instances of duplicated entries occurring. This may require the purchase of a newer payroll application to replace the existing system.

Part (b)

> **Top tips.** 'Continuity planning' and 'disaster recovery' are key terms which the examining team expect students to understand. A brief explanation of each was all that was required to achieve the first three marks available. Relating the significance of both terms to BeauCo should have been straightforward for those students that identified that the company runs a significant part of its operations using IT.

Continuity planning

Continuity planning is focused on ensuring the survival of an organisation and its operations in the face of short term adversity. Many internal weaknesses and external threats exist which if materialised could have a severe impact on an organisation's ability to achieve its long term objectives and ultimate survival. Events including natural disasters (eg fire and floods) and computer network failures (eg supply chain interruption) are likely to be highly detrimental to an organisation's operations.

Continuity planning is concerned with having in place courses of action directed towards combating and preventing the significant risks an organisation faces. Given the extensive use of computers in modern business, a strong focus of continuity planning is devoted to protecting IT assets (disaster recovery).

Most large organisations today produce business continuity plans which detail key parts of an organisation's operations to assist with operational recovery in the event of a risk materialising. Plans often include details about key personnel, customer and supplier contacts and related information about the entity's data back-ups.

Disaster recovery

Disaster recovery is part of continuity planning. It is predominantly concerned with the processes and procedures that an organisation uses to allow its IT systems to continue in operation in the event of a disaster occurring. In the event of critical functions being interrupted, a company's disaster recovery processes are directed at restoring the organisations operations within an acceptable time frame.

Significance to BeauCo

Continuity planning and disaster recovery are important for BeauCo due to the company's reliance on IT. BeauCo's operations are dependent upon on its online procurement and inventory management systems to enable the completion of customer orders. Furthermore, the company makes all of its sales through its website.

Such reliance on IT and information systems increases the potential impact that technology failure, malicious attacks on the company's website and natural disasters may have on BeauCo's IT performance.

Trading conditions

Current trading conditions in the computer components industry increase the likelihood that BeauCo could potentially suffer significantly in the event of such a risk materialising. Damage caused to BeauCo's website in the event of a malicious attack by a third party could potentially leave the company unable to take customer orders. The competitive nature of the market suggests that customers may choose to shop elsewhere should BeauCo's website be out of action for any significant amount of time. Any such problems with the company's website would need to be addressed as quickly as possible to avoid losing key customers.

BeauCo's disaster recovery plan could address such an issue by allowing orders to be taken over the phone while the designated IT team recover the website.

Similar problems could also occur should there be a technology failure with the online procurement system. An inability to order materials to meet demand will likely lead to lost custom and potentially leave the manufacturing department unable to operate.

Back-ups

At the current time BeauCo takes a back-up of all information stored on its computer system every three months. Taking a copy of all information is best practice as it allows the company to continue its operations with limited disruption should there be a systems failure. To maximise the effectiveness of this measure, BeauCo should look to ensure that a system back-up is taken much more frequently than at present, for example on a daily or weekly basis. It has become common practice in most industries that back up information is stored offsite in the event that the site of the company's IT infrastructure is destroyed by some form of disaster; fire or flood.

23 Finch Co

Text reference. The concepts of 'strategic alignment' and the four views model are covered in Chapter 9 of your BPP Study Text for exams from September 2015 to 31 August 2016.

Top tips.

Part (a): In order to help set the scene to your answer a short definition/explanation of the term strategic alignment was particularly useful technique to follow.

Part (b): The four views model has been developed to help organisations understand a wider range of areas that will require consideration when looking to improve a business system. Too often senior management only concentrate on the IT aspects when enhancing a business system. Using each view of the model in turn to help structure your answer here is a good approach.

Marking scheme

	Marks
Part (a)	
Up to 2 marks for a definition/explanation of strategic alignment	2
Up to 2 marks for exploring real world changes in shopping behaviour	2
Up to 3 marks for points made in support of the CEO's comment	3
	7
Part (b)	
1 mark for the correct application of the four views model	1
People:	
Up to 2 marks for a discussion on the lack of experience in project work	2
Up to 2 marks for a discussion on the lack of staff training	2
Up to 2 marks for a discussion on the lack of contingency	2
Up to 2 marks for a discussion on the lack of co-ordination	2
Processes:	
Up to 2 marks for a discussion on the lack of communication	2
Up to 2 marks for a discussion on the limited use of IT	2

	Marks
Organisational context:	
Up to 2 marks for a discussion on senior management support	2
Up to 2 marks for a discussion on role and responsibilities	2
Technology:	
1 mark for a discussion on the use of technology	1
	18
Total marks	25

Part (a)

Strategic alignment

Strategic alignment is concerned with ensuring that an organisation remains responsive to any opportunities or threats which may have an impact on its ability to achieve its objectives. Organisations need to continually scan the external environment to ensure that when significant changes arise that these are integrated into its strategies. Being proactive in adapting to change is central to survival.

CEO's comments

Andrew Finch's comments indicate that he has undertaken some environmental analysis of the grocery retail sector. Clearly, there have been significant changes to the way in which customers now wish to shop.

Changes in shopping behaviour

In recent years the global grocery retail sector has undergone some dramatic changes as companies try to position themselves in the best way in order to remain competitive.

The use of internet technologies has served as the main enabler of such developments. The increasing popularity of internet shopping in recent decades has seen most major grocery retailers develop their own online offering. Many supermarkets provide customers with the ability to purchase goods online with either the option of home delivery or collection from store ('Click and collect').

Other retailers have moved to supplement their online shop by introducing self service tills, allowing customers to reduce the amount of time that they spend in store.

Although the specifics are unknown, it is evident that competitors in Finch Co's market have embraced and integrated new technology into their operations. Andrew Finch believes this is largely behind the fall in his company's profits. If he is correct, this indicates that customers are prepared to switch retailers if they are easier to use. Such developments support Andrew's assertion that customers 'now expect more from us, convenience of shopping is what people want'.

As customers become more discerning and driven by the desire to save time while shopping, Finch Co's traditional focus on the quality of the in-store experience is likely to become less important to them.

The ability to give customers want they want in terms of convenience is a key part of remaining competitive in a particularly challenging industry. In the UK in recent years there have been numerous high profile cases of company's failing to move with the times and identify what customers want. This is a major concern for Andrew, illustrated by his comment that adaptation is central in avoiding the loss of customers to rivals.

The introduction of the 'click and collect' and new till systems coupled to Finch Co offering higher quality products are seen as ways of helping the company to remain competitive.

Part (b)

Four views model

People

Lack of experience in project work

The project committee consisted of three directors, none of which had prior experience in managing similar process improvement projects in the past. Although no details are given in the scenario, it would appear that the decision to introduce both systems at the same time was made with limited consideration of the potential implications that this may bring post-implementation. Market research and consultation with key stakeholder groups such as customers and staff may have helped to identify the potential issues before each system went live.

Furthermore, the IT department's level of experience in supporting such projects is unknown. Based on the limited use of IT in Finch Co historically this is likely to have been inadequate.

Lack of staff training

The committee's inability to understand a range of 'softer' issues in delivering a successful project has proven disastrous. The need for store level staff to receive full training on the new scanner system prior to it going live appears to have been overlooked. This sentiment was echoed by the shop worker who remarked of only having had 10 minutes training on the system in the morning, after the system had gone live for use by store customers. The

BPP
LEARNING MEDIA

inability of staff to resolve the problems customers were experiencing with the system led to a significant increase in customer complaints and lost sales as customers walked out in frustration.

Lack of contingency

Andrew Finch was heavily motivated by ensuring that Finch Co reduces its store costs as a way of reversing the decline in profits of recent years. However, the decision to make the majority of the checkout staff redundant appears to have been rather short-sighted. A contingency plan of retaining these workers and existing tills would have been advantageous, especially during the initial systems changeover. Such a move would have allowed for the operation of the stores to have continued while staff and customers became familiar with the new scanners. The apparent decision to go for a direct system changeover appears to have been a major contributing factor in the systems failure.

Lack of co-ordination

The introduction of the new 'click and collect' service appears to have been poorly forecast with more orders having been placed online than originally anticipated. The Operation Director's forecast of demand appears to have been determined by guesswork as actual online orders across all stores were 1,150,000 per month (5,000 orders × 230 stores) higher than predicted. There also appears to have been a lack of planning during the introduction of the 'click and collect' service. This is particularly evident as required staffing levels to run this service adequately appear to not have been considered. The quantity of orders placed has put the store staff under increasingly more strain, resulting in a poor customer experience. Customers have been unable to collect orders when due for collection as these have not been ready. This suggests a lack of store level co-ordination, as staff members do not appear to know what is expected of them.

Processes

Lack of communication

Finch Co appears not to have spent sufficient time communicating to its customers how the new till system should work. The significant increase in complaints from those customers made to queue in the aisles appears to have been particularly damaging to the Finch Co brand. Although, some checkout operators were retained to help customers download their purchases at the tills, it would appear that not enough staff have been made available to assist shoppers. The impact of this has reduced the quality of the customer experience when shopping in store. Clearly, the sight of customers leaving stores in disgust is likely to attract other customers to follow suit. Such controversy is likely to be exploited by Finch Co's competitors. Competitors may look to run promotional campaigns highlighting the superiority of their own customer experience.

This problem may have been largely avoided by having fully trained staff readily available to assist shoppers as they progress through the store. Demonstrations of how the system works could have been provided on the company's website to support customers.

Limited use of expertise

Finch Co's historic lack of IT in its business operations would appear to have been detrimental in its decision to develop its website by offering a 'click and collect' service. Although unclear from the scenario it would appear that no external specialist advice was sought by the project committee regarding the website upgrade. Clearly, it would have been beneficial to the project for such input to have been factored into any decision to improve the site. Guidance from an external third party may have helped Finch Co in improving its process for forecasting likely customer demand for this service.

It is worth noting that although Finch Co's approach to forecasting demand from its 'click and collect' service requires improvement, the company's upgraded website itself appears to have been a success. This is evident as the revamped website has been capable of handling 1,840,000 online orders per month (8,000 orders × 230 stores). This is particularly promising for Finch Co as it suggests that the 'click and collect' service has the potential to generate a significant amount of revenue for the company in the future provided the current in-store issues are resolved.

Organisational context

Senior management support

The management at Finch Co clearly need the new systems to work as the company has undertaken a significant capital investment in new technologies. Although, the CEO's message to the company was clear in stating that all

staff need to support the changes, this appears to have been the extent of any encouragement in using the new systems. Andrew Finch's belief that shop workers would learn how the new till system works through simply getting 'stuck in' has proven detrimental to the success of the project.

Finch Co's lack of innovation in the past is likely to have left some of its employees out of touch with modern technologies, meaning that the staff do not learn how to use the new tills as quickly and easily as the CEO had assumed they would.

Confusion over responsibilities

The confusion in store over the role and responsibilities of the shop floor staff indicates a lack of planning by the project team. If a store is to work efficiently then jobs and responsibilities need to have been defined in advance and there need to be sufficient staff available to do the work required.

Assigning store management set tasks such as overseeing the management of the new checkout system and 'click and collect' desk could have helped avoid the confusion among shop floor staff.

Technology

The technology employed in developing the two new systems would appear to be the most positive factor to come from the project. Although not mentioned, it would appear that the actual hardware used in operating the new till system and 'click and collect' ordering mechanism is working effectively.

Once the new till system is fully embedded, Finch Co should benefit from the ability to generate individual store sales reports in 'real time'. This may allow stores to boost sales. On days when sales fall below the stores intended target, managers may in a better position to influence demand by running in store promotions or changing store displays to attract customers.

The ability to take customer orders online may also help to attract new shoppers to use Finch Co on the basis of the convenience of the 'click and collect' service.

However, the success of both systems depends on the ability of Finch Co to address the people and process issues outlined above.

24 Chemical Transport

Text reference. Harmon's process-strategy matrix is covered in Chapter 9 of your BPP Study Text for exams from September 2015 to 31 August 2016. Customer relationship management systems are covered in Chapter 12.

Top tips.

Part (a) – this type of requirement has been seen before in P3 exams and, as they have been in the past, this part question was well answered in the majority of cases. If you are familiar with the process-strategy matrix you should be able to score highly on this requirement.

A significant number of students failed to notice that payroll should not be a complex process such as the one described in the scenario. The fact that the organisation has made it complex is a different matter. Similarly, is legal advice of strategic importance to a haulage company?

Easy marks. Part (a) gave well-prepared candidates the opportunity to pick up some easy marks provided you had learnt Harmon's matrix and were confident in applying this to the scenario.

Examiner's comment. In general this part question was very well answered, with a significant number of candidates scoring 13 marks or more. Alternate recommendations to those in the model answers (for example; whether to insource rather than outsource legal advice) were permitted if they were well justified.

Part (b) – always read the scenario carefully and ensure you tailor your answer to the company in question. Many students failed to fully understand that this is a B2B organisation which meant that many of the more 'generic' type answers given were not applicable and hence did not generate marks.

There was also a number of candidates who relied far too heavily on the 6Is. Again, such answers gained few marks as, not only were many elements of this not relevant to an organisation of this nature, they failed to address all the other elements of CRM. CRM is far wider than simply making use of the internet. The fact that the company already has a website in place was also often overlooked in answers such as these.

Marking scheme

		Marks
(a)	1 mark for each relevant point up to a maximum of 5 marks for each process area Three process areas required, giving a maximum of 15 marks	15
(b)	1 mark for each relevant point up to a maximum of 5 marks for principles 1 mark for each relevant point up to a maximum of 5 marks for the evaluation	10
		Total = 25

(a) Harmon's process-strategy matrix plots the strategic importance of a process and the complexity of that process along two axes to form a grid of four quadrants. For each quadrant, a different generic process solution is then suggested.

The three significant business process areas identified in the scenario will be considered in turn to determine where they fit in Harmon's process-strategy matrix and the resulting strategy that should be employed for each.

Payroll

In most organisations, payroll is a relatively uncomplicated process with limited strategic importance and, as such, would be fulfilled by an off-the-shelf software package. At CT the development and enhancement of bonuses and deductions has led to the payroll process becoming increasingly complex. A bespoke application has therefore been developed for this process.

However, it is noted that the drivers 'find the pay arrangements very confusing' and one has commented that 'it confuses rather than motivates us'. This suggests that CT would benefit from simplifying these arrangements and using the more standard off-the-shelf software approach. This would also be cost effective as updates for the regular and unpredictable legislative changes that affect payroll would be built into the contracted maintenance fee. Changes to a bespoke system are more likely to be time consuming and expensive in contrast. This was highlighted by the recent legislative changes which led to 'the IT team being fully occupied for three months, developing and testing the required modifications to the payroll system'.

The savings made by the simplified system could be offered to drivers therefore allowing CT to better reward their drivers and at additional cost to the company. This would likely improve the motivation and satisfaction of the drivers (who are key to CT's strategic success).

Legal advice

The nature of legislation is complex and changing and as such CT has outsourced this process to a specialist legal consultancy. CT has benefited from this advice but is concerned about the cost of this service and is now considering employing a full time expert in-house.

Finding such an expert may be difficult, however, as the individual will need a broad range of knowledge including chemical handing and transportation legislation, driving related legislation such as driving hours, and truck and trailer maintenance. Fees for non-compliance would be potentially very high and monitoring of all relevant legislation also could be very time consuming. Trying to find a single employee who could deal

with all the legal issues arising could be both expensive and risky. Retaining such a skilled individual in such a position with no clear career path may also prove difficult. Therefore it is questionable whether it actually would be any cheaper to hire an in-house lawyer than to use the consultancy.

The legal advice process can be placed on Harmon's process-strategy matrix as a process of high complexity and low strategic importance. The strategic importance is low because legal advice does not relate to the core business function, ie haulage. The appropriate strategy would therefore to be to continue to outsource this process to the specialist legal consultancy.

Delivery tracking web service

CT has agreed to upgrade its website to allow the chemical wholesalers (ie customers) to request and track deliveries in order to prevent the loss of contracts with the wholesalers who will otherwise look for alternative distributors. The fact that customers have asked for this service increases its strategic importance. It is also likely that such a system would be a beneficial part of CT's business strategy as it could be used to help extend the number of wholesalers it serves. This process is therefore of high strategic importance to CT.

This process is also likely to be fairly complex as the requirements are unlikely to be fully defined at this stage and could change as the needs of the wholesalers are discussed. There will also be security issues to consider, such as ensuring the details of competitors are kept separate and secure.

A highly complex and strategically important process such as this would be best addressed by the in-house development of a bespoke system. The expertise to do this already exists in house but the internal IT team are currently very busy with the payroll system. If the payroll system was simplified as suggested above and an off-the-shelf package installed, this would free up the time of the IT team allowing the resource to be used to develop this new bespoke system.

(b)   The current CT website is purely information based. Developing this website to provide delivery placement and tracking information is considered to be vital for customer retention as, without this, current customers may move elsewhere. Such a development may also assist in the acquisition of new customers, however, the business market is relatively small as in B2B (business to business) applications the buyers are generally large, but few in number.

Customer acquisition

The new website should be developed in line with the interests and requirements of the existing customers: the chemical wholesalers.

To attract new customers the new website should provide evidence of CT's expertise in chemical distribution within a stringent and fluctuating legislative environment. Examples and regular updates relating to recent legal requirements and challenges should be given to encourage repeat visits to the website. Testimonials from existing customers should be provided to reinforce the message.

CT's website is a B2B website and so no purchases will be made solely on the strength of the website. The role of the website in this case is to provide the potential customer with information and increase their confidence in CT to a point where direct contact will be made. To help achieve this, the website should look professional and avoid leaking information to competitors, such as CT's current customers or pricing levels.

The website should be optimised in search engines to ensure it can easily be found by potential customers. Purchasing sponsored links can also be useful in achieving this.

As a B2B business, the number of potential customers is unlikely to be great and so it should be fairly easy for CT to identify and target them. Any offline marketing material that is sent out to potential customers should promote the website and include details of the web address.

Collection of details of visitors to the site could be achieved by only making certain information available if an email address is input. This would allow CT to understand which companies are viewing their web pages and also could be used as the basis for promotion campaigns in the future.

Customer retention

The ability to place and track orders online is identified within the scenario as a key consideration in the retention of the existing customers. Improvements that would facilitate this could include helping the customers to plan deliveries in a way that minimises distribution costs, and assisting in the distribution of the chemicals directly to the end customer therefore helping reduce the costs of storage the wholesaler would otherwise have to pay. Fast online payments would also be of benefit to the customers.

If the website can be developed in such a way that integrates the systems of the supplier and the customer then customer retention will be greatly improved. This would provide the customer with a better service at a lower cost, but will also help to lock that customer in as it makes it much more difficult for them to switch suppliers. Linking the rest of the process (ordering, planning, payment and reconciliation) as well as extending the website would help CT to achieve this.

25 DRB

Text reference. Chapter 4 (Value chain); Chapter 11 (e-business, and supply chain management); Chapter 12 (e-marketing and customer relationship management).

Top tips. Requirement (a) contains three different parts: (i) draw the *primary* activities on the value chain; (ii) comment on the significant of them; (iii) comment on the value they offer to DRB's customers.

There are only 3 marks available for drawing DRB's activities on the value chain, so you need to answer all the parts of the requirement to score well.

However, the comments you make in (a) should also give you some ideas for (b) and (c).

Requirement (b) requires you to apply your knowledge of supply chain management to the scenario to explain how DRB can re-structure its upstream supply chain. Note again that there are two parts to the requirement: (i) to achieve growth; (ii) to tackle the current problems DRB is experiencing.

The changes required to tackle the current problems (managing in-bound logistics; dependency on a single supplier) are likely to be less dramatic than those necessary to achieve the growth required.

The examiner's solution includes an assessment alternative procurement models as possible sources of growth. The answer below looks as the possibility of using the independent marketplace as one such alternative procurement model.

Requirement (c), like (b), requires you to apply your knowledge to the scenario, and to identify ways DRB can achieve growth. As with (b) there are both relatively simple options – for example, increasing the amount of online advertising – and more complex options; changing from a supply led to a demand led business.

Easy marks. Drawing the primary activities on the value chain, and commenting on the significant of them should provide you with some easy marks for (a). (But make sure you put DRB's activities on the value chain; don't just draw a general value chain.)

Requirements (b) and (c) offer less opportunity for easy marks. There is little opportunity to display textbook knowledge here; the marks are available for applying it to the scenario under review. However, there is still a lot of merit in following a simple yet systematic approach – take a point from the scenario, assess its implications, suggest a solution, and justify it. There is quite a lot of material in the scenario itself to use to build an answer.

Marks

(a)   1 mark for each relevant point up to a maximum of 3 marks for the value chain

1 mark for each relevant point up to a maximum of 6 marks for the significance
and value of the primary activities

9

(b)   1 mark for each relevant point up to a maximum of 6 marks for identifying
upstream changes

1 mark for each relevant point up to a maximum of 4 marks for identifying how
these changes address problems experienced by DRB

10

(c)   1 mark for each relevant point up to a maximum of 6 marks for identifying
upstream changes

6
—
25

(a)   The value chain of the primary activities of DRB is shown below.

Handling and storing of fully configured inbound equipment	Re-branding of products	Customer collection	Local advertising	On-site technical support
Quality inspection	Re-packaging of products	Technician delivery and installation	Web based enquiries	Back to base support
Inbound logistics	**Operations**	**Outbound logistics**	**Marketing and sales**	**Service**

Inbound logistics

- Excellent **quality assurance** is required in inbound logistics.

- Quality assurance is essential for pre-configured equipment where customers have high expectations of reliability.

- High quality reduces **service costs**, and contributes to **customer satisfaction**.

Operations

- The re-branding and re-packaging operations **add little value to the customer**. They are a relatively minor component in DRB's value chain.

- They are currently being **undertaken in a relatively high cost country** – despite adding little value. DRB should re-consider the current arrangement.

Outbound logistics

- Customer feedback indicates that the installation **service is particularly valued by customers**. However, DRB's market is segmented into domestic and business customers, and the installation service only applies to the smaller (domestic) market.

- Nonetheless, most of DRB's larger competitors cannot offer an equivalent service so this is currently a **source of competitive advantage** for DRB.

- However, if DRB increases the amount it supplies outside its home region then it is likely this **level of service will be uneconomic to maintain**.

BPP
LEARNING MEDIA

Marketing and sales

- Sales and marketing are currently only minor activities at DRB. They **will have to be developed** if the company is to achieve its growth targets.

- The **limited functionality of the website** offers very little value to customers or potential customers.

Service

- Customer feedback indicates that after sales **service is particularly valued by customers**.

- Most of DRB's large competitors only offer an impersonal, off-short call centre service, so DRB's personal service is currently a **source of competitive advantage**.

- However, if DRB increases the geographic area which it supplies then it is likely this level of service will be **uneconomic to maintain**.

(b) **Reduce dependence on single supplier**

Currently DRB **only uses a single supplier** (ISAS), even though it does not have a long-term contract in place with them.

In order to achieve the ambitious growth target that Dilip Masood has set, DRB **will have to increase it sales levels** significantly. It is debatable whether a single supplier will be able to meet this increased level of demand.

DRB should look **to identify a wider range of suppliers** from which it can buy its products. DRB can continue to use web-based suppliers, but as part of their supplier selection they should consider the functionality of the suppliers' websites.

There will be costs associated with identifying and evaluating new suppliers, and establishing trading arrangements with them. However, these costs can be justified because they **remove the risks to DRB's business of sourcing all the products from a single supplier**.

Moreover, other **suppliers may have better systems in place to support and delivery tracking**, and having better control over these could generate savings for DRB in future.

Outsourcing re-branding and packaging to suppliers

DRB should seek to identify suppliers who are willing and able to re-brand and package their products with DRB material at the production plant.

The analysis of the value chain in part (a) identified that the **re-branding and re-packaging activities currently add little value to DRB's activities**. However, they are currently undertaken in a country where wage rates are high and so are likely to be relatively expensive.

If DRB negotiates for its suppliers to re-brand and package its products, it could make some significant cost savings, and instead **focus on the initiatives which deliver value** to their customers and their business.

Contract terms

Because DRB **has no long-term contract with ISAS** it has to pay when it places the order through a credit card transaction on the ISAS website. It does not appear to benefit from any volume discounts.

DRB needs to reconsider the decision not to negotiate any long-term contracts with its suppliers, and explore the possibility that it may be able to benefit from **more favourable payment terms if it commits to a long-term contract**.

However, any decision about long-term contracts needs to be made in conjunction with the decision to look at using additional suppliers. It may not be possible to enter into long-term contracts if DRB begins to trade with a number of different suppliers.

Forecasting of delivery dates

Currently, DRB is **not informed of the expected delivery date when it places an order,** and only receives this delivery information later through a confirmation e-mail from its supplier.

If DRB wishes to increase sales it is likely that they will **need a better planning system** to work out when in-bound products will be delivered.

Consequently, as part of the process for evaluating new suppliers, DRB should seek to **identify suppliers who are able to provide information about delivery dates** prior to purchase.

DRB should also look for suppliers who are able to **provide internet-based order tracking systems** to their customers. This functionality will allow DRB to monitor the progress of their orders.

Streamlining shipping process

Currently two different shippers are used to get products to DRB, and DRB has experienced a **number of problems with missing shipments**. It is time-consuming to track and follow up shipments which are feared missing and, more importantly, DRB has no rights to the goods in transit due to the nature of its contact of shipment with the supplier. Again, it cannot afford to have unreliable in-bound deliveries if it is trying to increase sales.

DRB should consider replacing the two supplier shippers with a **single contracted logistics company** which will collect the goods from the supplier and transport them directly to DRB.

This should reduce **problems with missing shipments**, but will also allow **greater visibility of the progress of the order from despatch to arrival**. It will allow DRB to plan for the arrival of the goods more accurately and schedule its re-packaging accordingly.

All the alternatives discussed so far are ways of refining DRB's existing procurement process. However, it is possible DRB could also achieve growth by introducing an alternative procurement model: the independent marketplace.

Independent marketplace

In the independent marketplace model, DRB place its requirement on an intermediary website.

These intermediary websites are **B2B electronic marketplaces** whose function is to facilitate trade by matching online buyers and sellers. Independent marketplaces allow potential customers to search products being offered by suppliers, and potential customers to place their requirements and be contacted by potential suppliers. In effect the marketplace acts as an online brokerage.

One of the main benefits of such marketplaces is that they promise **greater supplier choice with reduced costs**.

They also provide an **opportunity for aggregation** where smaller organisations (such as DRB) can get together with other companies that have the same requirement to place larger orders to gain cheaper prices (**economies of scale**) and **better purchasing terms**.

The technology in e-marketplaces is increasingly able to **match customers and suppliers automatically**, and therefore reduces the search costs associated with the sell-side model. Independent marketplaces are already quite common in the electronics industry because it is a highly fragmented industry.

This option would be worth considering at the same time DRB is looking to move from having a single product supplier.

Aggregation may also be an option for DRB at a physical level as well as in terms of e-commerce. It may be possible to set up some kind of consortium ordering, delivery and despatch facility – for example, a joint venture warehousing function.

(c) **Improve functionality of buy-side website**

At the moment DRB has a very simple downstream supply chain. Its website is an information source only, and does not have any **interactive facilities for customers to use**.

DRB should consider developing its website so that it shows **product availability**, and **allows customers to order and pay for products securely through the website**.

The website could also be integrated with a logistics system so that orders and deliveries can be tracked by the customer.

A number of DRB's competitors already have such systems so DRB needs to make these improvements to support its growth plans, or even to remain competitive.

Join an independent marketplace as a supplier

It may be beneficial for DRB to participate in independent marketplace websites as a supplier. By doing this it may be able to combine with other suppliers to bid for large contracts that it would not be able to take on individually.

B2C marketplace

DRB should also consider participating in B2C marketplaces such as Amazon. Many organisations use this as a route to marketplace.

Introduce online marketing

DRB only conducts sales and marketing activity through local advertising at the moment, and does not appear to do any online marketing.

However, DRB should consider using online marketing to generate new sales; for example using 'click through' deals (**banner adverts**) on other related sites. This will be particularly relevant if DRB starts selling on B2C marketplaces.

Inventory model

DRB currently uses a **push model supply chain**, which purchases products in advance, re-packages them and then stores them before selling them to customers. This means they can fulfil orders very quickly, but they incur **high storage and financing costs, because they hold high levels of inventory at any time**.

As the business grows, these storage and financing costs will also increase accordingly, as DRB's inventories rise further. This is likely to affect DRB's working capital management.

Consequently, DRB should consider ways of moving to a more **demand driven supply chain model**.

One way it could look to achieve this is to offer products on its website at a discount when they are purchased with specified delivery terms. This would allow DRB to supply to order rather than supply from stock.

However, if DRB is to be successful in moving to a demand-led system it will need to solve the problems it is currently experiencing with its upstream supply chain.

26 Perfect Shopper

Text reference. Chapter 4 (Value chain); Chapter 11 (Section 5 of Chapter 11 covers supply chain management).

Top tips. Requirement (a) asks you to describe the *primary* activities of the value chain of Perfect Shopper. There are 5 primary activities and 5 marks available, so this is a simple case of 1 mark per activity described.

However, be careful when classifying activities between 'Marketing & Sales', and 'Service.' Remember *Perfect Shopper's customers are the neighbourhood shops not individual consumers.* The examiner's answer shows promotions and special offers in Service because Perfect Shopper is providing the material as a service for the shops. Similarly, the ordering process is in marketing and sales, because it is the ordering process and the meeting with the sales representative which encourages the neighbourhood shops to buy goods from Perfect Shopper.

For requirement (b) you need to identify the problems Perfect Shopper is suffering before you can explain how it might re-structure its supply chain. 3 issues have been documented in the independent report showing the franchisees' discontent. But these alone will not provide enough points to earn 10 marks. So you need to look across the scenario as a whole, and keep in mind the value activities you have described in (a) to see how any could be re-structured.

You should adopt the same approach for (c), although as well as thinking of the value chain you should also think of the way Perfect Shopper is managing the franchise.

Again, remember that Perfect Shopper's customers are currently the neighbourhood shops, so one way of extending the downstream supply chain could be to also deal directly with the individual end-user consumers. The examiner's own answers include this option, and the answer below illustrates a couple of possible ways of doing it.

In practice, Perfect Shopper would need to evaluate the commercial logic of implementing such schemes before implementing them, but as the question asks how Perfect Shopper 'might restructure its downstream supply chain' disintermediation is an option you should include.

Easy marks. Requirement (a) is a relatively straightforward application of text book knowledge of the scenario. (b) and (c) required rather more application to the scenario. You have to identify what Perfect Shoppers problems are, and then decide how re-structuring the supply chain will address them. However, if you adopt a systematic approach – identify a problem, diagnose it, and suggest an alterative – you should be able to score quite well here.

Examiner's comments. This question was answered well by most candidates, and many explicitly referenced the case study scenario to their answers.

The only criticism that could be made was that some candidates wrote too much about the primary activities of the value chain. Some wrote two or three pages on this, when only five marks were on offer. Such lengthy answers caused candidates time problems later on, meaning some did not finish the paper.

Marking scheme

			Marks
(a)	Up to 1 mark for each part of the value chain up to a maximum of 5 marks	Max	5
(b)	Up to 3 marks for each relevant point relating to the scenario. Up to a total of 10 marks	Max	10
(c)	Up to 3 marks for each relevant point relating to the scenario. Up to a total of 10 marks	Max	10
			25

(a) The value chain of the primary activities of *Perfect Shopper* comprises:

Inbound logistics. Handling the bulk orders delivered by suppliers and storing them in bulk in purpose-built regional warehouses.

Operations. Splitting the bulk orders into smaller units; re-packaging, sealing and storing these smaller units.

Outbound logistics. Deliver the smaller units to neighbourhood stores every two weeks using specialist local haulage contractors.

Marketing and sales. Provide specially commissioned signs for the shops and personalised sales literature. Undertake the ordering process based on standing order agreed by sales representative.

Service. Provide specialist in-store display units for certain goods. Manage distribution of promotional material and leaflets for all shops.

(b) *Perfect Shopper's* upstream supply chain is relatively short. It makes bulk purchases of branded goods from suppliers and these are then delivered to *Perfect Shopper's* warehouses by logistics companies.

However, it is possible that by re-structuring its logistics arrangements *Perfect Shopper* could also improve brand recognition which is one of the issues raised by the franchisees.

Inbound logistics

At the moment, products are delivered from suppliers to the regional warehouses by **haulage contractors appointed by the suppliers**.

When *Perfect Shopper* was established, it decided not to have its own distribution network. However, it needs to review this decision now, in conjunction with a review of its outbound logistics arrangements.

Obviously there will be cost implications entering into a **contract with a logistics company**, but these may be balanced by a reduction in the price *Perfect Shopper* have to pay their suppliers now that they no longer have to incur the distribution costs. *Perfect Shopper* should perform a cost-benefit analysis to assess whether this option is financially viable.

However, a key benefit of *Perfect Shopper* having its own distribution contract is that it will be able to have the lorries and vans it uses **branded with its own logo**. This will significantly increase its brand visibility.

Outsourcing warehousing and packaging

If *Perfect Shopper* uses an integrated logistics contractor to manage the supply and distribution of their goods, it is possible they could also get the **contractor to supply storage and warehousing solutions for them**.

If this were the case, *Perfect Shopper* could **outsource all its distribution, warehousing and packaging activities to a single integrated logistics company**. It is likely that this will result the *Perfect Shopper* contract being a sizeable one for the logistics company, so *Perfect Shopper* should be able to negotiate a good price.

Nonetheless, *Perfect Shopper* would need to undertake a detailed cost-benefit analysis before deciding to proceed with this plan. Also it would need to **critically evaluate its core capabilities and competences**, to make sure it focuses on the areas most likely to generate competitive advantage for it.

However, if it did decide to proceed, *Perfect Shopper* could **re-position itself** as being primarily a **sales and marketing operation**.

Again, this would allow it more time to focus on improving its **brand awareness**, and **benchmarking** prices against the supermarkets which should address issues raised by the franchisees.

Ordering process

Perfect Shopper should also review **how it communicates orders with its suppliers**. The reliance on the supplier to arrange the delivery suggests that the process is a relatively straightforward one, in which case there may be opportunities for sharing information and allowing the suppliers access to forecast demand. This could be done through an **extranet system**.

Many companies have allowed suppliers access to their information to reduce costs and improve the efficiency of their supply chain, and it is likely that *Perfect Shopper* could benefit from adopting this process too.

Changing product range

The three ideas listed so far assume that *Perfect Shopper* continues to supply only branded goods.

However, it could re-structure its upstream supply chain more dramatically to commission the suppliers to **supply its own brand rather than buying branded goods**.

If this was the case, then the franchisees would be able to offer 'own brand' products to **compete more directly with the supermarkets** who also focus on own brand products. It is likely that the **range of products *Perfect Shopper* supplies its franchisees will increase** if it commissions its own brand.

This strategy would also **increase the visibility of the brand**.

However, if *Perfect Shopper* is contemplating this strategy, much more research is required into its viability before it is selected. For example:

The company will need to assess the prices it can negotiate with the suppliers to produce its own brand.

It will have to consider the extent of its product range, and whether it orders its own brand products alongside, or instead of, the existing brands.

It will have to consider the impact that supplying own brand goods instead of branded produce will have on the image of the company and the franchise.

It will have to undertake market research to identify whether the customers of the neighbourhood shops want to buy own brand products, or whether they prefer to buy branded goods.

(c) **Outbound logistics arrangements**

As we have identified in relation to the upstream supply chain, *Perfect Shopper* should revisit its logistics and distribution arrangements.

Currently, distribution to the neighbourhood shops is **carried out by local haulage contractors**. However, it may be possible for *Perfect Shopper* to negotiate a contract with one single integrated logistics company to carry out both its inbound and outbound logistics.

This **single contract will afford economies of scale**, but it should also provide opportunities for increased brand awareness if the delivery vehicles are branded with *Perfect Shopper*'s logo.

Shop ordering and delivery system

One of the key reasons for the discontent among the franchisees' is the inflexibility of the ordering and delivery system. This is characteristic of the '**push model' supply chain** which *Perfect Shopper* is currently using.

Perfect Shopper should consider introducing a much more **flexible ordering system**, in which shops can make **orders to match demand and deliveries can be made as required**.

However, again *Perfect Shopper* should assess the costs and benefits of such a change before committing to it.

The main reason why *Perfect Shopper* gets discounted prices from the suppliers is because it guarantees them bulk orders each month. However, if *Perfect Shopper* moves to a more **demand driven supply chain there is no guarantee it will still be able to make these bulk orders**. On the other hand, if it doesn't make the change the neighbourhood stores may leave the franchise because they are fed up with having to store excessive, unsold inventories as a result of the inflexible ordering system.

Either way, this scenario illustrates that *Perfect Shopper*'s downstream is going to reflect a **shift in the balance of power towards the neighbourhood stores**, because they are more able to dictate the terms on which they deal with *Perfect Shopper*.

Redeploy sales representatives

If a more flexible ordering system was introduced, there would be **no longer be a requirement for the three-monthly meetings** between the franchisees and the sales representatives. This should mean that either *Perfect Shopper* can **reduce the size of its sales team,** or else it **could redeploy some of them** on projects to **improve the branding and marketing** of the business.

IT systems

If *Perfect Shopper* does move to a demand driven supply chain model, it is likely that there will need to be improvements in IT systems to support it. The neighbourhood stores will need to place their orders over the internet, and then *Perfect Shopper* can consolidate the demand information from all the stores and make its orders from the suppliers.

EPoS tills and sales information

Perfect Shopper already produces tailored marketing material aimed at the end-user consumer. However, it could also **extend its downstream supply chain to include the customers in the neighbourhood stores** more directly.

If electronic point of sale (EPoS) tills were installed in the stores (if they are not already used) then the **stores could feed back sales information to a central data warehouse**, and this would allow *Perfect Shopper* to analyse sales information more closely.

This sales information could then be used both by the storekeeper for his own marketing, but also by *Perfect Shopper* for their tailored marketing material and for their re-ordering processes. If all the stores were connected to a central system in this way, **supplier orders could be generated automatically based on purchasing trends**.

However, if some storekeepers do not have EPoS tills they may not want to migrate to them. And other storekeepers may not want *Perfect Shopper* being able to see their sales figures, particularly as these would include information outside the products offered by *Perfect Shopper*. Either way, the implications of this EPoS initiative would need to be considered carefully so as not to damage goodwill of the franchisees.

Online sales

A second way *Perfect Shopper* could extend is downstream supply chain to **reach the end-user consumer is through establishing an internet-based sales service**.

It is unlikely that individual shopkeepers would be able to establish their own internet-based service. However, *Perfect Shopper* may be able to host an **online marketplace for all its franchisees**, through which the end-user customers can place their orders.

However, there could be a number of issues with this proposal, not least the scope of the online product range because *Perfect Shopper* does not offer a whole-shop service. Other potential issues are the extent to which people who normally shop at their local neighbourhood store will want to shop online; and the impact on the outbound logistics chain of having to deliver individual orders to customers' homes.

Given these concerns, *Perfect Shopper* may decide this strategy is not viable, but it is nevertheless an option it could investigate to see if it could improve the service it offers to its franchisees.

27 Independent Living

Text reference. The value chain is covered in Chapter 4 of the BPP Study Text for exams from September 2015 to 31 August 2016.

Top tips. Both parts (a) and (b) deal with the primary activities of the value chain only. Don't waste time considering the support activities or changes to them in your answer. Also, you should not have drawn the value chain.

Note that part (a) asks you to identify the current primary activities of the value chain for IL, while evaluating changes that could be made to those primary activities in order to improve competitive is the subject of part (b). Therefore, do not discuss any changes to the value chain in part (a) as you will not get any marks for it. Instead, use the time to carefully evaluate the existing value chain, and save the changes you would make to it for inclusion in part (b). Repeating the same information in both parts of the question will not generate marks.

Note also that there are two different contexts: simple, manufactured products, and bought-in products. Make sure you consider the activities for both.

Easy marks. The value chain is a core model which should be familiar to you. In part (a) up to 1 mark was available for simply identifying each of the primary activities – that is 5 easy marks! However, you don't get the marks for just naming them; they do have to be explained to get the marks available. An additional 2 marks were available for applying each activity to IL.

Examiner's comments. Many candidates answered part (a) fairly well, recognising that there were two value chains at IL. However it was also clear that a significant number of candidates were not familiar with the terminology and structure of the value chain.

		Marks
(a)	1 mark for identifying each primary activity (for example, inbound logistics) and up to 2 marks for discussing its application to IL in both contexts (metal scrap collection, supplier delivery) up to a maximum of	Max 10
(b)	1 mark for each significant point (for example, arrange bought in products to be delivered directly to the customer from the manufacturer) up to a maximum of	Max 15
		25

Part (a)

Independent Living (IL) supplies two kinds of products: simple items manufactured in house, such as walking frames and crutches, and larger bought-in items such as mobility scooters. The primary activities of the value chain for these two product sets are shown below:

Inbound logistics: Receiving, handling and storing the inputs.

Manufactured Products (MP): Collecting material from scrap merchants and storage of materials prior to use

Bought-in Products (BiP): Inbound logistics handled by supplier. Products stored in warehouse prior to use

Operations: Converting resource inputs into the final product

MP: Production, testing and packaging of the crutches/walking frames/other small products

BiP: Unpacking, testing and adding logo to products. Repacking and applying IL label to product

Outbound logistics: Storing the product and distributing to customers

MP and BiP: Storage of products, receipt of orders placed online and by telephone, and distribution of products to customers using national courier company

Marketing and sales: Informing the customer about the product, persuading and enabling them to buy it

MP and BiP: Promotional leaflets placed in hospitals, doctors' surgeries and local social welfare departments. Web-catalogue and online ordering system, and product advice and telesales

Service: Installing, repairing and upgrading products, and other after-care services

MP: Not required due to nature of product

BiP: Provided by original manufacturer

Part (b)

> **Top tips.** Remember that this is a **charity** and do make sure that your suggestions are relevant to the context. For example, one of the aims of the charity is to employ disabled people and so the operations cannot be changed too much.
>
> **Examiner's comments.** This part question was answered fairly well although the inappropriateness of some solutions in light of the charitable objectives was not sufficiently explored. Charities are an important part of the "not-for-profit" sector of the economy and their structure and objectives should be understood by candidates.

IL could make the following changes to the primary activities in the value chain to improve their competitiveness:

Inbound logistics:

Manufactured Products (MP):

- Request dealers store material until it is required. This would transfer the cost of storage to the dealer.
- Look into possibility of the dealers delivering metal. This may be cheaper than maintaining their own vehicle.

Bought-in Products (BiP):

- Use a specialist logistics company for inbound and outbound logistics, and possibly storage facilities. This would reduce costs due to economies of scale.

Operations:

MP:

- Difficult to change without compromising the core objective of providing work and income for the severely disabled. IL must retain this process to meet its objectives. This objective could be used as a source of differentiation for IL allowing customers to make an ethical choice.

BiP:

- Request manufacturers affix IL logo and test products then redeploy employees for example into order processing.

- Request manufacturers deliver directly to customers, reducing both delivery and inventory costs for IL.

Outbound logistics:

MP and BiP:

- Encourage use of the website (eg online discounts) to reduce costs and time involved in taking orders over the phone.

- Simplify the telephone ordering process by providing details of products to customers in advance (see marketing and sales).

Marketing and sales:

MP and BiP:

- A physical product catalogue could be produced.

- In addition to marketing leaflets, the product catalogue should also be left in hospitals, doctor's surgeries etc.

- Advertise in newspapers/magazines including details of how to obtain catalogue.

- Investigate possibility of installing Customer Relationship Marketing (CRM) systems to manage donors, for instance by contacting the donors to try to ensure they will continue giving.

- Charity status of IL and details of their work should be on all marketing literature to differentiate it from competitors.

- Website (and possibly tear off slip in adverts) should allow for readers to 'become a regular donor' or 'make a one off donation', thus encouraging donations as well as sales and widening their target market.

- Provide an email update facility. People visiting the website sign up to receive regular updates about the work of IL. These people could then also be targeted as potential donors or fundraisers for IL.

Service:

MP and BiP:

- Expand website to give general support on mobility and independent living.

28 Accounting Education Consortium

Text reference. E-marketing is the subject of Chapter 12 of the BPP Study Text for exams from September 2015 to 31 August 2016.

Top tips. Part (a) asked you to explain how e-marketing varies from traditional marketing. Although the question didn't asked you to mention any models or frameworks, you should have realised that the 6 Is was the relevant framework here.

An effective approach to answering this question was to take each 'I' in turn and then look at it in the context of the scenario.

You should have adopted a similar approach for Part (b) as well. In this case the relevant framework was the marketing mix (7 Ps) and so you should have looked at the 'P's in turn and looked at how e-marketing can help AEC vary its marketing mix.

To score well in the question overall you needed to ensure that you related your answers specifically to AEC, and also that the points you made in (b) did not repeat points made in (a). Using the different frameworks for each part of the question should have helped with this, but the examiner noted that a number of candidates still duplicated points between the two parts of the question.

Marking scheme

		Marks
(a)	Up to 2 marks for recognising the distinction between push and pull technologies in the context of the scenario	2
	Up to 2 marks for issues concerned with interactivity	2
	Up to 2 marks for issues concerned with intelligence	2
	Up to 2 marks for issues concerned with individualisation	2
	Up to 2 marks for issues concerned with independence	2
		10
(b)	Up to 4 marks for issues concerned with product	4
	Up to 3 marks for issues concerned with price	3
	Up to 2 marks for issues concerned with place	2
	Up to 4 marks for issues concerned with promotion	4
	Up to 2 marks for issues concerned with process	2

Credit will also be given for candidates who focus on other 'P's – physical evidence and people

15
25

(a) In traditional marketing media, such as advertising and direct mail, the marketing message is initiated by the **supplier sending out a message** to potential customers. However, there is limited interaction with the customer. In electronic media, **the customer plays a much more active role**, for example visiting a website to find out information about a course or seminar.

Interactivity – Interactivity is a key feature of electronic media, creating a dialogue between supplier and customer. Usually this dialogue is through e-mail exchanges. For example, AEC could use e-mails to provide customers with information about courses which may be of interest to them.

However, in order to do this AEC **needs to know the email address** of potential customers, and the courses they could be interested in. At the moment, AEC only collects personal information about people who wish to download study material; there isn't a facility on the website for **potential customers to register their interest** in a particular course, so that AEC can then send them further details about the course, and any special deals available to encourage them to book on the course.

In this respect, the functionality of AEC's website is more characteristic of traditional media (that is, sending out generic messages) rather than encouraging the interactivity which is characteristic electronic media.

Individualisation – Another characteristic of electronic media is that they allow marketing messages to be **tailored to specific market segments**, whereas with traditional media a single message is sent to all market segments.

For example, some of AEC's courses are for non-qualified candidates preparing for their professional exams while others are for qualified accountants fulfilling their CPD requirements. At the moment, AEC has a single website for all students. However, students could be asked to indicate which courses they are interested in (professional exams, or CPD) when they first visit the website, and then the **information could be filtered** so

BPP
LEARNING MEDIA

that only parts relevant to them are displayed on the screen, or they are taken to different screens depending on their interest.

The interactivity noted above also promotes individualisation. Once students have registered an interest in a particular course, or for a course in a particular location, subsequently e-mails individually relevant to them can be sent out advertising courses for related subjects in the nearest centre to them.

Intelligence – Because advertisers using traditional media do not engage in any dialogue with potential customers, they cannot use their marketing to find out anything about customers' requirements, and also which products or services are meeting them most effectively.

However, website software allows web owners to **record information every time a user clicks on a page**. For AEC, this would be useful to see which pages on its website (ie which courses) potential customers view most frequently. It would also be useful for AEC to see how the number of visitors to a web page translates into them signing up for a course of for study material.

If the **conversion rate from hits (visits) to sales** is low for particular products it suggests there is either a problem with the web page promoting that product (for example, it is not clear to follow), or with the underlying product itself (for example, potential customers are put off by the price of a course).

AEC could possibly even get more customer intelligence by including a **short survey on its website** asking visitors to the site for their feedback, on either the site itself, or the products AEC is offering.

Integration – Advertisers can use the intelligence which they gather from customers to add value to their products or services, by sharing the intelligence with other people across their company.

For example, at the moment only 10% of people who view AEC's downloadable study material proceed to purchase it. The online marketing team should discuss this low conversion rate with other areas of the business to assess whether there is anything that could be done to make the material more attractive to potential customers. These discussions could be with the authors of the material to discuss if it could be made more student-friendly, or with the finance department to see if any discounts or incentives could be offered to make the price more attractive.

Independence of location – By its nature, internet marketing has a global reach and so allows advertisers to access potential customers who were outside the reach of traditional media. Moreover, the internet is also accessible 24 hours a day, 7 days a week so it allows potential customers to find information about a company's products and services outside normal office hours.

The ability to communicate globally may be more useful to AEC for selling study material than selling courses. Although AEC has eight worldwide centres, it is only likely to be practical for students to attend these centres if they live relatively close to them. However, study materials can be sent to students wherever they live.

There are some practical considerations here though, which we will consider further in part (b). The procedures for booking courses do not support the 'global' aspect of the electronic media, for example, because customers cannot book a course online.

(b)   Electronic marketing offers a number of new opportunities which are not readily available, or affordable, using traditional marketing methods. We can evaluate how AEC can take advantage of them by looking at how they relate to some of the key elements of the marketing mix: product, price, promotion, place and process.

Product

AEC offers three different products for sale through its website: training courses for professional qualifications, training manuals for professional examinations; and CPD training courses.

Sample products – The website allows customers to **see a sample of the training manuals before they buy a product**, so that they can see first-hand the quality of the product they are buying.

At the moment, there is no similar way of assessing the quality of the courses in advance of purchasing them, not least because of their intangible nature. However, AEC could include some **video clips or web-casts** from previous courses on the website to give potential customers can get a flavour of the training provided. They could also include some **quotes from students** who have been on the most recent courses to endorse the quality of the courses.

Online courses – At the moment, the courses are only run from eight centres worldwide (three for CPD courses). This is likely to restrict the number of students who can attend courses to those who live relatively near to the course locations. AEC should consider whether the courses can be offered online through **web seminars** and **web casts**, supported by a **virtual learning environment** and **online tutors**. Even so, AEC may not be able to access a truly global audience, because customers will need **fast broadband access** to make these web seminars practical, but this option may allow AEC to increase its student numbers internationally.

Product size – At the moment, students pay a fixed fee of $180 which gives them access to a complete set of manuals for all the professional examinations. However, some students may not wish to purchase all the manuals at the same time. Therefore AEC should consider allowing candidates to buy individual manuals as an alternative to buying the whole set. (In part (a) we talked about customer intelligence. This is an area where AEC could benefit from customer research, to understand whether students would prefer to buy individuals manuals or to buy the whole set at once).

Product updates – It is likely that a number of AEC's training manuals will need updating each year to reflect syllabus changes or changes in legislation. AEC can use the website to publicise any such changes. Moreover, if it had a database of email address for students who had registered an interest in the material which was affected, AEC could send a message to the student telling them the new, updated version was available.

Price

Bulk discounts – In the section on price, above, we mentioned the option of allowing students to buy individual manuals rather than having to buy the whole set. However, if AEC takes up this option it could still offer a discounted fee for buying the whole set in one go.

Pay per access – At the moment, pay a one-off fee to download the material regardless of how much of it they want to use. An alternative approach may be allow students to pay 'on demand'. For example, they would only be charged when they access the material, and the level of the charge would depend on how many pages they access. The pricing structure could be explained on the website.

Price transparency – The internet allows potential customers to compare AEC's prices to its competitors very easily. Therefore AEC needs to make sure its prices are competitive in the marketplace.

However, this price transparency could also be problematic for AEC because it makes it harder to offer **differential pricing**. Candidates in poorer countries are going to be less able to afford the standard prices than candidates in richer countries.

AEC could consider **developing local websites for different countries** (with local domain names), translating the prices into local currency and possibly adjusting prices to reflect the income levels in the countries. If the content of the website was also translated into the local language, this, in conjunction with the local domain name would make it harder for people from other countries to compare prices internationally.

Dynamic pricing – It is much quicker and easier to change the price of products advertised on a website than it would be for prices advertised through traditional media. AEC could take advantage of this to vary the prices of its courses over time, in the same way that budget airlines do. For example, when a course first becomes available its price could be relatively cheap to encourage people to sign up. Then as the course becomes more fully booked the prices could rise. However, there remain a number of empty spaces on a course shortly before it is due to run, the price could be reduced to try to encourage late bookings.

Promotion

One of the main differences between electronic media and traditional media is the interactivity of the customer in seeking out information. Potential customers now use the internet to search for information about possible products.

Search engine optimisation – AEC needs to ensure that if potential customers enter a web search for accountancy manuals or courses then AEC's product offerings come near the top of the resulting listings.

The way AEC's website is constructed will affect the likelihood of it appearing on the first page of search engine listings.

Click throughs – AEC should also investigate the possibility of building links to its website from other sites. For example, where it offers professional qualifications it may be able to build a link from the qualification provider's website. Although AEC will have to pay a commission for the number of visitors who come to its site via the link, it should still prove a beneficial marketing tactic, because it will increase the number of visitors to AEC's website as well as improving its search engine ranking.

Currently, AEC's website appears to be a standalone site with no links to any other sites.

Banner advertising – AEC should also publicise its products and services through banner adverts. Although the logic behind these is no different to traditional press adverts, AEC advertising itself in more places will increase customer awareness about its products and services.

Place

Global reach – Although the internet allows AEC to communicate globally, in practice this global reach is likely to be more useful in selling the downloadable manuals than the training courses. Customers can download and print off the training manuals wherever they live.

However, there are currently only eight training centres worldwide, and of these only three offer CPD courses. Therefore, AEC's **training courses are only likely to be attractive to people who live relatively close to the centres**.

If AEC wants to maximise the global reach of the electronic media it offers, it will either need to consider opening new centres, or, as we have discussed earlier, provide courses and tutorials online.

Process

Website functionality – At the moment, AEC's website is predominantly only an information site; for example, students can find information about courses on the site, but **cannot book and pay for their course online**.

One of the features of the internet as an advertising medium is that operates 24 hours a day, 7 days a week. However, because course students have to contact an administrator to process their booking and payment details, this 24/7 flexibility is likely to be lost.

Interestingly, the website does allow students to pay for the downloadable material online, but AEC should consider adding the functionality to allow them to book and pay for their courses online.

Online queries – There is also no evidence that students can register any queries online. This is another feature which the marketing manager should consider adding to improve the consistency of the overall marketing mix.

29 ATD

Text reference. Least squares regression and time series analysis are covered in Chapter 2 of the BPP Study Text for exams from September 2015 to 31 August 2016.

Top tips. Part (a) – The fundamental issue at stake with this question was whether or not a company can reliably forecast future sales based on previous quarter sales. Past results provide no guarantee of future performance. Furthermore, for most companies, sales are likely to be affected by a greater range of factors than time alone. This undermines the usefulness of least squares analysis, as – for example – the impact of seasonal variations is not considered.

By contrast time series analysis does take account of seasonal variations which can be used in forecasting future values. The big issues with time series analysis is that no one universal approach exists in extrapolating trends.

Tutorial note. In respect of time series analysis the trend value of 148 provided in the answer is to illustrate the usefulness of time series as a method of predicting future values. It is important to note that 148 is an arbitrary figure, you could have used other figures here to help support your answer which would have been equally valid.

Marks

(a)   1 mark for each relevant point up to a maximum of 5 marks for an explanation of the least squares regression data. This may include:

– The expression of the equation (y = 125.022 + 1.84x)
– A predicted value using the equation
– The calculation of the coefficient of determination

1 mark for each relevant point up to a maximum of 5 marks for an explanation of the times series analysis data. This may include:

– A predicted value using a reasonable assumption
– Explanation of residual variation
– Explanation of seasonally adjusted values

1 mark for each relevant point up to a maximum of 5 marks for relevance of the approaches to ATD

15

(b)   1 mark for each relevant point up to a maximum of 10 marks

10

25

(a)   Historically, ATD's approach to forecasting its sales revenue has been determined by the sales manager through a combination of 'experience, intuition and guesswork'. This has resulted in increasingly inaccurate forecasts being produced. To combat these shortcomings ATD has now moved toward forecasting through the preparation of formal estimation methods – least squares regression and time series analysis.

Least squares regression

Least squares regression involves forecasting future values of 'y' according to the line of 'best fit'. This is the straight line which 'best fits' the data by minimising the differences between the actual values and those predicted by the calculated line.

Least squares regression requires one data set to be classed as being an independent variable with the other set classed as the dependent variable.

In the context of ATD, 'time' is the independent variable (denoted as x) and 'sales made' is the dependent variable (denoted as y). The intercept point on the y axis is denoted by a, which is the value of y when x equals zero. The gradient of the line (denoted by 'b') is the amount of the predicted change in the value of y for each change in the value of x.

The business analyst calculated ATD's line of best fit as:

y = 125.022 + 1.84x

This equation can be used to predict a value for the next quarter (2013 quarter 3):

y = 125.022 + 1.84(15)

y = 152.62

As 'b' is shown as a positive figure this illustrates that the sales trend is gradually going up.

The correlation between changes in the value of y and x can be measured statistically, using the coefficient of correlation 'r'. This has a value between -1 and +1, and the closer the value of r is to -1 or +1, the stronger the correlation between x and y. A value of -1 indicates that there is perfect negative correlation between x and y, while a value of +1 indicates a perfect positive correlation between both variables. As the value of x increases, the value of y also increases (and so the line of best fit is upward sloping). The information provided states that r is 0.253, suggesting a weak link connection between the two variables.

BPP
LEARNING MEDIA

The coefficient of determination (r^2) is the square of the coefficient of correlation. It measures the proportion of the total variation in the value of y that can be explained by variations in the value of x. At ATD the coefficient of determination is 6.4% (0.253 × 0.253), meaning only 6.4% of variations in sales (y) is caused by time (x).

This suggests that the two data sets are not closely related, and also suggests that the least squares regression analysis technique may not be appropriate for ATD in forecasting sales. The predicted sales figure for quarter three in 2013 is 152.62 which is significantly lower than the actual sales made in quarter three of the prior year of (169). The predicted sales figure is also not in line with the general sales trend which indicates that sales are gradually rising.

There are further problems which undermine using linear regression analysis for forecasting. There is an assumption that historical data can be used to forecast what will happen in the future. However, as illustrated above, this may not be appropriate. An additional problem with linear regression is that it looks to predict a straight line. However, the sales trend may not be a straight line.

It is also assumed that the value of one variable, y, can be predicted or estimated from the value of one other variable, x. In reality, the value of y might depend on several factors. In the case of ATD the underlining trend suggests that sales are rising over time. This may have been influenced by a competitor increasing their own prices which in turn has made ATD's offering more appealing.

Time series analysis

Time series analysis is concerned with defining trends through the calculation of a moving average. The trend series at ATD has been calculated by taking the average of quarters 1-4 and quarters 2-5 and comparing this against the actual sales achieved. The overall difference between the actual value and the trend is caused by seasonal variation + residual variation. The trend line can then be adjusted to reflect seasonal variations, thereby highlighting the residual variation for any individual quarter.

Future values can be forecast through the use of extrapolation techniques. This involves extrapolating the trend line and then adding or subtracting the seasonal variation as necessary. The main problem with this approach, however, is that no one universally agreed approach is used in extrapolating the trend.

If the trend value of quarter one of 2013 was 148, this would result in a predicted value of 133.3 (148 – 14.70). This is just under the actual recorded sales value of 137. By incorporating the seasonal variation into the predicted values, this could help ATD manage its inventory and production levels more accurately.

Time series analysis for use in forecasting does have its limitations. As with the least squares regression analysis, it is based on past data. Furthermore, it assumes that the seasonal variation for each season is the same amount each year which may not be correct.

However, unlike least squares regression, time series analysis does recognise the influence of seasonal variations which increases its usefulness.

Of the two techniques, time series analysis is likely to be the more appropriate for ATD in forecasting its future sales.

(b)

> **Top tips.** A good approach to adopt when attempting part (b) is to think about the behavioural benefits that using budgets can bring and then relating these back to the current issues ATD is experiencing.

What is a budget?

A budget can be viewed as an internal tool used by an organisation to assist in the achievement of its long term objectives. Budgets are commonly used in the short term to allow managers to take action regarding the resources within their functional areas of responsibility.

The main focus in ATD appears to be on achieving sales targets. The sales budget is therefore critical to the preparation of all other budgets. The level of anticipated sales will drive the organisation's requirements in terms of raw material levels and production staffing levels.

Benefits of budgeting

Accountability

A well-prepared budget will help an organisation to set realistic targets across all departments. This would support ATD in improving its approach to forecasting. Realistic targets place a degree of accountability on functional management for their departments, for example, the head of the production division can monitor the monthly spending on raw materials against the departmental budget. This is beneficial as it may allow the manager to take corrective action should costs rise beyond the intended level.

Where managers are provided with clear targets related solely to their area of responsibility this may serve to boost their morale, motivating them to work harder as their own performance can be closely measured against the budgets set. Central to improving motivation is to ensure that all targets set are robust and achievable, otherwise there is an increased risk that demotivation may occur.

Flexed budgets

In the event that sales targets are missed, it would help to assess divisional performance if divisional budgets were flexed accordingly. When sales targets are not met this will have a direct impact on the level of purchases needed to satisfy customer orders. In such instances the purchases budget should be flexed to reduce the level of materials needed this should lead to a more accurate indication of the production managers performance.

For example, ATD may miss its sales targets for a quarter however the production manager may still have been able to significantly reduce the target cost of raw material purchases. It would therefore clearly be wrong to ignore this factor when appraising the performance of the production manager.

The current approach adopted by the CEO at ATD appears to penalise departmental managers when sales targets are missed even though department managers cannot influence sales figures. This is illustrated by the comment made by the production manager, 'I am working tirelessly to keep costs down, but my only reward is that I cannot replace one of my best purchasing administrators who left in the last month'.

Motivation amongst the departmental managers may be further improved if they were able to participate in the budget-setting process. Departmental managers at ATD claim the current approach leaves them feeling 'powerless and undervalued'. However, allowing the departmental managers to be more involved in target setting would help to illustrate that their experiences and opinions are valued.

ATD may benefit from increased goal congruence as senior management can convey what is expected of departmental heads while also improving the understanding of target setting and co-ordination between departments.

Cost cutting at ATD

The CEO at ATD has been very bold in introducing the cost cutting measures in response to the missed sales targets. The decision to cut costs without formalising these in a budget means that the CEO has no way of knowing whether the cost savings are being achieved.

Moreover, the decision to 'ruthlessly cut costs' may actually prove to be detrimental to ATD's performance. The freeze on the recruitment of new staff may lead to a situation where departments are not able to operate effectively if they are under-staffed. The same is also true of the decision to cut back on the marketing initiatives. Reduced marketing is likely to result in fewer sales being achieved. To evaluate the effectiveness of the cost cutting measures the CEO should have specified cost reduction targets which could have been monitored through the use of variance analysis. This illustrates the need for a formal budgeting process at ATD.

In summary, short term cost savings are likely to adversely affect ATD's longer term performance and damage the company's chances of achieving its objectives.

30 CoolFreeze

> **Text reference.** The topics examined in this question are covered in Chapter 14 (finance) of your BPP Study Text for exams from September 2015 to 31 August 2016.
>
> **Top tips.** Note from the marking scheme that in order to gain all the marks available for this question you will have to explain how the spreadsheet has been constructed and the methods used as well as evaluating its use.
>
> Note that the requirement asks you to present your answer as a briefing paper for the managing director. You should therefore ensure you use the appropriate format to structure your answer and a suitable tone.

Marking scheme

		Marks
(a)	Spreadsheet construction: 1 mark for each relevant point up to a maximum of 5 marks	
	Analysis of spreadsheet model and explanation of moving average time series: 1 mark for each relevant point up to a maximum of 7 marks	12
(b)	Up to 3 marks for the flexed budget	
	Up to 2 marks for each appropriate variance up to a maximum of 8 marks	
	Up to 2 marks for the overall summary and other considerations (such as overhead costs)	13
		25

(a) **Explanation and evaluation of the forecasting spreadsheet**

Prepared by: Business Analyst

For: Managing Director, CoolFreeze

Date: January 2011

This briefing paper aims to explain and evaluated the forecasting spreadsheet you have provided.

The spreadsheet has been prepared using moving averages, a valid and well-established approach for analysing past results and forecasting the future.

Explanation of the construction of the spreadsheet

The technique used to construct the spreadsheet is based on average figures in the time series.

Column D is calculated by adding up the first four figures (56,70,74,60) and then adding this total to the total moved on by one quarter (70,74,60,60). This value is then divided by 8 (the number of values in the total calculation) to give the average value in column E. This represents the trend of the time series.

The figures in column F are the variation of the trend from the actual sales figures. These variations are analysed in part 2 where a seasonal variation is calculated.

This seasonal variation is then subtracted from the total variation of each quarter to determine the random or residual variation (column H).

Column I is a check column to ensure that the total of the trend plus seasonal plus random variation comes to the original sales figure.

It is hard to identify where the forecast figures come from. They are roughly in line with the observed trends and represent a very small increase on the previous year (less than 1% growth).

Analysis

Time series is based on historic data and cannot be used to predict sudden changes in the marketplace. However, the sales staff had already expressed doubts over the figures due to the weakening economy and the availability of cheap foreign imports. This indicates that a greater assessment of the external environment should have been carried out as part of the forecast.

The trend figures also indicated that growth had been weakening. Growth from 2006 to 2007 was around 11% (based on quarter 3 trend figure), yet from quarter 2 of 2008 to quarter 2 of 2009 growth was less than 1%. The final two actual sales figures for 2009 were, in total, the same as for 2008 (150 units). The forecasts did reflect this weakening, however there is little to suggest that the drastic fall in sales in quarter 2 of 2010 could have been predicted from the data alone.

In the last three quarters there was a sudden increase in the random variations. This may have indicated a change in the external environment and so perhaps should have been given greater consideration when the forecast was prepared.

The forecast could have been improved by using exponential smoothing (applying a series of weights to the data) so that the older data is given lighter weighting than the more recent data.

Overall, time series analysis is an established method of analysing past data to forecast the future, however, it is better suited to stable environments where historical data is likely to be representative. The concerns of the sales manager should have been taken into account and built into the forecast. The changes in the economic environment meant that the technique successfully used in the past produced optimistic forecasts that could not be achieved.

(b)

> **Top tips.** This question part deals with the relatively simple concepts of budgets and variances, however, remember that the majority of the marks here are not for endlessly carrying out calculations. You should be able to demonstrate that you understand what the variances are telling you and what this means in context of the scenario. You should be able to present this information clearly and draw sensible conclusions both for each variance calculated and for the results overall.

Despite warnings from the sales manager, there was no evidence that the budgeted sales figure for quarter two of 2010 of 83 units would not be achieved. Actual sales had been in line with budget for the past three quarters and there was no clear reason to change the forecast.

The budget can be flexed to see what would have happened had the planned level of output been 50 (actual sales) rather than 83 (planned sales). This is shown below.

Output (sales)	50 units
Sales revenue	$50,000
Raw materials	($17,500)
Labour	($16,250)
Fixed overheads	($18,000)
Operating profit (loss)	($1,750)

The below compares budget, actual and the flexed budget.

	Budget	Actual	Flexed budget
Units	83	50	50
Price	$1,000.00	$900.00	$1,000.00
Revenue	$83,000.00	$45,000.00	$50,000.00
Raw materials	($29,050.00)	($15,000.00)	($17,500.00)
Labour	($26,975.00)	($15,750.00)	($16,250.00)
Fixed overheads	($18,000.00)	($18,000.00)	($18,000.00)
Operating profit	$8,975.00	($3,750.00)	($1,750.00)

The following conclusions can be drawn from this.

Sales volume

The sales volume variance for quarter one is adverse. The sales manager is responsible for this, however he did raise concerns that the budget was too optimistic for the current climate.

Changes in the external environment appear to be the cause of this decline as customers are reluctant to invest in new machinery in difficult trading times and foreign imports provide a cheaper alternative.

Sales price variance

The sales price variance for quarter 1 is also adverse as lower prices have been charged. This is again the responsibility of the sales manager. It is likely that the prices have been cut to be in line with foreign imports. The sales manager warned that the imports were undercutting by around 10% and the lowering of prices from $1,000 to $900 would be consistent with this.

Materials variance

The materials variance is favourable (actual costs are lower than flexed budget). There could be two reasons for this.

1. The sales manager may have reduced the amount of raw materials used, however with a well-established product such as this it is unlikely.

2. The procurement manager may have negotiated lower prices for raw materials. This has offset some of the reduction in CoolFreeze's own prices noted above.

Labour variance

The labour variance is favourable (actual labour costs were lower than the flexed budget labour costs). Again there could be two reasons for this.

1. Labour costs may have been reduced by paying lower wages. This could be possible if some employees have left and been replaced by cheaper employees. Personnel would be responsible for this saving.

2. The number of hours required to produce each unit may have fallen. The production manager would be responsible for this saving.

Further information would be required to accurately establish who deserves the credit for this saving.

Overhead costs

Overheads have remained in line with the original budget.

Summary

It is not accurate to suggest that 'we have all made mistakes' as the majority of the problems lie with the sales volume and the sales price which are the responsibility of the sales manager.

Raw materials and labour costs have been well controlled with positive variances achieved. Overheads have also remained at their budgeted value.

31 Clothing Company

Text reference. Chapter 13 (Project management) of your BPP Study Text for exams from September 2015 to 31 August 2016.

Top tips. A sensible way to approach (a) is to identify the problems with the website re-design project and then think, firstly, what a business case is and how it could have helped prevent them and then, secondly, what a project initiation document is and how it could have helped prevent them.

The scenario identifies a number of problems to do with the objectives of the project and the project scope not being defined. You should use these as examples to illustrate how a business case and a project initiation document could have helped control the project.

Requirement (b) asks how effective *project management* could have further improved the project so it may be useful to consider the duties of a *project manager*, and then analyse how these could have helped this project. Planning, communication, monitoring and control, and quality control are all key responsibilities for a project manager, and likewise they are areas which would have benefited this project.

This is the approach which the answer below uses. However, an alternative approach would be to consider the stages of the project life cycle – definition, design, delivery, development – as a framework and consider what further improvements could have been made at each stage of the project.

Again, the scenario offers a number of ideas which are relevant for (b); so you need to make sure your answer is specifically relevant to this case rather than just being a general analysis of how project management can improve project processes and outcomes.

Note that (b) asks how both the *process* and the *outcomes* of the project could have been improved, so you need to address both of these aspects in your answer. When you plan your answer, you should treat each of them separately to make sure that you deal fully with both processes and outcomes.

Easy marks. The scenario highlights the problems that affected the project quite clearly, so you should use the scenario to help with (a).

In part (b), if you knew the duties of a project manager, it should be relatively easy to apply them to the scenario to see how the project could have been improved.

Examiner's comments. This question was poorly answered. While some candidates appeared to have a theoretical understanding of this part of the syllabus, they failed to apply their knowledge to the circumstances described in the scenario. The question did not ask for general descriptions of the contents of a business case and a project initiation document, but how they could have helped prevent some of the problems documented in the scenario.

Similarly, the scenario gave candidates plenty of opportunity for the basis of a good answer to the second part of the question. However, most candidates again opted for a restricted, theoretical answer which did not use the context of the scenario. Some candidates also repeated points from the first part of the question, failing to note that the requirement specifically asked for 'further improvements'.

Marking scheme

			Marks
(a)	Up to 2 marks for each relevant point relating to the scenario; up to a total of 15 marks	Max	15
(b)	Up to 2 marks for each relevant point relating to the scenario; up to a total of 10 marks	Max	$\frac{10}{25}$

(a)

> **Tutorial note.** The answer below starts with a summary of the contents of business case and a project initiation document, and how they are useful in project management. This is included for learning purposes, because when this exam was sat it appeared that very few students knew what a business case or a project initiation document should contain.
>
> You should not have included the same level of detail in your answer, although a brief summary of what each of the documents is and what they are used for would have been a good way to start your answer.

Business case. A business case is a summary of why the project is needed, what it will achieve and how it will proceed. Before a business case is approved, it should be evaluated to ensure that a project has value, that it will be properly managed, and that a firm has the capabilities required to deliver the benefits expected from the project.

Preparing a business case should ensure that the value and risks in the proposed project are made clear before it is undertaken and the delivery of the outcomes and benefits can be traced and measured. In this way, preparing a business case would have provided a frame of reference for the website re-design project which appears to have been lacking from the scenario.

Project initiation document. The project initiation document (or project charter) complements the business case and gives authorisation for work to be done and resources used.

A project initiation document should include the scope of the project in terms of project objectives and ultimate deliverables; project start date and finish date; project organisation including roles and responsibilities; and constraints and targets that apply to the project.

The initiation document also has an important role in internal communication within an organisation.

Preparing a project initiation document should ensure that a project has a complete and sound basis before there is any major commitment to the project; and it acts a base document against which the progress of the project can be assessed. This will be useful in dealing with any change management issues or viability issues.

Preparing a business case and a project initiation document would have addressed the following problems which affected the website re-design project:

Objectives and success criteria. The business justification of the project is poorly defined. The marketing manager (MM) identifies some general objectives such as 'increase sales revenue' and 'improve our market visibility' but these are poorly defined objectives because they are **not specific or measurable**.

For example, the MM should have prepared a **cost-benefit analysis** at the start of the project, quantifying how much the website would increase sales by as a result of the work done, and the timescale for the increase in sales. In preparing this analysis, the MM should also have explained the assumptions behind these figures, and to demonstrate how and the functionality of the website will increase sales volume.

It would also have been useful to prepare a **summary budget** for the project, because this would have shown the resources required to implement it.

The Board (or whoever is responsible for approving the business case and the budget) could then **challenge these assumptions before they commit resources to the project**, and by doing this they can prevent resources being invested in projects which are unlikely to benefit the company.

The business case and the cost-benefit analysis should be reviewed throughout the project to ensure that the project is not straying from its original justification.

Also, at the end of the project, the business **benefits should be reviewed against the original business** case to assess whether they have actually been delivered.

Because this project had no specific or measurable objectives set for it, it would have been impossible to assess the success of the project, even if it had not been withdrawn.

Project scope

The **scope of the project being undertaken is not clear.**

The term 're-design' has been **interpreted differently by the Board and MM**. The Board feel that a website 're-design' does not include development and implementation of new software, although MM feels that it does.

There is also **confusion about the scope of the project among the members of the project team**. The draft design produced by the image consultant was criticised for being too similar to the current website. MM and the product range manager 'expected it to do more.'

If a business case and project initiation document had been prepared, the scope would have been clarified in the process of preparing them.

Details of roles and responsibilities

It seems likely that the project sponsor is the MM, although this is not clearly stated. If a project initiation document had been prepared, it would have stated **who the project sponsor was**.

At meeting 4, the range manager makes a decision to accept a new design, but at meeting 5 this re-design was rejected by the MM. This incurs a cost in both time and resources, but was an avoidable problem, arising out of a **confusion over whose responsibility it was to approve new designs**.

If the project sponsor role had been properly defined and allocated (as it should have been in a project initiation document) then the range manager would have known he did not have sufficient authority to sign-off changes to the project deliverables.

In addition, if project roles had been formally allocated it is likely a **project manager would have been appointed** and made responsible for delivering the project. There is no indication of a project manager in the scenario, and the lack of a project manager is a major reason why the project will drift and take longer than anticipated.

Resources committed to the project

There is no evidence that the resources **available to the project have been discussed or agreed**. Consequently, problems emerge when the Board's decision to launch on 1 March causes the technical developer to express concern that he does not have enough developers to deliver the website on time.

In this case, the problem of not identifying resource requirements at the start of the project was compounded by not setting a project timetable either, which is what prompted to the Board to impose a deadline of 1 March.

Risk analysis

Well managed projects document potential risks to the project, and **identify the key risks which need to be managed**. Plans can then be prepared either to prevent significant risks from materialising, or for minimising the effect of them if they do occur.

There is no evidence of any risk management in this project, because **problems are dealt with on an ad hoc basis as they occur**. Non-compatibility of the website with the popular browsers should have been identified as a critical risk to the project, but it appears not to have been addressed until it was too late.

Assumptions and constraints

The scope of projects is often constrained by resources – usually **costs** and **time**.

In this project, **costs and budgets were not agreed at the start of the project**, not least because no cost-benefit analysis was prepared. Consequently, **no-one knew what the resource constraints in terms of costs were**, and cost were allowed to rise until the finance director intervened.

Project timetable

No timescale for the project was set at the start either. Consequently, the Board 'expressed concern' about the time taken to produce the re-design, and this led them to look more closely at the way the project was being conducted.

An **expected finish date** for the project should have been given in the project initiation document. This would then have provided a reference to judge whether the project was running behind schedule or not.

Schedule of work and project milestones

The project could have been made easier to manage by breaking it down into a series of stages, with an associated list of project milestones.

There is no evidence of any detailed planning for this project, and consequently there was no structure to the way the project was undertaken.

Technical constraints

The technical developer raised a number of issues during the project. At meeting 4 he 'explained that elements of the drafted re-design were not technically feasible.' This led to changes to the design which delayed the project.

Similarly, at meeting 6 he 'expressed concerns that the suggested design would not work properly with all web browsers'.

These delays and problems could have been avoided, if **technical constraints had been detailed** in the project initiation document.

(b)   Effective project management could have improved the process and outcomes of the website re-design project in a number of ways. Many of these **could have been achieved by having a project manager**.

Detailed planning

The project had no detailed plans, and this meant the project was very difficult to review and control. A **project needs a detailed plan as a baseline to review progress and performance**.

If there had been a detailed plan the process of delivering the re-designed website would have been much more structured. There are a number of practical applications which can assist project planning, for example:

- **Work breakdown structure**
- **Network analysis (critical path analysis)**
- **Gantt chart**
- **Project management software**

However, there is no mention of any of these being used in the scenario. If they had been there would have been far more control over the project, and consequently a far greater chance that the re-designed website would have worked.

Communication

The **Board were not kept informed about the progress of the project** and only became aware of problems when they realised the time being taken on it, and the finance director became concerned about the costs.

The Board should have been kept informed with any problems the project was facing. The re-designed website failed because the project team could not deliver to the timetable the Board imposed on them. However, if the Board's expectations of the project had been managed better, then a deadline may not have been imposed in this way.

Monitoring and control

The **failure to alert the Board to problems** with the website also suggests failure of monitoring and control by the project team, although this is exacerbated by the lack of a project plan to measure progress against.

Effective project management would have required the Board to be informed of the progress of the project. In his way they would have some control over the project and could **suggest actions to deal with problems and slippage in the project.**

However, the scenario suggests that all monitoring and control aspects of project management were completely absent from this project, meaning that the Board were unaware of any of the problems the project was suffering.

Realistic timescales

The budget and timescale which the Board approved on 4 January does not appear to take into account the complexity of the remaining work or the resources available to do it. Effective project management **requires realistic timescales to be established** so that a good quality product can be delivered at the end of a project.

Quality control

A consequence of the unrealistic timescale imposed by the Board is that the website was not ready for launch on 1 March. This lack of readiness was clear at the final meeting on 24 February, but the MM still decides to proceed with the launch.

Effective project management requires an understanding of the **trade-off between quality (functionality) and timeliness (deadlines)**. There may be times when it is better to deliver a good quality product slightly late rather than a poor quality product on time.

In this project, if the launch had been delayed slightly to give the technical developer time to make the software more robust and compatible with the web browser, the new website could ultimately have been successful – rather than being withdrawn completely, potentially writing off all the time and costs invested in it.

Appointment of deputies

Progress on the project was hampered by the **absence of key personnel at meetings 3 and 4** and the inappropriate sign-off by the product range manager of the technical design at meeting 4 in the absence of the technical developer.

This could have been avoided by **each of the key personnel having a deputy who could represent them at meetings** they could not attend, and who had a similar skill set to the person they were deputising for.

Leadership and teambuilding

The failure to appoint deputies may to attend meetings may also be symptomatic of the fact that the people carrying out the website project were working as individuals rather than as a team.

This is another area where having a project manager would have benefited the project, because a project manager would have encouraged the team to **work together more** and **communicate more effectively** with each other.

Flawed cost benefit analysis

The cost-benefit analysis which the MM belatedly produced is flawed in two key respects.

Firstly, there is **no supporting analysis to justify the assumptions** underpinning the benefits, and no sensitivity analysis showing the outcome if different levels of extra sales are achieved. In particular, there is no explanation as to why the year 4 and year 5 figures are higher than year 3. It is possible that these have simply been inflated to justify the project.

Secondly, the **future cash flows have not been discounted**. Future cash flows for all the projects that the clothing company is considering should be discounted at the same discount rate, so that the Board can **compare the expected returns on different projects**, and if necessary ration available capital according to the expected returns of each project.

32 Tillo Community Centre

Text reference. Project management is covered in Chapter 13 of your BPP Study Text for exams from September 2015 to 31 August 2016.

Top tips. Do not waste time writing all you know about the structure and content of a project initiation document in part (a). The question asks you to **analyse** how the document would have helped to address the problems identified in the scenario. Address each problem under a separate heading to focus your answer and maximise your score.

Marking scheme

		Marks
(a)	1 mark for each appropriate point up to a maximum of 13 marks	13
(b)	1 mark for each appropriate point up to a maximum of 12 marks	12
		25

(a)

A number of problems were encountered during the design and construction of the community centre which could have been better understood and perhaps resolved had a formal 'terms of reference' (project initiation document) been developed at the outset. These are discussed below.

Confusion surrounding the project's objectives

The local authority appears to not understand the difference between project objectives (in this case to build the centre by June 2011) and business objectives (in this case to deliver payback in four years as required by the Private/Public investment policy).

The project sponsor demonstrates this misunderstanding by calling for an inquiry into the performance of the project manager from the construction company due to the centre not delivering the anticipate benefits.

The project manager from the construction company is responsible for meeting the project objective of building the centre which he did so, ahead of schedule and within budget. He is not in control of the business objectives of that centre which extend far beyond its being built. Processes such as sales, marketing and the successful operation of the centre are required to meet these objectives and the project manager cannot be held at fault for this.

This problem stems from a failure of the local authority to distinguish between the objectives of the project and the wider business objectives that the result of the project (ie the building) will help to achieve. A failure to allocate responsibility to those wider objectives contributed further to this misunderstanding.

Future projects should clearly distinguish between project objectives and business objectives and the responsibilities for each should be allocated and communicated.

Quality of internal painting

Although most of the scope of the project was well defined, there appears to be confusion over the required finish quality of the internal painting and no documentation relating to this could be found. Now that the project is complete, this misunderstanding appears to be irreconcilable. The missing letter that the construction company claims sets out the intended finish was not counter-signed by the project sponsor. The construction company must ensure that this mistake is not repeated in future projects and that any subsequent adaptations or clarifications to the specification are fully documented and signed by both parties.

The local authority should also learn from this in future projects and demand that any changes are counter-signed by both parties to prevent such misunderstandings.

Failure to adhere to certain labour and sourcing requirements of the Private/Public policy

The new project sponsor raised concerns that the construction company had used subcontracted labour and had sourced less than 80% of timber used in the building from sustainable resources. These requirements of the Private/Public policy were not communicated to the construction company at the start of the project. In future, the local authority should ensure that any such requirements are incorporated into the terms of reference of the project to prevent the occurrence of similar misunderstandings.

Lack of accountability due to failure to define responsibilities

A project sponsor is responsible for decision making, provision of resources, considering and agreeing changes, promotion of the project within the local authority, and accepting the project upon its completion. This role was well understood by the original project sponsor. The successor, however, did not appear to understand her responsibilities suggesting that they had not been clearly defined within the local authority. Not only did she fail to focus on important issues such as determining where the responsibilities for delivering the business objectives lay, bust she also did not promote the project within the authority and subsequently tried to blame the builders for these failings.

To avoid future misunderstandings, responsibilities should be clearly defined and any failure to adhere to those responsibilities must be addressed.

Failure to define requirement for local authority resources and support in advance

Although most resources were well defined, this was overlooked and the lack of local authority staff willing and able to discuss disabled access meant that the contractors were left to handle this alone. The contractors did, fortunately, correctly interpret the relevant legal requirements and the new centre was deemed to meet accessibility requirements. However, this was very risky with serious consequences had the contractors misunderstood the requirements and such an approach should not be taken again in the future.

Resources and support such as this must be well defined in advance; with a back-up procedure in place should they be unavailable during the project.

(b)

Observable benefits

The realisation of observable benefits, such as increased staff morale, can only be determined by judgement or experience by someone who is qualified to make such an assessment. Staff morale could perhaps be assessed via an independent survey carried out both before and after the community centre is up and running, but the results of this and any benefit obtained can only be assessed once the project is complete and the building has been in place for some time.

The impact of benefits like this should never be devalued or underestimated, for example the increased motivation could well lead to reduced staffing costs as a result of lower staff turnover and the likely improvement in customer service may lead to the use of more facilities or more repeat visits.

However, such observable benefits should not be included in the business case. This is for several reasons:

It is not clear why the move to the new centre would bring about improved staff morale and motivation and there is no guarantee that it will do so. In reality, due to the upheaval of moving and the inevitable teething problems the new centre will experience, the reverse could very well be true at least in the short term.

If a satisfaction survey did indicate an improvement in staff morale and motivation, there would be no way of knowing if the move to the new centre was actually responsible for this shift as each employee will be affected by their own personal external factors which cannot be controlled for the sake of the survey.

The business case has included a benefit of £25k per year under staff morale, which presumably relates to increased customer usage and reduced staff turnover. However, if there is an increase in customer use, it would be impossible to determine how much of this could be attributed to the increased motivation of the staff rather than other factors such as the improved facilities. Staff turnover savings is also unlikely to be particularly high as the centre only employs 20 staff, 16 of which have been therefore for over 5 years. Combined with the ongoing deep recession faced by the country it would seem that staff retention is not currently a problem.

Measurable benefits

Measureable benefits, such as increased income, is an area of the business where performance could be measured, but the impact of the improvement cannot yet be quantified. Current income can be measured now and again in the future, however, we do not know with certainty how much income will be increased.

The basis on which the figures included in the business case were calculated needs to be established, and more information is needed to back up the large increases anticipated in years 3 and 4. It also seems unlikely that this benefit would be seen before the centre has had a chance to build up its reputation, nor that it would not be linked to any associated increase in costs.

Quantifiable benefits

Quantifiable benefits, such as energy savings, differ from measureable benefits because it is possible to quantify the degree of improvement before the change is actually made. Building constructed under the Private/Public investment policy arrangement must meet specific target energy levels and so the design of the building and the construction methods employed should ensure these targets are met. The likely energy savings can therefore be predicted fairly reliable by comparing these targets to the energy usage of the current building. Actual savings, however, can only be known once the building is operational.

Financial benefits

A quantifiable benefit can be converted to a financial benefit by applying a financial formula (such as cost or price) to that benefit. Assuming that the new building meets the minimum target energy levels, it might be possible to re-classify energy savings as a financial benefit. However, this would still be based on assumptions (for example, the new building may exceed the minimum levels required) and real energy savings can only be assessed once the building has been in use for some time.

A true financial benefit would be rental savings as the amount paid for both properties is known in advance. This is recorded corrected in the projected payback.

Overall, while measurable benefits are important and should be included within the business case, it is only appropriate to include financial and quantifiable benefits in the payback calculation.

Where measurable benefits are included in the business case, this should be supported with details of the underlying assumptions used to quantify these and information relating to the likely probability of the realisation of such benefits.

To improve the reliability of some benefits and potentially re-classify them as, at least, quantifiable benchmarking against similar centres could be carried out.

33 Lowlands Bank

Text reference. Project management is covered in Chapter 13 of the BPP Study Text for exams from September 2015 to 31 August 2016. Harmon's process-strategy matrix is covered in Chapter 9.

Top tips. Project management has been examined fairly regularly, and is a core part of the P3 syllabus. This question should not be too difficult if you have studied the material carefully.

As always, it is really important to use the material you are given and produce an answer that is specific to the LDB bank. Don't write everything you know about good project management in the hope you will gain some marks. Instead, read the material carefully and pick out the specific elements that have been used. Refer back to the material in your answer and provide specific quotes from the material to back up the points you make.

Examiner's comments. Part (a) was poorly answered in two ways. Firstly, too many candidates developed answers that discussed project management in general and did not apply them to the scenario. Second, a significant number of candidates seemed to answer a different question – identify the principles of good project management – to the one set in the examination.

Project management appears to be a significant area of weakness despite its relevance to accountants and real-world businesses.

Marking scheme

			Marks
(a)		Up to 1 mark for identifying an element of good project management (for example the allocation of a sponsor). Up to 2 marks for describing the significance of each of these elements within the context of the scenario up to a total of 12 marks	12
(b)	(i)	Up to 1 mark for each significant point (for example, describing the implications of a quadrant) up to a maximum of 4 marks	4
	(ii)	Up to 1 mark for each recommendation and up to 2 marks for the justification of each recommendation up to a maximum of 3 marks for each process initiative. Three process initiatives gives a maximum of 9 marks.	9
			25

Part (a)

The elements of good project management that helped make the branch rationalisation project successful include:

Experienced project manager: The project manager was experienced and had worked for the bank for many years. He was assigned to the project full time allowing him to focus entirely on the project.

Dedicated team: The project team were also seconded full time to the project. This prevents them becoming distracted by day-to-day pressures. Where project teams are also expected to continue with their usual role, the project is much less likely to succeed. This is because it has a long term focus, whereas day-to-day tasks usually require more urgent attention. The project will inevitably take a lower priority.

Mix of team: The team consisted of twelve members of staff, six of which came from each of the banks that existed prior to the acquisition. This meant that they had a good understanding of each of the banks, and that the team was 'politically' balanced, not favouring one over the other.

Project sponsor: The Operations Direction, a high ranking employee in LDB, was appointed as project sponsor. This indicates management support for the project and shows that they are committed to its success. His high level within the organisation also means that he has the authority to make key decisions relating to the project and authorise both decisions and expenditure. This prevents the project from drifting.

Defined objectives: The aims of the project were clearly defined and quantified at the start of the project (to cut the number of branches by 20% and branch employment by 10%). By doing this, it was easy to measure whether or not the objectives were met. It also meant that everyone involved in the project knew exactly what they were working towards.

Defined constraints: It was specified at the start of the project that there would be no compulsory staff redundancies. This meant that those working on the project were clear about what was outside the scope of the project and prevented the implementation of inappropriate solutions.

A timescale of 2 years was also set at the start of the project. This meant staff knew how long was available for them to complete the project and kept them focused. If there is no clear time frame, projects can easily expand or lose focus.

Potential slippage identified: The timescale was carefully monitored, and both potential slippage and its cause were identified and dealt with early on. This allowed for a revised schedule and deadline extension to be authorised.

Formal review: At the end of the project, both a benefits realisation review and a post-project review were carried out. This allowed the team to prove that the project's original objectives had been met. It also ensured any lessons learnt were fed back into the project management system, preventing future teams making the same mistakes.

Part (b)

> **Top tips.** The question asks you to recommend a solution from a choice of three that are given to you in the scenario. The three choices are outsourcing, purchasing a software package solution and bespoke development. In that case, you should not recommend that LBD automate a process, for example, just because that is the generic option suggested by Harmon's matrix.
>
> **Examiner's comments.** This part of the question was answered slightly better than part (a), although the suggested solutions were often unjustified any many marks could not be given for very brief answers.

(i)   Harmon's process-strategy matrix charts processes using their complexity on one axis, and their strategic importance on the other. These axes form four quadrants. Harmon recommends the following strategies for processes which fall into each of the quadrants:

Low strategic importance, low complexity: These are simple stable processes which add little business value. They should be automated in the most efficient way possible.

Low strategic importance, high complexity: These processes are complex and dynamic, but not part of the organisation's core competences. They are too complex to automate, so outsourcing is the best option.

High strategic importance, low complexity: These are simple but important processes that should be automated to improve efficiency and reduce cost.

High strategic importance, high complexity: These are complex, dynamic and high value processes which generate competitive advantage. They involve human judgement and expertise that cannot be automated. The strategy for this type of process should be careful process improvement focusing on the people involved.

(ii) 1. *The integration of two bespoke payroll systems currently operated by the two banks into one consolidated system*

Strategic importance: Low, although payroll is a necessary process, it does not add any significant value to the end customer.

Complexity: Low, simple, straight-forward process that can be automated to some extent.

Strategy: Purchase a software package solution and transfer data from both existing systems to the new one, however, any possible issues with transferring the data will have to be taken into consideration.

2. *The updating of all personal desktop computer hardware and software too reflect contemporary technologies and the subsequent maintenance of that hardware*

Strategic importance: Low, this process is unlikely to form part of the core competences of the bank.

Complexity: High, expertise will be required to carry out this process. Too complex to automate.

Strategy: Outsource the work to a specialist technology company.

3. *Development of processes, systems and software to support new private personal banking service for wealthy customers*

Strategic importance: High, as high net worth customers have been identified as an important growth area. This process could potentially be a source of competitive advantage.

Complexity: High, as this is a personalised service which will involve human interaction and judgement.

Strategy: Bespoke in-house development. The potential of this process to deliver high future profits suggests that it should be given high priority and resources should be focused in this area.

34 OneEnergy plc

Text reference. Ratio analysis and the use of financial information are covered in Chapter 14 of the BPP Study Text for exams from September 2015 to 31 August 2016.

Evaluation procedures for software packages are covered in Chapter 10.

Top tips. Although the question scenario provided a range of financial information, you should not simply have used this to calculate ratios. To score well in this question, you needed to assess what the ratios (and the financial information more generally) could tell you about the company's performance.

Examiner's comments. Overall, candidates produced reasonable answers to part (a). However, there was a wealth of information in the scenario that many candidates did not use.

Marking scheme

		Marks
(a)	Up to 1 mark for each non-ratio based observation up to a maximum of 5 marks	
	Up to 1 mark for each ratio based observation up to a maximum of 5 marks	
	Up to 3 marks for summary and integration of answer	13
(b)	Up to 1 mark for each relevant point up to a maximum of 3 marks for each failing	
	Four failings required	$\frac{12}{25}$

(a)   There are a number of aspects of Ritesoft's accounts which could have indicated cause for concern, and therefore should have prompted further investigation.

Goodwill – The **largest element of Ritesoft's non-current assets** is goodwill, rather than any tangible assets. This could be a problem for Ritesoft if it needs to raise additional funding, because lenders prefer to lend against tangible assets, such as property.

Also, Ritesoft's goodwill has **increased significantly** from 2007 to 2008 ($133k to $215k), and the reason for this increase needs investigation. It would suggest Ritesoft has made an acquisition, but the details of the acquisition and how it was financed need to be investigated further.

Increase in trade payables – Ritesoft's trade payables have increased proportionally significantly more than its receivables. This may indicate that Ritesoft **is trying to delay payments to suppliers** as a means of helping to finance its cash flow.

The fact that Ritesoft has **reduced its bank overdraft** may also support this suggestion. However, if suppliers start to think that Ritesoft is struggling to make payments as they fall due, then they may look to reduce Ritesoft's credit terms.

Increase in cost of sales – Sales revenue has actually increased by more than 10% between 2007 and 2008, but cost of sales has increased by slightly more, leading to a reduction in profit. It looks likely that increased staff costs are largely responsible for this cost increase, because the number of staff has increased from 70 to 90 (nearly 30%).

It would useful to investigate why **staff numbers have increased nearly 30%** yet turnover has only increased just over 10%. If Ritesoft has made an acquisition in the year, it may be that some of the staff came from the business acquired, but there is a risk there is now over-capacity in the combined business.

Retained profit – The extracts from the accounts show that no profit has been retained. This would suggest that the profit is being distributed to the shareholders, and will have to be investigated.

ROCE – The return on capital employed has almost halved, however the levels of actual profit have remained approximately the same. This indicates that the profit was maintained via a high level of borrowing.

Note that while comparing Ritesoft's financial information between the two years in the accounts can help evaluate its financial position, it would also be useful to compare Ritesoft's position with other companies in the software industry, and to see how its performance compares with the industry average. For example, it would be useful to compare Ritesoft's receivables and payables days with those of other companies in the industry.

(b)

> **Top tips.** The question asked you to examine four ways in which OneEnergy failed to follow a proper evaluation procedure in the **selection** of the software package. Unfortunately, a number of students who sat this paper instead chose to right about the features that make up good quality software and completely missed the points about the company failing to evaluate alternatives or the organisation structure of the supplier.
>
> **Examiner's comments.** Many answers to this part question were disappointing and disorganised. In many instances this seemed to reflect unfamiliarity with this part of the syllabus.

In addition to the failure to formally evaluate the financial position of RiteSoftware, OneEnergy failed to follow a proper evaluation procedure in the selection of the RitePay software package in the following ways:

Organisational structure and ownership

OneEnergy failed to investigate the company, its shareholders and directors. A Companies House inquiry, or perhaps even a simple Google search, would have highlighted the possible conflict of interest of the HR director. OneEnergy should then have either rejected the supplier, or obtained a formal declaration of interest from the HR director for inclusion in the supplier evaluation.

Functional requirements

The functional requirements of the software were not fully defined at the outset, leading to costly amendments and implementation delays. Both current and anticipated future requirements should be considered at the evaluation stage. Had this been done, the gap between the requirements and the software capability would have been identified. This would have allowed OneEnergy to assess how well the package meets the requirements, and how compromises might be managed.

Non-functional requirements

The **user-friendliness** of the software package was not evaluated, leading to users experiencing problems in understanding the terminology and structure of the software. User competences and expectations should be defined upfront for comparison against the software. This means the package can be properly assessed and any training costs can be built in.

Evaluation of alternatives

OneEnergy purchased the software without evaluating alternative solutions. This means they have no way of telling whether RitePay is the best solution for them. There may be other providers that better meet the needs of OneEnergy or provide better value for money. This will be of concern to shareholders who will expect the company to make best use of their money.

A formal **tender process** should have been carried out, allowing OneEnergy to directly compare the different solutions both against each other and against their own specific, pre-determined requirements.

35 Bridge Co

Part (a)

Text reference. Selecting software packages is covered in Chapter 10 of the BPP Study Text for exams from September 2015 to 31 August 2016.

Top tips. It is very tempting with a question requirement such as this rush in and to start to answer a different question to the one actually set. As the examining team's comments highlight, too many candidates simply went ahead and evaluated the problems that the Custcare software had caused Bridge Co. This was not what was required. What the examining team were asking for was a practical suggestion of a process for evaluating, selecting and implementing a software package solution and explaining how this process would have prevented the problems experienced at Bridge Co with the Custcare software.

When planning your answer to such questions it is often useful to take a step back and break the requirement down into its component parts. Using key words from the requirement is often a good way to get started, for example noting the words 'evaluation, selection and implementation' on your page. This is how we have structured our answer below. This approach should help to ensure that you keep your answer focused on the matter in hand and avoid unnecessary waffle.

Starting with evaluation, you could have asked yourself the question, if you were going to purchase a software package for personal use what would you need to do in order to evaluate whether this was the right option for you?

Given the likely costs involved you may require some form of plan to ensure that the software you choose ultimately does what you want it to. Failing to have a plan setting out what you want from a piece of software is likely to make it hard to know if the selected package will deliver the benefits that you require from it. In a business context such a plan is likely to take the form of a business case, which will provide a financial and non-financial evaluation of the proposed investment.

As this exercise illustrates, breaking down the requirements and prompting yourself with some general thoughts should make it easier to apply your knowledge to the scenario. The same logic can then be applied to the process of selection and implementation.

Easy marks. There was 1 mark available for each relevant point made up to a maximum of 15 for this requirement. As we discussed above it should have been possible to gain some of these marks by making some practical points about the three stages involved in the process of software procurement.

Marking scheme

		Marks
(a)	1 mark for each relevant point about stages in the process of software procurement up to a maximum of 15 marks	15
(b)	1 mark for each relevant point made for discussing the relative advantages of a software package over a bespoke solution up to a maximum of 10 marks	10
		25

Process for evaluating, selecting and implementing a software package

Stage One: Evaluation

Need for evaluation of options

The process of evaluation is focused on determining whether an 'off-the-shelf' software package would achieve its intended purpose. In the case of Bridge Co, such an evaluation is likely to focus on whether the Custcare software would have been appropriate to the needs of the company in automating its approach to CRM. Consideration of Harmon's process-strategy matrix could have been of some use at this stage. The scenario provides no insight into whether Bridge Co considered an alternative (for example outsourcing) approach to purchasing a software package. In terms of Harmon's process-strategy matrix , CRM software is likely to be relatively complex and of medium strategic importance.

The high initial purchase costs and subsequent fees suffered by Bridge Co in introducing the Custcare software indicate that a **fuller evaluation was needed prior to the purchase** decision being made.

Business case

In most organisations, it is standard practice that a business case is formed prior to the approval and commencement of a major project. A business case should set out the financial case for undertaking the project. This evaluation provides management with the opportunity to fully assess the merits and costs involved. At Bridge Co, all capital expenditure in excess of $20,000 needed to go through the company's internal authorisation process which included the submission of a formal business case.

In the case of the Custcare package, this process was not followed as Teri Porter managed to reduce the price of the software to fall under the capex threshold of $20,000. The lack of a business case resulted in a failure to consider the associated costs of introducing the software package. The cost of offering staff training on the new system was completely omitted as Teri Porter decided that she could personally train Bridge Co employees in how the application worked. Furthermore, the $10,000 cost of migrating data between systems had to be paid from Bridge Co's operational budget.

Business cases often act as a useful point of reference for management when determining whether a completed project has actually delivered the benefits intended at commencement. In this case, benefits are likely to have focused on the financial aspects of introducing the software, for example reducing Bridge Co's customer management costs. Intangible benefits here are likely to have focused on improving customer satisfaction through the creation of closer customer relations. Bridge Co's failure to produce a business case has left the company's management unable to assess whether the introduction of the Custcare software has actually resulted in any benefits at all.

Defining Bridge Co's requirements

It is evident from the scenario that Teri Porter was the driving force behind the decision to purchase the software. Teri's enthusiasm for the Custcare package was based on an assumption that Bridge Co's CRM requirements were similar to those of her previous employer.

Teri's assessment of the company's software requirements may, in part, have been correct, as Mick Kazinski commented that 'we were happy with the functionality and reliability of the Custcare software'. It is however, clear that consideration of the technical and performance requirements were completely overlooked. The slow running speed of the software resulted in the need for certain reports and queries to be aborted, while the 'inability to interface it to the order processing system' has damaged user confidence.

Bridge Co would have benefited from considering the type of relationship it, as a customer, would want from a software supplier. This should have helped management identify its own expectations in terms of supplier support and the ease of getting user support when needed as opposed to contacting the Custcare helpdesk in Solland outside of Deeland working hours. Mick Kazinski's frustration is evident commenting 'I just wish we had chosen a product produced by a company here in Deeland'.

Stage Two: Selection

Competitor offerings

Bridge Co's management would have benefited from the creation of an Invitation to Tender (ITT). An ITT is a document issued to potential suppliers which details the information about the project to be undertaken, in this case the provision of CRM software. Such information is likely to focus on the objectives and scope of the project as well as detailing the project imperatives. Issuing an ITT would have forced Bridge Co's management to consider using alternative suppliers to Custcare.

Such an approach may have shown that other suppliers were in fact better placed to meet the company's needs by offering a superior product to the software offered by Custcare. This would have also ensured that the process of selecting a software supplier was conducted thoroughly after due diligence.

Negotiations

It is evident from the scenario that the management at Bridge Co failed to fully assess the terms of the standard contract that they entered into with Custcare. Bridge Co has suffered as a result of this failing in two ways. Firstly, in the event of a conflict over contract terms between Bridge Co and Custcare the process for dispute resolution has been based on the laws of Solland not that of Deeland, which creates problems for Bridge because it is not familiar with commercial law in Solland.

The second issue with the contract concerns the fact that only Custcare employees are permitted to undertake data migration work, thereby restricting the ability of Bridge Co to hire in cheaper, third party experts. Bridge Co's management team should have undertaken a full investigation of the contract with a view to negotiating and amending these terms. Ultimately, amending contractual terms after agreement can be very difficult in reality.

Stage Three: Implementation

Training and data migration

Implementation is concerned with bringing the selected software into operation. Successful implementation of the new CRM software at Bridge Co would have involved effective user training, the provision of complete system documentation (for example a user help guide) and a fast and efficient process of data migration. Failing to pay for the Custcare run training courses clearly hindered Bridge Co's implementation of the system. This issue has been further compounded as Teri Porter has now left the company meaning that the only person supposedly able to use the software is no longer on hand.

Furthermore, the process of data migration had to be funded from Bridge Co's operational budget, which proved to be more expensive than it need have been. The incompatibility of the file formats between Bridge Co's existing software and the Custcare application, coupled with the slow running speeds, indicates that a process of user acceptance testing should have been conducted by staff at Bridge Co prior to taking full ownership of the Custcare software. User acceptance testing should have identified these deficiencies earlier on.

Part (b)

Advantages of adopting a software package compared with a bespoke software solution

Speed

One of the main advantages of selecting an 'off-the-shelf' software package is the speed at which it can be implemented. This is fundamentally due to the fact that the software is already in existence and only needs to be purchased. By contrast, a bespoke solution needs to be developed from the customers' requirements. This approach lengthens the lead time between identifying a need and implementing a solution. This situation was evident in the case of Bridge Co and the need for new CRM software, as the company's own IT department were unable to look at Teri Porter's requirements for 18 months. The Custcare package was available for use within 3 months.

Functionality

Standard software packages are very often produced in line with best practice requirements in particular industries. Furthermore, they generally have higher levels of functionality than maybe experienced when using a bespoke solution. As mentioned in part (a), the management at Bridge Co were impressed with the Custcare package. Mick Kazinski commented that 'it seemed to do all the things we would ever want it do and, in fact, it gave us some ideas about possibilities that we would never have thought of'. As Bridge Co had never used a CRM system before the purchase of the Custcare software gave the company the ability to instantly gain access to comparable systems operated by competitors in the construction industry.

Lower cost

Cost is often the main driver in attracting organisations to purchase a standard software package. Software packages are generally cheaper than bespoke solutions as the development costs are spread over a greater number of customers. The associated costs of developing bespoke software solutions are often prohibitive for many entities. This is illustrated in the scenario as the known financial cost to Bridge Co of purchasing the Custcare software (and associated data migration costs) amounted to $29,995. By contrast Bridge Co's own IT department quoted an internal transfer price of $18,000 for just defining the sales and marketing teams user requirements. It is highly likely that by the time the costs of developing and testing the bespoke solution had been completed that the total cost would have been significantly greater than the cost of the Custcare solution.

Higher quality

It is often the case with standard software packages that due to the higher number of customers using them that 'glitches' and problems are identified quicker after implementation, which in turn enables the software supplier to resolve them faster than may be possible in the case of a bespoke solution. In the scenario there appears to be no issue with the reliability and robustness of the Custcare software.

36 ASW

Marking scheme

		Marks
(a)	Up to 1 mark for each relevant point up to a maximum of 3 marks for each strategy	10
(b)	Up to 1 mark for each relevant point up to a maximum of 6 marks	6
(c)	Up to 1 mark for each relevant point up to a maximum of 9 marks	9
		25

Part (a)

Project Manager could request an extension to the deadline

Initial delays caused by CaetInsure – The early delays in the project were caused by the absence of key CaetInsure staff, and the changes in user requirements in the re-insurance module. This meant that the full system specification was sign off three weeks later than initially agreed.

However, the sales account manager suggested that this time could be made up in programming, which weakens ASW's case if they request an extension in the deadline now.

Nonetheless, the project manager could return to CaetInsure and tell them that it has not possible to catch up with the proposed schedule, and so the initial slippage caused by CaetInsure is going to mean that the deadline cannot be met.

New product launch – One of the reasons why CaetInsure insisted on the penalty clause is because they have linked the delivery of the software with the launch of a new product. We are not told how much CaetInsure have publicised the new product and the launch date, so it is possible that the launch date could be deferred without too much impact. In which case, the proposed product launch should not be seen as an obstacle to moving the deadline for the software product.

Reasons not to request an extension to the deadline

Delay has increased – The proposed delay is now longer than the three weeks incurred at the specification stage. Consequently, it will be difficult for the project manager to argue that the delay was caused by solely CaetInsure not ASW. If ASW have to accept at least part of the liability for the delay they will be liable to the penalty clause, either in part or in full.

Penalty clause – If ASW have to pay the penalty clause then this could seriously affect the profitability of the project.

Additional unexpected delays – If the project manager requests an extension to the deadline, he will have to be very confident in the revised deadline he proposes. If he subsequently has to request a further extension, ASW's credibility with CaetInsure could be severely damaged. As the project timetable does not allow any time for any faults to be corrected after systems testing or acceptance testing, it seems likely that there will be some further delays, because it is likely that some faults will be found during these tests.

Reduced scope of the software solution

Isolate re-insurance functionality – It appears that the re-insurance part of the system has been a cause of delays throughout the project, not least because this is likely to be one of the most complex parts of the software.

ASW's basic software package can be used immediately, and customisation and testing are only necessary to deal with specific customer requirements.

Deliver software in stages – Therefore, it may be possible to deliver the majority of the software on time, with the re-insurance functionality being added later. In this way, ASW can focus their resources on testing, documenting and training for the parts to be released first, allowing them to be delivered on time.

However, ASW need to assess whether this reduced functionality will affect the proposed new product which CaetInsure wants to launch. This is something which the project manager needs to discuss with CaetInsure as soon as possible. The project manager also needs to establish whether releasing the software in stages will have any other business impacts for CaetInsure.

Reasons for not reducing scope

Potential penalty clauses – The project manager needs to establish whether the penalty clauses may still be invoked if CaetInsure only receive a partial system. It may be necessary to renegotiate the contract to allow for a stepped penalty according to how much of the project remains outstanding at the original delivery date.

Additional costs – If the product is launched in stages, this will create additional costs for ASW in relation to **regression testing**. When the second phase of the software is added, ASW will have to carry out a detailed test to ensure that the new release does not unintentionally affect the software which has already been delivered.

Equally, introducing the new software in two phases could affect the **data migration**, and may require the data migration programmes being rewritten. This again could have cost implications.

Reduced quality of the software testing

Reduce testing of standard software – ASW could make up some time by reducing the length of time spent on System Testing.

It appears that much of the software is a standard package which is then tailored for specific functions. Consequently, large areas of the software will have already been tested before, by actual users in other businesses who are already using the ASW solution.

In addition, individual programs or modules for the CaetInsure package will have already been unit tested, before they are system tested. So, even if system testing is curtailed, no areas of the system will be completely untested, although some will not have been tested for functionality and usability.

Run system testing and acceptance in parallel – The overall time of the project remaining could be reduced by running system testing (by ASW testers) in parallel with acceptance testing (by CaetInsure testers).

Reasons for not reducing testing quality

Impact of faults found in acceptance testing – System testing would allow ASW to identify and correct faults in the product before it is given to CaetInsure. So if acceptance testing is run in parallel with system testing, CaetInsure's testers may find significantly more faults than they would otherwise expect to. This is likely to reduce their confidence in the software, and may even make them suspicious that ASW are cutting corners to try to make up time.

Issues with version control – If faults are being identified by both system and user acceptance testers at the same time this could cause problems in maintaining version control over the software. If versions of the software are released with faults which have already been reported and fixed in earlier releases, this could again lead to ASW losing confidence in the software.

Request more resources

Use more testers and writers – The current project plan does not indicate how many system testers ASW are planning to use, or how many authors are writing the user manual. It may be possible to add more resources so that the activities can be completed more quickly.

Automate and outsource – Alternatively, some of the testing could be automated or outsourced to specialist testing companies, thereby freeing up ASW's testers to focus on the most important areas of the software.

Reasons for not introducing more resources

Learning time – If new staff are added to the project team there could be a delay while the existing team members have to bring the newcomers up to speed. If the testing requirements are specified clearly and in detail, then new testers may be added quite quickly and with little disruption. However, if the requirements are not well specified, this learning process may be more time-consuming.

Slack time – In addition, there is some slack time between the scheduled completion of the user manual and the start of the training. Therefore, there is scope for some slippage to occur in writing the manual without delaying the overall project.

Cost – If additional resources are added to the project this will increase its costs above the original budget. This will reduce the profitability of the project, and if too many additional have to be added they may even make the project unprofitable.

Part (b)

There are potential limitations of all the solutions the project manager could use to deal with the slippage problem on the CaetInsure project. Therefore the project manager should look to reduce the slippage by **using several of the strategies** together, to combine the best aspects of each strategy.

Reduce scope – Instead, ASW should look to reduce the scope of the initial release, and introduce the software in two phases, with the re-insurance module being released in a second phase. The initial delays in the project were caused by the unavailability of CaetInsure's staff to sign off the system specification, particularly in relation to the re-insurance module, and so this will strengthen ASW's position in asking for the initial scope to be reduced.

Additional resources – The length of time taken for system testing could be shortened by adding additional resources to the project. However, the number of testers added needs to balance the costs incurred with the **level of risk** which would incur if the test coverage was reduced. If some areas of the system are essentially still 'off-the-shelf' they will need less testing than areas which have been substantially customised.

Rescheduling activities – At the moment, it appears that ASW are waiting for the system testing to be complete before they start writing the data migration programs. However, the migration programs for individual parts of the system could be written as those parts of the system pass their systems tests, rather than waiting to write the migration programs one the whole system has passed its system testing. ASW cannot reschedule the acceptance testing, because it is performed by CaetInsure.

Recommendation

On balance, and on the basis of the factors that he can control, the project manager should look to **add some additional resources to the project and reduce the test coverage in areas where risk is lower**. If the customer is prepared to accept a reduction in the initial scope to reflect past delays, without imposing a penalty clause, he should also ask for this, but this will be a bonus.

However, the project manager should not try to delay the initial delivery date, because the client has given significant importance to that date, and the penalty clauses could severely damage the profitability of the project.

Part (c)

A post-project review is a formal review of the project that examines the lessons that may be learned and used for the benefit of future projects. They help the organisation to avoid making the same mistakes twice.

Post-project reviews are carried out after the project has been completed and aims to measure the success of the project by considering:

- If the project was completed on time and within budget
- Whether the project was successfully managed, or if problems and bottlenecks were encountered
- If these problems could arise on future projects
- How well the team performed, both individually and as a group

The whole team should be involved in the post project review and the overall findings should be formalised into a report which should include the following.

- A **summary** of the findings highlighting any area where the process, structures and tools used to manage the project were unsatisfactory

- A **cost-benefit review** which compares the forecasted costs and benefits to actual costs incurred and benefits achieved

- **Recommendations** as to how the project management process could be improved

ASW have encountered significant problems with delays and project slippage which could result in the payment of costly penalties and compromised quality as the later stages of the project are likely to be rushed to improve the likelihood of completing the project on time. A post-project review could help ASW to identify the root cause of the problems and make changes to their processes to avoid similar delays in future projects. Possible improvements that such a review may help ASW make to their processes include:

Realistic time-scales. The review may identify that the time-scales defined at the outset and agreed with the client was not feasible, perhaps due to false assumptions or perhaps even intentionally ambitions in order to win the client given the stiff competition referred to in the scenario. In these cases delays would be inevitable. The finding would help ASW to revisit their planning processes to determine how more realistic estimates can be made.

Minimising client delays. The scenario states that the client caused three weeks delay at the sign-off stage. As the development by ASW does not begin until this stage is complete, it maybe found that timetabling delays could be avoided by excluding anything pre-sign off from the timetable, therefore making the start of 'week 1' the day that sign-off is obtained. However, in this case, the problem is that the client needs the software to tie in with the launch of a new product and so may not accept this approach. It is likely that the review would find that improved communication processes between ASW and their clients could avoid delays such as this occurring in the first place.

Clarity of information. The scenario states that the client caused three weeks delay at the sign-off stage and attribute blame for the slippage to the client for this reason. However, the post-project review may identify that the underlying reason for this stemmed from overly-complex information relating to the specification and system requirements provided by ASW. This may prompt ASW to find a simpler way of presenting this information to clients, thus reducing client confusion and associated delays.

Contract clauses. Penalty clauses written into the contract may mean that ASW are charged a significant financial penalty for delays that were out of their control (ie caused by the client). Although penalty clauses may sometimes be appropriate, ASW's experiences in this case should prompt them to carefully review the wording of any similar clauses required in subsequent projects. Clauses should be carefully phrased to ensure ASW are not liable where delays are caused by the client. This both ensures ASW are not unfairly charged for something out of their control and also protects them should a client decide to cause delays intentionally in order to benefit from the payout.

37 The Institute of Independent Analysts (IIA)

Part (a)

Text reference. Cost/benefit analysis and the terms benefit owner and benefits realisation are covered in Chapter 13 of the BPP Study Text for exams from September 2015 to 31 August 2016.

Top tips. The trick to answering this type of question well is to take the time to carefully read the requirement verbs. This was particularly important as you were asked for a 'critical evaluation' of the financial case for the proposed project. This requires you to adopt the mind-set of a qualified accountant, and means approaching the information provided in the scenario with professional scepticism. This involves closely questioning the detail in the project proposal. Ask yourself the following 'based on the information do the costs in the NPV and the assumptions on which they were determined seem realistic?' Although the solution set out below is structured differently, a useful approach that you could have adopted here would have been to classify the different costs/benefits under the headings of observable, measurable, quantifiable and financial. This approach may have helped to highlight that some of the benefits are not quantifiable and therefore should not have be included in the NPV.

This approach should help to ensure that you adequately query such proposals and avoid producing a generic answer.

Easy marks. There were 15 marks available for this requirement. Marks were awarded for making appropriate points in respect of the financial case of the featured project. 6 marks were on offer for points related to the costs of the project, with a further 6 marks for considering the benefits.

Provided that you had carefully read the scenario and focused your answer on both of these elements you should have been able to produce a balanced answer.

Examiner's comments. 'Similar questions using debateable data and assumptions to support a business case, have been posed in the past and they will be posed again in the future! However, a significant number of candidates were unable to critically evaluate the numbers, with too many candidates repeating the information in words…'the figures show that the initial software costs are $200,000', or passing some subjective assessment unsupported by information given in the scenario; for example 'the security figures look a bit high'. This question was the least popular of the option questions. Some candidates did get good marks, but too many produced inappropriate or sketchy answers that showed little understanding of costs, benefits, investment appraisal and the construction of a business case'.

Marking scheme

		Marks
(a)	1 mark for each appropriate point up to a maximum of 6 marks for issues concerning costs	6
	1 mark for each appropriate point up to a maximum of 6 marks for issues concerning benefits (including benefit classification)	6
	1 mark for each appropriate point in the overall evaluation up to a maximum of 3 marks	3
		15
(b)	1 mark for each appropriate point up to a maximum of 4 marks for each concept (benefit owner, benefits map, benefits realisation)	10
		25

General observations

The investment appraisal included in the IIA's business case indicates that project to introduce the computer-based assessment will generate a positive net present value (NPV) of $10,925. On this basis alone the project appears to be financially viable.

The basis on which the NPV working was prepared does, however, raise some concerns. The NPV uses a discount rate of 8%, no information is given as to why this figure has been used. The use of a lower rate may suggest that the IIA is attempting to manipulate the calculation to generate a positive NPV figure. Consideration should also be given to the length of time that the investment appraisal covers. This has been based on a period of seven years, which, while not technically incorrect, appears to be a long appraisal period for a software system. It may simply be the case that at the IIA the use of a seven year term is common practice. Confirmation of this will however need to be sought to ensure the validity of the investment appraisal.

Costs

Initial software costs

The initial software cost of $375,000 has been included in the IIA's NPV working. In addition to the software purchase cost the IIA is also intending to make a series of amendments to the software to reflect their bespoke needs. At the current time, a $25,000 charge has been included to cover these costs, however the exact nature of the changes required to the software are not currently known. This uncertainty increases the scope for the actual cost to be far greater than the $25,000 estimate.

It is particularly important that the IIA monitor the costs of amending the software to ensure that the final costs do not exceed the $25,000 estimate. Failure to monitor costs may undermine the IIA's business case. This issue is further compounded by the fact that the scenario makes reference to the problems in actually specifying the IIA's software requirements. This increases the scope for the projects completion to over run.

Software maintenance costs

The software maintenance costs are calculated as 10% of the final cost of the delivered project. Therefore, any increase in the software purchase and modification cost will result in a higher maintenance charge. This raises further doubts over the viability of the project, given that its NPV is only marginally positive.

Question bank costs

The IIA's current NPV working shows the total costs of developing a question bank for the project as being $100,000, split over year 0 and year 1. This represents the need for 2,000 questions to be initially produced, ($100,000/$50 fee per question written) with 100 questions being added each year thereafter. As the IIA have determined the number of questions needed to complete the question bank and have set the fee payable to the question writers these costs appear to be reasonably accurate.

However, as the question writers only receive their fees once the questions are successfully delivered to the question bank, it is seems unusual that the payment for the first 1,000 questions is shown in year 0. It is important the IIA confirm that this cost has been recognised in the correct period. Recognising these costs in the two subsequent years (year 1 and year 2) would actually result in an increased final NPV figure.

Security costs

The security costs appear reasonably definite, as these have been agreed in advance of the commencement of the project with an established security firm.

Disruption costs

Costs of $15,000 have been recognised by the IIA in years 1 and 2 in respect of the anticipated disruption to the organisation as a result of the project. While the inclusion of such costs in the NPV working appears to be prudent, it is clearly not realistic to attach a monetary amount to any decline in staff morale. As a result disruption costs should not be included when considering the viability of the project.

Benefits

Manual marker fees

The introduction of the new system will lead to a reduction in the IIA's marker fees as the current manual exam marking process will no longer be undertaken. Given that the current fees paid to markers is a known cost to the IIA, the figure per year of $125,000 represents an accurate saving. These savings are predicted to materialise in year 2, however the point at which these savings occur is likely to be unknown as the IIA is encountering problems specifying the requirements of the bespoke system.

Admin savings

As mentioned above in respect of the marker fees, the exact timing and amount of the administrative cost savings will be determined once the detailed system requirements have been finalised. In the meantime the IIA could conduct simulations to test the how the new computer-based assessment will impact the number of examinations staff likely to be required post-implementation. Such simulations should provide the management at the IIA with a better estimate of the cost savings to be realised.

Extra income

The extra income included in the investment appraisal represents the expected increase in student numbers attracted to the IIA due to the convenience of attempting computer-based assessments. However, the extra income is the IIA's 'best guess' at the amount of income which will result from this new assessment initiative. At present none of the IIA's competing institutions offer computer-based assessments. There may be some scope to determine and verify the anticipated uplift in student numbers if other professional bodies which offer similar forms of assessment can be contacted to provide some insight on this based on their own experiences. Clearly without further research the gradual increase in extra income between years 2 and 7 at present lacks credibility and can only be confirmed when the new system is fully implemented.

Summary

Based on the above evaluation it can be argued that the inclusion of the disruption costs and extra income in the IIA's investment appraisal increase the difficulty in assessing the viability of the project. In order for a more meaningful assessment to be carried out these two elements have been removed in order to produce a revised NPV working.

				Year				
Costs	0	1	2	3	4	5	6	7
Initial software	(200)	(200)						
Software maintenance			(40)	(40)	(40)	(40)	(40)	(40)
Question bank	(50)	(50)	(5)	(5)	(5)	(5)	(5)	(5)
Security			(20)	(20)	(20)	(20)	(20)	(20)
Total costs	**(250)**	**(250)**	**(65)**	**(65)**	**(65)**	**(65)**	**(65)**	**(65)**
Income/ savings								
Marker fees	0	0	125	125	125	125	125	125
Admin saving	0	20	30	30	30	30	30	30
Total benefits	**0**	**20**	**155**	**155**	**155**	**155**	**155**	**155**
Benefits less costs	(250)	(230)	90	90	90	90	90	90
DF (at 8%)	1	0.926	0.857	0.794	0.735	0.681	0.630	0.583
Present value	(250)	(212.98)	77.13	71.46	66.15	61.29	56.70	52.47

NPV (77.78)

The revised working now gives the project a negative net present value. Based on this, it is clear that the current project is not financially viable. It is important that, before a final decision is made, consideration is given to the non-financial benefits that the project may bring.

Part (b)

Top tips. When attempting questions such as these it is sometimes useful to break the question down into two parts. Firstly, you should consider what you know about each of the three terms (benefit owner, benefits maps and benefits realisation). As the question requires an explanation of each term it is critical that you provide this. If you are well prepared this should simply be a matter of illustrating your understanding of the theory. Secondly, (and perhaps most importantly) you need to link the theory back to the scenario. It may prove helpful to think about the

benefits that each of the three concepts could bring to the IIA. For example, by appointing a benefit owner this should help the IIA to ensure that a designated person has responsibility for realising the projects intended benefits.

Easy marks. There was 1 mark for each appropriate point up to a maximum of 4 marks (capped at a total of 10 marks) for each term mentioned in the question requirement. Providing a brief outline of each concept would have gained you some easy marks.

Examiner's comments. 'In general candidates knew little about benefit maps. They knew a little more about benefit owners, although it is the business that should own benefits, not the project manager. Benefits realisation has been the subject of a previous part question and candidates understood this concept relatively well'.

Benefit owner

A benefit owner is an individual or group who will gain advantage from a business benefit and who will work with the project team to ensure that the benefit is realised. Following the identification of the costs and benefits of undertaking a project, an owner is assigned to each individual benefit prior to it being stated in the business case. It is important to note that the project manager is not often the same person as the benefit owner. In the case of the IIA it would appear that project managers have historically failed to consider whether completed projects have delivered the intended benefit. The IIA director 'is concerned that project managers are just moving on to other projects and not taking responsibility for the benefits initially established in the business case'.

It is therefore important that the IIA appoints an internal benefit owner to assess the progress of the project. This role should involve making decisions to ensure that the required benefits are delivered. Failure to measure whether the project at the IIA delivers the anticipated cost savings will make it impossible to know if the project achieved its objective or not. As savings such as the administrative cost reductions have been determined using estimates, this increases the likelihood that the actual predicted savings will not be realised. The appointed benefit owner should therefore be able to ensure that the maximum level of cost savings materialise.

Benefits map

A benefits map is a useful tool which assists the benefit owner in understanding how to realise the intended benefit from a project. A benefits map can be linked back to the organisation's objectives to illustrate how the intended benefits will help the entity. For example reducing the marker fees may be part of the IIA's plan to improve profitability.

The benefits map should also help to indicate any new processes that will be needed in order to achieve the project's expected benefits. For example, IIA needs to determine the process involved in establishing the new bank of questions for computer-based assessments. Issues here are likely to include the development of a process for selecting appropriate external consultants to write new questions, and the process for returning questions to question writers which are in need of modification. Such tasks can then be included in the project plan, making it easier for the benefit owner and project manager to understand the steps that are needed to ensure that the promised benefits are delivered.

Benefits realisation

Benefits realisation occurs after the implementation of the project. It focuses on whether the finished project delivers the intended benefits set out in the business case. It is important to note that benefit realisation is also not solely restricted to benefits but should also consider the associated financial costs and time involved in undertaking the project. IIA's project to introduce computer-based assessments is due to take a period of 7 years, and as a result it is likely to be advisable to review the financial case for the project in stages. It is clearly more difficult to take action to correct benefits not fully realised if the project is reviewed in full at the end of year 7.

Benefits realisation may also bring to light previously unintended benefits. Such benefits should be fully considered, as there may be some scope to learn lessons from completed aspects of the project which can be used in the future when completing later stages. A common problem that benefits realisation presents is determining the factors which lead to a single benefit arising. For example the IIA believes that computer-based assessments will increase the number of candidates joining the institute. In reality, this correlation between the introduction of the new system and the increase in candidates may simply be down to the IIA running a new marketing campaign. As this example illustrates, correlation does not equal causation. Nonetheless, benefits realisation is still a value-adding activity, helping the benefit owner to monitor the realisation of a project's promised benefits.

38 Flexipipe

Text reference. Software requirements are covered in Chapter 10 of your BPP Study Text for exams from September 2015 to 31 August 2016.

Top tips. Part (a) requires you to **critically evaluate** the decision made be the CEO. The scenario provides you with information about the competitive environment in which Flexipipe operates, the nature of the project and internal processes and management. Address each factor under a separate heading to provide structure to your answer and make your script easy to mark.

Marking scheme

			Marks
(a)	1 mark for each appropriate point up to a maximum of 12 marks	max	12
(b)	1 mark for each appropriate point up to a maximum of 13 marks	max	13
			25

Part (a)

The decision to use a software package approach to automate the production process at Flexipipe was unlikely to succeed for a number of reasons. These are considered below.

Appropriateness of package solution

The innovative production process at Flexipipe provided the organisation with a distinct competitive edge over its suppliers. Package solutions, on the other hand, are widely available to all organisations and therefore it cannot create a competitive edge for an organisation.

A package solution is therefore unlikely to provide a perfect match to the process and the production process would be hindered by any package. This was proven to be the case as the flexibility and efficiency of the existing process could not be matched and so the competitive edge was lost.

Use of the Harmon process/strategy grid for the process could have led the organisation towards a more suitable choice. Flexipipe's production process can be considered to be both relatively complex and strategically important. Processes which fall into this category are best addressed via a bespoke software solution. Package solutions, such as that actually implemented at Flexipipe, would not be appropriate as these are typically better suited to straightforward processes that have lower strategic importance to the organisation.

Unstable and complex requirements

A key issue was the difficulty faced by Flexipipe in defining the requirements of the production process, commenting that 'what we do today, we might not do tomorrow; requirements are constantly evolving'. Selecting a software package against vague or incomplete requirements is very risky as key requirements could be missed or inappropriately addressed leading to problems which may be impossible to address further down the line.

There are several ways the lack of requirements could be addressed.

Flexipipe could request that the software vendor incorporates these requirements into their next release of the package. However, the vendor may not agree, and if they do, not only could this be extremely costly but the requirements would be made available to all again removing Flexipipe's competitive edge.

Flexipipe could request that the software vendor develops a tailored version of the package, however this is likely to be expensive (making a package no longer more competitive than bespoke software). Costs and maintenance problems are also likely to continue long term as the tailored version will need to remain compatible as new editions of the software and updates are released.

Flexipipe could attempt to find a manual work-around for the missing requirements, however this again would be costly and reduce the benefits they should have gained from a standardised software package.

In either case, the costs are likely to increase and/or the benefits gained be reduced.

The requirements of the process are also likely to change in the long term and there is no way of knowing if the software vendor will incorporate such new requirements into its package. This will again lead to issues of work-around or tailoring. As packages are selected on current requirements they are better suited to processes which rarely change (or only change in order to comply with legislative changes) than processes which are subject to long term change, such as the Flexipipe production process.

Lack of experience and established procurement process

This is the first time that Flexipipe have bought a software package for a non-standard application (such as payroll or accounts) and so there is no standardised or established package selection process in place. Given the high levels of importance and value of this process it was very risky to attempt to select a package without this prior experience with the aim of putting such a process in place 'as this project progresses'. Previous procurement problems have arisen due to their lack of expertise and relaxed approach in the past. For example short-term production problems arose when a key raw materials supplier went unexpectedly out of business. Despite experiencing this disruption, and the volume of work required, Flexipipe still employ only two full-time procurement staff who appear to have limited skill or experience in this area, and procurement process appears to be immature.

Long-term commitment to an external software provider is very risky as the supplier may go out of business (as happened here) or be sold and moving applications to a new supplier can be disruptive, expensive and technically difficult. A further risk is that a software supplier could be bought by a competitor of Flexipipe which would threaten long-term supply. Problems such as this do not tend to occur with bespoke packages as the software program code would belong to the company (ie Flexipipe), rather than the supplier, and the future development of that software would remain within its control.

Part (b)

> **Top tips.** Remember to identify issues relevant to the Flexipipe scenario. Simply discussing a generic evaluation process will not score well.

A formal software package appraisal process could have addressed a number of the issues experienced by Flexipipe.

Business case

Part of the appraisal process would involved producing a business case which would evaluate whether or not a standardised package is actually the most suitable solution for a process. As previously identified, this process would most likely have been better suited to a bespoke solution. The business case would have identified this and the package software idea scrapped early on.

Requirement specification

A formal software package appraisal process would require that process requirements are fully specified before the procurement of a solution can begin. If this could not be done, as was the case with Flexipipe, then it is likely this would have led to the scrapping of the package idea and re-consideration of a bespoke approach. The usability problems and missing requirements indicate that the requirements were not fully considered until the package was evaluated.

Formal and competitive tendering method

A formal tendering process would have given Flexipipe the best chances of identifying all suppliers who may be able to fulfil their requirements through exposure on internet tendering sites and in trade magazines. This was clearly not done as a post-project review found that there were at least three other suppliers that could have done this who were not considered at the time.

A formal process would have also created transparency in the process and would have prevented the situation at Flexipipe where a supplier was selected based on nothing more than it being seen during a visit to a software exhibition.

Evaluation against agreed criteria

A formal appraisal process would include the evaluation of the suppliers that submit tenders against specified criteria. This is to ensure that the supplier and the company can work well together as they need to be able to work together in the future. The customer will also need to be certain that the supplier has sufficient credentials and meets minimum requirements in areas such as liquidity, profitability and gearing. This would have to be balanced against the software that company was offering, ie a supplier may be well established and financially secure, but the package it offers may have only limited functionality. Formalised processes would be in place to ensure this is carried out fairly. Had this been done, it may have given Flexipipe some warning relating to the going concern of the selected supplier and directed it towards are more stable software provider.

Process for evaluation of solutions against requirements

In addition to evaluating the potential suppliers, a formal appraisal process would involve considering how well each potential solution matched the process requirements to ensure that the package selected is the one with the best 'fit'. While, in this case, it was unlikely that any package would have provided a good fit with the Flexipipe production process an understanding of the fit in advance would have helped them to negotiate with potential suppliers and perhaps find ways of filling those gaps. This may also have led to a greater level of tolerance for the functional shortcomings as these would have been fully known and understood prior to implementation.

Planned implementation

The users of the software were not given any training on the new software and they were expected to 'pick it up as they went along'. This is very risky and has perhaps been a factor in the perceived lack of usability of the software. A formal package software appraisal process would have required that the implementation of the software be considered as a key part of the process. This would have highlighted the need for training and guidance for the users and may have prevented this problem occurring.

39 Institute of Administrative Accountants

> **Text reference.** Project management is covered in Chapter 13 of the BPP Study Text for exams from September 2015 to 31 August 2016.
>
> **Top tips.** This question is about identifying the costs and benefits of implementing a computerised examining and marking system. Read the scenario carefully and you should find that lots of benefits and costs jump out at you. Also think about this from your own perspective and your own experiences of taking exams. Don't be afraid of stating the obvious with this requirement!
>
> Remember that costs are not just financial costs. Think about the controls over students not cheating in the multiple choice computer based exams and the reputational risk to the IAA if students do start cheating.

Marking scheme

			Marks
(a)	1 mark for each relevant point up to a maximum of 15 marks	max	15
(b)	1 mark for each relevant point up to a maximum of 10 marks	max	10
			25

Part (a)

Benefits

Reduction in the cost of exam centres and invigilation as this will no longer be needed for foundation level papers that now take place online. The scenario indicates that approximately 70% of these costs relate to foundation level papers, and some smaller centres that offer only foundation level exams are known to make a financial loss.

Reduction in bank charges on the overdraft incurred as a result of the peaks and troughs in the cashflow caused by the twice-yearly examination cycle.

Reduction in marking costs as all foundation papers will now be marked automatically.

Elimination of checking costs as foundation papers are marked automatically, whilst advanced papers are marked using marking software which totals the marks awarded by the marker automatically. Neither the marking of the foundation, nor advanced, papers will therefore need to be checked.

Reduction in central administration costs as temporary staff will not be needed to assist with the processing of results for foundations level exams.

Top tips. Note that the scenario clearly states that overtime for **permanent** staff is unpaid; therefore reduced overtime costs would **not** be a benefit in this case. The benefit here is the saving of the cost of **temporary** staff.

Courier costs will be eliminated completely.

Enhanced student experience as they will receive the results of the foundation exams immediately after completing their exam. The scenario indicates it currently takes 16 weeks to release the results to students and this has been the basis of much student criticism. It is also possible that the more efficient online marking of advanced papers, along with the time freed up by no longer having to mark and process foundations level exams, may reduce the wait time for these students also. The improved reputation may then lead to **additional income** as more people sign up to IAA than to study with the competitor.

Increased reach of foundation exams though being available 'any day, any time, anywhere' may lead to an increase in student registrations worldwide and hence **increased fee income**.

Increased income from repeat students. Students that fail the exam currently have to wait six months to retake their exam. The new system, however, would allow them to retake very quickly whilst the subject is still fresh in their mind. This may make them more likely to try again rather than to give up on the qualification.

Costs

Costs of preventing cheating

E-assessment creates a lot of potential for cheating at the fundamental level exams. This could happen in a number of ways.

- As the exams can be taken 'anywhere', including at home, there is a risk that the student could use text books or other study material to help them. It would be difficult and costly to implement a way of preventing students from doing this.

- Students could get someone else to do the exam for them. This can only be prevented by the identity checks that currently take place, meaning that invigilators (and their associated costs) may still be necessary after all.

- Centres, especially those where students are taught, or employed may help the student to get though the exam. The IAA will have to develop a way of ensuring this does not happen.

Reputational damage

IAA is a professional body and as such will be highly respected in the world of accountancy. If it is found that students are cheating then the exams will lose credibility and the reputation of the IAA could be irreparably damaged.

Cost of equipment

There will be a number of costs involved in obtaining and operating the technology required, including:

- Cost of the computers used for the exams and the associated software

- Cost of providing technical support to students should the technology fail or the computer crash during the exam

- Cost of licences for both the examining software and the electronic marking software

- Online support costs to ensure help is available to react when technology fails.

Cost of producing the multiple choice exam

A huge bank of multiple choice questions will have to be written in order to enable the exams to be run electronically in this way. This will involve a large upfront cost.

Ongoing costs will also be incurred as these questions will have to be regularly revised and updated.

Redundancy costs

Redundancy costs may need to be paid to existing IAA staff that are no longer required for checking.

Many of these costs will have to be incurred at the start of the process. This could be difficult for the IAA to finance as they are not a cash rich organisation.

Part (b)

> **Top tips.** If you have studied the project management section of the Study Text, you should be able to approach this part question without too much difficulty as it is mostly testing your knowledge of why a business case, benefits management and benefits realisation process are necessary in situations such as the one described in the scenario.
>
> Make sure you answer all three parts of this question – business case, benefits management and benefits realisation – in order to score the maximum number of marks for this question. However, make sure you apply your knowledge to the scenario. Don't just discuss the theoretical benefits of preparing a business case.

We have seen above that there are a number of costs, in addition to the benefits, associated with this project. The most significant one being the potential for cheating this new approach may bring.

If a formal business case is developed the **costs and benefits will have to be quantified** to lead to either a payback period, Internal Rate of Return (IRR) or Net Present Value (NPV) for the project. The project's features will have to be more accurately defined in order to realistically assess the costs and benefits. The project can then also be compared to other projects that the IAA might consider to see if it is still feasible given the poor cash flow situation of the Institute.

During the course of the actual project, the benefit will have to be managed to ensure it remains on track and the **anticipated benefit is actually realised**. It is likely that changes will have to be made to the requirements during the life of the project. If there is no proper benefits management system in place, the business case may not be revisited and so costs may spiral out of control and planned benefits may never materialise. Benefits management is necessary to ensure that the project is still justifiable given the changes that arise along the way.

After the project has been completed and e-assessment has been implemented, a formal benefits realisation review should be carried out to find out if the promised benefits have actually been delivered. This will force the project sponsor to carefully define the nature, timing and value of each claimed benefit to provide a yardstick to measure against.

The **enthusiasm for e-assessment** may mean that this project is adopted without sufficient consideration of the costs and benefits. This could potentially cause long-term problems for the organisation if these benefits never materialise or unexpected costs arise.

A formal business case and benefits management programme would ensure all costs and benefits are properly defined and monitored to ensure that benefits are actually realised. Ensuring the sponsor is formally responsible for the delivery of benefits should help prevent the development of business cases built on vague benefits which may never materialise.

40 Institute of Analytical Accountants

> **Text reference.** Process redesign is covered in Chapters 9 and 10 of your BPP Study Text for exams from September 2015 to 31 August 2016.
>
> **Top tips.** Take care when structuring your answer and give some thought to this before you begin to write. Well presented answers make it easier for the examining team to pick out relevant points and award you with marks.

When suggesting ways that the process can be re-designed, make sure you provide specific redesign options in the context of the scenario you are given. Making generic points such as 'merge swim lanes' or 'reduce handoffs' are insufficient and will not earn you marks.

Marking scheme

		Marks
(a)	1 mark for each relevant point up to a maximum of 15 marks	15
(b)	1 mark for each relevant point up to a maximum of 10 marks	10
		25

(a) **Re-design**

The process could be redesigned in a number of ways to solve the various problems with the existing process.

Problem	Consequences	Potential solutions
Bottleneck in the entering of questions into the question bank; there are too many questions for the amount of time the administrators have available. This is compounded by the fact that administrators are also not technical experts and therefore unable to check the accuracy of the material they have input.	Questions received back from reviewer cannot be updated with outcome, leading to frustration and delay. Quality of data – 1 in 10 has an error and so is unfit for purpose.	Employ more administrators to enter the data; however this would be costly and does not address the issues with quality. Delay question entry until the question has been accepted. This would mean time is not wasted inputting questions that go on to be rejected, and also prevents further errors that are made when updating questions with amendments following a review.
Too many handoffs between departments	Errors such as those mentioned above Delays and bottlenecks created	Reduce the number of swim lanes, perhaps by moving the tasks performed by the administrative department to the education department. This would reduce the number of errors as the education department has more technical expertise. However, this change is likely to be resisted by the education department, and also would mean reducing the number of administrators and employing more expensive employees in the education department. Changing the sequence so that the selection of the reviewer takes place before the questions are submitted so that all questions from one author are automatically sent to a specific reviewer. This would reduce the time spent forwarding questions, but it may remove the anonymity of the reviewer and so might not be acceptable to IAA. The task of raising a reject notification should be reallocated to either the administration or education department to remove the unnecessary involvement of the finance department.

Reengineering

Reengineering involves re-designing the process completely from scratch by focusing on the goals of the process. In this case the goal might be to have a bank of accurate, reviewed questions held in a computer system at minimal cost.

One way this could be achieved is to change the process so that the author enters the question directly into the computer system. This would both reduce the chances of mistakes (which should be picked up by the reviewer anyway should they occur) and transfer the input cost to the author, thereby removing the bottleneck and reducing administrative costs.

The reviewer would then be responsible for informing the author of the acceptability of the question. Accepted responses would automatically raise a payment notification to be sent to the finance department, and rejection would automatically generate a reject notification which is electronically sent to the author. Revision requests would also be automatically sent to the author so that the relevant amendments could be made and the question resubmitted for the second review process.

There may be some staffing implications with this reengineered process, as there would be much less need for administrators and potentially also educational staff. The involvement of finance personnel is also significantly reduced. There would inevitably be redundancies as a result of implementing such a process and therefore this solution is likely to be unpopular and difficult to implement.

(b)

> **Top tips.** Make sure you read the question properly and ensure you fully understand the requirements. A number of candidates answered this question by simply listing the advantages of a package solution – this was not what the question asked for. This question is actually asking you to discuss the implications of choosing this solution **for process-redesign** at IAA and your answer should therefore be focused specifically around this.

The purchase of a software package would provide a number of advantages to the IAA, including:

Speed of implementation. The package is already available and is used by a significant amount of other organisations, therefore the IAA only have to set up the software and populate it with data. This process is much faster than building a bespoke system which would require specification, development and significant testing. This is a significant advantage as the threat from competitors means that IAA are keen to implement the new solution quickly.

Software quality. The software has already been implemented at a number of significant examination boards. This suggests that the majority of faults will already have been found and corrected. This is a strong advantage over building a bespoke system which will not only require significant testing but, given the impossibility of finding all faults before implementation, is also likely to contain errors which could cause operational problems and costs. Reliability is essential for the IAA and so a tried and tested solution is important.

Try before you buy. Unlike bespoke software, which can only be tried by the users at the end of the building process, the users get to experience the solution before buying it. This means that any gap between the requirements of the IAA and the software solution can be evaluated prior to purchase. Any compromises the IAA may need to make in order to accommodate the package will be considered during the selection process, again prior to purchase. When users first try bespoke builds, it is not uncommon to find misunderstandings which need to be rectified. This problem is avoided when a standard software package is used.

Predicted maintenance costs. Maintenance fees are agreed in advance as part of the negotiations involved in putting package software in place. This will include further fault fixes as well as the implementation of new features that have been requested by the IAA and the wider user community. Although perhaps not specifically relevant to this situation, the maintenance fees would also cover legislative changes. However, this may be relevant for invoicing if there are changes to the tax policies in place.

With a bespoke package none of these costs would be included and the costs, for the fault fixing in particular, would be hard to predict.

Access to expertise. The software provider is likely to possess domain knowledge as a result of implementing the software at the various examination boards. They may therefore have additional ideas and possibilities that the IAA can benefit from that they may not otherwise have thought of. Bespoke systems are often limited by the experience of the organisation and it can be difficult for them to frame requirements in the abstract and to identify new ideas.

Initial cost. A software package is likely to be cheaper than a bespoke build, however, no specific information is included on this in the scenario. The main reasons for this are:

- Software is already built, so IAA can negotiate a better price the IAA will be contributing to the provider's profit margin rather than covering the costs of building the software.

- Cost may be negotiated or implemented on a fee-for-use basis, allowing the IAA to tailor the price paid to the number of students sitting their examinations. This is considerably cheaper than bespoke builds which are usually paid for in full on the delivery of the software.

Once implemented, the software package will significantly impact on the way the IAA operates in the future. Tailoring packages to fit specific organisational requirements is possible, but this approach is not recommended as the ongoing cost and difficulty of implementing updates and new releases can erode any competitive advantage that was gained through its development.

Although a package is unlikely to fit an organisation's requirement, the need to compromise is likely to be known at the start of the process, and differences between the requirements and the solution will form part of the package evaluation process.

Following the implementation of the package, a further implication will be the inevitable change in ways of working for the users. They will have to re-assess the ways in which they want to work and adjust to how the package allows them to work in practice.

Note that you may have interpreted this question slightly differently and therefore discussed the management process of installing a software package. The question was not intended to be answered in this way, however, if you have taken this approach you would still have been awarded some marks for doing this.

---

41 Pharmacy Systems International

Text reference. Strategic change is the subject of Chapter 8 of the BPP Study Text for exams from September 2015 to 31 August 2016.

Top tips. Part (a) asked you to analyse the nature, scope and type of change which the proposed strategy at PSI will involve. The terminology in the question should have highlighted that the relevant model was Balogun & Hope Hailey's matrix, whose axes are nature and scope of change.

There are a small number of marks available in this question for theoretical knowledge – explaining the nature and scope of change, but to score well you need to analyse the type of change PSI is facing.

The answer below takes each of the four quadrants of the Balogun & Hope Hailey's matrix and then assesses the situation at PSI to see which quadrant it fits best. As with many P3 questions, there isn't a definitive right answer – is the change adaptation or is it evolution? – but provided your argument is sensible and you support it with evidence from the scenario you will score marks.

Part (b) requires you to use 'an appropriate model' to identify and analyse the internal contextual features that could influence the success of the proposed changes at PSI. The most suitable model here was the contextual features model – which looks at time, scope, preservation, diversity, capability, capacity, readiness and power as features which can affect the success of a change programme.

We have used this contextual features model in the answer below, and the examiner used it in his model answers, but the cultural web is another alternative you could have used.

The marking scheme identifies that up to 3 marks are available for an analysis of each feature. So although there are 8 features within the contextual features model, you would not need to cover them all to score well in this question.

Easy marks. If you were familiar with the contextual features model, you should have scored well in part (b) because the scenario gave plenty of clues about things that could affect the success of the proposed change: for example, the company wants to move to a bigger marketplace even though they are struggling to meet the demand from their existing marketplace; software is key to the project, but the software director is unenthusiastic about it, and appears to be alienated from his fellow directors etc.

Examiner's comments. This was the least popular of the optional questions, and the candidates who did attempt it rarely scored more than half marks. It appeared that students were unfamiliar with the strategic change areas of the syllabus. However, despite a lack of familiarity with this part of the syllabus there were still plenty of clues in the scenario which could have provided the basis for an answer. A candidate could have crafted an answer out of the general points in the scenario without resorting to any specific published model.

Marking scheme

			Marks
(a)	Up to 2 marks for recognising that PSI is pursuing a diversification strategy	2	
	Up to 2 marks for explaining the nature of change	2	
	Up to 2 marks for explaining the scope of change	2	
	Up to 4 marks for exploring the types of change with particular reference to the situation at PSI	4	10
(b)	Up to 3 marks for an analysis of each feature that could influence the success of failure of the proposed strategic change at PSI; up to a maximum of 15 marks	3	15
	There are eight possible features in the contextual features model; a possible mark allocation (1 mark per point up to a maximum of 3 marks) for one of those features (time) is given below:		
	Explanation of possible effect of time		
	Recognition that time is not an issue at PSI – there is no evidence of a crisis that requires remedial action		
	Relatively long time to develop a new product given current time pressures		
	Impatience of the chief executive imposes arbitrary urgency		
	Conflict between chief executive and software development director over time allocation		
			25

(a) PSI currently sells to a specialist **niche market** – the retail pharmacy market. Therefore the proposed strategic change – to sell to the **general retail market** – represents a **significant change to PSI's product and its market**. In this respect, it represents a **diversification strategy**.

Nature of change – The nature of a change describes whether it is incremental or a one-off **'Big Bang'** change.

Incremental change builds on existing methods and approaches rather than challenging them. However, a **'Big Bang' change** involves a major change to existing methods, processes and cultures. Such an approach is usually required in times of crisis when rapid responses are required.

Scope of change – The scope of a change describes the extent of a change; the extent to which an organisation's business activities or its business model need changing. In this respect, a change can either be a **realignment** of a firm's existing strategy, or it can be a **transformational change** in which radical changes are made to the existing business model.

Types of change

Bringing together these different components of change means we can identify four different types of change: adaptation, reconstruction, evolution, revolution.

Scope of change

Nature of change		Realignment	Transformation
	Incremental	Adaptation	Evolution
	'Big bang'	Reconstruction	Revolution

Adaptation is a change where the existing model is retained, and the change only incurs incrementally. Because the proposed change at PSI represents a diversification of strategy, it is debatable whether the existing business model will remain valid.

The chief executive and the sales and marketing director may see the move to selling to the general retail industry as an adaptation of the existing model, but the software director's resistance to the change suggests that the change will involve a more significant transformation.

Reconstruction requires a significant, and rapid, change in the operations and process of an organisation often in response to crisis such as a long-term decline in performance. However, it does not involve any major change to the business model.

The proposed changes at PSI are borne out of a desire for growth, rather than in response to any critical problems facing the company. Therefore, they do not represent a reconstruction.

Evolution is an incremental process that leads to a new business model. Evolutionary change often arises as a result of business analysis, leading to a planned change.

This appears to be the case at PSI. The move into the generic retail market represents a **fundamental change in strategic direction** and it is likely that the company's processes and structure will have to change significantly to develop and sell the new packages successfully. However, the change has come about due the Chief Executive's **desire to grow the business rather than in response to external financial pressures**. Therefore the changes are likely to be relatively incremental rather than a sudden reconstruction of the business.

Revolution is rapid and wide ranging response to extreme pressures for change. It is likely to require a fundamental shift in the business model, and in the way a company operates. Although the proposed changes at PSI represent a diversification, they are not radical enough to represent a revolution.

(b)

> The marking scheme allows up to 3 marks for an analysis of each feature that could influence the success or failure of the proposed changes; up to a maximum of 15 marks. For tutorial purposes, the answer below includes all headings from the contextual features model because all of them are relevant here. However, the marking scheme – up to 3 marks for each feature – indicates that you would not have needed to include all 8 features to score well in this question.

The context of change

The context of change is provided by the organisational setting; this has many aspects and can therefore be very complex. However, this complexity can be approached in a manageable way by considering it under eight general headings proposed by Balogun and Hope Hailey, which we will analyse below.

Time

No need to rush – Many companies are forced into changes in response to difficulties they are facing in their business. However, PSI does not appear to be facing any financial problems are so time is not pressing in that respect.

Development time – Given that the software development team already appears to be under pressure to deliver and upgrade the current problem, it also seems unlikely that they will be able to develop the software package for the general market quickly. Therefore a longer time scale may be more realistic anyway.

Chief Executive's expectations – However, the chief executive wants to introduce the changes quickly to accelerate the growth of the company and makes it an attractive acquisition target. So the timetable for change could become a source of conflict between the chief executive and the software director and his staff.

Scope of change

Evolution or adaptation – We have already suggested in (a) that the proposed changes represent an evolutionary change, because the change from serving a niche market to serving a general retail market represents a substantial change of focus.

Changes to marketing mix – Moreover, PSI will need to develop new marketing skills for selling to a general market rather than to a specific niche market.

One possible threat to the success of the change is if the chief executive and the sales and marketing director underestimate the scope of the change.

Preservation

Software developers – The software development team are critical to the success of the proposed changes, and PSI's business more generally. Therefore it is vital that PSI **retains as many of its key software staff as possible**. However, the software developers are already under constant pressure to meet the demands of existing customers, and so if their workload is increased still further a number may decide to leave PSI.

If a number of key software developers leave PSI the whole change project could be jeopardised.

Software development director – Persuading the software development director to support the changes will also be crucial to their success. Not only is a supportive director more likely to lead to support from the software developers themselves, but the director will also need to play a key role in the design of the new product.

Diversity

Diversity of experience – The change process is likely to be made easier in companies which have diversity of experience, and so have experienced different ways of doing things. However, it appears that PSI has very little diversity and has been following a single, specialist, strategy for many years.

Therefore, it appears that the business' current experience does not support the chief executive's ambitious plans for expansion.

Diversity of expectations – The goals of the sales team and those of the software developers seem to conflicting. The sales team is making promises to customers that the developers are struggling to meet. As a result, quality standards are falling leading to customer dissatisfaction.

As the business expands, this scope for differences between the sales team and the developers will increase, and this could hamper PSI's efforts to enter the new market successfully.

Capability

Capability to manage change – Although the chief executive and the sales and marketing director are both keen on the proposed changes, the software development director and his team are far less so. The chief executive will need to **convince the software team of the merits of the proposals** so that they support the changes. If the software team remain unconvinced and unenthusiastic, the changes are unlikely to be successful.

Past experience – We do not know anything about the **directors' past experiences of managing change**. PSI has been relatively settled over the last three years, so if the directors do not have any previous experience of managing change this could hinder the proposals. Equally, we do not know if any of the software team has experienced change processes before, such that their experience could be used to increase the changes of success here.

Capacity

People – The software development director already wants to acquire further resources to support the existing product, and the quality of PSI's has recently been criticised at a user group conference. This suggests that PSI's software team is already working to capacity. Therefore, it is likely it will need to **recruit a significant number of suitably skilled new developers** to support the planned expansion. This will increase costs, but it will also take **time** – to recruit new staff, and to allow them to become familiar with PSI's systems.

This timetable may again be problematic for the chief executive if he wants to progress quickly, and PSI's product quality could suffer still further if developers have to start work on a product before they fully understand it.

Funding – We do not know the details of PSI's financial position, but it seems likely that it will have to increase its borrowings to fund the expansion. PSI is a private company, and so cannot raise capital through an issue of shares on the stock market. It could look to the current shareholders for additional funding, but that means essentially looking to the directors. The software development director is unlikely to fund changes he does not support, and the chief executive seems keener on getting money from a sale of the company rather than investing in it further. Consequently, PSI's plans could be constrained by the amount of additional loan funding they can raise from their banks.

Readiness for change

The software developers would prefer to improve the software package they offer existing customers rather than moving to this new generic package. Therefore it is likely that they will **resist the chief executives proposed changes rather than supporting them**.

Moreover, since PSI has been **growing gradually** over the last three years, there is little no evidence to suggest it is ready for the significant changes proposed.

Power

The **chief executive appears to be the dominant power** at PSI, supported by the sales and marketing director. However, in practical terms the success of the changes depends on the software team and the software development director.

The software development director appears justified in being cautious over the changes. However, there is a risk that the other directors will **force through the changes**, possibly even by buying out the software directors shares and replacing him with a new director. Such an aggressive strategy is unlikely to be successful, however, and could lead to PSI's revenues falling rather than the business growing.

42 Academic Recycling Company

Text reference. Leadership styles and the principles of job enrichment are covered in Chapter 15 of your BPP Study Text for exams from September 2015 to 31 August 2016.

Top tips.

Part (a) – Lots of information is given to you in the scenario and many marks can be gained in this part question simply by pulling out the relevant points from the scenario. Higher marks can also be gained if you use leadership theories to back up your answer, in particular stereotypical theory X and theory Y, Blake/Mouton grid and Tannenbaum manager centred leadership. Incorporating elements of each of these theories into your answer should help you to score highly in this requirement.

However, don't forget that as well as analysing Sully's leadership style before and after the training course, you also have to explain why the change in style was unsuccessful. For example, as well as the appropriateness of the different styles in relation to the workforce, how did the speed with which Sully tried to make the change affect its effectiveness?

Easy marks. Provided you have learned the recommended leadership theorists this question provided you with a good opportunity to apply your knowledge to the scenario.

Examiner's comments. This question was less popular than questions two and three, but candidates who chose to do it often adopted a good answer structure to this part question based on the requirement; before, after and reasons for failure. Many candidates recognised that the manager had moved from a stereotypical Theory X manager to a stereotypical Theory Y manager. Many answers made appropriate reference to management theory, and those citing contingency theory were particularly insightful, because the characteristics of those being 'led' were significant in the context of the second part of this question.

Part (b) – Presuming you are familiar with this area of the syllabus, you will be able to earn a number of easy marks here by simply explaining the principles of job enrichment. As ever though, to score highly, you will need to ensure you apply your knowledge to the particular scenario given; for example: what specific issues would be encountered by trying to implement job enrichment in the Contracts Office at ARC.

Examiner's comments. This part question was answered less well. Many candidates struggled to provide enough relevant information on job enrichment and also failed to apply it to the case study situation. It seems likely that its potential application was reduced at ARC by the fact that many of the people who it may have attracted have left the company. The characteristics of the led may make it very difficult for the manager to implement a job enrichment scheme. Remember, although a particular concept may generally be perceived as a good thing (job enrichment in this question), it may not necessarily be so within the described case study scenario. Candidates must always reflect the context of the scenario in their answers.

Marking scheme

		Marks
(a)	1 mark for each relevant point up to a maximum of 15 marks	15
(b)	1 mark for each relevant point up to a maximum of 5 marks for the principles of job enrichment and up to 5 marks for its application at ARC	10
		25

(a) **Prior to attending the course**

Sully Truin's original management style was autocratic and focused on tight control. This was because he believed that employees wished to avoid work and responsibility and therefore needed detailed direction and close control. The jobs of the employees therefore increasingly began to consist of simple, repetitive tasks which were carried out in accordance with well defined procedures. Other matters, even trivial ones, were escalated up to Sully for him to resolve. The escalation of these simple issues further reinforced Sully's opinion of the inadequacies of his employees and the need for tight controls in order to ensure their work got done.

The characteristics displayed by Sully fit in well with the Theory X style of manager described in McGregor's X and Y theory of leadership, particularly in light of his belief that employees are inherently averse to work.

Sully's approach of making a decision and then announcing it could be described as manager-centred leadership in terms of Tannenbaum's theory.

In terms of Blake and Mouton's grid, Sully's approach would be considered to be one of authority/obedience as he focused on task completion and led by dictating as to what needed to be done and how this should be achieved.

After attending the course

The course promoted a more democratic style of leadership which caused Sully to question his approach to management. He attempted to then implement a style in which subordinates are involved in task planning and leadership responsibilities are shared. This involved shifting to the right in the Tannenbaum model, and further towards a McGregor Theory Y manager.

Why the change of leadership was unsuccessful

There are a number of reasons why the change in Sully's leadership style was not successful. First, the speed of change was such that he radically changed his approach overnight. This will have been confusing for employees and will have made it very hard for them to understand what was expected of them under this new approach.

In addition, the employees were uncomfortable with the new style presented by Sully. The original approach was a fairly good match between the leader the subordinates and the tasks. Employees who had not liked Sully's tough-minded management approach will have previously left the organisation. The remaining staff are the ones who prefer to have their work clearly specified and tightly controlled. His style may also have influenced his choices when appointing new members of staff, selecting those that will fit in with his views and the culture of the organisation. The views of the staff can be seen in their suggestions that Sully reverts back to the original style.

The original approach would also appear to have been well suited to the tasks carried out by the employees for which he has developed a 'tight administration process' and has 'closely defined what needs to be done for each contract and how it should be monitored'. The processes are straightforward, but when quick decisions are required they are escalated up to Sully. He is experienced in making fast decisions and has sufficient authority to do so. When this decision making responsibility was moved to subordinates, they felt they lacked both the experience and the authority. They therefore consulted colleagues and the decision making process took much longer.

However, although reverting to the old style might be preferred by the employees, it does not solve the original problems faced by Sully. He is heavily relied upon to the point that it is damaging his health and preventing the company from expanding.

Many theorists have suggested that there is no one best way of leadership and that the style which is appropriate in any given context will depend on the nature of the work and the people involved. No management style is likely to fit all situations and the approach required will vary at different times depending on business needs. In order to resolve problems or get things done a democratic manager may, at some point, need to adopt an authoritarian approach and vice versa.

(b) Business systems generally consist of five activities: *planning, enabling, doing, monitoring and control*. In the scenario, the employees are responsible for doing and monitoring, while Sully takes controlling action when the monitoring indicates this is necessary.

Job enrichment includes several processes such as job rotation and job enlargement. In order for a job to be considered 'enriched' it must include an element of vertical amalgamation, ie the job must include some elements of responsibility for planning and control.

There are five core characteristics that enriched jobs should possess if they are to produce positive outcomes:

- The job requires the use of a **range of skills and talents**
- **Task identity**: the job includes all the tasks needed to complete an identifiable product or process
- **Task significance**: the job has an impact on other people's lives or work
- **Autonomy**: workers have a degree of discretion in scheduling and organising their work
- **Feedback**: workers are provided with information on the results of their performance

Sully's decision to provide employees with responsibility for responding to problems was a step towards job enrichment, however, it was done with such speed that two key problems arose.

The first was that it highlighted the knowledge and skills gaps of the employees. Sully could address this via coaching.

The second problem was that the employees were uncomfortable with the new levels of responsibility and they preferred the previous system of following established routines. The resulting anxiety led to procrastination and an eventual request for Sully to resume the original leadership style. The fact that the employees did not want more responsibility illustrates why jobs that have the potential to motivate will not necessarily do so. The employees at ARC appear to have been content in their previous role, whereas those that dissatisfied with the process have left the company.

In order for job enrichment to be successful at ARC, Sully will have to carefully assess his staff to determine which would be open to moving to this kind of role. It may be necessary to bring in new people from outside the company if it is to be a success.

If Sully wishes to further extend the jobs by including elements of planning and enabling, then even greater analysis of competencies, skills and willingness of the employees will need to be undertaken. However, were this to be done the employees could assist Sully in sourcing and securing contracts therefore helping to resume the growth of ARC.

43 ReInk Co

Text reference. SWOT and TOWS matrix analysis are covered in Chapter 4, and the contextual features of change in Chapter 8 of the BPP Study Text for exams from September 2015 to 31 August 2016.

Top tips.

(a) In order to give yourself the best possible chance of securing some easy marks it is important that you approach the question in a positive manner. The best way to avoid getting too bogged down in the detail of the question scenario is to start by reading the question requirements.

Once you have had a chance to read through the question requirements and gained an understanding of what the examiner is actually asking for it is likely that the paper will not seem as scary as it did at the first glance.

As you begin to read through the long section A scenario it is particularly useful to annotate the scenario text by picking out the key points. In this instance, part (a) required you to prepare a SWOT analysis for inclusion in a report to potential investors. As you read through the scenario you should have been noting the strengths, weaknesses, opportunities and threats relevant to ReInk Co. As you go through it is important to remember that strengths and weaknesses relate to factors internal to ReInk Co, whereas opportunities and threats come from the external environment. Annotating the text with a little note next to the respective point should help you to save time when it comes to writing up your answer at the end of the reading and planning time.

Easy marks. As illustrated by the examiner's comments, easy marks were available for applying the SWOT analysis model to the scenario. There were up to 6 marks available under each SWOT heading up to a maximum of 20 marks.

Examiner's comments. The examining team noted that in respect of the SWOT analysis requirement in part (a) candidates performed relatively well. The examining team highlighted that the main problem most candidates experienced concerned the misclassification of SWOT items. 'For example; classifying the financial situation of the company as a threat (presumably because it is a threat to the firm's existence), rather than as an internal weakness. Misclassified answers were given some credit, but in SWOT analysis classification is important, otherwise the analysis is just an unstructured list. Furthermore, some candidates gave relevant points, extracted from the case study, in their answers but actually did not classify them at all. This really is just copying parts of the scenario into an answer. Little credit could be given for such answers'.

Marking scheme

		Marks
(a)	1 mark for each relevant point. Up to 6 marks for each heading under the SWOT analysis up to a maximum 20 marks.	20
(b)	1 mark for each relevant point up to a maximum 14 marks.	14
(c)	1 mark for each relevant point up to a maximum of 3 marks for each quadrant of the matrix, up to a maximum of 12 marks.	12

Professional marks for the complete assessment required by Vi Ventures:
Up to 1 mark for appropriate quality
Up to 1 mark for fluency
Up to 1 mark for appropriate report tone
Up to 1 mark for professionalism of the complete answer

$\frac{4}{50}$

Part (a)

To: Management of Vi Ventures
From: A consultant
Date: June 2014

Standard assessment report of the strategic position of ReInk

Introduction

This report details the findings of a SWOT analysis conducted in relation to ReInk Co. It also considers the contextual features of strategic change and how these may shape the changes at Reink Co should Vi Ventures choose to undertake some form of investment. The report finishes with recommendations on the potential strategic options that ReInk Co could pursue. These recommendations were derived using a TOWS matrix.

Firstly, this report considers the internal strengths and weaknesses of ReInk and the external opportunities and threats the company is currently facing.

Strengths

Expertise

ReInk is renowned for its technological expertise and innovation in the process of refilling printer cartridges. This strength has been largely driven by the enthusiasm and expertise of ReInk's founder, Dexter Black. Dexter Black's reputation helped to attract technology experts to join the company, with many regarding the prospect of working for a leading expert in the field as being highly appealing. The ability to attract a skilled team of technologists is particularly important given the need for constant innovation in the printer consumables market.

Patent

ReInk currently has six years remaining of an eight year patent to protect its innovative process for refilling ink cartridges. This patent is a key strength as it prohibits competitors from developing copycat processes in the foreseeable future.

Department of Revenue Collections (DoRC) contract

ReInk has a long-term contract with Eland's Department of Revenue Collections (DoRC). This represents a significant strength, given that 20% of ReInk's $6m revenue comes from the DoRC. The government's drive to promote recycling in Eland potentially places ReInk in a strong position to win future contracts with other government departments.

Location in Eland

ReInk has historically been able to exploit its chosen location to help the company grow. Dexter Black's decision to establish ReInk in a declining industrial town has enabled the company to access government grants aimed at attracting hi-tech entities to set up operations in the area. The low-rental prices charged by local landlords has helped ReInk in establishing offices and a factory.

ReInk's location near an attractive area of countryside has helped the company to attract expert technologists to work for the company. This has been further supported by the low prices of residential property in the town which has allowed ReInk to offer prospective employees lower salaries, while offering a better standard of living than might available with competing firms. This is illustrated by the comment made by one of the expert technologists 'I took a pay cut to come here. But now I can afford a bigger house and my children can breathe fresh country air'.

Weaknesses

Financial position

ReInk's financial position is a major weakness. Recent moves by ReInk's bank (Firmsure) to reduce the company's overdraft appear to have been in response to the continued reporting of annual losses. Although ReInk has been successful in generating operating profits over the last three years, the need to make large interest repayments on its 'substantial overdraft' have wiped these profits out. Firmsure's decision to reduce ReInk's overdraft facility has created a cashflow crisis which has left the company unable to meet the next month's payroll payments. Unless the current situation can be resolved it seems unlikely that ReInk will be able to continue in operation.

Directors

Dexter Black has recognised that his lack of commercial expertise represents a weakness to ReInk. In response he decided to appoint two new directors (a sales and human resources director).The aim had been to boost sales and to enhance staffing practices. However, the appointments have not achieved the results originally intended. The technologists argue that the sales director's arrival has failed to increase sales revenue with some suggesting that 'he does not really understand the product we are selling'. Furthermore, the HR director's drive to cut staff costs has been poorly received, with some technologists commenting that the director 'clearly has no experience of dealing with professional staff'.

The current abilities of ReInk's management team can be regarded as representing a significant weakness.

Employee demotivation

The ongoing financial and management turbulence at ReInk is having a detrimental impact on employee motivation, particularly the technologists, with many seeking employment elsewhere. This represents a worrying development for ReInk as the company's technologists have been instrumental in creating its 'vital technical edge' over competing firms.

Promotion and marketing

ReInk currently lacks a strong, coherent marketing message. This is evident as the ReInk brand was not recognised by many of the consumer participants in the recent brand awareness survey. This can be explained in part by the company's narrow approach to marketing, which consists of promoting the ReInk brand through its website while excluding other channels of marketing. Furthermore, internet searches for the ReInk website are hard to distinguish from similar competitor services.

Opportunities

Recycling

There has been a recent increase in the number of 'green consumers' in the country of Eland. This represents a significant opportunity for ReInk, especially as its own business model is built upon reusing printer cartridges and refilling them with ink. The Eland government's commitment to recycling suggests that this trend will continue into the foreseeable future, thereby increasing demand for ReInk's services.

Underperforming economy

The ailing state of the economy in Eland is likely to support an increase in demand for recycling ink cartridges and represents a real opportunity for ReInk. The majority of commercial and domestic consumers in Eland own printers, with a significant number of people looking to reduce their printing costs.

Government contracts

The government in Eland is suffering from a fall in tax revenues, and in a bid to reduce costs the government is now requiring all departments to demonstrate value-for-money in purchases made. This requirement presents ReInk with an ideal opportunity to build upon the long-term relationship it already has with the DoRC, as further government departments are likely to be interested in using ReInk's services.

Threats

Legal challenges

Original Equipment Manufacturers (OEMs) have taken legal action against independent companies which provide cartridge refill services of OEM branded printer consumables. Such action has so far failed, with the government ruling that to make such services illegal would be anti-competitive. However, there is a threat that the OEMs may succeed with future legal bids as these larger companies continue to promote their argument to political parties in Eland.

New innovations

The printer consumables market in Eland is heavily technology driven. Players in the market are focused on developing 'innovations which make printing better and cheaper'. This represents a significant threat as new printer cartridge refilling processes may be developed which make ReInk's own processes more expensive or unappealing to customers. Furthermore, the patent on ReInk's refill process only has another six years to run, after which time competitors would most likely be able to develop their own version of the same technology. This could prove to be a real threat to ReInk, unless the company is able to enhance or develop newer processes to replace its existing approach.

Competition

The printer consumables market in Eland is highly competitive, due to a number of factors. The OEMs dominate the market and consist of a number of well-known household brands. Coupled to these larger players there are a large number of independent companies supplying printer cartridges. It is easy for new independent suppliers to enter the market, meaning that companies predominantly compete on price and customers show little brand loyalty to any one supplier. To combat the threat of independent players, the large companies such as Landy have taken to invalidating warranties on any Landy branded printers which are found to have used non-Landy ink.

Privatisation of the DoRC

The government in Eland is currently considering privatising the DoRC. This is potentially a significant threat to ReInk as the company currently derives 20% of it's $6m revenue from the DoRC. An independently run DoRC may choose to switch its supplier of reusable ink.

Part (b)

Top tips. This question requirement was quite unusual as the examiner provided candidates with the model to be used in answering the question – contextual features of strategic change. In such cases it is important that you use the model given in forming the basis of your answer, and so you should have used the component parts of the model as headings in your answer which could then be applied to the ReInk Co scenario.

Examiner's comments. 'The second part of the question asked candidates to evaluate the effect of contextual features on the introduction of strategic change at ReInk Co. These contextual factors are from the Balogun and Hope Hailey model and were specifically defined in the scenario. Although this model has been used in a number of past examinations, many candidates still seemed unfamiliar with it. They were forced to guess what each of the contextual factors is (although some are indeed easy to guess) and many answers made little reference to the scenario'.

In the second part of this report we shall consider the contextual features of change at ReInk. The framework used is based on the work of Balogun and Hope Hailey.

Time

The focus on time concerns the amount of time available for a change to be successfully implemented. The amount of time varies from organisation to organisation and is driven by a range of different factors. ReInk is currently experiencing extreme financial distress due largely to Firmsure bank's decision to reduce the company's overdraft. The current cashflow crisis will require Vi Ventures to invest quickly. Once an investment has been made Vi Ventures should have sufficient time to improve ReInk's future prospects, as steps can be taken to improve profitability and reduce the dependency on bank loans and the overdraft facility.

Preservation

In the contextual features model, preservation refers to the need to maintain certain elements of the existing organisation. Preservation commonly relates to safeguarding the competencies which give the organisation some form of competitive edge. At ReInk it is evident that retaining the skilled technologists represents an essential competency. As discussed earlier in the report the financial situation at ReInk has had a detrimental impact on employee motivation, with some technologists seeking alternative employment. Vi Ventures will need to reassure this group of employees about the financial viability of ReInk should the proposed investment be made. Attempts will need to be made to persuade the technologists to remain with ReInk.

Diversity

In the contextual features model, 'diversity' refers to the diversity of experience and opinion. Historically, ReInk has been predominantly focused on pursuing a strategy based upon the need for innovation in ink refill processes. As the sole shareholder this focus has been driven by Dexter Black's desire for technical innovation. Dexter's approach to business has been to recognise and reward employees who develop improved processes. However, it means there is a lack of diversity in opinion about the alternative strategies that ReInk could pursue. This suggests that, should Vi Ventures successfully invest in ReInk, any new ideas or proposed changes to the strategic direction of the company may be met with a degree of resistance by employees.

Capability

Capability relates to any previous experience that an organisation possess in managing change. In some cases organisations will have successfully managed change in the past and will have established the competencies and mentality among employees needed to implement future organisational change. Reink does not appear to have such competencies in place. Dexter Black has been unable to address the company's financial situation, with the appointment of the two new directors having failed to improve Reink's fortunes. Vi Ventures management expertise in improving the performance of struggling companies is a critical capability which Reink needs.

Capacity

Capacity is concerned with having the necessary resources needed to implement change. In this context, resources commonly relate to management and financial resources. As previously discussed, Reink lacks the capacity to make the changes needed. In order to successfully implement the change needed at Reink, Vi Ventures will need to make substantial financial and management investments in the company.

Readiness

Readiness relates to the readiness for change among the organisation's workforce. The degree of readiness for change will vary between organisations, with certain employee groups particularly resistant to the implementation of change. It is likely that Vi Ventures will encounter limited employee resistance to change at Reink given the high levels of dissatisfaction the technologists feel towards the current management team. Vi Ventures may experience greater resistance to change from the newly appointed directors as their role in the future of Reink is likely to come under close scrutiny. This is something which Vi Ventures will need to address carefully should the investment in Reink go ahead.

Power

In order for change to be successfully implemented it is necessary that there is an individual in place within the organisation with the power and authority to instigate the required changes. In the case of Reink, such an individual will need to be able to exert power from a position which is distinct from Dexter Black and the current management team. Achieving this position is likely to require Vi Ventures to put in place a new management team as part of the investment to achieve sufficient influence over the future running of Reink.

Scope

The scope of change will be dependent on the situation facing the organisation. In some cases a proposed change may require realignment with the prevailing management thinking at the time or may require a more far reaching transformational change to the entity's strategic direction. Balogun and Hope Hailey suggest the following matrix for determining the type of change required.

Scope of change

		Realignment	Transformation
Nature of change	**Incremental**	Adaptation	Evolution
	'Big bang'	Reconstruction	Revolution

Using the matrix as a guide it would appear that a Reconstruction change is needed to address Reink Co's financial decline. Reconstruction requires change to be implemented very quickly and often results in significant disruption throughout the organisation. Such change however does not ultimately alter what the business does (the paradigm). Common features of reconstruction change involve changing the structure of the organisation and making certain employees redundant in a bid to improve performance.

Part (c)

> **Top tips.** It is important to remember that the TOWS matrix quadrants consider internal strengths and weaknesses against external threats and opportunities. The model is intended to support the evaluation of strategic options. The four quadrants that you needed to use were:
>
> SO strategies employ strengths to seize opportunities.
>
> ST strategies employ strengths to counter or avoid threats.
>
> WO strategies address weaknesses so as to be able to exploit opportunities.

WT strategies are defensive, aiming to avoid threats and the impact of weaknesses.

It is important that you take note of the number of marks available when answering questions. In part (c) 1 mark was available for each relevant point up to a maximum of 3 marks for each quadrant of the TOWS matrix, up to a total of 12 marks. Taking note of the number of marks on offer should have helped to guide the amount that you needed to write in order to produce a well rounded answer. Candidates that spent too long writing about one or two of the TOWS quadrants did so to their detriment, enabling them to only realise a fraction of the marks on offer.

Examiner's comments. The examining team noted that part (c) was the answered least well by the candidates attempting the paper. A significant number of candidates got the TOWS matrix quadrants wrong , for example trying to find strengths to overcome weaknesses. Very few answers focused on strategic options with many 'preferring to describe a limited tactical response. Many candidates seemed to be familiar with the matrix but not with its application'.

This report concludes by considering the strategic options available to Vi Ventures should the proposed investment in ReInk be made. This analysis was conducted through the use of a TOWS matrix. A TOWS matrix contrasts different combinations of strengths and weaknesses against an organisation's opportunities and threats.

TOWS analysis

Strengths and opportunities (SO) option

An SO option is where the organisation's strengths are deployed to realise identified opportunities. The government in Eland is engaged in promoting recycling and environmentally friendly policies, while also emphasising the need for government departments to show value-for-money in purchasing. ReInk is in a good position to take advantage of these opportunities as the company offers 'green' printer cartridge solutions and has a long-term contract in place to provide services to the DoRC. Focusing on such a niche market by targeting public sector entities may help to improve ReInk's financial performance, while allowing the company time to address its key weaknesses in promotions and marketing.

Weakness and opportunities (WO) option

A WO option is focused on using identified opportunities as a means of reducing weaknesses. As previously discussed ReInk's attempts at building brand awareness to date has been poor. However, the increase in awareness among consumers of the need to recycle products represents a significant opportunity for ReInk. This opportunity is also being driven by the state of the economy in Eland, where consumers are seeking to reduce print costs. ReInk would be well placed to exploit these changes due to the nature of its refillable ink service, provided it can overcome its lack of marketing expertise.

Strengths and threats (ST) option

An ST option can be used to help an entity overcome external threats by using its internal strengths. ReInk operates in a market which requires the constant development of the latest printer consumables technology at increasingly affordable prices. This threat requires ReInk to pursue a strategy which utilises its competencies in technical innovation to keep ahead of its competitors offerings.

Weakness and threats (WT) option

A WT option aims to reduce an organisations weaknesses while allowing it to avoid threats. Such options predominantly defend the entities existing position. ReInk's greatest weakness concerns the state of the company's finances. This weakness means that in the short term the company will unlikely be able to compete with larger players in the printer consumables market. One such competitor, Landy, has issued clear statements to customers about invalidating printer warranties if they use non-Landy ink. Landy is also particularly aggressive in pursuing legal claims against independent companies which offer cartridge ink refills for use with its printers. ReInk could avoid the threat of legal action by not offering refill services in respect of Landy products.

Summary

In summary, based on the above analysis it is evident that ReInk operates in a highly competitive environment. The printer consumables industry is characterised by small independent companies offering printer and toner cartridges at low prices. Larger OEMs compete on the grounds of quality and innovation in printing. The nature of the environmental and economic climate in the country of Eland presents ReInk with some significant opportunities.

The contextual features of change applied to the prospective investment in ReInk highlight some interesting considerations. Vi Ventures will need to ensure any investment is completed relatively quickly given the state of the company's financial position, while ensuring that key competencies are preserved.

Finally, the TOWS matrix analysis highlighted that a number of options exist which Vi Ventures could implement in order to improve ReInk's performance.

> **Examiner's comments.** In respect of the 4 professional marks available for the report the examining team noted that the marks were given for the overall quality, construction fluency and professionalism. 'Issues considered here include vocabulary (is it appropriate to a professional report?), tone and approach (reflecting Vi Ventures as the recipient), fluency of argument and structure; and, finally, are there appropriate introductions and summaries?
>
> Overall, presentation was fairly good. However, the context of the report was often forgotten. It was for Vi Ventures; and this should have driven the tone and content of the report, particularly in part (b), where Vi Ventures need to be aware of their possible input into the strategic change process at ReInk'.

44 MachineShop

> **Text reference.** Methods of growth and the SAF model are covered in Chapter 6, and Porter's Diamond in Chapter 2 of the BPP Study Text for exams from September 2015 to 31 August 2016.
>
> **Top tips.** Part (a) of the question required three methods of growth to be evaluated. There are 18 marks available. There are three methods to discuss. So students should gauge that this means there will be about 6 marks for each method of growth. This is illustrated in the marking scheme presented below.
>
> A good approach here is to contrast MachineShop's growth strategy to date against the other methods mentioned. The scenario makes it clear that organic growth in Arboria has proven successful for the company, however, this is unlikely to be suitable for international growth.

			Marks
(a)	1 mark for each relevant point per method:		
	Internal growth: 1 mark per point	Max	6
	Acquisition: 1 mark per point	Max	6
	Strategic alliance: 1 mark per point	Max	6
			18

(b) 1 mark will be allocated for each relevant point and interpretation up to a maximum of 18 marks. It is expected that this will include a financial calculation for FRG. All financial calculations must be relevant. These will attract half a mark each and are likely to include:

Gross profit margin
Operating margin
ROCE
Gearing ratio
Interest cover

Financial calculations may also be included for LogsTrans/EngSup and these will be marked as follows (1/2 mark for each company):

Gross profit margin:	1/2 mark
Operating margin:	1/2 mark
ROCE:	1/2 mark
Gearing ratio:	1/2 mark

		Marks
Interest cover:	1/2 mark	
		18

Professional marks are allocated as follows:

Up to 2 marks for structure of report
Up to 1 mark for the clarity of the analysis
Up to 1 mark for the soundness of the conclusion — 4

(c) 1 mark for each appropriate point up to a maximum of 5 marks for
general points made about the model

1 mark for each appropriate point up to a maximum of 5 marks for points
that specifically relate to conditions in Arboria or Ceeland — 10

— 50

(a) **Internal growth**

Internal growth is sometimes referred to as 'organic growth'. It is achieved through the development of an organisation's competencies. MachineShop has followed this approach in Arboria to date, where it has been opening, on average, two new stores a month.

Appropriateness for MachineShop

Internal growth has proven to be particularly advantageous for MachineShop historically, allowing the company to use its competencies to secure a unique position in the market. MachineShop's position has enabled the company to develop in a market which it fully understands. Furthermore, at the current time there are few equivalent companies operating in Arboria, indicating that there is unlikely to be a suitable acquisition target available.

By developing organically MachineShop has been able to control the rate and speed of expansion to suit its own needs. Slower paced development has supported Dave Deen and the board of directors by ensuring that management time has been fully devoted to establishing the MachineShop brand in Arboria. An acquisition strategy may have served as a distraction to the board.

Continued internal growth would appear to represent the most appropriate form of expansion within Arboria at the current time, due in part to an apparent lack of suitable takeover targets in Arboria.

Conversely, acquiring an overseas entity may help to support Dave Deen's ambitious plans to build a worldwide brand. FRG in the country of Ceeland has been identified as a possible acquisition target. However, there are likely to be concerns over such a move as FRG unlike MachineShop predominantly sells larger machine tools to trade customers.

Internal growth can be beneficial for entities as the need to integrate operations with an acquisition target is not required. Cultural problems such as those MachineShop encountered when it acquired LogTrans and EngSup can therefore be avoided.

However, achieving international expansion via internal growth can prove particularly difficult. Establishing a presence in a new market from scratch and then growing the business is likely to take a long time.

Often national governments are keen to restrict foreign companies from entering fledgling domestic markets for fear of undermining home grown players. Historically, this appears to have been the case in the country of Ceeland as certain trading restrictions have only recently been removed. Internal growth for international expansion does not fit with Dave Deen's ambitious plan to create a worldwide brand in the near future.

Acquisition

An acquisition involves one entity taking ownership of another. Organisations which adopt this approach are often attracted by the speed of expansion that can be achieved in entering new markets. At the current time MachineShop is considering acquiring FRG in the developing country of Ceeland.

Appropriateness for MachineShop

By acquiring an established business such as FRG, MachineShop would achieve an instant presence in Ceeland. MachineShop would benefit from such a move as FRG is already established in a similar market to the one it presently operates in. MachineShop is likely to be drawn to FRG as the company already has its own depot and distribution network and sales team. MachineShop would be able to exploit FRG's understanding of social, cultural and legal factors when trading in Ceeland. This is a considerable benefit for MachineShop as the company would need to start from scratch if attempting to grow organically.

Acquiring FRG would allow MachineShop to meet Dave Deen's ambitious growth plans for the company, representing the first step towards developing a worldwide brand. It is likely that MachineShop would be able to realise economies of scale through becoming a larger entity. A larger MachineShop group should allow the business to operate more efficiently with reduced costs through bulk ordering of inventory. Dave Deen seems to believe this will act as a barrier to entry to potential competitors looking to trade in Ceeland.

MachineShop has, however, experienced problems when acquiring companies in the past. The acquisition of LogTrans was disrupted due to a personality clash between LogTrans' senior management and Dave Deen. The purchase of EngSup also led to poor engineer performance and customer complaints. To ensure a smooth acquisition, MachineShop needs to address its apparent inability to resolve cultural issues when integrating two businesses.

Strategic alliances

A strategic alliance is formed when two or more separate entities work together to share resources. The aim of such an alliance is to allow both entities to derive benefits through co-operation. In the case of MachineShop such an alliance with FRG would represent a form of 'co-specialisation'. Co-specialisation allows organisations to share each other's strengths, knowledge and expertise in a particular field or industry. An alliance between MachineShop and FRG would allow MachineShop to benefit from FRG's understanding of the local trading conditions in Ceeland.

Joint venture

A joint venture is a form of strategic alliance which goes a step further than simply sharing resources. This involves the establishment of a new organisation which is jointly owned and controlled by the parent entities.

Appropriateness for MachineShop

In the case of MachineShop, a formal joint venture with FRG would involve a new company being set up in Ceeland. FRG could provide the necessary distribution and sales network, whereas MachineShop could provide products and financial support.

Licensing

Alternatively, a licensing arrangement could be established with FRG whereby MachineShop hires space in FRG's branches. Such an approach would allow MachineShop to gain market share and build up its own presence in Ceeland. It represents a potentially lower risk strategy than entering a new market via an acquisition. In addition, such an arrangement could be entered into relatively quickly.

However, it is debateable whether Dave Deen would favour a licensing arrangement as it may not provide the opportunity to build MachineShop into the worldwide brand that he is pursuing.

The biggest problem for most organisations pursuing a joint venture strategy is finding an appropriate partner. It is not clear whether FRG would consider entering into an arrangement with MachineShop. Further research would be required to assess the situation. Failing to arrange an agreement with FRG may slow MachineShop's ambitious growth plans as an alternative partner would need to be found.

MachineShop's successes to date have in part been driven by Dave Deen's 'high national media profile'. Expansion through a joint venture may not provide him with the visible growth he is hoping to achieve. A potential drawback to any form of alliance is that this will involve working with partner organisations. This increases the risk of culture clashes between parties and the scope for MachineShop's 'unique competencies' to be copied.

(b)

Report

From:	Business Analyst
To:	The Board of MachineShop
Date:	9 December 2013
Subject:	Proposed acquisition of FRG

Introduction

This report will explore the potential acquisition of Fabrique Regle de Garrido (FRG) by MachineShop. The suitability, acceptability and feasibility of this proposal will be considered.

Suitability

The suitability of a proposal is concerned with whether or not it fits with the organisation's current market position and objectives. Expansion through acquisition allows organisations to achieve rapid entry into new markets. This would certainly appear to fit with Dave Deen's plans as he is interested in MachineShop achieving internal growth and building a worldwide brand.

The purchase of FRG appears to be suitable for MachineShop. FRG is an established player in the country of Ceeland where no direct competitors currently exist. It is also believed that acquiring FRG would result in MachineShop being able to achieve economies of scale while establishing barriers to entry to deter potential competitors.

In the event that MachineShop decided to establish its own chain of stores in Ceeland there would be increased potential that the company will encounter some resistance from consumers not keen on dealing with a foreign company. The suitability of the acquisition will in part be determined by MachineShop's ability to manage and integrate FRG into its operations. The previous acquisitions of LogTrans and EngSup may raise some concerns in this respect.

Acceptability

Acceptability is concerned with whether stakeholders will support a strategic proposal. Often the reaction of different stakeholder groups will be influenced by the risk and reward that the proposal offers. Primary stakeholders at MachineShop include Dave Deen and the board of directors. The board's attitude to business indicates that they are prepared to take risks to achieve growth.

A key part of determining acceptability involves conducting some financial analysis of the acquisition target. Based upon the financial information provided, the performance of FRG does not appear too attractive.

Comparison of MachineShop and FRG

	MachineShop	FRG
Gross profit margin	28%	16.67%
Operating margin	17%	8.89%
ROCE	17.5%	6.45%
Gearing ratio	15%	20.16%
Interest cover ratio	3.5	2.67

While the figures may help to provide a fuller assessment of FRG's performance is it important to understand that a straight comparison between both entities has limited value. MachineShop and FRG both target different customer groups. MachineShop predominantly sells to domestic customers as opposed to trade customers.

Direct comparison is also undermined as both companies operate in different countries. Ceeland is currently a developing nation whereas Arboria is a 'prosperous industrial' nation. Furthermore, MachineShop is a considerably larger entity, with turnover of $50 million compared to FRG's $9 million.

However, FRG's current position may represent an opportunity for MachineShop to improve FRG's fortunes should the acquisition go through. Consideration should be given to the fact that MachineShop has not previously acquired an overseas entity. MachineShop's experience in managing the acquisition of two Arboria based entities did not go smoothly. Dave Deen and the board would need to consider the impact of any cultural issues which may undermine the purchase of FRG.

MachineShop successfully financed the purchase of LogTrans and EngSup in Arboria, however, the proposed purchase of FRG would represent a far larger undertaking.

Feasibility

Feasibility involves assessing whether an entity has sufficient resources and competencies to implement a strategy successfully. MachineShop appears to have sufficient financial resource to acquire FRG. The company aims to achieve any such move through a mix of loans and retained profits.

Until a sale price for FGR is agreed, we cannot assess the financial feasibility of the purchase with any certainty. The process for valuing the company may take a significant amount of time as other stakeholder groups are likely to want to participate in any negotiations. The ownership of FRG is fragmented as it is owned by 30 shareholders, including a trade union. The trade union in particular is likely to want guarantees over members' workplace rights post-acquisition.

MachineShop has experienced issues in the post-acquisition phase of both the LogTrans and EngSup purchases. This may impact on the perceived feasibility of a move to acquire FRG. In the case of LogTrans, the company's post-acquisition performance suffered as a result of a dispute between Dave Deen and the senior management team at LogTrans. This resulted in the removal of this team. The purchase of EngSup resulted in problems with the service engineers not fully understanding the importance of good customer service. This required MachineShop to instigate organisational cultural changes.

As is illustrated below, the performance of both entities has reduced post-acquisition, which raises some concerns over MachineShop's ability to manage acquisitions successfully.

Performance analysis

	LogTrans 2012	LogTrans 2009	EngSup 2012	EngSup 2009
Gross profit margin	17.86%	21.54%	21.43%	23.08%
Operating margin	9.29%	10.77%	11.43%	13.85%
ROCE	9.56%	13.46%	12.50%	15.52%
Gearing ratio	14.71%	9.62%	9.38%	6.9%
Interest cover ratio	2.17	4.67	4.00	5.63

Conclusion

The acquisition of FRG appears to represent a suitable strategy to allow MachineShop to realise its growth objectives. However, questions remain over FRG's appropriateness as a potential target. FRG's financial performance is not particularly attractive when compared to MachineShop. It is also likely that due to FRG's current shareholder structure any acquisition will take a considerable amount of time to complete. Unfortunately, MachineShop's previous acquisitions have not been very successful. The domestic purchases of both LogTrans and EngSup resulted in significant upheaval immediately following their acquisition. On the balance of the information available it would appear that FRG is a high risk target. MachineShop may be better placed to consider alternative entities for any such move or give some consideration to pursuing the establishment of a joint venture with FRG.

(c)

Porter's diamond model

Porter's diamond model was developed to explore national competitive advantage. It is a particularly useful tool in understanding why companies operating in certain nations appear better placed to compete. The diamond consists of four key determinants.

Factor conditions

Factor conditions can be classified as being either basic or advanced. Basic factor conditions include unskilled labour and the natural environment, whereas skilled labour and the transport infrastructure are regarded as being advanced factors as these offer sustained advantages. Both types of conditions are deemed necessary if an organisation wishes to compete successfully in a particular industry.

In relation to Ceeland, the government has built up an effective road transport system which is cheap to use. The ability to easily distribute goods around the country is an attractive factor for MachineShop in considering whether to enter the market. MachineShop's interest has also been supported by the recent developments to Ceeland's digital communication network, since the ability to accept orders over the internet is a key part of its business model.

Demand conditions

Demand conditions are concerned with the level of demand by consumers for a particular product or service in a company's home market. The ability of an organisation to supply products and services to demanding discerning consumers in its home market may help when anticipating and satisfying buyer requirements in comparable overseas markets. This would appear to be a critical issue for MachineShop.

MachineShop has benefited in this regard by serving consumers in Arboria, where buyers are demanding and assertive. MachineShop would appear to be well positioned to exploit opportunities to expand into Ceeland, where consumers may be less demanding.

Dave Deen has suggested that a similar consumer society to Arboria is emerging in Ceeland. The decision by the government of Ceeland to lift restrictions on the type of machines permitted for use by citizens is likely to increase the demand for such machinery, thereby strengthening demand conditions. Prior to any venture into Ceeland, MachineShop would need to conduct full market research to ensure that the predicted social trends do occur.

Related and supporting industries

Related and supporting industries within a country are those which help to underpin the performance of organisations in a particular industry. MachineShop currently stocks products made by a supplier in Ceeland. The ability for a foreign entity such as MachineShop to source products of sufficient quality for sale in Arboria serves to make Ceeland even more appealing.

Firm strategy, structure and rivalry

The final component of the 'diamond' model concerns firm strategy, structure and rivalry. Porter identified that significant rivalry in a given market encourages competitors to continually develop their own products and services in order to maintain competitive advantage. MachineShop's success to date in Arboria has not been influenced by this factor due to a lack of competitors. As Ceeland's economy is still developing, domestic rivalry will also be lacking.

Government

Although not part of Porter's original model, the diamond has now been extended to reflect the potential importance of the Government in assessing the attractiveness of Ceeland to outside companies. Ceeland's government has invested heavily in its transportation infrastructure and information technology systems and has lifted restrictions on the type of machinery that can be used by domestic customers.

45 Network Management Systems

Marking scheme

			Marks
(a)	Up to 3 marks for each element of the PESTEL analysis up to a maximum of 15 marks		15
(b)	1 mark for each relevant point up to a maximum of 16 marks		16
	Up to 4 marks for clarity, structure and approach		4
(c)	(i)	Up to 2 marks for calculation and interpretation of gross profit margin, net profit margin and revenue per employee	
		Up to 1 mark for further appropriate points up to question part total of 9 marks	9
	(ii)	Up to 2 marks for time to payback issues	
		Up to 2 marks for identifying drawbacks and suggesting solutions	
		Up to four marks for issues about benefit identification and quantification up to maximum for question part of 6 marks	6
			50

(a) PESTEL analysis allows us to assess NMS's macro-environment in terms of the political, economic, socio-cultural, technological, environmental and legal factors affecting it.

Political

NMS is located in a prosperous country and is operating within a **stable political framework**, although a change in the political party in power could affect economic, monetary or fiscal policy.

Governments in industrialised countries look to **promote technology as a source of competitive advantage**. Tax incentives and grants are available for research and development or investments in new technology. Tax credits are also provided to offset company investment in research and development.

We can also see the **government's support for technological innovation** through the awards for technology which they make each year.

However, governments more generally act as **regulators of quality** in the industry. All new components being supplied have to be approved by the relevant government body in the country being supplied. This need for government approval may act as a **barrier to entry for potential new entrants** into the industry, although it may also be designed to protect domestic suppliers from foreign competition.

The current political environment also protects employees via legislation relating to employment hours, conditions and reward.

Economic

Economic cycle. The **economic cycle and business confidence will affect demand** in the economy, and, in turn, demand for NMS's goods. In 2010 the country suffered an economic downturn, and this led to many companies postponing technological investment.

The economic downturn may also cause customers to **postpone purchases**, however they may eventually have to invest in innovative products to gain cost and communication advantages.

Wage costs. NMS currently manufactures 40% of their components, but wage rates in Elsidor are high despite the economic downturn. Therefore, it is likely that NMS's **labour costs make its manufacturing costs more expensive** than competitors who source their components abroad and only assemble them in Elsidor.

Social

Recent years have seen significant increases in levels of **communication, information exchange and social networks**, and it is likely that these increases will continue. This means that the demand for companies supplying communication products and network systems will also continue to grow.

Although NMS's sales appears to be declining, it is likely that new social uses for telecommunications networks will **provide opportunities for growth in the industry sector as a whole**.

Technological

NMS is a **hi-tech business**, and technology is a significant factor in shaping the life cycle of existing products, and the introduction of new ones.

The hi-tech sector is extremely **innovative,** with new and improved technologies constantly emerging. NMS needs to be aware of this, and realise that the **product life cycles** for its existing products may be quite short.

NMS also needs to be constantly aware of any **new technologies** which competitors are introducing, and how this might affect the future of their own products. NMS should also consider how they can use new technologies in their own products.

Environmental issues

Organisations are encouraged by politicians and by legislation to **reduce pollution and emissions and to increase the amount they recycle**. Environmental issues are part of a company's broader corporate social responsibility.

Waste disposal may be a particular issue for NMS because they are dealing with electrical items. Regulation around the **disposal of electrical items** is becoming stricter, and this is increasing the cost of disposal.

Legal

NMS must work within the constraints of legislation relating to employer responsibilities and employee rights and so will have to evaluate the costs and benefits of doing so. Compliance costs could be saved by relocating to a country with less stringent requirements in these areas. This could be beneficial given the number of international competitors, some of which may be operating in countries with less legislation surrounding employment and other relevant areas.

(b)

Top tips. The requirement does not specify which models to use as a framework for your environmental analysis, but the answer below is based around Porter's five forces. This is the model which the examiner uses in his own answer. Because you had already been asked to undertake a PESTEL analysis is (a), you should not re-use this model in (b).

You should not describe or explain the five forces (or any other model you choose), and would not get any marks for doing so. Where you score marks is by using the theory to identify specific issues affecting NMS's position.

We are going to use Porter's five forces model as a framework for analysing NMS's competitive environment.

Bargaining power of customers

Data communication components

NMS is selling predominantly to **large international customers**, who demand **high quality and performance from the components, but at a competitive (low) price**. Large industrial customers are becoming increasingly cost conscious and this is likely to lead them to look reduce the price they pay for their components as far as possible. They are unlikely to put up with the late delivery of orders.

The **supplying industry is relatively fragmented**; NMS has less than 1% of the UK market share for this sector, and there are more than 20 supplier supplying it. This fragmentation of the market supply **increases the power that buyers have** over suppliers because it can compare a range of suppliers against one another and then choose the one offering the best deal. It is unlikely that NMS will be able to sustain good margins in this market.

Buyer power will be strengthened further during a **downturn in the global economy** because suppliers cannot afford to lose customers. The customer which accounts for 40% of NMS's sales will have a particularly strong bargaining position in any negotiations with NMS.

Network management systems

Although NMS still supplies to large end users, the customers have relatively less bargaining power in this market than in data communications components.

NMS is a **significant supplier** in this market, and **only faces two or three competitors**. Moreover, this is a specialist market where **bespoke solutions** are tailored to customers' specific needs, and this makes it harder for customers to compare potential suppliers on price grounds. In addition, the product purchase is likely to be only a small proportion of the buyer's overall investment in information and communication systems.

The fact that NMS is able to sustain gross margins of over 40% in this market shows that it has a relatively strong position in this market.

Bargaining power of suppliers

NMS manufactures 40% of the components used in its products, leaving the remaining 60% – including semiconductors and microprocessors – to be **bought in from global suppliers**. It is likely that these global suppliers are major companies, such as Intel, in which case supplier power will be significant.

Compared to these suppliers, **NMS is a very small company**, and so it will not have the power to exert any buyer pressure on them – either in terms of price or delivery terms.

NMS's lack of bargaining power with the suppliers is evident from the problems it has with the component deliveries which are resulting in delays to the manufacturing and assembly of its own products.

Labour can also be considered to be a supplier, and again this supplier has strong bargaining power as the scenario indicates that the small size and location of NMS makes it difficult for them to attract the key personnel necessary for future growth.

Threat from new entrants

NMS is operating in a hi-tech industry, and so one which is **capital and knowledge intensive**. This will mean there are **significant costs of entry** for any potential new entrants into the industry.

Moreover, particularly for the data communication components business, cost is an important decision-making factor for customers. This may be a deterrent for potential new entrants. They **will need to produce enough output to benefit from economies of scale**, otherwise their cost base will be higher than established competitors.

Equally, large international **customers may be cautious about moving to a new, unknown, supplier**. If the new entrants cannot secure a critical mass of custom then they will not be able to produce at high enough levels to benefit from economies of scale.

This uncertainty around user acceptance and future sales in the context of high initial investment and ongoing R&D investment in a hi-tech industry with short product life cycles may discourage new entrants from joining the market. The **need to offer a comprehensive support network** is an additional barrier to entry.

Government regulation. The need for government approval of new data communications equipment also acts a barrier to entry. Getting government approval is an expensive and lengthy process.

However, **NMS has shown that it is possible for smaller, innovative companies to secure a niche position** in network management systems market. There is no need for government approval in this market, and margins appear higher than in the data communications component market.

Nonetheless it is still a specialist market so any new entrants will need to acquire and demonstrate the **technical excellence needed to compete with the established players**. It is a low volume market, so there is unlikely to be capacity to sustain a high number of new entrants.

Rivalry among competitors

The two markets NMS competes in (data communication components, and network management systems) have very different levels of competition in them.

Data communication components market

The data communication components market is a **high-volume, low-margin market** with a number of businesses all competing to supply the large international customers. These customers can compare potential suppliers easily, and **switch between them relatively easily**, and so rivalry between suppliers will be intense. It is unlikely that NMS will be able to improve its margins in this area.

Barriers to exit (knowledge, skills and assets are industry specific) will make it difficult for an existing supplier to leave the industry. Therefore although margins are low, the suppliers are likely to remain in the industry and will maintain the high level of competition among suppliers.

Network management systems market

Rivalry among competitors will be **much less intense** in the network management systems market because there are only two or three competitors in this specialist market.

NMS is designing products specific to end users needs, and so it will be **much harder for users to switch** from one supplier to another.

However, to be successful going forward, NMS will need to ensure that it maintains the quality and reputation of its systems. It is currently able to pursue a strategy of **focussed differentiation** in this market place because it has a superior product which distinguishes it from its competitors, allowing it to charge a higher price for it.

Threats from substitute products

One of the characteristics of hi-tech industries is that they are prone to new technologies emerging and replacing established technologies. Product life cycles are becoming increasingly short in hi-tech industries. Consequently, it is important that companies in hi-tech industries are aware of any new product innovations that may pose a threat to their existing products.

NMS will need to ensure that if there are any technological developments in the industry it incorporates them into its own new products. The small size of NMS may prove critical here in allowing it to respond quickly and flexibly to any such changes.

(c)

> **Top tips.** Don't get too bogged down in the financial information when answering part (i), only perform relevant calculations and ensure you fully interpret and explain your findings in light of the scenario.
>
> When talking part (ii), you will need to evaluate both the method used to carry out the cost-benefit analysis, and the assumptions that have been made to calculate the figures that have been used within that analysis.

(i)   **Sales growth**

NMS has seen revenue increasing to a peak in 2009 but is now **predicting a 10% decline in sales in 2010 compared to 2009**. This is a major problem for the company, even if some of the decline is due to the economic downturn rather than performance issues specific to NMS. It would be useful to benchmark NMS's sales performance against some of its competitors to gauge how NMS is performing in relation to the rest of the industry.

One particular area of concern is that of new business being generated. In 2007, it stood at **73% of total sales**, but the forecast for 2010 shows an **order book of only 37% of total sales**. Although it is only a forecast and so may not be entirely accurate, the 2010 figure nonetheless suggests that NMS is struggling to generate new business, and this problem needs to be addressed as a matter of urgency.

Exports

Export sales form less than 10% of total sales, and this is worrying for a company operating in a global industry. Moreover, the 2010 forecast predicts a 20% decline in export sales, compared with a 10% decline in total sales. Therefore, it would appear that nothing is being done to increase export sales as a percentage of total business.

Cost of sales and gross profit

Although sales for 2010 are forecast to be marginally less than 2008, **cost of sales have risen 12% for the same period.** NMS needs to investigate the causes for this increase, which may have come from problems with supplier performance or subsequent problems with production scheduling. The increased cost of sales has meant **gross margin has fallen from 38.24% to 30.42% from 2008 to 2010**.

The scenario does not provide separate data on revenue and costs of sales for the three distinct business areas, however, it does suggest that the network management systems area generates 40% gross profit. This suggests the gross profit margin on data communication components is significantly lower.

Net profit margin

The net profit margin has also declined from **10.29% in 2008 to 7.52% in 2009 and again to 2.29% in 2010**. It could be that the 2010 decrease indicates a failure to bring operating costs under control following the sudden sales decline.

Sales revenue per employee

The number of staff employed increased until 2009 and in 2010 remains unchanged despite the falling revenue. This has caused the sales revenue per employee to fall from 113 in 2008 to 90 in 2010.

Overall financial position

Financially, the current position does not look good. Sales growth is slowing down, order levels are falling, and profitability is falling.

NMS's **internal processes** allow it to produce innovative products and meet end user requirements, but the operational and management control processes appear weak. The **planning and scheduling system** needs improvement to reduce the number of orders that are late. The **management accounting system** needs improving to allow management better control over costs.

(ii)   Ray has carried out a payback period calculation and has correctly determined that it will take 5 years for the machine to pay for itself. This is a legitimate approach to investment appraisal, however, there are two factors that Ray should bear in mind if he plans to make the decision based on this calculation.

Method of investment appraisal

The payback period method of investment appraisal does not take into account the time value of money. This means that future cash flows are not discounted. This is particularly important for NMS because the majority of the costs are incurred at the outset (year 0), however significant benefits do not accrue until the third and fourth years.

If Ray is satisfied with this method, then he must decide if 5 years is an acceptable timeframe and whether any other investments within the company would pay back sooner. This helps him to ensure that limited resources are directed towards the most lucrative investments.

Reliability of financial values

Ray has classified the expected benefits into three categories and a financial value has been attributed to each. However, not all these financial values are reliable.

Labour

Ray has estimated a reduction of $15,000 per annum based on observed performance as less labour will be required to use the machine. This is a tangible financial benefit which can be classed as a **quantifiable benefit** as there is sufficient evidence to reliably forecast the amount of benefit that will arise from the change. This financial value is therefore reasonably reliable.

Wastage

Wastage is currently measured, but it is **not possible to accurately predict** how much it will change if NMS switches to using the machine. This will be possible, however, once the machine is in active use at NMS. It is therefore a **measurable benefit**. Financial values based on these are less reliable than those based on quantifiable benefits.

Energy

Although energy costs are measured for the whole company, they are not measured for individual machines. The estimates that Ray has used can therefore only be based on an educated guess. Further, more savings after implementation cannot be reliably tracked back to the new machine and so are unlikely to be properly realised. This makes the financial values attributed to energy savings extremely unreliable.

46 The Ace Bicycle Company

> **Text reference.** The topics mentioned in this answer are discussed in Chapter 6 of your BPP Study Text for exams from September 2015 to 31 August 2016.
>
> **Top tips.** Do not be daunted by a single requirement worth twenty five marks. This indicates that there is plenty to say. Work methodically and plan your answer so that it flows logically from section to section. Also, take care: the mark allocation amounts to almost a quarter of your available time. Do not get carried away and spend too long on part (a)!
>
> **Easy marks.** You need to make sure you apply your knowledge of 'appropriate models' to the scenario, but there are a number of models which can help you here (BCG; Product life cycle; Ansoff; Strategy clock). Use them to evaluate how suitable the strategies ABC is pursuing are for each segment of the business.
>
> **Examiner's comments.** The examining team pointed out that an answer could have been based on other theoretical models, such as the product life cycle or *Ansoff's* product/market growth vector matrix. However, the BCG approach does seem particularly useful here for assessing ABC's portfolio.

		Marks
(a)	Up to 3 marks for report layout and structure	3
	Up to 5 marks for each evaluation of ABC's four types of bicycle (including the use of relevant models to support answer)	20
	Up to 2 marks for consideration of ABC's financial situation	2
(b)	1 mark for each relevant point up to 13 marks (Consideration may be given to the operational, financial and associated risks of establishing facilities in China)	13
(c)	1 mark for each relevant point up to a maximum of 4 marks for organic growth	4
	1 mark for each relevant point up to a maximum of 4 marks for acquisition	4
	1 mark for each relevant point up to a maximum of 4 marks for joint development	4
		50

Part (a)

REPORT

To: Colin Doncroft, Managing Director
From: Simon Gaskell, Management Consultant
Date: December 20XX
Subject: Evaluation of Ace Bicycle Company strategies

Introduction

This report is designed to consider the different **strategies** that Ace Bicycle Company (ABC) is following in its different markets and to **evaluate each of these individual strategies** given the information provided for the last two years and the current year's forecast figures.

In overall terms ABC has seen a **decline in demand** for its products, with demand expected to fall by 5% over the period. Although revenue is expected to increase in 2008/09 the direct costs are an increasingly large proportion of sales revenue and are expected to reach 84% of revenue in the current year, a rise of 14% over the period. Together with a dramatic expected increase in indirect costs of 54% over the period this has caused a significant fall in profits to an expected, and unacceptable low, of just 2%.

ABC has **four distinct market sectors** – racing bicycles, mountain bikes, health clubs and basic bicycles – with distinctly different strategies being followed for each market therefore I will consider each market in turn.

Background

ABC is a private, family owned company which is now a national producer of bicycles. Some of its products are sold under its own brand name whereas others are sold through a national retail chain under its retail brand name. Over the last few years ABC has seen its **market being eroded** with **increasing competition** from cheaper overseas imports. The overall UK market for bicycles is in decline and this has been made worse by the high value of sterling encouraging imports from foreign suppliers. However during this period ABC has been able to increase its share of domestic output by accepting lower profit margins in order to maintain sales. ABC concentrates its efforts solely on the bicycle market and has a **strong reputation** for reliable products.

Each individual market that ABC operates in will now be considered in turn in the light of this background information.

Racing bicycles

ABC has been making racing bicycles for many years and this area currently accounts for approximately 20% of its volume output and almost 60% of its sales revenue. This is the only sector of ABC's business where the volume of sales is expected to **increase** this year. This sector is by far the **most profitable** of ABC's market areas, but even though anticipated revenue has increased by 15% over the period considered, the **direct costs** of production have outstripped this with an expected increase of 25%. However, this area still remains profitable and although the bicycles are expensive to produce, some being custom made, the **distribution costs** in this sector are minimised by the policy of taking direct orders from amateur cycling clubs. These racing bicycles are marketed under the ABC brand name and have enhanced ABC's reputation.

ABC appears to have followed a successful strategy of **premium pricing** in this market and has **differentiated** the product by the policy of producing custom made bicycles. Despite the cost increases, the margins in this sector are still healthy with clear potential for volume and revenue growth. Any potential for increasing UK market share in this area or diversifying into sales of racing bicycles overseas should seriously be considered as this is clearly the most successful part of the current business.

This area of the business could be described as a **cash cow** according to the BCG growth-share matrix as ABC's market share is relatively high and the market is growing slowly.

Mountain bikes

ABC moved into this fashion area in the 1980s producing relatively cheap models and currently this sector accounts for 30% of ABC's output but only 16% of revenue. The volume of **sales is expected to decline by 8%** over the period considered and **revenue to decline by 5%**. However direct costs of production have increased each year and are anticipated to be 87% of revenue for mountain bikes in the current year. Despite increases in costs and decreases in revenue this sector remains **relatively profitable** in relation to other market sectors of the business.

About 75% of these mountain bike sales are made under the ABC brand name through **specialist bicycle shops**. The remainder of the sales are made through a **national retail chain** of bicycle and motor vehicle accessories stores under the retailer's own brand name.

ABC's pricing policy of charging relatively low prices for the mountain bikes is a strategy of **penetration pricing**; however, in order for this to be successful, ABC needs to be able to **compete on costs**. The increases in direct costs will tend to invalidate this policy as ABC does not appear to have the production capacity to achieve the **economies of scale** necessary to maintain profit margins as sales volumes decline and cheaper foreign imports pose a threat.

As ABC has been so successful in its premium pricing policy in the racing bike market, and the majority of the mountain bikes are also marketed under the ABC brand name, the company should consider **moving away from the low price market** for mountain bikes. If the mountain bikes produced are promoted as being of high quality based upon the well-respected **brand name** of ABC in the racing bike market, the company may be able to attract customers prepared to pay a higher price due to the quality of the product.

This area of ABC's business certainly appears to have potential but if changes in both the stabilisation of costs and marketing and pricing policy are not made it would appear that profits from this sector will continue to decline.

Exercise bicycles

The health club market for **exercise bicycles** plays only a small part in ABC's business currently with less than 5% of total volume sales. As this is a **niche market** it is possible to have a **premium pricing policy**; this sector has been consistently profitable over the period, although margins have reduced to an expected 11% for the current year. Part of the reason for the fall in profitability is, as with other areas of the business, the **escalation of costs** which in the current year represent 88% of the sales value of the exercise bicycles.

This market sector is different from ABC's other areas as it is a **diversification** into a different line of business. The exercise bicycles will have some similarities to the other bicycles manufactured but the market characteristics are very different. Health clubs are a completely different type of customer from those for the other sectors. Sales volume is expected to show a slight fall in the current year since ABC do not produce a full range of exercise equipment, which the market seems to prefer in its suppliers. Therefore ABC might consider **diversifying** into production of **other fitness equipment** such as running machines and cross trainers. This market appears to be potentially profitable but currently ABC is too small a player to take advantage of it in full.

Basic bicycles

The main product of the group, the basic bicycle, accounts for about 45% of the output volume and is therefore still the **core of the business**. However, the **margins** in this area are the main cause of ABC's overall fall in profitability. Sales volume has decreased by 7% over the past two years but sales revenue has fallen by even more, at 12%, as a result of reducing price in an attempt to maintain sales levels in the face of **increasing competition** from cheaper overseas imports. In the current year the margin has fallen to 2.4%, a drop of almost 80% over the two years. Two years ago the production cost per bicycle was £80 but this has increased to £83 per bicycle in the current year. In addition to this the selling price has reduced from £90 two years ago to £85 currently.

About 75% of these bicycles are supplied to a national retail chain supplying bicycles and motor accessories and marketed under the chain's own brand name. As ABC is heavily dependent upon the retail chain it may be that the retailer is forcing prices down using its **buying power**.

ABC's strategy in this market appears to have been one of competing on **both cost and price**. Unfortunately, it appears not to have worked. Prices are coming down and costs are rising. This area of the business is now being **subsidised** by the other more profitable but smaller markets.

There is no real brand association with the basic bicycles as the majority are sold under the retailer's brand name. Therefore it might be difficult for ABC to disassociate itself from the retailer and sell directly, although it may be possible to build on the brand association from the racing bicycle market. According to the BCG growth-share matrix the basic bicycle market could be categorised as a **dog** as the UK market in this area does not appear to be growing and ABC appear to have a relatively low market share.

If ABC is to improve profitability in this market it must decrease costs, probably move away from dependence on the retailer and attempt to **differentiate its product** in some way. Withdrawal from this market could be considered although as it is such a significant element of the business this may be a **dangerous strategy** and should only be considered when all other options have been examined.

Indirect costs

A further worrying area of the business is in the **escalating indirect costs**. Over the two years there has been a staggering increase of 54% in total indirect costs. **Distribution costs** are up by 43% although this may be understandable given the nature of the direct sales of the racing bicycles and exercise bicycles.

Administration costs have also increased by 25% over the last two years which, given the decrease in sales volumes, appears unusual.

Promotion costs have, however, fallen and this must be **rectified** if ABC is to capitalise on its brand name and increase sales volumes.

Loan interest is unavoidable but worryingly high as in the current year **interest cover is only 1.75 times**, a potentially dangerous level.

Conclusion

ABC currently has a wide range of strategies, a premium pricing policy for racing bicycles and exercise bicycles, and an attempt to be a cost leader at the lower end of the market with its basic and mountain bikes. **Production costs** must be brought under control before any rationalisation of strategies can be considered.

It would appear that ABC's strengths lie in its **strong reputation and brand** association in the racing bicycle market. If this can be extended to the **mountain bike market** and a premium pricing policy introduced here with **market differentiation based upon the quality of the product**, then this could produce significant improvements in the mountain bike market.

A further potentially successful market is that of the **health club equipment** if the production range can be extended. The basic bicycle market could be improved with more control of direct costs but as the UK market is not expanding and the strategy has been one of cost leader, which has not succeeded, then it may be necessary to consider withdrawal from this market.

It would appear that the future of ABC lies with the **quality products** as ABC does not appear to have the production capacity to achieve the cost economies necessary for a successful cost leader strategy at the lower end of the market.

Part (b)

When considering any potential investment many factors must be taken into account but when considering such a major change in strategy as the managing director is proposing then there must be a **wide ranging review** of the key factors.

Operations

Let us first consider the **operational aspects** of the development of a manufacturing or assembly facility in China. The proposal is based upon the **large demand** for bicycles perceived in the Far East, the **cheaper labour** which would reduce **production costs** and the reduction in **transportation costs**.

As far as the demand for bicycles is concerned, the view of the market appears to be that of the managing director and there is no evidence that any **market research activities** have been carried out. What type of bicycles are in demand in China and can ABC produce bicycles that satisfy this demand? If the bicycles required are not the same as those currently manufactured by ABC there may be significant costs involved in re-design and changes to the manufacturing processes.

The **labour cost** aspect must be put into perspective. Labour costs only account for 25% of the total production cost therefore the cheaper labour would only lead to a maximum decrease in production costs of 17.5%. The labour issue should be considered further – how does the **productivity** of bicycle manufacturing employees in China compare to that in the UK. If productivity is significantly lower in China then this could **wipe out any cost benefit**.

The **transportation costs** of bicycles from the UK to China are obviously significant. However, if the proposed facility is set up in China instead there are still likely to be significant transportation costs since China covers a vast area and demand is likely to be spread widely. This internal transportation cost should not be ignored.

ABC must consider other operational aspects of setting up a manufacturing facility in China. Can the correct **components** be purchased at a competitive price and be delivered on time? What type and amount of **marketing expenses** will there be? ABC must also question its **ability to run** such an operation as it has no experience in even trading with other countries, let alone setting up a full scale operation in one, particularly one as distant and unknown as China.

Finance

ABC must also consider **financial aspects**. ABC has very low profit levels currently and a large debt outstanding. How does it propose to **raise the finance** necessary for such a major investment? Would the finance be raised in this country or in China? Are there opportunities for a UK company to raise major finance in China? Would a joint venture with a Chinese company be a viable option?

Further financial problems will concern the **remittance of funds back to the UK** and any **foreign exchange risks** that ABC may face. Many countries restrict the amount of their currency that can be taken out of the country and as ABC is so short of funds it will clearly require any profits to be remitted back to the UK. ABC should also consider the foreign exchange risks that are associated with any form of trade with foreign countries. If the Chinese currency moves against sterling then ABC could be subjected to large foreign exchange losses.

Risk

Political risk is a further important area that should be considered. How stable is the Chinese government? What is their attitude to foreign investors, are they encouraged or are there sanctions which will make operations more difficult and expensive?

Analysis

Many of the key factors involved in this proposal can be addressed through a **PESTEL analysis** (political, economic, social, technological, environmental and legal aspects).

Analysis of **political issues** will be of great importance in a country such as China which has large state control. **Economic factors** will help to define the demand structure, inflation rates, interest rates and availability of finance.

Social factors will help to define the market, determine the type of bicycle required and clarify the potential customer and method of marketing and sale. From the **technological** viewpoint, particularly if there is a demand for ABC's more high-tech products, such as the racing bicycle, does the technology exist in China or must it be exported? **Environmental factors** will include designing the factory to minimise its impact on the environment, and maximise the safety of the workers in it. **Legal factors** will include dealing with suppliers, contracts for setting up a factory and employment issues.

Conclusion

The theory behind diversification for large companies is that there is no need for a company to do this simply to reduce the risk of just being in one industry as the shareholders are quite capable of doing this on their own behalf by owning a portfolio of shares. However for a private family owned company that is experiencing problems with profitability, a move into a new area is enticing. For ABC, given its core expertise, diversification should only be considered if it is believed that there are no future gains to be made from its current markets and that moves into non-core areas are likely to be successful.

Part (c)

> **Text reference.** The topics mentioned in this answer are discussed in Chapter 6 of your BPP Study Text for exams from September 2015 to 31 August 2016.
>
> **Easy marks.** There is little in the scenario that you can use in this answer, so you may proceed more or less on a textbook basis, which is generally easier than applying knowledge to scenario problems.

(i) **Organic growth**

Organic growth means setting up the operation purely with ABC's own resources. The benefits of such an approach are:

- Since ABC would provide all of the resources for the investment, the development can be scheduled according to its **own timetable** rather than that of a partner.

- Organic growth tends to be slower than setting up a joint venture and will be less of a **drain on the resources** of ABC, since it can set its own pace.

- As ABC is setting up the venture on its own **all profits will accrue to ABC** and do not need to be shared with any partner.

- As ABC is not reliant on any other party it will be able to expand its own **competencies and knowledge**.

- The development can to take place in an orderly manner with no pressures from third parties to introduce products early. ABC will be in control and can introduce its products to the market **as and when it deems appropriate**.

- There is no need for ABC to **integrate with a partner**, either organisationally or culturally.

- Organic growth is likely to mean **higher motivation for employees and managers** as they are in control of the operation without input from any other party.

(ii) **Acquisition**

A further way of setting up the operation in China would be to acquire a bicycle manufacturer in China. The benefits of this approach are:

- The project can get **started more quickly** as the acquired company will already have the infrastructure in place and the expertise and resources required.

- This approach may be **cheaper than organic growth** if the cost of setting up the operation from scratch was going to be very high. Also, an acquisition can sometimes be self-financing; this occurs if unwanted parts of the acquired entity can be sold at a profit.

- ABC has no experience of trade in China and therefore by acquiring a company already operating there they are also effectively **acquiring the knowledge and expertise required**.

- ABC may find that there are **barriers to entry into the market by organic growth** such as access to distribution outlets, building a brand name or obtaining necessary licences; by acquiring an already operational company ABC may be able to avoid these problems.

(iii) **Joint developments**

A further method of entering the Chinese market is to enter into some sort of joint venture with a Chinese organisation. The benefits of such a joint development are:

- The **cost of the investment would be reduced** as it would be spread between ABC and its partner.

- The **risk would also be lower** as it would be shared with the partner – if the venture were unsuccessful ABC would have less investment to lose.

- In many countries foreign operations are **treated with suspicion** by government and customers alike – if a joint venture with a Chinese organisation is set up then this would make the operation more politically and commercially acceptable.

- ABC should be able to enter the market much more **rapidly** in a joint venture than by organic growth.

- ABC will obtain the benefit of the partner's **market knowledge** and access the partner's current customer base and supplier network.

- By entering into a joint venture the partner is **avoided as a direct competitor**.

47 MidShire Health

Text reference. Project management is covered in Chapter 13 of your BPP Study Text for exams from September 2015 to 31 August 2016. Organisational culture is covered in Chapter 5 and organisational configuration is covered in Chapter 7. The three strategy lenses are covered in Chapter 1.

Top tips.

Part (a) (i) Note that there are three parts to this question. It asks you for the mistakes made by the project manager at each of the three stages: implementation, conduct and termination. Make sure you address all three areas. Using the stages as headings will help you to structure your answer.

Take care not to just repeat information from the scenario. Ensure you use this information to actually answer the question asked in the requirement. For example, while the fact that the doctors did not attend a meeting leads to problems in the planning of the project, this is not in itself a mistake made by the CEO. The doctors' absence occurred as a result of the mistakes the CEO made, such as failing to allocate team members to the project full time, and failing to communicate and manage the timetable of meetings to ensure all participants were present. Therefore, these are the issues you should identify, not the doctors' failure to attend the meetings.

Easy marks. Can be gained by using the scenario and pulling out the things that have gone wrong with the project management process.

Part (a) (ii) Note that this requirement covers both organisational culture and organisational configuration therefore you should include a discussion of each in your answer.

The use of models such as the cultural web will help you with this requirement, but do not rely too heavily on it. There is not necessarily something in the scenario for each of the elements of the web. Focus your answer on the relevant parts of the model.

Minzberg's stereotypical configurations model also provides a strong basis for the section of this requirement dealing with organisational configuration. For example, how is the configuration of the hospital likely to differ from the configuration of the CEO's previous organisation – a manufacturing company?

Examiner's comments. Too many answers followed the sequence of the meetings described in the scenario, repeating the same information and diagnosis, often accompanied by copying out sections of text directly from the scenario. There was a lack of analysis and organisation in many answers. This repetition of the same points also led to long answers which probably contributed to time problems later in the examination. In general, part (a)(i), concerning project management was better answered than part (a)(ii), on culture and configuration. This was largely because general points made about good project management were accompanied by appropriate illustrations from the scenario.

Top tips.

Part (b) Make sure that you are familiar with all areas of the syllabus and practice as many actual past exam questions as possible. Despite this question having already been asked in a previous exam a number of students did not appear to be familiar with the three strategy lenses.

Under the experience lens, a number of students took the approach that Terry was using 'strategy as experience' by trying to use the approach which had served him well in his previous job. This approach may also be valid providing that the answer then went on to note the reason why the strategy failed was because Terry's experience was not relevant in this kind of organisation.

Examiner's comments. There is an explicit learning objective on the three strategy lenses defined by Johnson, Scholes and Whittington (Study Guide section A1e) and a very similar question to the part (b) question posed here, was set in December 2008, concerning another public sector organisation, the National Museum. However, despite this, very few candidates scored good marks on part b of this question. Many candidates scored less than three marks, with answers that were often very sketchy and just rearranged the key words of the question.

Marking scheme

			Marks
(a)	(i)	1 mark for each relevant point up to a maximum of 18 marks	
	(ii)	1 mark for each relevant point up to a maximum of 18 marks	
		Up to 4 professional marks are allocated for the clarity, structure and logical flow of the answer	
		Total for requirement (a)	40
(b)		One mark for each relevant point up to a maximum of 10 marks	10
			50

(a)   (i)   **Project initiation**

There are a number of problems that arose during the project initiation stage which could have been prevented had a formal Terms of Reference (ToR) or Project Initiation Document (PID) been put in place. These issues relate to project objectives, scope and ownership.

Project objectives and scope

The objectives and the scope of the project are not clearly defined and seem rather confused. The scope could be considered to be either very wide, eg 'to implement a formal strategic planning system' or very narrow, eg 'to develop a comprehensive computer-based information system to record the outcomes and activities of the organisation'.

The various backgrounds and opinions of the members of the steering committee have also led to confusion around the project's objectives. Initially the main objective was stated by the CEO as 'to deliver health to the people of MidShire' but this was later revised to a narrower objective of 'effectively and efficiently treating disease'. In addition, these objectives do not really refer to the project specifically and are actually objectives that relate to the organisation as a whole. More detailed, specific objectives need to be formally agreed for this project if it is to be a success. These objectives should be documented in the Project Initiation Document.

Given that consultants were quickly appointed to implement a software system, it is likely that the project will be more focused on the technical solution. The distinction between the project's business objectives and the software system's technical objectives should be clearly defined and documented at the project initiation stage. Currently it would appear that the CEO is confusing the two, particularly given that the technical solution was selected before the business objectives themselves had been finalised.

 BPP
LEARNING MEDIA

Project ownership

Ideally one person, the project sponsor, should have overall responsibility for the project and that person should be the main decision maker and supporter of the project.

It is not clear in this case whether Terry Nagov is the project sponsor, of whether the intention is for the steering group to act as the project sponsor.

The project sponsoring role can be performed by a group, but this will only be effective if the group is united and work together for the same overall objectives. This is not the case here though. Not only are the group themselves disconnected, the scope and objectives of the project are also not clear, as discussed above. It is public knowledge that there is a high level of conflict within the group, therefore leaving the project without a clear and committed project sponsor. Without the clear leadership and support an effective project sponsor would provide, this project is much more likely to fail.

The role of the sponsor should have been carefully thought out and designed at the start of the project. This responsibility should have been clearly documented in the Project Initiation Document.

Conduct of the project

The issues encountered at this stage relate to the procurement process and group and stakeholder management.

Procurement process

As mentioned above, the software system was selected prior to the finalisation of the business objectives. This meant that once those objectives had been set it was found that the system was no longer a good match and significant bespoke work was required to make it fit for purpose. This was done at great financial expense and ultimately led to the failure of the project.

Best practice would have been to fully define the objectives and requirements prior to sourcing a software solution. Once the requirements are in place, a proper tender process should have been followed in which several companies were considered. The one which best fits with the requirements of the project at an acceptable price should be chosen for the job. The processes followed should be transparent and all decisions, and the reasons behind them, should be fully documented.

The system that was actually selected in this case had been originally developed for a bank. Had the above process been followed it may have been predicted that such a system would be unlikely to be suitable for use in a hospital.

Group and stakeholder management

The steering group is made up of three sets of employees: senior hospital doctors, hospital nursing managers and health support service staff. However, the level of power held by each of these groups is not equal. A fundamental mistake made by Terry was to fail to appreciate these differences in power.

The hospital doctors and the hospital nursing managers have similar opinions and this group appears to be dominant in terms of power. The CEO's views are generally supported by the health support service staff, however, this group would seem to be rather weak. These differences in power and culture will make it hard for this group to move beyond the 'storming' stage of team development.

The CEO could potentially have the power to help the group progress to the next stage, but by publically questioning the ethics of one of the hospital doctors, he further decreases the likelihood of the team achieving harmony. These actions also led to a formal complaint being made to the health minister of Etopia; an individual who had held little prior interest in the project but who has significant power to influence the outcomes.

Termination of the project

The quoted price of the software was not negotiated. It may have been possible to agree a lower price, particularly if the software could have been implemented in other health authorities and a fee for royalties could have been negotiated by MidShire Health. This would have helped the organisation to recover some of the cost of the investment. However, simply cancelling the project, as Terry Nagov did, meant that MidShire had no chance to rescue the project or to recover any costs.

Following the cancellation of the project there was no post-project review. This means that the lessons learned cannot be formally assessed and fed back into the project management system to prevent these mistakes being repeated in future projects.

(ii) **Organisational culture**

Culture consists of four layers: values, beliefs, behaviours, and taken-for-granted assumptions.

- **Values** – the mission of the organisation, perhaps documented within the mission statement.

- **Beliefs** – these are more specific. Beliefs are what we feel to be the case based on objective and subjective information.

- **Behaviours** – the way the organisation operates on a day-to-day basis.

- **Taken-for-granted assumptions** – the core of the organisation's culture. There is a discrepancy here between the vision the CEO has to 'deliver health' and the perception of the staff that the work relates instead to 'treating the sick'.

Aspects of the cultural web can be used to further analyse behaviours.

Stories

The stories in the organisation stem from the hospital doctors reinforcing their power status. The doctors do not appear to appreciate the value of the project, commenting in one meeting that they need to 'get back to their real work'.

They also do not appear to place much value on the role of the professional administrators as indicated by the reference to them as 'an unwanted overhead.'

Power structures

There is a hierarchy of power evident in the scenario with the hospital doctors at the top and the support staff at the bottom. The doctors highlight their respect for the support staff by walking out of a meeting when the support staff role and objectives were discussed.

The nurses have some degree of power, but not as high as that of the doctors. When the doctors are present at meetings, the nurses take the side of the doctors to create a powerful coalition allowing them to block the CEO's initiatives. When the doctors are not present the nurses are more co-operative and open to ideas, however, they then backtrack in later meetings when the doctors are again present.

The doctors have very favourable employment terms and a high level of freedom which is tolerated by the government. Although the nursing staff do not have this level of freedom, they have strong loyalties linking them to the doctors. The support staff, on the other hand, work under difficult circumstances for little or no recognition. This makes the support staff the most open to the changes suggested by the new CEO. As the doctors have the highest power, it is important that they support the new system if it is going to be successful. Terry therefore will need to find a way to get the doctors on side.

Control

The organisation does not appear to have much power over the hospital doctors. This is highlighted by the disclosure of confidential information to the press. This action is supported by the doctor's colleagues, and threats from doctors and nurses make it impossible for the CEO to pursue any disciplinary action.

Organisational configuration

Prior to his appointment as CEO at MidShire, Terry Nagov was CEO of a mobility appliances manufacturing company. This is a very different organisation to MidShire. A manufacturing company such as this is likely to fit the definition of a **machine bureaucracy**. The work carried out would be routine and repetitive. Production would be heavily automated and staffed by semi-skilled employees who follow procedures and standards. The management structure would be centralised with line managers responsible for achieving defined targets and objectives. As CEO of such a company, Terry would have held a lot of the power which is likely to be concentrated in the top management levels of the organisation.

Nagov had a very strong track record in the private sector and his skills should be valuable to Midshire, however they prove not to be as a result of his failure to understand organisational configuration.

MidShire Health undertakes very different work to a machine bureaucracy. The work is complex and relies on professional judgement and the application of skills built up over years of training. MidShire is dependent on these professionals (eg doctors) and as such will give them a high level of control over their own work. This kind of organisation is considered to be a **professional bureaucracy**.

Unlike a machine bureaucracy, which generates its own standards internally, a professional bureaucracy's standards are derived from the self-governing associations to which the professionals belong. For example the Institute of Hospital Doctors (IOHD) will play a key role in MidShire. Nagov failed to understand the role that this and other professional associations play in a professional bureaucracy when he caused offence to the professional staff by questioning the legitimacy of the advice offered by the IOHD.

By understanding the configuration of MidShire, Nagov should have been able to predict the response of the support staff to the formal planning initiative. As such staff are managed in a machine, top-down style, it could have been foreseen that these staff would be in support of the initiative. Their predictable response would have reduced the value they could bring to the working party and as such their inclusion in this group should have been questioned. In addition, the fact that the support staff are seen as subservient to the professionals would mean that their views would tend to be ignored in any discussion.

A further consideration is the fact that MidShire Health is a public sector organisation. This is very different from the private world previously inhabited by Nagov. It does not charge individual users for its services and instead is funded by taxation provided by the government. The organisation will be competing with other tax-funded organisations for resources and so will have to demonstrate the value for money the organisation provides in order to continue to secure funding. The government should therefore be a powerful stakeholder in MidShire Health but this power is reduced as a result of the powerful professions, the press and the public that defend the health service.

(b)   **Strategy by design** is a rational, top-down process where senior managers develop a planned course of strategic action. A system to implement this strategy is then put in place and supporting objectives are cascaded down through the organisation. It is a traditional and popular approach to strategic development.

This is the method that has been proposed by the CEO. It is possible that he has brought this approach with him following its successful use at his former company. The manufacturing environment in which he formerly worked would have been well suited to such an approach. A carefully designed strategy may appeal to the CEO in this new role as the controls and systems may help him to achieve good value for money: a key objective for a public sector organisation such as MidShire Health.

Strategy as experience sees strategy as an adaptation and extension of what has worked in the past. It is based on the experience and assumptions of influential figures in the organisation and the ways of doing things approved by the organisation's cultural norms. Strategy as experience is generally linked to incremental change and as such tends not to be appropriate for major change.

This approach is taken by the senior hospital doctors and nursing managers who are on the steering committee. Involvement on this committee has allowed them to propose an alternative vision based on their direct experience and perceptions and the initial vision was narrowed as a result. Professional managers can be publically undermined in organisations such as the IOHD and public support can often be gained.

This makes it difficult for fundamental changes in strategy to occur, and the CEO may be inexperienced in developing strategy in such an environment.

Strategy as ideas is an approach that emphasises innovation and the diversity of ideas. Strategy can emerge from the way people within the organisation handle and respond to the changing forces present in both the organisation and the environment. The role of senior managers is to create the context and conditions in which new ideas can emerge and the best ones survive and thrive.

A health support member of the steering committee attempted this approach in suggesting that 'preventing problems must be better than curing them'. However, this idea was quickly shot down by the hospital doctors and nursing managers suggesting that new ideas and innovation are unlikely to be encouraged in the culture of an organisation such as MidShire Health. Given their status within MidShire Health, doctors and nurses are likely to quash any ideas which might challenge their position therefore preventing such ideas emerging from within the organisation.

The three lenses should ideally support each other as certain issues may be seen through one lens but not through another. The approach that would appear to be most suitable to MidShire Health would be to develop a strategy through experience which is supported by ideas. The strategy by design approach which is favoured by the CEO is unlikely to be successful in an organisation of this type and culture.

48 Polymat Tapes

Examiner's comments. The compulsory question is the key to passing the examination. Candidates who fail to achieve at least 25 marks on Question 1 find it difficult to gain sufficient marks from Section B to compensate for a poor performance on the compulsory question. The scenario was of a multi-product manufacturing company supplying a range of industrial tapes to a wide variety of industrial and commercial customers. Many of their customers were large manufacturers themselves. There was therefore an emphasis on business-to-business relationships.

Marking scheme

		Marks
(a)	Evaluation of company performance	Up to 3
	Evaluation of each product group	Up to 6 each
	Use of appropriate models	Up to 5
		(Maximum 25 marks)
(b)	Source of competitive advantage – generic strategy	Up to 3
	Alternative growth directions	Up to 6
	Alternative methods for growth	Up to 3
	Preferred strategy – justification	Up to 5
		(Maximum 15 marks)
(c)	Consideration of culture change	Up to 3
	Models for creating change	Up to 3
	Measures for implementing change	Up to 5
		(Maximum 10 marks)
		(Total = 50 marks)

Part (a)

Text reference. The topics mentioned in this answer are discussed in Chapter 2 of your BPP Study Text for exams from September 2015 to 31 August 2016.

Top tips. The question asks you to use 'appropriate models' to support your analysis. As the examiner's comments below indicate there were a variety of models which you could have used.

You may also have wanted to use the BCG matrix. However, you should be aware that Johnson, Scholes and Whittington advise that the BCG matrix should be used on **strategic business units**, not products. In this question, you are analysing a single company with a range of products, therefore you should be cautious in using the BCG matrix here.

To: Richard Johnson, Managing Director, Polymat Industrial Tapes Ltd

From: External consultant

Date: December 20XX

Introduction

There is cause for concern at PIT. At company level the return on sales is falling, with a disproportionate increase in fixed costs. Close analysis of the performance of the individual factories and product groups reveals further disturbing developments, as well as some cause for optimism.

Analysis of specific product groups

Cable Jointing Tapes

This product group is registering a sound increase in year-on-year sales, clearly exceeding the increase in the cost of sales with a consequent **improvement of the gross margin** from 40% in 2001/02 to a forecast 45% in 2003/04. There appears to be a link between the consistently high R&D spend and successful development of profitable products that meet customer requirements. **Market share** is high and consistent.

PVC Industrial Tapes

This group seems very stable, with gross margin again forecast at a healthy 45% in 2003/04 and a steady if slow growth in sales. The **decline in market share** does give cause for concern, perhaps reflecting the impact of low cost tapes. In addition, R&D expenditure is low, which seems to indicate that there is little prospect of product innovation to grow the market for the products of this division.

Paper Masking Tapes

Sales are declining and costs are increasing, particularly those associated with transport. **Market share** is being maintained, but costs cannot be allowed to spiral out of control in order to achieve this at any price. Despite the investment in a modern factory, this division is constrained by the terms of the operating licence with the US, and its inability to achieve an efficient low cost operation.

Models that could be used to analyse PIT's performance include Porter's five forces (looking at the level of competitive rivalry PIT is facing) and the BCG matrix, which emphasises the relationship between market share and profitability.

Although the BCG matrix is best applied to the balance of business units in a corporate portfolio, rather than products, we still think it offers a useful insight here. A company with a portfolio of business units could expect a range of growth profiles in the various industries with which it is associated. There is little evidence however to suggest that PIT has any products (business units) in high growth sectors.

In terms of the three product groups, the *Paper Masking Tapes* group has a respectable market share compared to its main competitor, but it more closely resembles a 'dog' than a 'cash cow' because of its declining profitability and spiralling costs. Moreover, the fact that there is **excess capacity in the industry** and sale of low price tape by the American competitors means that PIT has a relatively weak competitive position in this market. It is difficult to see how this division could be turned around without radical cost control measures.

Closer analysis of the tape groups could suggest that *PVC Industrial Tapes* are reaching the **mature stage** of their **product life cycle**, with stagnant profits and static sales. There appears little chance of significant growth in this market, and PIT is likely to face increased competition from its low cost competitors. It is possible, however, PIT could differentiate itself on grounds of quality – as it has done with the car manufacturers.

A respectable market share together with improving margins, supported by significant R&D, suggests that the *Cable Jointing Tapes* division has the potential to move into the 'star' category, assuming that market growth can be assured (there is nothing in the scenario however to indicate that this is possible). The fact that the **US competitor** has a strong brand and is an **aggressive innovator** is cause for concern because new product innovations could severely weaken PIT's position in this market.

Porter's generic strategies

Competitive strategy involves a choice between being the lowest cost producer (cost leadership), making the products different from competitors in some way (differentiation) or specialising in a segment of the market (focus, using cost leadership or differentiation). *Porter* believes that firms must choose one of these, or be regarded as 'stuck in the middle'. It could be said that PIT is 'stuck in the middle', with few if any claims to be a cost leader. Only in its Cable Jointing Tapes division does it have products differentiated to meet the needs of cable manufacturers.

PIT's products are aimed at a wide range of customers – from large multinationals to DIY enthusiasts and, consequently a large range of distribution channels are used. This has promoted inefficiencies: transport costs need to be brought under control and the value chain for each division needs examination for the benefits that are being delivered.

Information for management decision making – organisational knowledge

There is a lack of detailed management information on the **profitability**, or otherwise, of PIT's product range. The links between sales and marketing and the R&D teams seem *ad hoc* and underdeveloped and there is little co-ordination of the overall R&D effort. **Organisational knowledge** is not currently shared.

It should be noted in this context that knowledge and 'knowledge workers' are increasingly recognised as significant factors in the determination of competitive advantage, and PIT should consider the development of a system that encourages the sharing of its significant organisational knowledge. This will eliminate duplication of effort in accessing information, encourage a consistent approach to product management and facilitate employee co-ordination. This will be particularly valuable in the effort to **better understand customer requirements** and **promote innovation**.

Conclusion

Many of PIT's products are **mature**, and suffering from severe **price competition**. A strategy is needed to ensure the survival and growth of the company. The product life cycle is instructive in this regard: opportunities for innovation should be sought out to extend the life of products and create new ones.

Part (b)

Text reference. The topics mentioned in this answer are discussed in Chapter 6 of your BPP Study Text for exams from September 2015 to 31 August 2016.

Examiner's comments. Part (b) gave the opportunity to discuss strategic options. Here the BCG matrix and the invest/harvest/divest options were relevant, together with a consideration of Ansoff's growth options. Useful consideration was often given to whether the value chain of the firm should stay the same, as there were clear prompts from the scenario to consider whether the centralised warehouse and in-house transport service were really adding value to the company's products. There was often a reluctance to choose a preferred strategy as requested.

Strategies need to be evaluated by PIT according to their **suitability** to the firm's strategic situation, their **feasibility** in terms of resources and competencies and their **acceptability** to key stakeholder groups. From the scenario, it appears that radical change to either products or markets is unlikely to occur, but there is a need to establish which products can be developed, and for which customers.

Product market strategies involve the determination of which products should be sold in which markets, by market penetration, market development, product development and diversification. Any analysis of PIT's performance to date should lead to withdrawal from unprofitable markets, divestment of poorly performing products and a closing down of company activities which are adding little value, thereby releasing resources to be redirected to value-adding spheres of activity.

Examining each of the divisions in turn:

Cable Jointing Tape products with a lower cost base, but PIT has the advantage that its products already meet demanding quality standards so there may be resistance on the part of **satisfied customers** towards moving to a competitor. **Innovation** is likely to be a key differentiating factor in the future for this division, and the way to retain competitive advantage, but the question of whether product innovation in a mature market is a realistic strategy should be asked. Sustained look to offer the most likely opportunity for improved **market penetration** and **market**

development, through links with cable manufacturing customers. There may be an opportunity to **develop PIT's brand** as part of an attempt to stave off aggressive US competition.

Paper Masking Tapes is a product group without much scope for improved performance. Its cost base is higher than its major competitor, it has significantly lower market share and its access to product and process innovation is limited because of the arrangement with the American manufacturer. In addition there is significant overcapacity, and tape supplied to the automobile industry is under **severe price pressure**. **Divestment** would be a sensible option.

PVC tape products look to be a **product group with some potential**, with healthy margins and sales increases. Competition is increasing from competitors competitive advantage may involve **process** (rather than product) **innovation**. Certainly, PIT needs to look closely at its **value chain** and its customer base.

PIT needs to review the value of operating its own **warehouse and transport system**, which together involve the commitment of significant resources. More evidence is needed on the precise benefit that such an arrangement brings for the company. The scenario indicates that it has merely added to overheads and done very little to add any value for customers or the company.

A range of strategic options is open to the company, but much more information is needed on revenue and costs. From the above analysis however is does appear that an exit from Paper Masking Tapes, closing the warehouse and outsourcing the transport function would contribute to a successful business strategy.

Part (c)

Text reference. The topics mentioned in this answer are discussed in Chapter 8 of your BPP Study Text for exams from September 2015 to 31 August 2016.

Top tips. Part (c) was looking for ways the culture inside the firm could be changed – the process of change rather than any marketing actions and decisions. Culture and culture change has been a favourite area in previous papers.

References to the cultural web, and the different styles of change management could both have been useful here.

Examiner's comments. Parts (c) and (d) were the parts which typically gave the most problems but offered the candidate an opportunity to think creatively about what was required. Lewin's force field analysis and change process was by far the preferred model for explaining how the process might be managed, and there was encouraging evidence of its being better understood and more effectively applied to the problem.

Culture at PIT is production led. This is evidenced by the use of graduate chemists, the organisational structure of the company into factories specialising in their own product range, and separate R&D programmes. There is no overall mechanism for reporting, for example, the performance of the various divisions in terms of customer satisfaction or detailed product/market analysis. R&D should be closely co-ordinated with marketing because customer needs, as identified by marketers, should be a vital input to new product development.

Favoured models for stimulating change such as is required here include *Lewin's* **force field analysis** and three stage change process (unfreeze, change, refreeze). It is important to recognise that there is likely to be resistance to any change, so the culture shift has to be well thought out and implemented.

Unfreeze is the most difficult stage of this process, concerned mainly with selling the need for a marketing orientation to the staff of PIT, who may regard it as unimportant. They need a **motive** for changing their attitudes – this may be provided by demonstrating the negative effects of a lack of adequate marketing focus for the future of the company. A failure to stimulate the market has certainly had a detrimental effect upon the performance of **Retardon**, and paved the way for competitors.

Change is mainly concerned with identifying the key features of a new marketing orientation, communicating it and encouraging it. The new ideas must be shown to work. **Refreeze** implies the consolidation or reinforcement of the new behaviour. This could involve an **action plan** including timescales for particular activities (such as staff training on how to use a new customer database), milestones and the allocation of responsibilities.

Measures to increase the exposure of all types of staff to marketing, and the setting up of appropriate customer information systems leading eventually to a proper customer database, will help. Marketing has a key role to play in the effective implementation of new products but requires these changes to information provision.

BPP LEARNING MEDIA

The change from a technology driven culture to a marketing led one is likely to be a fairly major one for PIT. It is likely that the core **assumptions and behaviours of the company** will have to change to accommodate it. In addition, the changes will need to happen relatively quickly rather than filtering in incrementally.

Consequently the management are likely to have to adopt a **transformational style** to direct and enforce the changes.

49 Shoal plc

Text reference. 'Change management is covered in Chapter 8 and the BCG matrix is covered in Chapter 6 of the BPP Study Text for exams from September 2015 to 31 August 2016.

Top tips. The marks are allocated equally to each of the three companies considered in the scenario (ShoalFish, ShoalPro and ShoalFarm) so ensure that you dedicate an equal amount of time to each company.

There is a lot of information given in the scenario for you to draw on when answering this question, so you should be able to score lots of marks here and get the exam off to a good start.

A number of candidates chose to apply SWOT analysis to this question rather than BCG and generally did not score as highly. Don't automatically assume that SWOT is the answer to every question about company performance! Read the information you are given carefully before deciding which is the most appropriate model to help you frame your answer.

The fact that ShoalFish is the sixth largest fleet in the Western Ocean, does **not** give it a high relative market share. Many students overlooked the fact that the relevant axis on the BCG matrix is **relative** market share, not simply market share, and so incorrectly concluded that ShoalFish has a high market share.

Also, note that there are eleven other companies in the portfolio not described here. Some students answered this question as if there were only three companies in the complete Shoal portfolio.

Marking scheme

				Marks
(a)	1 mark for each relevant point up to a maximum of 5 marks for each company			
	There are three companies giving a maximum of 15 marks for this part of the question		Max	15
(b)	(i)	1 mark for each relevant point up to a maximum of 13 marks		
		Up to 2 additional professional marks allocated as follows: 1 mark for the *identification* of an appropriate model, 1 mark for the *justification* of an appropriate model	Max	15
	(ii)	1 mark for each relevant point up to a maximum of 8 marks		
		Up to 2 additional professional marks allocated as follows: 1 mark for the cogency of the analysis and 1 mark for the overall application to the case study	Max	10
(c)	1 mark for each relevant point up to a maximum of 10 marks			
			Max	10
				50

Part (a)

ShoalFish

PESTEL analysis indicates that fish stocks are rapidly declining (environmental) and the government has imposed fishing restrictions (political) with which ShoalFish have to comply.

Using the BCG matrix, ShoalFish has the characteristics of a dog. It has a small (12%) market share and the market itself is declining (5% over two years). Profits are also declining, although the 2009 gross profit margin (4.9%) is higher than in 2008 (4.7%) possibly indicating that the company has managed to reduce operating costs in line with the turnover.

However, despite being an apparent dog, disposing of the company may not be in Shoal plc's interest as it perceives there are synergies between ShoalFish and the other companies in the Shoal plc portfolio; it provides 40% of the fish used by ShoalPro, and it will directly supply the Captain Haddock restaurants post-acquisition therefore keeping the cost of raw materials down.

Shoal Plc must determine whether it can tolerate the declining performance of ShoalFish for the sake of the supply chain to the other companies in the group. If this is not feasible, a possible alternative may be to lease or sell their boats to individual owners with the guarantee of sales to Shoal plc companies. The scenario indicates that owner-skippers account for almost half of the boats in the western oceans so this could be a viable alternative.

ShoalPro

ShoalPro is a mature organisation that is still expanding (market growth of +2% from 2007 to 2009). It holds 40% of market share and so is likely to be the market leader. Although a significant percentage of its fish is provided by ShoalFish it is increasingly processing fish for other companies.

It is a profitable company, and gross profit margins have increased from 10% in 2007 to 10.6% in 2009. This suggests that revenues are increasing faster than costs.

These characteristics (high relative market share; slow growth) in the BCG matrix suggest ShoalPro is a cash cow.

PESTEL analysis indicates that ShoalPro operates in an area of high unemployment which attracts national grants (political and economic), and ShoalPro has access to a skilled local workforce (socio-cultural). The high unemployment rates suggest that Shoal Pro is likely to be able to recruit skilled workers relatively cheaply.

ShoalPro is a key part of Shoal plc and should be retained and maintained.

ShoalFarm

ShoalFarm is a fairly recent addition to the Shoal plc group and has a low market share (10%) of a growing market. ShoalFarm is growing at a slower rate (+12% from 2007 to 2009) than the market as a whole (+20% over same period).

PESTEL analysis shows that there is a favourable ethical perception of this market (socio-cultural) but the company faces difficulty in finding acceptable sites (environmental).

In 2007 ShoalFarm had the highest gross profit (14%) of these three companies. This declined to 12.7% in 2008 before recovering slightly to 13.3% in 2009.

ShoalFarm has the potential to be a significant provider to both ShoalPro and the Captain Haddock restaurants, and could replace fish supplies from ShoalFish if the latter continues to decline.

ShoalFarm could be classified as a question mark (problem child) in the BCG matrix as it requires further investment to allow it to become a key player in a significant market place. If Shoal plc is happy to provide this investment, then ShoalFarm should be expanded and developed. If it does not wish to take this risk, then it may be better to divest itself of this company.

The three companies are closely linked in the value chain, however there are conflicting environmental forces that both reduce the dependency between the companies and encourage the synergies of a vertically integrated group. The proposed acquisition of Captain Haddock could lead to additional synergies, but only if the correct relationships are set up between the companies.

Part (b)

(i)

For a change programme to be successful it must be designed in line with the context in which it will be implemented.

Captain Haddock's financial performance is rapidly declining and the concerns over breaking bank covenants has led to the resignation of both the chairman and the managing director. Any strategic change programme that is implemented by Shoal plc will have to be implemented very **quickly**.

Captain Haddock has a strong brand, excellent staff and highly regarded staff training programmes. These **competencies need to be retained** and so Shoal will have to ensure suitable policies are put in place to retain staff and re-affirm the brand.

Change is easiest in **diverse** organisations where there is a variety of experience, views and opinions, as existing norms and practices are more likely to be challenged. This is unlikely to be the case at Captain Haddock where there is a 'tradition of recruiting staff directly from schools and universities'. Shoal will need to bring in the required diversity whilst remaining sensitive to the views of the employees of Captain Haddock.

For change to be successful, the **capability** to manage that change needs to exist. Captain Haddock has little change management experience, however Shoal does have the relevant experience and capability to successfully implement change. This is the first time, however, Shoal has moved into the restaurant industry and has no experience in this sector. Their experience from other sectors may not transfer.

Change is expensive so Shoal will have to consider the resources it has available to support the change. This is the **capacity** for change. Captain Haddock has no resources available so the change, and the outstanding bank covenants, will have to be financed by Shoal.

Readiness for change is an important consideration and it is clear that Captain Haddock will be receptive to the change. Two senior managers have already left and employee representatives have indicated that the staff are looking for a leader to guide a demoralised workforce.

Shoal plc will need to identify who will have the **power** to bring about the change and ensure that person is given sufficient power to implement those changes. This power will come from Shoal plc, rather than the existing management at Captain Haddock.

Finally, the **scope** of the change will have to be considered.

		Scope of change	
		Realignment	**Transformation**
	Incremental	Adaptation	Evolution
	Big Bang	Reconstruction	Revolution

(With "Nature of change" labelling the rows.)

Adaptation does not require a new paradigm and proceeds step by step.

Reconstruction can also be undertaken with an existing paradigm but requires extensive and rapid action. This is the most appropriate approach for the change at Captain Haddock. There is nothing fundamentally wrong with Captain Haddock's business so the paradigm doesn't need to be changed. However, rapid action needs to be taken to reverse the disastrous diversification programme which Captain Haddock has undertaken.

Evolution is an incremental process that leads to a new paradigm.

Revolution is rapid and wide ranging responses to extreme pressures for change.

(ii)

An appropriate strategy for managing the change at Captain Haddock would be a **turnaround** strategy as this is appropriate when fast change is needed to deal with a decline in financial performance and changing market conditions.

Successful turnaround strategy focuses on getting the **existing business right**, not diversifying into new markets or businesses. Shoal will have to divest the company of its loss making real estate and stock market activities.

There are seven elements that form the basis of a turnaround strategy.

- **Crisis stabilisation** – costs need to be reduced and revenues increased. This could be achieved through the synergies achieved through ShoalFish directly supplying the restaurants. Improving productivity and reducing direct costs is likely to be more successful than reducing overheads.

- **Management changes** – a new chairman and chief executive will need to be found. Cost savings will also be made as a result of the resignation of the previous post-holders. The replacements should be less expensive as reducing the cost of senior management is a feature of a turnaround strategy.

- **Communication with stakeholders** – support by the stakeholders is vital for a change programme to succeed. Employees already appear to be supportive of the change and the banks are also likely to be in favour of the acquisition by a large and trusted parent company.

- **Attention to target markets** – a lack of focus is a common cause of decline and there is evidence that this may have happened with the 'disastrous diversification'. Target markets must be clearly defined and the Captain Haddock brand will have to be emphasised to re-establish itself in its traditional market.

- **Concentration of effort** – resources should be concentrated on the best opportunities to create value. Poor performers, or those not focused on the target market, should be eliminated and none-core activities outsourced. The acquired land should be sold if possible.

- **Financial restructuring** of Captain Haddock is required. Shoal will make an initial investment of $15 million to meet the short-term cashflow problems and improve liquidity. This is not a significant amount compared with the gross profit of approximately $11 million per year that Captain Haddock should be able to deliver, based on the performance of other companies in this sector.

- **Prioritisation** – the eventual success of the change will depend on Shoal's ability to prioritise necessary activities and to deliver fast, significant improvements.

Part (c)

> **Top tips.** This part question is mostly just testing your **knowledge** of the approaches to creating value with only limited application. Therefore it should have been possible to pick up easy marks here. However many students had limited knowledge in this area and so did not score highly. This shows the importance of being familiar with all areas of the syllabus.
>
> Note that 'portfolio manager' is a specific role for a corporate parent and you should describe this role here. It is not a cue to repeat topics such as the BCG matrix from part (a).

Johnson, Scholes and Whittington identify three approaches to value creation that the corporate parent might adopt:

Portfolio manager

Portfolio managers seek out and purchase undervalued companies, improve their performance and sell them on at a premium. Improvement is usually achieved through asset stripping, by disposing of underperforming elements or by installing new management. In all circumstances, value is extracted from the company.

Portfolio managers keep their own costs low and provide few central services, the Strategic Business Units (SBUs) are generally autonomous and are judged by financial results. The portfolio manager adds value though investment, standard setting and performance monitoring.

This approach is not suitable for Shoal plc.

Synergy manager

This approach creates value through the **shared use of resources and competencies**. It works on the principle that the whole is worth more than the individual parts that make it up.

This is a relevant approach for Shoal plc as it is clear from the scenario that synergies are valued by the organisation.

Synergies can arise in two ways, first by applying common skills across the business, and secondly through one company being the customer of another (as ShoalPro is to ShoalFish).

Where one company is the customer of another, there is a risk that inefficiencies may arise and each company's objectives may become confused. For example ShoalFish may not control its costs as it knows ShoalPro is a guaranteed customer. ShoalPro may, as a result, be unable to meet its profit objective. If the SBU business managers cannot identify 'what is in it for them' then this approach may not work.

In relation to knowledge sharing synergies, Shoal plc must be aware that it knows very little about the restaurant industry yet is planning to acquire Captain Haddock. This company is very different from the rest of the companies in the Shoal group and so planned synergies may never arise.

Parental developer

In this method value is created via the competencies of the **parent.** An example might be where the parent has a strong brand name that is globally recognised and associated with quality and value.

The parent identifies businesses that are not fulfilling their potential but may be able to if they were associated with the brand. The brand name opens the business up to a wider market of people who are already familiar with the brand and so place the same trust in that business as they do the brand itself.

This approach focuses on providing companies with the competencies of the parent, rather than achieving synergies, and so is not an appropriate approach for Shoal plc.

50 Bonar Paint

Text reference. Chapter 1 (Strategic position); Chapter 2 (Environmental issues; including Porter's five forces and PEST analysis); Chapter 4 (value chain) and Chapter 6 (Strategic options; including Ansoff's matrix).

Top tips. The scenario provides you with useful information about the company and you should use this to ensure that your answers relate specifically to Bonar Paint.

You should use relevant theoretical models as frameworks for the ideas you glean from the scenario. There are a number of models which you could use here. Porter's five forces is the one specifically referred to in the marking guide, but thinking through a PESTEL or SWOT analysis would also be useful. Equally, a consideration of the value chain could remind you that costs are too high, while Ansoff's matrix could indicate possible future opportunities for the business.

However, the question does not require you to describe or explain any of these theories and you would not gain any marks for doing so. What you would get marks for is *using* relevant theory to analyse the issues raised in the scenario, and then using them to assess the strategic position.

You should also use the financial information presented in the scenario to draw some conclusions about Bonar's performance, and whether it was attractive for a management buyout. Note there are two distinct parts of the requirement: (i) an assessment of Bonar's strategic position; (ii) an assessment of Bonar's attractiveness for a management buyout.

Easy marks. You should realise from the scenario that the company is facing a considerable number of challenges, and so using some of the models noted above you should be able to assess how the challenges Bonar is facing affect its strategic position.

The financial information presents you with some simple data, yet marks are still available for considering the implications of it: for example, assessing the impact of static sales and declining gross margins.

Marking scheme

		Marks
(a)	Up to 3 marks each for each relevant point relating to performance analysis	
	Up to 3 marks for each relevant point relating to Bonar's attractiveness for a management buyout	
	Up to 5 marks for use of appropriate models	20
(b)	Up to 2 marks for each relevant point for advantages of product/customer divestment	
	Up to 2 marks for each relevant point for disadvantages of product/customer divestment	15
(c)	Up to 2 marks for each advantage of a formal mission statement for Bonar Paint	
	Up to 2 marks for each disadvantage of a formal mission statement for Bonar Paint	
	Up to 5 marks for the role which a formal mission statement can play in the strategic planning process	15
		50

(a) It is very important for the management team to make an assessment of the business' performance over recent years and its future prospects as they are considering a management buyout (MBO) of the business. This assessment will determine not only a fair price to pay for the business, but also whether the MBO is attractive at all.

Static sales

Bonar paint's financial performance over the last three years has been disappointing. **Sales have declined** slightly, while the **cost of sales have increased**. The cost of sales increase may reflect inefficiencies in

production caused by the large product range, and the small batches used in production. Production is also labour intensive, reflecting the lack of investment in production technology and machinery. Finally, distribution costs are also high due to the policy of delivering to each and every customer.

Declining margins

The combination of static sales and increasing costs has meant that gross profit has declined by 14% over the three years. Net profit has declined even more, falling from £1.37m (13%) in 2004 to £0.4m (4%) in 2006. If these figures are indicative of a longer term trend then they should be a cause of concern for any future owners.

Reliability of forecasts

Interestingly, the **projected figures** for 2007 show an **upturn in both sales and margins**. However, it will be important for the senior management team to understand the assumptions behind these figures, and to gauge how realistic they are. In particular, they need to understand why the decline in profits for 2004-6 is replaced by a forecast increase in profitability for 2007-8. It is possible that Jim and Bill have presented an **optimistic picture of the business** to make it seem more attractive to potential buyers than it actually is to try to raise the sale price.

The company is operating in an **increasingly competitive environment**. The management team need to consider the threats this poses to the business, because those threats could affect the basis of the forecasts going forward.

Assessment of product range

One of the key factors in the business' performance going forward will be the attractiveness of its product range to customers.

The current process of developing products in response to customer demand without any independent product development process means that Bonar has built up a **very wide product range**.

However, the increasing size of the product range has not translated into increased sales or profitability. This suggests that Bonar's product range is now **too wide** and should be reduced to a more manageable level.

Impact of product range on costs (and level of inventory held)

The extent of the product range means that Bonar has to hold **high levels of inventory**. This means that Bonar's **working capital requirements** are likely to be higher than a potential buyer might like.

We have already noted how the small batch size which accompanies the extensive product range is contributing to the **high cost of sales**.

Value chain and understanding of costs

As part of their analysis of the business, the senior management team need to look critically at the costs incurred by the business and work out whether any efficiencies can be made.

The large product range, the small production runs, and delivering direct to customers for all orders all suggest that costs are higher than they could be. If this is the case, then by **increasing cost efficiencies** the net profit margin of the business could be improved.

Bargaining power of customers

Many of Bonar's customers are large international manufacturers. They will want to secure the best price they can for the goods they buy from Bonar, and this will put **pressure on Bonar's margins**.

At the same time, Bonar must continue to satisfy its customers' needs so that they do not shift their custom to its competitors. A key issue for the MBO team to consider will be the level of customer loyalty which they can secure after any buyout, because this will be important in projecting future sales.

Bargaining power of suppliers

The raw materials Bonar uses are sourced from large chemical companies, so it is **susceptible to any price increases** they may impose. Bonar's relatively small size compared to its suppliers puts it in a weak bargaining position against any price increases, especially after the change in ownership.

When taken together, Bonar's relatively weak bargaining position compared to both customers and suppliers means that its **gross margins could be under threat** going forward.

Threat of new entrants

The management team should also consider the threat of any new competitors entering the market, which could reduce sales and margins further.

However, Bonar may get some protection from competitive rivalry by its focus on low volume, specialist paints. It has developed a **niche market position** for itself.

This market is unlikely to be attractive to larger competitors. However, this may in turn indicate that it is not a market which offers significant opportunities for growth in the future.

Future product innovation

The success of Bonar's future product innovation will be **crucial to the longer term success of the business**, especially if Bonar is operating in a niche market with limited opportunities for growth.

Currently, **R&D spending is low**, suggesting that it is viewed as a low priority for the business.

Moreover, although Bonar has a good reputation for R&D in the past, it does not have a formal R&D process for developing new products. The **lack of any structured new product development** may now be contributing to the weak sales performance.

Conclusion

Bonar's attractiveness to a management buyout will depend, in part, on the **price** the senior management team can negotiate to buy it for. If the **price is inflated by optimistic future sales forecasts**, then it will not be attractive.

However, the senior management team also need to consider the **underlying position of the business**, and whether it is a viable, profitable business going forward. If the management team need to raise bank finance to fund their buyout they will also need to demonstrate the viability of the business to their bankers.

The viability will depend on what impact lower gross margin percentages from customers and suppliers may have on results. It will also be dependent on the levels of customer loyalty and customer retention Bonar can achieve after the buyout, because this will be important in **sustaining underlying sales**.

It is likely that Bonar will be operating in a niche market, with an increasingly competitive environment around it, so **opportunities for sales growth are limited**. Consequently, the business' ability to reduce costs is very important in considering its attractiveness for a buyout.

Ultimately, the attractiveness of the business will be determined by the **expected future profitability**, and this will reflect both **sales, gross margins, and cost control**. If the senior management team are not convinced that these three factors can be secured, then they should not proceed with the buyout.

(b)

Text reference. Chapter 4 (Value chain, and product portfolio)

Top tips. As with part (a), the scenario should provide some useful context here. It identifies the differing opinions of the three members of the senior management team so this should offer you some context in which to consider Roy's strategy.

Also, the scenario notes on more than one occasion the problems Bonar is currently having with its cost control so you should recognise this as the key motive behind Roy's strategy, and then use the value chain model as a framework for your answer, in particular the primary activities of the value chain.

You could also draw on the ideas in the product portfolio to think of the implications of reducing the product range.

It is important to recognise exactly what the question is asking for. You are asked to assess the **advantages** and **disadvantages** of both the **product range** and the **customer base**. So your answer should cover four different aspects: (i) advantages of reducing the product range; (ii) disadvantages of reducing the product

---

range; (iii) advantages of reducing the customer base; and (iv) disadvantages of reducing the customer base.

Easy marks. Although you are not asked to describe the value chain in your answer, if you had thought about the components of it, in particular the primary activities, you should be able to generate some sensible ideas in conjunction with the information you were provided in the scenario.

Roy's strategy is based on controlling costs, as opposed to providing customer service or repositioning Bonar in the market. Instead he is looking to **simplify the value chain** within the business. However, before implementing his strategy it will be necessary to consider the potential impact it will have on the business.

Advantages of reducing product range

Economies of scale in processing. Currently, the extensive product range means that Bonar produces a large number of small batches of each of the different products. By reducing the product range, it would be able to use process **larger batch sizes**. It will produce fewer batches but each of them will be larger. This will mean Bonar can benefit from economies of scale in processing.

Increased automation, and staff savings. The current manufacturing process is very labour intensive, with little investment in production technology. By increasing batch sizes, and reducing the number of batches produced, Bonar should be able to have a more automated process. On the one hand, this may speed up the production process, but more importantly, it should also mean that **fewer staff are required** in the manufacturing process. This should mean that Bonar can make **savings on labour costs**.

Economies of scale in procurement. Reducing the product range should also mean that Bonar can reduce the number of different chemicals and other raw materials it needs as inputs into the manufacturing process.

Reducing the range of inputs required should allow Bonar to make **larger orders** from its suppliers, with the option of **improved price and delivery terms** from them as a result.

Reduced inventory levels. The reduction in the number of deliveries coming in should **simplify the inbound logistics** arrangements of the business.

Equally, the reduction in the number of different chemicals required in the manufacturing process, should reduce the **inventory levels of raw materials** the business holds.

More importantly, reducing the product range will also reduce the inventories of finished goods which are held. Bonar currently holds high **inventory levels of finished goods**. These are only required because of the long lead times associated with the current batch production process. Simplifying the production process will should allow Bonar to improve **product availability**, thereby reducing the need to hold high levels of inventory.

Improved working capital management. Reducing inventory levels will reduce Bonar's working capital requirements and will release cash for the business. This could be very important if the management buyout goes ahead, and the business becomes **highly geared**.

Improved reliability. The reduced product range should allow Bonar to improve both product reliability and also reliability of deliveries to its customers. In an increasingly competitive market this will be important because a reliable product offering will improve customer retention. If Bonar becomes confident in its reliability, in time it will be able to use this as a **competitive advantage** to try to increase market share.

Lower product failures and warranty claims. The reduced range should reduce the level of product failures and with it the cost of any warranty claims against the company.

Disadvantages of reducing product range

Loss of sales – By reducing the product range, Bonar may suffer a reduction in sales. Before introducing the changes Roy has proposed, Bonar should look at the **distribution of sales across their product range**. If it is the case that a small number of products constitute the vast majority of total sales, then by discontinuing the products which contribute little to sales the impact will be minimised. If, however, all the product ranges contribute equally, reducing product range could have a greater negative impact on sales.

Therefore, before discontinuing any products from the product range it is important that Bonar have accurate information about the sales and contribution to profit generated by each product.

Complimentary products – There may be some products, which although they do not generate significant sales or profits in their own right, are **bought in conjunction with other better selling ranges**. There is a risk that if the first product is discontinued, the customer will not buy the main product from Bonar either because they are looking to buy the whole range of paints they need from one supplier.

Again, this means that it will be important for Bonar to identify any products which act as compliments, before deciding which to discontinue.

Customer service issues – Reducing the range of paints available may reduce the level of customer service Bonar can offer its customers. There is a risk that if Bonar do not meet all their customers needs, as they have done historically, the customers may move to a different supplier.

Advantages of reducing customer base

Reduced distribution and delivery costs. By reducing the number of customers it delivers to Bonar will be able to simplify its outbound logistics arrangements considerably, and also make significant savings in delivery costs.

Improved reliability in delivery. If Bonar is delivering to a smaller number of customers, planning and scheduling the deliveries should become easier. Bonar will also be able to factor in a contingency for delays and hold-ups into the schedule.

Disadvantages of reducing customer base

Loss of sales – By reducing its customer base, Bonar may suffer a reduction in sales. Before introducing the changes Roy has proposed, Bonar should look at the **distribution of sales across its customers**.

If it is the case that a small number of customers provide the vast majority of total sales, then if Bonar continues to serve these and stops serving the others, the negative impact on sales will be minimised. This is likely to be the case given that Bonar deals with some major industrial customers who will be key accounts for the firm.

Also, if Bonar subsequently uses distributors to service the smaller customers it will not lose their business altogether, but it will have to **share the margin earned from them with the distribution partner**.

However, before making any decisions about reducing the customer base it is important that Bonar has accurate information about the sales and contribution to profit they receive from each customer.

Reaction of sales force – The changes may be resented by the sales force if they have built up good relationships with a number of customers who they will no longer serve. If the sales team are demotivated as a result, there is a risk that sales made to the remaining customers will also suffer.

Impact on reputation – Bonar currently has a reputation for supplying directly to each and every customer, and this may be an attribute which distinguishes if from its competitors. If it stops doing this, and makes some customers use a distributor, there may be some negative publicity within the industry.

(c)

Text reference. Chapter 1 (Mission statements)

Top tips. The question tells you that Bonar Paint 'has had no formal strategic planning process'. This should indicate that there will be some advantages from introducing the process for the first time. Equally, it should alert you to some of the potential disadvantages of a mission statement being prepared by people with no prior experience of planning. And given that the senior managers will probably be busy negotiating the buyout, is preparing a mission statement really the best use of their time?

Note that although the question talks about developing a 'formal mission statement' you need to discuss the advantages and disadvantages of having a mission statement as compared to not having one. It is not asking of the relative merits of a 'formal' statement as compared to an 'informal' one.

Note again that there are two parts to the requirement. Once you have considered the advantages and disadvantages of developing a mission statement, you then also need to consider how it can be used in the strategic planning process. Although the majority of the marks available in this question will be earned by discussing the advantages and disadvantages of a mission statement, do not forget to comment on what role it could play in Bonar's strategic planning process. Make sure your answer is consistent with the advantages, or possibly the disadvantages, you have identified earlier.

> **Easy marks.** Missions, goals and objectives are a key part of setting business strategy so you should have been able to identify some advantages from developing a strategy, and then how it can be used in the strategic planning process.

The management buyout will be a significant change for Bonar, and so it will be important for the new owners to make clear their strategy for the business and what they expect from their staff. They may look to use a mission statement to summarise the purpose of the business going forward.

Advantages of developing a formal mission statement

Goal congruence

Determine direction – A mission statement will determine the direction of the business after the buy out, and focus attention on achieving the stated strategy and direction. It will focus the business' efforts on a single goal, as expressed in the statement.

Unified strategy – The three members of the senior management buyout (MBO) team each has a different view of how Bonar Paint should develop after the buyout. Creating a mission statement will force the buyout partners to reconcile these differences and to determine a unified strategy for the business.

Communication – Bonar Paint will need to communicate its business model and strategy going forward after the MBO: for example, what is its business, its products and its markets? This strategy should be clearly communicated in a mission statement.

Determine market approach

Basis of competition – The mission statement will determine the basis on which Bonar Paint competes in the industry, for example whether it wants to be a specialist paint maker which creates a strong brand and a reputation for customer service, or whether it wants to be a low-cost producer.

It is important for Bonar to establish the basis on which it wants to compete because of the fragmented nature of the paint industry – from branded international manufacturers offering luxury, high-end paints, to low-end manufacturers producing own label paints for DIY stores. There is a danger that without a clear strategy Bonar Paint will be left **stuck in the middle**, and will see its profitability fall as a result. This is particularly important as the paint industry is seen as mature, and so margins will come under increasing pressure.

Consistency of offering – A mission statement will help Bonar Paint ensure that all aspects of its business are consistent with the basis on which it is competing in the market. For example, if Bonar Paint decides it wants to focus on the high-end market, then all its processes, from manufacturing the paint itself, to customer service and delivery must be of sufficiently high quality to support this strategic position.

Satisfy key stakeholders

Identify key stakeholders – One of the key elements of a business' purpose is to satisfy the needs of stakeholders, and a mission statement should help a business achieve this purpose. However, before a business can begin to assess the needs of stakeholders it first needs to **determine who the key stakeholders are**.

Keep key stakeholders satisfied – Alongside the MBO team, the **banks** which provided loan funding for the MBO, Bonar's **employees** and **customers** are all key stakeholders. Therefore Bonar's future direction after the buyout needs to keep them satisfied in order for the business to be successful.

The mission statement should demonstrate how Bonar Paint will serve its customers and reward its employees, recognising that **customer loyalty** and **employee loyalty** will be very important as the business undergoes a change of ownership.

Disadvantages of developing a formal mission statement

Wasted time

Time consuming. Creating a mission statement will be time consuming, especially as Bonar Paint has never had one before and so it will need to be developed from nothing. If the mission statement does not generate any positive results in terms of corporate values and profitability, then the time spent will have been wasted. This is especially important given the number of other issues which need addressing at Bonar Paint.

Identifying priorities. The senior management team will have a number of practical issues – for example, ensuring that they pay a fair price in the buyout, securing funding from their banks and working out how they are going to control and mange the business going forward. Whilst developing a mission statement could be useful in guiding the strategic planning process, it is debatable whether it is a top priority at the moment. Spending too much time developing a mission statement could deflect attention from more pressing issues.

May be ignored. There does not appear to be any history of formal planning at Bonar Paint – for example, there is no formal process or new product development and paints are developed in response to customer demand. Consequently, a mission statement as part of a formal strategic planning process, may be alien to the company and may ultimately be ignored.

Too restrictive

Deter innovation. Bonar Paint has a good reputation for product innovation and developing new high performance paints. This is one of the company's strengths, but if a mission statement imposes more a prescriptive approach to planning, these qualities of innovation may be lost.

To be successful going forward, it is likely that Bonar Paint will need to balance its innovative qualities and skills at new product development with an overall company strategy. However, that strategy could be one which emerges and adapts over time, depending on changes in the external environment. In this context, a mission statement as part of a formal planning process may not be appropriate, because it may actually prevent the company taking advantage of new opportunities which arise.

Role of mission statement in the strategic planning process

Fits with rational planning model. Mission statements can play an important role in the strategic planning process, but they are most suitable for companies which follow the full rational planning model. In such companies, a mission statement can influence the way a company implements its planned strategy and it can act as a reference document against which future business plans can be judged.

Limited impact on its own. However, it appears Bonar Paint does not have a formal strategic planning process in the way the rational planning model suggests. Without that kind of context and support, a mission statement on its own will have little impact on the strategic planning process.

51 Hammond Shoes

> **Text reference.** Financial performance and ratio analysis are covered in Chapter 14 of your BPP Study Text for exams from September 2015 to 31 August 2016. Strategic choices are covered in Chapter 4.
>
> **Top tips.** Part (a) requires you to **analyse** the financial position of the company. Use the data provided in Figure 1 to calculate performance ratios such as ROCE, gearing and interest cover. Do not forget to comment on the respective ratios and what they mean for the business.
>
> You are also required to **evaluate** the proposed investment. Use the cost, income and probabilities provided in the scenario to calculate expected values.

		Marks
(a)	1 mark for each appropriate point up to a maximum of 14 marks	14
(b)	1 mark for each appropriate point up to a maximum of 20 marks	
	Up to 4 further marks are available for the style, structure and clarity of answer	24
(c)	One mark for each appropriate point up to a maximum of 12 marks	12
		50

(a) Financial analysis

The financial analysis of Hammond Shoes (HS) is considered below under the key headings of profitability and gearing.

Profitability

The impact of the cheap imports can be clearly seen in Figure 1 as both revenues and gross profit have fallen significantly over the four years.

The gross and net profit margins have declined steadily over the years, as shown below

	2007	2009	2011
Gross profit margin	23.5%	20.0%	17.9%
Net profit margin	8.2%	4.7%	2.9%

The company have failed to keep costs under control and, while sales have fallen by $150m over the four years (approximately a18% decrease), cost of sales have only decreased by $75m (approximately 11.5%). It is likely that this has been caused by reacting to reduced demand by reducing labour. Given the large redundancy payments required by law in Arnland and HS's heavy use of local labour it is likely that this was a costly exercise.

The Return on Capital Employed (ROCE) has also plummeted from 24.14% in 2007 to just 6.45% in 2011.

Gearing

The capital structure of HS has changed significantly over the last few years, no doubt causing concern to this generally risk averse organisation. In particular:

- Long term borrowings have dramatically increased.

- Retained earnings are declining reflecting the higher dividends taken by the family.

- Traditionally the social values of the family have been reflected in the company's very low level of gearing which was only 6.9% in 2007.

- By 2011 the company was much higher geared having risen to 22.5%.

- While this gearing level is still relatively low, the speed with which these changes have occurred should be of concern to the senior management of HS.

A further concern linked to gearing arises by considering the way the company manages its trade receivables and trade payables.

Goods in Arnland are normally supplied on 30 days credit and back in 2007 HS had no problem in meeting this, however, the time taken on average to pay their suppliers has more than doubled. Over the same period, trade receivables have slightly reduced as shown below:

	2007	2009	2011
Trade payables (days)	28	43	63
Trade receivables (days)	38.65	38.93	36.50

This would indicate that HS appear to be using their suppliers as a source of free credit on top of the bank loads they have taken out in the last few years.

Financing costs have also risen over the last few years. This has directly affected profits and has also caused the interest cover ratio to plummet from 14 to 1.33.

This financial analysis backs up the worrying picture presented in the scenario. Profits are falling and HS is struggling to make the fast cost cuts needed to survive. It is becoming increasingly reliant on external finance which will undoubtedly be a cause of great concern to the owners (on ethical grounds) as well as to their suppliers who are unlikely to remain loyal to HS should the worrying trend of increasingly late payment continue.

Investment analysis

The senior management appear to have accepted that the company will continue to experience low sales despite investing in new production facilities. They then only anticipate a 30% chance of sales increasing if there are favourable changes in the environment. This pessimistic view of the company is reflected in both of the scenarios they have developed.

The lower labour costs and increased productivity are projected to provide net benefits of $15m over the first three years ($5 per year) in both scenarios.

The two scenarios then split to look at the likely outcomes depending on whether low demand continues (Scenario 1) or higher levels of demand are experienced (Scenario 2). The anticipated value of the benefits each of these scenarios would provide are shown below:

Scenario 1:

Probability of continued low demand	0.7
Net benefits per year	$5m
Total benefit for years 4-6 ($5 × 3)	$15 m
Expected value of benefits ($15 × 0.7)	**$10.5m**

Scenario 2:

Probability of higher demand	0.3
Net benefits per year	$10m
Total benefit for years 4-6 ($10 × 3)	$30 m
Expected value of benefits ($30 × 0.3)	**$9m**

Total expected benefits ($15m + 10.5m + 9m) $34.5m

The total expected benefits of $34.5 is below the cost of the proposed investment $37.5. This suggests that this investment would not be financial viable unless the second scenario actually materialises in which case the total benefits would be $45m ($15m + $30m).

It must be noted, however, that the projection covers only the first six years and, given that the last upgrade was carried out twenty years ago, it is likely that net profits would continue for many years beyond these six. However, it becomes increasingly difficult to predict net benefits beyond that six year timescale.

(b)

> **Top tips.** The question does not require that you use a particular framework to answer this question. The answer below uses the TOWS matrix as it can be linked clearly to the SWOT analysis provided in the scenario. You may have chosen to use an alternative framework such as the Ansoff matrix or the strategy clock. Such approaches are equally valid and you will still earn marks if you chose to use such a method.

The TOWS matrix is a positioning approach to strategy which builds upon the SWOT analysis and categories strategic options under the following headings.

- SO strategies employ strengths to seize opportunities.
- ST strategies employ strengths to count or avoid threats.

- WO strategies address weaknesses so as to be able to exploit opportunities.
- WT strategies are defensive, aiming to avoid threats and the impact of weaknesses.

The alternative strategic options that Hammond Shoes (HM) could consider are discussed within this framework below.

Employ strengths to seize opportunities

- HS could attempt to exploit the opportunities of increased customer spending and consumerism in Arnland through building on its strong retail expertise. This could be achieved by selling complementary goods or competing products in its stores and thus obtaining a cut of the profit margins of its competitors and helping to preserve the long-term future of the shops.

- An additional strength of HS is that it owns land both in Petatown and in the disused factory in the north. Along with the retail expertise these two strengths could take advantage of the opportunity of rising consumerism by developing retail villages on this land. There is a strong trend towards 'safe' shopping experiences of this kind in Arnland and this development would provide customers with this valued and sought out experience. There are currently no HS retail stores in either of the towns where these sites are located and so this strategy could be combined with the product diversification described above.

- The opportunity of the internet as a preferred method of purchasing could be addressed though the application of the company's software expertise to the development of an innovative e-commerce site. This would also provide the company with the opportunity to make sales outside of Arnland, opening up markets that have never been within the reach of HS and perhaps significantly widening the customer base.

Employ strengths to count or avoid threats

- A key threat to HS is that is facing competition from organisations with lower production costs who can undercut the prices that HS need to charge. Presuming that HS cannot lower its production costs, it could compensate for this by employing its strengths in retail, shoe design and distribution software. It might be possible for innovate production and retail systems to be combined and extended in order to provide economies of supply. This might lead to a reduction in storage and supply costs which would reduce the overall costs faced by HS.

- A further strength of HS is its extensive property portfolio which could perhaps be used to provide short term finance to HS. This may see the company through to a time where overseas production becomes just as expensive as domestic production due to the rising cost of fuel and pressure to raise the pay and conditions overseas. By selling or leasing some of its property HS might be able to remain in business until these changes occur and the competitive playing field is once again levelled.

Address weaknesses so as to be able to exploit opportunities

- The weaknesses of outdated production facilities and the cost of production could be simultaneously overcome by investing in the upgrade of production machinery. This would improve productivity, and so reduce unit costs, while also reducing energy costs through the use of modern equipment. The board has suggested that overcoming these weaknesses would allow HS to continue to compete in their existing market.

- The opportunity of appealing to the rising number of green consumers in Arnland might also be exploited through the reduced energy costs achieved through the overcoming of the current production weaknesses. The energy efficient process would be likely to raise the appeal of these products to ethical consumers who may already have some support for the company given that its products are produced locally rather than transported many miles at significant cost to natural resources. The marketing department of HS could incorporate details of their 'lowered carbon footprint' in order to increase the appeal of their products to this segment of the community.

- The weakness of the expensive production process could be converted into a strength by building on the negative publicity recently given to the competitors that use cheap and exploited labour. This could be done by ensuring the country of origin is a key message in HS's manifesto, backed up by details of its commitment to local jobs and communities and minimising energy consumption and pollution via short shipping distances. This may lead to an increase in appeal of the products to people who are willing to pay a premium for ethically sourced products.

Avoid threats and the impact of weaknesses

- The threat of cheap imports and the high cost of labour weakness could possibly be avoided were HS to consider diversifying into footwear products which have lower raw material demands or where a premium can be charged due to either product quality or appropriate branding. For example, children's shows use less raw material and, on the whole, require less precision. This is an appealing market as children's feet grow quickly meaning that their shoes must be regularly replaced and parents wish to avoid the permanent damage to their children's feet which could arise as a result of wearing inappropriately sized shoes. Retail strengths such as the extensive product knowledge of HS staff and excellent customer care could be employed to support this approach. Re-branding of HS as primarily a children shoe supplier would reinforce the new message, while a scaled back selection of adult shoes would still be available as cross-sale products which could be purchased impulsively by parents visiting with their children.

- Other possible niches might be high quality fashion shoes for which customers may be prepared to pay a premium. Appropriate marketing and a degree of exclusivity would be required to support this approach. Aside from the premium that can be charged, this market is also appealing as customers who buy shoes in line with fashion are likely to make replacement purchases regularly as the fashion seasons come and go.

(c)

> **Top tips.** Make you answer specific to the scenario. For example, outline the general importance of a mission statement (shapes the overall direction and purpose of an organisation) and then comment on what it could mean for Hammond Shoes. At present it appears that the core values of the company are implied, but not explicitly stated – a mission statement would enable Hammond Shoes to communicate its beliefs to customers, suppliers and employees.

An organisation's mission is its basic purpose; what it is for and why it exists. It defines the overall direction and purpose of an organisation. A mission statement is a formal document that state the organisation's mission. They are published within organisations to promote desired behaviour: support for strategy and purpose, adherence to core values and adoption of policies and standards of behaviour. Critics, however, argue that they are can be full of generalisations and little more than public relations exercises that are ignored in practice.

Most organisations tend to take the approach of using a short strap-line backed up by a more in-depth details of what the organisation is about, its stakeholders and how it wishes to interact with those stakeholders.

Defining a mission statement also allows an organisation to communicate its core values, either within the mission statement itself or in subsidiary statements, web resources or corporate reports. Core values inform customers and suppliers about the way an organisation chooses to carry out business.

Hammond Shoes (HS) appears to have very strong values (such as secure jobs and good working conditions) however, it would seem that these values are not well communicate – even internally to its own senior management. This was illustrated by their suggestion of closing the Petatown production plan and outsourcing production to reduce costs. The quick dismissal of this proposal by the Hammond family highlighted their continuing commitment to the community of Petatown, a core value of which the senior management were seemingly unaware.

Explicate statement of the core values of HS would help the organisation to prevent future misunderstandings and ensure that business is carried out in the way the organisation believes it should. Such a statement would also communicate these values to external parties such as customers and suppliers. Some customers may share similar values and so chose HS as a way of supporting local business.

Objectives are statements of specific outcomes the organisation wishes to achieve. They should translate the mission into specific goals relating to the more operational running and should be consistent not only with the overall message of the mission but also with each other. Often such objectives are expressed in financial terms (eg profit levels) or in marketing terms (eg target market share), however JS and W recognise that unquantifiable objectives (eg being a leader in technology) are equally valid. HS has a number of such objectives including the provision of education for employees and providing good working conditions. However, not all objectives should be of this kind and it is necessary that management do have some quantified and prioritised objectives to work towards rather than constantly work towards vague, immeasurable objectives.

Setting up such objectives would provide HS with the opportunity to bring the work of the various departments, managers and employees into line with the overall objectives and develop an understanding of how their roles fit into the organisation's mission at an individual level. The scenario illustrates a lack of communication of the objectives down through the organisational layers and represents a key weakness of the business that could be responsible for any number of internal failings. For example, linking the requirement to pay suppliers within 30 days to the core objective of fair treatment of suppliers may have prevented the payment of suppliers slipping to over 60 days. As is stands, HM fails to meet this important corporate objective.

Overall it can be seen that HS do not have a clear mission statement backed up by clearly defined objectives. This needs to be considered urgently, and alongside the strategy review, to ensure this is fully in place and communicated when the new strategy goes live.

52 EcoCar

Text reference. Environmental issues, including the PESTEL model and Porter's five forces are covered in Chapter 2 of your BPP Study Text for exams from September 2015 to 31 August 2016.

Issues related to outsourcing are covered in Chapters 4 and 9 of your Study Text.

Top tips. Remember that the PESTEL model should be used to evaluate the **external** environment, therefore marks relating to the strengths and weaknesses (internal factors) of the company will not earn marks. A number of candidates made this error, particularly in relation to the internal technology of EcoCar.

Some candidates also wasted time describing the historical closure of Leopard Cars and the industrial decline of the area, rather than focusing on the consequence of this for the current strategic analysis, ie the likelihood of the government continuing to provide grants to the area. This demonstrates a common P3 student error of failing to analyse what the models are telling us and the consequences, rather than just writing out sections of the scenario under the relevant PESTEL heading.

Marking scheme

			Marks
(a)	1 mark for each relevant point up to a maximum of 16 marks Up to 4 professional marks	Max	20
(b)	Up to 1 mark for each appropriate point up to a maximum of 15 marks	Max	15
(c)	Up to 1 mark for each appropriate point up to a maximum of 5 marks for each of: lack of control and co-ordination; research and development – succession and learning; and understanding of risk	Max	15
			50

(a)   The environmental analysis will be carried out using the PESTEL model to consider the political, economic, social, technological, environmental and legal factors that affect EcoCar.

Political position

EcoCar has received significant support from the government in the form of tax incentives, grants and interest free loans. The government has also supported green technology by heavily taxing cars with high CO_2 emissions whilst funding the development of 130 charging centres nationwide where EcoCars can be recharged.

EcoCar must monitor the government's continued commitment to green technologies and environmental protection, as well as the policies of the political opposition.

Economic position

EcoCar is both more expensive and has poorer acceleration and speed than the rivals, and sales are driven by the social factor of compassion for the environment. EcoCar must monitor the state of the economy and disposable income levels as significant changes may mean that consumers are no longer prepared to pay a premium price for an environmentally friendly car that has poorer performance than conventional alternatives.

Social factors

EcoCar's customers are 'green' consumers who are concerned about the use of oil – a non-renewable energy source – in conventional cars and the effect of CO_2 emissions on climate change. These people have changed their buying approach based on their belief that their own choices really do make a difference to the future of the Earth.

EcoCar would therefore suffer if scientific evidence that, for example, CO_2 is essential to the survival of the planet or a similar reverse in thinking came to light.

The general views of society also may change away from a green mindset towards a more immediate and self-centred buying approach. Such a trend would be a significant threat to the survival of EcoCar. Trends such as these must be monitored by EcoCar.

Technological factors

EcoCar is a technology driven company and its success depends on its ability to innovate. It is therefore important that it monitors any advances in technology. Particularly, EcoCar should be aware of any improvements to lithium-ion batteries that may make them cheaper, lighter or more powerful as such developments will allow EcoCar to improve their product.

However, EcoCar should also be aware of any alternatives to lithium-ion batteries which could emerge (eg hydrogen) as such alternatives may create a threat to the viability of EcoCar.

Environmental factors

Continued scientific evidence that environmental damage is caused by CO_2 emissions.

Continued concern for the environment to prompt the existence and growth of green customers.

Willingness of customers to continue to pay a premium for environmentally friendly cars.

Legal factors

A number of general laws on car safety have been put in place by the government with further legislation expected. EcoCar must monitor this and ensure it complies with these laws.

This PESTEL analysis highlights a number of threats which EcoCar should consider and, via risk management processes, they must ensure suitable controls are put in place to reduce the risk surrounding these threats. The risks of alternative technology emerging or green consumers declining must also be considered and managed where possible.

Porter's five forces model will now be used to analyse the external industry in which EcoCar operates. EcoCar must define the scope industry when using this framework to analyse where the company can expect to face competition. The industry could be considered to be the car industry as a whole, or just the sector of the car industry that is focused on reducing emissions, or the entire transport industry.

Five forces

Threat of substitute products

There are a number of alternatives and hybrids are either under development or already available. EcoCar must monitor and keep up with changes occurring in the technological environment. The threat from substitutes is relatively high as there is no clear successor to conventional petrol or diesel cars.

In addition, it is possible that a car may not be needed at all, other valid substitutes for such green transportation include cycling, walking and public transport.

Threat of new entrants

There is a constant threat of new entrants to the market as the successor to conventional cars has not yet become clear. However, there are significant barriers, in the form of high capital investment costs which prevent others entering the environmentally friendly car market. EcoCar have overcome these barriers with the help of Universal Motors, who provided some capital investment, and grants and interest free-loans provided by the government.

This governmental assistance is unlikely to be available in all counties and regions as they specifically relate to reducing the high levels of unemployment in the specific area in which EcoCar operate. Funding on the scale of that provided by Universal Motors may also not be available to potential competitors.

Further barriers to entry are the lack of skilled labour with car-building expertise and the processes that Professor Jacques has patented.

Bargaining power of suppliers

The bargaining power of suppliers is unclear. It is likely that their power will be high in an industry with a specialised product of this nature as switching between suppliers can be difficult. This is particularly true for smaller suppliers, such as EcoCar, which has little bargaining power. However, EcoCar is now owned by Universal Motors which may have more influence and hence use its power to help EcoCar negotiate favourable contracts with suppliers and reducing the bargaining power those suppliers have over EcoCar.

Labour can also be considered to be a supplier, and there is an increasing shortage of skilled labour available. This has lead to an increase in labour rates causing EcoCar to consider outsourcing the production of one of their models.

Competitive rivalry

There is likely to be high competitive rivalry in the car industry as a whole due to the high fixed costs and cost of leaving the industry. However, EcoCar is part of a specialised segment of the market dealing with minimal environmental impact cars. This sector of the market is still immature and differentiated, therefore the competitive rivalry within this sector is likely to be lower than in the car industry as a whole.

Regardless of the way in which EcoCar decides to define the industry in which it operates, it should identify the risks it faces from existing competitors and ensure they are dealt with via the company's risk management processes.

Bargaining power of customers

If the industry is considered to be the car industry as a whole, the switching costs for the consumer are relatively low as they can just purchase an alternative car; they are not locked in to a specific company. However, EcoCar is purchased by customers who are driven by the environmental cleanness of the car, rather than the cost. This type of green customer may not be actively seeking a cheaper alternative and, despite knowing they exist, will not purchase them to avoid compromising their green beliefs.

(b)

> **Top tips.** Don't give a generic list of general advantages and disadvantages of outsourcing. Although this will generate a few marks, the majority of the marks will be awarded for direct application to the scenario. In particular, do not overlook the quantitative data provided – many candidates failed to make full use of this and so missed out on marks.

Case for outsourcing

If we consider the EcoLite in isolation from the other EcoCar products we can see the main benefits that would be achieved by outsourcing its production. The relevant supporting information is shown in Figure 1 below.

	EcoLite
Selling price per car ($)	6,999
Variable cost per car ($)	4,500
Weekly demand (cars)	6
Production time per car (machine hours)	8
Contribution (6,999 – 4,500)	2,499

	EcoLite
Contribution per machine hour (2,499/8)	312
Production time (6 × 8)	48

Figure 1: Information relating to the in-house production of EcoLite

The cost of manufacture quoted by the potential outsource provider is $3,500 which is cheaper than the $4,500 variable cost of manufacturing this car at the existing site, therefore saving EcoCar $1,000 per car. There is also a transport cost of $250 per car associated with the outsourcing option which reduces this saving to $750, however, this still suggests that outsourcing the production of the EcoLite is more attractive than retaining production in house.

The high variable cost of in-house production is partly due to the high labour and inbound logistics costs. These costs are driven by the labour skills shortage and the highly congested roads in Midshire and so look likely to continue to rise. As a result of the high costs even the most profitable combination generates only a relatively small profit margin. Figure 2 shows more information about the entire Eco Range.

	Eco	EcoPlus	EcoLite
Selling price per car ($)	9,999	12,999	6,999
Variable cost per car ($)	7,000	10,000	4,500
Weekly demand (cars)	6	5	6
Production time per car (machine hours)	9	10	8
Contribution	2,999	2,999	2,499
Contribution per machine hour	333	300	312
Production time	54	50	48

Figure 2: Information relating to the current production of the EcoCar range

The case for outsourcing is further supported by the fact that EcoCar is unable to meet the demand for its products using its current facilities. The production capacity at Lags Lane is 112 hours which is 40 hours short of the 152 (54 + 50 + 48) hours of demand. This demand could be met and profits could be increased if the outsourcing option is taken.

A further consideration is that the Eco and the EcoPlus have 95% of the same components and one is a slightly more luxurious version of the other and so are likely to have similar production processes. The EcoLite, however, shares only 70% of the components of the other cars and as such is likely to be the best choice for outsourcing. This would reduce overheads as parts specific to the EcoLite would not need to be built or stored at Lags Lane. The scenario suggests this overheads saving would be $1,250 per week.

Case against outsourcing

The most profitable combination of products produced using the current system is as follows:

	Cars produced	Hours of production	Contribution
Eco	6	54	$17,994 (6 × $2,999)
EcoPlus	1	10	$ 2,999 (1 × 2,999)
EcoLite	6	48	$14,994 (6 × $2,449)
		112	$ 35,987

If the EcoLite is outsourced, the most profitable combination would be as follows:

	Cars produced	Hours of production	Contribution
Eco	6	54	$17,994 (6 × $2,999)
EcoPlus	5	50	$14,995 (5 × 2,999)
		104	$32,989

This combination gives a total contribution of $32,989 which is less than the forecast $33,750 weekly overhead cost and utilises only 104 production hours leaving 8 production hours unused. This may mean that the Lags Lane site may no longer be viable in the future once EcoLite is outsourced.

It my be possible to address this by changing to a three-shift pattern to increase production capacity to 168 hours (7 days, 3 shifts of 8 hours each) per week. This would mean that demand (152 hours) is met leaving 16 hours (168 – 152) available for maintenance, however, the labour shortage may mean that this is not possible. EcoCar would have to determine whether or not this is feasible and if they consider the 16 hours of maintenance time to be sufficient.

EcoCar receives grants to help it continue to produce a car in an area of high employment, therefore if the production of one of the cars is outsourced, this funding could be lost. Additionally, the scenario states that many people in the local region are proud of their car making heritage and show this support by purchasing EcoCar's products. If one of these cars is outsourced, sales in this area may fall.

EcoCar's customers are environmentally conscious individuals who chose to purchase these cars for social and moral reasons. These people may no longer view the company so highly if they outsource the production of one of their cars therefore taking employment away from the area. They may see the decision as being driven by money rather than morals and decide to no longer support EcoCar. An additional concern for these customers would be the use of non-renewable energy to transport cars from the outsourced production facility back to Erewhon, which may undermine the environmentally focused brand of the company. Such customers may no longer consider EcoCar to be the ethical choice and, again, sales may fall as a result.

Overall, outsourcing would be more financially viable than producing EcoLite in house, as long as the Lags Lane factory is not expected to make a profit. However, given the green nature of the product, there could be significant consumer and political backlash to this approach which could lead to a loss of grant funding as well as causing irreparable reputational damage to the company.

(c)

> **Top tips.** Again, with this requirement it is important to read the question and the scenario clearly to understand exactly what it is asking of you. The first part 'lack of control and co-ordination' should focus mainly around budgets and the budgeting processes in place, the second part 'research and development – succession and learning' should focus on human resource development, and the final part 'Understanding the risk' should focus on risk management processes. Note that risk is also covered in the P1 syllabus and the knowledge gained here can also be used and applied to this question.
>
> Responses to this question were mixed with some candidates scoring very highly and others scoring very low marks or missing it out altogether.

Lack of control and co-ordination

The company's current budgeting process is very basic and focuses on agreeing values rather than co-ordination and monitoring. A comprehensive budgeting process should be implemented to:

- **Improve control** as deviations from the plan can be identified early and appropriate action can be taken. This would have prevented the ordering of excessive components as it would have been identified as a major deviation from the plan and action would have been taken. The associated increase in costs and reduction in profit margin would then have been avoided.

  Training costs are also perceived to be out of control. A proper budgeting process would help to bring these costs back under control.

- **Facilitate co-ordination** across the departments and activities of the organisation. The scenario indicates that production was halted due to a lack of an important sub-assembly due to the lack of co-ordination between production, procurement, inventory and finance. This could have been avoided with appropriate budgeting procedures.

- **Facilitate planning** by promoting forward thinking and identifying forthcoming problems. For example the public row and potential legal action from the supplier could have been avoided by putting finance in place to address cash flow problems.

Research and development – succession and learning

EcoCar is a technology led company and so research and development (R&D) has been central in its success to date. However, there is no R&D succession planning in place and the senior managers are getting older. Also, despite the high levels of technical expertise held by the senior managers, they have only limited people skills. Their lack of recognition of the graduates and failure to motivate them has led to the company losing skills and potential as those graduates left the organisation. The existing R&D culture also appears to be preventing the recognition or exploitation of technical opportunities.

In order to retain their intellectual lead in this industry, EcoCar must greatly improve its approach to Human Resource Development (HRD). Proper HRD processes should be established to encourage a culture of **investing in learning**. This will require a shift in mindset away from concern over the cost of training towards a view of long-term training as an investment in the organisation. The capability of staff is a valuable asset for an organisation as technologically focussed as EcoCar.

Improved HRD is also likely to increase the loyalty and commitment of the EcoCar staff, therefore reducing the cost of staff turnover. Therefore investment in learning and the learning organisation are key concepts in succession planning from within the organisation.

The learning organisation concept is also one of the best ways of challenging the existing culture of an organisation. This is essential at EcoCar where the founders appear to have run out of steam and require new contributors to strategy.

Understanding the risk

EcoCar appear to recognise risks yet, other than discussing them, appear to do very little about them. Senior managers appear to be individually risk averse yet as a group they seem to be taking increasingly risky decisions.

A proper risk management system should be put in place to ensure that risks are identified, documented and assessed for likelihood and impact on a risk register, and that suitable policies and controls are put in place to eliminate, or reduce the impact of those risks.

Risk is also related to corporate governance and so EcoCar should consider establishing a main board risk committee to ensure that significant risks faced by the organisation are regularly reviewed by the board.

There are four strategies for dealing with risk once it has been identified:

- **Risk avoidance**. This involves removing the risk by transferring it to another party. This approach could be taken by EcoCar should it go ahead with the outsourcing proposal as some of the risk would be passed to the outsource provider.

- **Risk reduction**. This involves putting controls in place to reduce the likelihood of the risk occurring. For example, EcoCar could reduce the risk of employees divulging technical information could be reduced by setting up strict contractual terms of employment with harsh penalties.

- **Risk mitigation**. This is often associated with risk reduction and involves establishing a response procedure should the risk occur. In the example above, discovery of the disclosure of information could be mitigated by taking immediate legal action against the employee.

- **Risk recognition and absorption**. This is when it is accepted that certain risks will arise just as part of the organisation's day to day business. These risks are continually monitored but no specific action is taken unless they go beyond acceptable levels.

53 Oceania National Airlines (ONA)

Text reference. Chapter 4 (Strategic capabilities; SWOT); Chapter 6 (Strategic options). Chapter 8 (Managing strategic change).

Top tips. Requirement (a) asks you to evaluate the strengths and weaknesses of ONA and their *impact on its performance*. It is important that you link the strengths and weaknesses you identify to the business' performance. And it is also important that you consider financial as well as operational factors. The examiner identifies financial factors (such as margins, liquidity, and gearing) as being crucially important, so to score well in this question you need to include a range of financial strengths and weaknesses.

The requirement expressly states that opportunities and threats are not required in your answer, so you should not have included them.

You could adopt a 'freeform' approach to this question, using the scenario to generate strengths and weaknesses. This is the approach we have taken in the answer below.

However, as the question is about ONA's internal capabilities (strengths and weaknesses) you may prefer to use the 9 Ms model as a guide to prompt you for potential strengths or weaknesses.

In the text box at the end of the answer to part (a) we have provided an illustration of how you could have used this approach to help you. The relevant 'M' is included in square brackets at the start of each factor.

Requirement (b)(i) is a knowledge-based requirement, based on Bowman's strategy clock. Although there are no marks available for referring to the strategy clock itself, you should use it as the basis for your answer.

Requirement (b)(i) is also useful preparation for Part (b)(ii). Your explanation of what a 'no frills' strategy is, in conjunction with the strengths and weaknesses you have identified in (a), should provide you with some clear indicators as to why a 'no frills' strategy is not suitable for ONA. Part (b)(ii) requires you to evaluate a strategic option, so you should use the criteria for strategic choice (suitability, acceptability, feasibility) to structure you answer.

As well as looking at the appropriateness of the strategy in operational terms you should also consider its suitability in terms of cultural fit. The CEO refers to 'an unnecessary and bloody revolution', which may suggest something of the nature and scope of the change required to introduce a 'no frills' strategy.

Notice that the requirement for (b)(ii) tells you that there are 3 professional marks available. These are for the appropriate use of evidence, and drawing the main themes together. The marking guide also indicates that a further 3 marks are available for a conclusion supporting the CEO's view.

Requirement (c) asks you to identify and evaluate the strategic options ONA could consider to address its current weaknesses. Note the two parts of the requirement: (i) identify; (ii) evaluate. In your evaluation, you should mention the limitations of the options you identify as well as their advantages.

The answer below uses the ideas of differentiation and focused differentiation from Bowman's strategy clock as its framework. However, the examiner indicated that other frameworks (such as Ansoff's matrix) would also have been acceptable, as would a freeform answer evaluating a range of options in terms of their suitability, acceptability and feasibility. However, note that you will not gain any marks for simply mentioning any of the theories themselves. Rather you should use them to structure your answer.

Whichever model you choose, however, you need to make sure your answer is specifically related to ONA. Notice that, as with (b), there are professional marks available for the style and structure of your answer as well as the impact and justification of your business arguments.

Easy marks. The scenario highlights a number of strengths and weaknesses which you can use in the 20 mark part (a) without needing any specific text-book knowledge. If you work through the scenario highlighting points that represent strengths or weaknesses, and then explain them, this should yield some easy marks.

Examiner's comments. Most candidates answered part (a) reasonably well.

However, not enough use was made of the financial data. Relatively easy marks were available for calculating and interpreting standards ratios.

Also, some candidates wasted time explaining frameworks and models, rather than evaluating the strengths and weaknesses of ONA.

Part (b) of the question was answered less well. The question asked why moving to a 'no-frills' strategy would be inappropriate for ONA.

Too many answers were neutral in tone and did not carry sufficient conviction about the inappropriateness of such a move.

Part (c) was looking for strategic options and encouraged candidates to explain the strategic check or any other appropriate framework. Unfortunately, some candidates did not pitch their answers at a strategic level, focusing on piecemeal operational improvements instead. This limited the number of marks they could score.

Marks

(a) Up to 2 marks each for each identified strength up to a maximum of 10 marks for strengths
Up to 2 marks each for each identified weakness up to a maximum of 10 marks for weaknesses

20

(b) (i) Up to 1 mark for each relevant point up to a maximum of 4 marks

(ii) Up to 2 marks for each relevant point concerning the inappropriateness of a no-frills solution, up to a maximum of 10 marks
Conclusion supporting the CEO's view: up to 3 marks
Professional presentation of coherent argument: up to 3 marks

20

(c) Explanation of alternative strategies: up to 2 marks for each significant point up to a maximum of 8 marks
2 marks are also available for professional presentation and coherence of the complete answer

10
──
50
══

(a)

Tutorial note. The marking guide identifies that there are 'up to 2 marks' available for each identified strength, and each identified weakness, up to a maximum of 10 marks for each part. So in theory 5 each of strengths and weaknesses well explained and evaluated could secure the 10 marks for each part.

You should not have limited yourself to 5 strengths and weaknesses, and should have included as many relevant points as you could in the time available. However, the answer below includes more strengths and weaknesses than you would be expected to include in your answer because we have tried to provide a comprehensive list of many of the relevant points you could have made.

Strengths

Brand. ONA has a strong brand identity, particularly with the citizens of Oceania. A recent survey indicated that ONA was the airline of choice for the residents, for both regional flights and international flights. This brand strength should help **create customer loyalty**, and in turn **sustain customer demand**.

Regional presence. The citizens of Oceania are proud of their airline and feel that it projects a positive image of Oceania. This again should help **promote customer loyalty** and **sustain sales**.

Customer service. ONA provides excellent customer service, and has won industry awards for both its customer service and its in-flight meals. This excellence helps ONA **differentiate itself from some of its competitors**, and may allow it to charge **premium pricing**.

Employees. ONA is perceived as an excellent employer in Oceania. As a result, its **employees are highly motivated and courteous**. This helps maintain the high levels of customer service it offers.

Safety record. ONA has an excellent safety record, and has had no fatal accidents. Although the safety record is unlikely to increase sales in its own right, it is a feature which ONA can use to highlight the quality of its product.

Flight scheduling. ONA's flight schedules in the regional sector are **convenient for business travel**. Convenient scheduling will increase ONA's attractiveness for business people, so will **increase demand in the lucrative business market**.

Passenger occupancy in business class. ONA has very **high passenger load factor for business class customers in the regional sector.** This is likely to reflect the convenient flight scheduling noted above.

In both the regional and international sectors, ONA's business class load factors are higher than its standard class. This suggests ONA is strong in the business market, and this should be good for revenues. Although we do not know the relative pricing structures of the two classes, it is likely that business fares will include a premium over standard class.

Gross profit margin. ONS's gross profit margin has **remained relatively constant** from 2004 to 2006. (2004: 37.04%; 2006: 36.98%). This suggests ONA is **maintaining its business mix between premium and standard class fares**, and also maintaining its load factors. If load factors fall it is likely that cost of sales (for example, fuel costs) will increase as a percentage of revenue, thereby reducing the gross margin.

Long term liquidity. The company's **gearing ratio** has remained relatively constant from 2004 to 2006, which suggests that the company has not needed to borrow any additional money from lenders, and that its **long-term liquidity is relatively solid**. This is also illustrated by the fact that ONA has been able to **reduce the value of interest bearing long-term loans** by more than the reduction in its cash and cash equivalents over the period.

Receivables collection. ONA's trade receivables is low (2006: 29 days; 2004: 31 days), which is beneficial for cash flow. However, trade receivables tend to be low in the airline industry as a whole, because customers pay in advance of flying.

Weaknesses

High cost base. ONA pays above industry average salaries, offers excellent benefits and has a very generous pension scheme. Whilst these features help sustain employee motivation, they are likely to make ONA's **cost base less competitive than its rivals**. For example, Table 2 in the scenario illustrates that ONA **pilots' salaries are more than 10% higher** than the average in the low-cost airline sector.

Declining wage productivity. Although revenue has only increased 4.8% from 2004 – 2006, wages and salaries have increased 15% over the same period. Consequently the ratio of revenue to wages and salaries costs has fallen from 4.33:1 to 3.95:1. This again suggests that ONA's costs are less competitive than they could be.

No outsourcing. ONA also **provides all of its catering in-house**. This again may mean that it has a higher cost base than other airlines who have outsourced their catering contracts. Specialist catering companies will be able to generate economies of scale in food provision which ONA will not be able to match.

Ageing fleet. The average age of ONA's **fleet is much older than that of its low-cost rivals**. The older fleet is likely to require more maintenance – again suggesting that ONA's costs are likely to be higher than their rivals.

Fleet utilisation. ONA uses its planes for **less hours per day than the low-cost airlines**. This may be due its **scheduling arrangements**, or because ONA's planes need **more maintenance time**. However, either way, lower asset utilisation rates are another indication that ONA's cost base is likely to be **less competitive than its rivals**.

Low frequency of flights in the international sector. ONA only makes one flight per day on average to each destination. This low volume makes it very difficult for the company to gain any **operational economies of scale in the international sector**, and so will be another cause of costs being higher than they could be.

Composition of fleet. ONA's fleet comprises planes **made by three different manufacturers**. This is a legacy of the fleets which the two separate companies – Transport Oceanic and OceaniaAir – used before the merger. However, the Airbus 320 and Boeing 737 are both short-to-medium range commercial aircraft, with **very similar passenger capacity** (see Table 1 in the scenario). So, in effect, they are competitors to each other. Having two aircraft types instead of one suggests is likely to mean that ONA's **servicing and maintenance costs are greater than they would be if they standardised the planes used**. Again, ONA will not be able to benefit from any economies of scale.

Slow growth rate. Between 2004-6 world-wide passenger air travel revenue increased by 12%, and revenue from air travel to Oceania increased by 15%. Over the same period, ONA's passenger revenue only increased 4.6%.

Limited functionality of website. Although ONA allows customers to book flights online, it **does not allow them to check in online**, whereas some of its competitors do. This means that customers who value the convenience of being able to check in online may choose not to fly with ONA.

Sources of revenue. ONA's low-cost competitors generated 84% of their sales revenue through **online sales**, and only 4% through **commission sales**. ONA generates approximately 45% of its sales revenue through each channel. Because travel agents retain part of the revenue from commission sales as their commission, ONA would increase the revenue it retains if it adjusted the sales mix away from commission sales and into online sales.

Passenger occupancy in standard class. ONA's average passenger load factors in standard class are much lower than its low-cost competitors, **especially in the international sector**. If load factors decline, ONA's margins will also decline, because it will still incur the costs of the flight (fuel, flight crew etc) but will not be earning revenue from the empty seats.

As noted in the 'strengths' above, ONA's **load factors in standard class are lower than in business class**. This suggests there may be a weakness in capacity planning; and that for some flights it may be beneficial to re-assign standard class seats to business class.

Declining net profitability. ONA's **net profit before tax has fallen 25%** over the period 2004-6 (2004: 80; 2006: 60), despite revenue increasing slightly.

Over the three year period 2004-6, **profit before interest and tax** has fallen from 12.1% to 9.7%, and the **net profit before tax has fallen** from 9.9% to 7.1%. These figures highlight the problem that high and increasing costs are damaging the profitability of the business.

Declining ROCE. ONA's ROCE has fallen from 10.7% (2004) to 9.4% (2006). This again **reflects declining net profitability due to costs** increasing more quickly than revenue. ONA's **asset turnover** (sales/capital employed) **has actually increased** over the three year period, meaning that costs are a key problem area behind the business' declining financial performance.

Current ratio. ONA's **current ratio has fallen** from 1.24 (2004) to 1.05 (2006). A falling current ratio may indicate that the company will struggle to meet its debts when they fall due.

Alternative approach to (a)

Strengths

[Methods] – **Safety record** – ONA has an excellent safety record, and it can use this record to highlight the quality of its airline.

[Methods] – **Customer service** – ONA has received awards for its customer service levels and the quality of its in-flight meals. This helps differentiate it from its competitors, and may allow it to charge premium pricing.

[Men] – **Courtesy and motivation of employees** – ONA is perceived as an excellent employer in Oceania, and its employees are highly motivated and courteous. This helps maintain the high levels of customer service it offers.

[Make-up] – **Brands** – ONA has a strong brand identity, particularly with the citizens of Oceania. This brand strength should help create customer loyalty, and in turn sustain customer demand.

[Markets] – **Business class occupancy** – ONA has a very high passenger load factor for business class customers in the regional sector. This is likely to reflect ONA's flight schedules in the regional sector which are convenient for business travel. Convenient scheduling will increase demand in the lucrative business class market.

[Markets/Methods] – **Promotional offers** – ONA offers special promotional fares for customers who book online. If ONA increases the proportion of customers who book online it can reduce the number of administration staff needed to support the bookings process, thereby reducing costs.

[Money] – **Long term liquidity** – ONA's gearing ration has remained relatively constant from 2004 to 2006, which suggests it has not had to borrow any additional money, and therefore that its long-term liquidity is relatively solid.

Weaknesses

[Men]/[Money] – **High wage costs** – ONA's salaries are above the industry average, and ONA also offer very generous benefits and pensions. Whilst this helps keep employee motivation high, it makes ONA's cost base less competitive than its rivals.

BPP
LEARNING MEDIA

[Men]/[Money] – Salary increases – Wages and salaries have increased 15% over the period 2004-6, although revenue has only increased 4.8% over the same period. This again suggests ONA's costs are less competitive than they could be.

[Machinery] – Composition of fleet – On average, ONA's fleet is much older than the fleets of its low-cost rivals. An older fleet is likely to require more maintenance, again suggesting ONA's cost base will be higher than its rivals. Also, ONA's fleet comprises planes made by three different manufacturers. This will further increase ONA's maintenance costs compared to what they would have to pay because they will not be able to benefit from the economies of scale they might enjoy if they had a single supplier.

[Machinery] – Fleet utilisation – ONA uses its planes for fewer hours per day than the low-cost airlines. This may reflect scheduling arrangements, or it may be because ONA's planes need more maintenance time. Either way, the lower utilisation rates will again reduce the competitiveness of ONA's cost base.

[Methods] – No outsourcing – ONA provides all of its catering in-house. This means it may incur a higher cost base than other airlines who have outsourced their catering contracts to specialist caterers who benefit from economies of scale.

[Methods] – Website functionality – ONA's website does not allow passengers to check in online whereas some of its competitors' websites do. Passengers who value the convenience of online check-in may therefore choose to fly with one of the competitors instead of with ONA.

[Methods] – Sources of revenue – ONA's low cost competitors only generate 4% of their sales through commission sales (travel agents). ONA generates about 10 times this figure. Because travel agents retain part of the revenue from commission sales as their commission, ONA's profitability is lower than it would be if it adjusted its sales mix away from commission sales into online sales.

[Money] – Reduction in net profit – ONA's bet profit before tax has fallen 25 over the period 2004-6, despite revenue rising slightly. This highlights how ONA's high and rising costs are damaging financial performance.

[Money] – Poor working capital management – Alongside the fall in profitability, ONA has also suffered a fall in its current ratio from 1.24 (2004) to 1.05 (2006). If the current ratio continues to fall, this suggests the company will struggle to pay its debts when they fall due.

(b) (i) A no frills low-cost strategy **combines low price with low perceived value added**, and **focuses on price-sensitive market segments**. Price is the key element of competitive strategy.

A no frills strategy is a **cost leadership approach**, and this is the case in the airline industry where no frills airlines such as EasyJet or Ryanair (in the UK) or SouthWest (in the USA) adopt a low cost pricing strategy. The characteristic features of these airlines are low fares and basic service levels, coupled with high load factors.

A no frills strategy also requires **very tight management**; efficiency levels must be kept high so that the cost base remains low.

No frills strategies usually exist in markets where buyers have high power and/or low switching costs, because in these markets it is **difficult to build customer loyalty**. A no frills strategy does not attempt to build significant customer loyalty.

A no frills strategy may also provide a means for **new entrants to enter a market segment**. If the major providers are competing on a non-price basis, the low-price segment will provide an opportunity for small, new players to avoid the major competitors initially. The new players can achieve market entry through a no frills strategy, and use it to build volume (market share) before moving on to other strategies and challenging the established players.

(ii) In order for a no-frills strategy to be appropriate for ONA it must be suitable, acceptable and feasible.

Suitability of cost structure

ONA's structure is not suited to a no-frills strategy. Many of the airline companies which have used the 'no frills' strategy have been **new entrants to the market**. They have **very low overheads** and have used the 'no frills' low-cost approach to **gain market share** before moving on to alternative strategies to cement sustain their position in the industry.

A key element in their strategy is achieving a **low cost base to sustain their low cost strategy**.

The evaluation of ONA's strengths and weaknesses in (a) has identified that **ONA does not have a low cost base**. It pays wages above the industry average and maintains overheads such as a catering department that its low-cost competitors do not have.

Also, ONA's aircraft utilisation rates are lower than its competitors, its fleet is older than its competitors, and it uses aircraft made by three different manufacturers. These factors all suggest that its **costs are relatively higher than its competitors**. And because ONA prides itself on its safety record it will be reluctant to reduce maintenance expenditure at the risk of compromising safety.

ONA creates its **competitive advantage through the quality of service** it offers customers, rather than through low costs.

In this respect, a no frills strategy will not be suitable for ONA.

Changes to business model, culture and operations
Given the context of ONA's operations, it seems highly unlikely that it can achieve the changes to its cost based which would be required for it to become a no frills low-cost budget airline without significant changes to its business model, culture and operations.

Suitability of reducing customer service levels

Low-cost budget airlines usually do not offer customer services such as free in-flight meals and drinks, and they do not allocate passengers to specific seats.

ONA **prides itself on its in-flight customer service**, and has gained prestige an public relations exposure from it, winning the Regional Airline of the Year award.

If ONA moved to a 'no frills' strategy, it would need to abandon its tradition of excellent customer service. This is **unlikely to be a suitable strategy** for ONA because it damages one of its core competencies.

Risk to load factors. There is also a danger that ONA's existing customers may object to the decline in customer service levels in which case load factors could fall. A strategy which leads to a fall in load factors would **not be acceptable for ONA**.

Cultural change. Moving to a no frills strategy would not only require a major cultural change at ONA, sacrificing the strengths of the organisation and the competencies of its employees, but it would also **lead to redundancies**. There would be significant redundancies in the catering department, and there may also be redundancies in the numbers of cabin crew employed.

These redundancies could prove difficult and time-consuming to implement in a **heavily unionised organisation**, and would also **damage its reputation** on the island, since most of its **employees are residents of Oceania**.

In this respect, moving to a no-frills strategy will **not be feasible or acceptable for ONA**.

Feasibility of revising flight schedules

ONA currently only has, on average, one flight per day to each city in the international sector. In order to benefit from economies of scale and become a volume carrier in this sector, ONA would have to **extend its flight network, flight frequency and fleet size significantly**. We do not how whether ONA has sufficient funding available to achieve this, which means the **feasibility of such a strategy** would need to be investigated.

Moreover, ONA has only expanded gradually since its formation, and only added three aircraft to its fleet between 2004 and 2006. Therefore, a significant, rapid fleet expansion may be **unacceptable to the culture of the organisation** which prefers gradual change to rapid transformation.

Acceptability of changing selling channels

On average, 'no frills' low-cost airlines achieve 84% of their sales online. However, ONA only achieved 40% of their regional sales and 60% of their international sales online.

If ONA is to become a 'no frills' airline, it will need a **major change in its sales channels**.

It is difficult to know whether this change will be an acceptable strategy. The low percentage of regional online sales suggests that the **citizens of Oceania may be more comfortable buying through third parties** such as the travel agents rather than buying directly online.

Acceptability of using regional airports to reduce costs

Many no frills airlines fly into airports that offer cheaper taking off and landing fees. However, these are often **relatively remote from the cities** they serve. This remoteness may be acceptable to leisure travellers, but not to **business travellers** – and business travellers are ONA's key customers in the regional sector.

Given that one of ONA's strengths is the high passenger load factors is achieves for regional business travel, a strategy which involves moving to airports which are less convenient for business travellers is **unlikely to be suitable or acceptable**.

Conclusion

The CEO's decision to reject a 'no frills' strategy for ONA appears to be justified.

It would require major changes in the structure, cost and culture of the company which would be difficult to justify, and which do not appear suitable, acceptable or feasible for ONA.

The extent of the changes required would represent a **revolution** rather than an **evolution** of existing processes. However, a revolution is normally only required when a company is facing a crisis and needs to change direction quickly.

There is no evidence to support the need for such a radical transformation. Although net profit has declined over the three years 2004-6, the company's **financial position is still relatively healthy**, and there is no evidence that the company is a takeover target for any predators.

It can be argued that a more **incremental approach to change will be more beneficial**, building on the strengths of the organisation, its existing brand, and the competencies of its employees.

If ONA really wants to move into the no frills sector it would be better advised to set up a new low cost brand to do this – rather than trying to restructure its existing business model.

(c)

Tutorial note. The answer below is based mainly on Bowman's 'Strategy clock' and the use of differentiation strategies. However, (c) is an option generation question and so you could equally use Ansoff's matrix or Lynch's market options matrix to generate ideas for growth strategies. Alliances are a popular growth strategy in the airline industry, and considering Lynch's matrix might have reminded you about this.

Two alternative strategies ONA might consider are **differentiation** and **focused differentiation**.

Differentiation

By adopting a differentiation strategy, ONA can seek to provide service that offer different benefits from those offered by its competitors.

If these **benefits are valued by customers** they will lead to an increase in passenger numbers. This will improve ONA's market share and seat utilisation.

Differentiation may also be attractive to ONA because it may allow it to charge a **price premium**. Because ONA's product offers added value compared to its low cost competitors (free in-flight food and drinks, allocated seats), passengers may be willing to pay more to fly with ONA.

However, the **success of the no frills airlines shows that not all passengers do value these premium products**; instead some want to fly as cheaply as possible rather than paying extra for in-flight hospitality.

Therefore, a **basic differentiation strategy may not be suitable** for ONA given the **two separate markets** it serves – business class and standard class travellers. It is likely that business class travellers will be more receptive to the premium service than the standard class travellers. Consequently, ONA should consider a **focused differentiation** strategy rather than a broad-based differentiation strategy.

Focused differentiation

A focused differentiation strategy looks particularly **suitable for the regional sector.**

ONA already has a strong market presence in this sector, and this strategy would allow it to build on these strengths.

ONA should consider the following initiatives to improve its product offering for the regional business class market:

- **Change seat configuration and provide more space.** ONA should consider changing the **balance in seat numbers between business and standard class.** The *average* load factor for regional business class travel was 90%, which suggests that some regional flights were fully booked or over-subscribed. However, the overall seat occupancy is lower than this. So ONA could convert some of the leisure travel seats to business class. Although this will **reduce passenger numbers overall**, the low load factors in standard class suggest that there is sufficient spare capacity to be able to absorb this change, and overall revenue will increase as a result of the change.

- **Faster check in arrangements**. ONA should look to speed up the process of booking and checking in because business class travellers are likely to value easier and quicker checking in. In this respect, ONA should investigate the possibility of **introducing automated self-service check-in kiosks** in the airport departure areas, or an online check-in facility.

- **Supporting services**. ONA should look to provide **passenger lounges** for its business passengers with **internet and fax facilities** so that they can work while waiting for their planes.

- **Loyalty schemes**. ONA should consider providing loyalty schemes aimed at business travellers. Brand loyalty is one of the aspects that differentiates a premium product from a 'no frills' alternative.

- **Convenient scheduling**. Although 'most flights' are already timed conveniently for the business traveller, ONA should seek to ensure that this is maintained.

Although this focused differentiation strategy is aimed at the business customer, it is also likely that some aspects of it will be valued by some leisure travellers in the regional sector. Given the strong regional brand, and the nature of the leisure travel in this sector (families visiting relatives) it seems unlikely that there will be a significant decline in leisure travel in the regional sector as a result of making business class a premium product.

International sector

ONA's strategic choice in the international sector is less clear. ONA's customer profile is more evenly matched between business and standard class travellers, and it is competing with strong 'no frills' competitors.

ONA could still pursue a basic differentiation strategy; however this in itself will not address the key problem which it faces in this sector – **low flight frequency**.

Alliances. The problem of low flight frequency could be addressed through seeking **alliances with established airlines** which already serve the same countries as ONA. **Code share agreements** in which a flight operated by one airline is jointly marketed as a flight for one or more other airlines are common in the airline industry, and they would provide ONA with a quick and easy way of increasing flight frequencies.

However, when looking at potential code share partners ONA will need to ensure a **good cultural fit** with its partners. If it is pursuing a differentiation strategy then code sharing with 'no frills' airlines would not be a suitable option.

Operational efficiency

Whatever strategy ONA adopts to try to boost revenues, it must still review its operational efficiency and cost efficiency. **Management of costs is important, even though ONA is not using cost advantage as a competitive strategy**. We have suggested ONA should adopt a differentiation strategy to secure a high price premium, but for this to benefit net profitability ONA will have to keep costs under control.

We have already mentioned the possibility of **increasing the functionality of the website to reduce costs**, but two other key areas for ONA to review are the composition of its fleet, and its employee levels.

Fleet. We already mentioned that standardising the fleet will reduce maintenance costs. However, ONA could also get significant benefits from moving to a **newer, more fuel efficient fleet**. But, against this, ONA

would need to balance the financing implications of leasing a new fleet, or the capital implications if they choose to buy any new planes outright.

Employee levels. We have also noted in (a) that employee productivity is declining. While customer service staff and cabin crew are essential to provide the **quality of service appropriate to premium pricing** it is **important that ONA does not overstaff**. Employee costs, alongside fuel costs, are the two biggest costs of running an airline so it is important ONA monitors wage costs to ensure that any increases in wage costs are justified by revenue increases.

54 ABCL

Text reference. Porter's five forces model and acquisitions are both covered in Chapter 6 of the BPP Study Text for exams from September 2015 to 31 August 2016.

Stakeholder mapping is covered in Chapter 5.

Top tips. Make sure you read the question properly! This question clearly steers you towards using Porter's five forces model as a basis for your answer. Despite this, some candidates instead chose to use Porter's diamond. This makes answering the question more difficult than it need be, although marks were still awarded for relevant points made.

Structure your answer clearly, using the five forces as headings and, as usual, make sure anything you include under each of these headings is specifically relevant to the material provided in the case study. For example, do not waste time simply listing the five forces at the start of your answer.

Make sure that you are clear as to what might be classed under each of the five forces. In the exam some candidates showed a misunderstanding of what might be considered a substitute and suggested that the other providers in the market were substitutes. These other firms are actually rivals and so should be discussed under the force 'threat of rival companies', not 'threat of substitutes'. Substitutes are alternative products from a different industry, not competitors within the existing industry.

Examiner's comments. Many candidates answered part (a) relatively well, showing an understanding of Porter's framework and an ability to apply it to the case study scenario.

Marking scheme

		Marks
(a)	1 mark for each significant point (for example, access to supply channels) up to a maximum of 20 marks	20
(b)	1 mark for each significant point (for example, issue of poor credit control) and up to 1 mark for each supporting calculation (for example, accounts receivable – 71 days and rising) up to a maximum of 16 marks Up to 4 additional professional marks for structure, persuasiveness and a coherent conclusion supporting the acquisition of Ecoba	20
(c)	1 mark for each significant point (for example, classification of stakeholders, power/interest) up to a maximum of 10 marks	10
		50

Part (a)

Threat of new entrants: If a new supplier enters the market, existing suppliers may lose market share and profitability. ABCL is the new entrant in this case, and will have to overcome the following barriers to entry:

Dominant providers: The market is dominated by three suppliers who are powerful enough to have forced a similar new entrant out of the market. They will be likely to retaliate if ABCL attempts to enter the market in its own right.

Employer contracts: 60% of student fees are paid by their employers. These employers have contracts and existing relationships with the already established firms. ABCL would have to work especially hard to attract these clients away from their current provider.

Accreditation: The existing providers hold Gold certification from accrediting body EloBa. It would be difficult for ABCL to compete in this market without that level of accreditation to assure customers of tuition standards. In addition, obtaining such certification will not only be costly, but will take over a year to achieve. This is long enough for ABCL to have already been forced out of the market.

Well established brands: The big three providers in the industry have well established brands, supported by extensive marking. Lots of investment would be required for ABCL to build a brand which could compete and attract loyal customers away from those established brands.

Threat of substitutes: Substitutes reduce demand and can potentially lead to the product/service becoming obsolete. ABCL will not want to invest in an industry that could be easily substituted. The substitutes in this market are:

Self study: 40% of students attend no training at all and study alone, as there is no legislative requirement to study with an accredited provider. Training providers can therefore be substituted by self study.

E-Learning: this is acknowledged, but not yet carried out, but the big three firms. If ABCL have experience in e-learning, it may be possible for them to enter the market using this differentiated product to generate competitive advantage. This would also be significantly cheaper as would make savings on premises, utilities, lecturing staff etc.

Blended learning: One of the smaller providers has recently launched a blended tutor and e-learning course with the aim of attracting self-studying students on to a course by offering them a cheaper and possibly more flexible way of studying.

Bargaining power of customers: If customers a have high level of bargaining power, then they have the ability to drive down prices or improve quality by playing suppliers off against each other. There are two different types of customers in this market; individual students, and corporate clients who fund students in their employment. The two customer groups have different levels of bargaining power, corporate clients having more than individual students. In this market the following issues arise:

Corporate contracts: There are 15 major corporate clients making up approximately 60% of the market. These mostly use the big three training providers, and the case study indicates that they are starting to play them off against each other in order to drive down their prices. This indicates a high level of customer bargaining power.

Purchase of provider: One of the large clients recently purchased one of the smaller training providers and is now able to carry out all its training in-house. This shows high customer power and raises the threat that suppliers will be purchased by customers.

Low switching costs: Neither corporate nor individual students appear tied-in with the training providers and the cost of switching between them is relatively low. This gives the customers high power. Individual students can easily move elsewhere if they are not happy with the training they receive, and corporate clients can move to another company if they are not getting value for money or are unhappy with the pass-rates of their employees.

Standardised products: The training firms all provide a very similar service, and so it is easy for customers to change providers. The levels of certification provides assurance over standards, however, all three large firms all hold Gold certification meaning there is little to differentiate them from each other. Again, this places the customer in a strong bargaining position.

Bargaining power of suppliers: If suppliers have high levels of bargaining power, they can raise their prices, or reduce the quality of their service. The suppliers in the case study are the lecturers, their power is determined by the following:

Limited supply: Competent lecturing staff are limited and so hard to find.

Supplier choice: The lecturing staff have choice of who to work for and can easily move between rival training providers.

These factors mean that the suppliers are powerful and can demand higher wages in order to retain them.

The Big 3 firms themselves also have some supplier power as they dominate the industry. The industry is much more concentrated than the industries they sell to, meaning that they will have influence over price, quality and supply terms.

Threat of industry rivals: The number and size of existing rivals, and the way they react to each other and to new entrants must be understood before moving into a new market. The important issues for ABCL are:

Dominant suppliers: There are three dominant suppliers who are on good enough terms to co-ordinate a response to any new entrant. They will protect their market and ABCL can expect a strong fight-back if it attempts to enter the market organically.

Smaller providers: There are 20 other providers in this market, accounting for approximately 20% of the market share. This indicates that the dominant suppliers are tolerant of these smaller rivals.

Differentiation: The service provided by the existing suppliers is very similar, and once Gold certification has been awarded to the suppliers there is little to differentiate them from each other, and so little to prevent customers moving between them.

Part (b)

Top tips. Despite the large amount of financial information provided in this question don't spend all your time calculating endless ratios, especially if you don't then go on to use them in your report. Only calculate those ratios you need and interpret them within the context of the scenario.

The marking scheme indicated that "up to 1 mark was available for each supporting calculation". In order to gain the full mark you would have to use the calculation in your report to make a relevant point, stating what that calculation showed. Marks were awarded on the basis of ½ a mark for a calculation and ½ a mark for the comment on it.

The non-financial information given in the scenario is equally as useful as the financial information you are provided with. You should have used the non-financial information provided to assess how easily Ecoba could be acquired in comparison to the other dominant firms in this market.

The financial information would indicate that, in contrast to the other two dominant suppliers, Ecoba would not be the most attractive acquisition target available. However, you should have also noticed that the other two companies would be very unlikely to accept any acquisition bids, which could lead to ABCL paying an excessive price for the company. Ecoba, on the other hand, should be relatively easy to acquire, given that it is almost wholly owned by a single shareholder who is approaching retirement.

You should also have noted the opportunities for the new management to improve the efficiency of the company, particularly in relation to the payment of suppliers and chasing up debt. This is attractive to an acquiring company as they can make quick changes which improve efficiencies leading to cost savings, and potentially higher profits.

The requirement asked you to **evaluate** the attractiveness of Ecoba as an acquisition target, and so the criteria of suitability, feasibility, acceptability could have been relevant. However, don't simply railroad your answer into this formulaic approach.

Easy marks. The requirement asks you to produce a report. There are four easy marks available here for using an appropriate report format, a persuasive style and coming to a coherent conclusion. Use headings in your report to help the examiners mark your paper, and draw their attention to your conclusion.

Examiner's comments. Candidates answered part (b) relatively well, calculating and using financial information that had been signposted in the scenario.

An evaluation of the attractiveness of Ecoba as an acquisition target for ABCL

Prepared by: Business analyst, Xenon Ltd

Date: March 2009

Introduction

Further to the interim report produced by Xenon Ltd (referred to from this point as us or we) in January 2009, ABCL asked us to evaluate the attractiveness of Ecoba Ltd as an acquisition target.

This report will:

- Consider the three main suppliers in the market, demonstrating why Ecoba is the most feasible target for acquisition.

- Look at Ecoba in more depth, evaluating the attractiveness of the company as an acquisition target.

Analysis of the market and feasibility of acquiring a BACTI training company in Erewhon

Three main providers dominate the industry in Erewhon: CATalyst, Batrain and Ecoba. They are each considered below to establish their feasibility as acquisition targets for ABCL.

- CATalyst

    - CATalyst is a wholly owned subsidiary of the Tuition Group.

    - The Tuition Group noted in its annual report that CATalyst is core to its strategy and a source of significant growth.

    - It is unlikely that the Tuition Group would consider selling CATalyst, except for a premium price.

- Batrain

    - Batrain is a private limited company with shares equally divided between eight founding members.

    - This structure would suggest that any proposed acquisition would be immediately dismissed or lead to extensive negotiations between the shareholders which would draw out the process to an unacceptable timeframe.

    - Four of the eight shareholders are under 40 years old, and as such are unlikely to want to give up their interest in the company.

- Ecoba

    - Ecoba is also a private company, but is almost entirely (95%) owned by founder, Gillian Vari.
    - Gillian is approaching retirement age and may be persuaded to sell Ecoba.
    - Smallest of the three dominant suppliers, but has enjoyed significant recent growth.

The respective ownership structures means that of the three dominant suppliers in this industry, Ecoba is clearly the most feasible acquisition target.

Detailed analysis of Ecoba as an acquisition target

The analysis below looks more specifically at Ecoba as an acquisition target for ABCL using the financial information provided for 2007, 2008, and for its competitors, as well as the other information provided in the scenario. Supporting calculations can be found in the Appendix at the end of this report.

Financial performance

Ecoba is the smallest of the three dominant companies and has both the smallest revenue and profit figures of the three.

However, revenue increased by almost 30% between 2007 and 2008. This was joined by an increase in retained earnings, and an increase of 40% in cash and cash equivalents. Although this looks positive, the increase in cash and equivalents could be a result of the slow payment of lecturers.

Profitability ratios (Sales revenue to capital employed, Gross Profit Margin and Net Profit Margin) also showed improvements in 2008, however the margins are the lowest of the Big 3 firms. This could be caused by weak controls over costs.

The liquidity of the company (based on the current ratio) is stable and in line with its competitors.

The gearing of the company is much lower than its competitors, and has reduced further in 2008.

This information suggests the company is becoming more profitable, and successful, however analysis of earlier years would be necessary to establish if this is a trend or an anomaly.

The low level of gearing suggests the company has significant unused borrowing capacity.

Operational performance

Ecoba is currently suffering efficiency problems, particularly in relation to the payment of suppliers and chasing up debts. This is evidenced from the average payables settlement period and average receivables settlement period, both of which increased in 2008. In addition, both of these figures are approximately double the equivalent figures for their competitors.

There is a clear opportunity here for the new management, who could benefit from making rapid changes, to improve the efficiency of Ecoba's admin department. This could lead to significant cost savings and increased profitability of the company as well as improving the goodwill among lecturers.

Conclusion

Ecoba is an attractive target for acquisition by ABCL and would provide a cost-effective entry into the BACTI market. This is because:

- It is profitable, and the increase in both its revenue and profitability suggests the company is still successful.

- There is significant unused borrowing capacity that could be used by the new management.

- It provides the opportunity to make efficiency improvements which could lead to significant cost savings and increased profitability of Ecoba.

- The structure of the company suggests it would be relatively easy for ABCL to acquire.

Appendix

The below calculations support the figures quoted in the report.

Increase in revenue: $\dfrac{22,000-17,000}{17,000} = 0.294 = 29.4\%$

Increase in cash/cash equivalents: $\dfrac{21,000-15,000}{15,000} = 0.4 = 40\%$

Profitability ratios

Sales revenue to capital employed:

2007: $\dfrac{17,000}{5,375} = 3.16$

2008: $\dfrac{22,000}{5,850} = 3.76$

Gross profit margin:

2007: $\dfrac{3,250}{17,000} = 0.19 = 19\%$

2008: $\dfrac{4,500}{22,000} = 0.20 = 20\%$

Net profit margin:

2007: $\dfrac{750}{17,000} = 0.044 = 4.4\%$

2008: $\dfrac{1,000}{22,000} = 0.045 = 4.5\%$

Liquidity ratios

Current ratio:

2007: $\dfrac{4,590}{4,935} = 0.93$

2008: $\dfrac{6,470}{6,920} = 0.93$

Gearing ratio

Gearing:

$$2007: \frac{225}{225+5{,}100} = \underline{0.042}$$

$$2008: \frac{200}{200+5{,}100} = \underline{0.037}$$

Part (c)

> **Top tips.** Don't spend a long time describing Medelow's matrix; there is only 1 mark available for this! The requirement asks how ABCL can manage the specific stakeholders in the scenario, so your time should be focused on this instead.
>
> Note that the stakeholder analysis takes place after Gillian Vari has sold/left the company so she is no longer a key stakeholder. A number of candidates in the real exam thought she was.
>
> The competitors (ie CATalyst and Batrain) are also stakeholders and it would have been valid to include these in your answer also.
>
> **Examiner's comments.** Most candidates answered this part question relatively well, with appropriate use of the Mendelow matrix often leading to high marks.

There are a number of stakeholders in Ecuba Ltd that will be affected by the change in management, although not all stakeholder groups will be impacted to the same degree.

Stakeholder management will help during the transition period, but the extent of management required will differ between stakeholder groups. Stakeholder mapping looks at the levels of power and interest of each stakeholder group and recommends an approach for managing them based on those levels. This approach has been applied to the stakeholders of Ecoba below:

Customers – Corporate

Concerns: The corporate clients will want to be assured that they are still getting value for money. Their contracts were negotiated with the old management, and two large customers have only recently changed to this training provider and may be tied in for a specified period. One of these large customers identified specific lecturers as a reason for giving their business to Ecoba, and will need to be assured that they are still there.

Power and interest: These customers are key players as they have both a high level of power, in that they could move their business to the competition, and high interest due to the high value of the contracts.

Approach: This stakeholder group will have to be actively managed during the transition period. Their retained custom is crucial to the success of Ecoba and any strategy taken by the new owners must, as a minimum, be acceptable to these stakeholders. A possible way in which they could be managed would be appointing a dedicated account manager to each of the corporate clients.

Suppliers – Lecturers

Concerns: Although their jobs are fairly secure due to being named suppliers in the contract, they will be concerned that their working environment and structure of their roles will change under the new management.

Power and interest: They have some level of interest as the way they carry out their job may be affected, but a high level of power as they could move to a competitor.

Approach: These stakeholders will need to be kept satisfied to prevent them leaving the company. Paying their invoices more quickly may help to keep them onside.

Employees – Admin staff

Concerns: The main concern of the admin staff will be keeping their jobs. The pressure currently on the team has led to late payments of suppliers and failure to chase up debt. This will attract attention from the new owners.

Power and interest: High level of interest, but little power.

Approach: These employees will have to be kept informed about the proposed changes.

Customers – Individual

Concerns: Individual students are concerned with passing their exams and are unlikely to have much interest in the takeover, providing the standards of education do not drop.

Power and interest: Low levels of both power and interest as they are largely unaffected.

Approach: These stakeholders require very little management as they are mostly unaffected by the takeover. Resources would be better applied to managing other stakeholders.

Certifiers – EloBa

Concerns: EloBa previously awarded Ecoba Gold level certification. They will need to be satisfied that these standards are still met under the new management if they are to retain this level of certification.

Power and interest: The accreditation body has a high level of power as it could withdraw the accreditation at any time, significantly affecting the reputation and student numbers of Ecoba. The information provided gives no indication as to their current levels of interest.

Approach: This stakeholder needs to be managed carefully and the main approach should be to keep them satisfied. However, they are stakeholders with high power and are capable of developing higher interest levels if they become concerned about the new ownership and becoming a key player. If this happens, this group will require much more active management.

55 Wetland Trust

Text references. The relevant chapters for this question are Chapter 1 (mission statements) Chapter 2 (environmental issues), Chapter 4 (strategic capability) and Chapter 5 (stakeholder expectations, ethics and organisational culture).

Top tips. This question does not request any one specific model and provides the opportunity to give a very wide ranging model. Candidates that used a number of models to look at the position of the organisation from a number of perspectives scored highly.

Note that this question is asking you to evaluate the **current strategic position** of the Wetland Trust, not to identify potential solutions.

Examiner's comments. Part (a) was well answered, using a wide range of appropriate models and frameworks. PESTEL was widely used but there is insufficient in the case study scenario to completely answer the question using this framework.

Marking scheme

		Marks
(a)	1 mark for each relevant point up to a maximum of 21 marks, up to 4 professional marks	25
(b)	1 mark for each relevant point up to a maximum of 15 marks	15
(c)	1 mark for each relevant point up to a maximum of 10 marks	10
		50

(a) **Assessment of the strategic position of WET**

Prepared by: Business Analyst
For: Sheila Jenkins
Date: January 2011

I have conducted an assessment of the current strategic position of WET. This assessment looks at the environment in which WET operates, the strategic capability of the charity, the expectations of the stakeholders of WET, and the charity's organisational mission.

Environmental analysis

I have assessed the environment by using the PESTEL framework.

Political position

The government of Arcadia is under pressure to increase taxation in order to meet the rising public expenditure. An outcome of this is that the government has changed the taxation rules for claiming GiftHelp.

Under the new rules GiftHelp can only be claimed on donations made by Arcadian taxpayers rather on all donations as was the case in the past. This will mean that WET will now have to implement changes to the donation system to ensure the relevant information is claimed from donors. There will be admin costs involved in doing this.

WET's income is also likely to fall as a result of these changes as GiftHelp (a payment from the government of 20% of the donation to represent the income tax the donors/members would have paid) will no longer be received for donations made non-taxpayers and non-Arcadians.

A further fall in income is also likely as there is evidence that 30% of people do not give the correct details. GiftHelp cannot be claimed on these donations.

Economic position

Following a number of years of growth Arcadia is now in recession. This will affect the amount of disposable income available to the citizens of Arcadia. As charity giving is not an essential item it is highly likely that less donations will be made. Those donors who can still afford to give to charity may switch to supporting social care charities that are likely to be under much greater pressure in times of recession. Members also may choose not to renew their membership due to financial hardship.

The economic downturn may also affect the amount available from government as evidenced by the tax clamp down as they will have less resources to spread around. They may wish to spend funds tackling issues such as homelessness before looking to support the environment. Priorities change during a recession.

Social factors

Arcadia has a well educated population which will be likely to understand the importance of protecting the environment and natural habitats for future generations. As such they are likely to be supportive of the work of WET.

Technological factors

There is little information in the scenario relating to technology issues in the wider environment.

Environmental factors

Climate change is occurring in Arcadia and rainfall has dropped significantly. This has severe implications for the continued existence of the wetlands and the habitats they support which WET exists to protect. WET must remain vigilant and support any initiatives that could reduce climate change or increase rainfall.

Legal factors

As a charity, WET will have to comply with the laws of the Charities commission. WET must remain aware of any changes required in legislation and ensure their continued compliance with these laws.

In addition to the PESTEL analysis, some elements from Porter's five forces model can provide further information about the environment in which WET operates. This can be done both by looking at the charity sector as a whole, and also by considering wetland protection as a sector.

Threat of new entrants

Charities as a whole face a constant threat from new entrants and barriers to entry are fairly low. The Government have refused to reform the Charity Commission rules and establishing a new charity remains relatively easy.

Wetland preservation on the other hand has high barriers to entry as WET already own all the remaining natural wetland in Arcadia and creating artificial wetland is extremely expensive. Rival charity WWTFT attempted to create artificial wetland and has been unable to raise the necessary funds to do so.

Threat of substitutes

The threat of substitutes is high as WET competes for disposable income and people can decide to either stop donating to use the money elsewhere, or donate to other charities such as the social care charities mentioned in the PESTEL analysis above. Switching costs between charities are very low.

Competitive rivalry

The level of the threat from existing rivals in the **charity sector as a whole** is high as there are many other charities to chose to donate to.

The level of competitive rivalry is much lower in the **wetland preservation sector** as WET is the dominant charity. It has an established brand, a well-known and charismatic leader and has all the remaining wetland in Arcadia under its control.

Strategic capability

I have assessed the strategic capability of WET by identifying the strengths and weaknesses of the organisation.

Strengths

- WET owns all the natural wetlands in Arcadia. This is a unique tangible resource which is difficult for competitors to replicate.

- WET has knowledgeable and experienced human resources, many of whom work for WET for free.

- WET is a strong brand which is recognised by 85% of Arcadians according to a recent green consumer survey.

- Dr Abbas is a well-recognised charismatic leader and public figure. This is another unique resource which competitors would find difficult to imitate.

Weaknesses

- Poor access to the wetlands for members and poor facilities on site. This makes them uninviting to members and does not encourage them to continue to renew their membership of WET.

- The way in which volunteers are utilised by WET needs to be revised to ensure the resource is used in the most efficient and effective way. The current poor management of the volunteers has led to them feeling under-valued and their numbers are starting to reduce as a result.

- Marketing and sales is a well-known weakness of WET. This reduces both the number of new donors and members and the number of existing customers that continue to support the charity.

- IT systems are causing a number of problems for WET due to restricted and cumbersome processes.

This illustrates that WET have some impressive strengths, some of which are unique resources which competitors would struggle to replicate. However, these resources need to be better exploited as the weaknesses demonstrate that they are not currently deployed in the best possible way for the success of WET.

Expectations, mission and purpose

We will now look at what people expect from WET. This is particularly important due to the recent change in the ethical stance of the organisation.

In order to survive, WET is dependent on two key stakeholders; members and volunteers, both of which are currently declining. Dr Abbas has recognised that this is because WET has failed to take sufficient account of the needs of these people and this must be improved going forward. The main expectations of these groups are:

Members expect better access to the wetlands and more information relating to the activities of WET.

Volunteers expect to be treated more professionally, feel higher valued and allowed to participate in decision-making. The contribution of these stakeholders is of upmost importance during this time of recession as it may become necessary to reduce paid staff. WET should also appreciate that the recession will affect the lives of the current volunteers as well as themselves and may need to rethink the decision not to pay travelling expenses which may be a factor in the decline in the number of volunteers.

The consultation exercise with members and volunteers is likely to have caused an expectation among them that the new leadership culture of WET will be more open and democratic.

The original mission statement of WET was to preserve, restore and manage the wetlands in Arcadia. However, given the recent changes at WET it would be the ideal to revisit the statement to address the expectations of the key stakeholders. For example, many volunteers and members appear to view saving the wildlife of the wetlands as a higher priority than protecting the wetlands themselves. A new mission statement such as 'to protect the wetlands and the wildlife they support' may be more relevant for the majority of members and volunteers.

(b)

Top tips. Make sure you are as specific as possible with identification of the faults, simple observation such as 'there are problems with the computer system' are unlikely to generate marks.

Look for the root cause of the problems, not just the symptoms that arise from these faults.

Examiner's comments. Candidates failed to spot glaring errors in the process and so many answers were too general and did not gain the marks on offer.

There are two key faults in the process which have led to a number of adverse consequences for WET:

Sales and marketing receive renewal confirmation before payment has cleared

This has led to the sending out of membership cards and booklets to members prior to their payment clearing. Once this is received, the member would conclude that their payment had cleared and therefore would not respond to any request for payment. This may be why there is a low rate of response to payment requests.

Where these membership details are sent to members whose payments may have not cleared, those members may accidentally receive a year's free membership.

These members, however, would be recorded in the system as 'lapsed' and would not be requested to renew the following year. It is likely that this is why some members are not receiving renewal notices.

Reminder notice is sent out one week before renewal irrespective of whether the renewal is actually 'in progress'

This has led to renewal reminders being sent out to those members whose payments are awaiting clearance. This means that reminders are received by members whose payment will clear, or possibly already has. Those whose payments do not clear will also receive this letter however, as mentioned above, given that they have already received their membership pack they will assume it did clear and ignore the renewal.

From receipt of the payment, it takes Finance 5 days to notify the membership department that payment has cleared, and there is a backlog of cleared notifications awaiting entry to the computer systems. This means renewal reminders may also be sent in error to members whose details have not yet been updated by the membership department.

Members received their card and booklet before payment has cleared and these people will also receive a renewal letter.

The people receiving these unneeded renewal letters may view this as wasteful and inefficient. This may cause the members to leave WET in favour of another charity that they perceive to be more efficient that will put their donation to maximum use.

Possible solutions

Notification to sales and marketing department

Finance should only send notification of a membership renewal to the sales and marketing department after payment has cleared to ensure only fully paid members receive the membership card and booklet.

Review reminder letter process

Renewal reminders should be only sent to individuals that have not responded to the renewal notice. This can be done by updating the membership system when a payment is received to show that it is being processed. This will reduce wastage and improve customer perceptions of WET.

However, this will involve a change to the computer system and add more work to the already pressurised membership department (there is already a backlog of cleared payments). It will also involve a further handoff between the finance and membership departments which increases the risk of error and further delays.

The problems can also be reduced by employing more staff in the membership department, however, this will increase administration costs.

Handoff reduction

The current system involves many handoff which increase the time taken to carry out processes as well as increasing the risk of error and cost of the process. Reducing swim lanes would reduce these handoffs.

One way this could be achieved would be by the finance department entering membership details of cleared payments into the system themselves rather than notifying the membership department that the payment has cleared. However, the finance department would require access to the system, appropriate training and sufficient resource to deal with the backlog.

Bring payment validation forward in the process

Payment validation should be part of the primary activity, rather than a separate activity as it is currently.

Early validation could be achieved by offering the member the option of making their payment online using credit/debit cards. This would eliminate the problem of errors in the details provided as the details would be immediately validated by the card provider. This would mean that WET would receive the money quicker and would reduce the number of finance requests, therefore also reducing costs and possibly headcount in the finance departments.

To do this the internet site will have to be developed to be capable of taking secure payments. This will involve both initial costs and transaction fees from the provider of the financial solution.

Direct debits

Customers should be encouraged to set up Direct Debits for their membership, an incentive such as a small reduction in annual membership may encourage customers to chose this option. Direct debits then allow for automatic renewals to take place which do not require any action from the customer. The customer would have to opt out of membership rather than opt in as they do under the current process, therefore action is only required if they chose **not** to renew their membership. This should both improve member retention and reduce administration as those memberships can be quickly and easily processed with no need to send out reminder letters therefore easing the pressure on the membership department and reducing administrative costs.

In order for this to happen changes will need to be made to the membership computer system.

(c)

> **Top tips.** Make sure you answer the question that was actually asked. This question is actually about the acquisition, retention and extension of customers with a focus around the ways that email and website technology can be used to support this. Many candidates chose instead to answer the question 'what are the advantages of email and website technology'. This meant that their answers lacked focus and many valid points were missed.

Email and website technology can be used for the acquisition, retention and extension of customers in the following ways:

Acquisition

Global reach

Websites are accessible to locations beyond those which can be reached by other means. This means that WET could widen its base of donors by making their cause known and accessible to people beyond Arcadia. The website also provides a channel of information 24/7 – it is not constricted by working hours and means that information is available to potential donors at whatever time suits them.

Online payment

The website can be set up with secure payment facilities so that potential members can sign up to membership or make a donation online. This is fast and convenient, which should lead to an increase in members and number of donations made as the easier that WET can make this process for potential members/donors, the more likely it is that they will actually act on their decision to sign up or donate.

Existing members could also be encouraged to renew their membership online.

Web discounts and incentives

To attract members via the website, special discounts or other special offers (such as a welcome gift) could be offered as an incentive to sign-up online. This means that web hits can be quickly converted into members by encouraging them to act on the idea straight away.

This could also be done to encourage donations, for example by offering a small token such as a free car sticker for all donations made online.

A members area can also be used as an incentive. This is an area of the website that provides members with various resources, offers and discounts. It is locked to the general public and accessible only via member log-in.

A referral scheme is an incentive that would help both acquire new customers and retain existing customers. For example, the member can invite a friend to join and earn credit, such as 30% off their membership renewal price, 14 months for the price of 12, or a free T-shirt from the online shop.

Experience of a wetland

Potential members and donors can experience the wetland 'live' via a webcam showing current activity at the site. This allows them to see for themselves what they are supporting and demonstrates why their help is needed.

Targeted emails

Mailing lists of similar organisations, for example other wildlife and environmental charities, could be obtained to identify potential customers who are likely to be sympathetic to the needs of WET. Targeted emails could then be sent to these individuals based around the information known about them.

Data collection

Data can be collected from the website to identify people who have visited the site. This data can be used as a basis for future targeting of those visitors to encourage them to donate or to sign up as members.

Banner advertisements

Banner advertising for WET could be used on search engines, or other websites, which if clicked will direct the user to the WET website.

Retention

Customer profiling

WET should gain an understanding of the specific needs and interests of individuals and target them accordingly. Customer segmentation (eg potential customers, donors, members and volunteers) is one approach as each segment will require different information so communication should therefore be tailored to those needs. Providing separate areas on the website for members and volunteers helps to ensure each group gets the information most relevant and of highest interest to them.

Profiling can also be done at a more individual level based on information known about them personally and their interests.

Online communities

Online communities and forums can be set up within the WET website itself to allow members and volunteers to communicate with each other and discuss topics of interest. It also encourages them to actively participate in the organisation.

In addition, such communities provide WET with the opportunity to find out more about what is important to its customers, any problems they may have with WET, or features/services that they want but do not currently receive. This helps WET to enhance the member experience and therefore reduce the number on members that choose not to renew. Valuable information for targeting of communications can also be gleaned from this.

Links to social networking, such as a Facebook group and Twitter updates etc help to communicate with members and the wider public.

Ease of renewal/direct debit

To increase the chance of renewal customers could be encouraged to sign up for direct debit. This means that at renewal time no action would be required for the membership to continue into another year, action would only be required if they chose **not** to renew. This makes it more effort to end support than to continuing.

Encouragement of participation in the organisation

Exiting customers can be encouraged to participate in the organisation via feedback sections in the website, as with online communities this helps WET improve the services offered.

Further participation can be offered via online petitions and lobbying of government. This helps members feel that they make a genuine difference to the Wetlands and the success of WET in protecting them.

Extension

WET branded products and reinforcing the brand

WET products (T-shirts, hats, mugs etc) could be offered in the online shop section of the website. To further increase revenue when a customer makes a purchase, the suggestion to 'add a donation to your basket' could be made before the transaction is completed. A similar suggestion to 'show your support for WET and add this to your basket' could be made as part of the membership payment and donation process.

Branded products also act as advertising and reinforce the brand.

Cross-selling related goods and services of interest to the WET customer

The online shop could also include products which are not specifically sold by WET themselves but are of interest to the customers, eg books relating to the Wetlands or Wetland wildlife. These orders would be fulfilled by a separate company, eg Amazon, from whom WET would receive commission.

56 Institute of Information Systems Architects

Environmental analysis is covered in Chapter 2 and methods of growth are discussed in Chapter 6 of the BPP Study Text for exams from September 2015 to 31 August 2016. Harmon's process-strategy matrix is explored in Chapter 9.

Important note. These answers are the examiner's illustrative answers, showing the level of technical content candidates should aim to achieve in an answer.

However, because these answers are designed as a teaching aid, they are **much longer than would be expected from a candidate** sitting this paper under examination conditions.

Marking scheme

			Marks
(a)	Up to two marks awarded for identifying macro-environmental influences in each of the six PESTEL areas – even if justifying the lack of influence	12	
	A further five marks are available for candidates who have extended their argument in selected areas of the framework. It must be accepted that each area of the PESTEL framework will have a differential effect and that candidates will interpret this in various ways	5	
	A further three marks are available for professional marks	3	
			20
(b)	One mark for each relevant point, up to a maximum of 10 marks within this, there is a maximum of five marks available for identifying appropriate principles	10	
			10
(c)	Up to four marks available for the description of the Harmon process strategy matrix	4	
	Up to four marks for the application of the matrix to the situation faced by the IISA	4	
	Up to two professional marks	2	
			10
(d)	One mark for each valid point up to a maximum of 10 marks within this, there is a maximum of five marks available for each option	10	
			10
			50

Part (a)

The PESTEL framework may be used to explore the macro-environmental influences that might affect an organisation. There are six main influences in the framework: political, economic, social, technological, environmental and legal. However, these types are interlinked and so, for example, political developments and environmental requirements are often implemented by enacting laws. Candidates will be given credit for defining the main macro-environmental influences that affect IISA, rather than classifying these influences into the PESTEL framework. In the following answer, it is assumed that social (socio-cultural) and technological influences will be the most significant drivers of change.

Political

The IISA is situated in a country with a relatively stable political system. All political parties in this country appear to value and promote education. Tax incentives and Government schemes help companies and individuals gain appropriate qualifications. Like many countries, the Government is committed to the promotion of lifelong learning to help its citizens develop and adapt to changing labour circumstances. There are periodic initiatives, such as

Investors in People and the Skills Task Force, established to 'ensure that Britain has the skills to sustain high levels of employment, to compete in the global marketplace and to provide opportunity for all'. Furthermore, the Government itself is a major consumer of labour and a large procurer of training. It continues to demand that employees have appropriate qualifications and that suppliers have a well-qualified work force. Many of its Information Technology (IT) suppliers use certification as a way of demonstrating that their workforce is well qualified and this assists them in successfully bidding for government contracts. Having said all this, British Governments have largely taken what has been referred to as a voluntarist approach, with organisations left to finance and organise their own training and development. Other countries have a more interventionist approach; for example, using a payroll levy which is directly used to fund training.

Economic

The IISA is situated in a relatively stable economic environment, where interest rates are relatively low and living standards are high. In general, system architects, like all IT staff, enjoy a good income. If their employer does not support their interest in professional accreditation (and this is unlikely – see below) then it is feasible for the individual to fund their own training and examinations. However, the IISA will have to be aware that this may not be possible in some of the countries which they are targeting. Hence they will have to monitor this situation.

Social (or socio-cultural)

The IISA is operating in a country and sector where people tend to already have a good education and the scenario suggests that many candidates studying for the IISA Diploma already have a degree. There is evidence to suggest that candidates currently perceive that getting the Diploma will enhance their career prospects. The IISA will need to monitor this and ascertain whether this perception is correct and, if it is, ensure that this message is communicated to prospective candidates. The overseas markets targeted by the IISA also have high levels of education and are countries where professional qualifications are highly valued.

There has also been the emergence of competency and skill frameworks with human resource functions linking personal development and job roles to clearly defined competencies. Research evidence suggests that competency frameworks have a wide range of use including a more structured approach to training and development. The IISA is likely to benefit from linking its qualification to a published framework. The Skills Framework for the Information Age provides a common reference model for the identification of the skills needed to develop effective Information Systems (IS) which makes use of Information Communications Technologies (ICT). It is a simple and logical two-dimensional framework, consisting of areas of work on one axis and levels of responsibility on the other. It directly refers to skills in systems architecture and so some link to the IISA qualification appears both feasible and desirable.

Organisations have been increasingly influenced by writers who believe that the strategic capability of an organisation often lies in the day to day activities that people undertake in the organisation. Consequently, developing an individual's ability to recognise the importance of what they do and the contribution it may have to the strategic capability of the organisation is important. The IISA should benefit from this value that organisations give to improving capability. In many organisations there is a link between developing competency, delivering training, and supporting professional certification. Human Resource Development has become a significant force in organisations. Jeffrey Gold has suggested that 'it carries the prospect of unleashing the potential that lies within people, allowing employees to contribute and indeed transform strategy'. Peter Senge's promotion of the 'learning organisation' has also been very influential. He suggests that the organisations that will excel in the future will be those that that encourage people to continually 'expand their capacity to create the results they truly desire, where new and expansive patterns of thinking are nurtured, where collective aspiration is set free and where people are continually learning how to learn together'. It can be argued that investment in appropriate qualifications can help nurture this.

Technical (or technological)

The introduction of computer-based assessment has been a major influence on many examining boards. They have been able to roll out examination schemes worldwide using centres (such as those provided by Prometric (www.prometric.com)) that provide the technical infrastructure, software and security required to successfully deliver computer-based assessments. Candidates for such examinations appreciate the objectivity of much computer-based assessment as well as the provision of immediate results. Although the Board of the IISA has rejected computer-based assessment, it must maintain a watching brief on its flexibility and functionality, particularly if it wishes to expand worldwide. It is likely that such software will be developed to support much more sophisticated question types.

The introduction of examination workflow systems is much newer, allowing conventional handwritten examination scripts to be scanned into a computer system and then distributed electronically to markers. Such systems eradicate the need for couriers and so remove the cost and security risks associated with the physical movement of scripts. Furthermore, markers can be geographically remote. E-marking software allows scripts to be partitioned, allowing answers to be distributed to specific markers. For example, the answers to Question 1 of this examination might only be sent to experts in business process modelling. E-marking software also guarantees anonymity, so that markers are marking a particular question cannot see the name, examination centre or even marks from other answers on the script.

Increased use and availability of electronic media may mean that options are available for moving away from conventional handwriting in examinations. The production of answers in a word processed format could be fed directly into examination script workflow software and be subjected to e-marking.

Environment

Environmental issues continue to have an impact on organisations, as they are encouraged by politicians and legislation to reduce their emissions and improve their recycling. The cost of disposal is also increasing. The IISA is currently a significant user of paper (for its paper-based examinations) and it currently has to pay for secure storage and disposal. The cost of this is rising and will continue to rise. Paperless examinations will increasingly be seen as environmentally friendly and cost effective. However, if a move to paperless examinations is not feasible, the organisation may commit itself to the publicised recycling of its examination scripts.

Legal

The IISA is working in a country where there are many laws defining employer responsibilities and employee rights. It is likely that regulation will continue and the IISA will, like all organisations working in the European Union (EU), have to evaluate the benefits and cost of working within such legal structures. Some organisations seek to gain advantage by moving to countries where regulation is more lax, thereby avoiding the compliance costs incurred by their competitors. The IISA is potentially a relatively footloose organisation, so moving to a less regulated regime might provide cost advantages. It promotes itself as an *international* organisation (although all of its examinations are currently held in the UK), so moving from the UK may actually give out a positive message.

Part (b)

A strategic alliance takes place when two or more organisations share resources and activities in order to pursue a particular strategy. This approach has become increasingly popular for a number of reasons. In the context of the IISA, it would allow the organisation to enter into a marketplace without the large financial outlay of acquiring a local organisation. Furthermore, it would avoid the cultural dislocation of either acquiring or merging with another organisation. The motive for the alliance would be *co-specialisation,* with each partner concentrating on the activities that best match their capabilities. Johnson, Scholes and Whittington suggest that co-specialisation alliances 'are used to enter new geographic markets where an organisation needs local knowledge and expertise'. This fits the IISA requirement exactly.

The exact nature of the alliance would require much thought, and indeed different types of alliance might be forged in the three markets targeted by the IISA. A *joint venture* is where the new organisation is jointly owned by the parents. This is a formal alliance and will obviously take some time to establish. The IISA will have to contribute finance and resources to the newly-established company, but such costs and resources should be much less than those incurred in an acquisition. However, joint ventures take time to establish and it may be not be an option if the IISA wants to quickly move into a target marketplace in order to speedily arrest its falling numbers. A *licence agreement* could be an alternative, where the IISA licenses the use of its qualification in the target market. This could be organised in a number of ways. For example, a local organisation could market the IISA qualification as its own and pay the IISA a fee for each certificate and diploma issued. Alternatively, the qualification may be marketed by the local organisation as an IISA qualification, with the IISA paying the organisation a licence fee for every certificate and diploma it issues in that country. This requires less commitment from the IISA but it is likely to bring in smaller financial returns, and affords less control over how the qualification is marketed. Furthermore, if the qualification is successful, there is the risk that the local organisation will develop its own alternative so that it gains all the income from the transaction, not just a percentage of the transaction fee.

At first sight, the strategic alliance appears very appropriate to the IISA's current situation. The licensing approach is particularly attractive because it seems to offer very quick access to new markets without any great financial commitment and without any cultural upheaval within the IISA itself. However, the uptake of the qualification is unpredictable and the marketing and promotion of the qualification is outside the control of the IISA. The IISA may find this difficult to accept. Furthermore, the IISA will only be receiving a fraction of the income and so it must ensure that this fraction is sufficient to fuel growth expectations and service the newly qualified members in other countries. Finally, there is often a paradox in organisations where internal development has been the strategic method adopted so far. An organisation used to internal development and control often finds it difficult to trust partners in an alliance. Yet trust and co-operation is probably the most important ingredient of making such strategic alliances work.

Part (c)

Organisations operate using many different processes, most of which could benefit from investigation and improvement. A classification of the complexity and value of these processes helps organisations develop an appropriate response to requests for their improvement. **Figure 1** is a process-strategy matrix adapted from Paul Harmon's book *'Business Process Change'*.

Figure 1: Matrix – Complexity and importance of processes

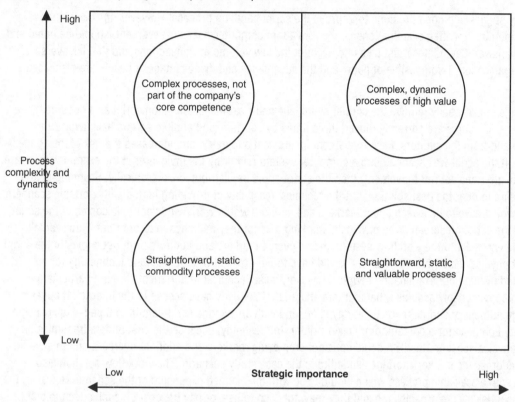

The matrix in **Figure 1** can be used to classify business processes. The vertical axis shows the complexity and dynamics of the process. Some processes are very straightforward (such as sorting mail) and do not change very much. In contrast, other processes have complex business rules and involve elements of judgement. Such decisions may also be dynamic in that they have to continually respond to changes in the environment. The horizontal axis shows the strategic importance of the decision. Some processes (such as payroll) are enabling processes and contribute little to the products or services that the organisation provides. In contrast, other processes are very important to the success of the organisation.

Processes in the lower left hand quadrant are relatively straightforward and should be automated using standard software packages or perhaps outsourced to a specialist computer services company. Processes in the lower right hand quadrant are also relatively straightforward but may offer an important competitive edge. Such processes have to be made as efficient as possible and may then be automated using either a software package or a bespoke solution. Processes in the upper left hand quadrant are complex processes that have to be done but do not add much to the organisation's product or services. These processes may be difficult to automate successfully and perhaps should be considered for outsourcing to an organisation that specialises in this type of process. The processes in the top right hand quadrant are high value but are difficult to automate. Setting examinations might be an example for this quadrant of the matrix.

In the context of the IISA, evidence suggests that the script handing system is arguably a relatively high complex process but it is of little strategic importance. Evidence of its overall complexity is provided by the problems reported in the case study scenario, such as:

- Loss of scripts during transfer by courier
- Poor maintenance of marker and auditor addresses and records of availability
- Incorrect and delayed publishing of examination results

The IISA may wish to investigate the outsourcing of examination distribution and administration. Some logistic companies may offer this, but the most likely source of such a service is another examination body which already has appropriate systems to support its own examinations. The IISA is based in a country where there are significant examination boards providing a range of services to schools and colleges. They have the systems in place to support high volume processing of the type required by the IISA.

Part (d)

Candidates may suggest a range of options to improve the script handling process. However, the decision to continue with open book written examinations, and not to adopt computer-based assessment, should be noted and reflected in the answer. Candidates must take into account the low volume of transactions and the risk averse nature of the organisation. Two possible options, and the advantages and disadvantages of each, are discussed below.

The first option is to essentially remove the courier swim lane and treat the examination script as a document in a workflow system. All scripts are currently moved three times by couriers, and audited scripts have two further movements, to and from the auditors. Each movement incurs cost and delay, and increases the risk of losing the physical script. If the script was scanned into a computer system (either by the invigilator at the examination centre or by HQ Admin after one courier movement) then the script could be distributed electronically. Scanning by the invigilator appears to offer the best solution, but the technical feasibility of providing high quality portable scanners to invigilators would have to be investigated. Markers and auditors would work with electronic copies of the script, either marking the script on screen or by physically marking a script they had chosen to print out. However, all marks would be entered into the workflow system and so even if markers and auditors print out copies of the script they would not physically distribute it. Markers would have to be provided with appropriate technology for downloading and printing out examination scripts. However, these technical requirements are not particularly onerous. It can be reasonably assumed that markers and auditors already have access to the internet. It appears that the average number of scripts marked per day is 10, and with an average script length of 6 pages, sixty pages per day is a very light load for a contemporary laser printer. Interestingly, because the cost of data transmission is not related to physical location, the IISA could consider employing markers and auditors overseas and this would allow them to address the marker shortage alluded to in the case study scenario. The work flow solution also provides them with a scaleable process which would cope with the planned expansion of the scheme. However, the IISA is noted as a risk averse organisation and they may not wish to use, or pay the cost of, such a technology dependent solution. The transmission of scripts across the internet may also raise security issues which would have to be addressed.

The second option is to retain the physical scripts but to reduce their movement by relocating markers or auditors or reducing the direct involvement of HQ Admin. For example, scripts may be sent directly from the invigilator to the marker and from the marker to the auditor. This would remove one transport of scripts (for scripts not requiring audit) and a further movement for scripts requiring audit. However, such time and cost savings may not be too attractive given the problems of maintaining marker and auditor addresses and availability. It could be argued that removing HQ Admin from this process is very risky as it removes important controls performed by full-time employees of the IISA. Markers and auditors are sub-contracted resources. An alternative to reducing the involvement of HQ Admin is to move the physical location of marking or auditing. For example, the role of marker and invigilator might be combined so that people who have invigilated the examination are also paid to mark the scripts and to submit them to HQ Admin. The process may be further streamlined by inviting auditors to HQ to perform their auditing. These two changes would reduce the physical movement of scripts to one move (invigilator/marker to HQ Admin). Furthermore, this movement would take place AFTER the scripts were marked and so markers/invigilators could be asked to physically record their marks before sending the scripts. Hence, there is a fail safe system if the scripts are lost. The script scanning option does not offer this (unless scripts are scanned by the invigilator at the examination centre). This second option is technically less risky and expensive than the script scanning option and so might be a more appropriate solution in an organisation which is noted as being risk averse.

57 The National Museum

Text reference. Environmental analysis (PESTEL) is covered in Chapter 2 of the BPP Study Text for exams in September 2015 to 31 August 2016; the cultural web is covered in Chapter 5, and the strategic lenses are covered in Chapter 1.

Top tips. Part (a) asks you to analyse the museum's macro-environment using a PESTEL analysis. Although you should have structured your answer using the PESTEL headings – political, economic etc – the most important thing here is to identify the main macro-environmental influences that affect the museum, rather than to spend too long debating which heading they fit in. Often, the influences are inter-linked, so for example, political developments may also influence legal issues through new legislation being implemented.

Although you shouldn't have spent too much time debating which headings influences fitted into, you should have recognised that some were more important than others, and spent more time analysing the more important aspects.

However, you must remember that a macro-environmental analysis only looks at the external environment in which the museum operates, so you should not have spent time discussing any internal factors (eg strengths or weaknesses) affecting the museum's performance. Any such discussions of internal factors would score no marks.

Although requirement (b) doesn't prescribe that you use a specific model, the reference to 'organisational cultural issues' should have been a clue that the cultural web will be very useful here. The scenario gives quite a clear picture of the aspects of the museum's existing culture, and there is a clear suggestion that the new Director General's strategy was unsuccessful because he failed to understand the museum's culture.

The model answer below uses the cultural web as a framework for exploring the failure of the Director General's strategy from a cultural perspective. However, the examiner indicated that students who explored the cultural perspectives using a different framework would still be given credit – provided they linked the cultural issues they identified to the failure of the Director General's strategy.

In requirement (c) you should have examined the insights offered by each of the lenses and then applied them to the strategy process at the museum. A useful approach might be to compare the strategy under the director general's new regime with the strategy process under the old regime, and to consider which lenses the two approaches fit with.

Note both requirement (b) and requirement (c) offer 2 professional marks for the clarity and coherence of your answer. This highlights the importance of careful planning before writing your answer.

Easy marks. The scenario highlights a number of environmental factors which you can use in the 20 mark part (a) without needing any specific text-book knowledge. If you work through the scenario highlighting factors that will influence the museum, and then explain their influence/impact, this should yield some easy marks.

Marking scheme

		Marks
(a)	Up to 2 marks for identifying appropriate macro-environmental influences in each of the six PESTEL areas – even if it is justifying the lack of influence. A further 8 marks are available for giving credit to candidates who have extended their argument in selected areas of the framework. It must be accepted that each area of the PESTEL will have a differential effect.	20
(b)	Up to 2 marks for each significant cultural factor identified by the candidate up to a maximum of 8 marks.	
	Up to 2 marks for an explanation of how each factor contributed to the rejection of the Director General's proposals, up to a maximum of 10 marks. This includes any ethical issues raised within the cultural analysis.	20
(c)	Up to 8 marks for the insights offered by the lenses into the case study scenario.	
	Up to 2 professional marks are available for the overall clarity and coherence of the analysis.	10
		50

Part (a)

Political

Funding and funding changes – The museum is currently 90% funded by direct grants from government, meaning that the government's decision to **gradually reduce that funding over 5 years** will have a major impact on the National Museum.

The **government and the opposition party have both agreed** that museums' reliance on government funding should be reduced, and so it appears that these funding reductions are unlikely to be reversed in the near future.

The **Board of Trustees recognised the implications of these changes**, which is why they appointed a new Director General to help the museum adapt to this new funding regime. However, senior staff at the museum appear not to have realised the potential significance of the funding changes, and opposed the Director General's plans.

Heavier funding cuts threatened – The government's response to the Director General's resignation has been to threaten further funding cuts, and to increase the political influence on the running of the museum by appointing more of the trustees. If the government's threat to impose heavier funding cuts is carried out, this could have serious implications for the museum's cashflow, and in the worst case, could even threaten its ability to continue operating.

Trustee appointments – The government's appointment of trustees is important to the museum. The two government-appointed trustees supported the Director General's proposals, and they were the only trustees who did so. The government is now threatening to appoint more of the trustees itself, thereby making it more likely that the museum will comply with the political vision of how museums should be run.

Performance measures – Going forward, the museum's government funding will be linked to certain performance measures – such as disability access. These measures will have a major impact on the museum's outlook. The museum will no longer simply be a guardian of the Heritage Collections, as it has historically seen itself, but it will have to meet a number of targets if it wishes to retain any government funding.

Economic

Economic exposure – When the museum was substantially government funded, it has been largely sheltered from any changes in the economic environment. Funding appears to have been stable, increasing to reflect inflation each year, and based on the Heritage Collections held by the museum.

However, the reduction in the level of government funding will mean that the museum will be increasingly exposed to commercial pressures. For example, it will have to generate revenues through admissions, and this revenue will be affected by the relationship between price and visitor numbers. The problem of sustaining revenues will be made harder if **visitor numbers continue to fall**, as they have done between 2004-7.

Ticket pricing – One of the key issues the museum will have to address is the price it charges visitors. Historically, visitors have been used to paying only a nominal entry charge. If prices are set too high, people will not visit the museum, particularly the lower social classes which the government is keen to include. However, if prices are set too low, they may not generate enough revenue to make good the shortfall in government funding.

New revenue opportunities – The Director General identified that the museum will have to look at new revenue opportunities, for example by increasing the commercial income through poster sales and souvenirs.

Social

Social inclusion – The Government is keen that museum attendance increases among the lower social classes and among younger people. However, visitor figures indicate that the proportion of young people visiting the museum is actually decreasing. In 2004, the number of visitors aged 30 or under was 35%; by 2007 this figure had fallen to 21%. The museum will need to reverse these trends if it is not to suffer further funding cuts.

The museum needs to identify ways it can become **more attractive to younger people or lower social classes**. The Director General suggested offering free admission, but it is also likely that the museum will need to make its exhibits more **interactive and approachable**. The Director of Art and Architecture's comments about confusing 'popularity' and 'historical significance' suggests that the museum has tended to ignore the wider public. However, this attitude will need to change in the light of the changed funding status.

Urban decline and local geographical context – The decline of the local neighbourhood around the museum may **deter fee-paying visitors**. Therefore the museum will need to ensure that visitors feel safe on their way to and from the museum, for example, improving security around the museum if necessary.

Location and visitors – It is likely that the museum's visitors are mainly middle class people, but the decline in the local neighbourhood means these are the people who will be moving away from the area.

However, while this is a problem for the museum on one hand, on the other hand it means that the neighbourhood around the museum is increasingly housing more of the people the government wants it to encourage as visitors. Therefore, if the museum can create **linkages with its local community** this could help it to **achieve the social inclusion the government wants** to promote.

Conversely, if the problem of middle class visitors not wanting to visit the area becomes too bad, and therefore visitor numbers drop still further, the museum may ultimately have to consider **relocating from its current site** to one in an area which is perceived to be safer to visit.

Technological

Increased coverage of artefacts – Currently, only 10% of the museum's collection is on display, with the remainder in storage. However, a proportion, if not all, of this remaining 90% could be displayed through a virtual museum online.

Increased visitor accessibility – A virtual museum would also allow **reduce problems with the physical accessibility** of the museum. People from all round the country, and internationally, could read about the collections and view the online displays through a virtual museum. The virtual museum could also benefit some disabled people who cannot physically visit the site.

A virtual museum also allows people to view the museum's collections from the comfort of their own homes, if they have concerns about the safety and security of the neighbourhood around the museum.

E-marketing – The museum could also use technology to increase the **scope of its marketing activity**. For example, if it collects a list of email addresses of regular visitors, it could **notify them of special exhibitions** which may be of interest to them – either in the virtual museum or the physical museum. As an initiative to attract younger visitors, the collections could also **publish blogs**, highlighting some of their more interesting features, and illustrating their relevance to younger people.

Electronic commerce – One of the government's targets for the museum is to increase its level of electronic commerce. On the one hand, this could be achieved if online visitors pay a **subscription fee to view the virtual museum**; on the other hand, the museum could have an **online shop** where visitors can buy replica items and souvenirs through a secure payment facility.

Environmental

Upkeep of building – The museum building is over 150 years old, and requires continual repair and maintenance. It is likely that an old building is less energy-efficient than a modern, purpose-built one would be, and therefore the museum's heating costs may be higher than they could be.

Alterations to building – The museum has had to make alterations to its building to comply with disability and health and safety legislation. It is likely that these alterations were relatively expensive. However, they have been criticised as being out of character with the rest of the building. The museum faces a dilemma here – it has to make its building compliant with the legislation, whilst trying to preserve the fabric of the existing building.

The criticisms about these alterations to the building, plus its energy inefficiency may encourage the museum's Board to consider moving to a modern, purpose-built site; particularly in conjunction with concerns about the decline of the museum's neighbourhood.

Legal

Access requirements and safety legislation – We have already noted that the museum has had to make alterations to its building to comply with legal requirements for disability access and health and safety legislation. If the government is keen to encourage social inclusion, further changes may be required – for example, including all public notices in a variety of languages or in Braille.

Furthermore, if the proposal to convert the staff dining room into a restaurant is adopted, the museum will need to ensure it complies with the relevant hygiene standards which govern food being served to the public.

Trustees and charity law – The museum is a charity and is run by a Board of Trustees. The Trustees are responsible for ensuring that the museum complies with the charity law in its country, and that it conforms to the charitable purpose for which it was established.

Moreover, in order to preserve its charitable status, a charity needs to be seen to be providing a benefit for the public at large. This may help explain why both the government and the opposition are keen that the museum should be as socially inclusive as possible.

Part (b)

> **Top tips.** To score well in this requirement you need to identify the relevant cultural issues at the museum, and then explain why they have led to the failure of the Director General's strategy.
>
> A sensible approach would be to use the cultural web as a framework for your answer, and within each aspect of the web to identify the relevant cultural issues and then explain their impact on the strategy.

One of the main reasons why the Director General's strategy at the National Museum failed was because **he failed to understand its culture** and therefore the way its staff behaved. The museum's culture can be assessed by looking at its **cultural web**.

Symbols

Symbols are the **representations of an organisation's culture** – for example, the offices (visual symbols) and the titles (verbal symbols).

At the museum, symbols such as the **dedicated dining room** and **personal assistants for the heads of sections** indicated that these people were considered very important.

The **status of professor** conferred on those section heads with responsibility for Heritage Collection provides a further layer of status within the cohort of section heads themselves.

It appears that it was important for the academics to be able to **demonstrate their position and their importance in the organisation** through the symbols attached to their position.

Threats to status – The suggestion to **close the heads' dining room and remove their personal assistants would have involved removing two of these key status symbols,** and would therefore have been very unpopular with the sections heads. Furthermore, by making such a suggestion and challenging their status, the Director General would have immediately made the section heads hostile to any other suggestions he might have had.

Power structures

The power structures of an organisation reflect who has the real power in an organisation, and who has the greatest influence on decisions and the strategic direction of that organisation.

Historically, the **academics who head up the sections containing Heritage Collections** have dominated power at the museum. These section heads constitute three of the five directors on the Board.

Equally, the **Trustees** have historically all been people well-known and respected in **academic fields** relevant to the museum's collections.

Consequently, the **power at the museum lay with people with an academic interest in the collections.** Until recently, the government has also effectively allowed the academics to be essentially autonomous; the government has simply provided funding for the trustees to distribute.

Threat to power structure – However, the **appointment of a non-academic as a full time Director General represents** a threat to this power base. Moreover, the DG's **proposed Board contains only one academic** (Director of Collections) out of six directors.

Therefore, the existing directors and academics will see the DG's proposals **as an attack on their power, and they will inevitably resist this.** The fact that the DG is a non-academic makes this perceived attack on their power even worse.

Organisational structure

Although the organisational structure reflects the formal structure of an organisation as well as the informal lines of power and influence, in practice it is likely to reflect the power structures.

This appears to be the case at the museum. **The museum's management are seen largely as administrators who are subservient to needs of the collections.** The title 'Director of Administration' for the Director in charge of finance, marketing, personnel, and visitor services suggests this imbalance in the power and influence between the collections and the operational aspects of the museum.

Proposed reshaping of priorities – The fact that the DG's **proposed board** includes a 'Finance Director,' a 'Visitor Services Director,' a 'Director of Resources,' and a 'Director of Information Services' **illustrates a significant reshaping in the priorities of the museum,** and so again is likely to be unpopular with the section heads.

Control systems

The control systems of an organisation concern the way that organisation is controlled. They include financial systems, quality systems and rewards. Looking at the areas which are controlled most closely can indicate what is seen as most important to an organisation.

Allocation of budgets – The budgets at the museum again reflect the **dominance and importance given to the Heritage Collections**.

However, these controls suggest a **fairly inflexible environment**. The smaller sections only receive a small percentage of the budget each year, which means there is **little opportunity for them to acquire new artefacts or to grow**. In effect, it appears that the system is designed to sustain the importance of the sections with Heritage Collections.

The DG could have used this disparity to try **persuade the heads of the smaller collections of the potential benefits of the proposed budget allocations**, and thereby to get them to support him. However, he does not appear to have done this.

Inward-looking focus – The museum's controls indicate an inward-looking focus (budgets to maintain the collections), rather than a focus on any external indicators, such as visitor numbers of accessibility. This also indicates that the museum is not used to having to measure performance, and, perhaps more importantly, is not used to using performance as a means of allocating rewards.

Change of approach – In the context of control systems, the DG's proposal is likely to be unpopular for two different reasons:

(i)   It is using an **external measure** (visitor numbers) to allocate budgets, and it allocates the budget on **actual performance** rather than status.

(ii)   It could be seen to be **challenging the superiority and status of the sections with Heritage Collections** in, by offering smaller sections the chance to increase their budgets.

Given that the heads of the sections of the Heritage Collections are also the Directors who the DG has proposed be demoted from the Board, these changes to the budget are likely to aggravate them still further.

Rituals and routines

The behaviour and actions of people in an organisation signal what is considered acceptable behaviour in that organisation.

The Directors seem to think it is acceptable to **lobby individual Trustees** to express their concerns with the DG's proposals.

Perhaps more importantly, the Directors seem to think it is **acceptable for them to write letters to the press and appear on television** to promote their views and gather support in opposition to the DG's plans.

Lobbying to resist changes – Although the DG was brought in specifically by the Trustees to help the museum adapt to its new funding position, the Directors have then tried to block any of the changes he has suggested to try to achieve this. It appears that the Directors feel that by lobbying the external media they can create sufficient pressure to resist the proposed changes.

Given this **blatant hostility to his proposals**, it was perhaps inevitable that the DG's strategy would fail.

Stories

Stories are used by members of the organisation to illustrate the sorts of things it values.

In the museum, the **stories reinforce the impression given by its symbols.** We have already seen how the symbols illustrate the status given to the heads of sections; in turn, the stories and the way the heads of section talk about other people reinforce their own sense of self-importance.

For example, the Director of Art and Architecture **dismisses the idea of linking budgets to visitor numbers** by suggesting that the **public are undiscerning**, and therefore cannot really be expected to appreciate the value of the collection.

Furthermore, this story also reinforces the control systems aspect that the museum has no concept of results, as measured by the public actually wanting to come and visit its collections.

Academic interests vs. commercial management – Overall, the stories reinforce the idea that the museum's **staff do not really value management and commerce**. The anonymous reference to the new DG as an 'ex-grocer' can be taken as an attempt to denigrate his commercial background, suggesting that the **established academic principles of the museum are somehow superior** – although the governments funding changes mean that without becoming significantly more commercial the museum is facing financial ruin.

The paradigm

The manifestations of culture in the cultural web (symbols, power structures etc) combine with the set of assumptions which are taken for granted in an organisation (the paradigm) to define an organisation's culture.

At the museum, the paradigm reinforces the idea that the **museum exists for the good of the nation,** and that its **value lies in guarding the nation's heritage** and culture, as defined by the museum's own experts. Importantly, the subservience of finance and management to the artefact collections also suggests that the museum has **not yet realised the significance of the government's funding changes.**

But perhaps more importantly, the paradigm does not give any **recognition to visitors or customers,** and making the museum a more commercially successful organisation. These are major changes, and it will take time for the museum to adapt to them.

Challenging the paradigm – However, perhaps the overriding reason why the DG's strategy failed is that it involved making a number of major changes to the museum in a short space of time, and the museum's senior management viewed these changes as challenging their position, rather than realising how vital some of them were in allowing the museum to deal with the government's funding proposals.

Part (c)

Strategy as design

Top-down process – The design lens suggests strategy as a top-down process in which senior managers establish a clear and **rational course of strategic action** as a result of **analysing and evaluating strategic options and constraints**.

Senior management responsibility – The design lens considers that it is senior management's responsibility to devise the strategy for an organisation, leaving lower levels of management to deliver the operational actions required by the strategy.

Clear objectives – The design lens assumes that an organisation has clear and explicit objectives, and that it uses strategy and objective setting to move towards those objectives.

In the case of the National Museum, the government has taken a much increased role in objective setting, by linking the museum's funding to the achievement of certain objectives.

Lack of consultation – The new Director General was responsible for trying to establish a strategy within those objectives. And it appears he has done this in a top-down manner, in which he has not consulted his staff. For example, **staff were particularly critical of the lack of consultation,** feeling that the proposals had just been handed down from on high with no input from them.

This imposition of a strategy 'from on high' is indicative of a design lens view of strategy. However, in this case, the new Director General had little alternative to this approach, because the change in government funding policy required a major shift in the museum's strategy.

Strategy as experience

Adapting current experience – Strategy as experience views strategy as an adaptation and extension of what has worked in the past. It does not look to change the existing strategy but to adapt it, and build on it. Therefore, changes are often **incremental** as an organisation adapts to new opportunities or threats in its environment.

No change in paradigm – One of the key features of this lens is that sees strategy as being **based in the experience and assumptions of influential figures** in an organisation, thereby **fitting within the paradigm**.

It appears that the process of strategy development at the **National Museum has historically followed this pattern**, being led by the experience and assumptions of the section heads.

However, one of the problems with this strategic perspective is that the **assumptions become inherent in an organisation** and it becomes very difficult to change them. This appears to have been the case at the museum.

The major changes being imposed by the government suggest that a **change in the museum's cultural paradigm is needed**, meaning that strategy as experience is no longer an appropriate approach.

Strategic drift – Equally, given the change of paradigm, it is unlikely that the existing management would have been able to deliver a strategy that meets the government's requirements. The section heads have become so comfortable with the prevailing approach that **they have let the museum's strategy drift**.

This is why a new Director General needed to be brought in to **develop a new strategy**. And because a new strategy was needed, the **strategy as experience approach would have been inherently unsuitable** for him to follow.

Strategy as ideas

Emergence of ideas – This approach to strategy emphasises innovation and the need for new ideas. These ideas can **emerge from all levels of an organisation**, not just from senior management.

Ideas in a time of change – The ideas lens suggests that strategy can emerge from the way people in an organisation respond to changing forces in the organisation and the environment.

So, the macro-environment factors facing the museum could be seen as catalysts for change. For example, the need to meet new technological objectives should generate ideas for how to develop a virtual museum.

Context for ideas – However, for an organisation to be successful at generating ideas there must be a culture and context which encourage staff to generate ideas and to embrace change.

But this does not appear to be the case at the museum. The museum appears to be dominated by a small number of section heads who are more interested in protecting their own interests and preserving their own symbols of power, than cultivating new ideas.

No drivers for change – Another factor which has reduced the need for new ideas has been the protected economic environment in which the museum has historically operated. Because the museum has been largely government funded, there have been no incentives to develop new ideas which might have increased revenue.

The change in government funding policy is likely to require the museum to become more innovative going forward.

Strategy at the museum

Historically, the museum has followed the **strategy as experience** lens. However, the government-imposed changes mean that this was not an option for the new Director General.

He elected to pursue a **strategy as design**, which appeared to be the obvious choice given the scale of the change required. However, because the Director General was not sensitive to the museum's cultural web his strategy was not successful.

In this context, he may also have been able to employ the some aspects of **strategy as ideas** to encourage section heads and other staff to suggest alternative proposals themselves. In that way, they would have felt more included in the strategic process, and would have been more supportive of it.

It is likely that the section heads whose sections contained Heritage Collections would always have wanted to preserve the status quo, but others may have been more receptive to a new regime which would have allowed their sections to gain increased funding.

58 GreenTech

Marking scheme

			Marks
(a)		1 mark for each relevant point (strength, weakness, opportunity or threat) up to a maximum of 12 marks	12
(b)		1 mark for each relevant point about Lewis-Read's proposal, up to 5 marks 1 mark for each relevant point about Fenix's proposal, up to 5 marks 1 mark for each relevant point about Ag Wan's proposal, up to 5 marks 1 mark for each relevant point justifying the selection of Ag Wan's proposal, up to a maximum of 6 marks Up to 2 professional marks	20
(c)	(i)	1 mark for each relevant point. (A relevant point can be a deficiency or a correction, so if a relevant deficiency is identified, as well as a relevant correction for it this can score 2 marks)	10
	(ii)	1 mark for each relevant point Up to 2 professional marks	8
		50	50

(a) **SWOT analysis of greenTech**

Strengths

Financial position – greenTech has grown steadily, and has been consistently profitable since its foundation. As a result it has accumulated a cash surplus of $17 million.

Competitive strategy – greenTech has followed a clearly defined strategy, as a focussed differentiator, in a specific market niche.

Core competencies – greenTech has accumulated significant technical know-how and competencies in 'green' technologies.

Management team – The management team have been in place since the company was founded, and so greenTech has a stable management team with extensive knowledge of the business.

Established brand – Market research indicates that 70% of the global electronics industry uses greenTech components somewhere in their products. This should mean than greenTech has established a strong brand name in the market, which in turn can support its strategy as a focussed differentiator.

Weaknesses

Low marketing expenditure – Although marketing expenditure has increased significantly from 2006-8, it is still very low, being just over 0.3% of revenue in 2008.

No marketing spend on fully assembled green computers – greenTech does not spend any of its marketing budget on promoting fully assembled green computers. Although these currently only generate a small proportion of greenTech's revenue, they could be an opportunity for growth if they were marketed better.

Ordering process – The current process for ordering and configuring computers has a number of deficiencies which result in greenTech losing potential sales.

No manufacturing capacity – greenTech has no manufacturing capability and so is vulnerable to problems in the chain.

Management team – The management team have been in place a long time now but there is a danger they are running out of ideas for the company. greenTech has accumulated a large cash surplus, but it does not appear to know what to do with it.

Opportunities

Government policy – The government has just announced a preferential procurement policy for energy efficient computers. This should allow the 'green' segment of the market to continue to grow.

Growth of green consumption – Society is becoming more environmentally conscious, and so consumers are increasingly looking to buy environmentally friendly products. This is likely to increase the number of people looking to buy 'green' components.

Growth into new sectors – Although greenTech has so far concentrated on selling to the electronics industry, the increase in environmental awareness should mean that companies in other industry sectors look to produce products that are quiet, recyclable and low emissions. This should provide opportunities for greenTech to supply components for them.

Interactive technology for developing prototypes – The current process for producing fully assembled computers is not interactive. However, technological developments should allow customers to construct virtual prototypes of the computers they want, and, in future, possibly also other electronic equipment.

Threats

Supplier bargaining power – Because greenTech has no manufacturing capability it is vulnerable to suppliers increasing their prices or to other problems which could occur in the supply chain.

Competitive rivalry – Although greenTech's sales are increasing, it is still a relatively small company and so is unlikely to be able to compete with the established global suppliers of fully assembled computers.

Barriers to entry to new markets – The fact that there are already large global suppliers who supply the market for fully assembled computers may act as a barrier to entry into the market. These global suppliers will benefit from economies of scale in production and distribution, for example, which greenTech is unlikely to be able to match.

(b)

Briefing paper

The purpose of this briefing paper is to provide an evaluation of each of the three proposals put forward for the future development of greenTech. It will then identify the chosen strategy and explain why this is the best strategic option for greenTech to pursue.

Lewis-Read's proposal

Lewis-Read is suggesting a **market penetration** approach, in which greenTech **gains market share** through **increasing its marketing activity**.

Lewis-Read's proposal only seems to focus on the **market for fully assembled green computers**.

Growth opportunities – The logic behind their proposal is likely to be that this **market will grow rapidly**, as domestic and commercial customers look to buy more environmentally friendly computers.

This growth will be further enhanced by the **government's procurement policy** which will promote energy efficient computers.

Low start point – At the moment, greenTech's **sales of fully assembled computers are very low**, and greenTech does not devote any of its marketing expenditure to promoting 'green' computers. This lack of marketing and promotion may well explain the relatively low sales of fully assembled green computers. Consequently, Lewis-Read's proposal would be that greenTech **increases its marketing expenditure** in order to take advantage of the opportunities in a growing market.

Competing with customers – However, if greenTech starts selling computers directly to home users and companies it will be **competing directly with two of its customers**, who are medium-sized computer manufacturers. GreenTech needs to be aware of the risk that these two manufacturers will stop using greenTech as a supplier if it becomes a direct competitor. It needs to consider the potential loss of sales to the manufacturers compared to the potential new sales from marketing its own fully assembled green computers more vigorously.

Fenix's proposal

Fenix are suggesting a **product development** approach, in which greenTech aims to offer a **more comprehensive product range**.

Buy manufacturing capability – A key aspect of the Fenix proposal is that it looks to **protect greenTech's supply chain**. Currently greenTech has no manufacturing capability and so is vulnerable to a supplier raising prices, terminating its contract with greenTech, or even going out of business.

Fenix argues that if greenTech had its own manufacturing plant it would remove these risks. Also, having its own manufacturing plant might allow greenTech to reduce its supply costs compared to having to buy in components.

Acquisition – greenTech will either have to set up its own manufacturing plant or acquire one. Fenix suggests that acquisition is the more practical option, because it will take a lot of time and money to set up a manufacturing plant organically. Acquiring an existing manufacturing company will provide a much quicker solution, although, since greenTech's management have **no experience of making acquisitions**, it will also bring its own problems.

In addition, as acquisition could prove to be expensive. There are a lot of costs involved in buying a new company, particularly if the directors of the target company resist the acquisition. Although greenTech have a large surplus, the management will have to ensure they have sufficient funds available to finance the acquisition.

Evidence suggests that over half of all acquisitions fail. If greenTech implements this strategy, it must be prepared to face a number of challenges, such as compatibility problems and resistance from the target company and its customers, if it is to succeed.

Professor Ag Wan's proposal

Exploiting core competencies – Professor Ag Wan's proposal suggests that greenTech should look for ways of using its **core competencies** with green technology in other industries, or with other products.

Professor Ag Wan is suggesting that greenTech finds **new uses for existing products and knowledge**.

Change in approach – However, this requires greenTech to make quite a significant change to the way it looks at itself: instead of being a supplier of components, it will now become a **supplier of ideas and technology**.

However, making this move will allow greenTech to **compete in the market for green technology as a whole**, rather than being restricted to a single market sector: electronics.

Rise of green consumers – There is an increasing number of consumers who want to buy from companies which demonstrate 'green' credentials and have sustainability policies. This growth of 'green' consumers will support greenTech as it exploits its competencies in green technologies.

Government policies – Government policies will also support the growth of the green technology market. For example, as tougher laws on emissions and waste disposal, the demand for green products should increase.

Market research – If Professor Ag Wan's proposal is to be successful, then greenTech will need to identify suitable new market sectors to move into. Therefore, greenTech should use some of its surplus cash on market research to identify the most lucrative potential markets to enter.

Justification of selection

Lewis-Read's solution is not suitable or feasible

Feasibility – Lewis-Read's solution aims to take advantage of the large potential market for green computers, recognising that it is currently under-promoted and under-sold. However, the computer market is very competitive, and dominated by global brands, and so it is unlikely that greenTech will have sufficient marketing funds available to make a significant impact in the market.

Suitability – In the first instance, greenTech might be able to maintain a niche position, selling its 'green' computers at a premium price. However, it is likely that the major suppliers could soon produce computers that compete directly with greenTech, meaning greenTech no longer differentiates itself from its competitors, forcing it to reduce its prices.

By producing its own computers, greenTech would also potentially come into conflict with the two medium-sized computer manufacturers it currently supplies components to. This could mean they stop buying components from greenTech.

Fenix's solution is not acceptable

Fenix's suggestion would have the benefit of reducing greenTech's reliance on its suppliers, and could allow it to reduce costs. However, it would involve greenTech acquiring another company, and historically greenTech has grown organically rather than by acquisition.

GreenTech has no experience of acquiring or integrating companies, and the management team seem quite conservative and risk-averse. Therefore the **risks involved** in making an acquisition are unlikely to be acceptable to them.

Ag Wan's solution

By contrast, Professor Ag Wan's solution which allows greenTech to continue to exploit its key competencies and know-how is **acceptable**. It is **feasible** because it does not appear to require any significant funding or additional resources. And the fact that it allows greenTech to use its competencies in a new and exciting way, which could be motivating for staff, also make it a **suitable** strategy.

Furthermore, Professor Ag Wan's solution seems to accept that most of greenTech's current activities are will fellow electronics companies or enthusiasts, and it will continue that tradition. Transactions are likely to remain primarily business-to-business.

(c)

> **Top tips.** The second part of Part (c) asked you to analyse the relationship between process design and strategic planning using the context of greenTech to illustrate your analysis. This is a difficult question and many students struggled with this in the exam. The examiner used Johnson, Scholes and Whittington's strategy lenses as a basis for his answer. Most students, however, took a similar approach to ours.
>
> **Examiner's comments.** Most candidates provided good answers to part (i) showing good business analysis skills. Part (ii) was poorly answered with many candidates providing only cursory answers.

(i)   **Current deficiencies**

Low conversion rate – 40% of customer enquiries do not proceed any further after the delivery and payment details have been sent to the customer. This should be a major concern to greenTech because it means a considerable amount of time and effort is being wasted by both greenTech and Xsys, preparing quotes which are not taken up.

The scenario does not tell us why customers do not take up the quotes they are given, but it alludes to the fact that the **price** may be higher than the customer wanted or that the **delivery date** was later than expected.

If the delivery times are an issue, then greenTech needs to look at ways at reducing the time taken to build and deliver the computers, by improving the processes illustrated in the swim lane diagram.

Delay between enquiry and confirmation – Another reason for the low conversion rate could be that delays occur in the various **email exchanges** between Xsys, greenTech and the customer, and in that time the customer changes their mind about buying a computer.

In which case, it would be useful if there was a better interface between greenTech's website and Xsys's systems, so that customers can see prices directly, and could make **a firm commitment** that they want a computer much earlier in the process.

Timing of credit check – A further 20% of orders are rejected at the credit check, which occurs after a customer has placed an order. This again means greenTech incurs wasted time and effort preparing delivery and cost details for customers with poor credit histories, and therefore who it will not sell to.

The problem here is that the credit check is performed too late in the ordering process, and so greenTech should look to bring the credit check **forward to the start of the ordering process**.

Missed delivery dates – Currently greenTech and Xsys provide customers with two delivery dates: the first given when the customer makes an initial order, and the second when the order is confirmed. However, this causes problems because the delivery date initially agreed at the start of the process cannot always be met to when the order is confirmed. This slippage from the initial delivery date is customers' biggest complaint.

However, if the delays between ordering, payment and credit checking were removed, it would **no longer be necessary to provide two delivery dates**. Instead, Xsys could provide a single delivery date at the start of the process.

Testing and delivery – A further inefficiency in the current system is that once Xsys has built the computer, the logistics company (EIM) delivers the computer to greenTech for testing, and then, after testing, greenTech couriers the computer to the customer.

There is no reason why greenTech needs to do the testing rather than Xsys. Therefore, it would be **more efficient for Xsys to test** the computer after it has built it, and then there could be a single logistics shipment to deliver the finished computer from Xsys to the customer.

(ii)   *Process follows strategy*

Process design is necessary to help an organisation implement its strategy. In effect, processes are required to help an organisation achieve its **objectives** and **goals**. The new strategic direction followed by greenTech will require the **design of new processes** to help them carry out business-to-business transactions with potential new customers. This demonstrates how process follows strategy.

Process leads strategy

However, processes can also lead strategy. Existing processes, goals and measures may not be aligned with strategy because some part of the **strategy is operationally unfeasible**. In this case, the processes would be modified to make them workable, and the strategy would also be modified to accept this.

Strategic change

Changes resulting from process re-design can be both small and **incremental** or **significant shifts** in strategy. GreenTech's change is significant, and they will have to re-evaluate the decision to follow the chosen strategy if they change their strategic position.

Mock exams

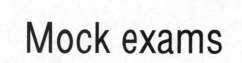

ACCA
Paper P3
Business Analysis

Mock Examination 1

Question Paper	
Time allowed	
Reading and planning	**15 minutes**
Writing	**3 hours**
This paper is divided into two sections	
Section A	**ONE compulsory question to be attempted**
Section B	**TWO questions ONLY to be attempted**

During reading and planning time only the question paper may be annotated

DO NOT OPEN THIS PAPER UNTIL YOU ARE READY TO START UNDER EXAMINATION CONDITIONS

Section A – This ONE question is compulsory and MUST be attempted

The following information should be used when answering question 1

Question 1

Introduction

Rudos is a densely populated, industrialised country with an extensive railway network developed in the nineteenth century. This railway network (totalling 6,000 kilometres), together with the trains that ran on it, was nationalised in 1968 and so became wholly owned by the government. By 2004, RudosRail, the government-owned rail company, was one of the ten largest employers in the country. However, in that year, the general election was won by the Party for National Reconstruction (PRN) with a manifesto that promised the privatisation of many of the large publically-owned organisations, including RudosRail. The PNR argued that there had been a lack of investment in the railway under public ownership and that the absence of competition had meant that ticket prices and costs (particularly labour costs) were too high for the taxpayer to continue subsidising it. The combination of high ticket prices and large public subsidies was very unpopular. As a result the government split the railway network into eight sections (or franchises) and invited private sector bids for each of these eight franchises. Each franchise was for ten years and was for the trains, tracks and infrastructure of each section. Each franchise would be awarded to the highest bidder.

The East Rudos franchise, one of the eight franchises, was awarded to Great Eastern Trains (GET), a company specifically set up to bid for the franchise by former members of RudosRail's management. It was the only independent company to win a franchise. The other seven franchises were awarded to companies who were subsidiaries of global transport groups and, initially, were largely financed through investment from the parent companies. In contrast, GET was primarily financed through loans from the government-owned Bank of Rudos. The ten-year franchise started in 2006. GET is an unquoted company, owned by its management team.

GET – the early years

The first three years of the GET franchise was extremely successful, both in terms of profits and passenger satisfaction. This was partly due to government subsidies to help ease the transition of the network from public to private ownership. However, it was also due to the skill and knowledge of the management team. This team already had significant operating experience (gained with RudosRail) and they adapted quickly to the new private sector model. GET was the most profitable of the new franchises and it was held up as an example of successful privatisation. Its investment in new trains and excellent reliability record meant that it quickly built up a well-respected image and brand. GET uses a series of television advertisements to promote its services. These feature an old lady arriving at various stations and texting her family that she has 'arrived safe and on time!' In a recent consumer survey these advertisements were rated as both memorable and effective.

In the newly privatised rail system many passenger journeys crossed franchise boundaries, so that a journey often involved the use of two or more franchise operators. GET developed an innovative booking and payment system that also automatically reallocated revenue from fares between franchise holders. It also allowed Internet booking and gave discounts for early booking. This system was so successful that GET now uses the system to process the bookings of three of the other franchise operators. GET is paid on a transaction basis for the bookings that it processes on behalf of these other franchisees.

The fourth and fifth years of GET's operation were not as successful. No government subsidies were paid in those years and economic problems in the country led to a fall in passenger numbers. Financial information for GET for 2010 is provided in Figure 1. Figure 2 provides data for the rail industry as a whole in Rudos.

Figure 1: Selected information for GET in 2010

Extract from the statement of financial position: all financial figures in $m

ASSETS		
Non-current assets		**$m**
Property, plant, equipment		2,175
Intangible assets		100
	Total	2,275
Current assets		
Inventories		275
Trade receivables		10
Cash and equivalents		300
	Total	585
Total assets		2,860
EQUITY AND LIABILITIES		
Share capital		550
Retained earnings		110
Total equity		660
Non-current liabilities		
Long-term borrowings		2,000
Total non-current liabilities		2,000
Current liabilities		
Trade and other payables		199
Current tax payable		1
Total current liabilities		200
Total liabilities		2,200
Total equity and liabilities		2,860

Extract from the statement of comprehensive income

All financial figures in $m

Revenue	320
Cost of sales	(210)
Gross profit	110
Administrative expenses	(40)
Profit before interest and tax	70
Finance cost	(60)
Profit before tax	10
Tax expense	(1)
Profit for the year	9

Extract from the annual report

Number of employees	3,010
Number of rail kilometres	920

Figure 2: Financial information for the Rudos rail industry as a whole

Measure	National rail industry average
ROCE	4.50%
Operating profit margin	10.00%
Gross profit margin	22.00%
Current ratio	2.1
Acid test ratio	1.2
Gearing ratio	48%
Revenue/employee per year	$85,000
Number of employees per rail kilometre	4.1

Current position

Despite the apparent success of GET, there has been considerable criticism of the overall privatisation of the railway. Much of this criticism is concentrated in two of the geographical areas where the franchisees have struggled to provide an efficient and economic service. The government has appointed auditors who are reviewing the operation of these two franchises and a government minister has stated that 'terminating the franchise and opening it up to re-bidding has not been ruled out as an option'. A major rail accident in Rudos (with many fatalities) has also led to concerns about safety and led to new legislation being enacted. Further safety legislation is expected concerning the relaying of track and all franchisees will be expected to implement the requirements immediately.

In 2009, the PNR was returned to power, but with a reduced majority. The leader of the main opposition party originally suggested that the railways must be re-nationalised if he were to gain power. However, he has since moderated his view, although he suggests that 'they should return a significant percentage of their profits to the taxpayer'. Road transport has also suffered under the PNR government, with many of the roads in the country heavily congested. Fuel costs have increased to reflect increasing scarcity, causing many companies to face spiralling transport and storage costs. For the first time in the country's history, an ecology (green) party has won seats in the government, capitalising on the growth of the 'green consumer', particularly in urban areas.

International rail developments

The pioneering privatisation initiatives in Rudos have been observed by other countries and many have adopted similar policies. Recently, the Republic of Raziackstan announced that it intended to privatise its railway network. Raziackstan is approximately five hours' flying time from Rudos and is part of the former eastern trading bloc. It is a country where there is currently very little health and safety legislation. Although there is also little employment legislation, public service jobs are traditionally viewed as safe, and employees perceive that a 'railway job is a job for life'. At present the railway network, which is 1,500 kilometers long, employs 8,000 employees generating revenues of $180,000,000. The country itself still has a limited technological and financial infrastructure, with only an estimated 20% of the population having access to the Internet. However, all political parties are united in their desire to privatise the railways so that money can be invested elsewhere in the country, for example, for providing better health care.

Because of the poor condition of the railway, the proposal is to retain and upgrade the rail tracks under public ownership. However, the trains and infrastructure, such as stations, will be privatised. The government is looking for letters of intent from private companies who are willing to take over the complete network (excluding the tracks).

A stipulation of the contract is that the bidder should have a significant industrial presence in the country. For some time GET has been interested in acquiring the company that undertakes most of the track and train maintenance in Raziackstan. This company SOFR (Society Fabrication de Raziackstan) was established in 1919 and has a long tradition of engineering. GET has used the company to refurbish some of its equipment and they have been delighted with the results.

The board of GET now senses a great opportunity. It would like to combine the speedy acquisition of SOFR with a bid to run the rail network in Raziackstan. In fact, early informal indications from the Raziackstan government suggest that the bid will be successful if SOFR has been acquired by GET as no other prospective bidders for the network have yet come forward.

Required

(a) Using appropriate models and frameworks, analyse GET's current strategic position from both an internal and external perspective. **(20 marks)**

(b) GET's proposed strategy is firstly to acquire SOFR and then the franchise to run the rail network of Raziacstan. You have been asked to provide an independent assessment of this proposed strategy.

Write a report evaluating GET's proposed strategy. **(16 marks)**

Professional marks will be awarded in part (b) for appropriate structure, style and fluency of the report.

(4 marks)

(c) Critical Success Factors (CSFs) and Key Performance Indicators (KPIs) are important business concepts in the context of franchising rail services.

Explain and discuss these concepts in the context of GET and the rail industry. **(10 marks)**

(Total = 50 marks)

Section B – TWO questions ONLY to be attempted

Question 2

iCompute was founded twenty years ago by the entrepreneur, Ron Yeates. It initially specialised in building bespoke computer software for the financial services industry. However, it has expanded into other specialised areas and it is currently the third largest software house in the country, employing 400 people. It still specialises in bespoke software, although 20% of its income now comes from the sales of a software package designed specifically for car insurance.

The company has grown based on a 'work hard, play hard work ethic' and this still remains. Employees are expected to work long hours and to take part in social activities after work. Revenues have continued to increase over the last few years, but the firm has had difficulty in recruiting and retaining staff. Approximately one-third of all employees leave within their first year of employment at the company. The company appears to experience particular difficulty in recruiting and retaining female staff, with 50% of female staff leaving within 12 months of joining the company. Only about 20% of the employees are female and they work mainly in marketing and human resources.

The company is currently in dispute with two of its customers who claim that its bespoke software did not fit the agreed requirements. iCompute currently outsources all its legal advice problems to a law firm that specialises in computer contracts and legislation. However, the importance of legal advice has led to iCompute considering the establishment of an internal legal team, responsible for advising on contracts, disputes and employment legislation.

The support of bespoke solutions and the car insurance software package was also outsourced a year ago to a third party. Although support had been traditionally handled in-house, it was unpopular with staff. One of the senior managers responsible for the outsourcing decision claimed that support calls were 'increasingly varied and complex, reflecting incompetent end users, to lazy to read user guides.' However, the outsourcing of support has not proved popular with iCompute's customers and a number of significant complaints have been made about the service given to end users. The company is currently reviewing whether the software support process should be brought back in-house.

The company is still regarded as a technology leader in the market place, although the presence of so many technically gifted employees within the company often creates uncertainty about the most appropriate technology to adopt for a solution. One manager commented that 'we have often adopted, or about to adopt, a technology or solution when one of our software developers will ask if we have considered some newly released technology. We usually admit we haven't and so we re-open the adoption process. We seem to be in a state on constant technical paralysis.'

Although Ron Yeates retired five years ago, many of the software developers recruited by him are still with the company. Some of these have become operational managers, employed to manage teams of software developers on internal and external projects. Subba Kendo is one of the managers who originally joined the company as a trainee programmer. 'I moved into management because I needed to earn more money. There is a limit to what you can earn here as a software developer. However, I still keep up to date with programming though, and I am a goalkeeper for one of the company's five-a-side football teams. I am still one of the boys.'

However, many of the software developers are sceptical about their managers. One commented that 'they are technologically years out of date. Some will insist on writing programs and producing code, but we take it out again as soon as we can and replace it with something we have written. Not only are they poor programmers, they are poor managers and don't really know how to motivate us.' Although revenues have increased, profits have fallen. This is also blamed on the managers. 'There is always an element of ambiguity in specifying customers' requirements. In the past, Ron Yeates would debate responsibility for the requirement changes with the customer. However, we now seem to do all amendments for free. The customer is right even when we know he isn't. No wonder margins are falling. The managers are not firm enough with their customers.'

The software developers are also angry that an in-house project has been initiated to produce a system for recording the time spend on tasks and projects. Some of the justification for this is that a few of the projects are on a 'time and materials' basis and a time recording system would permit accurate and prompt invoicing. However, the other justification for the project is that it will improve the estimation of 'fixed-price' contracts. It will provide statistical information derived from previous projects to assist account managers preparing estimates to produce quotes for bidding for new bespoke development contracts.

Vikram Soleski, one of the current software developers, commented that 'managers do not even have up-to-date mobile phones, probably because they don't know how to use them. We (software developers) always have the latest gadgets long before they are acquired by managers. But I like working here, we have a good social scene and after working long hours we socialise together, often playing computer games well into the early hours of the morning. It's a great life if you don't weaken!'

Required

(a) Analyse the culture of iCompute, and assess the implications of your analysis for the company's future performance.   **(13 marks)**

(b) iCompute is currently re-considering three high level processes:

    (i)   Advice on legal issues (currently outsourced)
    (ii)   Software support (currently outsourced)
    (iii)   Time recording (in-house, bespoke software development)

    Evaluate, using an appropriate framework or model, the suitability of iCompute's current approach to **each** of these high level processes.   **(12 marks)**

(Total = 25 marks)

Question 3

HomeDeliver is a nationwide company that sells small household goods to consumers. It produces an attractive, comprehensive catalogue which it distributes to staff known as catalogue supervisors. There are 150 of these supervisors in the country. Each supervisor has approximately 30 part-time home based agents, who then deliver the catalogue to consumers in their homes. Agents subsequently collect the catalogue and any completed order forms and forward these forms to their supplier. Payment is also taken when the order is collected. Payment is by cash or cheque ant these payments are also forwarded to the supervisor by the agent. At the end of the week the supervisor returns completed order forms (and payments) to HomeDeliver. Order details are then entered into a computer system by order entry admissions at HomeDeliver and this starts an order fulfilment process that ends with goods being delivered directly to the customer. The supervisors and the agents are all self-employed. HomeDeliver rewards supervisors on the basis of how many agents they manage. Agents' reward packages are based on how many catalogues they deliver and a commission based on orders received from the homes they have collected orders from.

In August 2010 HomeDeliver decided to replace the physical ordering system with a new electronic ordering system. Agents would be provided with software which would allow them to enter customer orders directly into the computer system using their home personal computer at the end of each day. Payments would also be paid directly into a HomeDeliver bank account by agents at the end of each day.

The software to support the new ordering system was developed in-house to requirements provided by the current order entry administrators at HomeDeliver and managers concerned with order fulfilment and invoicing. The software was tested internally and by the order entry administrators. At first, both the specification of requirements and initial software testing progressed very slowly because order administrators were continuing with their normal operational duties. However, as project delays became more significant, selected order administrators were seconded to the project full-time. As a result the software was fully acceptance tested by the end of July 2011, two months behind schedule.

In August 2011 the software was rolled out to all supervisors and agents. The software was claimed to be easy to use, so no formal training was given. A large comprehensive manual with colour screenshots was attached as a PDF to an email sent to all supervisors and agents. This gave detailed instructions on how to set up and use the software.

Unfortunately, problems began to appear as soon as the agents tried to load and use the software. It was found to be incompatible with one particular browser, and agents whose computers used that browser were advised to use an alternative browser or computer. Agents also criticised the functionality of the software because it did not allow for the amendment of orders once the had been submitted. It emerged that customers often contacted agents and supervisors to amend their order prior to it being sent to HomeDeliver. This was no longer possible with the new system. Many agents also claimed that it was not possible to enter multiple orders for one household. However, HomeDeliver confirmed that entering multiple orders was possible; it was just not clear from the software, or from the instructions provided, how this could be achieved.

Most of the agents were reluctant to print off the manual (preferring to read it on screen) and a significant number claimed that they did not receive the email with the manual attachment. Agents also found quite a number of spelling and functionality errors in the manual. At certain points the software did not perform in the way the manual stated that it would.

Internal standards at HomeDeliver require both a post-project and a post-implementation review.

Required

(a) Explain the purpose of each of the following: a post-project review, a post implementation review and a benefits realisation review. **(6 marks)**

(b) Evaluate the problems and the lessons that should be learned from a post-project review and a post-implementation review of the electronic ordering system at HomeDeliver. **(12 marks)**

(c) HomeDeliver does not have a benefits management process and so a benefits realisation review is inappropriate. However, it does feel that it would be useful to retrospectively define the benefits to HomeDeliver of the new electronic ordering system.

Identify and discuss the potential benefits to HomeDeliver of the new electronic ordering system. **(7 marks)**

(Total = 25 marks)

Question 4

The Institute of Solution Developers (ISD) offers three basic certificates in Information Technology; Software Engineering; and Solutions Architecture. ATL is one of the many training companies certified by the ISD to offer training courses to prepare candidates for these three certificates. ATL has, traditionally, taught these courses over five days culminating in a multiple choice examination. It has differentiated itself in the marketplace by offering high quality training in well-equipped training centres. Its prices are slightly higher than its competitors, but it is well regarded by both candidates and employers. ATL also provides training courses through sales intermediaries known as training brokers. These brokers negotiate a reduced fee with ATL and then add a profit margin to determine the price that they charge the end customer. All ATL courses are run in Eothen, an established industrial nation with a high standard of living.

In the last six months, ATL has developed an e-learning course for the certificate in Information Technology. There are three main reasons for this development. The first reason is to allow candidates to prepare for the examination in a flexible way, studying 'at their own pace in their own place'. Currently, courses are only run in Eothen and each certified course takes five days. In contrast the e-learning product will be delivered over the internet. The second reason is to provide a cheaper route to the qualification. Courses places currently cost $950 per person. Finally, ATL wishes to exploit a global market. It believes that there is a very large market for e-learning for this qualification, particularly in countries where disposable income is less than in Eothen. It feels that overseas customers will be sensitive to price, but they have no estimate of this sensitivity.

Eothen, itself, is in a period of economic decline and the top 500 companies, which are specifically targeted by ATL, are reducing their training budgets. Figure 1 shows the results of research from Midshire University into the relationship between average training spend per employee and companies' gross profit. Data given below is from 10 of the 500 companies targeted by ATL. Statistics produced by the Eothen government suggest that the average gross profit of the top 500 companies in Eothen will fall to $50m next year. In this analysis, the independent variable (gross profit) is x, which is being used to estimate a dependent variable y (average annual training spend per employee).

Company	Gross Profit ($m) (x)	Average annual training spend per employee ($) (y)	Analysis
A	50	900	The regression line for the two variables is defined by
B	100	1,050	y = 616.23 +3.939x
C	120	1,500	
D	30	750	And correlation by
E	15	600	
F	130	1,500	r = 0.801
G	55	850	
H	20	400	
I	40	500	
J	300	1,500	

Figure 1: Training spend analysed against gross profit

The e-learning product has been specified by an experienced lecturer and developed by a business analyst. The latter will also be responsible for supporting students once the product has been released. ATL is the first company to produce an e-learning product for the ISD market. It wishes to quickly build on its success and to offer e-learning for the other two certificates – Software Engineering and Solutions Architecture.

Each certificate examination costs $125 and is available on demand in test centres all over the world. This makes it very accessible to the countries that ATL are targeting. The managing director of ATL has also discovered the following analysis of nationwide e-learning sales published by Training Trends, a respected Eothen-based publication. Here the independent variable is time (x) and e-learning sales is the dependent variable (y).

Year	Quarter	Period (x)	e-learning sales ($m) (y)	Analysis
2008	3	1	2.65	The regression line for the two variables is defined by
	4	2	2.66	
2009	1	3	2.74	y = 2.38 + 0.12x
	2	4	2.84	
	3	5	2.86	And correlation by
	4	6	2.97	
2010	1	7	3.15	r = 0.958
	2	8	3.25	
	3	9	3.55	
	4	10	3.75	

Figure 2: E-learning sales in Eothen analysed by quarter (source: Training Trends)

The period column has been inserted to facilitate the regression analysis.

Required

ATL needs to determine the price (or prices) of its e-learning product:

(a)   Identify and discuss the factors that need to be taken into consideration when pricing the e-learning product.
(15 marks)

(b)   Figures 1 and 2 provide important, independent, statistical data:

Evaluate the potential of each set of statistical data for use in the pricing decision for the e-learning product, particularly highlighting any limitations in using such data. **(10 marks)**

(Total = 25 marks)

Answers

**DO NOT TURN THIS PAGE UNTIL YOU HAVE
COMPLETED THE MOCK EXAM**

Plan of attack

Remember to use your 15 minutes' reading time wisely. We suggest you first scan through the paper to identify where your strong questions are, and which section B questions you are more likely to score well on. You can then start planning your first question. It is really important you plan all your answers carefully before starting to write.

As a rule, we would recommend that students start with the compulsory Section A question before moving on to the two Section B questions they want to answer. However, you can start with a Section B question if you prefer to because you feel it is a particularly strong question for you. If you do, though, remember that you must only spend 45 minutes on each section B question.

Question 1 is a fairly typical case study question. Effective use of the reading and planning time will help you with this question. Read the requirements carefully, making sure you have a clear understanding of what you are expected to do. Read the scenario several times. You should read actively, highlighting the points that are relevant to the requirements and making notes in the margin of the question paper.

Part (a) asks you to analyse the current strategic position of a railway franchise from both an internal and external perspective. This should lead you to use models to assess the environment (such as PESTEL and Porter's Five Forces) and also to look at the internal capabilities of the company via a review of strengths and weaknesses. Lots of information is given in the scenario to help you with this.

Part (b) asks you to evaluate a proposed strategy that the company is considering. A sensible approach to use when asked to evaluate options faced by an organisation is suitability, acceptability and feasibility.

Part (c) asks you to explain and discuss the concepts of Critical Success Factors (CSFs) and Key Performance Indicators (KPIs) in the context of the organisation given. If you have an understanding of what these concepts are, this requirement should not cause you too many problems.

Question 2 asks you to analyse the culture of an organisation that develops software. The scenario includes a lot of useful information and using a model such as the cultural web will help you extract these points.

Part (b) asks you to evaluate the approach the organisation is taking with three of its high level processes. This requirement should be less problematic than part (a) and you should be able to quickly score plenty of marks here.

Question 3 requires you in part (a) to explain the purpose of a post-project review, a post-implementation review and a benefits realisation review. Presuming you have learnt these terms this should be quick and easy to answer. If you are in doubt over the meanings of these terms, this may not be the best question to choose as you will also need an understanding in these areas to successfully answer part (b).

Part (b) asks you to evaluate the problems that occurred and lessons learnt that would be identified by the post-project and post-implementation reviews,

Part (c) is quite straightforward and simply requires you to identify the benefits the organisation would gain from the new electronic ordering system they have developed.

Question 4 asks you to identify and discuss the factors that need to be taken into consideration when setting the price of a product. You are also provided with some statistical data and asked to discuss the usefulness and limitations of this data.

This could be a good choice if you are confident in your knowledge of regression analysis and the pricing decision.

Question 1

Marking scheme

		Marks
(a)	1 mark for each appropriate point up to a maximum of 20 marks.	max 20
(b)	1 mark for each appropriate point up to a maximum of 16 marks.	max 16
	1 mark each for report structure, style, and fluency up to a maximum of 4 professional marks	max 4
(c)	1 mark for each appropriate point up to a maximum of 10 marks.	max 10
		(Total = 50 marks)

Part (a)

External analysis

The external environment of GET can be analysed using elements of the PESTEL framework.

Political

GET has been strongly influenced by the government as the company exists as a direct result of the election of the PNR and the subsequent privatisation of the rail network.

The government is also considering terminating the failing franchises and re-opening bidding. This will also be of interest to GET.

The opposition government were originally in favour of re-nationalisation of the rail network but have now changed their opinion and would instead take a larger proportion of the company's profits. This means that, if this party were to be voted in, GET's profits would fall dramatically or, if they were to revert to their original policy, GET's existence would be threatened. GET should continue to monitor the views of the main opposition party and take action to influence these opinions where possible.

Economic

Rudos has in the last couple of years slipped into an economic recession which has led to a fall in passenger numbers. Combined with the end of government subsidies this has had a significant impact on the profitability of GET. GET must monitor the economic state of Rudos and revise its passenger number predictions to be in line with economic indicators.

Environmental

The roads in Rudos are becoming increasingly congested and fuel prices are spiralling out of control as a result of the increasing scarcity of oil. The impact on the environment of this kind of travel is therefore high and customers may be more likely to switch to rail travel in order to limit the damage they cause.

Social/Cultural

The rise of the 'green consumer' is evidenced in Rudos by the ecology party winning seats in the government for the first time in the country's history. This suggests there is a degree of green awareness in the country and may mean that customers are more likely to chose to travel methods that are more energy efficient and limit the impact on the environment. Rail travel would therefore appeal to such consumers and this message should be reflected in GET's strategy and marketing materials.

Legal

GET's costs are currently rising as a result of the increased legislation of safety that has recently been enacted. In addition, increased legislation relating to track relaying is also expected and GET and the other franchises will have to take immediate action to implement the requirements made. This is likely to have a significant effect on the profitability of GET as it unlikely that these costs would have been anticipated at the time of winning the contract for the franchise.

A further factor that GET will have to consider is the worldwide trend towards privatisation. GET should monitor other countries who may plan to make similar changes to its rail network and remain alert for any opportunities that may present themselves abroad.

Elements of Porter's Five Forces model will now be used to analyse the external industry in which GET operates.

Threat of substitute products

The main substitute for rail travel is driving on the roads. The scenario indicates that the PNR have failed to invest in the road network which has led to heavy congestion on the roads. Combined with the spiralling fuel costs (due to the increased scarcity of oil) this makes road travel much less appealing.

This threat therefore is reducing as rail travel is both congestion free and may not use oil. GET should ensure this is reflected this their strategy and marketing materials.

There may also be a degree of threat from air travel companies and, particularly in the current economic climate, the decision not to travel at all.

Bargaining power of customer

The bargaining power of the customers is weak. They have little choice but to use GET if they wish to travel by rail through the East Rudos area and so are not in a strong position to bargain down the prices. The problems with the road network, discussed above, further reduce the choice of the customer and hence further reduce their bargaining power.

Threat of new entrants

The franchise contracts have been awarded for ten years and so it is not possible for new entrants to join the market whilst these contracts are in place. This is a strong barrier to entry to this market.

Competitive rivalry

The franchise set up means that there is no rivalry from existing firms as the network is divided into geographical areas. As such, if a customer's intended journey passes through the East Rudos area, the customer will have no choice but to use GET.

Internal analysis

This internal analysis focuses first on the strengths and then the weaknesses that currently exist within GET.

Strengths

The management team of GET gained significant operating experience with Rudos Rail and went on to quickly adapt their skills to the new privatised model to the extent that it became the most profitable of the franchises and was help up as an example of successful privatisations. These internal competences will be invaluable should they choose to exploit opportunities elsewhere.

GET developed an innovative booking and payment system which has been extremely successful and is now used by three other franchise operators for which GET receives a payment for each transaction processed. This is both a strong internal competence and a steady stream of revenue which is unlikely to have been anticipated when the contract was originally won.

In 2010, GET's profit margin was 34% (110/320) which is well above the 22% profit margin for the industry as a whole. GET's operating margin on 22%(70/320) is also higher than the 10% for the industry as a whole. This would indicate that GET's overheads are well controlled.

The liquidity of GET can be demonstrated by the current ratio of 2.93 (585/200) and acid test ratio of 1.55 ((585 − 275)/200) demonstrating that GET is capable of meeting its short-term liabilities. The acid test ratio is also higher than the industry average of 1.12 which shows it is better able to do this than most in the industry.

The efficiency of GET could be analysed by looking at the revenue generated per employee. This shows GET generates (320,000,000/3,010) $106,312 which is significantly higher than the $85,000 revenue/employee of the industry as a whole. This shows each employee of GET generates much more income than the average employee working in the industry.

Efficiency can also be measured by looking at the productivity of the employees per kilometre of track. Employee per kilometre for GET is (3010/920) 3.27 which demonstrates that GET's employees are more productive than the Rudos average which has 4.1 employees per kilometre.

GET has invested in new trains and has established a strong record for reliability. These have helped GET to quickly establish a strong image and brand which is highly rated by both customers and peers.

Weaknesses

GET is a franchise company and as such is very vulnerable to external factors that can impact upon its profitability and existence. Although the team has a lot of experience within the rail industry, it has few external influences and so appears to have difficulty in obtaining external ideas and experience from different industries or countries. This could affect its ability to create a long term-future for GET.

GET is geared at 75% (2000/(550 + 110 + 2,000)) which is high in comparison to the industry level of 48%. This reflects the way that the company was initially funded. This may be concerning to their bank should they face economic difficulties.

GET's Return on Capital Employed (ROCE) is 2.63% (70/(550+110+2,000) = 70/2,660) which is likely to be concerning to shareholders as this is relatively low in comparison with the industry average of 4.5%.

Part (b)

> **Top tips.** Although you are not asked for any particular model or framework in this question, using the Suitability, Acceptability, Feasibility framework will help you to structure your answer and draw out relevant points.
>
> Don't make the mistake of repeating lots of the information you have already given in part (a) as this is unlikely to earn you many marks.
>
> A number of candidates misunderstood what exactly was being asked in this question and provided an answer which discussed the pros and cons of franchising. This was not the intention of this question and these candidates scored very badly in this requirement.
>
> **Easy marks.** Don't forget that there are four professional marks available for this question. You are asked to produce a report for the management of GET, so take the time to format your answer carefully and use an appropriate style and tone for the intended audience of that report.
>
> **Examiner's comments.** A good approach to this part question would have been to evaluate the strategy in light of any SWOT analysis derived from part (a). Part (a) should have been used as a springboard for part (b).

Written by: A.Candidate

Date: 11 November 2010

Introduction

This report independently assesses the proposed strategy of GET to acquire both SOFR and the franchise for running the Raziackstan railway services by establishing the suitability, acceptability, and feasibility of this decision.

Management summary

This report finds that the proposed strategy appears to be a suitable approach for GET, however, the assessment of the acceptability and feasibility of this strategy highlighted a number of risk and funding issues. This might suggest that a lower risk strategy, such as waiting for the failing franchises in Rudos to be re-opened for bidding, could be preferable.

Suitability

Suitability looks at the fit of a proposed strategy with the current strategic position of the organisation. The suggested strategy of bidding for the rail franchise is Raziackstan appears to make sense in this context in a number of ways.

It would allow GET to exploit strengths it has developed in running a privatised railway, in particular the competences of the management team and the ticketing system it has developed. This strategy would also address the weakness associated with being a one-contract company as it is at present. This would mean that GET would no longer be dependent on winning the Rudos contract when it is again offered for bidding and would possibly have greater longevity as a company.

An associated risk that this strategy may address is the potential of changes in the political climate of Rudos which could have a significant impact on the profitability, and even threaten the existence of the franchise. In contrast, Raziackstan appears to be a more stable environment with less political uncertainty and lower levels of employment and safety legislation.

Currently, more staff are employed per kilometre of track in Raziackstan (5.33) than at GET (3.27) and revenue per employee in Raziackstan is $22,500 compared with $106,000 at GET. These two measures both demonstrate that there is scope for increasing the efficiency, and therefore the profitability, of the Raziackstan rail network. This could be very appealing for GET as it could allow it to raise profitability without raising ticket prices.

The acquisition of SOFR may also allow GET to spread its risk by investing in a potentially expanding market at the neglected rail network is upgraded.

There are also potential synergies between SOFR and the franchise operation in Rudos, however, the key functionality of the software (cross-charging) is irrelevant in Raziackstan as the network will be allocated to only one private operator. Another key function of the software is the capability for internet booking. This will also be less important in Raziackstan as only 20% of population have access to internet, although this may become more important in the future.

Acceptability

A strategy will be acceptable if it provides sufficient return, without excessive risk and is appealing to the stakeholders of the organisation. Acceptability is affected here by risk levels which could be high for a number of reasons.

There is a mismatch between the experience of GET, which involves controlling both the trains and the tracks, and the franchise model that is proposed for Raziackstan, which would involve controlling trains only while the tracks remain under state control. GET has no experience of operating under this kind of model and the mismatch of experience may lead to difficult to resolve conflicts between GET (trains) and state (rails).

Another factor that increases the riskiness of this proposed strategy is the fact that the GET management team has no experience of working outside Rudos and it is likely that the culture in Raziackstan is likely to be very different. In Rudos, railway jobs are perceived to be 'a job for life'. This is unlikely to be the case in Raziackstan and there may therefore be a number of culture clashes to contend with. This may prevent efficiency gains from being achieved.

A further issue is that the GET management team has no experience of running an engineering company such as SOFR. Attempting to do this, especially within a different culture, could therefore be difficult.

A final concern that the stakeholders are likely to hold is the risk that the Raziackstan strategy could distract GET from running their profitable East Rudos franchise and so causing a fall in its performance.

Feasibility

For a strategy to be feasible, the organisation must have sufficient competences and resources (including funds) to be able to deliver it.

GET does have some cash, however the analysis in part (a) above indicated that this organisation is already highly geared and as such it is unlikely that the Bank of Rudos (who financed the franchise in Rudos) would wish to loan increased amounts to this company, particularly as it is to be used for an international investment.

Raziackstan has a financial infrastructure which is immature and as such is unlikely to be able to provide a source of funding to GET.

GET may also have concerns relating to the profitability and security of investment in medium and long term, particularly if the government change their strategy on rail privatisation.

Other resources and competences GET may require for this strategy such as engineering expertise may have to be developed. In addition, although GET have rail franchise experience, they have no experience of operating in Raziackstan.

Conclusion

Although the proposed strategy of bidding for the Raziackstan rail franchise and acquiring SOFR appears well suited to GET there are a number of risks involved and the company may struggle to secure sufficient funds to implement this strategy. A less risky strategy, such as waiting for the re-opening of bids for the failing franchises in Rudos, may be better approach for this organisation.

Part (c)

> **Top tips.** Careful reading of the scenario should lead you to the main areas valued by the GET customers. For each of the points, thinking of a way these could be measured will lead you to the associated KPI.
>
> Using the balanced scorecard as a basis will help you to identify a number of other KPIs that GET could use to measure their performance.

Critical success factors (CSFs) are product features that are **particularly valued by customers**. These are therefore the areas in which the organisation must excel in order to outperform their competitors.

As discussed in part (a) above, the competition can be considered to be road travel, air travel, and choosing not to travel at all.

GET's current marketing campaign centres around the message 'safe and on time'. This fits with the customer centred approach of CSFs, however, customers may also value other aspects such as cleanliness, affordability, environmental impact, security and convenience (timetabling). It is likely that different groups of customers will value certain features higher than others, for example leisure travellers may value safety and affordability whereas business travellers may value punctuality.

Key performance indicators (KPIs) are quantifiable measurements that management can use to monitor and control progress towards achieving its CSFs. They represent the targets that the organisation needs to achieve. For example, GET may class a train as 'on time' if it arrives in the station within 5 minutes of the planned arrival time and so would consider it had achieved the KPI wherever this was met.

The other CSF currently used by GET relates to safety and this could be measured in terms of the number of accidents or fatalities that have occurred on their tracks.

The CSFs and KPIs discussed above relate to customers, which is one of the four focuses of the balanced scorecard; a system for measuring performance based on non-financial as well as financial measures. Many companies may have KPIs relating to the other three focuses. For example:

- Financial: A target return on capital employed

- Internal business processes: Target number of trains that should be in use at any particular time (asset usage)

- Learning and growth: Targets for improving the skills of the workforce via training and development

In practice, organisations tend to overuse the term CSF and it is used to describe a range of elements, not just those that directly impact the customers' buying decision. The problem with this is that, although non-customer focused CSFs may improve internal processes, these will have no bearing over the customer decision to buy.

The CSF of safety could well be compromised in the proposed plans in Raziackstan to split responsibility for track provision from rail travel provision. The situation in Rudos when all responsibility lies with the franchise holder makes the responsibility for safety much clearer.

Question 2

> **Text reference.** Organisational culture is covered in Chapter 5 of your BPP Study Text for exams from September 2015 to 31 August 2016.
>
> **Top tips.** Using the Cultural Web as a framework is a good approach as this will help you structure your answer and help you identify the relevant information provided to you in the scenario. To score highly you should make sure that, as well as picking out the relevant points, you state what effect this is currently having on iCompute and the long-term effect this might have should the behaviour continue.
>
> **Examiner's comments.** In general, candidates spent too long providing detailed descriptions of the culture rather than producing an analysis of that culture and its implications for iCompute.

Marking scheme

		Marks
(a)	1 mark for each appropriate point up to a maximum of 13 marks.	max 13
(b)	Up to one mark for the suggested framework Up to 4 marks for each high level process	
	Up to a maximum of 12 marks for this part question	max 12

(Total = 25 marks)

Part (a)

The cultural web model can assist in understanding the culture at iCompute as follows.

Stories

Stories circulate between the employees of an organisation and often relate to the history of the organisation and can be very indicative of the issues that exist.

Stories at iCompute revolve around the weakness of the current management which is presented in comparison with the management of the past.

Symbols

Logos, language and terminology, offices, cars and titles used commonly within an organisation are all symbols which give clues towards the culture of an organisation.

At iCompute the main language and symbols are dominated by technology. Possessing gadgets such as the most up-to-date mobile telephone is not only considered to be important but is also seen as a reflection of the individual's technical competence.

Playing computer games is referred to as a typical after-work activity. Combined with the culture of long-working hours this could be potentially viewed as devise.

There appears to be a constant distraction cause by technological objectives and new alternatives seem to cause doubt and delay. This was referred to by one of the managers as a 'state of constant technical paralysis'.

Another manager suggests that customers are viewed as either incompetent or lazy due to their need to make calls to the support team, indicating a need to refocus managers towards customers.

Routines and rituals

Routines and rituals relate to 'the way we do things around here'.

At iCompute, there is a culture of long working hours and male-oriented after-work activities such as playing football and playing computer games. This culture would quickly alienate any member of staff that may prefer to go home to undertake family commitments, or who do not have interest in taking part in such activities.

Such a male focused culture likely to contribute to company's difficulty in recruiting females and also to its high first year labour turnover. The culture therefore is contributing to the need to incur high recruitment and training costs.

Control systems

In contrast to the technical focus of iCompute, there is a limit to how far technical expertise is rewarded. In order to be promoted, it is necessary for the technical staff to move into management and the evidence given in the scenario suggests that this is not always successful. There is the general view that the manages are technically out of date and any technical work they produce is generally viewed with contempt and quickly replaced.

The management of iCompute have recognised that there is a lack of measurement systems to permit adequate control, however, the recent attempts to introduce a system that would improve time recording has been met with anger from the software developers.

Paradigm and conclusion

When iCompute was first established, it was an entrepreneurial organisation with a strong work ethic focused around innovation and aggressive management. The organisation now appears to have superficially matured, but the analysis of the culture within the organisation would suggest that this is not actually the case.

Managers appear to avoid problems by failing to negotiate with customers, outsourcing problematic functions such as software support, and attempt to gain control by installing formal computer systems.

The culture has directly impacted on the ability of the organisation to attract and retain female staff and has created high levels of staff turnover by as only a particular 'type' of employee will be suited to an organisational culture such as this.

In order for iCompute to move forwards and recruit a more balanced and stable workforce, the culture of the organisation must change. The focus must move away from the technology-centric attitudes towards a more business focused approach.

Note that although the cultural web has been used in this model answer, the question did not ask for any specific model or framework to be used. You might, therefore, have taken an alternative approach to answering this question. There are a number of frameworks and perspectives through which the culture of an organisation can be assessed and you will still be awarded marks if you have chosen a different approach.

Part (b)

The Harmon process-strategy matrix aims to ensure that the most important areas are addressed when a process is redesigned. It does this by plotting the complexity and strategic importance of each area within a grid and suitable options are provided for each of the four quadrants of the grid. This approach will be used to assess the three high level processes that are currently under consideration at iCompute.

(i)   **Advice on legal issues**

This is currently outsourced and the development of a bespoke system to bring it in house would be risky. The scenario mentions litigation between iCompute and two of its customers which demonstrates that contracts would need careful wording and advice to ensure legal disputes are appropriately managed.

To do this, iCompute would need to recruit and motivate a suitable in-house legal team which could be both difficult and costly. The current system of outsourcing external provision of this process is more likely to provide iCompute with experienced experts who keep up to date in this fast moving and complex field.

Within the Harmon process-strategy matrix, this process can be classified as high complexity/low strategic importance. Therefore, the best approach for this high level process would be to continue to outsource.

(ii)   **Software support**

Software support was originally an in-house service but was later outsourced. Poor customer feedback has indicated this was a bad decision. In addition, service is a primary activity on the value chain and as such directly influences customer perceptions and will have an impact on the likeliness of repeat purchases. Poor feedback from end users will influence future software buying decisions which means that in the Harmon process-strategy matrix, this process can be classified as relative complexity/high strategic importance. Therefore, the best approach for this high level process would be to bring in back in-house and support this with an automated solution.

(iii)   **Time recording**

Some of iCompute's contracts are billed on a time and materials basis, and so accurate time recording data which details how long employees have worked on certain tasks is necessary for prompt and accurate billing.

iCompute has taken the decision to develop software in-house to support this process, however, this may not be the best use of internal resources which could instead be employed on external fee-earning contracts. Furthermore, time recording is not a problem unique to iCompute and so it is highly likely that software packages have already been developed.

Within the Harmon process-strategy matrix, this process can be classified as relatively simple/low strategic importance. Therefore, the best approach for this high level process would be to either buy an off-the-shelf software package or to outsource.

Note that the question again did not ask for any specific framework to be used and so you may not have chosen to use the Harmon process-strategy matrix. Credit will be given for any appropriate alternative framework.

Question 3

Note that there are only two marks for each of the types of review. Don't spend too long writing whole pages for each as you will not gain any further marks for doing so. Stick to the key points relating to what they, when they should be carried out, and what is done with the findings.

Easy marks. There are 6 easy marks on offer in part (a) of this question for simply repeating knowledge you have learned about the purpose of post-project reviews, post-implementation reviews and benefits realisation analysis. Unfortunately, it appeared that a number of candidates failed to earn these marks due to an apparent confusion over what is involved in each of these reviews and when exactly they should take place.

Marking scheme

			Marks
(a)	1 mark for each relevant point up to a maximum of 2 marks for each type of review and up to a maximum of 6 marks for this part question	max	6
(b)	1 mark for each relevant point up to a maximum of 6 marks for each type of review. Two types of review, giving a maximum of 12 marks for this part question.	max	12
(c)	1 mark for each relevant point up to a maximum of 7 marks	max	7

(Total = 25 marks)

Part (a)

Post-project review

The post-project review takes place on completion of the project and may be considered to be the final stage of the project after which the project is signed off and the team officially disbanded.

The post-project review aims to evaluate the success of the project itself, not the success of the product delivered by that project. It will look at the processes followed and decisions made during the project to determine what both went well, and what problems and barriers were encountered. These findings are then fed back into the organisation's project management process as lessons learned to ensure the same errors are not repeated in future projects and therefore improve subsequent project management at the organisation.

Post-implementation review

The post-implementation review aims to evaluate the product that the project has produced and as such will take place some time after the working solution (in this case the electronic ordering system) has been implemented and been in use by the organisation. This gives the users time to work with the new product and feedback their experiences into the formal review.

The focus of this review will centre around the fitness for purpose of the working solution and will both determine the approach for fixing the identified fault and recommend ways in which such faults could be avoided in the future. These lessons learnt will be fed back to the product production process.

Benefits realisation review

The benefits realisation review involves returning to the business case for the project and determining whether or not the costs were accurate and also if benefits identified at the outset were actually delivered by the project. This review can only be carried out, therefore, once the product produced by the project has been delivered.

It is likely that this review will take place at a later date than the post-implementation review due to the long-term nature of many benefits. In reality, the benefits realisation review may actually be a series of reviews where the long-term costs and benefits identified in the business case are monitored.

The lessons learned from the benefits realisation review will feed into the organisation's benefits management process.

Part (b)

Post-project review issues

Issues that may have been raised by the post-project review, and the associated lessons learnt which should be fed back into the project management process, are summarised in the table below.

Issue	Lessons learned
Project slippage Employees were originally only allocated to the project on a part time basis whilst also continuing to carry out their normal duties. This led to significant project slippage occurred which could not be rectified completely even when staff were allocated to the project full-time. This late decision led to delivery of the software two months behind schedule.	Appropriately qualified staff should be allocated to projects on a full-time basis from the outset. Failure to do so may cause the project to fall behind schedule.
Lack of consultation Although internal stakeholders were identified and consulted during the life of the project, it would appear that external stakeholders (such as catalogue supervisors and agents) were not consulted at all. As a result, their requirements (such as the need to be able to amend an order) were not built into the software. This also caused them to have very little understanding of the software before it was implemented, increasing the difficulty of their transition to the new system.	Both internal and external stakeholders should be included within the stakeholder analysis. External stakeholders should be included in the in requirements gathering process where appropriate.
Failure to run a pilot project prior to roll-out Rather than running a pilot project involving only a few supervisors and agents, the software was rolled out to all supervisors and agents from the outset. This meant that it was not possible to identify and fix faults prior to roll out. There should have been a risk assessment process to determine the scope of the project and its implementation. The scope should then have been defined in the project initiation document.	A risk assessment relating to the scope of projects should be carried out. Project managers should consider mitigating the risk by reducing the scope.

Post-implementation review issues

Issues that may have been raised by the post-implementation review, and the associated lessons learnt which should be fed back into the software development process, are summarised in the table below.

Issue	Lessons learned
Software faults and omissions There were a number of faults and omissions within the system, including the omission of the order amendment facility which has already been considered. The system failed to work with a popular browser suggesting the testing was insufficient as testing should be carried out using a range of browsers. The review needs to look into the reasons for this and determine why these faults were not identified prior to the release of the software. Wider acceptance testing including part time and home-based users may have helped to identify these problems.	Testing of new software should be considered over a number of different browsers. Wider acceptance testing which includes a range of different users should take place. The testing should take place in the environments in which the software will be required to work.
Documentation faults The documentation was provided to the self-employed users of the system in PDF format and is described as a large colour document. This is inappropriate as it is not reasonable to expect these people to print such a document at their own cost. As a result, this was not done, the manual was therefore not properly read and their ability to use the software suffered as a result. In addition, the PDF was provided to users as an email attachment and a number of users claimed to not receive the manual at all. This suggests this was not the best method of distribution for such a document. Finally, the manual contained a number of spelling and functionality errors. This reduces confidence in both the document and the software to which it relates.	The method of distribution of software instructions should be carefully considered to ensure it is appropriate to the needs of the user. Documentation should be carefully proof read and technically checked to minimise the risk of errors.
Lack of formal training No formal training was given to employees as it was considered that the software was easy to use. However, the evidence in the scenario, relating to the inability of the system to support multiple orders per household, would suggest that this was not in fact the case. An additional consequence of the lack of training was that faults (such as browser incompatibility) were not determined early on.	Training should be carried out in order to: • Pass on the necessary skills and knowledge • Build rapport with users • Allow early identification of possible faults or issues with the software

Part (c)

Top tips. A careful read through of the scenario should help you identify a number of benefits that could be gained by HomeDeliver as a result of the new electronic ordering system.

Don't make the mistake made by a minority of candidates by misreading this as an e-marketing requirement. A discussion relating to the 6Is is not relevant and is unlikely to earn many marks.

HomeDeliver might receive a number of benefits from the new electronic ordering system, including the following.

Staff savings

Fewer, if any, administrators will be required leading to significant staff costs savings. These savings should be easy to quantify.

There should also be a reduction in the staff costs incurred for catalogue supervisors as the amount of work required of them will fall significantly with the new system suggesting that less of them will be required. However, as each supervisor will now co-ordinate more agents costs may actually increase in the current reward system (where supervisors are rewarded based on the number of agents they administer). The contractual agreement may therefore need to be changed for such savings to arise.

Improved cashflow

With the new system, money will be sent daily rather than only at the end of the week, hence improving the cashflow at HomeDelivery which will then increase investment income or reduce borrowing costs. This benefit should be easy to quantify.

Improved customer service

Customer service and associated customer satisfaction should increase as the new system will allow the customers to receive their items faster. This is because orders are entered daily rather than weekly. Although this is a benefit for the customer, HomeDelivery is also likely to benefit from this as improved customer satisfaction should create more repeat business, increased numbers of customers and fewer cancelled orders (due to the reduced waiting time). These benefits may be difficult to reliably quantify in advance.

Question 4

Text reference. The concepts of price and price setting is covered in Chapter 12 of your BPP Study Text for exams from September 2015 to 31 August 2016. Regression analysis is covered in Chapter 2.

Top tips. Price, as part of the marketing mix, has been given more importance in the revised syllabus and this is the first time that it has been examined in this context. You should be able to generate a number of marks by thinking about what generic factors companies might wish to consider when setting a price for a new product. However, to score highly you will need to make sure you properly relate it to the scenario in question.

Examiner's comments. This question was an unpopular choice with very few candidates choosing to answer it. A general lack of knowledge was evident in both parts (a) and (b) of this question.

Marking scheme

			Marks
(a)	1 mark for each relevant point up to a maximum of 15 marks	max	15
(b)	1 mark for each relevant point up to a maximum of 10 marks	max	10
			(Total = 25 marks)

Part (a)

When setting the price (or prices) of the e-learning product, ATL will need to consider the pricing objectives; customer demand for the e-learning product and the ability of the customers to buy the product; assumptions used in costing the product and the associated policy; and the pricing strategy that ATL select. These areas are considered below.

Pricing objectives

ATL's pricing objectives must be carefully aligned with their overall corporate and marketing objectives. The organisation is described as having 'differentiated itself in the marketplace by offering high quality training in well-equipped training centres'. It is also mentioned that its strong reputation with both candidates and employers allows it to be able to charge higher prices than those of its competitors. It is likely price of ATL's e-learning software will directly reflect their 'premium' image.

Other objectives, such as targeting market share (a key reason for developing the software is to provide a cheaper route to the qualification), exploiting a global market (which is likely to be very sensitive to price) or generating sufficient cashflow to develop similar products for their other qualifications, should also be given consideration when the price of this software is set.

ATL is the first company to produce an e-learning product for the ISD market and as such may choose to use price and market share as a method of establishing barriers to entry to this new market.

Customer demand and the ability to pay

The price sensitivity and demand of customers is assessed for the three main customers that ATL wish to target.

The first consumer group consists of **individual customers** (B-C) who will purchase the e-learning course over the internet from all over the world are likely to be very sensitive to price. However, the size of this market and the elasticity of demand is not known.

The **top 500 companies of Eothen** (B-B) are being targeted by the e-learning product and ATL has obtained data on their current training spend which we are given in Figure 1. This data can be used to help establish price that the companies are willing to pay and the level of demand from this type of consumer. E-Learning is becoming popular in Eothen and the demand can be estimated using the data provided by Figure 2. However, it is also likely that these customers will make multiple purchases and so will expect discounts. This will need to be taken into consideration.

The final group of customers is the **third party reseller** (B-B) who now wish to offer e-learning services. These suppliers will need to make a margin and this will have to be factored into the price.

Costing assumptions and policy

As well has having a strong understanding of its continuing costs, ATL will have to determine the attitude the company has towards recovering the costs already incurred in the development of this product. Although these costs could be considered to be sunk costs, it may be possible to attempt to recover this investment if the right margins and costing approaches are selected.

A key advantage of providing e-learning is the low variable cost involved of each sale. As most of its costs are fixed in the short term, ATL should have great price flexibility therefore allowing it to set a price that allows it to maximise its revenues.

Other fixed costs, such as employing a dedicated support staff, are harder to predict as they are directly associated with both the level of demand and the usability and effectiveness of the software; the easier the product is to use and the better it is at preparing students for the exam, the lower these costs will be. It is likely that costs such as these will be stepped fixed costs although how this will work is difficult to predict.

The price will also reflect a contribution to the overhead costs of ATL as a whole such as finance, administration and human resources.

Selection of a pricing strategy

There are a number of pricing strategies that may be relevant to ATL.

- **Negotiated pricing** is accepted in the company's traditional market and therefore may also be appropriate to the e-learning package

- **Secondary market pricing** may also be a reasonable pricing strategy given that one reason for developing the software was to target overseas students where levels of disposable income may be lower. This pricing strategy would reflect the local economic conditions might be exploited.

- **Reference pricing** may be used as this would help to indicate the position of the e-learning course against the traditional classroom training which is offered as an alternative.

- **Bundle pricing** could also be appropriate. For example, the examination fee could be included as part of the package when the online course is purchased.

ATL must keep in mind that the selection of the price is not the end-all and changes can often be quickly made to reflect the actual trading conditions once the product goes live. Price is the most flexible and convenient way of adjusting the marketing mix.

Part (b)

> **Top tips.** Don't let the large amounts of financial information throw you and don't get too bogged down in it. Take the time to carefully read and understand the data, then develop an answer that explains what the information is showing, and how it can help iCompute to set the price for its e-learning course. Then go on to explain the limitations of this data. You should be able to earn a few by listing the generic problems with linear regression analysis.

Both Figure 1 and Figure 2 use linear least squares regression and correlation to describe the relationship between the variables.

Figure 1 shows the relationship between the gross profit of the company (the independent variable – x) and the average training budget per employee per year (the dependent variable – y). This therefore shows that the amount an organisation will spend on training its employees will depend, in part, on the profitability of that organisation. This analysis can therefore help ATL to predict how much the corporate customer would be willing to pay for a product. This is a vital element of the pricing process.

Figure 2 shows the relationship between time (the independent variable) and e-learning sales (the dependent variable). It uses least squares regression in order to establish a trend line in the data which could be used by ATL to help predict the demand for the product in the future. This is also a key element of the pricing process.

Least squares regression determines a line of best fit though historical data. The regression equation ($y = a + bx$) can then be used to predict changes in y from changes in x. The correlation coefficient (r) assess the extent to which the forecasts based on the line of best fit can be relied upon. The value of r ranges from 1 (perfect positive correlation) to -1 (perfect negative correlation), with 0 being no correlation.

In Figure 1, the regression equation is given as $y = 616.23 + 3.939x$. We are also told that the government statistics suggest that the average gross profit of the top 500 companies will be $50m next year. This is the x figure to be used in the equation above. This gives a predicted training budget of $813 per employee. This is lower than the current course fees of $950 which are charged for traditional courses.

Using the same equation for the sample data for the ten companies shown, the average annual gross profit is $86m and so the predicted spend on training is $955. This suggests that there will be pressure on prices in the coming year, particularly for traditional courses, which is likely to make e-learning an attractive solution in fulfilling their training needs.

Figure 2 can be used to estimate the demand for e-learning products overall by extrapolating the trend line, for example in 2011 quarter 4 spend can be predicted as $4.06m ($y = 2.38+(0.12 \times 14)$). However, this kind of extrapolation may not be that reliable as it involves predicting values that are outside of the scope of the sample.

Care must also be taken in the interpretation of the data as thee are a number of limitations to the linear least squares regression and correlation technique. A key problem with this technique is that it provides a straight line fit where the data appears to suggest that a curve may be more appropriate. The possibility of an upward curve trend is visible in Figure 2 where sales seem to increase disproportionately in the final four quarters.

Another problem with this technique is that correlation is simply a statistical measure. It does not proof a link or imply any meaning between the data.

The coefficient of determination is calculated as a way of expressing the strength of the relationship between the two variables and is calculated as r^2. For figure 1 this is therefore ($0.801^2 = 0.64$) which suggests that 64% of variability in the average training spend per employee is due to gross profit. The remaining 36% will be due to other factors.

Consideration must also be given to the sample used in Figure 1, both in terms of the sample size and how representative of the population this can be considered to be. Only 10 of the 500 top companies are used in the sample which is a relatively small proportion on which to make assumptions relating to the population as a whole.

ACCA
Paper P3
Business Analysis

Mock Examination 2

Question Paper	
Time allowed	
Reading and planning	**15 minutes**
Writing	**3 hours**
This paper is divided into two sections	
Section A	**ONE compulsory question to be attempted**
Section B	**TWO questions ONLY to be attempted**

During reading and planning time only the question paper may be annotated

DO NOT OPEN THIS PAPER UNTIL YOU ARE READY TO START UNDER EXAMINATION CONDITIONS

SECTION A – This ONE question is compulsory and MUST be attempted

The following information should be used when answering question 1

Question 1

Introduction

The EA Group has a portfolio of companies that currently specialise in alternative energy supply and associated products and services. It grew out of Power of the Sun (POTS) Co, one of the pioneers of solar heating, which still remains an autonomous company in the Group. The profits generated by POTS funded the initial development of the Group, which now comprises 12 companies. Only four of these companies are considered in this scenario.

Power of the Sun (POTS) Co

POTS Co was one of the first companies to realise the potential of solar powered energy solutions and it pioneered the use of the technology, particularly in government and city council (public sector) buildings. From 1995 to 2005 its net profit regularly exceeded 15%. Recent results for the company are shown in Figure 1. The approximate size of the overall market is also given (sector turnover).

All figures in $m	2011	2010	2009	2008
Sector turnover	357·00	357·00	356·00	355·00
POTS sales revenue	107·10	100·00	96·10	88·80
Gross profit	22·50	21·00	22·10	22·20
Net profit	7·50	7·00	8·70	9·80

Figure 1: Selected data for POTS Co

Although POTS was the main source of the profits which drove the expansion of the EA Group, many employees within POTS feel that it is now relatively neglected. Consumer surveys suggest that the brand is not as well recognised as it was and respondents who did recognise it saw it as a tired and traditional brand. Many of its most gifted managers have been promoted into the EA Group headquarters or other companies within the Group. It was expected that their expertise, gained with POTS, would help improve the performance of acquired companies. However, despite this loss of valuable resources, POTS still has recognised expertise and many valuable contacts and contracts in the public sector which the EA Group has been able to exploit. These contracts, particularly with city councils, have allowed the company to retain a significant presence in the solar powered energy market at a time when competitors have withdrawn from, or scaled down, their operations.

Neach Glass

The EA Group acquired Neach Glass in 2005. Neach Glass was founded by Kevin Neach to provide high quality glass products. These were used in the original solar panels developed by POTS and a close relationship was built up between Kevin Neach and the managing director of POTS, Ken Nyg. Ken later became chief executive officer (CEO) of the EA Group. The glass panels continue to be used in POTS products. In 2005, Kevin Neach informed Ken Nyg that Neach Glass was on the brink of going into administration. As a result, the EA Group acquired the company to help secure the supply of a vital component in the POTS product. Since that time, financial and management resources have been invested in Neach Glass in an attempt to improve market share and profitability. Some of POTS's best managers have been transferred to the company. Data for Neach Glass is shown in Figure 2. Again, the estimated size of the total market is shown as sector turnover.

All figures in $m	2011	2010	2009	2008
Sector turnover	88·00	89·00	89·50	90·00
Neach turnover	7·94	7·12	7·16	6·30
Gross profit	1·45	1·28	1·22	1·07
Net profit	0·72	0·57	0·57	0·45

Figure 2: Selected data for Neach Glass

ENCOS

In 2007, Ken Nyg recognised that other alternative energy sources other than solar power were becoming increasingly important. Council managers were increasingly requesting a combination of power sources with control systems that could be used to switch the power source to reflect the most economic combination of sources. As a result of this, the EA Group acquired ENergy COntrol Systems (ENCOS), a company with innovative control systems for monitoring power use and matching it to the most suitable and cheapest source of supply. ENCOS was acknowledged as a technical leader, but had little marketing expertise and few contracts in the public sector. ENCOS's control systems have sophisticated mathematical algorithms which are now used in many private sector applications. It has an excellent record in profitable delivery, with each contract carefully estimated and a detailed analysis of gross profit reported per contract. Financial data for ENCOS is shown in Figure 3. The market sector turnover is again given.

All figures in $m	2011	2010	2009	2008
Sector turnover	81·00	76·00	71·50	70·00
ENCOS turnover	21·00	17·00	14·30	13·30
Gross profit	5·00	4·00	2·75	2·55
Net profit	3·35	3·00	1·85	1·65

Figure 3: Selected data for ENCOS

Steeltown Information Technology

Steeltown City Council is the second largest city council in the country. Two years ago, responding to government initiatives to outsource non-core activities, it decided to outsource its information technology department to the private sector. The department developed and implemented bespoke in-house systems to support the departments of the council (housing, education, social services etc). Trade unions in the council mounted a vigorous campaign against the plan and employees were overwhelmingly against it. Many of the employees had worked for the council for many years and had experienced a stable work environment. However, this opposition hardened the council's resolve and they forced through the plan, citing the union's restricted working practices as a major problem. The council invited private sector companies to tender for the work and resources of the department.

The EA Group were keen to broaden their technological services to the public sector and saw this as an opportunity to acquire an organisation that could spearhead its growth. As Ken Nyg said 'we must avoid being too narrow in focus. We started out in solar energy, before broadening out into other energy sources and services. We now wish to broaden again into information technology services in general and the acquisition of the Steeltown City Council's information technology department is a perfect vehicle for this. We see clear technology synergies with ENCOS who are technical leaders in control software design and development.'

Steeltown Information Technology, as the company is now called, has entered into a ten year exclusive contract with Steeltown City Council to supply information technology services. The contract price is based on current costs, plus inflation, plus a 5% gross profit margin. The contract will be renegotiated after five years, when it is expected that savings made by the company can be passed on to the council.

The IT director and his deputy, who both vigorously opposed privatisation, have not been transferred to the new company. They both took voluntary redundancy from the council. Other managers are philosophical, glad that the uncertainty of the last two years was behind them. One manager commented that although 'he was against outsourcing in principle, now the sale has been agreed, let's get on with it'. Very few new systems have been developed in the last two years whilst the future of the department was being discussed. There is now a backlog of applications to develop for a number of council departments. Users in these departments usually find it very difficult to specify system requirements in advance and there have been very few successfully implemented IT solutions.

Although the Steeltown City Council contract is on a cost plus basis, managers who have always been budget and service-driven will be expected to profitably deliver solutions to other potential customers in the public sector.

As part of preparing for strategic change at Steeltown Information Technology, the EA Group wishes to benchmark its performance. They have been provided with the information given in Figure 4.

	2011	2010	2009	2008
User satisfaction (1)	48%	46%	45%	44%
Faults reported	200	250	375	425
User satisfaction (nationwide) (3)	45%	44%	44%	43%

Figure 4: Data for Steeltown City Council information technology department

(1)   Measured by internally constructed and analysed user surveys at Steeltown City Council
(2)   Measured by reported faults in software at Steeltown City Council
(3)   Reported by city councils throughout the country

As another part of their preparation for strategic change at Steeltown Information Technology, the EA Group also wish to understand the contextual factors that will affect such change. They want to explore these factors before they firm up their proposed strategy for the newly acquired company.

Required

(a)   Analyse the performance of each of the four companies described in the scenario and assess each company's potential future contribution to the EA Group portfolio of businesses.   **(24 marks)**

Professional marks will be awarded in part (a) for the clarity and structure of the answer.   **(4 marks)**

(b)   Time, scope, capability and readiness for change are four contextual factors that affect strategic change.

Evaluate the potential influence of these four factors at Steeltown Information Technology on any strategic change proposed by the EA Group.   **(12 marks)**

(c)   Discuss the principles, together with the advantages and the disadvantages, of benchmarking in the context of Steeltown Information Technology.   **(10 marks)**

(Total = 50 marks)

Section B – TWO questions ONLY to be attempted

Question 2

Moor Farm is a large estate in the rural district of Cornaille. The estate covers a large area of forest, upland and farmland. It also includes two villages, and although many of the properties in these villages have been sold off to private homeowners, the estate still owns properties which it rents out. The estate also has a large mansion house set inside a landscape garden designed in the 19th century by James Kent. The garden, although now overgrown and neglected, is the only surviving example of his work in the district. The estate was left as a gift to a charitable trust ten years ago. The trust is based at the estate. A condition of the gift to the trust was that the upland and forest should be freely accessible to visitors.

The estate has a manager, four full-time staff and 45 volunteers. These volunteers undertake most of the work on the estate, including the continuing excavation of Kent's original garden design. They are happy, well-motivated and fully support the current manager who is due to retire in the very near future. Three of the volunteers have become acknowledged experts on land management, through their work on the estate. Government grants for initiatives such as tree planting, protected pasture land and rural employment have been received by the estate in the past. However, a recent change in government means that this funding is unlikely to continue. This will also affect funding for the maintenance of the mansion. It was built almost 80 years ago when the climate of the area was much colder and drier. Recent warm wet winters have caused the fabric of the building to decay and increased the cost of maintaining it.

The estate has appointed a new manager who is due to take over the estate when the current manager retires. She is working alongside the current manager so that she understands her responsibilities and how the estate works. As a one-off project, she has commissioned a stakeholder survey which has requested information on the visitor experience to help with a planned re-design of the estate's website. The website is generally thought to be well structured and presented, but it receives fewer visitors than might reasonably be expected. It provides mainly static information about the estate and forthcoming events but currently users cannot interact with the site in anyway.

Here are some extracts from the survey:

'I live in one of the villages and I am angry about visitors crowding around the village attractions – the tearooms, the craft shops, the souvenir stalls. We feel that we are prisoners in our own village and the traffic is terrible.' **Homeowner, from a village on the estate**

'We had a good day, but the weather was awful. If we had known it was going to rain all day, then we probably would have postponed the visit until a fine day. It spoilt a family day out. ' **Visitor with small family**

'We were very disappointed, on arrival, to find that the family fun day was fully booked.' **Visitor who had travelled 100 km with two small children to visit a special event**

'We all love it here, but we didn't know you had a website!! We almost had to type in the complete website address before we found it! I am sure more people would come if they could only find the website!' **Visitor aged mid-20s**

'As usual, we had a great time here and took great photos. It would have been nice to be able to share our pleasure with other people. We would recommend it to anyone who loves the outdoors.' **Visitor – family with teenage children**

'We met the volunteers who were excavating the buildings in the landscape garden. They were so helpful and knowledgeable. They turned something that looked like a series of small walls into something so much more tangible.' **Visitor – elderly couple**

'I was disappointed that I was not allowed into the farmland with my dog. As a human being, I have the right to roam. It is a basic human right.' **Visitor – elderly female dog-walker**

'We are regular visitors and we really want to know what is going on! There are many of us who would like to really be involved with the estate and help it thrive. We need more than just occasional questionnaires.' **Visitor – hiking group**

'We came out for a nice walk and ended up dodging cyclists. Next time we will go somewhere where they are not welcome.' **Visitor – hiking group**

'As a farmer, I am appalled with the reckless attitude of some dog walkers. Last week, I lost two sheep, ravaged by dogs that should not have been off their leads.' **Farmer – estate tenant**

'I'm a volunteer and I love it here. We are a happy, social group of people. I hope the new manager is not going to change things.' **Volunteer**

Required

(a) Evaluate the strategic position of the estate with specific reference to the expectations of stakeholders, to the external environmental factors beyond the control of the estate and to the strategic capabilities of the estate itself.

(15 marks)

(b) Discuss how the website could be further developed to address some of the issues highlighted in the survey.

(10 marks)

(Total = 25 marks)

Question 3

Emile Gonzalez is an industrial chemist who worked for the government of Pablos for more than 20 years. In his spare time, he continually experimented with formulating a product that could remove graffiti from all surfaces. Graffiti is a particular problem in Pablos and all previous removal methods were expensive, dangerous to apply and did not work on all surfaces. After many years of experimentation, Emile formulated a product that addressed all these issues. His product can be applied safely without protective clothing, it removes graffiti from all surfaces and it can be produced economically in small, as well as large, volumes.

Three years ago, Emile left his government job to focus on refining the product and bringing it to market. He formed a limited liability company, Graffoff, with initial share capital funded by his savings, his family's savings and a legacy from a wealthy relative. He is the sole shareholder in the company, which is based in a factory in central Pablos. The company has filed two years of results (see Figure 1 for extracted information from year (2), and it is expected to return similar net profit figures in its third trading year. Emile takes a significant dividend out of the company each year and he wishes that to continue. He also wishes to remain the sole owner of the company.

Four years ago, Emile was granted a patent for the formula on which his product is based and a further patent on the process used to produce the product. In Pablos, patents are protected for ten years and so Emile has six further years before his formula becomes available to his competitors. Consequently, he wants to rapidly expand the company and plans to lease premises to create 30 new graffiti removal depots in Pablos, each of which will supply graffiti removing services in its local region. He needs $500,000 to finance this organic growth of his company.

Emile does have mixed feelings about his proposed expansion plan. Despite the apparent success of his company, he prefers working in the laboratory to managing people. 'I am just not a people person', he has commented. He is aware that he lacks business experience and, despite the technical excellence of the product, he has failed to build a highly visible brand. He also has particular problems in the accounts receivables department, where he has failed to address the problems of over-worked and demotivated employees. Emile dislikes conflict with customers and so he often offers them extended payment terms to the dismay of the accounts receivables section, who feel that their debt collecting effectiveness is being constantly undermined by his concessions. In contrast, Graffoff pays bills very promptly, due to a zealous administrator in accounts payable who likes to reduce creditors. Emile is sanguine about this. 'I guess we have the money, so I suppose we should pay them.'

In Pablos, all goods are supplied to customers on 30 days credit. However, in the services sector that Graffoff is trading in, the average settlement period for payables (creditors) is 40 days. One supplier commented that 'Graffoff is unique in its punctuality of payment.'

Emile is currently reviewing how to finance his proposed organic growth. He is unwilling to take on any further external debt and consequently he has also recently considered franchising as an alternative to organic growth. In his proposed arrangement, franchisees would have responsibility for leasing or buying premises to a specification defined in the franchise agreement. The franchise would have exclusive rights to the Graffoff product in a defined geographical region.

The Equipment Emporium has 57 superstores throughout the country selling tools and machines such as air compressors, generators and ventilation systems. It is a well-recognised brand with a strong marketing presence. It focuses on selling specialist products in bright, well-lit superstores. It has approached Graffoff to ask whether it can sell the Graffoff product through its superstores. Emile has rejected this suggestion because he feels that his product requires proper training if it is to be used efficiently and safely. He sees Graffoff as offering a complete service (graffiti removal), not just a product (graffiti removal equipment) and so selling through The Equipment Emporium would be inappropriate.

Figure 1: Extracted financial data for Graffoff's second year of trading, reported at 31 December 2011

Extract from the statement of financial position: as at 31 December 2011

Extract from the statement of financial position: as at 31 December 2011

All figures in $'000:

ASSETS	
Non-current assets	
Property, plant and equipment	1,385
Intangible assets	100
Total non-current assets	1,485
Current assets	
Inventories	100
Trade receivables	260
Cash and cash equivalent	30
Total current assets	390
Totals assets	1,875
EQUITY AND LIABILITIES	
Share capital	1,500
Retained earnings	30
Total equity	1,530
Non-current liabilities	
Long-term borrowings	250
Total non-current liabilities	250
Current liabilities	
Trade and other payables	75
Current tax payable	20
Total current liabilities	95
Total liabilities	345
Total equity and liabilities	1,875

All figures in $'000:

Revenue	1,600
Cost of sales	(1,375)
Gross profit	225
Administrative expenses	(100)
Finance costs	(15)
Profit before tax	110
Income tax expense	(20)
Profit for the period	90

Required

(a) Evaluate the franchising option being considered by Graffoff, highlighting the advantages and disadvantages of this approach from Emile's perspective. **(10 marks)**

(b) Johnson, Scholes and Whittington have identified franchising as a form of strategic alliance.

Evaluate how other forms of strategic alliance might be appropriate approaches to strategy development at Graffoff. **(7 marks)**

(c) A consultant has suggested that Graffoff should be able to completely fund its proposed organic expansion (at a cost of $500,000) through internally generated sources of finance.

Evaluate this claim. **(8 marks)**

(Total = 25 marks)

Question 4

World Engines (WE) is one of the largest producers of aircraft and ship engines in the world. It has assets in excess of $600bn. It is currently considering improvements to its marine engine production facilities. These improvements include the introduction of specialist hardware and software engine testing technology. Two companies have been shortlisted for supplying this technology.

Amethyst is a well-established company whose product provides sophisticated testing facilities and costs $7m. The software that supports the product is written in a conventional programming language. The solution is widely used, but it is relatively inflexible and it has an out-of-date user interface. Amethyst has been trading profitably for 20 years and currently has an annual turnover of $960m.

Topaz is a relatively new company (formed three years ago) whose product is more expensive ($8m) but it offers significant advantages in high volume performance and stress testing. It has a modular software design that allows it to be easily maintained and upgraded. It is written in a relatively new powerful programming language and it also has an attractive and contemporary user interface. Topaz currently has a turnover of $24m per year. Some WE executives are concerned about purchasing from such a young, relatively small company, although externally commissioned credit reports show that Topaz is a profitable, liquid and lightly geared company.

On a recent evaluation visit to Amethyst, WE's complete evaluation team of five people, including the financial specialist, were killed when their aircraft crashed on its approach to landing. It was a small, 12 seat commuter aircraft that was flying the WE team on a short 100 km flight from the international airport to a small rural airport close to Amethyst's base. It later emerged that small commuter airlines and aircraft were subject to less stringent safety procedures than larger aircraft used by established airlines.

Later that year, one of the divisional directors of WE was given responsibility for picking up and running the testing technology evaluation project. He has found the following table (Figure 1) produced by the financial specialist in the evaluation team who was killed in the air crash. The divisional director recalls that these returns were based on 'tangible benefits resulting from the two options. The returns reflect the characteristics of the two products. Topaz produces better returns if demand for testing is high, but is less effective in low demand circumstances. This is a reflection of the fact that the two solutions differ slightly in terms of their functional scope and power'.

Figure 1: expected returns for three demand and supplier combinations.

Option	Supplier	IF High demand	IF Low demand
A	Amethyst	$3m per annum	$0·5m per annum
B	Topaz	$4m per annum	$0·1m per annum

The divisional director also recalls a workshop convened to consider future market demand.

'Demand in the marine industry is currently affected by global economic uncertainty and it is increasingly difficult to predict demand. I remember that we were also asked to estimate demand for our marine products for the next six years. We eventually came up with the following figures, although it was relatively hard to get everyone to agree and debate at the workshop became a little heated'.

- High demand for six years: probability p = 0·4
- Low demand for six years: probability p = 0·4
- High demand for three years, followed by low demand for three years: probability p = 0.2

These figures are confirmed by a document also recovered from the air crash site. 'As I recall', said the divisional director, 'the financial specialist intended to develop a decision tree to help us evaluate the Amethyst and Topaz alternatives. However, there is no evidence that he ever constructed it, which is a pity because we could have taken the procurement decision on the basis of that decision tree'.

Required

(a) Develop a decision tree from the information given in the scenario and discuss its implications and shortcomings.

Ignore the time value of money in your analysis. **(9 marks)**

(b) The divisional director suggests that the procurement decision could have been taken on the evidence of the decision tree.

Discuss what other factors (not considered by the decision tree analysis) should also be taken into consideration when deciding which option to select. **(6 marks)**

(c) WE executives are concerned about the risk of Topaz, as a relatively new company, going out of business. They have also expressed concern about the loss of the evaluation team in a fatal accident and they believe that this should lead to a review of the risks associated with employee travel.

Discuss how **each** of the above risks (supplier business failure and employee travel) might be avoided or mitigated. **(10 marks)**

(Total = 25 marks)

Answers

DO NOT TURN THIS PAGE UNTIL YOU HAVE
COMPLETED THE MOCK EXAM

A plan of attack

We've already established that you've been told to do it 101 times, so it is of course superfluous to tell you for the 102nd time to **take a good look at the paper before diving in to answer questions**.

The next step

You may be thinking that this paper is a lot more straightforward than the first mock exam; however, having sailed through the first mock, you may think this paper is actually rather difficult.

Option 1 (Don't like this paper)

If you are challenged by this paper, it will be best to get the optional questions done before tackling the case study. Don't forget though that you will need half the time to answer the case study.

- **Question 2** is not as simple as it may first seem. Beware of over-reliance on PESTEL or Mendelow's matrix in part (a). Ensure you read this requirement carefully and be sure you understand exactly what you are being asked to do before you start. You can score well in (b) however by looking at the complaints raised by the customers of the estate and linking this to improvements that could be made to the website.

- **Question 3** is a good choice and offer lots of chances to score highly, particularly in parts (a) and (b), if you have good knowledge of franchising and strategic alliances. Take care with part (c) though and ensure the question you answer is actually the one that was asked.

- Part (a) of **Question 4** offers lots of easy marks if you are strong on decision trees. Part (b) follows on from this and again offers the chance to score well. There are 10 marks for (c), many of which can be earned by application of logic. If you keep focused and plan your answer carefully there is the potential to score very well on this question making it a very good option to select.

- In part (a) of **Question 1** make sure you analyse all four of the companies. Leaving out Steeltown means you will not be able to get a quarter of the marks on offer. The best approach to part (b) is, for each of the four contextual factors given, to first define the factor and then link the factor back to information given in the scenario. If you were unprepared for requirement (c), have a go anyway. It's always better to get something down on paper and give yourself the chance of a few marks than to leave it out completely.

Option 2 (This paper's all right)

Are you **sure** it is? If you are then that's encouraging. You'll feel even happier when you've got the compulsory question out of the way, so you should consider doing **Question 1 first**.

- **Question 1** part (a) offers 24 marks and there are four companies to assess. This means there will be only six points on offer for discussion of each company so beware of spending too long on this section analysing each in great depth. Chances are that you will make enough suitable points in only a few paragraphs per company. The pages you continue to write beyond this will generate no additional marks and may put you at risk of not having enough time to complete the rest of the paper.

- **Question 2** offers the chance to score highly in part (b) by considering what features could be added to the website to address the concerns raised in the scenario. Note that the majority of the marks are for part (a) however and that this part question is not as easy as it may first seem. It is about the conflict and expectations of stakeholders – not management of them via Mendelow's power/interest grid. There is also insufficient information provided for PESTEL and SWOT to be used as the sole tool of analysis. A broader and well structured approach is needed for this question to be answered well.

  If you are confident of your knowledge of franchising and other forms of strategic alliance, **Question 3** is a good applied question to choose.

- **Question 4** will test your understanding of decision trees, but there are lots of opportunities to score well in this question if you are strong in this area. It pays to be slightly wary of (c), as you'll have to carry out a substantial amount of quantitative analysis to back up any claims you make – single line suggestions won't be enough.

Once more

You must **allocate your time** according to the marks for the question in total, and for the parts of the questions. And you must also **follow the requirements exactly**.

Finished with fifteen minutes to spare?

Looks like you slipped up on the time allocation. However if you have, make sure you don't waste the last few minutes; go back to **any parts of questions that you didn't finish** because you ran out of time.

Forget about it!

Forget about what? Excellent, you already have.

SECTION A

Question 1

> **Text reference.** Portfolio planning is covered in Chapter 6, the contextual features model in Chapter 15 and benchmarking in Chapter 4.
>
> **Top tip.** This is a portfolio analysis question which should lead you towards using the BCG matrix to help you structure your answer and determine a suitable strategy for each of the companies. Make sure you address all four of the companies as the marks are split evenly between them.
>
> Take note of the mark allocation when answering questions. There were a maximum of six marks available for each of the four companies. A number of students made far more points than the marks on offer, leading to them scoring very highly on this section but later experiencing time problems later in the paper. A few candidates earned over 20 marks on this part question yet still failed the examination overall.

(a)   **Power of the Sun (POTS) Co**

POTS was the main source of the profits which drove the expansion of the EA Group and enabled it to make acquisitions such as ENCOS and Neach Glass possible. However, in recent years POTS has become less profitable:

Gross profit has fallen from 25% (22.20/88.80) in 2008 to 21% (22.5/107.10) in 2011.

Net profit is now less than half of that of the company's peak and has fallen in line with gross profit from 11.04% (9.80/88.80) to 7.00% (7.5/107.10).

Market growth has also slowed down, reflecting the greater selection of alternative energy suppliers and options that are now available. However, it is noted that POTS has retained a significant presence and market share of the solar powered energy market as other competitors have withdrawn from, or scaled down, their operations. The market as a whole grew by only 0.5% in the last two years, however, POTS managed to increase its market share from 25% to 30%.

This high market share should allow POTS to keep its unit costs below those of its competitors, and it is likely that POTS is a cash cow. However, the group has concerns that this company is being neglected and the fall in profits would support this. The removal of the best managers to work in the newer acquisitions is also likely to have affected the morale within POTS.

Customer surveys have also highlighted an issue with the brand of the company being perceived as a tired and traditional brand. An overhaul of the brand and the operation of the company to assist in publically reaffirming the group's commitment to POTS would be beneficial if the group is still committed to solar energy as an important energy source.

Neach Glass

Neach Glass produces high quality glass products and began its relationship with the EA Group as a key supplier to POTS. In 2005 Neach Glass was on the brink of going into administration but was then purchased by EA group to help secure the supply of a vital component of the POTS product. However, despite the financial and management resources that have been invested in Neach Glass since it was purchased, performance has failed to improve.

While both gross and net profit margins have seen some improvement (gross profit from 16.98% to 18.26% and net profit from 7.14% to 9.07%), but this is still relatively low.

The market share of Neach Glass has increased from 7% (6.30/90.00) in 2008 to 9% (7.94/88.20) in 2011, but the market itself has declined by 2% in the last four years.

This would indicate that this company is a dog. EA Group has been unable to fix its problems and it would perhaps have been better to purchase the company as only a short term solution until an alternate supplier could be found. EA Group should consider divesting Neach Glass.

ENCOS

ENCOS was acquired when it became apparent that alternative energy sources other than solar power were becoming increasingly important. This company was acknowledged as a technical leader, but it had little marketing experience and few contracts in the public sector. EA Group was ideally placed to be able to bring these skills and contacts to ENCOS and it would appear that the acquisition has been successful.

Gross and net profit margins have both increased (gross profit from 19.17% to 23.81% and net profit from 12.41% to 15.95%) and net profit continues to grow disproportionately to revenue. This suggests that operating costs are falling. In absolute terms, these returns are the highest of the four companies included in the scenario.

The market has grown by 15.71% over the four years, and the market share of ENCOS has increased from 19% to 25.93%. This indicates that ENCOS is a potential star, however, further information would be needed to determine if this is actually the case.

There are clear synergies between ENCOS and POTS and it would appear that the company has performed even better since it was acquired by EA Groups than it did as an independent company.

Steeltown Information Technology

The outsourcing of Steeltown City Council's information technology department was in response to a government initiative to outsource non-core activities. This initiative means it is likely other councils will follow this example, and the industry of 'public sector technology' can therefore be assumed to be a growing market. The response of the trade unions would indicate Steeltown's outsourcing programme was one of the first examples of such outsourcing and so it can be reasonably assumed that, at present, Steeltown Information Technology has a reasonably large share of this market. This company is also potentially a star.

No financial figures are available, but the cost plus contact that was negotiated would suggest that relatively modest profits will be reported for at least the first five years.

While EA has experience of gaining contracts within the public sector, it has no experience in doing this in relation to information technology and systems. The extent to which the skill is transferrable to this is not yet known. EA also has no experience of acquiring a public sector organisation and achieving the level of change required to shift the deep-rooted culture and to transform the company into a private sector company that is driven by profit.

This acquisition has allowed EA group to broaden its profit base and to enter a new market. The problem here is that the acquired company, Steeltown Information Technology was not itself yet established in that new market.

The level of synergy between this company an ENCOS does not appear to be great given that they operate in different markets and have very different aims and objectives.

(b)

> **Top tips.** The issues explored in this question are four of the eight contextual factors, identified by Balogun and Hope-Hailey, which strategically influence strategic change. To score well on this part question, you will need to be familiar with this model and the specific definition of the factors. For example, 'time' relates to how much time is required to carry out the time not, as a number of students suggested, whether or not it is 'time for a change'. Also, 'capability' refers to the capability to manage the change, not to run the business.

Time

The amount of time available to implement changes can sometimes be a critical factor if action needs to be taken very quickly in order to ensure the short term financial viability of the organisation.

Time does not appear to be critical for Steeltown Information as the contract with the city council is for ten years and it will only be renegotiated after five years. It is not therefore vital for change to be implemented at a fast rate. Present levels of resources at Steeltown Information Technology are likely to be maintained for the next five years, potentially allowing EA plenty of time to implement the change.

Scope of change

Change can be considered to be either realignment, which can be generally accommodated within the current culture, or transformational, which requires a significant shift in the culture to take place. The Steeltown Information Technology change would appear to be transformational. Work is currently budget driven and inward focused and the management have limited private sector experience. This change will involve shifting away from these core assumptions.

Given that time is not critical, as shown above, this change can be made incrementally in order to gradually shift the paradigm over a reasonable long period of time. This type of change is known as evolution.

Capability

The level of experience of managing change that exists within an organisation will impact on how that change is implemented. It will be easier to implement a change if the managers have successfully managed other changes in the past, and the workforce is used to change.

Given the level of opposition that was seen at the start of the process, it is very unlikely that the workforce have much experience of change. One of the driving forces for this change was the fact that established work practices are written into trade union agreements.

EA itself has plenty of experience of managing change in organisations that they have acquired; however, the acquisition of Neach Glass did not appear to be particularly successful. This would indicate that the capability of EA to manage the change may not be high as it may seem.

Readiness for change

The attitude of the organisation towards the change will affect the way the change is made. The extent to which the change is either welcomed or resisted will have a significant impact on the way the change is approached and managed.

The scenario shows that there was initially a significant degree of resistance to the change as trade unions campaigned vigorously and employees were overwhelmingly against it. However, after the sale went through, the need for change began to be accepted and understood. The general feeling now appears to be one of being resigned to the fact that the changes will go ahead and it would be better to just get on with it. This should make it much easier for EA to successfully implement the change.

(c)

Benchmarking involves gathering data to allow current performance to be identified and evaluated against best practice or past performance.

The benchmarking information provided to EA Group by Steeltown is based on historical data. Historical benchmarking is an internal comparison of current against past performance. The data provided shows that the number of faults reported has decreased continuously between the years of 2008 and 2011. This has been matched with a steady increase of user satisfaction. This suggests that the software produced by Steeltown is becoming more reliable.

However, this trend could also be due to less new systems being developed in the past two years. New systems are much more likely to contain faults than established systems which will have been reviewed and fine-tuned to iron out any such glitches.

In addition, the overall figures seem quite low, even though the data was collected and analysed by the technology department. Satisfaction surveys measured externally would generally be preferable.

It would be difficult for Steeltown Information Technology to benchmark against competitors as a suitable sector to compare it with would have to be chosen. Published government statistics with other public sector organisations would appear to provide the best comparison, however, the results would still have to be treated with care as it may not be known if the same assessment criteria were used by the other councils. Following the privatisation Steeltown Information Technology has become unique. Therefore finding a similar organisation against which benchmarking could be carried out is virtually impossible.

EA has suggested ENCOS as a possible benchmark, however the focus of development has been so different than comparisons may mean very little. ENCOS reports on profit per contract, whereas Steeltown Information Technology has only one client. It is also unlikely to have any relevant data given that profitability was not an objective of the organisation.

A further issue with industry comparisons is that the whole industry may be performing badly or losing out to technologies or industries that could satisfy customer needs in a different way.

The problems encountered with industry benchmarking have encouraged organisations to seek best practice comparatives wherever they can be found. This is known as best-in-class benchmarking and involves making comparisons with similar features or processes in other industries. It has been suggested (Johnson, Scholes and Whittington) that this approach can have a shock effect on complacent managers and lead to dramatic improvements, however, the specific nature of software development may make it difficult to identify any such comparisons.

Furthermore, there are problems with benchmarking overall.

- Benchmarking tends to focus on doing things right rather than doing the right thing, ie, efficiency not effectiveness. A process can be efficient but its output may not be useful. This can mean the organisation continues with a strategy which is already flawed.

- Benchmarking does not identify the reasons why performance is at a particular level, whether good or bad. It could be that improvements have occurred as a result of external environmental factors rather than anything in particular the organisation has done.

It would seem that benchmarking effectively would be difficult at Steeltown Information Technology. Short-term, it may make more sense for the organisation to focus instead on improving processes and employee motivation in order to successfully implement and manage the change.

SECTION B

Question 2

Marking scheme

		Marks
(a)	1 mark for each relevant point up to a maximum of 15 marks	**(15 marks)**
(b)	1 mark for each relevant point up to a maximum of 10 marks	**(10 marks)**
		(Total = 25 marks)

(a)   When developing the strategy for Moor Farm, it will be important to ensure the expectations of stakeholders, the external environmental issues beyond the control of the estate, and the strategic capability of the estate itself are all taken into account. These are considered below.

Expectations of stakeholders

There are many stakeholders involved with Moor Farm, a number of whom have conflicting views. These views will all have to be considered as part of the formulation of any proposed strategy for the estate.

A key stakeholder group is the **volunteers** who make up 90% of the workforce. Their objectives will not be the same as the paid staff and these objectives will need to be understood, because if the new strategy does not meet them this may alienate the volunteers. Were this to happen, the estate could be left without the majority of its workforce and be unable to operate. Volunteers are difficult to replace as, unlike paid workers, they can not be attracted via increased salaries. It would also take their replacements a significant amount of time to build up the same level of experience and knowledge held by the existing volunteers.

The interests of **customers** will also have to be taken into consideration. However, in the case of Moor Farm, there are a number of different customer groups and the needs and interests of these groups are in conflict with one another. For example, it is noted that there is conflict between the needs of dog walkers and farmers, as well as between walkers and cyclists. When the estate was left as a gift to the charitable trust it was done so under the condition that the upland and forest should be freely accessible to visitors. This stipulation makes the exclusion of potential customers difficult. As such it will be necessary to formulate a strategy which is sensitive to the customers' conflicting needs without breaking this condition.

The private homeowners from the surrounding villages are unhappy about the increasing number of visitors to the Moor Farm estate and the traffic implications of this.

External environmental issues

There are a number of external environmental issues that may affect the estate and so it will need to constantly scan the environment for such issues and develop strategy that reflects those external changes.

A key external issue (out of the control of the estate) is the recent change of government which is likely to result in a cut or the removal of the funding provided to the estate. The government will have to be closely monitored and action, such as lobbying, may need to be taken.

The changing climate also appears to be having an effect on the mansion situated on the estate which is suffering from decay as a result of the recent warm wet winters. This is having a significant impact on maintenance costs to the estate and may also affect visitor numbers as people don't like to visit in the rain.

The 'rights' of individuals also appear to be of increasing concern to the population of the country. For example, some individuals believe they have the 'right to roam' on private land, however, this is in violation with 'rights' of farm owners, or other land users such as cyclists. This social trend and the associated conflicts will need to be reflected in the planned strategy.

Strategic capability

For any strategy to succeed, it will need to reflect the organisation's internal resources and competencies. The estate has a significant amount of land and property and the mansion is set inside a landscaped garden which is the district's only surviving example of the work of James Kent. This is a unique resource and therefore the strategy should aim to exploit this.

Another internal capability would appear to be a happy workforce of volunteers, some of which have exceptional land management skills. It is therefore important to ensure they are included in, rather than alienated by, strategic change. Their concerns about the new manager changing things must be taken into consideration, and leadership style planned accordingly to prevent a drop in morale. The new leader will need to build on the success of her predecessor whilst being sensitive to the leadership style the previous leader employed.

(b)

> **Top tips.** This was a well answered requirement and candidates generally scored well on this part of the question. As usual, you should avoid generic lists in favour of using information given in the question (for example, it is mentioned that the website is difficult to find with search engines).
>
> Candidates that failed to pass this part of the question tended to over-rely on the 6Is and provided a number of general points that could not be backed up with a relevant example.

There are a number of ways in which the website could be further developed to address some of the issues highlighted in the survey.

Search engine optimisation

A key problem noted with the website is the difficulty in finding it: "We didn't know you had a website. We almost had to type in the complete website address before we found it!" If people cannot find the website, it doesn't matter how good it is, it will not do its job. Moor farm needs to determine what terms are most directly relevant, for example 'moor farm', 'walking' 'hiking' 'rural' and 'Cornaille' are possibilities, and ensure they are included in such as a way to optimise search engine listings. There is conflicting advice as to the best way to achieve this. Sponsored links could be a good approach for a charity organisation such as this estate.

Weather feed

Some visitors have commented that the weather spoilt a good day out. A live weather feed on the home page of the website may help prevent this from happening, so that visitors that require better weather can plan their visit to suit their needs and gain more enjoyment from their day at the estate. Webcams placed at a number of points around the estate would allow visitors to view the estate 'live' and make an informed decision on conditions. The pictures from the webcam could also be supplemented by photos and videos of the estate 'at its best' in good weather conditions, perhaps encouraging people to visit the estate.

Online booking

The estate occasionally holds events, the details of which are provided on the website. However, the stakeholder survey highlighted the disappointment of a family that had travelled 100km to the estate, only to find that the event was sold out. Improving the interactivity of the website to allow online booking and payment would allow families to secure their tickets before setting out. They would also prevent a wasted trip in the situation of the event being fully sold out.

Introducing online booking would also allow the estate to predict demand prior to the event allowing it to adjust the scale and make any alterations as necessary. Cash flow will also be improved as payment will be received in advance.

Feedback

There does not appear to be the facility on the existing website for customers to post comments, photos or recommendations. Such feedback both helps to attract new customers to the estate, and also helps the estate to understand where improvements can be made to better meet customer demand.

The knowledge and enthusiasm of the volunteers could also be captured in the form of a blog describing what they are doing and what is currently going on at the estate. Social networking sites such as Twitter could be linked to this.

Online community

The stakeholder survey highlighted that there are a number of regular visitors to the estate who are keen to know what is going on. However, it would seem they are not getting this information at present. This could be solved via the website by setting up a community which can be joined online. The members will then be sent e-newsletters, regular updates and special offers. A section of the website could be dedicated to this community, and members can access it by logging in to their account.

In addition to meeting the demands of the regular visitors, establishing an online community would provide the estate with the opportunity to build a marketing profile of likely visitors and better understand what different visitors want from the estate.

Question 3

Text reference. Franchising, and other types of strategic alliance, are covered in Chapter 6 of your BPP Study Text for exams from September 2015 to 31 August 2016.

Top tips. Make sure you relate your advantages and disadvantages back to the information given in the scenario. A list of generic points is unlikely to score highly.

Some candidates attempted to use the Johnson, Scholes and Whittington framework of suitability, acceptability and feasibility. This framework did not really suit the information given in the scenario and as such these answers were generally weak.

A number of candidates were also confused about franchising and restricted their answer to a franchise just offered to one company: the Equipment Emporium.

Marks

(a)   1 mark for each appropriate point up to a maximum of 10 marks   **(10 marks)**

(b)   1 mark for each relevant point up to a maximum of 7 marks   **(7 marks)**

(c)   1 mark for each relevant point up to a maximum of 8 marks

The evaluation of the claim may include:

Receivables calculation: 1 mark
Value of reducing receivables to norm: 1 mark
Payables calculation: 1 mark
Value of increasing this to the norm: 1 mark   **(8 marks)**
    (Total = 25 marks)

(a)   Franchising would involve independently run businesses entering into a franchise agreement with Graffoff to purchase training, equipment and materials, in exchange for an exclusive geographical franchise area.

Advantages

Emile's original expansion plan involved purchasing or leasing appropriate premises. If the franchising option is taken then this would instead be done by the franchisees, therefore, this option would allow Graffoff to avoid these payments.

The substantial upfront payment that would be received from the franchisees would provide funds which Emile could then use for either investment or dividend payments.

The franchisees would also be responsible for the operational costs of their franchise, again allowing Graffoff to avoid such costs.

Franchisees are often motivated by the fact that they run their own business, and the responsibility for motivating their staff also lies with them. This would make the franchising option attractive to Emile as it would allow him to avoid employee motivational issues, which he has acknowledged is not his strength.

A further advantage of the franchising option is that Emile would not have to raise finance or manage the period of expansion. He could continue to run Graffoff in much the same way as he is currently.

Disadvantages

A key disadvantage is that it is likely that short-term and long-term returns to Graffoff will be lower than if the depots were directly owned or leased. This is because the majority of the profits will be taken by the franchisees. Graffoff will also be dependent on income from materials supply and a relatively small percentage of the annual sales of the contract.

The upfront fee paid by the franchisee will be the same whether or not the franchise turns out to be successful, but any continuing income is completely dependent on its success. Therefore it is important that franchisees are selected appropriately and carefully controlled. It would seem that Graffoff has no experience of this, or any systems in place to control and audit performance. Investment and development of such systems is therefore necessary prior to the launch of the franchise scheme.

Graffoff currently has a very low profile, and Emile has so far failed to build a highly visible brand. A franchise scheme, which relies heavily on branding, will not succeed unless this is rectified. Emile could attempt to do this by employing marketing expertise and launching vigorous campaigns.

Attracting franchisees in the first place may be difficult if potential franchisees recognise that sales volumes will be difficult to maintain once the patent has expired. However, Emile has strong product development capabilities so he could aim to improve the product to extend the patent, rather than focusing on business expansion.

(b)

A strategic alliance involves the sharing of resources and activities by two or more organisations in order to pursue a strategy. Materials, skills, innovation, finance and access to markets can often be accessed more readily via collaboration than by a single organisation alone.

Franchising is one form of strategic alliance, however, there are other forms of alliance that Emile could consider. He will most likely be interested in co-specialising given that Graffoff has strengths in product design and development but weaknesses in marketing, retail and finance. This could be achieved with the following:

Joint venture

This is where the two companies jointly set up and control a new organisation and is often a way of entering a new geographical area. In this case however expansion will be within the same country. At present, there is no possible organisation that could be considered for a joint venture and setting up a contractual relationship once a suitable company is found could be a lengthy process.

Emile may also find it difficult to give up the amount of control necessary for the joint venture to succeed given his entrepreneurial spirit.

Network arrangement

This is where two or more organisations work in collaboration without a formal relationship. Emile has already rejected the offer made by The Equipment Emporium to sell his product in their 57 stores on the basis that his product requires proper training.

Emile might consider going back to them and offering to set up small outlets in their stores where the product could be demonstrated and sold in exchange for payment of a fee to The Equipment Emporium. This would have a similar effect to organic growth but without the high investment. The Equipment Emporium's stores are already set up and already benefit from a well-recognised brand with a strong marketing presence.

This arrangement would seem ideal as it draws on both partners' expertise and would allow Graffoff's expansion to occur rapidly.

A common problem relating to informal arrangements such as this involves concerns that one party would steal the other's ideas. However, this does not seem likely in this case as The Equipment Emporium is focused mainly on products rather than services, and Graffoff has no interest in becoming a general machine superstore.

(c)

Emile is committed to paying high dividends, therefore the possible sources of internal finance open to him are tighter credit control and delayed payment to suppliers. Reduced inventory may also be an option, but no information relating to this is given in the scenario.

Tighter credit control

Customers are given a 30 day payment term, however, the average time taken for them to pay their debts is 59 days [(260/1,600) × 365 = 59.31].

If credit control is tightened up and the average is brought down to 30 day approximately $128,500 could be released for funding.

Reducing the average to 40 days – the industry standard – would release approximately $84,500.

To achieve this, significant improvements would have to be made to the accounts receivable procedures; a department which is currently both under-staffed and poorly motivated. Some of these gains therefore would most likely be offset by the cost of increased staffing.

Emile also dislikes conflict with customers. This is why he has allowed the extended payment terms to occur. A change to enforcing the 30 day payment terms could create difficulties and put a strain on relationships with customers. If this is to be done, Emile will have to stop undermining the accounts receivable department with offers of such generous terms.

Delayed payment to suppliers

On average, Graffoff takes only 20 days to pay its suppliers [(75/1,375)×365 = 19.91]. This is far quicker than the industry standard of 40 days. If the company were to delay its payments so that they were only made after 40 days approximately $75,500 could be released for investment.

There is no reason why this change could not be put in place as the fast payment appears to be simply due to the 'zealous administrator in accounts payable who likes to reduce creditors'. It is also noted that Graffoff is 'unique in its punctuality of payments'.

Even if payments are only delayed to 30 days (the normal credit terms for the country), $38,000 would still be realised.

If these changes were made to both tighten credit control and delay payments a total of $204,000 could be raised resulting in a short-term, one-off acceleration of cash inflow.

Debt Factoring

This would involve a third party taking over Graffoff's debt collection. Factoring companies will generally pay 80% of approved trade receivables in advance, which would translate to an immediate cash input of £208,000. Given the existing problems with credit control, this could be an attractive alternative. It could potentially also address the motivation and staffing problems in the accounts receivable section.

However, regardless of the option chosen, it is not possible for internal finance resources to raise the full $500,000 that would be needed for the organic growth plan. The consultant's claim is therefore incorrect and some external funding would also be needed.

However, it would seem that internally raised finance could be sufficient to finance either franchising, or an opportunistic alliance with The Equipment Emporium.

Question 4

Text reference. Decision trees and expected values are covered in Chapter 13 of your BPP Study Text for exams in September 2015 to 31 August 2016.

Top tips. If you have a good understanding of how to construct a decision tree and use this to calculate appropriate expected values, there is the opportunity to score very highly in part (a).

Marking scheme

		Marks

(a)   Up to 5 marks for the decision tree analysis and decision tree diagram

Typically this will include (up to a maximum of 5 marks)

Diagram of the decision tree: 1 mark
Expected income from Amethyst: 1 mark
Expected value of Amethyst: 1 mark
Expected income from Topaz: 1 mark
Expected value of Topaz: 1 mark
Conclusion (Topaz): 1 mark

Other marks (up to 4 marks) including subjective nature of probabilities, sensitivity
analysis, only part of the procurement decision   **(9 marks)**

(b)   1 mark for each relevant point up to a maximum of 6 marks   **(6 marks)**

(c)   1 mark for each appropriate point up to a maximum of 5 marks for software vendor
issues,1 mark for each appropriate point up to a maximum of 5 marks for
employee travel issues, maximum of 10 marks for this sub-question.   **(10 marks)**

(Total = 25 marks)

(a)

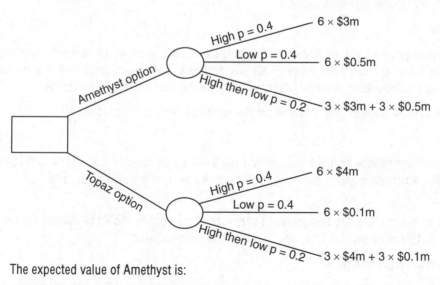

The expected value of Amethyst is:

($18m × 0.4) + ($3m × 0.4) + ($10.5m × 0.2)

= $10.5m **minus** cost of $7m

= **$3.5m**

The expected value of Topaz is:

($24m × 0.4) + ($0.6m × 0.4) + ($12.3m × 0.2)

= $12.3 **minus** cost of $8m

= $4.3m

The decision tree shows that Topaz has the higher expected value and therefore is the option that should be chosen.

However, there are limitations to making an investment decision based solely on the decision tree analysis as the analysis is only based on information that was available at this point in time.

The decision tree is based on probabilities that have been determined in the workshop rather than on actual past statistical data. There was debate and heated discussion in attempting to agree these figures, demonstrating the subjective nature of the data on which the analysis is based. WE should determine the sensitivity of the outcome to slight changes in the assessments of these probabilities.

The predicted returns may also be slightly inaccurate as the basis upon which these have been estimated is unclear. Again, a sensitivity analysis of the outcome to slight changes in the returns would be beneficial. The Topaz option in particular would benefit from this. The high demand predicted value of $4 represents around 78% (ie 9.6/12.3) of the total expected value of the option. If annual returns have been overestimated by, for example 10%, ($3.6m rather than $4m per annum) then Topaz would no longer have the higher expected return and as such would no longer be considered to be the best option.

There may be scope for negotiation with the potential software suppliers in regards to prices and structure. Any such possibilities may significantly affect the expected value of the two options.

The decision tree, therefore, should be only one of a range of factors and analyses on which the procurement decision is actually based.

(b)

> **Top tips.** This requirement asks you to consider other factors which are not reflected in the decision tree, therefore, do not waste time repeating the same financial justification stated in part (a). There are a number of features that can be picked out of the scenario here, such as the intangible benefits offered by Topaz. Applying a common sense approach to what other factors you might wish to consider were you really making this decision, such as the risk of each option, can also help you to generate marks.

In addition to the decision tree analysis, a number of other factors should be taken into account when making the purchasing decision. These include.

Intangible benefits

As well as the financial returns identified above the non-tangible benefits, such as the contemporary user interface offered by Topaz, should be considered. This is important as such an interface may be more user-friendly and provide a better user experience, which will increase the worth of the system to WE.

Intangible benefits of both Amethyst and Topaz should be identified and documented.

Risk assessment

A risk assessment of both options should be carried out and the findings documented. It is likely that, as an established supplier, Amethyst would be a much less risky choice than the smaller Topaz, a relative newcomer.

This risk, and any other risks that may be associated with each of the options should be documented in the business case so that it can be considered when the ultimate decision is taken.

Relative impact on the organisation

The two options operate very differently and the level of functionality and scope offered by the two products are unlikely to have the same implications for the company in terms of the degree of change they would inflict, the effect they would have on organisational processes and responsibilities.

Effective selection procedure

All features associated with each solution should be weighted by importance so that all factors are taken into consideration. As well as financial viability, factors to consider should include the level of support available, process certification, user group effectiveness and so on. The extent to which the system is fit for purpose, its usability, flexibility and design will also have to be taken into consideration.

(c)

> **Top tips.** This part of the question focuses on risk and notes two risks: supplier selection and employee travel. The marks are split equally between these two risks, so ensure you spend a similar amount of time on addressing each.

Supplier business failure

While Topaz has been shown to be low geared, liquid and a profitable company, it is still a relatively new company and has only a small turnover in comparison to WE. For these reasons WE is concerned about its long term viability and stability.

The continuing success of Topaz is important to WE given that it is considering entering a long-term relationship with the supplier. If WE is employing a risk avoidance strategy Topaz would therefore not be considered as a supplier.

If WE were to go select Topaz, the following steps could be taken to mitigate the impact of this risk.

- Lodging the software as an escrow agreement, ie storing the source code with an independent third party. This would ensure that WE (and other customers of Topaz) would have access to the source code allowing them to maintain and support it.

- In-house expertise in the Topaz product's programming language could be established at WE. There are two reasons for doing this:

  1. To facilitate the development of a long-term in-house software application that could be used to replace the software elements of the Topaz product.

  2. To allow the escrow agreement to be enacted should Topaz go out of business. Access to the software code will be more beneficial if the in-house team is able to pick up the software, maintain it and develop it.

- The size and purchasing power of WE is significant enough that it could consider purchasing Topaz should the company experience difficulties. This would secure the supply of the software to WE and may also allow them to supply the software to competitors.

WE should also develop a contingency plan which could involve switching to a different software provider or developing their own in-house team. Monitoring Topaz's financial performance could be linked into this plan to ensure this is done on a continuing basis, rather than just at the time of purchase. This is especially important when the system purchased from the supplier is business critical to the purchaser, as interruptions to supply may have significant consequences.

Risks associated with employee travel

A number of steps should be put in place by WE to reduce the likelihood of events similar to the fatal air crash reoccurring, and to minimise the impact of any such incidents which may occur.

- The entire evaluation team were in the aircraft that crash landed and as such all detailed knowledge relating to this purchase was lost with them. WE should develop a policy which prevents key employees from travelling together.

- The aircraft involved in this accident was a small commuter plane and as such may have less robust safety procedures than the more mainstream airlines. This journey may also have been possible by rail or car. WE should ensure that the level of risk involved with different methods of transport is considered when travel arrangements are made.

- It is unclear whether this journey was actually necessary. It is possible that the objectives could also have been met via web-conferencing. WE should establish a method of looking at all journeys and eliminating any that are found to be unnecessary, therefore avoiding travel and reducing the risk of travel accidents occurring.

- WE should establish a method of ensuring that all work is fully documented, clearly filed and easily accessible so that other employees can easily pick up the work in the event that a member of staff, or the whole team, is killed or seriously injured in such circumstances.

BPP
LEARNING MEDIA

ACCA
Paper P3
Business Analysis

Mock Examination 3 (December 2014)

Question Paper	
Time allowed	
Reading and planning	**15 minutes**
Writing	**3 hours**
This paper is divided into two sections	
Section A	**ONE compulsory question to be attempted**
Section B	**TWO questions ONLY to be attempted**

During reading and planning time only the question paper may be annotated

DO NOT OPEN THIS PAPER UNTIL YOU ARE READY TO START UNDER EXAMINATION CONDITIONS

Section A – This ONE question is compulsory and MUST be attempted

The following information should be used when answering question 1

Question 1

Roam Group Co

Roam Group Co (The Roam Group) was formed in 2009 when the owners of Stuart Roam Road Transport decided to create a group structure to facilitate the acquisition of companies. The CEO of The Roam Group is Sir John Watt, a highly experienced businessman and he has a financial director and an operations director to assist him. The objectives of The Roam Group is to acquire companies which fit well with its existing companies, which would benefit from being part of the Group and which would also bring benefits to companies already in the Group. The Roam Group is a very lean operation. Besides the three full-time directors, it only has two full-time administrative employees. There are currently three operating companies in the Group: Stuart Roam Road Transport, Stuart Roam Warehousing and Stuart Roam Rail. The managing directors of all three operating companies also sit on the board of The Roam Group. Each of these operating companies has significant autonomy within the Group.

The Roam Group, like all the operating companies in the Group, has the majority of its shares owned by the Roam family. Financial information for the operating companies is given in Table One. The Roam Group and its operating companies are all based in the country of Meeland.

Stuart Roam Road Transport

Stuart Roam Road Transport (SRRT) was founded in 1955 by Stuart Roam. It has grown to be the largest road freight company in Meeland, with over 2,000 trucks. It specialises in the haulage of consumer food and drink and it has significant contracts with most of the large supermarket chains. There are no toll roads in Meeland. Taxes for roads are levied through a fuel tax and an annual road fund licence. The managing director of SRRT is Stuart Roam junior, who was originally employed by his father as a driver. He still drives a truck for one day every month, so that 'he never loses touch with the business'. SRRT's distinctive red and white trucks are seen all over the country, and all carry the company's catchphrase 'All roads lead to Roam'. They have attracted a fan club, whose members spot the trucks on the road and record their movements on a dedicated internet site. These so-called 'New-Roamantics' have themselves become famous and, partly as a result of this, Stuart Roam has become a household name and is the most recognisable brand in the road transport industry. To maintain a modern fleet, SRRT replaces its trucks every three years. It wants to ensure that they are reliable, efficient and that they project a modern image which is attractive to their customers.

Stuart Roam Warehousing

The growth of company outsourcing and consumer internet purchasing made it increasingly clear that SRRT's customers wanted an integrated transport and storage solution. The Roam Group acquired a number of warehouses from its customers who wished to divest themselves of this part of their operations. In 2009, it consolidated these, together with a number of small warehousing companies it had acquired, into a company called Stuart Roam Warehousing (SRW). The 2010 figures shown in Table One represent the first year that the company traded in its current form. Nationwide, it owns 4 million square metres of warehousing, with its warehouses painted red and white and prominently displaying the Stuart Roam logo. The warehouses are efficient and highly automated. However, development land for warehouses is getting more difficult to find and acquisition costs of the land are also increasing. The average price for warehouse development land in Meeland is now $20,000 per hectare. A hectare is 10,000 square metres.

Stuart Roam Rail

Increasing fuel costs, increasing road congestion and concern about the environmental consequences of road transport caused The Roam Group to look at opportunities offered by rail transport.

In 2010 The Roam Group purchased the Freight Direct Rail Company (FDRC). FDRC was formed in 2000 when the government of Meeland privatised the rail freight business. FDRC had struggled to survive in a business dominated by two large companies who shared the lucrative bulk freight contracts (coal, iron ore and oil) between them. The

FDRC board welcomed The Roam Group acquisition and the locomotives were quickly painted in the red and white corporate colours and FDRC was renamed Stuart Roam Rail. However, despite experienced managers being transferred into the company from other companies in the Group, Stuart Roam Rail (like FDRC) has struggled to make a significant impact in the rail freight sector. Most of its customers are at locations which are not directly accessible by rail. Furthermore, the lucrative bulk rail freight contracts (coal, iron ore and oil) are in products which companies within The Roam Group have no experience in. It is still unclear whether the movement of consumer food and drink to multiple locations (The Roam Group's core business) is suited to rail transport. Furthermore, it has also been difficult for The Roam Group's senior management to understand the culture and economics of the rail freight business. The railway tracks, which are still owned by the state, are subject to very close control and monitoring and Stuart Roam Rail's use of these tracks is directly charged. There has also been a failure to recognise that train driving requires far greater skills and training than truck driving.

However, on the positive side, Stuart Roam Rail has developed an innovative mini-container system which can easily transfer goods between trucks and trains and it also effectively uses warehouse space. Furthermore, most of the supermarkets, attracted by a green image, are very supportive of the rail initiative and wish to be associated with it.

	2013		2012		2011		2010		2009	
	Roam	Industry	Roam	Industry	Roam	Industry	Roam	Industry	Roam	Industry
Stuart Roam Road Transport										
Revenue	575	2,050	565	2,025	550	2,015	520	2,050	500	2,000
Operating profit	10.80%	9.98%	10.75%	9.95%	10.80%	9.93%	10.45%	9.50%	10.25%	9.57%
ROCE	12.25%	11.50%	12.15%	11.45%	12.05%	11.45%	11.95%	11.30%	11.95%	11.35%
Stuart Roam Warehousing										
Revenue	315	3,200	275	3,010	270	3,050	255	2,950	250	2,850
Operating profit	14.55%	14.50%	14.25%	14.15%	14.20%	14.25%	14.00%	14.25%	13.85%	14.15%
ROCE	14.50%	14.15%	14.25%	14.10%	14.15%	14.10%	13.95%	13.90%	13.95%	13.85%
Stuart Roam Rail										
Revenue	112	3,150	110	3,000	105	2,850	105	2,650	105	2,500
Operating profit	4.75%	12.45%	4.50%	12.35%	4.85%	12.25%	4.95%	12.75%	5.15%	12.85%
ROCE	3.50%	8.75%	3.65%	8.55%	3.75%	8.55%	3.85%	8.35%	3.85%	8.25%

Table One: Financial data for operating companies in The Roam Group.

The performance of the company is shown under the columns headed Roam. Industry figures (provided by Freight Line International) are shown under the columns headed Industry. Operating profit and ROCE figures are averages for the industry while revenue figures are totals. All revenue figures are in $million.

Note 1: Stuart Roam Warehousing first traded in 2010. The 2009 figure is compiled from companies which were consolidated into Stuart Roam Warehousing.

Note 2: Stuart Roam Rail was formed after the takeover of FDRC. 2011 was the first reporting period for Stuart Roam

Rail. The 2009 and 2010 figures are for FDRC.

Note 3: The standard payment terms in Meeland is payment within 30 days of the invoice date.

Godiva airport

The Godiva airport is situated on the outskirts of Boleyn town where SRRT already has three transport depots and warehouses. The airport occupies a site of 450 hectares and it has two tarmac runways, four hangers and a small terminal/flying club facility. The airfield is exclusively used by private flyers and two flying clubs. The airport is adjacent to the motorway which connects North and South Meeland. Financial information for Godiva airport is given in Table Two.

All figures in $000s	$
Assets	
Non-current assets	
Property, plant and equipment	6,000
Goodwill	250
Total non-current assets	6,250
Current assets	
Inventory	550
Trade receivables	80
Cash	370
Total current assets	1,000
Total assets	7,250
Equity and liabilities	
Share capital	2,550
Retained earnings	250
Total equity	2,800
Non-current liabilities	
Long-term borrowings	4,050
Current liabilities	
Trade payables	120
Short-term borrowings	250
Current tax payable	30
Total current liabilities	400
Total liabilities	4,450
Total equity and liabilities	7,250

Statement of profit or loss

	$
Revenue	975
Cost of sales	(700)
Gross profit	275
Administrative expenses	(125)
Finance costs	(100)
Profit before tax	50
Tax expense	(10)
Profit for the period	40

Table Two: Godiva airport – extracts from financial statements – 2013

The Roam Group has recently issued the following press release from Sir John Watt:

The Roam Group is pleased to announce that it has signed an initial agreement to purchase Godiva airport from the Godiva Airport Company for the sum of $7m, funded from retained profits from within the Group. We see this as a natural extension of our transport capabilities. Road, rail and air have long been complementary forms of transport and we are pleased to be able to offer our customers all three, using our innovative mini-container system as an effective transhipment method between transport modes. We also hope to attract a no-frills airline to the airport, encouraged by low landing fees and a population of over 150,000 people living within 20 miles of the airport. Godiva Airport Company will become an operating company within The Roam Group, and renamed Stuart Roam Air.

In a critical article on the proposed airport acquisition in the financial press, an independent aviation consultant has provided national performance statistics for airports of a similar size and type to Godiva airport (see Table Three).

Operating profit margin	Return on Capital Employed	Current ratio	Acid test ratio	Gearing ratio
17·5%	8·5%	2·25	1·50	40%

Table Three: Average national performance figures for medium-sized light aviation airports: 2013

He has also cast doubt on Sir John Watt's statement about attracting a no-frills airline to the airport. He says that a local regional population of at least 500,000 people is required to make such a service attractive. He believes that the population of the Boleyn area is much too small to make passenger services economical.

Required

(a)   Write an independent report which:

(i)   Evaluates the current performance and contribution of each of the three current operating companies in The Roam Group portfolio and assesses their relative significance in its future strategy. **(21 marks)**

(ii)   Evaluates the proposed acquisition of Godiva airport.   **(15 marks)**

Professional marks will be allocated in part (a) for the clarity, structure, logical flow and appropriate tone of your answer.   **(4 marks)**

(b)   A Business Analysis research student has suggested that Stuart Roam Road Transport (SRRT) pursues a hybrid strategy of offering a price lower than its competitors, whilst simultaneously attempting to achieve differentiation.

Required

Discuss how both elements of this route to competitive advantage (price and differentiation) might be achieved by Stuart Roam Road Transport.   **(10 marks)**

(50 marks)

Section B – TWO questions ONLY to be attempted

Question 2

Stella Electronics (SE) owns a chain of electrical retail stores throughout the country of Arborium. The company sells to the general public through its stores and website. It has outsourced three areas of a business process to Terra Call Generale (TCG), a call centre specialist based overseas. They handle, on behalf of SE, the following calls:

- Customers requesting service contracts
- Customers requesting refunds for goods purchased from the SE website
- Customers with technical queries about the products they have bought.

The business process for handling these calls is given in Figure 1.

SE is currently reviewing the renewal of the TCG contract in the light of customer complaints about:

- The time taken to complete a query
- The frustration caused by the need to provide a reference number and password
- The problem of understanding the accents of the people in the call centre.

Unemployment is rising in Arborium and there is increased resistance to services being outsourced and offshored to companies such as TCG. SE is aware of the growing hostility of customers to such arrangements.

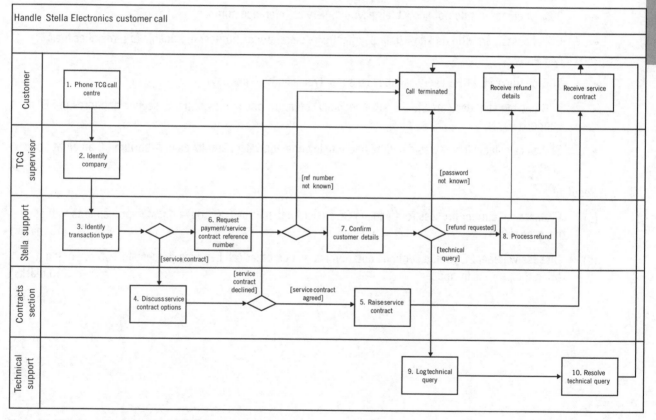

Figure 1: Business process for handling a Stella Electronics customer call

Call centre processing (TCG) – to be read in conjunction with Figure 1

1. The process is initiated by a customer phoning the TCG call centre.

2. TCG offers call centre services to a number of companies. The supervisor asks the customer which company they are phoning about. Calls for SE are routed to Stella support. Calls for other companies are routed to other support teams (not shown here).

3. The TCG support operator asks the customer what their call is about. Three transaction types are possible.

4. Callers who wish to discuss a service contract are passed immediately to the contracts section. Service contract options are discussed and if the caller decides to buy a service contract, then this is raised in the next activity in the process (5: Raise service contract).

5. Raise service contract and details are emailed to the customer. If the caller decides not to have a service contract, then the call is terminated.

6. For all other transaction types, Stella support asks the customer for their payment reference number or service contract reference number. If the customer cannot supply either of these, then the call is terminated. If the reference number is provided, then the support team member enters it into the computer system.

7. The computer system retrieves customer details and these are confirmed by the support team member with the customer. These details include a password which the customer has to give. Failure to give the correct password leads to the call being terminated.

8. If the password is correct and the customer requires a purchase refund, then the refund is processed and details emailed to the customer and the call is terminated.

9. If the password is correct and the customer has a technical query, then the call is passed to technical support who log and then resolve (process 10) the query before terminating the call.

Further information:

- TCG provides a 24 hour/7 days per week service. There are 600 calls per 24 hours from SE customers.

- 60% are technical queries, 25% are requests for refunds and 15% are for service contracts.

- 30% of customers do not know their payment/service reference number.

- 5% of customers who do know their payment/service reference number are unable to remember their password.

- TCG charges SE $1 for every call they take (so, typically $600 per day).

- TCG has ten staff dedicated to SE: six in technical support, one in the contracts section and three in SE support.

- SE has calculated that it would cost $50 to employ one equivalent employee in Arborium for an eight hour shift.

Required

(a) Evaluate the current process for handling SE's customer calls at TCG and suggest improvements to that process at TCG. **(15 marks)**

(b) Discuss whether SE should continue outsourcing its customer call handling process to TCG or should it bring the process in-house. **(10 marks)**

(25 marks)

Question 3

This information was taken from an internal newsletter of The Knowledge Partnership LLP (TKP), a company which offers project and software consultancy work for clients based in Zeeland. The newsletter was dated 2 November 2014 and describes two projects currently being undertaken by the partnership.

Project One

In this project, one of our clients was just about to place a contract for a time recording system to help them monitor and estimate construction contracts when we were called in by the Finance Director. He was concerned about the company supplying the software package. 'They only have an annual revenue of $5m', he said, 'and that worries me.' TKP analysed software companies operating in Zeeland. It found that 200 software companies were registered in Zeeland with annual revenues of between $3m and $10m. Of these, 20 went out of business last year. This compared to a 1% failure rate for software companies with revenues of more than $100m per year. We presented this information to the client and suggested that this could cause a short-term support problem. The client immediately re-opened the procurement process. Eventually they bought a solution from a much larger well-known software supplier. It is a popular software solution, used in many larger companies.

The client has now asked us to help with the implementation of the package. A budget for the project has been agreed and has been documented in an agreed, signed-off, business case. The client has a policy of never re-visiting its business cases once they have been accepted; they see this as essential for effective cost control. We are currently working with the primary users of the software – account managers (using time and cost data to monitor contracts) and the project support office (using time and cost data to improve contract estimating) – to ensure that they can use the software effectively when it is implemented. We have also given 'drop in' briefing sessions for the client's employees who are entering the time and cost data analysed by the software. They already record this information on a legacy system and so all they will see is a bright new user interface, but we need to keep them informed about our implementation. We are also looking at data migration from the current legacy system. We think some of the current data might be of poor quality, so we have established a strategy for data cleansing (through offshore data input) if this problem materialises. We currently estimate that the project will go live in May 2015.

Project Two

In this project, the client is the developer of the iProjector, a tiny phone-size projector which is portable, easy to use and offers high definition projection. The client was concerned that their product is completely dependent on a specialist image-enhancing chip designed and produced by a small start-up technology company. They asked TKP to investigate this company. We confirmed their fears. The company has been trading for less than three years and it has a very inexperienced management team. We suggested that the client should establish an escrow agreement for design details of the chip and suggested a suitable third party to hold this agreement. We also suggested that significant stocks of the chip should be maintained. The client also asked TKP to look at establishing patents for the iProjector throughout the world. Again, using our customer contacts, we put them in touch with a company which specialises in this. We are currently engaged with the client in examining the risk that a major telephone producer will launch a competitive product with functionality and features similar to the iProjector.

The iProjector is due to be launched on 1 May 2015 and we have been engaged to give advice on the launch of the product. The launch has been heavily publicised, a prestigious venue booked and over 400 attendees are expected. TKP have arranged for many newspaper journalists to attend. The product is not quite finished, so although orders will be taken at the launch, the product is not expected to ship until June 2015.

Further information:

TKP only undertakes projects in the business culture which it understands and where it feels comfortable. Consequently, it does not undertake assignments outside Zeeland.

TKP has $10,000,000 of consultant's liability insurance underwritten by Zeeland Insurance Group (ZIG).

Required:

(a) Analyse how TKP itself and the two projects described in the scenario demonstrate the principles of effective risk management. **(15 marks)**

(b) Describe the principle of the triple constraint (scope, time and cost) on projects and discuss its implications in the two projects described in the scenario. **(10 marks)**

(25 marks)

Question 4

Noble Pets is one of four companies which dominate the pet food market in the country of Brellia. Between them, these four companies share 90% of the market. Noble Pets was established in 1930 in the market town of Milton. Its factory (plant) was updated in 1970 with new canning and labelling technology. However, further developments and expansion to the factory site were prevented by the rapid growth of housing in Milton. The factory, which was once on the edge of the town, is now surrounded by modern housing development. The town is also relatively remote from the motorway network which has been developed in Brellia since 1960. Trucks transporting goods in and out of the plant have to negotiate relatively minor rural roads and also have to pass through the town centre of Milton, which is often very congested. Furthermore, the large 44 tonne trucks which Noble Pets and its competitors use, wherever possible, to distribute cans of pet food to wholesalers and supermarket distribution centres are banned from the centre of the town. Thus distribution out of the Milton plant is undertaken with smaller 36 tonne trucks, which are less cost-effective. However, residents find even this size of truck too large, complaining that they keep them awake at night.

The Milton plant is solely concerned with the production of moist pet food. Raw foodstuff and empty unlabelled cans are brought into the plant, where the foodstuff is cooked and put into cans which are then labelled and distributed to wholesalers or supermarket distribution centres. Many of these distribution centres, like Noble Pets' competitors, are now located on or near the motorway network. Although the recipe for the pet food is very similar to its competitors, Noble Pets has a reputation for producing a quality product. This quality has been promoted ever since the company's formation by clever marketing campaigns which stress the importance of giving your pet good food, and the superior nature of Noble Pets' products to its competitors. This has traditionally been supported by free fact guides and information promoting responsible pet ownership and nutrition. The company now has a website dedicated to giving advice and guidance. This advice appears to be unbiased, although recommended solutions to pet problems often involve Noble Pets' products.

Noble Pets is currently reviewing its operations and has asked external consultants to assess the Milton plant from a value chain perspective. It has provided the following table (Table One) to help in that analysis. Average figures for its competitors are also provided.

Production cost of a six can pack of moist pet food	Milton Factory	Competitor A	Competitor B	Competitor C
	$	$	$	$
Raw foodstuff costs	.10	.10	.09	.15
Cost of cans	.05	.10	.06	.05
Direct labour costs	.25	.25	.30	.24
Production costs	.30	.25	.20	.26
Transport costs (good inward)	.15	.10	.10	.12
Transport costs (good outward)	.10	.05	.05	.08
Sales price (to customer)	1.25	1.15	1.10	1.20

Table One: Direct costs of the Milton plant compared to major competitors

Dry pet food is an alternative to moist pet food. It is packaged in bags and it is in the form of a biscuit. Many people who buy pet food prefer the dry food because it does not smell and can be left in the pet's bowl for longer. Noble Pets also produces dry pet food, but not at its Milton plant. It would like to reduce costs at Milton but it is concerned that the demand for moist pet food will not justify such investment. Consequently, it has also asked the consultants to look at the pet food market as a whole and to forecast demand for moist pet food for the next three years (2014, 2015 and 2016). It is aware that new technology is available (and is already being used by its competitors) which offers more efficient and reliable canning, but it is not sure that it is worth investing in.

The consultants have identified the following information provided by the Pet Food Industry Group.

Years	Year (x)	Moist pet food (000s tonnes) (y)	Dry pet food (000s tonnes)
2007	1	370	292
2008	2	350	307
2009	3	331	321
2010	4	325	329
2011	5	315	341
2012	6	310	351
2013	7	310	359

Table Two: Production of pet food (2007–2013)

A linear regression analysis has been conducted for the moist food production. Time (years) is represented as x (the independent variable) and moist pet food volume as y. The linear regression analysis has identified the following values of a, b and r for the relationship between time and moist pet food production.

a	b	r
369·5714	−9·86	−0·94432

Noble Pets currently has a market share of 30% of the moist food market, a share which has remained unchanged since 2007. It has three sites. As well as the Milton plant it has two other plants. These two plants combined have an annual maximum capacity of 40,000 tonnes of moist pet food.

Required

(a) Evaluate the strengths and weaknesses of the Milton plant from the perspective of the primary activities of a value chain analysis. **(15 marks)**

(b) (i) Analyse trends in the pet food industry. **(5 marks)**

(ii) Forecast demand for moist pet food for the next three years, as required by Noble Pets, using the regression formula given and comment on the validity and implications of that forecast.

(5 marks)

(25 marks)

Answers

DO NOT TURN THIS PAGE UNTIL YOU HAVE COMPLETED THE MOCK EXAM

A plan of attack

We discussed the problem of which question to start with earlier, in 'Passing the P3 exam'. Here we will merely reiterate our view that question 1 is nearly always the best place to start and, if you do decide to start with a Section B question, **make sure that you finish your answer in no more than 45 minutes**.

In part (a)(i) of **Question 1** it is important that you recognise that there are two parts to the requirement. You need to ensure that you devote sufficient time assessing the performance of the three group companies covered in the scenario. The best approach to adopt for part (a)(ii) is to use the SAF model as a framework when considering the proposed acquisition. Part (b) asked for a discussion of how one of the group company's featured in the question could achieve competitive advantage by pursuing a hybrid strategy (price and differentiation). It is particularly important that you avoid confusing the issue of offering low prices with low cost.

Question 2 may appear to be a difficult question at first glance. Try to not be deterred by the swim lane diagram, this has been included to help you answer the question. Ensure you read this requirement carefully as part (a) consists of two requirements. You can score well in part (b) by contrasting the advantages and disadvantages to SE of continuing to outsource its customer call handling process against bringing the process in-house.

Question 3 is a good choice if you are familiar with risk management. To score well in part (a) it is essential that you demonstrate how effective risk management principles are being followed at TKP and during the two projects outlined in the scenario. Application of your knowledge here is key. In part (b) it is particularly important that you discuss the implications of the triple constraint in relation to the two projects described. To score well here you need to recognise that the constraints on both projects are very different.

Part (a) of **Question 4** offers the opportunity to gain some easy marks provided you are familiar with Porter's Value Chain model. To score well it is important that your answer concentrates on strengths and weaknesses. The first section of Part (b) requires a methodical approach when analysing trends in the pet food industry. A good approach here is to consider trends in both moist and dry pet food as well as the underlying trend in the industry as a whole. The second requirement of part (b) is likely to be more challenging if you have not devoted sufficient time to studying regression analysis.

SECTION A

Question 1

Text reference. The BCG matrix, Ashridge model and the SAF success criteria are all covered in Chapter 6 of the BPP Study Text for exams from September 2015 to 31 August 2016.

Top tips. Part (a) of the question requires the completion of a report, therefore it is crucial that you give appropriate consideration to the lay out and structure your work. You should have noticed that there were 4 professional marks available for the clarity, structure, logical flow and tone of your report. You should be familiar at this stage in your studies with the importance of getting the marker on your side. In this context the use of appropriate headings and short, punchy sentences are what the marker wants to see.

Part (a)(i) asked for two things, firstly an evaluation of the current performance and contribution of the three Roam Group companies and secondly an assessment of their relative significance in the group's future strategy. As you can see from our solution below we have structured our answer into three parts, each of which focuses on each group company. To ensure that both elements of the question are answered sufficiently, two headings have been used which focus on current performance and contribution and the significance of each company to the group in the future.

There were 21 marks available for this requirement. These were split equally between the three companies, capped at 7 marks each. It was important that you did not spend too long analysing any one company as you ran the risk of running out of time later on in the exam.

When considering performance and contribution it is important not simply to use the financial information provided in isolation. The financials should be used to help you explain why the company has performed in a certain way and should be used in conjunction with the scenario information provided. To score well on this part of the question you needed to go further than simply stating that revenue has gone up 'by x%' and ROCE is worse than the industry average. To get more from your answer the use of appropriate theoretical models will give you more to talk about. As the question focuses on assessing a portfolio of group companies the use of the Boston Consulting Group matrix and Ashridge model should provide a useful structure for your work.

Part (a) (ii) required an evaluation of the proposal to acquire Godiva airport. It is important that you read the question carefully at this point as Godiva is an airport and not an airline. Failing to make this distinction is likely to have led to the inclusion of irrelevant points in your answer. In the event that Godiva had been an airline you would have been justified in highlighting the synergies that exist with Roam's current capabilities in logistics and transport. However, this was not the case.

To avoid producing a superficial evaluation of the proposed strategy, it is important that you think critically about whether the acquisition represents a sensible move by a group of companies which have no background experience or expertise in operating an airport.

This type of requirement lends itself nicely to the use of the SAF model. The SAF model considers the appropriateness of a proposed strategy from three perspectives, suitability, acceptability and feasibility. This is the framework that we have used in our answer below. Structuring your work in such a way should help to ensure that you consider the proposal from different viewpoints, it should also help to ensure that you have a sufficient amount to talk about. However, it is worth noting that you could have attempted the requirement without using a formal model and still gained the marks on offer. In order to score well on this requirement you needed to use the financial information provided about Godiva airport as there were 6 marks available for the correct calculation and interpretation of a number of ratios including ROCE, gross profit margin, liquidity and gearing.

Part (b). The final requirement asked for a discussion of how Stuart Roam Road Transport could pursue a hybrid strategy of offering low prices while attempting to differentiate in order to achieve competitive advantage. It was particularly important that you avoided confusing the issue of offering low prices with low cost. By focusing on cost you may have been tempted to apply your knowledge of Porter's generic strategies to the question. This was not required. By contrast the use of Bowman's strategy clock was appropriate here as it considers how the issues of perceived added value and price interact to determine strategy.

In order to score well on this question you needed to ensure that you focused your answer on Stuart Roam Road Transport and avoided a general discussion of the Roam Group as a whole. Furthermore, it is important that you give consideration to how both a low price strategy and differentiation could be used together. On the face of it such a strategy may seem destined to fail, however, careful consideration of the scenario suggests that such an approach maybe viable, for example, we are aware that the road haulage market is barely growing and that Stuart Roam Road Transport is the dominant player in the market for consumer food and drink products. Therefore, a low price strategy supported by the profile gained from the New Roamantics fan club is likely to be a good way to attract customers from competitors and gain market share.

Easy marks. The 6 marks on offer in part (a)(ii) for the correct calculation of the ratios and subsequent interpretation were a source of easy marks.

Examiner's comments. The examining team highlighted in part (a)(i) that the main problem most candidates experienced concerned the misclassification of the group companies when applying them to the BCG matrix. 'Many candidates related each company to the Boston Box, or (less frequently) to the Ashridge model. The biggest misclassification related to Stuart Roam Rail. Because it was underperforming, many candidates considered it, in BCG terms, a dog. However, the rapidly expanding market, indicated by the performance figures, is significant here and Stuart Roam Rail is really a question mark, because it appears to have the right market conditions to grow, but it is failing to do so.'

Part (a)(ii) which focused on the proposed acquisition of Godiva airport was adequately answered my most candidates. 'Most answers included the obvious financial ratios that could be calculated from the information provided (ROCE, gross profit percentage, operating margin, gearing and liquidity ratios). Very few answers picked up on the trade payables and trade receivables figures, which suggested that Godiva airport was using its suppliers as a source of free credit. Much was made of the non-financial challenges facing the acquisition, particularly given the Group's experience in the rail industry. So, overall, answers were adequate but rarely spectacular, with many answers just not making enough points to get the marks on offer.'

The examining team reported that part (b) was particularly poorly answered. As the examining team's comments highlight it is important that you read the question requirement carefully to avoid including unnecessary detail in your answer. 'Very few answers used the context of Stuart Roam Road Transport to illustrate the elements of a hybrid strategy. Some candidates also included examples from one of the other companies in the group, or from the proposed acquisition of Godiva airport, all of which were outside the scope of the question. The requirement was explicitly and solely related to Stuart Roam Road Transport.'

(b)   1 mark for each relevant point up to a maximum of 10 marks.

Part (a) (i)

Report

To: The Board of Roam Group Co
From: A N Consultant
Date: December 20X4
Subject: Evaluation of group performance and proposed acquisition of Godiva airport

This report provides an evaluation of the current performance and contribution of three group companies which make up the Roam Group (Stuart Roam Road Transport, Stuart Roam Warehousing and Stuart Roam Rail). The second half of the report considers the proposed acquisition of Godiva airport.

Stuart Roam Transport

Performance and contribution to the Stuart Roam Group

Stuart Roam Road Transport (SRRT) is a key part of the group. In 2013 SRRT generated more than half of the group's revenue, 57.39% and 54.8% of its operating profit. SRRT is the largest road haulage company in Meeland and it has built up extensive experience in the haulage of consumer and food and drink products. The company's success to date is characterised by the company's ability to win contracts to provide road haulage services to most of the large supermarket chains in the country.

Between 2009 - 2013 revenues in the road haulage market only rose slowly (2.5%) . However, during this period SRRT achieved revenue growth which led to its market share increasing from 25% to 28%. SRRT would therefore be classified as a 'Cash Cow' using the Boston Consulting Group matrix. The operating profits generated by SRRT are marginally higher than the industry averages. This is positive as SRRT is generating profits which it can reinvest in its own operations or those of other Roam Group companies.

Significance of SRRT

The current Managing Director of SRRT, Stuart Roam Junior is the son of the founder of the company and has a strong connection to the company. This is evident as he insists on driving a truck one day every month. The desire to not lose touch with the business indicates a commitment by the Managing Director to understand the operational issues facing SRRT.

The management at SRRT have been effective in creating a recognisable a brand image for the company. The distinctive red and white livery used on SRRT's trucks combined with the company's catchphrase 'All roads lead to Roam', has attracted a fan base of loyal truck spotters known as the 'New-Roamantics'. This has helped to raise the profile of the company, making SRRT a household name. SRRT's brand image is further underpinned by the company's policy to replace its trucks every three years, this helps to project a modern image which is attractive to customers.

SRRT would be classified as a 'Heartland business' using the Ashridge portfolio model. As the Roam Group was formed by the owners of SRRT in 2009, the fit between the parent and strategic business unit is strong. SRRT's performance and significance means it should be retained in the group.

Stuart Roam Warehousing

Performance and contribution to the Stuart Roam Group

During the period 2009 to 2013 Stuart Roam Warehousing (SRW) achieved a 26% increase in revenue. This is particularly promising since the warehousing market as a whole grew by 12.28% over the same period. The company's revenues make up 31.4% of the group's total revenue.

SRW has achieved marginal growth in its market share since 2009 (8.77%) increasing this to just under 10% (9.84%) in 2013. The company is performing slightly better than the industry average with regards to ROCE and operating profit margin. In 2013 SRW contributed 40.47% of operating profit to the Stuart Roam Group.

Applying the Boston Consulting Group matrix, SRW could be classified as either a Star or a Question Mark. The final classification will be determined by whether or not the company's 10% market share is considered 'high'. Regardless of the classification, both 'Stars' and 'Question marks' require capital expenditure in order to maintain / build on their position. Building on SRW's current position is however likely to be constrained by the difficulty in finding new warehouse space. Such investment is likely to be supported by profits generated elsewhere in the group ie by SRRT.

Significance of Stuart Roam Warehousing

SRW would be classified as a 'Heartland business' using the Ashridge portfolio model. The fit between the company and the Stuart Roam Group would appear to be good. In this case the parent has a good feel for the strategic business unit. As the group grew from SRRT the skills and expertise gained in road haulage fit well with the opportunity to provide customers with an integrated transport and storage solution.

The national spread of the company's warehouses which are painted in the Stuart Roam colours and display the Stuart Roam logo help to reinforce the group's brand image. The growth in internet shopping by end consumers, coupled to increased demand for outsourced solutions to warehousing would have likely been key drivers for management in making the decision to enter this market. SRW therefore represents an important element in the group's offering.

Stuart Roam Rail

Performance and contribution to the Stuart Roam Group

Since 2009 revenues in the rail freight market have rapidly increased year on year; and between 2009 -2013 they grew by 26% ($650m). Concerns over increasing road haulage fuel costs, road congestion and the environmental consequences of continued road usage have all contributed to this growth.

Stuart Roam Rail (SRR) is a small player in the rail freight market in Meeland. It's market share is in decline. In 2013 the company held a market share of 3.56%, compared to the 4.2% held in 2009. Unlike the revenue growth experienced in the market as a whole SRR only achieved growth over the period of 6.6%. The company's operating profits and ROCE have also been significantly lower than the annual industry averages. Since the Roam Group's acquisition of SRR in 2010 the company's performance has steadily worsened, with both operating profit and ROCE declining. It could be argued that Stuart Roam's involvement in the rail business is having a detrimental impact on the company's performance.

In the context of the BCG matrix, SRR would be classed as a Question Mark. The company's failure to increase its market share in a growing industry represents a worrying development and requires further investigation. The company is small in comparison to the two large companies, this increases the difficultly of realising economies of scale. The situation is compounded further as the Roam Group does not have experience or expertise in operating bulk rail freight contracts for coal, iron, ore and oil. This increases the difficulty for SRR in winning such contracts from established players in the market.

Furthermore, the decision to distribute consumer food and drink products to supermarkets by rail may not be entirely appropriate given the inability of retailers to access the rail network at all locations. Finally, senior management at the Roam Group do not appear to not fully understand the culture and economics of the rail freight business. Unlike the road system in Meeland which is free to access, the country's network is subject to a usage charge administered by the state owned supplier. Coupled to this has been the failure to appreciate the level of skill and training required to be a train driver.

Significance of Stuart Roam Rail

SRR could be classified as a value trap business using the Ashridge portfolio model. SRR initially appeared attractive to the Group as it offered the opportunity to enter a new sector in the transport industry. In practice it has not been as successful as the Group hoped, this is due, in part to the differences in the skills and competencies needed to operate a rail freight company.

Ventures such as SRR should only be retained if they can be moved into the Heartland; this will require the Stuart Roam Group to acquire new skills and resources.

On a positive note, the company has developed an innovative mini-container system which can easily transfer goods between trucks and trains and helps to use warehouse space effectively. This potentially represents a significant opportunity for SRR as a number of supermarkets are keen to support the new system due to its 'green', environmentally friendly credentials. This increases the scope for the company to implement a new approach to distribution if deliveries can be made to regional railway stations with goods being immediately transferred onto haulage trucks for the final leg of their journey to supermarkets.

Summary

SRRT and SRW are Heartland businesses and should clearly be retained. The acquisition of FRDC in 2010 however appears to have been misjudged as the rail company is classified as a value trap business. Senior management at the Roam Group will need to give careful consideration to how they transform the company into a Heartland business. The focus of this effort is likely to concentrate on addressing the company's underlying problems.

Part (a) (ii)

The following section of this report evaluates the proposal to acquire Godiva airport. The proposal has been considered using the SAF criteria of suitability, acceptability and feasibility.

Suitability

The Group needs to consider whether the acquisition makes sense given its current strategic position.

Synergies

Taking a high level view it arguably appears to be a sensible move given the group's established operations in transportation. This is backed up by the comments made by Sir John Watt, 'road, rail and air have long been complementary forms of transport and we are pleased to be able to offer our customers all three'. However, a closer look at the proposal is likely to raise some doubts. As outlined in the first half of this report the anticipated similarities between road haulage and rail have not been fully realised, this calls into question whether extending the range of transport options further will succeed.

Wide spread of locations

Arguably, Roam Group's focus on transporting consumer food and drink products via road and rail on behalf of major supermarkets is unlikely to lend itself to air freighting goods to supermarket stores. Due to the wide dispersion of airport locations it seems highly unlikely that these would be close enough to the end destination (supermarket store) to be worth the associated hassle of setting up operations. The suitability of the proposal would partially rest on the ability of the mini-container system to be integrated for use with aircraft.

Environmentally friendly

Furthermore, given the supermarkets support for more environmentally friendly modes of transporting goods it seems highly unlikely that they would be keen to use an airfreighting service.

Experience and expertise

It is important however to note that the current proposal is to purchase an airport and not an airline. Sir John Watt's press statement implies the future establishment of an airline at some point but fails to go any further than this. This raises an interesting consideration about the suitability of the proposal, namely the fact that at present the Roam Group does not have any experience or expertise in operating an airport.

Demand for 'no-frills'

Sir John Watt's proposal highlighted an intention to attract a 'no-frills airline to the airport', however, at the current time it is unknown whether such an airline would be interested.

The article by the independent aviation consultant raises doubts whether a 'no-frills' airline would be attracted to Godiva airport given the relatively small local population around the site. Arguably, if there was sufficient demand we might expect that a no-frills airline would already be operating from the airport.

Acceptability

The acceptability of a strategy depends on expected performance outcomes and the extent to which these are acceptable to stakeholders. Such returns may be both financial and non-financial in nature.

Financial performance

Determining the financial performance of Godiva airport is made harder as no comparative financials have been provided beside the extracts for 2013. However, the national performance statistics supplied by the aviation consultant for similar sized airports provide a useful guide for measuring relative performance.

In 2013 the airport site was valued at $6m, this is to be expected as this represents the company's main asset. This valuation suggests that the $7m to be paid by the Roam Group to acquire the airport represents a reasonable price. One of the issues facing SRW in (part (a)(i) concerned the increasing lack of land available in Meeland to be used for warehousing. Godiva airport occupies a site of 450 hectares, based on the market rate the land alone is worth $9m ($20,000 × 450 hectares). As the airport is located near the motorway purchasing the site for warehousing is likely to highly acceptable to the Group given the price.

Profitability

Godiva airport is a profitable entity, the company generated a profit after tax of $40,000 in 2013. The airport achieved a gross profit margin of 28.21% and an operating profit margin of 15.38% in the year (compared to the industry average of 17.5%). Interestingly, Godiva airport achieved a higher operating profit margin than all of the Roam Group companies in 2013.

By contrast Godiva airport's ROCE of 2.19% (earnings before tax and interest / total assets less current liabilities) is far lower than the industry average of 8.5%. This indicates that the airport has required a significant level of investment in Godiva airport to generate very low returns.

Liquidity & Gearing

Godiva airport has a positive liquidity position with a current ratio of 2.50 compared to the industry average of 2.25. However, it appears to have a very high inventory balance. When this is stripped out from current assets results Godiva's acid test ratio of 1.125 is lower than the national average of 1.50.

The airport is more highly geared (59.12%) than the industry average (40%). This is driven by significant long-term borrowings of just over $4m.

Receivables and payables

The standard payment terms in Meeland require payment within 30 days of the invoice date. In 2013, Godiva airport was receiving payment from trade receivables in 30 days (80/975 × 365), however, it was only paying its own suppliers after 60 days on average (120/700 ×365). This is likely to raise some concern over the airports ability to manage its cash flow. Further investigation into this apparent discrepancy is required as Godiva takes just over twice the accepted standard payment terms in Meeland .

From this limited financial analysis it is apparent that Godiva's performance is somewhat mixed. Although it is profitable, the company is hindered by a significant long-term debt which has resulted in a relatively low ROCE.

Risks of acquisition

In order for the acquisition of Godiva airport to be deemed acceptable careful consideration needs to be given to the level of risk attached to the proposal.

Financial risk

Given the Roam Group's financial resources the initial purchase cost of acquiring the airport is likely to represent a small investment. In the event that Godiva airport incurred operating losses post-acquisition these should be covered by profitable group companies. Although the financial risk to the Roam Group appears to be low, consideration needs to be given to the potential impact that funding an acquisition would have on other group entities.

As discussed in the first half of this report, both SRR and SRW could both be classified as 'Question Marks' per the BCG matrix. The process of developing Question Mark business units into Stars often requires significant levels of investment. Clearly, acquiring Godiva airport will lead to a reduction in funds available to support other business units. There is an inherent risk that employees working in existing Roam Group companies may become demotivated and resent the acquisition at a time when the funds may have been spent more appropriately elsewhere.

Shareholders

At present the Roam family hold the majority of the shares in the Roam Group. Their interest in road haulage continues to be particularly strong given the family's close connection with SRRT. As a result it is highly plausible that the shareholders may regard an airport purchase as straying too far from the groups original direction.

Feasibility

Feasibility asks whether a proposed strategy can be implemented and, in particular, if the organisation has adequate strategic capability to implement it. In order to understand whether a strategy is feasible it is important to consider the Roam Group's competencies.

The Roam Group clearly has built up a high level of expertise in the provision of road haulage services through the operation of SRRT and has extended its operations into warehousing. However, it has been unable to deploy these competencies as effectively at SRR. There is a danger that the acquisition of Godiva airport could lead to a similar situation – as the competencies required to run an airport do not exist within the Roam Group.

Conclusion

As the analysis indicates, the purchase of Godiva airport represents a poor investment for the Roam Group at the current time. The Roam Group does not possess the necessary competencies needed to undertake the proposed strategy. Although, the Roam Group are in a position to fund the acquisition, the impact that such a move would have on shareholders and the other group companies increases the undesirability of the proposal.

Part (b)

Low Price

Pursuing a low price strategy involves management's willingness to accept lower profit margins on the goods or services sold. The acceptability of such an approach to pricing may be linked to the organisation's ability to sell greater quantities of its goods/ services than competing firms or may be driven by the ability of other group companies to subside a particular business unit.

Cross-subsidise

As SRRT is part of a group this may allow a low price strategy to be implemented. SRW is generating positive returns which could be used to cross-subsidise SRRT selling its services at a lower price.

Gain market share

At the current time there is little scope for growth in the road haulage market. Since 2009 the market has only grown by 2.5%, meaning that continued growth can only be achieved by SRRT taking market share from competitors. A low price strategy may therefore help SRRT to undercut smaller rivals and drive them out of the market. SRRT appears to be well placed to resource and sustain a price war certainly in the short term.

Differentiation

Differentiation can be achieved in a number of ways including the creation of a product or service which is hard for competitors to copy, the exploitation of unique competencies or resources, and through re-investing profits.

Integrated service

SRRT may be in a position to differentiate its offering to those of it's competitors through the provision of a complete transport service which may help to reduce the desire of customers to switch transport providers. The Roam Group's involvement in road and rail transport coupled to warehousing gives a significant amount of flexibility to customers which is hard for competitors to copy in the short term. Imitation of such a service is likely to be possible but may prove prohibitive given the level of investment needed to match the Roam Group's current position.

New-Roamantics

The New-Roamantics fan club represents a key point of difference between SRRT and its rivals and should be exploited. The group's interest in SRRT has helped to make the company a household name. Customers are not likely to purchase services from SRRT solely because of the company's fan base, however, it may help to keep SRRT in the minds of potential customers. Indeed some potential customers may be keen to realise the indirect benefits of being associated with such a well known brand. The management at SRRT should therefore look to encourage the New-Roamantic movement to help support the company's image.

SECTION B

Question 2

Text reference. Business process change is covered in Chapters 9 and 10 of the BPP Study Text for exams from September 2015 to 31 August 2016.

Top tips. Part (a) of the question is made up of two components. Firstly, you are required to evaluate the current call handling process for SE's customer calls and secondly, you are asked to suggest how the process could be improved. In order to produce a meaningful evaluation it is of critical importance that you read through the detail in the scenario carefully, picking out those parts of the process which seem cumbersome or unnecessary. A good approach to adopt when faced with a swim lane diagram and the narrative detail around a process is to go through both of these at the same time. Taking a moment to read the detail while reviewing the visual aid should help you to better understand the stages involved in a process.

From an initial scan of the scenario information it is apparent that the current call handling process involves too many stages and too many handoffs between the sections featured, especially as the call centre has one fundamental purpose – to handle customer queries.

Clearly, any improvements you suggest should help to address the deficiencies you have identified as part of your evaluation of the current process. Practical suggestions here should address the need to reduce the number of handoffs between sections, for example providing SE customers with a direct, dedicated telephone number for each query type (technical, contracts and Stella support). There are a number of different points you could have made in answering this part of the question, some of these have been included in the solution below. If you made certain points in your answer which are not included in our solution this does not invalidate your response. Provided the points you made are legitimate you would have been given some credit. Above all you need to ensure that any suggestions you make are practical and relate to the call handling process. To avoid producing an answer which overlaps with part (b) it is important that you make a distinction between the two requirements. Part (a) is specifically focused on operational issues in the processes featured, whereas part (b) takes a strategic view as to whether the company featured should continue to outsource its customer call handling or bring it back in-house.

Part (b) required a discussion on whether SE should continue its outsourcing arrangement with TCG or whether the process should be brought in-house. This type of question requires a balanced answer, where you consider the advantages or disadvantages to SE of outsourcing contrasted with bringing the process in-house. The question scenario gives further information which you should have used to assess the financial case for outsourcing the process. While the financial considerations were important you need to avoid focusing only on the cost of outsourcing compared to the cost of in-house solution. The scenario information gave strong indications that there is a growing resistance in Arborium to companies outsourcing services to third parties overseas, coupled to the fact that SE is experiencing an increase in the number of customer complaints it receives concerning the current call handling process. These factors should have provided you with additional points for inclusion in your answer.

Easy marks. Part (b) of the question presented the opportunity to gain some easy marks provided you were confident in using the scenario information to assess the benefits to SE of continuing its outsourcing relationship contrasted against the case for bringing the process in-house.

Examiners comments. Part (a) required an evaluation of the current process for handling customer calls at TCG and required suggestions of improvements to the process. The examining team reported that 'generally, answers were better on suggestions for improvement than on the evaluation of the current process. Too much of the evaluation was general and did not use the data provided in the scenario. However, despite this, answers were generally quite good, suggesting that the scenario and the question requirements were both well understood.'

Part (b) required a discussion on whether SE should continue to outsource customer call handling or bring the process in-house. As the examining team's comments illustrate to score well on such questions it is important that you give sufficient consideration to both the financial and non-financial issues. 'Candidates should have been able to show that the financial case for outsourcing remained very strong. However, other factors, such as negative feedback from customers and the importance of service as a primary activity in the value chain, might suggest that non-financial factors might lead to the company bringing this process back in-house. This part of the question was worth 10 marks. Again, many answers were too general and did not use the data provided (or incorrectly used it) and so many of the points made in candidate answers were insubstantial. Candidates often claimed that 'outsourcing is generally cheaper' but did not offer evidence to support this from the actual scenario, even though the evidence was there.'

Marks

(a) 1 mark for each relevant point up to a maximum of 8 marks for
evaluation of the problem.
1 mark for each relevant point up to a maximum of 8 marks for
suggested improvements.

15

(b) 1 mark for each relevant point up to a maximum of 10 marks
1 mark will be allocated for the correct calculation of the daily cost of
delivering the service in-house

<u>10</u>
<u>25</u>

Part (a)

Evaluation of the process for handling SE's customer calls

The role of the supervisor

At present when a customer calls the SE call centre they initially speak to the TCG supervisor, who connects the call to the Stella support team. The supervisor has to distinguish which company the caller requires as TCG provides call centre services to a variety of companies. The role of the supervisor in the process fails to enhance the customer experience, and can be regarded as a non-value adding activity.

Reference and password

Customers contacting the call centre to discuss refunds and technical queries are required to provide their payment reference number or service contract number. Failure to supply these leads to the call being terminated. If correctly provided, the customer's details are retrieved, at this point the customer is expected to provide a password. Failure to provide the required password leads to the termination of the call. At present the caller is not made aware of the need for these items until partway through the call. Clearly, at present these items are requested too late in the process. Failure to complete the call wastes the customers' time and increases the waiting time for other customers attempting to get through to the call centre.

Cost of terminated calls

The daily cost to SE of calls not resolved as a result of customers failing to provide the reference and password is $172 per day, see Working 3. Failing to resolve customer queries increases the number of customer complaints SE receives.

Staffing levels

It would appear that the service contracts section is understaffed. At present there is only one operative designated to handling the 90 daily calls (15% of the 600 calls are for service contracts). Six operatives work in the technical support section and handle 60% of the queries (360 daily calls), and three operatives work in the Stella support section handling 25% of queries (150 daily calls). If comparable staffing levels to the two other SE sections were used then the service contract section should have the equivalent of one and a half operatives.

Bottleneck

There is evidence of a 'bottleneck' in the existing call handling process. At the current time all callers regardless of the section required are connected to one of the three operatives in the Stella support section before being redirected. This anomaly and the shortfall in staff in the service contracts section goes some way to explain the increase in the number of customer complaints because they increase the time taken to complete a query.

Solutions

Removal of the supervisor

SE could issue different telephone numbers for each of the three support sections via its website, in-store literature and product documentation. This would remove need for a TCG supervisor and help to speed up the time it takes

for the customer to get assistance. Such a move would also help enhance the image SE projects as three dedicated telephone numbers would give the impression to customers that they are actually dealing with SE and not a third party.

Reference and password details

SE should request the customer's payment/ service reference and password earlier in the call handling process. Callers requiring a refund or technical support should be made aware of the need for such items when they first make a call. This could be achieved through the use of an automated reminder on the call menu choice when the customer makes an initial enquiry. Furthermore, this information could also be displayed on SE's website.

In the event that the TCG supervisor role remains then such a reminder could be issued to customers at this point in the call. The use of memorable information could potentially be introduced as an alternative to passwords. In the event that a customer cannot remember their password the operative could request the customer's date of birth or mothers maiden name instead. This would avoid calls being terminated if the customer is unable to remember their password.

Automated telephone system

The call handling process could be further enhanced through the use of an automated call management system. Such a system would allow the caller to select the options from a call menu which would direct the call to the appropriate SE support section. This would help customers ensure that their call is handled by the required section.

Staffing levels and Multi-skilled operatives

TCG should be able to identify from historic call data the busiest call times in a typical week for each of the SE support sections. This data could be used to determine the number of workers needed at particular times. TCG could then flex the number of staff needed in a section to reflect the anticipated number of calls.

Although the feasibility of this option would need to be fully explored, there may be scope for TCG to train the operatives to deal with customer queries regardless of the SE support section required. This would serve to reduce the number of handoffs between sections and help simplify the complete process.

> **Tutorial note:** There were a range of valid points that you could have made here. Although, not mentioned in the answer above, it would have been appropriate to mention the introduction of a FAQs page on SE's website. Such a move would help to answer commonly asked customer queries thereby reducing the total number of calls received.

Working 1

Daily cost of customers failing to provide a reference number

TCG receives 600 calls a day from SE customers.

60% of customers call for with a technical query

25% of customers call for a refund

30% of customers do not know their payment/reference number

TCG charges SE $1 for every call taken (regardless of whether caller's issue is resolved)

Therefore:

600 calls a day X 85% X 30% X $1 = $153 per day (153 people a day do not know their reference number)

Working 2

Daily cost of customers failing to provide a password

5% of customers do not know their password

600 calls a day less 153 being those unresolved (W1) X 85% X 5% X $1 = $19 per day (19 people a day do not have their payment/reference number and password)

Working 3

Total cost of failing to provide a payment/ reference number and password

$153 (W1) + $19 (W2) = $172

BPP
LEARNING MEDIA

Part (b)

Outsourcing and TCG

At present TCG provides SE with a call handling service 24 hours a day, 7 days a week. In the following discussion it is assumed that SE require the service, (whether provided in-house or by a third party) to operate on the same 24/7 basis.

Financial considerations

Staffing costs

SE currently pays $600 a day to TCG for the provision of 10 operatives to manage the company's call centre operations. SE have determined that it would cost $50 to employ a worker with equivalent skills in Arborium to work an eight hour shift. In order to cover a 24 hour period this would cost $150 (3 employees at eight hours per shift × $50). In the event that SE employed 10 people this would generate a daily cost of $1,500. Based on this calculation alone it is evident that the decision to continue to outsource using TCG makes financial sense ($600 v $1,500).

> **Tutorial note:** It is not clear from the scenario whether the 10 staff that would be required by SE to operate the call centre in-house are available for an entire 24 hour period or whether their work would be split over the three eight hour shifts. In the event that the 10 members of staff were expected to operate the call centre over a 24 period this would in fact give a total daily cost of $500 and not $1500. Clearly, a daily cost of $500 would make bringing the process in-house more attractive when compared to the outsourced cost of $600.
>
> Had you arrived at a cost of $500 and recommended bringing the call centre in-house you would have gained the marks on offer.

Infrastructure costs and operational expenses

It is important to note that the above calculation does not take account of the required infrastructure that SE would need if the call handling process was brought back in-house. Expenditure will include the costs of purchasing or renting offices, telephones, desks and chairs. Operational expenses will include charges for electricity and heating, and property rental charges (in the event that office space is not purchased). The inclusion of these costs strengthens the financial case to maintain an outsourcing relationship with TCG.

Operational considerations

Process improvements

Before the decision is made on whether or not to continue with TCG, the management at SE should explore options for redesigning the current set up of the call handling service. Improvements to the documentation supplied to customers when they purchase a SE product may help to reduce the number of technical queries made. Furthermore, most companies have frequently asked question (FAQs) pages on their websites to assist customers with product queries, this is something SE could look to introduce.

There may be scope to direct customers (via the company website) that require a refund to their nearest SE store. While this would help reduce the demand for telephone queries, the benefits would need to be considered carefully against the impact on the customers' experience of purchasing from SE. After all the call centre deals with refund requests when the customer has made a purchase from the SE website, and has therefore purposefully avoided making the same purchase in one of SE's retail stores.

The management at SE could also consider whether customer requests for service contracts could be provided online. Clearly, requests for service contracts of a more complex nature are likely to require a dialogue between the customer and SE, and as a result may reduce the appropriateness of moving this service online.

Such operational improvements at SE could reduce the need for TCG to have the same number of call handling operatives working in the centre. Any cost savings here could be passed on to SE and would strengthen the argument for retaining a relationship with TCG. Equally, in the event that the number of customer calls could be lowered through the introduction of the improvements mentioned above there would be less need for customer service operators, meaning that SE could look to bring the call centre back in-house if the cost savings were deemed financially viable.

Value chain considerations

Customer experience

An important consideration for the management at SE concerns the impact that the current outsourcing arrangement with TCG is having on the customer experience. Service is a primary activity in the value chain, and can be particularly important in shaping how a company's offering is perceived by customers.

The number of customers complaining about not being able to understand the accents of the people working in the TCG call centre is rising, coupled to complaints that queries take too long to process. Furthermore, there is a growing resistance in Arborium to services being outsourced and offshored to companies like TCG. In the event that SE continues to outsource this increases the risk that some customers may decide to switch where they purchase their electrical goods. As a result SE could look to bring the call centre operations in-house staffed by people from Arborium. The management at SE could use this opportunity as a PR exercise, promoting the company as a supporter of employment in Arborium.

Conclusion

From a financial perspective, SE's outsourcing deal with TCG offers a lower cost solution than managing the call handling process in-house. It is evident that SE could look to make the current call centre arrangement with TCG more cost effective through instigating a series of process improvements. However, the management at SE need to consider the longer term implications of continuing to use TCG as the quality of the customer experience appears to be worsening. As a result there may be scope for SE to use the current situation to bring the call centre back in-house to Arborium on the grounds of doing the 'right thing' to appeal to customers resistant to dealing with overseas third party service providers.

Question 3

Top tips. Part (a) of the question asked for an analysis of how TKP itself and the two projects featured in the scenario demonstrate the principles of effective risk management. In practical terms to score well on this question it is vitally important that you identify the points in the scenario which demonstrate effective risk management and avoid simply explaining the term with little application to the scenario.

This question illustrates the importance of studying the whole P3 syllabus, as risk management is one of those areas which has not been as regularly examined as other areas. Failure to have devoted sufficient time to understanding the key components of risk management prior to attempting the question would have put you at a significant disadvantage and may have restricted your options when choosing your section B questions in the exam.

A good approach to adopt before starting the question is to consider what constitutes effective risk management. You may recall from your studies that risk management involves a series of stages (including identifying and assessing risks, planning and recording risk responses and taking steps to eliminate such risks) you could have looked to use these in structuring your answer. However, if you were unable to remember these, it would have been just as effective to think about what you would need to do manage a given risk. Ultimately, risk management is concerned with identifying the risks associated with undertaking a particular project, and putting in place policies to eliminate or reduce them.

In the suggested solution below, our answer has been built around three key headings which cover: risk assessment, risk management strategies and the continuous nature of risk management. In order to produce a good answer here you need provide a little detail under each heading about what constitutes each of the risk management stages you mention. It is, however, of critical importance that you link the theory back to TKP and the two projects. When considering appropriate risk management strategies you could have used the four strategies of avoidance, transference, reduction and acceptance, and then applied the theory to TKP. For example, it was appropriate to mention that TKP's use of a professional liability insurance policy was an example of risk transference.

A good way to conclude your answer was to highlight that effective risk management does not just cease when all current risks have been identified and recorded. Risk management is a continuous process and as such will require TKP to continue to monitor the risks the two projects face.

The requirement for part (b) was split into two parts. Firstly, you were asked to describe the principles of the triple constraint (scope, time and cost) in relation to project work and secondly to discuss its implications for the two projects featured.

The triple constraint in project work is covered in Chapter 13 of your BPP Study Text for paper P3. This required you to provide a brief description of each element of the triple constraint. As you can see from the solution below we have also mentioned the 'fourth constraint' of quality which is sometimes included in such discussions. This was a prime opportunity for you to display your knowledge.

The second part of the question required you to apply your knowledge to the two projects under review. It should have been clear that the constraints of each project were significantly different. For example, the issue of time in order to complete project 1 was not as critical as in project 2 where a launch party for a new product had been heavily publicised has occurring on a particular date.

Examiner's comments. The examining team reported that most candidates that attempted part (a) answered the question relatively well. 'There were clear links between the elements of risk management and the circumstances described in the scenario. However, some candidates spent too much time here framing general answers on good project management, which was not what was required.'

Although, there were 10 marks available for part (b) this requirement was not well answered. 'Too many candidates focused on describing the three elements of the triple constraint, with little linkage to the projects described in the scenario. When links were made, they were often wrong, with most candidates failing to correctly identify the main driver within each project (cost, time) and how these impinged upon the other two facets of the triple constraint. Overall, candidates did not score well in this part question.'

Marks

(a)   1 mark for each relevant point up to 15 marks

15

(b)   1 mark for each relevant point up to 2 marks for principles
        1 mark for each relevant point up to a maximum of 4 marks for each project.

10
25

Part (a)

Risk assessment

Effective risk management involves a series of stages some of which are considered here in relation to TKP and the two projects under review. Initial risk management involves the identification, and assessment of risk. Risk assessment is largely focused on determining the probability that a risk event will occur and the consequences that may arise as a result. A variety of assessment techniques can be used to analyse the likelihood of a risk event occurring, including subjective measures such as exercising personal judgement and the use of statistical methods.

TKP adopted a statistical approach to risk assessment in project 1 when they analysed the failure rate of software companies operating in Zeeland. In the previous year 10% of software companies with annual revenues of between $3m and $10m ceased trading. Determining this percentage and comparing it against the 1% failure rate of software companies with revenues of more than $100m per year led to TKP's client selecting a software solution from a large, well-known supplier. Although the risk was not completely removed, as large companies also fail, the chances of a well-known software supplier ceasing to trade are significantly reduced.

Risk management strategies

Once risks have been identified and assessed appropriate risk management strategies can be deployed. Dealing with risk involves four strategies; avoidance, reduction, transference and acceptance.

Avoidance

A risk avoidance strategy involves avoiding those activities that carry risk. In the case of project 1, TKP's client could have avoided the risk of choosing a software supplier likely to fail by simply not making a software purchase at all. This risk could also have been avoided by TKP's client had they ordered a bespoke, in-house software solution instead. It is evident that TKP itself also pursues a risk avoidance approach as it only undertakes 'projects in the business culture which it understands'. As a result TKP does not undertake assignments outside of Zeeland.

Transference

Risk transference involves passing risk on to another party. This is often achieved through the use of insurance. TKP itself has taken out a consultant's liability insurance policy to protect the firm from claims up to the value of $10,000,000 for issuing poor advice. Due to the inability to assess the likely impact of potential future claims the pursuit of a risk transference strategy using an insurance company seems highly appropriate. Although TKP is liable to pay the insurance premiums when they fall due these costs are clearly outweighed by the benefit and peace of mind that such insurance policies offer the firm's management.

It is also evident that TKP transferred risk in project 2. The developer of the iProjector sought TKP's advice on establishing a worldwide patent on the device to reduce the risk that competitors will copy the product. Due to a lack of specialism in this area TKP referred the client to a company with expertise in patent protection, thereby transferring the provision of the advice to a third party.

Reduction (mitigation)

Risk reduction is appropriate in cases where a risk cannot be removed but the likelihood of the loss occurring can be reduced in some way. In project 2, TKP has identified that the manufacturer of the chip used in the client's iProjector product has been trading for less than three years and has a very inexperienced management team. To avoid future problems resulting from this TKP has suggested that an escrow agreement be established between the client and the chip manufacturer. This is an example of a risk reduction strategy, as an escrow agreement would require the chip manufacturer to place the design details of the chip with a suitable third party. In the event that the chip manufacturer ceased trading TKP's client would still be able to gain access to the chip used in producing the iProjector. The nature of this risk to TKP's client is likely to be high as failure of the supplier could critically damage production of the iProjector.

As a short term risk management strategy TKP has also suggested to the client that significant quantities of the chip be held in inventory to alleviate concerns over the company's supply chain.

TKP are also pursuing a risk reduction strategy in project 1, in response to concerns over the quality of data being migrated between the existing time recording software and the new application. In the event that the quality of the data migrated is poor, TKP has established a 'strategy for data cleansing' to avoid future problems when new system comes into use.

Acceptance

A risk acceptance strategy is where a potential risk is accepted in the hope or expectation that the incidence and consequences can be coped with if necessary. Risk acceptance is usually appropriate where the likelihood of a risk occurring is deemed low or the consequences of it happening are insignificant or if it is not possible to mitigate / transfer the risk. In project 2, the client is 'concerned that a major telephone producer will launch a competitive product with functionality and features similar to the iProjector'. Although this risk is of justifiable concern to the client, in reality there is very little that can be done to stop a competitor producing a similar product to the iProjector. In such cases the only realistic option here is to accept the risk.

Continuous process

Once various risk strategies has been determined, they are then planned and put into action. However, this is not the end of the process as risk management is an ongoing activity. Procedures are necessary to regularly review and reassess previously documented risks. In the case of project 2, the risk that the chip manufacturer could cease trading should be closely monitored. TKP's client may wish to make use of a company checking agency. Organisations such as Company Check in the UK provide data on companies using a variety of sources, including local Gazettes and Companies House. The agency could monitor the manufacturer's financial performance, and notify TKP's client of any significant deterioration in it. This will allow TKP's client to take appropriate action to protect its interest. For example in the event that the chip manufacturer went into terminal decline, it could begin the process of gaining access to the chip design details held under the escrow agreement.

Most organisations maintain a risk register as a means of recording and monitoring identified risks. Both of TKP's clients could look to use a risk register to assign the management of a particular risk to a given individual; such individuals are sometimes referred to as a 'risk owner'.

Part (b)

Triple constraint

Scope, time and cost are normally regarded as the yardsticks against which project success is measured. These elements may also be referred to as the triple constraint.

The scope of a project means that all the work that was specified has been done and all the deliverables have, in fact, been delivered.

Cost means that the project should be completed without exceeding the authorised expenditure.

Time is concerned with the point at which the project should be delivered. The progress of the project must follow the planned process, so that the 'result' is ready for use at the agreed date.

In some cases it may be appropriate to add a fourth constraint; quality. Quality means that the end result conforms to the project specification and is deemed 'fit for purpose'; in essence the result achieves what the project was intended to.

These factors all have an impact on how a project should be managed.

Project 1

TKP's client in Project 1 has made it company policy of 'never re-visiting its business cases once they have been accepted' as this is regarded as being essential for 'effective cost control'. The budget of the project is fixed, which indicates that cost is the key constraint in Project 1. Ensuring that actual costs remain in line with the budget is more important than the scope of the project and the time it takes to complete.

There is no mention that time is immediately critical to the success of the project, this is supported by the fact that the completion date of May 2015 is an estimate and not a set deadline. Furthermore, as Project 1 is an internal business project, any delays to completion are unlikely to have an adverse impact on customers.

The impact that the project has on employees will vary. The primary users of the software include the account managers and those workers in the project support office. In the event that the project's completion were delayed these individuals would be directly affected. However, most employees are unlikely to be affected at all by the switch to the new system as they will simply engage with a 'bright new user interface' when the system goes live.

In many ways the scope of the project is set, as the software package will simply deliver the expected features which make-up the application, in this case the ability to record time and cost data. The quality of the end result should also be good as the client has simply purchased a software package used by many other companies.

Project 2

By contrast, the launch date of the iProjector product in Project 2 has been announced and this therefore means that the project deadline is fixed. This indicates that time is the key constraint in Project 2. The makers of the iProjector have heavily promoted the launch and have even gone to the lengths of booking a prestigious venue to host 400 attendees at the products launch party. Although, formally launched with orders being taken on 1 May 2015, the iProjector does not ship to customers until June 2015. This raises some interesting considerations around the scope of the iProjector project as the product at the current time is not quite finished. Due to the shorter time frame it is possible that the iProjector displayed at the launch party may not quite be the finished item if minor defects still remain. Clearly, such quality issues will need to be explained to those individuals attending the launch in order to avoid an embarrassing situation where those in attendance refuse to place an order for the product.

To ensure such a situation does not arise, it is important that the main features of the iProjector are ready for the launch party. Features here are likely to include the ability of the iProjector device to display a high definition image. In order to ensure a successful launch of the product the company should make sufficient funds available to address any technical deficiencies as soon as possible as time and not cost is the key constraint.

Question 4

Text reference. Linear regression is covered in Chapter 2 of the BPP Study Text for exams from September 2015 to 31 August 2016.

Top tips. Part (a). It is important that you remember that Porter's Value Chain looks at operational activities within a company and does not focus on the strategic choices of the entity. For example, the fact that the Milton Plant featured in the question is only concerned with the production of moist pet food is not a weakness in its value chain. Furthermore, you are only asked to consider the Milton plant from the perspective of the primary Value Chain activities. As a result any attempt to analyse the plant using the support activities of the Value Chain model would gain you no marks and only wastes valuable time. As we have seen in other questions a good approach when applying a model to a scenario is to use key parts of the model to help structure your answer, in this case using the primary activities as headings. When faced with a question like this it is particularly important that you go through the scenario carefully. Most students find it useful to identify and classify the different types of primary activities by annotating the question scenario as they read through. This approach is particularly useful as it should cut down on the need to re-read the scenario information.

This question also required you to evaluate the strengths and weaknesses identified in the Milton plant's primary activities. You need to remember that both strengths and weaknesses are internal factors and do not come from the external environment like opportunities and threats. Clearly, to talk about hypothetical opportunities and threats not featured in the scenario would gain no credit. When considering strengths and weaknesses it is often useful as you read through the scenario to ask yourself; What do Noble Pets and in particular the Milton plant do well? What is it good at? What is it not so good at? What problems does the Milton plant currently face?

The scenario included competitor cost data which should have helped to give you something to talk about. For example, how do the Milton plant's costs compare to its competitors? Does this data indicate any potential strengths or weaknesses?

Such prompts may help you to generate points when considering the different primary activities.

Part (b) was broken down into two separate requirements, it is therefore important that you deal with each in turn and think carefully about how they relate to each other as to avoid making the same point in both (i) and (ii). The first requirement asks you to analyse trends in the pet food industry, whereas part (ii) is looking specifically at Noble's forecast and the implications of that forecast in how it organises its production capacity.

In Part b (i) it should have been clear that you needed to use the information provided by the Pet Food Industry Group at this point. As there are only 5 marks available for this part of the question it is important that you do not get too bogged down in the detail. Before you put pen to paper you should take a moment to familiarise yourself with the data provided. At this point it should be instantly clear that demand for moist pet food is declining, while demand for dry pet food is increasing. This should form the basis of your answer. In our solution below we have structured our answer in three parts by considering trends in the moist and the dry pet food market, as well as considering trends in the market as a whole. Structuring your work in such a manner should help to keep you focused on the requirement, avoiding the temptation to write too much.

Part (b) (ii) is likely to be more challenging. The final requirement is formed of two parts firstly you are asked to forecast demand for moist pet food for the next three years using the regression formula given and secondly to comment on the validity and implications of your forecast. In order to make a reasonable attempt at this part of the question you need to understand the component parts of the regression formula and how they interact. There is very little need to perform lots of calculations as the question provides you with the values of a, b and r.

To score well you need to comment on the forecast demand that you calculate, at this point you need to ensure that you comment on the reasonableness of your forecast and highlight any implications that this has for the future of Noble Pets and the Milton plant.

Easy marks. Part (a) represented the opportunity to score some easy marks. There were a number of fairly obvious weaknesses highlighted in the scenario, so provided you read through the detail carefully you should have been able to use these when answering the question.

Marking scheme

			Marks
(a)	1 mark for each relevant point up to a maximum of 15 marks		15
(b)	(i)	1 mark for each relevant point up to a maximum of 5 marks	
	(ii)	1 mark for each relevant point up to a maximum of 5 marks.	
		This may include 1 mark for arithmetically correct forecasts and 1 mark	
		for explaining the coefficient of determination.	10
			25

Part (a)

Evaluation of the strengths and weaknesses of the Milton plant

Porter's Value Chain analysis focuses on those activities which go into providing a product or service. Value Chain analysis consists of support activities and primary activities. Primary activities consist of five elements; inbound logistics, operations, outbound logistics, marketing and sales, and service.

Inbound logistics

Inbound logistics involve receiving, handling and storing inputs into the production system. Activities commonly undertaken involve warehousing, transportation and inventory control.

At the Milton plant, inbound logistics are focused on getting the raw foodstuffs and empty unlabelled cans needed into the plant prior to the production of pet food. Milton appears to be paying competitive prices (15 cents per unit) for both raw foodstuffs and empty cans compared to the costs incurred by Competitors A, B and C. As a result Noble Pets' procurement process can be regarded as a value chain strength.

By contrast the transport costs paid to get goods to the Milton plant are higher than all three of the main competitors. The Milton plant incurs transport costs for goods inwards of 15 cents per unit produced compared to the 10 cents paid by Competitors A and B and the 12 cents paid by Competitor C respectively. This is likely to be due to the location of the Milton plant, which unlike the competitors' plants is not positioned near the motorway network. The positioning of the Milton plant can be regarded as being a significant weakness as 'trucks transporting goods in and out of the plant have to negotiate relatively minor rural roads', which coupled to road congestion in Milton town centre is likely to cause reduced fuel economy of delivery lorries.

Operations

Operations are focused on converting resource inputs into a final product. Operations at the Milton plant are centred on producing pet food. Activities involve the cooking of raw food stuffs, and canning and labelling of the final product.

At present the Milton plant incurs 25 cents of direct labour cost per unit produced, which is broadly in line with Noble Pets competitor costs. However, its production costs are higher, with the Milton plant paying 30 cents per unit compared to Competitor B which incurs the lowest cost among the 4 competitors of 20 cents per unit. This difference is likely to be due in part to the age of the technology used by Noble Pets in canning its products as these are now becoming increasingly inefficient. The Milton plant was initially set up in 1930 and was subsequently updated in 1970 with new canning and labelling technology, however further expansions and upgrades have been prevented since this time due to the development of residential housing around the plant.

As most of the equipment in the plant is now at least 40 years old it is highly likely that the Milton plant will fail to achieve further economies of scale in its production operations.

Outbound logistics

Outbound logistics is concerned with storing the product and its distribution to customers. In the case of the Milton plant distribution is focused on getting finished products to a number of wholesalers and supermarkets. The associated costs of distributing products to the end customer are illustrated by the transport costs outward. In respect of the Milton plant the transport costs incurred are higher (10 cents per unit) than those paid by competitors who pay between 5 to 8 cents per unit. As mentioned earlier (in relation to inbound logistics) this is likely to be due in part to the type of roads around the Milton plant which contributes to increased costs.

This situation is compounded further as Noble Pets are required to use the less cost-effective 36 tonne trucks when making deliveries to wholesalers and supermarkets in Milton town centre. This is due to a ban on the use of larger, more efficient 44 tonne trucks in the town. By contrast Noble Pets' competitors are better positioned to make deliveries using the larger vehicles as the location of their factories do not need to pass through Milton town as regularly.

Noble Pets logistics operation is also disadvantaged as residents in Milton have started to complain that the use of even the 36 tonne trucks is keeping them awake at night. This could cause Noble Pets reputational damage in the longer term if more appropriate delivery trucks are not introduced.

Marketing and sales

Marketing and sales involves informing customers about the product and persuading them to buy it. Such activity usually entails various forms of advertising and promotion. Noble Pets is renowned for its 'clever marketing campaigns which stress the importance of giving your pet good food'. As a result marketing can be regarded as being a significant strength to the company. Noble Pets charges a higher selling price per unit that Competitors A, B and C. This is important as price is an essential element in marketing products. The fact that Noble Pets charges customers a higher price helps to support the reputation it has built for selling quality products. This message is somewhat reinforced by the companies name 'Noble', which provides connotations of a superior, better quality item. Despite a higher selling price the Milton plant still only generates a profit margin of 30 cents per six can pack. This is exactly the same as the firm's competitors who have lower costs.

Service

Service in this context commonly refers to after sales service, following a purchase of a product. Activities here usually relate to installing products, repairing them, upgrading them and providing spare parts. At Noble Pets the provision of free fact guides and a website dedicated to giving advice on pet ownership and nutrition can be classified as the service element in the value chain.

The advice presented by Noble Pets appears to be unbiased, however, the recommended solutions to pet problems often involve Noble Pets products in some way. As a result this increases the likelihood that customers will purchase Noble Pets products and not those of competitors. Service can therefore be regarded as a significant strength at Noble Pets.

Part (b)(i)

Trends in the pet food industry

Moist pet food

The information provided by the Pet Food Industry Group makes it clear that sales of moist pet food have been steadily decreasing between 2007 and 2013. In 2007 55.89% of all pet food produced in Brellia was of the moist variety, by 2013 this had fallen by almost 10 percentage points to 46.34% (see **Working 1**). The period between 2007 and 2010 saw the greatest decline in moist pet food sales. Since this time the decline in sales has slowed.

Dry pet food

By contrast dry pet food has experienced a gradual increase in sales. Between 2007 and 2013 sales of dry pet food as a percentage of all the pet food produced increased from 44.11% to 53.66% (**see Working 2**). The boost in sales of dry pet food has most likely been supported by a growing preference among pet owners to use dry pet food as it does not smell (unlike moist pet food) and can be left in the pet's bowl for longer.

Overall market

As illustrated by **Working 3** the total amount of pet food produced between 2007 and 2011 fell. In 2013 total pet food production rose to 669,000 tonnes, the highest level since 2007. This indicates that the pet food market has reached the maturity stage of the industry lifecycle. The market is dominated by four entities. Between them these four share 90% of the market, with Noble Pets holding a 30% share. As a result growth can only be achieved by taking market share from each other. Competitive rivalry is likely to be intense amongst the market participants given low customer switching costs.

Working 1

Moist food

Year	Moist pet food as a % of total pet food produced	Production (000s tonnes)	% change year on year in production
2007	55.89% (370/662 × 100)	370	
2008	53.27% (350/657 × 100)	350	-5.4% (350 – 370/370 × 100)
2009	50.77% (331/652 × 100)	331	-5.4% (331 – 350/350 × 100)
2010	49.69% (325/654 × 100)	325	-1.8% (325 – 331/331 × 100)
2011	48.02% (315/656 × 100)	315	-3.1% (315 – 325/325 × 100)
2012	46.90% (310/661 × 100)	310	-1.6% (310 – 315/315 × 100)
2013	46.34% (310/669 × 100)	310	0% (310 – 310/310 × 100)

Working 2

Dry food

Year	Dry pet food as a % of total pet food produced	Production (000s tonnes)	% change year on year in production
2007	44.11% (292/662 × 100)	292	
2008	46.73% (307/657 × 100)	307	5.1% (307 – 292/292 × 100)
2009	49.23% (321/652 × 100)	321	4.5% (321 – 307/307 × 100)
2010	50.31% (329/654 × 100)	329	2.5% (329 – 321/321 × 100)
2011	51.98% (341/656 × 100)	341	3.6% (341 – 329/329 × 100)
2012	53.10% (351/661 × 100)	351	2.9% (351 – 341/341 × 100)
2013	53.66% (359/669 × 100)	359	2.3% (359 – 351/351 × 100)

Working 3

Year	Total production (000s tonnes)
2007	662
2008	657
2009	652
2010	654
2011	656
2012	661
2013	669

(ii) **Regression analysis for moist pet food sales**

There are no marks available for stating the key elements of the linear regression analysis formula. This has been included as a learning aid when reviewing the solution below.

Linear regression analysis formula: $Y = a + bx$

Y is the dependent variable (in this case moist pet food volume is dependent on the independent variable)

X is the independent variable (time)

a is the intercept of the line on the y axis

b is the gradient of the line

Forecast demand for the next three years

Using the linear regression analysis provided at Noble Pets:

$Y = 369.5714 - 9.86x$

As 'b' is denoted by a negative figure (-9.86) this indicates a downwards slope of the curve. In order to forecast the demand for moist pet food over the three years from 2013 we change the value attached to each year. As 2013 was year 7 in respect of x (the independent variable), 2014 will become year 8, 2015 becomes year 9 and 2016 becomes year 10. These figures can then be used to forecast demand for each year as follows:

2014 (Year 8)

$369.5714 - (9.86 \times 8) = 291$

2015 (Year 9)

$369.5714 - (9.86 \times 9) = 281$

2016 (Year 10)

$369.5714 - (9.86 \times 10) = 271$

Comment

The values calculated in the working appear to be too low given that demand in 2011 was 315,000 tonnes and 310,000 tonnes in 2012 and 2013. As a result these demand forecasts do not appear realistic.

The correlation coefficient r is negative (-0.94432) this is in line with expectations given the decline in the production of moist pet food. The coefficient of determination is the square of the correlation coefficient. It measures the proportion of the total variation in the value of y that can be explained by variations in the value x. In this case the coefficient of determination is 0.89174, this means that 89% of the variation in demand for moist pet food can be explained by the passage of time (which is quite a high correlation). It should however be noted that time alone is unlikely to be the only factor contributing to such variations. Factors including opposing moves by competitors and buyer behaviour are likely to have also had an impact.

Implications

Estimates of demand figures over the next three years appear more likely to be closer to 300,000 tonnes than to those forecast in the linear regression, given the gradual decrease in the decline for moist pet food up until 2013. The management at Noble Pets will need to consider the impact that demand at this level would have on any future investment in the Milton factory. In the event that Noble Pets maintains its 30% market share it should have demand for at least 90,000 tonnes (30% × 300,000 tonnes) of moist pet food.

At present Noble Pets two other plants have a combined annual maximum production capacity of 40,000 tonnes, meaning that the Milton plant would have demand for around 50,000 tonnes per annum over the period 2014-2016.

ACCA's exam answers:
June and December 2014

June 2014 exam – ACCA's exam answers

1   (a)   Introduction

This first section of the required report analyses the internal competencies of ReInk (in terms of its strengths and weaknesses) and the external environment which the company currently operates in. This environment creates opportunities for, and threats to, the organisation.

Strengths

Technological expertise is a significant strength of the company. It has successfully developed an innovative process for cheaply and successfully refilling ink cartridges. The technical elements of this process have been patented, which gives the company a further six years protection. The technical expertise of Dexter Black is acknowledged by his staff and his competitors. Many of the senior technical employees have been attracted to ReInk by the opportunity to work with an acknowledged expert in the field. Most of the skilled, experienced staff still remain at ReInk, although many are now seeking job opportunities elsewhere (see weaknesses).

The long-term contract with the government Department of Revenue Collections (DoRC) is an important asset. As well as providing 20% of the company's revenues, it also helps promote the legitimacy of ReInk as a significant and reliable supplier. Selling into other government departments may be a significant opportunity (see opportunities)

Location: Although ReInk is a high technology company, its operations are in a declining industrial town and are relatively cheap. Indeed, Dexter was originally attracted to the town by government grants and a rent-free period. Although this has now expired, the rent remains low. Furthermore, property prices in the area are also cheap, and the area offers a good standard of living. This means that staff can be attracted by relatively modest salaries, as one commented, 'I took a pay cut to come here. But I can now afford a bigger house and my children can breathe fresh country air.' In a market place where companies primarily compete on price, low production costs are important.

Weaknesses

The major weakness which has to be immediately addressed is the *financial state of the company*. Although ReInk is making a small operating profit, it is undermined by the need to service a considerable debt. The recent decision by Firmsure bank to reduce the company's overdraft facility has created a cash flow crisis which threatens the continued existence of the company. Capital needs to be injected into the company so that it can meet next month's payroll obligations.

Weak management team: The technological expertise of Dexter has been acknowledged. However, he has little commercial expertise or experience and the directors he has appointed to address this weakness have failed to deliver. The technologists at the company also have little faith in their management team, claiming that the sales director 'does not really understand the product' and the HR director 'clearly has no experience in dealing with professional staff'. The overall competence of the management team can be classified as a company weakness.

Demotivated staff: The employees are proud of their achievements and respect the technological expertise of Dexter. However, the attitude of senior management and the obvious financial problems of the company have combined to demotivate and demoralise them. A poorly thought out programme of cost cutting and staff regrading has compounded this attitude, and many are resigned to the company failing and are actively looking for other jobs.

The final weakness concerns *poor brand awareness*. Although ReInk is a technological leader, the public has little knowledge of its services and capabilities. Marketing has focused on the website, to the detriment of all other channels, where the company is up against competitors who appear to offer similar services and also have very similar trading names.

Opportunities

The continued decline of the economy provides a significant opportunity for ReInk. Both domestic and commercial users will be looking to reduce their printing costs and so the market place should be growing. Indeed, ReInk will have to monitor the economy to detect any upturn which could adversely affect the demand for its product.

Increased awareness of the need to reuse and recycle products should also provide the company with significant sales opportunities. The number of 'green consumers' is growing within the country. These consumers may have particular concerns about using printer cartridges which can only be used once, or which are expensive to recycle.

Government contracts: The economic problems in the country have accentuated the need for government departments to show value-for-money, as well as demonstrating excellent reuse and recycling practices.

Threats

Legal threats: It is important for the organisation to continually scan the legal environment to identify potential threats. Original Equipment Manufacturers (OEMs) have failed in their attempts to make refilling their products illegal. However, they continue to lobby political parties to change the law, citing their need for income from printer consumables to fund their investment in advances in printer technology. The company also has to be aware of threats to their patented process, or indeed to patents which might threaten their competitive edge.

Technical threats: Threats will continue to emerge from new technology. These threats might be to produce reusable ink services at a lower cost, or indeed to remove the need for ink replacement all together. The printer industry is very technology driven and ReInk will have to continuously monitor new innovations and product announcements to see if its services and products are threatened.

Competitive rivalry: The print consumables industry is very competitive. Entry costs into the industry are relatively low, and companies largely compete on price. This is partly why OEMs, with their higher costs, find it difficult to compete in this market. Consequently, they largely compete on quality and the generation of fear amongst consumers that unauthorised products could damage their printers, and, if they do, their printer warranty will be invalid. Thus it is an extremely competitive environment, with relatively low brand loyalty. If the potential damage to printers is overlooked, then there are no switching costs in moving to a different consumables supplier.

Finally, *the government is considering privatising the DoRC.* This could jeopardise the continuation of the contract to supply this department with reusable ink products and services, on which ReInk is highly dependent as it contributes 20% of its revenue.

In summary, the company is operating in a very competitive industry where OEMs also compete aggressively on non-price criteria. However, economic and environmental issues provide ReInk with opportunities for growth if they can properly harness their strengths and address the financial and management weaknesses of the company.

(b)   Introduction

The second part of this report looks at the contextual features which will have to be taken into consideration if strategic change is to be successfully implemented at ReInk.

Time: refers to the amount of time available to implement change. An organisation which faces immediate problems has a quite different context for change than one which is stable enough to be able to plan carefully for incremental change over a number of years. ReInk has pressing financial problems and so Vi Ventures (VV) will have to move quickly to make their investment. However, once that investment is made, VV will then have some time to make the changes necessary to address the financial performance of ReInk. For example, investing in initiatives to increase brand awareness and increase sales which will increase the company's operating profit.

Preservation: In most change situations there is a need to preserve some elements of the current organisation. In particular, the change will have to safeguard the competencies which are vital if the change is to succeed. In the case of ReInk, these are the skills and experience of the technologists. These employees are key to the success of the company, but have become demotivated and restless, and some are actively looking for other jobs. If VV makes their proposed investment in ReInk, then they must move swiftly to reassure the senior technical staff and dissuade them from leaving the company.

Diversity: Diversity refers to *diversity of experience.* Change can be assisted by a significant degree of diversity of experience, views and opinions within the organisation. It is hampered by a homogenous view, formed from pursuing the same strategy for years. The latter seems more likely at ReInk. The focus has been on technical excellence and innovation. There are no clear groups offering a different perspective. If the proposed investment does take place, then VV can expect some resistance to change as they bring in new ideas and directions.

Capability: Capability concerns the experience the organisation has in managing change. Some organisations have experience of effectively managing change and also have a workforce which has readily accepted and implemented these changes. At ReInk, the opposite appears to apply. The management team has been unable to formulate any changes which have improved the financial performance of the company. Moreover, the changes they have implemented have not been accepted by the workforce and indeed have led to a fall in staff motivation. VV's experience of implementing change will be an important capability which they will bring to ReInk.

Capacity: Change programmes require management and financial resources. Capacity for change is concerned with whether the organisation has sufficient resources to effect the required change. In some circumstances, the organisation might have the *capability* to undertake the change, but they do not have the resources (*capacity*) to carry it out. At ReInk, the current management do not have the capability or the capacity. VV will have to invest financial and management resources to successfully implement strategic change.

Readiness: Readiness for change refers to how changes will be welcomed in the organisation. There may be certain employee groups who are resistant to change and will hamper the progress of change programmes. This appears unlikely at ReInk. The technologists are likely to positively embrace change as they are very disillusioned with the expertise of the current management team. VV should have little problem in convincing this group about the need for change, particularly as VV will be anxious that their competencies are *preserved* within the company. The most difficult group might be the current management team. Except for Dexter, it seems unlikely that they will have a role in the future. VV should be aware of this and ensure that the acquisition takes place in a way which does not alienate this group. Otherwise, the investment may not go ahead, as the management team protect their position, even if this is at the long-term detriment of the company.

Power: For change to be successful there has to be someone in the organisation who has the power to effect the desired changes. This again will influence the terms associated with VV's proposed investment. Given the situation, they need to be in a position in ReInk where they have such power, unencumbered by the current managing director or current members of the management team. They have to have an appropriate shareholder structure in place as part of the investment agreement, otherwise they may not be in a position to bring in the changes which their competencies and finances should allow.

Scope: A proposed change may just need to realign the organisation within the current organisational beliefs or assumptions. Alternatively, it may require fundamental transformational change. *Transformational change* is usually associated with an elemental change in strategic direction. The scope of change is often associated with the nature of change. *Incremental change* takes place over a longer period of time, *'big bang'* takes place very quickly, and is typically needed when the organisation is facing crisis or needs to change direction very quickly. The scope and nature of change can be represented in the following table:

Nature of the change		Scope of the change	
		Realignment	Transformation
	Incremental	Adaptation	Evolution
	Big Bang	Reconstruction	Revolution

VV probably needs to implement **Reconstruction** change at ReInk. This type of change is rapid and usually brings about a great deal of upheaval, but it does not fundamentally change the paradigm of the organisation. It is typical of a turnaround situation where there is a need for major structural changes to deal with a decline in financial performance.

In summary, VV needs to be aware of the context of change at ReInk before it finalises its investment and the terms of that investment. It needs to ensure that it has the *power* to speedily implement the required changes and *preserve* the competencies of the company. It will bring important *capabilities, capacity* and *diversity* of experience to a company which lacks them. In return, it will find a company which generally is *ready for change* and should welcome it, although vested interests in the current management team will have to be carefully considered during negotiations on the terms of the proposed investment. Finally, it will need to *reconstruct* ReInk, quickly implementing the required changes, but not fundamentally changing the nature and direction of the business.

(c) Introduction

This final section of the report uses a TOWS matrix to generate strategic options. Each quadrant of the matrix is used to identify options which address a different combination of internal factors (strengths and weaknesses) and external factors (opportunities and threats).

External factors	Internal factors	
	Strengths (S)	Weaknesses (W)
Opportunities (O)	SO	WO
Threats (T)	ST	WT

TOWS analysis of ReInk:

SO – this quadrant is used to generate options which use the strengths of the business to take advantage of identified opportunities. The government of the country is committed to environmental policies and demonstrating value-for-money. ReInk has a product which fulfils both of these criteria and it also has a track record in the sector, through its contract with the DoRC. A strategy of focusing on a market niche of government and public sector organisations may be very lucrative and generate good short-term results. It will take time to address the weakness of brand awareness (see WO), but focusing sales and marketing on a well-defined business-to-business sector should be much easier.

WO – is concerned with options which take advantage of opportunities by overcoming weaknesses in the organisation. The growth of the green consumer has been recognised as an opportunity. In general, individual consumers are increasingly keen to recycle products, particularly if it also brings economic benefits, as they are likely to be affected by living in a country which is experiencing continuing economic decline. ReInk can offer reusability and cost savings. However, its brand awareness is low. Addressing this weakness should allow it to take advantage of the opportunities offered by the green consumer movement. Like many WO options, this is a medium-term initiative.

ST – this quadrant is used to generate options which use strengths to avoid or counter threats. One of the threats which affect ReInk is the continual technology development from an industry which is committed to deliver better and cheaper technology. Continual research of the technical environment, combined with internal innovation, reinforces the need for a strategy which is committed to continual product development. It particularly needs to ensure that new patented processes are in place when its current patent runs out. Like many ST options, this is a medium-term initiative.

WT – is concerned with generating options which minimise weaknesses or avoid threats. These are primarily defensive, aiming to avoid threats and the impact of weaknesses. To a large extent, the weaknesses identified in the SWOT analysis are being addressed by inviting investment and participation from Vi Ventures. However, it is unlikely that the company will ever have the financial strength and brand awareness of the large OEMs which it is competing with. One of these companies (Landy) is aggressive in its statements about warranty and is litigious. Avoiding this company in the marketplace, by not offering refills for its products, could be a reasonable defensive strategy.

In summary, there are viable strategic options in all quadrants of the TOWS matrix. In many respects, the investment of money and expertise by VV represents a reasonable initial strategy in the WT quadrant. The WO and ST quadrants seem to both offer medium-term initiatives. However, the analysis of the SO quadrant, focusing sales and marketing on a well-defined business sector (government and public sector organisations), appears to offer achievable short-term success which would help address the profitability of the company and offer VV early rewards for its investment in ReInk.

2   Tutorial note: *A number of different legitimate approaches could be used to answer this question. The structure used here is based on the one produced by Ken Garrett in his article on Business Strategy and Pricing, published in the February 2011* Student Accountant. *However, alternative frameworks are acceptable as long as appropriate points are made.*

(a)   Mission and marketing objectives

Pricing is ultimately part of an organisation's strategy. It should reflect the organisation's self-perception and its feeling about its position in the market. Marco wants to position iTTrain as a quality provider to the business market. Does his suggested price of $750 per delegate reflect this? It could be argued that this is a reasonable price as long as other factors support it. He is not providing a 'no frills' service to self-financed candidates, so his price can reflect this. His main benchmark is AQT, and he is suggesting a price which undercuts their list price ($900), and their discounted price ($810), so his company theoretically offers the same (or better) quality at a more competitive price.

Pricing objectives

In the short term, there can be a variety of pricing objectives. Sometimes, irrespective of long-term objectives, the need to survive and increase short-term cash flows will dictate price cuts. At present, Marco is not in this position. He wishes to establish iTTrain in the market place, and he is looking for short-term modest profitability. His price should reflect this.

Costing and financial analysis

Tutorial note: *The financial analysis may be undertaken in a variety of ways and appropriate credit will be given to alternatives. In the following analysis, Marco's suggested price of $750 per delegate is used as a basis of the analysis. Expected contribution is calculated by using the values from AQT.*

Figure 1 shows the contribution for class sizes of three to nine delegates on a course. iTTrain will not run courses with fewer than three delegates, and the training rooms at CityCentre have a maximum capacity of nine delegates.

The expected contribution per course has been calculated using the probabilities derived from courses at AQT. The delegate fee is $750.

Course length   3 days   All financial figures in $

Probability	Delegates	Lecturer	Room	Manual*	Lunch	Total cost	Income	Contrib	Exp contrib
0·15	3	450	250	60	30	2,250	2,250	0	0
0·21	4	450	250	80	40	2,300	3,000	700	147
0·25	5	450	250	100	50	2,350	3,750	1,400	350
0·19	6	450	250	120	60	2,400	4,500	2,100	399
0·07	7	450	250	140	70	2,450	5,250	2,800	196
0·08	8	450	250	160	80	2,500	6,000	3,500	280
0·05	9	450	250	180	90	2,550	6,750	4,200	210

*Manual cost is per delegate per course   Total expected contribution   1,582

Figure 1: Contribution for class sizes of three to nine delegates

The expected contribution per course is $1,582.

Thus the breakeven on a course basis is $65,000/1,582 = 41·09 courses.

The company plans to offer 40 courses per year. If the contribution per course is $1,582, then iTTrain will make a small operating loss (40 x $1,582 = $63,280 – $65,000) = ($1,720).

A consideration of the profitability at different delegate volume levels is also instructive, showing that an average attendance of six delegates per course is required to achieve operating profitability assuming that 40 courses a year actually do run. In other words, classes have to operate at a minimum of two-thirds capacity, on average, for the company to be profitable if only 40 courses actually run during the first year.

All financial figures are in $

Number of delegates	Contribution	Fixed overheads	Operating profit (loss)
3	0	65,000	(65,000)
4	28,000	65,000	(37,000)
5	56,000	65,000	(9,000)
6	84,000	65,000	19,000
7	112,000	65,000	47,000
8	140,000	65,000	75,000
9	168,000	65,000	103,000

A number of options might be considered:

–   To increase the price towards their nearest competitor. For example, assuming the same attendance pattern as above, increasing the price towards that of their nearest competitor (AQT), at just under $800 per delegate, would maintain their competitive price advantage while potentially increasing the expected value, realising a modest profit. (Note that sensitivity analysis could be undertaken to verify this using the same method used to calculate the expected value based on a delegate price of $750.)

- Decreasing costs: The lecturer and training room rates are standard rates. It may be possible to agree bulk booking discounts. A 5% discount on lecturing and room booking rates increases the expected contribution per course to $1,687·00 (assuming a course fee of $750). On 40 courses, this gives an expected income of $67,480, producing an operating profit $2,480, returning a modest operating margin of 3·68% (2,480/67,840).

- An exploration of other scenarios which combine increasing the price and decreasing the costs.

- Revisiting overheads, although little information is given in the scenario about this. Marco might be prepared to take less income from the firm in its formative years.

The financial analysis suggests that the $750 delegate fee suggested by Marco appears to be too low to produce the modest profit he would like. It also has to be recalled that the analysis is based on statistical probabilities which are from a well-established training company. Marco has to consider the likelihood of a newly formed training company initially having the same attendance pattern as an established company such as AQT.

Importantly, he has also assumed that all 40 scheduled courses will run. This assumption has to be examined and the sensitivity of profitability to only a certain proportion of courses running has to be explored. Consideration might also be given to the likely proportion of under-subscribed courses at the price actually set. At first sight it appears that a course which does not attract enough delegates will not incur any cost, because all training provision costs are variable. However, there may be cancellation costs associated with the training venue and the freelance lecturer.

Competition

It appears that price is not the only determinant of consumer selection, otherwise the cheaper training providers would dominate the market. Consumers are clearly also affected by non-price factors such as quality of the training and the quality of the place (where the training is provided). Consequently, Marco can price the training at the price he has suggested because there is considerable evidence that consumers (particularly corporate buyers) are willing to pay that price (or more) to get a service which they are satisfied or delighted with.

Consumers

Suppliers have to keep in mind how much consumers are willing to pay. Evidence from AQT suggests that corporate customers (iTTrain's target market) are able to pay the price which Marco has suggested. In contrast, the cheaper 'no frills' training providers appear to appeal to self-financed customers for whom price is an issue. The existence of training brokers as intermediaries in the supply chain does complicate the situation. If Marco wishes to offer them a margin as great as AQT, then he has to reduce his price (to training brokers) to $675 per delegate, which will obviously affect contribution.

Controls

The market is not subject to any legislative pricing controls.

Setting prices

As stated before, Marco wishes to set prices to show a short-term modest profit.

Strategic approaches (tactics or ploys)

A number of tactics or ploys can be used within the pricing strategy, for example: price skimming, penetration pricing, product-line pricing, etc. None of these appear to be particularly appropriate to iTTrain. However, many training companies (like airlines) provide 'early-bird' (early booking) discounts in an attempt to quickly reach a critical mass. Early-bird payments also improve cash flow. iTTrain might also wish to consider 'late booking' discounts, perhaps through training brokers, to provide extra contribution in courses which they are already committed to run.

Summary

Taking all factors into consideration, the suggested price of $750 per delegate appears to be broadly acceptable, except for its likely impact on the financial performance of the company as a whole, specifically the achievement of Marco's modest profit objective. He should consider raising the price to just under $800 per delegate, which gives him some margin of safety, particularly if costs can be reduced through bulk discounts. It also provides more leeway with the discounts he will have to give to training brokers. To some extent, Marco can experiment with the price level. It is the most flexible part of the marketing mix. In business nothing will remain constant. The economy, taste, innovation and competitor actions will change constantly, forcing prices to be continually reappraised. In reality most companies are price-takers, rather than price makers and Marco's pricing approach will have to reflect this.

(b) The **physical environment** in which the service is offered is often central to the consumer's understanding of the service and to their satisfaction or enjoyment of the service. It must reflect customer expectations and the overall brand positioning. Marco has taken this into consideration in the selection of the CityCentre training centre as his course venue. As a result, delegates should experience a physical environment which reflects the quality of the teaching and course documentation. Marco also has the opportunity to give prospective buyers a feel for the physical environment by providing a virtual tour of the location on iTTrain's website. Physical evidence of good quality documentation and teaching can be provided through sample hand-outs and a sample teaching presentation. In the niche which Marco is trying to position iTTrain, physical evidence of the quality of the company is very important.

Most services require direct interaction between the consumer and the **people** who represent the service provider's organisation. In conventional terms, employee selection, training and motivation are significant considerations. Most

successful businesses devote time and resources to managing their customer-facing staff. In the context of iTTrain, this is particularly significant. One of the most important people in the process, the lecturers, are not employees of iTTrain, they are self-employed contractors. Marco must ensure that lecturers are properly briefed, conduct themselves correctly and act in such a way that is consistent with the quality branding. Formal audits (observation of courses, feedback questionnaires) will be both a source of control and of marketing material (delegate testimonies). Marco also has to recognise that although he might make the initial sale, many subsequent sales may be down to the customer's enjoyment of the course and pass rates, and central to this will be the performance of the lecturers.

The **process** which surrounds the service is often perceived, by the customer, as part of that service. There is a significant difference between purchasing a product and a service. The service is often consumed only once (course attendance) whilst a product (such as a computer) might be used many times. The service often requires direct interaction between the person ordering and consuming the service and the service provider (the lecturer). In contrast, the producer of a computer seldom meets the customer. Service is often abstract and transitory and this can accentuate the consumer's expectations and their reflections on the success of the experience. They often perceive that the ordering process, the ease of payment and the accuracy of joining instructions are part of the service and include them in their assessment. Thus Marco must ensure that all the processes which precede and follow the actual teaching process are effective and customer focused.

3 **(a)** *Tutorial note: The structure of this answer is just one way which Bridge Co could have procured the software package in a structured way. Other answers with an appropriate approach will be given credit.*

Stage One: Evaluation

This is concerned with establishing whether a commercial off-the-shelf software package would be an appropriate way of automating the CRM requirements. A framework such as the Harmon process – strategy matrix could be used. There is no evidence in the scenario that any alternative (outsourcing, bespoke software development) to the software package approach was considered. Generally, CRM applications are likely to be relatively complex and of medium strategic importance. Consequently, by chance, a software package approach does appear a reasonable response, although it would have been beneficial for that decision to stem from a proper evaluation, rather than the whim and the will of the new sales and marketing executive.

Stage Two: Business case

This stage would require the definition of a formal business case, including a financial evaluation of the proposed investment. This was avoided by negotiating the price down to below the capex threshold at Bridge Co. If this had not been done, then a business case would have been required. The failure to produce a business case has two consequences. First, it meant that no other likely costs associated with the software purchase were ever considered. These were either avoided (such as the training costs) or had to be funded out of the operational budget (the cost of data migration). Second, and more importantly, there was no attempt to establish what benefits the Custcare CRM package offered the organisation. These could have been financial benefits (so could be compared with costs using an appropriate investment appraisal technique) or they could have been intangible benefits (such as improved customer satisfaction). Both tangible and intangible benefits could have been subject to a benefits realisation review at the end of the project, to see whether the anticipated benefits had materialised. The failure to document the anticipated benefits in advance means that although the software is being used, there is an air of disappointment and deflation about the project outcome.

Stage Three: Requirements definition

This stage is concerned with defining the requirements which the software package is to be evaluated against. No formal requirements definition was performed at Bridge Co. Teri was enthusiastic about the product, based on her experience at her previous company. She felt that the requirements would be very similar at Bridge Co. In fact, she was proved correct, as far as the functional requirements were concerned. The sales and marketing staff appear to be quite happy with the features of the software and, indeed, it has provided valuable functionality which they did not anticipate. However, important non-functional and technical requirements were missed. These concerned the technical interface with the order processing system and the overall slow performance of the software. Performance and interface requirements should have been part of the requirements specification which the package was evaluated against. More thought could also have been given to supplier requirements: what Bridge Co would like from the supplying company. This would have prompted thoughts about support requirements and also the geographical location of the supplier. At the end of the interview Mick says, 'I just wish we had chosen a product produced by a company here in Deeland.' This could have been one of the evaluation criteria.

Stage 4: Evaluation of competing products

The need to compile and issue a formal Invitation to Tender (ITT) would have required Bridge Co to consider alternative products and suppliers. Even just following the capex requirements at Bridge Co would have forced the sales and marketing department to consider three competitive responses to their requirements. This was not done, no alternatives were considered. It may have been possible to find a solution which did fulfil the technical interface requirements and achieved the required performance. However, even if this were not possible, and Custcare remained the best solution, the formality of the ITT process would have allowed Teri to demonstrate that the package had been selected after proper consideration of alternatives. It would have introduced an element of due diligence and transparency which is missing from the project.

Stage 5: Contract negotiation

Once a potential solution is identified, a detailed investigation of the contract is required to remove or amend clauses which the customer is unhappy about. Contracts are usually framed in favour of the software supplier. It is at this stage that Bridge Co would have identified two issues which subsequently caused problems. First, the legal jurisdiction of the contract; this could have been changed, through negotiation, from Solland to Deeland. Second, the restriction on who can be employed as contract staff on Custcare projects. Again, this would probably have been removed after negotiation (or a preferential contract rate agreed). Contractual arrangements are very difficult to change retrospectively. They need to be reviewed before the purchase is completed. If insurmountable problems occur (for example, a reluctance to vary a clause), then the customer can legitimately withdraw at this stage, citing the unacceptable risk the clause exposes them to.

Stage 6: Implementation

Effective training, appropriate documentation and successful data migration are central to the success of the project. Proper consideration of them also contributes to the business case (stage 2). Omitting training has been a false economy at Bridge Co, leading to too much use of an inadequate support agreement. Data migration had to be separately funded and turned out to be disproportionally expensive.

(b) The Custcare solution did provide a quick solution to the CRM requirement at Bridge Co. *Speed of implementation* is a claimed advantage of commercial off-the-shelf software packages and this is valid in this scenario. It would be at least 18 months before the IT department could even start to look at the sales and marketing department's requirement. In contrast, the Custcare solution was up and running within three months.

The Custcare solution did provide comprehensive functionality. The sales and marketing department were impressed with the package. It did all the things they wanted it to do and it also gave them ideas and possibilities which they would never have thought of. Software packages have the advantage of incorporating *industry best practice* within a broad, comprehensive functionality. Custcare allows an organisation without a CRM, such as Bridge Co, to quickly get up to speed and to offer services as least as good as some of its competitors.

Despite the extra costs of data migration, the software package does appear to offer a relatively cheap solution. In general, software packages, where the cost of development and maintenance is shared amongst many customers, are *usually much cheaper* than bespoke alternatives. The Custcare solution has still cost less than $30,000. The internal IT department has quoted a price of $18,000 just for requirements analysis. Given that they still have to develop and test the solution, this suggests that the overall cost will be much greater than the money spent on the Custcare solution.

There have been no complaints about the robustness of the Custcare solution. The only difficulties concern its failure to meet certain requirements, and the problems of support and training. In general, software packages are of *better quality* than bespoke alternatives. The package has been extensively used by many users in a range of organisations and problems will have been progressively identified and solved. It is impossible to exhaustively test bespoke solutions, so they are often beset with robustness and reliability problems, particularly in the period just after implementation.

The two problems reported by Mick are relatively easy to solve. A piece of bespoke software could be developed as a bridge between the CRM and the order processing system. This *bridge* would import files from the CRM system in one format and then convert them into the format required by the order processing system, and vice versa. The performance of the software could be addressed by improving the specification of hardware at Bridge Co, or by scheduling jobs so that complex reports and queries are run when the system is not busy, for example, overnight. These solutions are not ideal, but provide a reasonable way forward. Overall, the software package approach still seems a reasonable way forward.

4 (a) Overview

The table presented in the scenario suggests that the project is currently financially viable. It returns a net present value of $10,925. However, the basis of the discount rate selection could be questioned. Although there is little information in the scenario about this, it might be felt that it has been set artificially low to produce a positive NPV. Also, the duration of the investment appraisal is quite long (seven years). Three and five year appraisals are more common. So again, the basis of this could be questioned. Perhaps seven-year investment periods are common at the IIA, but this needs to be investigated and confirmed.

It would also be beneficial to perform a sensitivity analysis on the data. A relatively small change in the initial cost of the software makes the NPV negative.

Costs

Software costs

Although the software package has a fixed cost, the IIA wishes to make a number of significant bespoke amendments. The actual detail of these amendments is still under discussion. They are currently estimated at $25,000 and this cost is part of the year 1 payment. However, this estimate may change once the detail of the requirement is agreed. The IIA must keep bespoke requirements under review to ensure that costs do not rise substantially, invalidating the financial business case for the investment. The scenario also suggests that there are problems in defining the detail of the requirement and these may lead to project delays, meaning that benefits may not begin to accrue until year 3 (or beyond), which will seriously affect the financial viability of the project. The final delivered cost of the project will also determine the maintenance cost, as it is

calculated at 10% of the final delivered software cost. So, an increase in the initial cost of the software will also have long-term implications which may again affect the overall viability of the project.

Question bank costs

External consultants are to be paid a fixed fee for each question they successfully deliver to the question bank. The current estimate is for the initial delivery of 2,000 questions (with payments spread over year 0 and year 1) and then the subsequent update and amendment of 100 questions per year. These costs are within the control of the IIA and so appear reasonably definite. However, it is unclear why a question bank cost of $50,000 would be incurred immediately (year 0) as question setters are only paid on the acceptance of their question. This demands further investigation. If it is incorrect and the costs are actually incurred in years 1 and 2, then the NPV of the project will be increased.

Security costs

This is a definite cost; a fixed price has been agreed with a security firm who have guaranteed it for the duration of the project.

Disruption costs

The IIA believes that implementing the new assessment system will lead to a temporary reduction in productivity and staff morale in the examinations department. They have estimated that this will cost them $15,000 in year 1 and 2 of the project. However, this is really an intangible cost and is impossible to accurately predict in advance.

Benefits

Reduced marker costs

The reduction in marker costs can be accurately predicted. Manual marking will not be required once the new assessment method is in place. In Ward and Daniel's terms this is a *financial benefit*, and it can be accurately predicted in advance. The only issue may be the timing of the benefits, given the current problems in specifying the bespoke system requirements.

Reduced administrative costs

The reduction in administrative costs is difficult to predict accurately in advance because the undefined bespoke software amendments will affect the administration of the assessment process. However, by simulating the new work process, it should be relatively easy to forecast how many administrative posts will be lost and at what cost. Thus, using Ward and Daniel's classification, this is either a *financial* (at best) or *quantifiable* (at worst) benefit. The IIA should revisit their cost saving estimates as soon as the bespoke element of the software is agreed.

Increased student numbers

The final benefit is extra income from increased student numbers attracted by the convenience of computer-based assessment. It is difficult to put a credible value on this in advance of the project. At best, using Ward and Daniel's classification, this is a *measurable* benefit. It concerns an aspect of performance which is currently being measured (student numbers), but it is not possible to estimate how much performance will improve when the computer-based assessment system has been implemented. It may be possible to get credible evidence from other professional bodies which have implemented computer-based assessment to support this, but there is no evidence that this has been done. It is the IIA's best guess.

Summary

There is a strong argument for taking disruption costs and increased student numbers out of the financial appraisal of the project. It is difficult to put credible values on these in advance of the project. The effect of doing this (for information) is shown below.

All figures in $000s				Year				
Costs	0	1	2	3	4	5	6	7
Initial software	200	200						
Software maintenance			40	40	40	40	40	40
Question bank	50	50	5	5	5	5	5	5
Security			20	20	20	20	20	20
Total costs	250	250	65	65	65	65	65	65
Income/Savings								
Marker fees	0	0	125	125	125	125	125	125
Admin saving	0	20	30	30	30	30	30	30
Total benefits	0	20	155	155	155	155	155	155
Benefits – costs	(250)	(230)	90	90	90	90	90	90
Discount factor	1	0·926	0·857	0·794	0·735	0·681	0·630	0·583
Present value	(250)	(212·98)	77·13	71·46	66··15	61·29	56·70	52·47
						Net present value		(77·78)

The net present value is now less than zero, so there is no financial case for the project. However, this does not mean that the project should not go ahead. IIA management may feel that intangible benefits make the investment worthwhile and so the project may be progressed.

(b) A *benefit owner* is someone who has responsibility for defining, agreeing and delivering a benefit defined in the business case. Without benefit owners, benefits are unlikely to happen. It is very unlikely that the project manager responsible for a change project (as alluded to by the IIA director) would be the benefit owner. Their responsibility is to deliver the project, not to operationally run the outcome of the project. This must be the responsibility of the business and so the benefit owner should be a person who has authority to make business decisions which help deliver the benefits. Many projects which have promised cost savings have not delivered them because no-one had responsibility for making those savings. It is very important that the IIA appoints a benefit owner for the administrative cost reductions. First, because the extent of those savings cannot be reliably estimated due to problems in requirements definition and, second, because someone has to actually make these staff cuts when the new system is in place to deliver the benefits promised in the initial business case.

A *benefits map* helps the benefit owner determine what has to be put in place to deliver the promised benefit. The map can also be used to show how the benefits relate to the objectives of the organisation. For example, increased student numbers may be part of improving the accessibility of the qualification. Benefits may require business changes and *enabling changes* which have to be put in place to deliver the benefit. For example, the eventual elimination of marker costs (a benefit) will only be achieved once a question bank has been defined (an identified cost). A process will have to be put in place to define how questions will be commissioned, how they will be evaluated and how they will be entered and maintained in the question bank. These business and enabling changes require tasks which will have to be estimated and scheduled in a project plan. They form the link between the IT enabler (the software solution) and actually delivering the benefit. The benefits map shows exactly what has to be done to actually deliver the promised benefit.

Benefits realisation is a post-implementation activity which actually compares the delivered benefits with the promised benefits (and costs) forecast in the business case. This is another key role for benefit owners. Also, because of the nature of the financial case (where benefits are delivered annually), it is useful if benefits realisation is a series of reviews. The primary objective is to establish which benefits have been delivered and which have not. Undelivered benefits are investigated and remedial action may be taken. Unanticipated benefits may have also emerged and these are also considered in the reviews. Lessons learnt are fed back into the *benefits management process*. It is often very difficult to disaggregate benefits as time passes. For example; an increase in student numbers may be due as much to the improvement of marketing, to the decline of competing institutes or to demographic change, as it is to computer-based assessment. However, benefits realisation remains worthwhile, if only to stress that someone has to have continuing responsibility for realising the promised benefits which justified the financial investment made by the organisation.

1 **(a)** 1 mark for each relevant point. Up to 6 marks for each heading under the SWOT analysis up to a maximum of 20 marks.

(b) 1 mark for each relevant point up to a maximum of 14 marks.

(c) 1 mark for each relevant point up to a maximum of 3 marks for each quadrant of the matrix, up to a maximum of 12 marks.

Up to 4 professional marks for the complete assessment required by Vi Ventures; up to 1 mark for appropriate quality, up to 1 mark for fluency and up to 1 mark for appropriate report tone and up to 1 mark for the professionalism of the complete answer.

2 **(a)** For the non-financial analysis: 1 mark for an appropriate point up to a maximum of 9 marks. For the financial analysis, up to a maximum of 10 marks. There is a maximum of 16 marks for the complete part question.

   – Table of figures showing values for different class sizes (2 marks)
   – Expected contribution per course (2 marks)
   – Breakeven analysis (2 marks)
   – Course running value and implication (1 mark)
   – Options for flexing (2 marks)
   – Assumptions (2 marks)

(b) 1 mark for each appropriate point up to a maximum of 3 marks for each part of the marketing mix. Three parts are specified (physical evidence, people and process), so there is a maximum of 9 marks.

3 **(a)** 1 mark for each relevant point about stages in the process of software procurement up to a maximum of 15 marks.

(b) 1 mark for each relevant point made for discussing the relative advantages of a software package over a bespoke solution up to a maximum of 10 marks.

4 **(a)** 1 mark for each appropriate point up to a maximum of 6 marks for issues concerning costs. 1 mark for each appropriate point up to a maximum of 6 marks for issues concerning benefits (including benefit classification). 1 mark for each appropriate point in the overall evaluation, up to a maximum of 3 marks.

(b) 1 mark for each appropriate point up to a maximum of 4 marks for each concept (benefit owner, benefits map, benefits realisation). Up to a maximum of 10 marks.

December 2014 exam – ACCA's exam answers

Professional Level – Essential Module, Paper P3
Business Analysis

1 (a) (i) Introduction

The Roam Group currently consists of three operating companies: Stuart Roam Road Transport, Stuart Roam Warehousing and Stuart Roam Rail. Roam Group Co (The Roam Group) is a corporate holding company which facilitates the acquisition of operating companies in the Group. This first part of the report evaluates the performance and contribution of each of the three current operating companies and assesses their relative significance in The Roam Group's future business strategy. The portfolio analysis references two significant models: the Boston Box (or BCG matrix), suggested by the Boston Consulting Group, which uses a classification based upon a company's market growth and market share, and the *parenting matrix* of the Ashridge Portfolio Display which focuses on the fit between the company and its parent.

Stuart Roam Road Transport

Stuart Roam Road Transport (SRRT) is a central part of The Roam Group. Not only does it reflect the original business purpose of the Group, but it is also a fundamental part of its current business strategy, linking customers to rail, warehouse and, potentially, airports. It is also the largest revenue generating part of the Group, contributing 57·39% of the Group's revenues in 2013 and 54·83% of its operating profit. The company has extensive experience in road freight and it is now the dominant company in this business sector. There is also a clear emotional attachment to the industry, with the managing director taking time out once a month to return to everyday trucking. It has an outstanding brand image, promoted partly through significant non-corporate initiatives (the New-Roamantics), which give it free high-profile promotion. The brand image is supported by a clever catch phrase painted on every truck and by the ownership of a modern, reliable, efficient fleet of trucks. In terms of the Ashridge portfolio model, partly because of the historical development of the group, SRRT is definitely a heartland business.

The road freight market has experienced relatively little growth over the last four years (2·50% growth). SRRT has increased its market share over this time (from 25·00% to 28·05%), with a 15% increase in revenues. In Boston Box terms it is a cash cow, although fairly low margins reduce the amount of money it can produce for investment in itself or in other companies in the Group. These relatively low operating profits appear to be typical for the industry sector, with SRRT consistently performing slightly better than industry averages.

Stuart Roam Warehousing

Stuart Roam Warehousing operates a number of efficient, automated warehouses around the country. The physical size of these warehouses provides another opportunity for promoting the brand image and colours of The Roam Group. There is clear synergy with the road transport operation. Indeed, the Group probably had little hesitation in entering this sector of the market. Powerful external forces (including the growth of outsourcing, the growth of internet shopping and retailers requiring an integrated logistics solution) meant that the business case would have been overwhelming.

As a whole, the sector is expanding. The market has grown from revenues of $2,850m to $3,200m dollars in four years – a growth of 12·28%. Stuart Roam Warehousing has experienced a 26·00% growth in this time period, although their market share is still less than 10% (9·84%). Operating margins are slightly higher than the road transport sector and the ROCE is also higher. Stuart Roam Warehousing contributes over 40% (40·47%) of the operating profit of the whole Group. In the Boston Box analysis, there is a practical problem in defining what is meant by 'high', so the company is either a question mark or a star depending on the assessment of its market share. However it is classified, it needs further nurturing and investment. In the context of the Ashridge portfolio model, the company appears to be a heartland business. The Group has a good feel for the business and there seems to be a good fit between the business opportunities and the characteristics and capabilities of the Group as a whole. Overall, its financial performance is largely in line with industry averages.

Stuart Roam Rail

The rail freight market appears to be expanding rapidly. There is a 26·00% rise in industry revenue between 2009 and 2013. Perhaps this reflects the increasing cost of road transport, increasing road congestion and fears about the environmental impact of road transport. However, Stuart Roam Rail is a very small player in this market. It has failed to match growth (only 6·6% growth over this period) and its market share has fallen (from 4·20% to 3·56%). Its financial performance is relatively poor, reporting lower operating margins and ROCE than the industry averages. Importantly, the acquisition of FDRC by the Group does not seem to have made a positive impact. In fact, despite an increase in revenues, overall financial performance appears to be worse. In 2010 (the last year the company traded as FDRC), the company reported an operating profit of 4·95% (4·75% in 2013) and a ROCE of 3·85% (3·50% in 2013). This decline in performance is important to bear in mind when considering the possible acquisition of Godiva airport.

In Boston Box terms, Stuart Roam Rail is definitely a question mark (problem child, wildcat). The Group needs to investigate why the company is failing to grab an increasing market share of a rapidly expanding industry. There are at least three possibilities contained within the scenario. Firstly, the company is small and will find it difficult to match the economies of scale enjoyed by the two large rail freight companies. This probably contributes to high operating costs. Secondly, the company has no expertise in the bulk freight contracts (coal, iron ore, oil) which dominate the Meeland economy. This will make it difficult to take these contracts from the current incumbents. Finally, it is unclear whether the transport of consumer food and drink is really suitable for rail transport. The company is distributing to supermarkets, many of which are unlikely to be directly accessible to the rail network. Road transport is a much more flexible alternative.

There are also cultural problems within The Roam Group. The company is used to dealing with a transport method where the medium (roads) is free and drivers are relatively unskilled. In the rail network the transport medium (rails) is charged on a usage basis by a monopoly supplier. Train drivers have to undergo extensive training and are constrained in their route selection. Road and rail are both methods of transport, but they have quite different characteristics. In the context of the Ashridge portfolio model, this cultural problem might suggest that the company is a value trap business. It is typical of a company which initially appears attractive because there appears to be opportunities for the parent to add value. Value trap businesses should only be included in the strategy if they can be moved into the heartland. This will probably only be possible if new skills, competencies or resources are gained by The Roam Group.

However, on the upside, the company has developed an innovative mini-container system for transferring goods from road to rail and for storage in the warehouse. Also, the supermarkets, aware of the demands of the green consumer, are attracted to rail alternatives and perhaps see this as the primary way of distributing in the future, particularly if loads can be quickly transferred onto road vehicles for the last part of the journey from the railhead to supermarket.

Conclusion

In summary, SRRT and Stuart Roam Warehousing are both heartland businesses. However, the similarities between rail transport and distribution and road transport and distribution may have been misjudged. The rail company is potentially a value trap business and the Group will have to reconsider how to move it into the heartland. In Boston Box terms, it is also a problem child (question mark, wildcat) and so their strategy for moving it into the heartland must also address the underlying reasons why market share is falling in a rapidly expanding business sector.

(ii) Introduction

This section of the report considers the proposed acquisition of Godiva airport in the context of its suitability, acceptability and feasibility.

Suitability

The suitability of a strategy addresses the circumstances in which the organisation is operating – its strategic position. Here we have to ask the question, does the acquisition of Godiva airport by The Roam Group make sense? It does appear to be appropriate at a very superficial level – provided by Sir John Watt in his press release. Road, rail and air are all means of transport with different strengths and weaknesses. However, analysis has already revealed (part (i)) that the similarities between road and rail are much less than might be expected. This is particularly true from a customer perspective. Supermarkets tend to have many individual sites, convenient for road transport but not for rail. There are still doubts whether rail can be used as a significant way of distributing consumer food and drink from the warehouse to the supermarket. The integrated mini-containers represent a possible solution, but the cost of unloading and loading at the rail terminal might make their extensive use unlikely on cost grounds. Even if the mini-container system can be extended to aircraft, airports are relatively few and far between, making distance to supermarket sites even more of an issue. Furthermore, air freighting consumer goods is unlikely to deliver the economies of scale associated with rail freight, or to appeal to the eco-sensibilities of the supermarkets.

However, this broad consideration of the complementary nature of transport alternatives hides another, more fundamental issue. The Roam Group is considering buying an airport, not an airline. This is roughly analogous to buying a station (or set of stations) for Stuart Roam Rail or a portfolio of toll roads for Stuart Roam Road Transport. Sir John Watt's statement does appear to imply the purchase, use or formation of an airline sometime in the future, but that is all. The Roam Group has no experience in running airports and although they intend to offer the opportunity to 'no-frills' airlines to offer scheduled passenger services from the airport, there is no evidence that any airline is currently interested in this option. Indeed, the relatively sparsely populated hinterland of the airport makes it difficult to imagine that there would be much demand for such services. If 'no-frills' airlines were to fly out of Godiva, it seems likely that they would have done so by now.

Acceptability

The acceptability of the strategy is concerned with expected outcomes in terms of return, risk and shareholder reaction. Returns are the benefits which stakeholders would expect to get from the strategy, both in financial and non-financial terms.

The financial performance of the airport can only be assessed from the snapshot of its 2013 performance. It would have been useful to have been given access to data for previous years. However, the industry average performance figures given by the aviation industry consultant can give some measure of the airport's relative performance. Unsurprisingly, the primary asset of the company is the airport site itself which is valued at $6m.

Trading profitability appears quite reasonable. The gross profit margin is 28·21% and an operating profit margin 15·38% (compared to a 17·50% industry average). Indeed, the operating profit compares favourably with the companies currently in The Roam Group. It is much better than, for example, Stuart Roam Rail. However, it has taken significant investment to generate these returns and the Return on Capital Employed (ROCE) is much lower than the industry average. Even if the ROCE calculation excludes interest costs in its calculation (as in Atrill and McLaney), it is still only 2·19%, a very low return. In contrast, liquidity is relatively good (a current ratio of 2·50 – average 2·25), although there appears to be a disproportionally high inventory value. When this is excluded, the acid test ratio is only 1·125, compared to an industry average of 1·50. Gearing is higher than the industry average (59·12% compared to 40%). Finally, in a country where the normal payment period is 30 days, the airport is achieving this for receivables, but is paying in over

60 days (62·57 days). This needs to be investigated further. It might be due to administrative incompetence or to cash flow constraints, with suppliers providing free credit.

Overall, the financial situation is mixed. The airport is trading quite reasonably, but its performance is affected by long-term debts which contribute to a high gearing and a low ROCE. The acid test ratio is of some concern, particularly as customers are paying on time, but payments to suppliers are over twice the accepted payment norm in Meeland.

Risk concerns the probability and consequences of the failure of the acquisition. From the perspective of the resources of the Group, the cost of the acquisition is relatively small and any operating losses could easily be absorbed. A failed acquisition would not be catastrophic for the Group. However, the case has already been made for further investment in Stuart Roam Rail and Stuart Roam Warehousing (two potential problem children) and these may be partially starved of funds due to money being invested in the airport. Managers and employees in other companies may become demotivated by investment in, what might appear to them, an ego-driven vanity project.

The shareholders might also be ambivalent towards the purchase. The Roam family still own the majority of the shares. Their hearts appear to be in road freight, and an investment in an airport might be a step too far.

Feasibility

Finally, feasibility is concerned with whether an organisation has the resources and competencies to deliver a strategy. The issue of financial resources has been considered in the previous section. However, a consideration of competencies is particularly relevant here.

There seems little doubt that the company has significant competencies in road transport and it has been able to adapt these to warehousing. However, these competencies have not proved useful in the rail transport industry. Indeed, since the acquisition of FDRC, the performance of the company has deteriorated. This makes it doubtful that The Roam Group will be able to turn round the performance of an airport – an organisation which is not directly involved in transport. The appropriate competencies are just not in place.

Conclusion

It is the final point about competencies which reinforces the view that the purchase of Godiva airport is an inappropriate strategy and a poor investment for the Group. The company can clearly afford the purchase price of the airport, and absorb any subsequent operating losses, but this will be at the cost of reducing shareholder value and reduced investment and performance in other companies in the Group. Money and management focus would be much better spent on improving the market share of Stuart Roam Warehousing and the overall performance of Stuart Roam Rail. From a suitability perspective, the acquisition does not make sense because it does not appear to address the requirements of customers. It is surprising that someone as experienced as Sir John Watt is advocating this acquisition.

However, one final point must be raised. Perhaps the acquisition is not about airport and 'no-frills' airlines; or indeed, about air freight at all. In a country where land for warehousing is getting scarcer and more expensive, Godiva airport offers 450 hectares of land. At commercial warehousing costs, this would cost $9m to buy. At the offer price of $7m, The Roam Group is getting a discount of about 22% on normal land values. Perhaps land is at the heart of the purchase, particularly as the airport site is next to a motorway and a town where SRRT has three depots and warehouses. The declared strategy might not be the real motive. Getting cheaper land for warehouse development might be the real reason for this acquisition, and from that perspective, it makes a lot more sense, particularly if it frees up existing Roam sites within the town which can be sold for housing or office development.

(b) Johnson, Scholes and Whittington identify four ways of sustaining a price-based strategy: to accept reduced margins, to win a price war, to reduce costs or to focus on specific segments of the market. Elements of all of these might be discerned from the case study scenario. Indeed, the company's focus on consumer food and drink for supermarkets is a continuing example of the last of these strategies. However, this model answer focuses on possibilities offered by reduced margins and a price war.

An organisation pursuing elements of a low price strategy may be prepared to accept a reduced margin, either because it can sell more volume than its competitors or because it can cross-subsidise that business from other business units in the portfolio. The Roam Group can pursue both these options within the context of Stuart Roam Road Transport. It is a dominant player in the road transport market place (generating high volume and revenue) and it is generating good returns in the warehousing business which could be used to cross-subsidise the transport section. It is generally accepted that margins are relatively low in road transport, so reducing operational margins still further might force rivals to exit the business. Market growth is relatively static (2·5% over the last five years), so continued growth requires SRRT to take market share from its rivals. A price war might also achieve this aim. The company is financially sound and evidence suggests that it has greater financial resources than many of its competitors. If it chose to, SRRT should be able to initiate, sustain and win a price war with short or medium-term losses in contribution driving competitors out of the market.

With respect to differentiation, Johnson, Scholes and Whittington offer three ways of sustaining differentiation: creating difficulty of imitation, pursuing imperfect mobility and the re-investment of margin. Two of these are considered here. Imperfect mobility of resources or competencies can be achieved in a number of ways. Two approaches might be applicable at SRRT. It can attempt to increase the difficulty and cost to the customer of switching its supplier. The integration of road transport, warehousing and rail transport using the mini-containers developed by the company might be a key feature here. Nobody can match this flexibility at present (particularly with the eco-friendliness of rail travel which is especially attractive

to supermarkets). It may be possible to imitate it, but it will require considerable investment. However, what is virtually impossible to imitate is the contribution of the New-Roamantics. This is not a carefully crafted management initiative but a group which has spontaneously developed through a shared interest in the Stuart Roam trucks. It is a unique way of promoting the brand. It is unlikely that customers will buy solely because of it, but it does ensure that Stuart Roam is always in their consciousness and there is a certain aspect of fame by association. Subtly encouraging and rewarding this club will maintain an important differentiator between the Stuart Roam Road Transport company and its rivals.

2   (a)   Issues with the current process

–   There are too many handoffs in the current process, particularly given the need to connect to each section by telephone. It seems likely that bottlenecks will form around these handoffs.

–   The role of the supervisor is particularly redundant from the perspective of Stella Electronics (SE). Enquiries for other companies should not be part of their process and, from their perspective, the supervisor adds no value.

–   The payment or service contract reference number and the password are requested relatively late in the process. The need to have these available could have been flagged earlier in the process, perhaps at first contact with the supervisor.

–   On average, 153 people per day (600 calls x 0·85 x 30%) do not know their reference number. This means that SE is billed $153·00 per day for calls which are not resolved. It also wastes the end customer's time and money and is a potential source of complaint and dissatisfaction.

–   On average, 18 people (17·85) per day ((600 – 90 – 153) x 5%) do not know their password. This means that SE is billed $18 per day for calls which are not resolved. It also wastes the end customer's time and money and is, again, a potential source of dissatisfaction and complaint.

–   Although the split of staff across the sections seems reasonable at first sight (six people in technical support for 60% of queries, three people in Stella support for 25% refunds, and one person in the contracts section for 15% of queries), this masks two problems. Firstly, the contracts section is disproportionately understaffed (it should have 1·5 staff) and, secondly, and, more importantly, 100% of the calls have to pass though the three people in Stella support. This must be a bottleneck, and is likely to be the main reason for the poor service experienced by the end customer.

Potential solutions

Tutorial note: *There are a range of potential solutions. Some ideas are presented below, but other legitimate answers will be given credit.*

–   A dedicated phone number could be given to SE customers to eradicate the need for a TCG supervisor.

–   Different phone numbers could be given to SE customers for the three different types of query. Thus there will be a dedicated refund line, a dedicated contracts line and a dedicated technical support line.

–   Staffing levels could be changed to reflect the frequency of calls. For example, an extra person could be provided in the contracts section, although this does not address the support bottleneck.

–   The role of routing calls could be performed by an automated telephone system. For example, option 1 could be refunds, option 2 for technical queries and option 3 for service contracts. This would also provide a mechanism for handling other types of queries (option 4), which could be the responsibility of the supervisor if his or her role is retained.

–   Customers requesting refunds or requiring technical support could be informed earlier in the process of the need to have their contract reference number and password ready. This could be given in the automated reply (see point above) to the initial phone call or menu choice selected or it could be requested by the supervisor, if this role is retained. The need for this could also be prominently displayed on their company's website.

–   Multi-skilling staff so that they could effectively handle any part of the process would reduce handoffs. It may be difficult to include technical support in a multi-skilled role, but it certainly seems feasible to merge the refund and service contract roles. Reducing the number of swim lanes is an effective way of improving a business process.

(b)   The financial case for outsourcing still remains very strong. At present, the cost to SE is $600 per day for a service provided by 10 people, giving a 24 hour service. SE has calculated that it will cost $50 to employ a person with similar competencies in Arborium for an eight hour shift. This produces a 24 hour cost of $150. If SE continues to employ 10 staff, then the total cost will be $1,500 per day. There would also be capital costs of re-establishing the infrastructure to provide the support service, including telephones, office furniture and training costs. There will also be operational costs, such as electricity and office rent and property charges.

So a like-to-like switch back to an in-house support unit seems impossible to justify on cost grounds. However, SE could consider alternative ways of dealing with calls. Technical queries could be addressed by improving support documentation (reducing the demand for queries) and by publishing frequently asked questions (FAQs) on its website. Email support could also be offered. The processing of refunds and the handling of service contracts could be provided by an online process. This seems particularly suited to refund processing. Contracts, which appears to require a dialogue between the customer and SE, seems less of a candidate for this. Improvements in query handling might also allow SE to reduce the number of people working in the centre to a level where the cost of the service would be roughly the same as the outsourced equivalent.

The cultural context of outsourcing needs consideration. Outsourcing, and particularly offshoring, appears to have a negative impact on customers who, as well as having difficulty in understanding the call centre staff based in different countries, increasingly view offshoring as a way of exporting employment. As the number of people out of work in Arborium continues to grow, so the pressure increases on companies to bring work back in-house. SE might be able to make some marketing or public relations capital out of bringing support back in-house and into the country.

Service is a primary activity on the value chain. It is a key point where customers interact with an organisation and form their opinions about it. At present, many customers have a negative view of SE informed by their contact with the TCG call centre. Queries take too long to process and there are problems in understanding the call centre staff. SE needs to consider whether it is wise to outsource such a customer-focused activity. Perhaps the support activities (information technology, procurement) of the value chain are better candidates for outsourcing.

However, it also has to be recognised that support is not a core activity of SE. It is primarily an electronics retailer. It might be reasonable to conclude that a company such as TCG, dedicated to providing call centre support, should give a better service, leaving SE time to focus on its core competencies and activity.

In the short term, it would seem sensible to introduce improvements at the TCG call centre. The service is already relatively cheap and could be made cheaper by reducing the number of calls (through improved documentation and website support) and by reducing the number of calls which are not resolved. In the longer term, SE might wish to re-consider the wisdom of outsourcing a customer-facing service and they may, on ethical grounds, wish to invest in jobs in the country where most of their customers are. Publicising this socially responsible decision might also boost sales.

3   (a)   The first stages of risk management are the identification, descriptions and assessment of the risk. This assessment is primarily concerned with the *likelihood* of them occurring and the *severity of impact* on the organisation or project should they occur. Sometimes the likelihood is a subjective probability, the opinions of experienced managers or experts in the field. On other occasions, there is some statistical evidence on which to base the assessment. For example, in project 1, TKP identified that 20 IT software companies with annual revenues between $3m and $10m went out of business last year. This represented 10% of the total number of software companies reporting such revenues. Its report to the client suggested that there was a 10% chance of the current preferred supplier (who had a turnover of $5m) ceasing business and this would have a significant short-term support implication. This compared to a business failure rate of 1% for software companies with an annual revenue exceeding $100m. The client felt that the probability of supplier failure was too high, so eventually bought a software solution from a much larger, well-known, software supplier. In this case, the likelihood of the risk led the client to changing its procurement decision. The risk itself does not go away, large companies also fail, but the probability of the risk occurring is reduced.

The *avoidance (or prevention) of a risk* is a legitimate risk response. In project 1, the client could avoid the risk 'failure of the supplier' by commissioning an in-house bespoke solution. Similarly, TKP itself avoids the risks associated with trading in different cultures, by restricting its projects to clients based in Zeeland.

There are three further responses to risks.

Risk mitigation (or risk contingency) actions are what the organisation will do to counter the risk, should the risk take place. Mitigation actions are designed to lessen the impact on the organisation of the risk occurring. In project 2, TKP recommends that the producers of the iProjector should establish an escrow agreement with the company which produces the chip which enhances the quality of the projected image. It was agreed that design details of this chip should be lodged with a third party who would make them available to the producers of the iProjector should the company which owned the enhanced image technology cease trading. This is a mitigation approach to the risk 'failure of the supplier'. The supplier is relatively high risk (less than three years of trading, inexperienced management team), and the product (the iProjector) is completely dependent upon the supply of the image enhancing chip. The failure of the business supplying the chips would have significant impact on iProjector production. If the escrow agreement had to be enacted, then it would take the producers of the iProjector some time to establish alternative production. Consequently (and TKP have suggested this), it might be prudent to hold significant stocks of the chips to ensure continued production. In such circumstances, the need to mitigate risk is more important than implementing contemporary just-in-time supply practices. In some instances a mitigation action can be put in place immediately. In other instances risk mitigation actions are only enacted should the risk occur. The risk has been recognised and the organisation has a rehearsed or planned response. For example, in project 1, TKP has identified 'poor quality of current data' as a risk associated with the migration of data from the current systems to the proposed software package solution. It has established a strategy for data cleansing if that risk actually materialises. Importantly, the client knows in advance how to respond to a risk. It avoids making a hasty, ill-thought out response to an unforeseen event.

Risk transfer actions are concerned with transferring the risk and the assessment and consequences of that risk to another party. This can be done in a number of ways. TKP itself has liability insurance which potentially protects the company from the financial consequences of being sued by clients for giving poor advice. TKP has identified this as a risk, but is unlikely to be able to assess either the probability of that risk occurring or establishing meaningful mitigation measures to minimise the effect of that risk. Consequently, the responsibility for both of these is transferred to an insurance company. They establish the risk, through a series of questions, and compute a premium which reflects the risk and the compensation maximum which will have to be paid if that risk occurs. TKP pays the insurance premiums. TKP itself also transfers risks in project 2. It is unsure about how to establish patents and so it refers the client to another company. Transferring avoids the risk associated with 'establishing the patent incorrectly' and the financial consequences of this.

Finally, risk may be identified but just accepted as part of doing business. *Risk acceptance* is particularly appropriate when the probability of the risk is low or the impact of that risk is relatively insignificant. Risks may also be accepted when there are no realistic mitigation or transfer actions. In project 2, the producers of the iProjector are concerned that there is 'a risk that a major telephone producer will launch a product with features and functionality similar to ours'. This is a risk, but there is little that can be done about it. Risks of competition are often best accepted.

The discussion above is primarily concerned with deciding what action to take for each risk. Once these actions are agreed, then a plan may be required to put them into place. For example, establishing an escrow agreement will require certain activities to be done.

Risks must also be monitored. For example, in project 2, the risk of supplier failure can be monitored through a company checking agency. Many of these companies offer a continuous monitoring service which evaluates financial results, share prices and other significant business movements. Reports are produced, highlighting factors which may be of particular concern. Risks will also disappear once certain stages of the project have been completed and, similarly, new ones will appear, often due to changes in the business environment. Many organisations use a risk register or risk log to document and monitor risks and such logs often specify a risk owner, a person responsible for adequate management of the risk.

(b) Every project is constrained in some way by its scope, time and cost. These limitations are often called the **triple constraint**. The scope concerns what has to be delivered by the project, time is when the project should deliver by, and cost is concerned with how much can be spent on achieving the deliverable (the budget). Quality is also an important feature of projects. Some authors include quality in their triple constraint (instead of scope), others add it as a further constraint (quadruple constraint), whilst others believe that quality considerations are inherent in setting the scope, time and cost goals of a project. How a particular project is managed depends greatly on the pressures in the triple constraint.

In project 1, the reluctance of the company to re-visit the business case means that the budget (or cost) of the solution is fixed. The implementation date might be desirable, but it does not seem to be business critical. It is an internal system and so any delays in implementation will not affect customers. It will also be a relatively seamless transition for most employees in the company. They already record the time record details which the new system will collect and so all they will see is a changed user interface. Only the direct users of the output (account managers and the project office) will be affected by any delay. The scope of the software package is also pre-defined. If it fails to meet requirements, then the users will have to adjust their expectations or business methods. There is no money to finance customisation or add-on systems, so in this sense the scope of the solution is also fixed. The quality of the software, in terms of its reliability and robustness, should also be good, as it is a popular software solution used in many large companies.

In project 2, the launch date is fixed. It has been heavily publicised, the venue is booked and over 400 attendees are expected, including newspaper journalists. Thus the time of the project is fixed. However, although orders will be taken at the launch, the product is not expected to ship until a month after launch. Thus the scope of the product shown at the launch date might be restricted and inherent quality problems might not yet be solved. Any defects can be explained away (this is a pre-production model) or, more effectively, they may be avoided by ensuring that the product is demonstrated to attendees, not used by them. The project manager must ensure that key functionality of the product is available on launch date (such as producing an image of a certain quality), but other functionality, not central to the presentation (for example, promised support for all image file formats) could be delayed until after the presentation. The company should make extra funds available to ensure that the launch date is successful.

4 (a) There are five primary activities in the value chain: inbound logistics, operations, outbound logistics, sales and marketing and service. Each of these is now considered in turn.

Inbound logistics are activities associated with receiving and storing the inputs to the production process. In terms of the costs identified in the scenario, inbound logistics are concerned with raw foodstuff costs, the costs of cans and the transport costs (goods inward). In two of these areas (raw foodstuff costs and can costs) Noble Pets appears to be competitive. However, goods inward costs are higher than any of its competitors. The fact that raw foodstuff costs and can costs are competitive makes it seem unlikely that the high goods inward costs are due to procurement failings. What seems more likely is that the location of the factory makes transport costs higher. Travelling on relatively minor rural roads and negotiating the congested town centre and the growing suburbs of Milton will affect the fuel economy of the trucks which make deliveries to the plant. This will place Noble Pets at a disadvantage compared with competitors who may be located adjacent to major motorways. There is also some reputational damage caused by complaints from local residents kept awake by the trucks.

Operations are concerned with the production activities associated with turning inputs into their final form, outputs. Production at Noble Pets involves the processing of the raw materials, canning and labelling. In the context of the scenario, these are represented by production costs and direct labour costs. Direct labour costs are roughly in line with its competitors. However, production costs are higher. This is probably associated with the ageing technology of the plant itself. Although it was innovative when it was installed 40 years ago, technology changes have meant that there are more reliable and efficient alternatives available. The physical site is also constrained by housing developments which were built subsequent to the plant. Thus the original plant could not be expanded to obtain any further economies of scale.

Outbound logistics are the activities involved with distributing the product to the customer, in this instance the wholesalers and supermarkets. This area is represented by transport costs (goods outward) included in the table given in the scenario. Like inward logistics, these transport costs are higher than Noble Pets' competitors. This is again partly due to the nature of the roads which lead to the factory and to the congestion in Milton. It also seems very likely that most of the company's customers have relocated to locations which have good road links. Wholesaler and supermarket distribution centres are relatively flexible and footloose and most locate to easily accessible locations. A further problem with outbound logistics is the size of the trucks which can be used to carry the final product. The larger 44 tonne vehicles are banned from Milton town centre, so the company has to continue using the less cost-effective 36 tonne trucks. Again, it is likely that its competitors will be benefiting from the lower unit transport costs offered by the larger trucks.

Sales and marketing is concerned with the activities which make the buyer aware of the product (marketing) and also provide a means by which the buyer can purchase the product (sales). No details of the costs of sales and marketing are provided in the table. However, marketing is an acknowledged strength of the firm and has allowed the company to command a premium price for its products. The term 'noble' itself has positive connotations and appeals to the buyers' sense of duty to feed their pets with what appears to be a superior product. This is significant, because the firm is targeting the buyers of a product who are, in this case, not the consumers of that product. In fact, the consumers' feedback is probably restricted to the pet's reluctance to eat the food. So advertising campaigns which stress the need for people to give their pets the best and that the best is provided by Noble Pets are very effective. Interestingly, the trend to move from moist foods to dry foods (discussed in part (b)) has been driven by buyers wanting more convenient foods rather than the preferences of the pets themselves.

Service activities are designed to support or enhance the product. Normally, these include services such as installation, repair, training and part supply. In the context of Noble Pets, this can be perceived as the factual information sheets and website designed to promote responsible and appropriate pet ownership. Although the advice is product neutral, its association with Noble Pets enhances the reputation of the company and makes it more likely that consumers will buy its products. The apparently unbiased advice which Noble Pets gives to the community is again an acknowledged strength of the company.

Summary

Noble Pets is a company trapped by its location and its technology. These have led to high transport costs and uncompetitive production costs. It may be possible to address the latter by installing new equipment which is more efficient and reliable, but the business case for replacing all the moist food production facilities depends on future trends in the relative popularity of dry and moist foods. However, it is difficult to see how the company can reduce its transport costs if it remains at the current site. Perhaps it has to continue relying on strong branding and praiseworthy service to allow it to charge a premium price for a product to buyers who are unaware that its content is really very much the same as its competitors' cheaper alternatives.

(b) **(i)** It is immediately clear from Table Two that the sales of moist pet foods are decreasing and the sales of dry pet foods are increasing. The decline in moist foods was particularly severe in the period 2007–2010. Since then, the downward curve has flattened out. The rate of increase for dry food sales has decreased in the last few years, but it is still showing healthy year-on-year growth. This change in pattern is due to the buyers of product requiring something which does not smell and can be left for longer in the pet's bowl.

The total sales of pet foods are worth closer examination.

| Year | Moist food | | Dry food | | Total |
	Production (000s tonnes)	Percentage	Production (000s tonnes)	Percentage	Production (000s tonnes)
2007	370	55·89%	292	44·11%	662
2008	350	53·27%	307	46·73%	657
2009	331	50·77%	321	49·23%	652
2010	325	49·69%	329	50·31%	654
2011	315	48·02%	341	51·98%	656
2012	310	46·90%	351	53·10%	661
2013	310	46·34%	359	53·66%	669

This shows that, overall, pet food sales declined from 2007 to 2011 and only in 2013 rose above the 2007 level (and even then, by only just over 1%). Thus Noble Pets has been competing in, at best, a stagnant market dominated by four companies. The only way that any of these companies can grow is to take market share from each other and hence (in Porter's terms) competitive rivalry is high, compounded by low switching costs from one brand to another. It is probably these strains within the industry which has prompted Noble Pets management to ask the Milton plant to review its value chain.

The Milton plant has also suffered from a change in buying tastes. In 2007, moist pet foods accounted for 55·89%. In 2013, this figure had reduced to 46·34%. Although Noble Pets' share of this market remains the same (30%), this is a reduction in real terms of 18,000 tonnes of production (from 111,000 to 93,000 tonnes).

(ii) The regression analysis for moist food sales suggests the following line of best fit.

$$Y = a + bx$$
$$Y = 369·5714 - 9·86x$$

The negative value of b shows that the slope of the curve is downwards. Substituting values for 2014 (8), 2015 (9) and 2016 (10) into this equation gives the following (rounded) forecasts.

2014: 291   2015: 281   2016: 271

These values do appear to be too low, given the flattening out of demand in 2011, 2012 and 2013. The line of best fit is influenced by the rapid decline in the first four years of the analysis. Thus these forecasts appear too pessimistic when extrapolating the linear line of best fit.

The correlation coefficient r is negative (–0·94432), which is what would be expected given the production decline. The coefficient of determination of 0·89174 (r^2), suggests that 89% of the variation can be explained by the passage of time or, more sensibly, by some factor or factors which have changed over this time – such as buyer behaviour. However, the correlation coefficient measures the strength of the linear relationship, and there does appear to be some obvious curve in the original data values.

Although the market for moist food has declined rapidly in the last few years, this decline appears to have been arrested. However, the steepness of this decline, in the early years of the analysis, has meant that the line of best fit produces estimates which appear too pessimistic. A free-hand extension of the curve joining the actual data points is likely to give estimates of over 300,000 tonnes for the next three years. This will have to be taken into account when deciding any further investment in the Milton plant. If Noble Pets retains its 30% share of the market, it still has a demand for 90,000 tonnes of moist pet foods. The other two factories producing moist pet food are relatively small, producing 40,000 tonnes between them. Thus a detailed financial analysis can reasonably be based on a demand of at least 50,000 tonnes in the period 2014–2016, even if the other plants work at full capacity.

1 **(a)** **(i)** 1 mark for each relevant point up to a maximum of 7 marks for each company in the Group, up to a maximum of 21 marks for the answer. Within the analysis, marks may be given for the correct calculation of market share change (1 mark), market size change (1 mark) and appropriate classification using a portfolio analysis model (1 mark).

(ii) 1 mark for each relevant point up to a maximum of 15 marks. Within the analysis, it is possible for the candidate to calculate and interpret a number of financial ratios. Marks will be allocated for the correct calculation and interpretation of gross profit margin, net profit margin, ROCE, liquidity, gearing, payables and receivables, up to a maximum of 6 marks.

Professional marks: Up to 1 mark each for the clarity, structure, logical flow and appropriate tone of the answer.

(b) 1 mark for each relevant point up to a maximum of 10 marks.

2 **(a)** 1 mark for each relevant point up to a maximum of 8 marks for evaluation of the problem. 1 mark for each relevant point up to a maximum of 8 marks for suggested improvements. A maximum of 15 marks for this part question.

(b) 1 mark for each relevant point up to a maximum of 10 marks. 1 mark will be allocated for the correct calculation of the daily cost of delivering the service in-house.

3 **(a)** 1 mark for each relevant point up to 15 marks.

(b) 1 mark for each relevant point up to 2 marks for principles. 1 mark for each relevant point up to a maximum of 4 marks for each project. Maximum of 10 marks in total.

4 **(a)** 1 mark for each relevant point up to a maximum of 15 marks.

(b) **(i)** 1 mark for each relevant point up to a maximum of 5 marks.

(ii) 1 mark for each relevant point up to a maximum of 5 marks. This may include 1 mark for arithmetically correct forecasts and 1 mark for explaining the coefficient of determination.